Ireland in an Increasingly Unequal World

Editor
Colm Regan

Peadar Cremin, Marie Cullen, Pauline Eccles, Rachel Hayhow, Anne Leahy, Stephen McCloskey, Sean McDonagh, Colm Regan, Roger Robinson, Jean Somers, Roland Tormey, Sinéad Tynan and Liam Wegimont.

Cartoons by
Martyn Turner

Photographs by
Carol Lee

Published by Dóchas,
The Assembly of Irish Non-Governmental Development Organisations

75:25
is dedicated to the memory of Ken Saro-Wiwa, Barinem Kiobel, John Kounien, Baribor Bera, Saturday Dobee, Felix Nwate, Nordu Eawo, Paul Levura, and Daniel Bgokoo murdered by the Nigerian Government in 1995 for their defence of the Ogoni people and their homeland.

Dóchas and Development Education Centre, Birmingham would like to acknowledge the contributions of the following:

Anna Farrell, Dóchas

Tom Ryder, Deirdre Farrell, the members of the Development Education Working Group and the Executive of Dóchas, Frank McGuinness, the staff of DEC, Birmingham, Brian Davies and Brendan Walsh in CAFOD and John Dornan in SCIAF, Calypso Theatre Company, Giancarlo Ramaioli of Public Communications Centre, the members of the Northern Ireland Development Education Forum and Ian Caprani, Gerry Fenlon and Charlie O'Reilly of Genprint.

Dóchas and Development Education Centre, Birmingham gratefully acknowledge the financial support of the member agencies of Dóchas, CAFOD, SCIAF as well as the Development Directorate of the European Communities, Brussels and the National Development Education Committee, Dublin.

Designed by Public Communications Centre (Ireland)
Printed by Genprint (Ireland)

Published by and available from:
Dóchas, 59 Deerpark Road, Mount Merrion, Co.Dublin.
ISBN 0 9516077 1 5

CONTENT

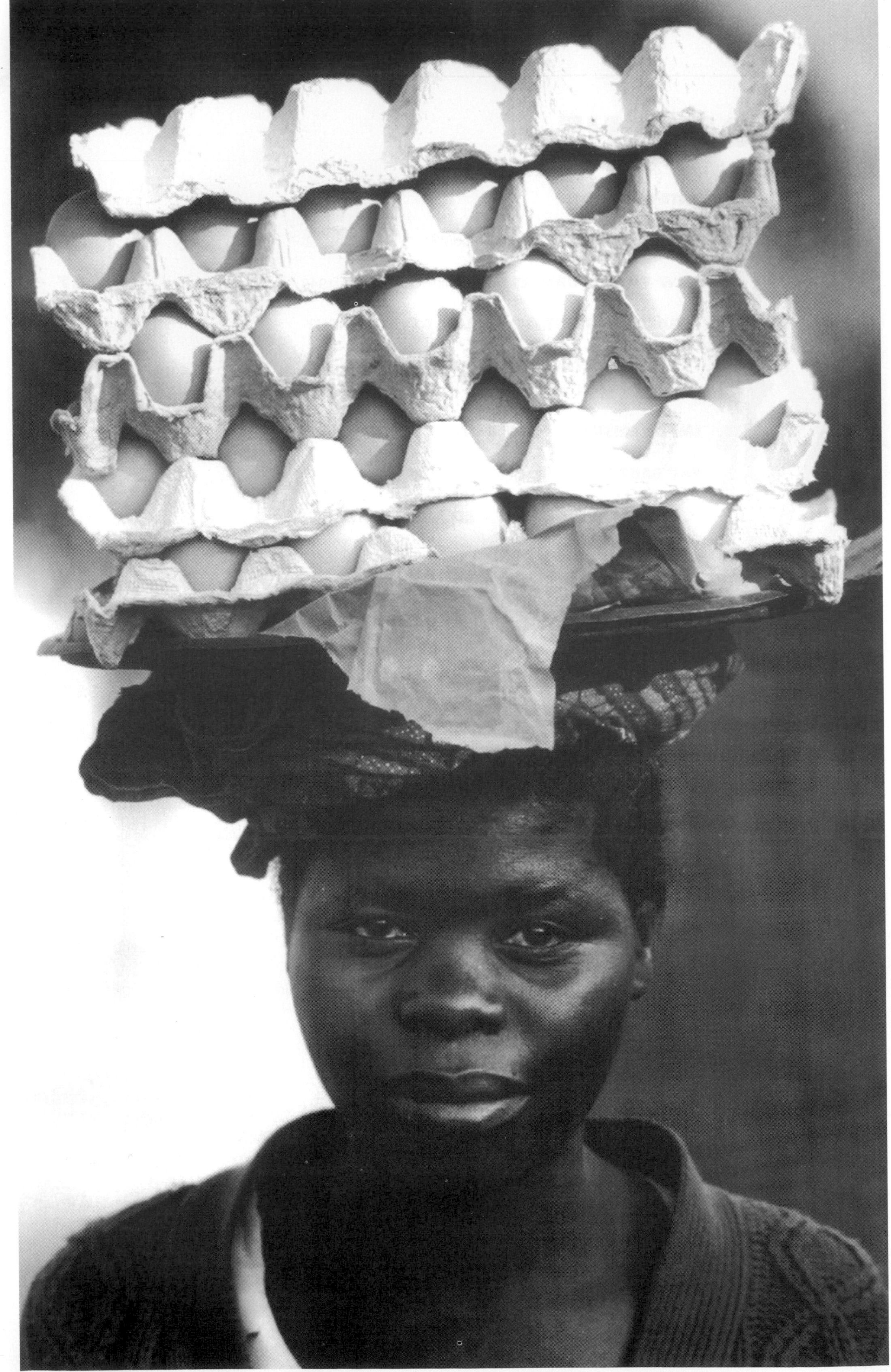

INTRODUCTION

Development education seeks to open eyes, ears and hearts. As we enter the 21st century, our world is increasingly interpreted for us by others - the image manufacturers of television, newspapers, advertising and merchandising. The dominant message is that, despite its malfunctions, our model of development is basically sound or at least as sound as human ingenuity can make it. Not only does such a message serve (both consciously and unconsciously) to perpetuate inequalities and injustices it also posits simplistic answers to complex political problems and, ultimately, it ensures the non-participation and exclusion of millions.

Development education seeks to challenge this worldview - that this is the way the world inevitably is, and, apparently ever will be. It encourages people to see and examine the realities of injustice. It seeks to open hearts and minds to the way the world really is and it proclaims that 'it doesn't have to be like this'. It highlights the fact that injustice is not accidental, but the direct result of human action and inaction at individual, collective and institutional levels.

Development education seeks to build upon peoples' innate sense of justice and the human potential for change; upon the stories of people world-wide and the various traditions of transformation which have helped them map out new and better options. It not only imagines a different and better world, but, through education and dialogue, it seeks to enable people to begin to build it.

Simply stated, development education is justice education with a global perspective.

Traditionally development education has been associated with one particular model of education which sought to explore and extend three core dimensions - ***information*** (about global issues and challenges); ***skills*** (the encouragement and strengthening of skills for global citizenship) and ***attitudes*** (challenging ignorance/prejudice and fostering tolerance and understanding). Because of its roots in the development movement (and the dominant influences of development studies and development co-operation), development education, in its early years, was heavily dominated by an information based approach. It paid scant attention to questions of educational philosophy and practice. In more recent years, this approach has changed significantly and a considerable body of development education thought and strategy now exists (For example, see DEC (1981), Hicks and Townley (eds. 1982), Korten (1990), Richardson (1990), Leahy (1995) and Fountain (1995).

Today, development education is increasingly understood to embrace at least ***six core dimensions - A justice and a global perspective; an action dimension; the use of***

participative methodologies; the linking of both local and global understandings and actions and the development of imagination, visions and values. Some of the key questions posed by development education within these dimensions are outlined in the diagram below.

DEVELOPMENT EDUCATION KEY QUESTIONS

The Justice Perspective

how is the world just or unjust?
who gains? who loses?
why does Injustice continue? how is it maintained?
is injustice inevitable? unavoidable?
how does it relate to me? us? how do I understand it?

Using Participative Methods

why is participation important?
what can I learn from others? share with them?
what are the benefits/difficulties of working together?
what skills and approaches do we need for participation?
how do we build the practice of participation?

The Global Perspective

how am I linked to others throughout the world?
how do my/our actions affect them and vice-versa
where/how does Ireland, Britain, Europe fit into the world?
how do we see/portray others and vice-versa?
what can we learn from others?

Linking Local and Global

why should we link local and global issues?
are they really the same?
what are the benefits of linking? its disadvantages?
how do I/we do it?
what are the key linkages between Britain, Ireland and the wider world?

An Action Dimension

how can I/we help to improve things?
how does change come about?
what skills/experiences/opportunities help me/us to decide what actions are appropriate?
what are others doing and how can I get involved?
can we really change things?

Developing Imagination, Vision and Values

how could things be different?
what's our vision/values for the future? how do we describe and share them?
what steps do we take to get there?
where can we seek inspiration?
how do we educate our social imaginations?

While 75:25 has been consciously developed as an information based resource, it has, nonetheless, been written and designed with ease of access and use firmly in mind. Bearing in mind that 75:25 is not a methodological handbook, we believe that the information it presents can be readily adapted to the methodologies referred to above (see section below on *Using 75:25* for some general ideas).

As with previous editions, this third edition has been written for use by teachers, senior secondary students, undergraduates, adult and youth educators, journalists, those developing educational materials and activists. It has been designed as an introduction to development and justice issues for the interested reader and as a resource into which users can 'dip' using different chapters or sections within chapters as appropriate.

75:25 is based upon a number of key ideas and principles which have informed both its content and approach. Amongst these key ideas are the following:

- *Education is a crucial and integral part of the global development and justice agenda. Development education involves not just the provision of information but also actively engages with the educational process itself as well as with the needs, capabilities and perspectives of learners of all ages. The simple provision of information and the generation of 'awareness' is not, in itself, a sufficient condition for change.*

- *Development is a complex, contradictory and controversial process. There is no such thing as an agreed definition of development or an agreed strategy to achieve it. Development education tries to present and explore different perspectives and approaches but it does this in the knowledge that change towards a more equal and just world is one of the priority challenges of the millennium.*

- *Many of the sources of information and analysis currently used by teachers and students remain solidly Eurocentric and ideological. Development education seeks to challenge this perspective and to do so on the basis of presenting the views and perspectives of Third World writers and activists.*

- *Development (or underdevelopment - a word which is, unfortunately, unfashionable today despite the overwhelming evidence of its accuracy) is a global human process in which all societies and people participate. Development is not something which happens 'out there' in the Third World but is, rather, a process which envelopes us all on a daily basis. Development is not something pursued by 'experts' (although one would be forgiven for believing this to be the case given the prominence afforded to their views), but by all of the world's citizens. Such a perspective allows development education to explore issues at both local and global levels and to develop methodologies and perspectives for achieving this.*

- *Development education seeks to affect positive change towards a more just and equal world but it does so in a spirit of exploration and discovery, debate and discussion. It recognises that how change comes about and how the participation of all involved are crucial to its success are as important as the change itself. Development education thus opposes the imposition of solutions from whatever source they arise. It also operates within the assumption that the vast majority of the world's people want and support change for the better. In this context, 75:25 is therefore about crucial world citizenship issues and challenges.*

The first two editions of 75:25 were entirely 'Irish Affairs' but this third edition has become a joint venture. Over the past decade, an increasing number of projects have led to a greater appreciation of the value of joint work and of a comparative approach (see Regan and Sinclair (1986a and 1986b) and Bridle and McCarthy (eds.1993). This edition has benefited greatly from being developed collectively. Needless to remark, this development was not without its difficulties and challenges!

In designing a 'big island' edition (as one of our editors coined it) to accompany the Irish one, we assumed that the chapters on local issues in both islands would only be included in their respective editions. But, as the text developed, it became clear that there was considerable value in incorporating both chapters in each edition. We hope you agree.

By definition, 75:25 is not comprehensive. Like all good development education, it does not contain the answers - it provides the sources of the questions, a map of the debates and the dialogue which is the prerequisite for a globally educated people. The issues highlighted, the information presented and the analyses offered reflect the many choices and values of authors, editors and commentators. In this context, 75:25 is offered in a spirit of exploration and discussion and as a contribution to a vital global debate.

Colm Regan - Dóchas
Scott Sinclair - Development Education Centre, Birmingham.

REFERENCES:

Marge Bridle and Stephen Mc Carthy (eds.1993) **Colonialism, Conflict and Community: cross-curricular themes in the classroom,** Dublin and Birmingham, Trocaire and Development Education Centre.

Development Education Centre Birmingham (1981) **Priorities for Development: A Teachers Handbook for Development Education,** Birmingham.

Susan Fountain (1995) **Education for Development: A teachers Resource for Global Learning,** London, Hodder and Stoughton.

David Hicks and Charles Townley (eds. 1982) **Teaching World Studies: an introduction to global perspectives in the curriculum,** London, Longman.

Anne Leahy (1995) **Challenges for Change: Development Education in 'Disadvantaged' Youth Work,** Dublin, Development Education for Youth (DEFY).

Colm Regan and Scott Sinclair (eds.1986a) **Half the Lies are True: Ireland/Britain - a microcosm of international misunderstanding,** Dublin and Birmingham, Trocaire and Development Education Centre.

————— (1986b) "Learning from the Past? History and Development Education" **International Journal of Educational Development,** Vol.6, No.2, pp.127-131.

Robin Richardson (1990) **Daring to be a Teacher,** Stoke-on-Trent, Trentham Books.

READ, DISCUSS, ACT

Some ways of using 75:25

Groupwork

While reading and using 75:25 alone will prove stimulating and rewarding, it is perhaps best used in a group situation. As well as constituting a body of knowledge, development education also embraces a methodology in which groupwork features centrally. Groupwork is important in that it helps participants to grow in appreciation of the rights and values of others, while learning the skills of groupwork. It encourages discussion, fosters questioning and helps us to express our ideas while appreciating and listening to those of others.

A basic methodology for groupwork could involve the following:

- reading a chapter or a section from a chapter prior to discussing it in a group
- discussion of individual and group reactions to it, what individuals found particularly informative, challenging etc.
- dividing the information within a chapter between different groups allowing that group to become an "expert" in that dimension and to study and discuss it in detail and then sharing each group's information with the larger group. This facilitates the sharing of large amounts of detail within a group.
- encouraging the identification of areas where supplementary information is required
- using creative methodologies to present the information to others (posters, role-play, collages, creative dialogue etc.
- identification of appropriate actions by individuals and groups which might follow

75:25 presents a lot of facts, ideas and opinions. It is by no means exhaustive on any one topic, nor does it cover all topics. It is important to remember that there is no single answer to many of the questions posed.

For additional ideas on groupwork see Anne Wilkinson Hayes (1993, 2nd ed.) ***It's Not Fair: a handbook on world development for youth groups,*** London and Dublin, Christian Aid and Trocaire. Two particularly useful resources for a general approach to methodology in development education and to using information are SEAD (nd) ***Using Knowhow: Learning from Case Studies of Community Empowerment in Scotland and South Africa,*** Edinburgh, SEAD and TIDE (1995) ***Development Compass Rose: a consultation pack, Birmingham,*** DEC.

Debating the Issues

75:25 provides ample raw material for debating many of the key issues relating to global justice and development topics. The sections on definitions of aid (page 160), on capital punishment (page 121), on the causes of hunger (page 107) and on the benefits or disadvantages of transnational companies (page 189) are presented with such an activity in mind. The material in other chapters can be adapted to a similar format. Many of the pages of 75:25 contain different and often conflicting views on important issues e.g. viewpoints on population growth and its impact, definitions of development. Such pages provide a direct stimulus to debate and as such can be photocopied and distributed for group use.

Cartoons, graphs and photographs

Martyn Turner's cartoons have become an important part of the content and approach of 75:25. Not only do they draw immediate attention to issues and to connections between issues, they are also a source of intense debate and argument. Martyn's original 75:25 cartoon (on the cover) has been the source of much argument and disagreement. The cartoons in this edition will, no doubt, act as a stimulus to additional debate. Some very basic activities for using cartoons include identifying and describing the theme (this alone can stimulate discussion!); sharing opinions on the cartoons; questioning a cartoon; ranking sets of cartoons and, of course, drawing your own cartoons. For additional ideas about the role of cartoons in education see Colm Regan, Scott Sinclair and Martyn Turner (1988) ***Thin Black Lines*** and (1994) ***Thin Black Lines Rides Again,*** Birmingham, DEC.

Equally Carol Lee's photographs provide a basis for discussion in much the same way. Reading a photo, labelling it, using keywords to describe it, ranking sets of photographs, questioning and storytelling around photographs have all become basic development education activities. For additional or detailed activities see ***Southern Exposure: Photographs by Carol Lee*** (1995), Dublin, Public Communications Centre; VSI Development Education Group (1996) ***Images from the South: an exhibition of Photographs by Shahidul Alam,*** Dublin, Voluntary Service International and DEC (1987) ***What is a Family?,*** Birmingham, DEC.

Using the Case Studies

75:25 contains many case studies which attempt to describe the human dimensions of the various issues presented. Frequently the case studies present the viewpoints of people involved in their own words. As such they can form the basis for creative essay writing, for drama and role-play and for storytelling. The case studies can also be used as an introduction or follow-on to the use of simulation games - for example, the case studies and the general information included in chapter 13 could complement the use of the ***Trading Game*** (see ***It's Not Fair*** above). Many of the case studies could also form the basis of language sessions or activities with direct translation work or dialogue development.

The graphs and statistics can also be used in much the same way.

Using the Resources and Addresses Sections

75:25 has included a brief list of useful resources and addresses for additional information/ideas. It has not been possible to include all the resources available or all the addresses necessary. The organisations and resources listed are an excellent starting point for taking the whole exercise further.

75:25 has not been written as a text book or as an extended essay - it is designed as a basic resource book. It provides many opportunities for the creative use of information and analysis.

DEVELOPMENT
What's it all about?

Colm Regan

"The process of development, the fate of the people going through it, is a global drama. It is the story, often tragic, of billions of individual lives, their hopes and frustrations, their efforts and their failures, their sufferings and their conflicts. It is perhaps the central story of our time. One that concerns, directly, three quarters of humanity, and ought to concern the other, industrialised quarter much more than it does, if only because its inhabitants live in relative comfort on a planet in which there is so much staggering poverty."

Paul Harrison in ***Inside the Third World*** (1993)

Introduction

"*Brazil has done well but the Brazilians have not"* is a phrase often cited to illustrate a key issue in debates about the nature and impact of development today. It refers to the reality that for many millions of Brazilians, perhaps the majority of the population, the very real, if uneven, growth which the economy has experienced over the past three decades has not automatically translated (as was traditionally assumed) into a better quality of life. This is a phenomenon which has also characterised the economies of many "developed" societies in recent years and has lead to the use of the phrase *"growth without development"*. This experience directly challenges many of the basic assumptions not only of the theory of development but also many of the strategies adopted to try to achieve it. At the core of the debate are arguments about what precisely do we mean by development and who should define it.

In contemporary world affairs, the term *"development"* is one of the most often used yet most frequently debated and ill-defined words. Alongside other key words such as *"growth"* and *"expansion"* or, more recently *"community"*, it has become, in the popular mind, a very positive and much sought after goal. Almost everyone is in favour of development but when it comes to defining the term, our problems and disagreements emerge.

Debating Development

Until very recently, the primary importance of economic growth in bringing about development was taken for granted. Economic growth and development were seen as synonymous in many people's minds and in much of the development literature. However, growing economic, social and environmental problems in many industrialised countries (and the recent increase in levels of poverty) and the obvious failure of much of development in the Third World has fuelled a major development crisis. Not only is there widespread criticism of the strategies used to achieve development but also of the very concept itself. Such criticisms arise from a very wide range of sources - from the poor, from environmentalists, from the women's movement, from church sources, from international institutions and from various political groups.

The debate about development and particularly about its human dimensions and consequences is as much about the developed world as it is about the Third World. In much of western Europe, with rising unemployment, major balance of payments problems, the growing marginalisation of the poor, serious regional and social inequality and increasing environmental damage, many observers and critics now argue that it is time to redefine what precisely we mean by development.

Many would argue that we have lost the core values by which development was traditionally defined and that there is now a major debate about what key concepts such as *"community"* and *"society"* really mean. There is also a vigorous debate about who should define such terms and about the exclusion of increasing numbers of people from the development debate. Others argue that a lack of realism, hard work and discipline are holding everyone back - that traditional values and strategies, based upon local or national communities are an anachronism and that the new international driving force for change is the *"global market"*.

There is also widespread debate about strategies for development. Many argue that goals such as the elimination of poverty (which was agreed as a global prerogative at the 1994 Social Summit in Copenhagen) will have to await expansion within the economy while others argue that that very expansion, given current inequalities, is actually creating inequality. Such debates within Ireland and Britain mirror those taking place internationally - is human and social development to be ultimately derived from economic development or is the former a prerequisite for achieving the latter?

In the Third World, the much heralded triumph of capitalism over communism and the re-emergence of a *"New World Order"*, has not produced the predicted peace and development dividend. Critics argue that continued adherence to a western concept of development has not lead to a better life for all, especially the poor and powerless. They argue that alternative paths to development, based on different values (which are often in conflict with dominant western values) are urgently needed. The stark contrast between a world where mass hunger and starvation continue while hundreds of millions of pounds continue to be invested in the arms trade, is seen as one key indication of how development has gone tragically wrong.

Before attempting to outline what development might mean, it may be useful to briefly review some of the dominant definitions which have guided development strategies over the past four or five decades.

Rapid economic growth along western lines

Following the Second World War, development was defined, in the words of one commentator, as *"...a rapid and sustained rise in the real output per head and attendant shifts in the technological, economic and demographic characteristics of society"*. This definition tended to emphasise the total value of economic production to the neglect of the role of the individual in development. Since it was believed that western market economies had achieved *"rapid and sustained growth"*, then it logically followed that Third World societies should follow the western path of development.

The most famous expression of this view of economic development was put forward by American economist Professor Walt Rostow who argued that each country, no matter when or where, had to pass through five stages on the road to development.

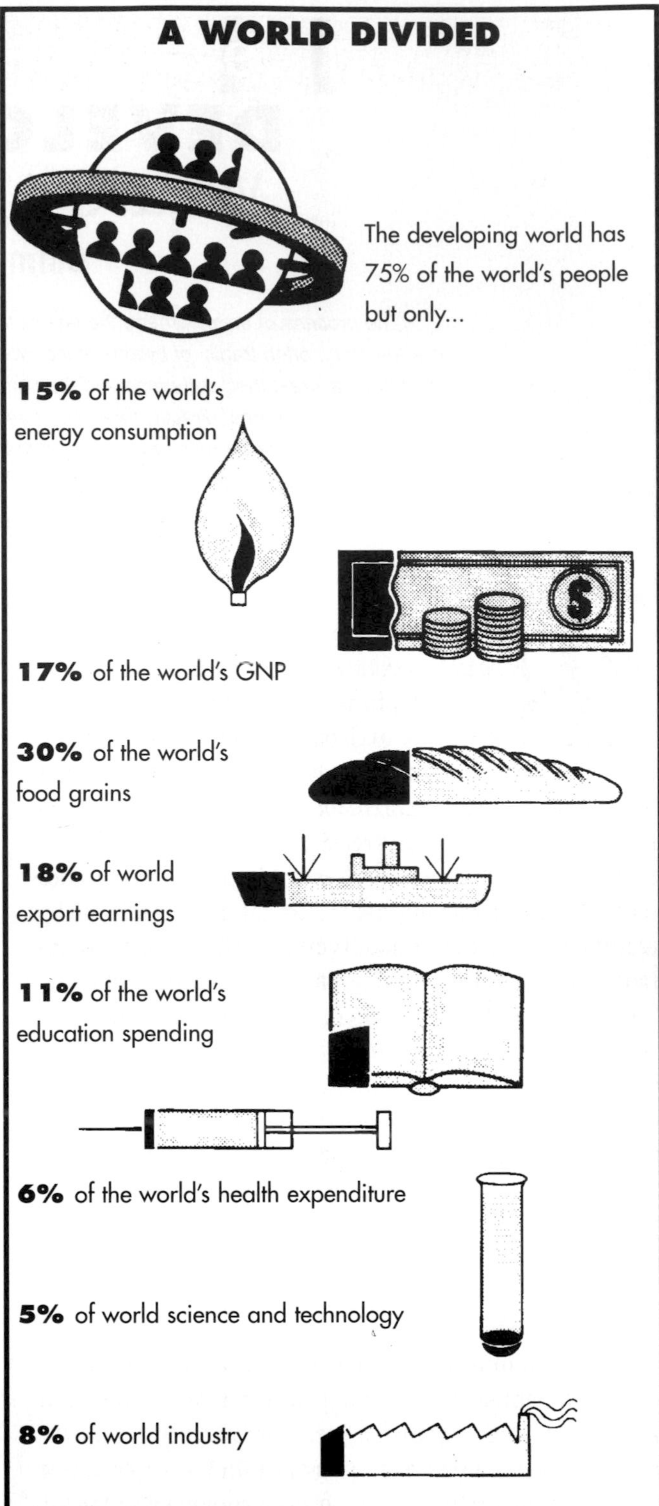

A WORLD DIVIDED
The developing world has 75% of the world's people but only...
15% of the world's energy consumption
17% of the world's GNP
30% of the world's food grains
18% of world export earnings
11% of the world's education spending
6% of the world's health expenditure
5% of world science and technology
8% of world industry

These were:

* the traditional society
* the preconditions for take-off
* the take-off
* the drive to maturity
* the age of high mass consumption.

Defining Development

The influential economist Dudley Seers has identified three vital aspects of development which, he argued, could be posed as questions:

1. What has been happening to poverty in the country under study?

2. What has been happening to unemployment?

3. What has been happening to inequality?

He argued that if all three had been declining from high levels, then, beyond doubt, it could be said that development had been taking place. Later he added a fourth factor - whether a country had increased its self-reliance in economic as well as in technological, social and cultural affairs, although he failed to adequately address the environmental dimension.

For the philosopher Denis Goulet, there are three goals which should underpin development:

1. Life Sustenance (food, health, shelter, protection etc.)

2. Esteem (the promotion of respect for all)

3. Freedom (not only in political, but also in social, cultural, economic and spiritual matters).

Thus, for Goulet, we need to be concerned about the values and the ethics base of development.

DEVELOPMENT - A SHORTHAND DEFINITION

Development

Development *is about people*

Development *is about people making choices*

Development *is about people making choices based on values*

Development *is about people making choices based on values about the quality of life.*

In its 1994 Human Development Report, the United Nations Development Programme incorporated a major change in emphasis within the concept of development by presenting an overall definition in terms of human security. This concept was defined at seven different levels reflecting many of the debates and approaches of recent years:

Economic Security - a basic secure income (not automatically linked to employment), social safety nets for the poor, access to land or adequate credit, fair wages and reasonable working conditions, adequate housing etc.

Food Security - physical and economic access to food, improved storage and distribution systems, programmes focused upon those most at risk etc.

Health Security - adequate nutrition, clean safe water and sanitation, basic healthcare facilities with equal access for all, investment in health, focus on most vulnerable groups etc.

Environmental Security - policies to protect the environment, provision of clean, safe environments, action against pollution, awareness of future consequences of current actions etc.

Personal Security - protection against the violence of the state, other states, other groups of people (ethnic violence), other individuals, of men towards women etc.

Community Security - protection from communal or ethnic attack, protection for indigenous people and cultures etc.

Political Security - protection against political repression, torture, violation of human rights, the right to vote etc.

In introducing the notion of human security as a comprehensive overview of development, the UNDP commented:

"Human security is therefore not a defensive concept - the way territorial or military security is. Instead human security is an integrative concept.
It acknowledges the universalism of life claims...It is embedded in a notion of solidarity among people. It cannot be brought about through force, with armies standing against armies.
It can happen only if we agree that development must involve all people."

Rostow and his colleagues identified these stages in the history of various countries and, where the pattern did not fit, identified intermediate or alternative stages. In the case of India, for example, which appeared stuck between stages 2 and 3, they identified a *"stage of long delay"*. In Rostow's model, development was seen as equivalent to the stage of high mass consumption and applicable to all countries irrespective of history or culture. It was also assumed that the United States had achieved this last phase of development and was thus the model which others should aspire to.

This view of development was extended in modernisation theory, which sought to isolate those key factors which could help the developing world to repeat the experience of western societies. The emphasis was on identifying the economic, social, psychological and political characteristics of developed societies through which, it was assumed, they had developed and then applying them to the Third World. Western Europe was viewed as developed and thus offered a model or image towards which developing societies should strive. Since the drive for individual wealth and prosperity was seen as the engine of growth in Europe, then development strategy was designed to promote wealth-generating behaviour among individuals.

Emphasis was placed on industry rather than agriculture, urban growth in place of rural, the promotion of consumption and personal wealth before social or collective well-being. It was assumed that if Gross National Product (GNP) grew, then the well-being of each person would inevitably rise also. Developing countries seemed set to re-create the European experience of development and would soon (and, inevitably) achieve modernisation or development. Despite the obvious flaws of such an approach, this view of development, or, at least the assumptions which underlie it, still informs much of development practice today even though development theory has moved on. The same can be said about much media coverage, public discussion and, in some cases, aid.

Development as structural change

Building on the work of earlier thinkers, many Third World writers and movements, particularly from the 1960s onwards, began to put forward a fundamentally different view of development and, crucially, underdevelopment. While accepting many of the arguments of those concerned with distributive justice, they argued that mechanisms to redistribute income or to overcome underdevelopment were doomed to failure unless they addressed directly the underlying economic and social structures of society. They argue that underdevelopment is not the *"original condition"*

Debating Development and Underdevelopment

"Development must be redefined as an attack on the chief evils of the world today: malnutrition, disease, illiteracy, slums, unemployment and inequality. Measured in aggregate growth rates, development has been a great success. But measured in terms of jobs, justice and the elimination of poverty, it has been a failure or only a partial success."

Paul Streeten, World Development Institute, 1985.

"Underdevelopment, far from constituting a state of backwardness prior to capitalism, is rather a consequence and a particular form of capitalist development known as dependent capitalism."

Political Scientist Theotonio Dos Santos, 1969.

"Normally, development theorists should be trained to test their models by observing what they do to people, since human welfare is theoretically the goal of development. 'People' in this context means not the well-off, well-fed elites but poor and hungry majorities whose fundamental needs are presently not being met. When the reigning development model, or paradigm, has been applied for decades and has failed to alleviate human suffering and oppression - or, worse still, has intensified them - it should be ripe for revolution."

Political Scientist Susan George, 1988.

"Whenever you are in doubt...apply the following test. Recall the face of the poorest and weakest man whom you have seen, and ask yourself if the step you contemplate is going to be of any use to him. Will he gain anything by it? Will it restore him to a control over his own life and destiny?"

Mahatma Gandhi

"The process of development consisted...of moving from traditional society, which was taken as the polar opposite of the modern type, through a series of stages of development derived essentially from the history of Europe, North America and Japan - to modernity, that is, approximately the United States of the 1950s."

Writer John Toye, 1987.

"The challenge of development ... is to improve the quality of life. Especially in the world's poor countries, a better quality of life generally calls for higher incomes - but it involves much more.
It encompasses as ends in themselves better education, higher standards of health and nutrition, less poverty, a cleaner environment, more equality of opportunity, greater individual freedom, and a richer cultural life."

The World Bank, 1991.

"Underdevelopment as it is encountered today in Spanish America and elsewhere is the product of history... Underdevelopment is part of the same process which produced development...it is only from an examination of the forces of history i.e. of the historical uses of power, both political and economic - that one may obtain an insight into the origin of underdevelopment."

Historian Keith Griffin, 1979.

"Sustainable development is development that meets the needs of the present without compromising the ability of future generations to meet their owns needs...meeting essential needs depends in part on achieving full growth potential, and sustainable development clearly requires economic growth... it can be consistent with economic growth provided the content of the growth reflects the broad principles of sustainability and non-exploitation of others."

World Commission on Environment and Development (Brundtland Commission), 1987.

"In other words, sustainable development is economic growth that has somehow been made more equitable and environmentally careful. However, since growth itself is not sustainable, the concept (of sustainable development) is a dangerous contradiction in terms."

Economist Richard Douthwaite, 1992.

"It is no use offering us tired old trade-offs and crooked-looking production functions whenever we talk about income distribution and employment. It is no use dusting off old theories and polishing up old ideas and asking us to go and try them again. It is time that we take a fresh look at the entire theory and practice of development"

Economist Mahbub ul Haq, former Pakistan Planning Minister, 1976.

"Development = economic growth + social change"

Former UN Secretary General U Thant, 1962.

"Sustainable human development is development that not only generates economic growth but distributes its benefits equitably; that regenerates the environment rather than destroying it; that empowers people rather than marginalising them. It gives priority to the poor, enlarging their choices and opportunities, and provides for their participation in decisions affecting them. It is development that is pro-poor, pro-nature, pro-jobs, pro-democracy, pro-women, and pro-children."

UNDP Administrator, James Gustave Speth, 1994.

of any society but rather represents a distortion of the development process as a result of human intervention in both the past and present. Development and underdevelopment are therefore part of the same process and are seen as arising from the dominant economic and social system in different parts of the world.

In this view, development has come to be defined primarily as economic, political, social and cultural independence with an explicit commitment to social justice and to equality in the distribution of wealth and resources. Power and power relations come to play a central role in development. Lack of political, social, economic or cultural power or gross inequality in the distribution of resources are therefore seen as the prime characteristics of underdevelopment.

Historically, there have been many variants in this approach, as indeed is the case in all other approaches to the development debate. Development as structural change has been a very strong element in the philosophy of liberation movements; it has long been a part of world-wide socialist thinking and is a central tenet of Marxism; it forms a part of radical religious thinking and philosophy and it also informs some variants of the women's movement and the Green movement today.

Development as liberation

For many writers in various religious and cultural traditions, development has come to be defined as *"liberation"*. They have emphasised the ethical aspects of the development debate. The emphasis is on the integrity and humanity of each person and on the creation of circumstances in which such traits can be realised. In this view, development comes to mean liberation from those forces - economic, political or social - which obstruct the development of people. The traditional view of growth is seriously challenged because it is argued that over-concern with material well-being creates just as many problems as it solves. Even the so-called *"developed"* world is seen as under- or over-developed or even mal-developed. For

Figure 1:1

SELECTED COUNTRIES: SOME DEVELOPMENT INDICATORS

Country	GNP per capita 1993 (US)	HDI Ranking 1995	Life Expectancy 1993 (years)	Under 5 Mortality Rate (per 1000 births)
Mozambique	90	159	46.5	282
Bangladesh	220	146	52.2	122
China	490	94	70.5	43
Georgia	580	66	73.0	28
Bolivia	760	113	60.5	114
Romania	1,140	72	69.9	29
Jordan	1,190	98	67.3	27
El Salvador	1,320	112	65.2	60
South Africa	2,980	93	62.2	69
Malaysia	3,140	57	70.4	17
Gabon	4,960	114	52.9	154
Greece	7,390	25	77.3	10
Ireland	**13,000**	**21**	**75.0**	**7**
United Kingdom	**18,060**	**10**	**75.8**	**8**
United States	24,740	8	75.6	10
Switzerland	35,760	2	77.8	8

Attempting to measure the immearusable - development

The need to design a universally acceptable measurement of development which includes social, political, environmental and cultural factors is obvious, although in practice it has proved very difficult to achieve. In recent years there has been renewed interest and debate around this issue, especially amongst various UN agencies and academic commentators. Some of the debates around these issues are briefly introduced below. They do not supplant discussions as to the relative value of different definitions of development or how it is best achieved.

GNP and its critics

Given that economic well-being is so central to development, the most traditional measure of development has been Gross National Product per capita (GNP per capita). There are a number of major problems associated with this measurement of development. Chief amongst them is that it tells us nothing about the actual or real distribution of wealth amongst people in an economy and it does not include wealth generated in the unofficial or "informal" sector. Thus while it could be said that GNP per capita is a real measure of economic development at the national level, it is purely theoretical at the individual level. This, however, is a criticism levelled at any "average" measurement.

Another criticism of GNP as a measure (and, by implication, of all economic measurements) is that it assumes that economic wealth equals development and it takes no account of social, political and cultural dimensions. As part of an attempt to introduce the social dimension, the Overseas Development Council of the US Government introduced, in 1977, the Physical Quality of Life Index (PQLI). The PQLI measures life expectancy, infant mortality rates and literacy levels. These are measured on a scale from 0 to 100 - 0 being the worst performance in each category in 1950 and 100 representing the best performance expected for the year 2000. These indices are then averaged.

UNICEF

UNICEF, on the other hand has argued strongly for the use of the death rate of children under 5 years (per 1000 live births - U5MR) as a key measure of development as it indicates the trend with regard to the welfare of children. UNICEF argues that the measure has a number of distinct advantages:

* It measures the end result of the development process rather than one of its inputs e.g. school enrolment rates.

* The U5MR also reflects the end product of a number of inputs such as the nutritional health of mothers, levels of immunisation, availability of maternal health services etc.

* The U5MR is more accurate as a general measure because it is less affected by issues of wealth and poverty.

While the U5MR is a vital component in the measurement of development, it has not become a universal measure because of its limited scope and the fact that it is largely focused on comparisons between, rather than within, countries.

Human Development Index

In 1990, the United Nations Development Programme (UNDP) published its first Human Development Report which introduced the Human Development Index (HDI). The HDI combined life expectancy, educational attainment (adult literacy rate and mean years of schooling) and income (purchasing power expressed in parity dollars) into a composite index. This allowed for comparative studies of both economic and social dimensions of development between countries. The 1993 HDI also began to examine the situation between different groups within countries.

Despite all of this work, the Human Development Report for 1994 argued:

> *"A priority in the years ahead must be to improve human development statistics - at country, regional and international levels. The statistical map of human development still has too many blanks. Too many indicators are missing. Too much information is outdated. And too many statistics are not collected or analysed separately for different population groups - for men and women, for urban and rural, for rich and poor (particularly the growing populations of urban poor) or for different races or ethnic groups."*

Human Rights

In 1992, Charles Humana developed yet another measurement of development based upon human rights concerns. He attempted to include those rights which could be accurately defined and measured. This would, he argued, not only deepen our appreciation of another key dimension but would also help to establish a base line for monitoring human rights. On the basis of his work, as updated by the **New Internationalist Magazine,** the 10 countries with the best human rights record in 1993 were - *Finland, Aotearoa/New Zealand, Denmark, Germany, the Netherlands, Czechoslovakia, Hungary, Norway, Belgium and Switzerland* - while those with the worst record were - *Burma, Iraq, Sudan, North Korea, China, Iran, Libya, Angola, Afghanistan and Saudi Arabia.*

Who is measuring development is another key issue which needs to be addressed.

for writers in this tradition, societies which have highly developed material bases but which lose touch with the spiritual dimension are seen as maldeveloped. Many crucial human traits have been lost or abandoned in such *"mal-development"*. The development philosopher, Denis Goulet, argues that because people in many parts of the developed world have so much material well-being, they have to strive hard to retain their humanity.

This view of development has been echoed in liberation theologies which have highlighted not only the economic, social and cultural aspects of development but also the spiritual and cultural. The rejection of growth and materialism for its own sake reflects the concerns of many major world religions and philosophies for many years.

Gender, Culture and the Environment

In recent years, writers and commentators on development issues have had to take increasing account of the views and arguments of the women's movement and the environmental movement. This has happened as a direct result of the growth in numbers of both movements and of an explicit focus upon the impact of development thinking and strategies upon women and the environment. In addition, this trend has strengthened a growing focus upon groups who have been significantly absent from mainstream development debates. It is no longer possible for development strategies to ignore the gender, environmental or cultural dimensions of various policies.

While such foci contribute to a more rounded and sensitive definition and concept of development, they have also posed many fundamental questions about the underlying assumptions and perceptions of much of development theory. They have, for instance, highlighted some of the hidden and, previously unexplored, costs of economic development models (e.g. the *"deferred costs"* of environmental damage, the *"hidden"* labour of women or the inter-generational dimension of the idea of environmental sustainability has challenged the *"here and now"* approach of many). Those addressing the cultural dimensions of development have also contributed to this challenge in emphasising the cultural imperialism of much of development theory and the *"Euro/Ethno - centrism"* of much thinking and writing.

A NOTE ON NUMBERS

Discussions of development often involve the use of very large numbers - millions and billions are commonplace in the vocabularies of politicians and economists. It is worth trying to visualise a million to get some idea of the reality. If a million people stood in line one metre apart the line would be about 1,000 km long, so the population of Ireland would stretch across the Atlantic, and that of the UK more than once around the world at the equator. If these people walked past you at the rate of one per second, a million people would take about twelve days, Ireland nearly two months and the UK a couple of years.

Counting Money

At a national or international scale, money soon gets into billions (thousands of millions). A billion US dollars would give every person in Birmingham $1,000 each, everyone in Ireland $250 or in the UK $20, the USA $5, China $1 or the world 20 cents each.

Sums of money can be presented in different ways depending on the image you want to give. Suppose the UK has a monthly trade deficit of £2,500,000,000 and in the same month the government announces a new grant to inner cities of £1,400,000. How will the government present this information? ***"There was a trade deficit of only £2.5 billion this month" or "a deficit of £2,500 million" or "We have agreed a new grant of £1.4 million for inner city community projects" or "a grant of £0.0014 billion"?*** *The way information is collected and presented can be highly political.*

Roger Robinson, Development Education Centre, Birmingham

Learning from the Human Development Index

According to the Human Development Index, the top ten performers in human development between 1960 and 1992 were - Malaysia, Botswana, Republic of Korea, Tunisia, Thailand, Syrian Arab Republic, Turkey, China, Portugal and the Islamic Republic of Iran.

Examining the relationship between the HDI and GNP per capita is revealing. In 1994, some countries - Angola, Guinea, Namibia, Saudi Arabia and the United Arab Emirates - had a world ranking based upon income which was far ahead of the HDI ranking showing that they still have considerable potential to translate income into improved well-being. Other countries - China, Colombia, Costa Rica, Cuba, Guyana, Madagascar and Sri Lanka - had a HDI ranking ahead of that for GNP thus showing that they have made a more judicious use of income.

The HDI is a composite index measuring three indicators (life expectancy, educational attainment and income)- so some countries may do well on one index but not so well on another. For example, Switzerland ranks number 2 on the HDI but only 21st on tertiary education enrolment while the Republic of Korea ranks number 4 on the HDI but only 18th when it comes to life expectancy.

Examining income disparities within countries in the 1994 report is also revealing. In industrialised countries, Belgium and Germany do relatively well while Canada, Switzerland and Australia do not. Within the developing world, Brazil and Botswana perform poorly while China, Sri Lanka and Jamaica do relatively better.

One of the most significant differences revealed in the HDI is that between men and women with the former doing better on almost every socio-economic indicator, except life expectancy. According to the 1994 Human Development Report, all countries treat women worse than men but some countries do less badly than others. Japan, Canada, Switzerland and Hong Kong fare badly when gender disparity is examined whereas Sweden, Denmark, Finland and New Zealand do relatively better. In industrialised countries, gender discrimination shows up mainly in employment and wages whereas, in developing countries, discrimination is more broadly based in employment, education, nutrition and health.

The HDI can also illustrate trends and issues within and between countries. For example, the disparity between blacks and whites in South Africa is four times larger than in the United States; regional disparities between the North-east and the South in Brazil are considerable - 17 years in life expectancy, 33% in adult literacy and 40% in GDP per capita, and regional disparities in Nigeria are amongst the worst in the world.

Like all attempts to measure development, the HDI has serious limitations which must be kept in mind. Its origins are political in that it represented an attempt to refocus attention on health and education - in place of the traditional economic focus. As with all average indicators, it runs the risk of avoiding examining differences between classes of people rather than countries or regions. The HDI highlights relative rather than absolute development thus under-appreciating the progress of poorer countries.

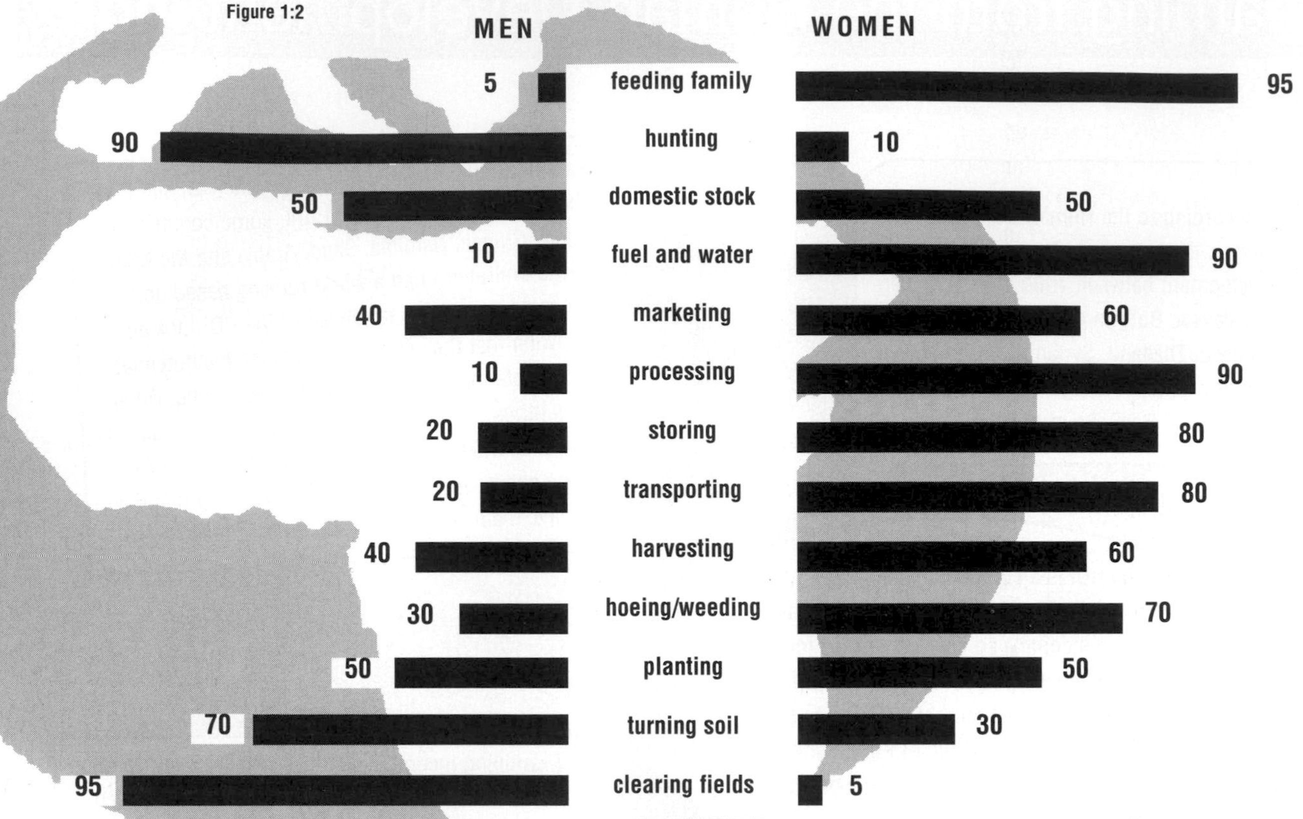

Source: Commonwealth Secretariat

Debating Keywords and Ideas

Brazilian educator and activist, Paulo Freire has reminded us frequently of the importance of the name we give to a process or event - naming something is an intensely political act. No-one should therefore be surprised that there are vigorous debates underway for many years as to how to label the poorer countries of the world. The choice of labels reflects a host of perceptions, values, understandings and positions. There are apparently purely technical phrases such as ***"middle income"***, ***"newly industrialised"***, etc.; there are other, less neutral phrases such as ***"developing"***, ***"industrialising"***, ***"North-South"*** etc., and there are overtly political phrases such as ***"Third World"*** or ***"colonised world"***. The history of the debate about what to call the poor of the world tells us much about the politics of development itself.

Today, the phrase which is most often used is ***"developing world"*** or ***"developing countries"*** - a phrase which has a double implication. One, it gives the impression that the Western world is already developed and that the poorer world is now developing in the same direction. Many object to this phrase as they believe it contradicts the reality for many of the world's poor, who have increased in number while the gap between rich and poor worlds continues to widen. Two, the phrase ***"developing world"*** denies a reality described by many writers and labelled by Andre Gunder Frank and others as ***"underdeveloping"***.

Other phrases which have been used in recent decades include ***"primitive"***, ***"backward"***, ***"undeveloped"***, ***"less developed"***, ***"emerging"***, ***"rapidly developing"*** and ***"industrialising"***. More recently the phrase ***"North-South"*** has become popular. Clearly all of the phrases capture something of the essence of the debate but they also reflect the values of those proposing them. Various writers and researchers have argued for a division into 4 worlds (Wolf-Philips) or 6 worlds (O'Connor) while the World Bank divides the world into 5 categories - low-income countries, middle-income countries, industrial market economies, capital surplus oil exporters and non-market industrial economies. Other models and perspectives have added to the growing list of labels (and the analyses which lie behind them) including ***"Core and Periphery"*** which refers to geographical and economic inequality both within and between countries and ***"Majority / Minority Worlds"*** which is based upon identifying people and social or economic groups rather than countries.

The writers in 75:25 make use of various phrases reflecting their own preferences and understandings. In this chapter, I have made use of the phrase ***"Third World".*** For many this phrase is unacceptable for a variety of reasons. Firstly, it might imply some kind of development ***"pecking order"*** - first, second and third; secondly, it lumps together very economically diverse countries such as Brazil, Ethiopia and Bangladesh; and thirdly, it pre-supposes two other ***"worlds"*** - one of which no longer exists. In response to this it is often pointed out that the phrase ***"Third World"*** (coined in France in the 1950s) was never seen as an economic category - rather it was envisaged as an essentially political phrase - one which united together those who were opposed to colonialism. As one writer, Peter Worsley put it:

> *"What the Third World originally was, then, is clear: it was the non-aligned world. It was also a world of poor countries. Their poverty was the outcome of a more fundamental identity: that they had all been colonised."*

In defence of the phrase ***"Third World",*** a number of other points can be made. Firstly, there is a pressing need to keep the agenda of the poorest peoples of the world to the forefront of political debate and discussion, particularly at a time when events in Eastern Europe threaten to downgrade it. Secondly, there is a tendency in many currently fashionable phrases to negate the distinctiveness and specificity of specifically ***"Third World"*** issues and to lump everything into one big development basket. Thirdly, many people of the poor world often refer to themselves as the ***"Third World"*** and this fact should not be lost sight of. It is also useful to remember the fact that the phrase is well understood popularly in the industrialised world. Finally, the original intent in the use of the phrase ***"Third World"*** - drawing attention to the disparity in the distribution and use of world power - is still entirely relevant. In fact, real power may now be concentrated even more in the hands of the Western world than it was in the 1950s.

In conclusion it may be worth quoting two Third World sources on this issue of definition. One is Algerian writer Franz Fanon (author of the classic **Wretched of the Earth**):

> *"We know that it (the Third World) is not a homogeneous world; we know too that enslaved peoples are still to be found there; together with some who have achieved a similcrum of phoney independence; others who are still fighting to obtain sovereignty and others again who have obtained complete freedom, but who live under the constant menace of imperialist aggression...Thus the unity of the Third World is not yet achieved. It is a work in progress..."*

The other is Egyptian economist Ismail-Sabri Abdalla:

> *"All those nations which, during the process of formation of the existing world order, did not become rich and industrialised...A historical perspective is essential to understand what is the Third World, because by definition it is the periphery of the system produced by the expansion of world capital."*

For additional discussion on this issue see chapter 3.

The debate about development is a debate about people not things

DEVELOPMENT - SOME REALITIES

"We too are falling..."

"In the black community of Vertente, in the Brazilian North East, 60 families live crowded onto 5 hectares of drought-stricken land. It is April, and six months since the last rain fell. The only water supply is a trickle of a stream, where it can take four hours to fill a bucket. Dusk is falling and a shining green humming bird hovers in front of an enormous purple bud on one of the few banana trees that keep the community going. As it grows dark, sounds seem louder: children's voices, birdsong, the rustle of banana leaves. 'The banana trees are falling, because they only have one leg', says one old man. 'A man has two legs to support him, but now we too are falling.' The pot-bellied children gather round to dance, as the adults talk of their endless struggle for farms big enough to feed their families. At the moment they are sharecropping, meaning a large portion of whatever pitiful crop they harvest must go to the landlord. There is good soil lying idle nearby, but they dare not farm it for fear of reprisals. A greater proportion of Vertente's children die than anywhere else in North-eastern Brazil.

Duncan Green **Faces of Latin America** (1991), London, Latin American Bureau.

COMMENT

Many poor communities throughout the North East of Brazil have infant mortality rates comparable to the worst for Sub-Saharan Africa, in this the world's 9th largest economy. In recent years hundreds of rural workers leaders have been assassinated for organising and lobbying in favour of rural dwellers rights.

Progress for women is progress for all...

"The Kassassi Women's Agricultural Development Association (KWADA) started in 1976 as a small-scale initiative by a group of village women in a poor and isolated area of Sierra Leone. The main occupation of the village is subsistence farming, and many young people have left for the towns. In an effort to create opportunities for their children, and to increase their farming revenue, a group of women looked at the potential of a nearby area of communal swampland. They joined forces to drain and clear it, dividing about 80 acres into individual farms to provide food for their families. Another 20 acres is farmed communally on a rota basis, growing rice, groundnuts and cassava. The communal land is seen as central to the members' livelihood. The sale of the first harvest provided funds for second and subsequent cultivations. Now the produce is communally owned and sold at a fair price to members in the 'lean season' when no crops grow.

Although the association is run by women, it includes the whole community in its projects, in particular girls and boys who can earn money to pay their school fees by working on the farms. For the women involved, the benefits are not purely economic. 'Women are more vocal, and consider themselves as part and parcel of society, getting involved in the decision-making of the village.' This is the view of Sally Formah-Kamara, who has helped the project establish links with the group Scottish Education and Action for Development who have established a 1% Women World-wide Campaign."

Women and Work, Susan Bullock (1994), London, Zed.

COMMENT

In both adult literacy and school enrolment, the gaps between women and men were halved between 1970 and 1990 in the Third World. Women's literacy increased from 54% of the male rate in 1970 to 74% in 1990.

"Before, it was a silent life..."

"Before, it was a silent life between men and women. They never spoke to one another, not even husband and wife. Neighbouring women would pass the evenings chatting and spinning, and you would talk with other women at the wells or the grinding stone. Women never spoke in the presence of men: they'd be ashamed and above all scared that they'd be beaten...So women kept their ideas to themselves, even if these would have been a help to the community. Women are never allowed to inherit the land of their husband. As this is normal here, women never complain, thinking 'that's how things are'. Nowadays, the radio is a major source of information...

We now have women who preside over meetings in the village, in the local area and even in the towns. They have all been democratically elected... Development projects have helped women greatly in their work, through meetings and by helping them to visit different areas and exchange ideas about different social structures."

62 years old Fatimata Sawadogo from Ouahigouya in Burkina Faso, **At the Desert's Edge: Oral Histories from the Sahel,** quoted in Cross, N. and R. Barker (Eds.) (1992), London, Panos Publications.

COMMENT

According to the United Nations, the adult literacy rate has increased by more than one-third since 1970 but there are still 1 billion adults who are illiterate and 600 million of those are women. Illiteracy rates amongst women in rural areas are highest, sometimes as high as 85%.

"THE GAMINES OFFER A PARABLE..."

"In the press of pedestrians on Bogota's main artery, Carrera 10, a smart young professional raises an arm to halt a cab. His palm stretches out and his grip on the neat, leather-cased folding umbrella he carries is loosened. Suddenly, like a greyhound from its trap, a tattered, barefoot figure in a jacket three sizes too big shoots out, weaves under the man's arm, wrenches free the umbrella and is away...

That was the first glimpse I caught of Fabio, just eleven years old, whose innocent cartoon-like face under a basin of raven black hair looks three years younger still. He left home when he was eight because his stepfather used to beat him with an iron bar. Since then he has been one of Bogota's army of five to ten thousand - no one knows exactly how many - urchins or gamines, who live, sleep, beg, sing, steal, fight, love, hate and often die on the streets of a heartless city. In this naked confrontation of the poor with the affluence of the rich, the gamines offer a parable for all Third World cities."

Inside the Third World,Paul Harrison (1993), London, Penguin (3rd edition).

COMMENT

The United Nations estimates that by the year 2000, over 2.1 billion, or 66%, of the urban dwellers of the world will live in the Third World. If current trends continue, only 2 of the world's 20 largest cities (Tokyo and New York) will be in the developed world in the year 2000.

THE WATER THAT BRINGS NEW LIFE

"In the coastal villages of Kwale district in Kenya, women have, for many years, carried out the daily chore of collecting and carrying water from the local wells. The work is backbreaking and often dangerous. Each family has an average of eight members requiring a canful of water each. The average distance from village to well is nearly 3 kilometres. Often the water is contaminated and also it frequently dries up.

Since the mid 1970's, a local Kenyan organisation, KWAHO (Kenyan Water for Health Organisation), has been active in organising a community-based project to provide over 100 boreholes yielding reliable and clean water. This is part of a broader Kenyan government project to provide water for all by the year 2000 and to ensure its benefits for all, especially women.

According to a local worker Rose Maluma, 'Water is life - almost everything revolves around it. If the water is not clean, it is bound to undermine the people's health. And if the people aren't strong enough to work, they cannot contribute to development. It's as simple as that'.

While the Kenyan Government is providing engineering and technical solutions to water needs, it is not equipped to deal with the social and cultural aspects of water and sanitation provision. This is where KWAHO becomes involved. It emphasises self-help and strong community involvement. Without it, they argue, projects are less likely to satisfy real local needs. It has helped organise and support local community involvement in the project.

Apart altogether from the installation of water pumps, the project has also involved health and education workshops. KWAHO does not underestimate the problems of achieving its goals.

Based on chapter 6 of Harry Bhaskara et al (1989) **Against All Odds: Breaking the Poverty Trap,** London, Panos.

COMMENT

The provision of clean, safe water throughout the Third World has increased by more than two-thirds over the past twenty years.

"NOW, IN SOUTH-EAST ASIA, WE SAW IT AGAIN..."

"Two months earlier Eric Pepper and I had followed Pope John Paul on his return to Poland, where we had seen Auschwitz for the first time. Now, in south-east Asia, we saw it again. On a clear, sunny day with flocks of tiny swifts, the bravest of birds, rising and falling almost to the ground, we drove along a narrow dirt road at the end of which was a former primary school, called Tuol Sleng. During the Pol Pot years this school was run by a Khmer Gestapo, 'S-21', which divided the classrooms into an 'interrogation unit' and a 'torture and massacre unit'. People were mutilated on iron beds and we found their blood and tufts of their hair still on the floor. Between December 1975 and June 1978 at least 12,000 people died slow deaths here: a fact not difficult to confirm because the killers, like the Nazis, were pedantic in their sadism. They photographed their victims before and after they tortured and killed them and horrific images now looked at us from walls; some had tried to smile for the photographer, as if he might take pity on them and save them. Names and ages, even height and weight, were recorded. We found, as in Auschwitz, one room filled to the ceiling with victims' clothes and shoes, including those of many children.

However, unlike Auschwitz, Tuol Sleng was primarily a political death centre..."

Heroes, John Pilger (1986), London, Pan.

COMMENT

During the four months April-July 1994, over 1 million Rwandans were murdered and a further 2.5 million forced to flee their homes due to political conflict in Rwanda.

A NEW FOCUS: THE POOREST 40%

A hypothetical country with a population of ten people in which five people receive an income of $100 per year and the other five receive $10,000 a year would have an average annual income of over $5,000 a year. Per capita GNP - the conventional indicator of a country's economic development - may therefore say very little about the standard of living of the poor. If, as UNICEF has recently argued, the development effort should be refocused on the poorest groups, then better indicators of their economic well-being are needed to guide and measure that effort.

From this point of view, the GNP per capita of the poorest 40% of a country's population would clearly be a more meaningful figure. Unfortunately, such a statistic does not exist for the majority of countries.

Development as Displacement - a Mozambican Refugee Camp in Malawi

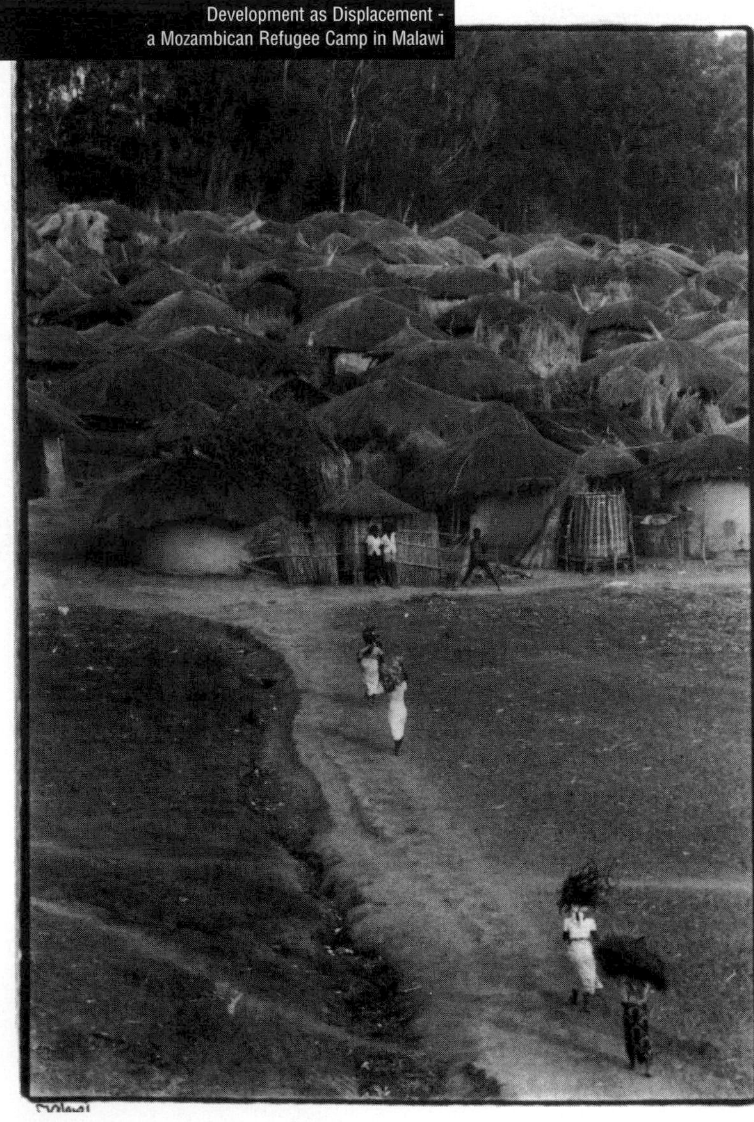

Figure 1:3 uses the available information on the 1992 per capita GNP of the poorest 40% in 16 nations. Column 1 shows the country's overall average GNP per capita, Column 2 shows GNP per capita of the poorest 40%.

As an indicator of economic development focused on the poor, the table quickly shows its value:

- It shows, for example, that although the overall GNP per capita of Kenya is double that of Bangladesh, there is no difference between the two countries when we look at the per capita GNP of their poorest 40%
- Similarly, Brazil has an overall GNP per capita which is 2.5 times that of the Dominican Republic, but the per capita GNP of the Dominican Republic is almost equal to that of Brazil.
- Venezuela's overall GNP per capita is 4 times as high as that of Bolivia but the % of per capita GNP to the poorest 40% in each country is about the same.
- Mexico's overall GNP per capita is a little higher than that of Venezuela, but the per capita GNP of Mexico's poorest 40% is less than that of Venezuela.

Figure 1:3

COUNTRY	GNP PER CAPITA IN 1992 US$	% TO LOWEST 40% OF HOUSES (1981 - 1992)
Hong Kong	15,710	16.2
Argentina	6,170	
Korea	7,220	19.7
Chile	2,780	10.5
Venezuela	2,920	14.3
Mexico	3,510	11.9
Brazil	2,810	7.0
Peru	1,350	14.1
Dominican Rep.	1,070	12.1
Indonesia	680	20.8
China	480	17.4
Guatemala	1,000	7.9
Bolivia	750	15.3
Bangladesh	220	22.9
Uganda	180	20.6
Kenya	330	10.1

Souce: UNDP (1995). Human Development Report, Oxford University Press.

THE SEVEN DEADLY SINS OF DEVELOPMENT

In 1989 UNICEF published a list of seven deadly sins which it argued were gaining ground in the 1980s despite the hard won lessons of the 1960s and the 1970s. These were:

Development without infrastructure

Most of the cost-effective techniques now available, from immunisation to oral rehydration therapy, new seed varieties to hand pumps, are of little value without a reliable delivery mechanism for informing and supporting the majority in using them.

Development without participation

Sustained development ultimately depends on enhancing people's own capacity to improve their own lives and to take control over their own destinies.

Development without women

The women of the developing world are responsible for producing and marketing most of its crops; they also carry the main responsibility for food preparation and home-making, for water and fuel, for nutrition and health care, for hygiene and for the education of the young. Yet in development assistance efforts to date, most of the education and training, the technology and the inputs, the investments and the loans, have gone to men.

Development without environment

Fifteen years ago, it was widely thought that the environment was an industrialised world problem, a function of affluence, and of little relevance to the developing world. Today, the deforestation of lands, the erosion of soils, the silting of lakes and rivers, the new propensity to drought and flood, and industrial disasters, have shown that the environment is also a Third World problem.

Development without the poor

The challenge of reaching the very poorest is the greatest challenge in social development. Over the last ten years, almost every initiative - large or small - has come up against the same problem of reaching the unreached. Even the most serious and politically difficult attempts at shifting priorities in favour of the poor - via primary schools or adult literacy campaigns, rural clinics or supplementary feeding programmes - have often failed to reach substantial numbers among the very poorest groups.

Development without the do-able

Experts in the various disciplines of development, who must take much of the credit for the knowledge base now available, must also take some of the blame for the failure to implement that knowledge on a significant scale. It is the task of shaping today's knowledge into plans which are capable of attracting what political will is available; politicians must be handed not the blunt instrument of undifferentiated knowledge but the sharp axe of the 'do-able'.

Development without mobilisation

The task of development in the decade ahead is, in large part, the task of putting today's knowledge at the disposal of the majority. A communications revolution has given the developing world an unprecedented capacity to put new knowledge at the disposal of the majority.

UNICEF argues that respecting these principles and avoiding the seven deadly sins could double the effectiveness of development projects in the decades ahead.

Source: UNICEF (1989) **State of the World's Children Report,** Oxford University Press.

Figure 1:4

FOUR DECADES OF PROGRESS

INCOME

GNP per person (1980) dollars	1950	1980	1993
Industrial countries	4,130	10,660	23,090
Middle-income countries	640	1,580	3,425
Low-income countries	170	250	380

Average annual growth (%)	1950-60	1960-80	1980-93
Industrial countries	3.1	3.3	2.2
Middle-income countries	2.5	3.3	0.6
Low-income countries	0.6	1.7	3.7

HEALTH

Life expectancy at birth (years)	1950	1993
Industrial countries	67	76
Middle-income countries	48	69
Low-income countries	37	62

EDUCATION

Adult literacy rate(%)	1950	1976	1990
Industrial countries	95	99	99
Middle-income countries	48	72	82
Low-income countries	22	39	59

▼ References

Susan George (1976) **How the Other Half Dies,** London, Penguin.

Denis Goulet (1971) **The Cruel Choice: A New Concept in the Theory of Development,** New York, Athenum Press

Duncan Green **Faces of Latin America** (1991), London, Latin American Bureau.

Paul Harrison (1993) **Inside the Third World,** London, Penguin (3rd edition).

Janet Henshall Momsen (1991) **Women and Development in the Third World,** London, Routledge.

Instituto del Tercer Mundo (1993/94) **Third World Guide,** Montevideo.

M. Todaro (1994) **Economic Development,** London, Longman

United Nations Development Programme (1994) **Human Development Report,** Oxford University Press

UNICEF (1994 and 1995) **State of the World's Children Report,** Oxford University Press.

Paul Vallelly (1992) **Promised Lands: Stories of Power and Poverty in the Third World,** London, Fount/Christian Aid.

Kevin Watkins (1995) **The Oxfam Poverty Report,** Oxford, Oxfam.

NEW WORLD ORDERS?
The Third World Since 1945.

Colm Regan

"If the 1960 were characterised by the great hope of seeing an irreversible process of development launched throughout what came to be called the Third World...the present age is one of disillusionment"

Samir Amin ***Maldevelopment,*** (1990).

Introduction

The period from the beginning of the sixteenth to the end of the nineteenth century witnessed the emergence of an inter-related world system, tied together as never before and divided into two distinct groups of nations, those of the dominant North and those of the dominated South. There were few areas or peoples within what became the Third World who were not radically affected by this new world order. Their economies, social structures, political processes, cultural traditions, environments, religions and development paths were fundamentally altered and, in most cases, deformed. Some of the specific consequences of colonialism are commented on below by Galeano, Nehru and Udo. The reality of this *"New World"* is well-illustrated in the case of the island of Java which became the *"property"* of the Dutch East India Company and, in the words of local historian K.M. Panikkar *"The island of Java became a plantation of the Company, and the relations between the sovereign, which the Company now claimed to be, and its subjects were in substance those of planter and coolie, in which the former was not merely the employer of labour, but also the authority invested with the rights of life and death...*

...Java had become a vast coffee estate...It was a far reaching revolution that the plantation-system introduced...Previously, the Dutch had only been merchants buying the spices and rice...The changeover into a plantation-economy involved the actual exploitation of labour...in fact, 'estate-management' over a whole country..."

FOR SALE:

- One half-breed negress of the Cabinda race, for the sum of 430 pesos. Knows rudiments of sewing and ironing.
- Leeches, recently arrived from Europe: prime quality. Four, five and six vintes apiece.
- Carriage. Will sell for five hundred patacones, or exchange for one negress.
- One negress, thirteen or fourteen years old, free of vices; of the Bangala race.
- Small mulatto, eleven years old, knows rudiments of tailoring.
- Essence of sasaparilla, two pesos per bottle.
- One nursing female. To be sold without offspring, has good and plentiful milk.
- A lion, tame as a dog, will eat anything; a bureau and chest, both of mahogany.
- Maid, free of vices and disease, of the Conga race, approximately eighteen years of age; also a piano and other pieces of furniture, all at reasonable prices.

Advertisements from Uruguayan newspapers of 1840, twenty-seven years after the abolition of slavery. Quoted in Eduardo Galeano (1991) The Book of Embraces, London, Norton).

With the overthrow of colonialism, this division of the world clarified itself further in the twentieth century into a wealthy North (including the Soviet Union) and an impoverished South. The ending of the Cold War was seen by many as providing the possibility of ending this divide (at least politically if not economically or socially) and ushering in a "new world order" which could provide the basis of a more equitable and peaceful world system and which would move away from the old world created by colonialism and from the arguments and disagreements over its impact and consequences. Given the reality of international development today and the growing gap between rich and poor, this is now a vision in tatters and is one challenged by many writers and commentators.

Modern World Economy

The basis of the modern world economy which we now have was laid in the years immediately following the Second World War in the light of the economic crisis which affected most industrial countries in the 1930s and the experience of the war itself, particularly the human rights abuses which characterised the period. The world's dominant powers resolved to rebuild western economies and to establish institutions which would create the basis of global governance in the future. The Bretton Woods Agreement was a conference attended by 44 nations (18 from the Third World) but was dominated by the United States and Britain. The Third World was represented by mostly Latin American countries. The Agreement led to the establishment of four major institutions which have retained huge influence in world affairs to this day. These were the **International Bank for Reconstruction and Development** - now known as the World Bank (providing long-term finance for development), the **International Monetary Fund** (providing short-term finance); the **United Nations** (an international forum for debating and resolving international issues) and **The General Agreement on Trade and Tariffs (GATT)** (for regulating international trade and commodity prices - now known as the World Trade Organisation).

Given the geographical, political and economic power of the western world in 1945 it is no surprise that the Bretton Woods Agreement represented the interests of the developed world. In the wake of this agreement, international politics became dominated by the competition between the United States and the Soviet Union, to the neglect of priority consideration of developing country issues. GATT, for example did little to stabilise commodity prices as the United States insisted on access to cheap raw materials. The United Nations was, in theory, a forum where the interests of developing countries could be voiced and pursued but increasingly, the UN became a "talking shop" with little influence in economic affairs. The latter became the almost exclusive domain of the Organisation for Economic Co-operation and Development (OECD) and, more importantly, the G7 (a group made up of the UK, the USA, Germany, Canada, France, Italy and Japan).

The "Golden Years" of the 1950s and 1960s

This "restructuring" of the world economy fuelled considerable economic growth in the developed world and provided a model of successful development which was seen by many observers and "experts" as the way forward for the Third World. Annual average growth rates in the developing world of over 5% for East Asia, 4% for Latin America and even 3% for Sub-Saharan Africa seemed to justify such optimism. It was assumed that the benefits of such growth would "trickle down" to the poor. A very considerable amount of private investment went into the Third World, particularly from the corporate sector, at this time and while this boosted economic performance indictors, it did not, by and large, increase local capacity and often simply by-passed the poor. Nonetheless, impressive levels of industrialisation were recorded in some Latin American countries and in

There have been real and effective changes for women and children over the past thirty years but much needs to be done

THREE WRITERS ON COLONIALISM IN THREE CONTINENTS

LATIN AMERICA

"Undoubtedly gold and silver were the main motivating force in the conquest, but Columbus on his second voyage brought the first sugar-cane from the Canary Islands and planted them in what is now the Dominican Republic. To the Admiral's joy they rapidly took hold. Grown and refined on a small scale in Sicily, Maderia and the Cape Verde Islands, and purchased on the Orient at high prices, sugar was so precious to Europeans that it figured in the dowries of queens. It was sold in pharmacies, weighed out by the gram.

For almost three centuries after the discovery of America no agricultural product had more importance for European commerce than American sugar. Canefields were planted on the warm, damp, littoral of Northeast Brazil; then in the Caribbean Islands - Barbados, Jamaica, Haiti, Santo Domingo, Guadeloupe, Cuba, Puerto Rico - and in Veracruz and the Peruvian coast, which proved to be ideal terrain for the "white gold".

Legions of slaves came from Africa to provide King Sugar with the prodigal, wageless labour force as required: human fuel for the burning. The land was devastated by the selfish plant which invaded the New World, felling forests, squandering natural fertility, and destroying accumulated soil humus. The long sugar cycle generated a prosperity as mortal as the prosperity generated by the silver and gold of Potosi, Ouro Preto, Zacetecas, Guanajuato. At the same time, directly or indirectly, it spurred the growth of Dutch, French, English and the United States industry."

Uruguayan writer Edwardo Galeano in Open Veins of Latin America, (1973), New York, Month Review Press.

ASIA

"The techniques of British rule which had already been well established were now (after 1857) clarified and confirmed and deliberately acted upon. Essentially these were: the creation and protection of vested interests - bound up with British rule .... The princes and the big landowners were the basic vested interests thus created and encouraged. But now a new class ... grew in importance. This consisted of the Indian members of the services, usually in subordinate positions. Indians so employed were so dependent on the British administration and rule that they could be relied upon and treated as agents of that rule ....

By giving greater importance to the Indian states then they had ever had before, by encouraging one group against another .... All this was a natural and understandable policy for a foreign imperialist power to pursue, and it is a little naive to be surprised at .... But the fact that it was so must be remembered if we are to understand subsequent developments .... Nearly all our major problems today have grown up during British rule and as a direct result of British policy. A significant fact which stands out is that those parts of India which have been longest under British rule are the poorest today. Indeed some kind of chart might be drawn up to indicate the close connection between length of British rule and progressive growth of poverty .... there can be no doubt that the poorest parts of India are Bengal, Bihar, Orissa and parts of Madras Presidency; the mass level and standards of living are highest in Punjab".

Statesman and writer Jawaharla Nehru in The Discovery of India, (1960), New York, Doubleday Anchor.

AFRICA

"New industrial crops, including cocoa, coffee and cotton, were introduced during the colonial period when the production of palm oil and groundnuts was also stimulated. The high prices in the world market for these crops brought considerable income to African farmers who were largely responsible for industrial crop production in British colonial territories. In French and Belgian territories, large areas of land were allocated to foreign companies for establishing plantations of cocoa, rubber, coffee and oil palms.

The development of food crops received little or no attention from the colonial administrators in spite of the periodic famines that featured all over tropical Africa .... The colonial administrators did not initiate but merely accelerated the change from subsistence to export-based agriculture .... What colonial governments achieved in this direction was to intensify the production of cash crops by imposing taxes to be paid in cash as well as by forcing some Africans to cultivate such crops on their farmlands or to provide labour on European-owned plantations.

Industrial development was suppressed as being contrary to the economic interests of the metropolitan countries just as the British Board of Trade had discouraged cotton cultivation in Ghana in 1951. The result was that indigenous manufacturing technology, which had been disrupted during the slave trade, was further handicapped and eventually suffered total eclipse. An increasing range of manufactured goods was supplied to the colonies while goods from countries like Germany and Japan were debarred from entering territories like Nigeria and Ghana. Today some countries have not moved much further in the field of industrialisation, but still supply raw agricultural products to Europe in return for industrial goods."

Nigerian geographer Reuben K. Udo in The Human Geography of Tropical Africa, London, Heinemann Educational.

East Asia (in what were termed the Newly Industrialising Countries - NICs).

At the same time, the terms of trade went seriously against developing countries with an estimated decline of 25% between 1951 and 1965. This was happening at a time when primary commodities (usually raw materials) made up to 70% to 90% of developing country exports and while manufactured goods made up to 50% to 60% of imports. In these circumstances, it was inevitable that serious balance of payments problems would emerge alongside demands that social development be given a higher priority. The economic development which did occur at this time was seen to be limited to a selected number of countries and, within those countries, to selected groups of people. It became clear that the development of the economy was not the same as the development of the people. It also became increasingly clear that the models/strategies for development that had supposedly fuelled growth in the developed world would not work equally well in the Third World.

Debt-led Growth in the 1970s

The growth at all costs model of development was replaced, to a significant degree, with one more oriented towards social provision, employment and redistribution of the benefits of increased growth. The decade of the 1970s also witnessed the substantial rise in the debt problem in many developing countries - a problem which has caused so much damage in the 1980s and a reversal of so much of what was achieved in the 1960s in areas of key basic needs. The 1970s witnessed significant decreases in employment in traditional agriculture (from 32% in 1960 to 16% by 1980) and, therefore, increased unemployment in rural areas; and also increasing migration to cities and the growth of vast slums and serious problems of urban under/non-employment. This led many organisations to promote the notion of labour intensive industrialisation. Focus also began to emerge on the role of women in development both within the household economy and also in the wider economy. Rapid urbanisation also led to significant increases in employment in the "informal sector" - in jobs and very small scale activities not recognised in formal statistics or in the formal official economy.

The first "oil crisis" of 1971 helped turn the terms of trade further against developing countries already at a disadvantage in exporting poorly priced primary commodities. This occurred at a time of growing protectionism in developed countries in response to increased unemployment. The availability of "cheap" loans as a result of oil revenues being deposited in western banks led to a culture of lending

at low interest rates to Third World countries. By the end of the 1970's, interest rates began to rise again, causing major crises in many developing countries. By the mid 1980s, 38% of developing country debt was owed by Latin American countries, 23% by East Asian countries and 12% by Sub-Saharan African states. By the beginning of the 1980s, social development had significantly slowed down, debts had mounted up, interest rates continued to rise and the prospects for development were much reduced throughout the Third World.

The "Lost Decade" of the 1980s

The impact of the 1980s on development in the Third World was well summarised by the South Commission in 1990:

> *"...a large part of the cost of controlling inflation and introducing structural change in the North was borne by the South. Developing countries had to pay out more and more to service their debt while receiving less and less for their exports. As these contrasting movements aggravated their financial difficulties, commercial banks decided to stop lending them new money, and the result was the international debt crisis of the 1980s"*

(The South Commission, The Challenge to the South, Oxford University Press)

The processes described by the South Commission led to a situation where the net flow of resources was reversed from earlier decades to one from South to North alongside a decrease in investment in developing countries and a net outflow of profits. Allied to this was the continuing decline in the value of primary commodities between 1980 and 1988, the real price of the 18 most important non-oil commodities exported by developing countries declined by 25% and continued protectionism in developed country markets. The impact of these trends was severe in many Latin American countries which had borrowed heavily and catastrophic in many Sub-Saharan African countries where debt service payments represented an even higher percentage of GDP. Per capita incomes in both Latin America and Africa actually declined in the 1980s and the sectors which suffered most were health, education, infrastructure and communications. One sector which continued to increase spending was arms purchases. Many countries also began to experience the impact of structural adjustment programmes forced upon them by the IMF.

The Third World and the Cold War

World politics in the period between 1945 and 1990 were overwhelmingly dominated by competition and conflict between East and West - between the United States and its allies and the Soviet Union and its allies. This conflict affected almost every aspect of international development from the models it proposed to the strategies it promoted and the groups and states it affected. This conflict inevitably extended into the global arena and affected all Third World states. It is often claimed that the massive military edifices created on both sides provided an uneasy balance of power which delivered peace since 1945. Viewed from the perspective of the Third World and the over 140 conflicts which have occurred there - the so called "proxy wars of the superpowers" - nothing could be further from the truth. In short, the increasingly important North-South agenda has had to take a poor second place and be subsumed by the dominant East-West agenda.

The fall of the Berlin Wall in 1990 symbolised the end of the Cold War and the beginning of the New World Order with a huge anticipated "peace dividend" (an estimated $935 billion between 1987 and 1994) which could be used to redress the development imbalance between North and South. This has not been the case and according to one researcher, Michael Renner, the peace dividend *"...disappeared into a gigantic fiscal Bermuda Triangle"* - into balancing budgets in the developed world. The ending of the Cold War is seen by some commentators as an opportunity for the Third World to pursue its interests and objectives while for others, it is simply an opportunity for the West - the United States, Japan and the EU - to increase their stranglehold on the Third World. According to Egyptian Samir Amin:

> *"The axis of the new world conjuncture is Western capitalist aggression against the Third World peoples with the aim of subordinating their further evolution to the demands of redeployment of transnational capital."*

In contrast to this view is that of writer John Ravenhill who argues:

> *" The changing global agenda... offers a growing number of issues on which there are mutual interests between North and South and on which the co-operation of Southern countries will be necessary if the industrialised countries are to attain their goals. For individual Southern*

countries there will be opportunities to engage in strategies of issue linkage (between, for example, debt, environmental and market access questions) to improve their bargaining position with the industrialised countries."

Other commentators point to the fact that any benefits of the new world order will be very unevenly experienced within the Third World with large numbers of countries and peoples simply excluded, particularly in Sub-Saharan Africa and South Asia and also in the context of the continuing dominance of Transnational Companies.

Assessing the arguments around the "New World Order", Professor Noam Chomsky concludes:

"...thus we refer euphemistically to developed and developing societies, or the North-South divide. Though the full picture is complex, in its essentials the divide is real enough. It has deepened in recent years, quite sharply in the 1980s..."

Assessing the impact of the period on the poor, American researcher Alan Durning comments:

"The histories of rich and poor diverged particularly sharply in the eighties. For industrial nations, the decade was a time of resurgence and recovery after the economic turmoil of the seventies. For the poor, particularly in Africa and Latin America, the eighties were an unmitigated disaster, a time of meagre diets and rising death rates."

In the context of the comments of both Chomsky and Durning, the reality of the gap between rich and poor and its impact are graphically illustrated by the table of wealth distribution in Brazil between 1981 and 1990 and the story of the impact of debt in the 1980s on one community in Peru as described by Oxfam:

"In the old days, we provided soup for a few hundred people. Then, in 1990, we had 'stabilisation'. Prices went up more than 2000 per cent. Look around you, you can see what stabilisation has meant. Look at the children hawking on the streets, when they should be in school; look at the numbers of people we are feeding; look at the numbers sleeping on the streets; look at the conditions in our slums. Has 'stabilisation' made things better?"

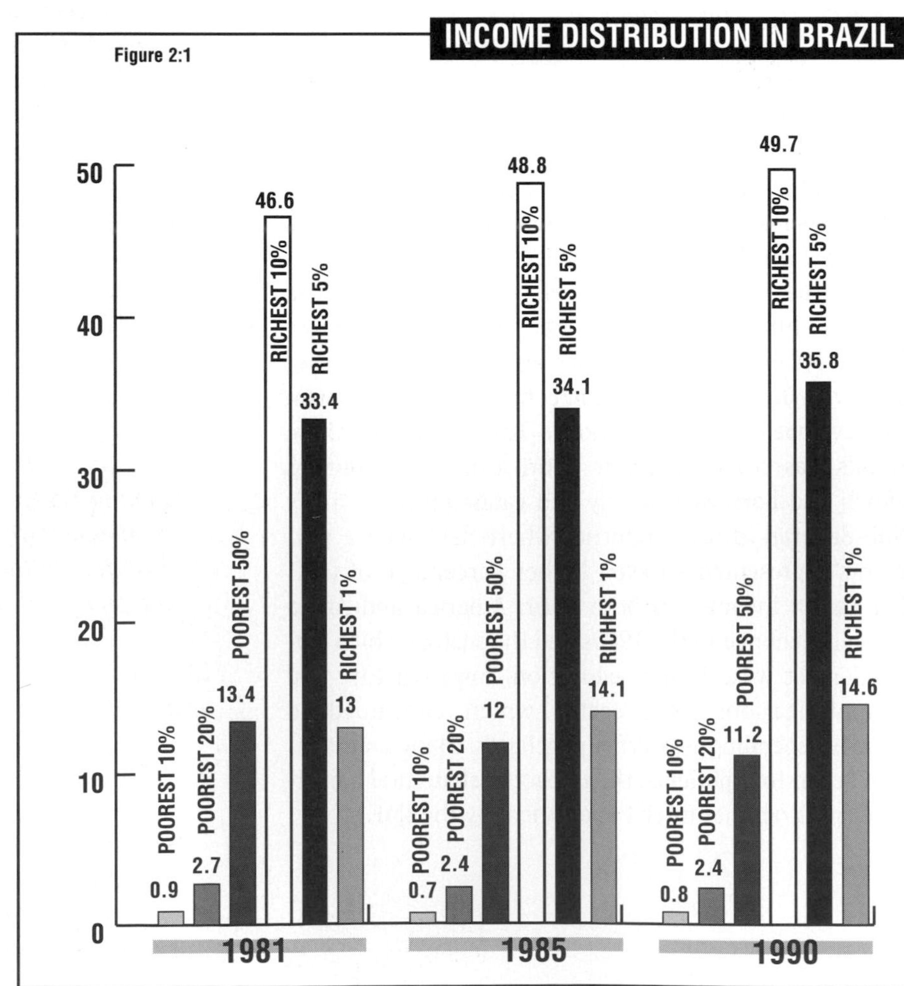

Source: World Bank (various years) **World Development** Report, Oxford University Press.

REWRITING HISTORY

"For a long time, all kinds of myths and prejudices concealed the true history of Africa from the world at large. African societies were looked upon as societies that could have no history".

These are the words of UNESCO director Amadou Mahter M. Bow in the introduction to Volume Seven of the *General History of Africa* initiated by UNESCO. In this introduction he is describing a process of history writing which has, until recently, remained unchallenged. It is a view of history which concentrates on *"great leaders",* key battles, great thinkers, etc. and places little emphasis on the bulk of people. The writing of history has frequently written out the role of the poor, women, racial minorities or indeed any group which challenged the predominant power systems. The *General History of Africa* is but one example of how the oppressed are beginning to reclaim history.

The *General History* was conceived as a major attempt to rewrite Africans back into their own history. It began in 1965, with Volume Seven being published in 1985. Some of the comments and arguments put forward to justify the project are worth noting and clearly have implications for history writing in many places and contexts.

"Since the European Middle Ages were often used as a yardstick, modes of production, social relations and political institutions were visualised only by reference to the European past."

"... there was a refusal to see Africans as the creators of original civilisations which flowered and survived over the centuries in patterns of their own making and which historians are unable to grasp unless they forego their prejudices and rethink their approach".

"... the continent of Africa was hardly ever looked upon as a historical entity ... The Sahara was often presented as an impenetrable space preventing any intermingling of ethnic groups and people or any exchange of goods, beliefs, customs and ideas ....

"Another phenomenon which did great disservice to the objective study of the African past was the appearance, with the slave trade and colonisation, of racial stereotypes which bred contempt and lack of understanding and became so deep-rooted that they distorted even the basic concepts of historiography."

The *General History of Africa* is published jointly by Heinemann and UNESCO in English, French and Arabic and in African languages such as Kiswahili, Hausa, Fulani, Yoruba and Lingala.

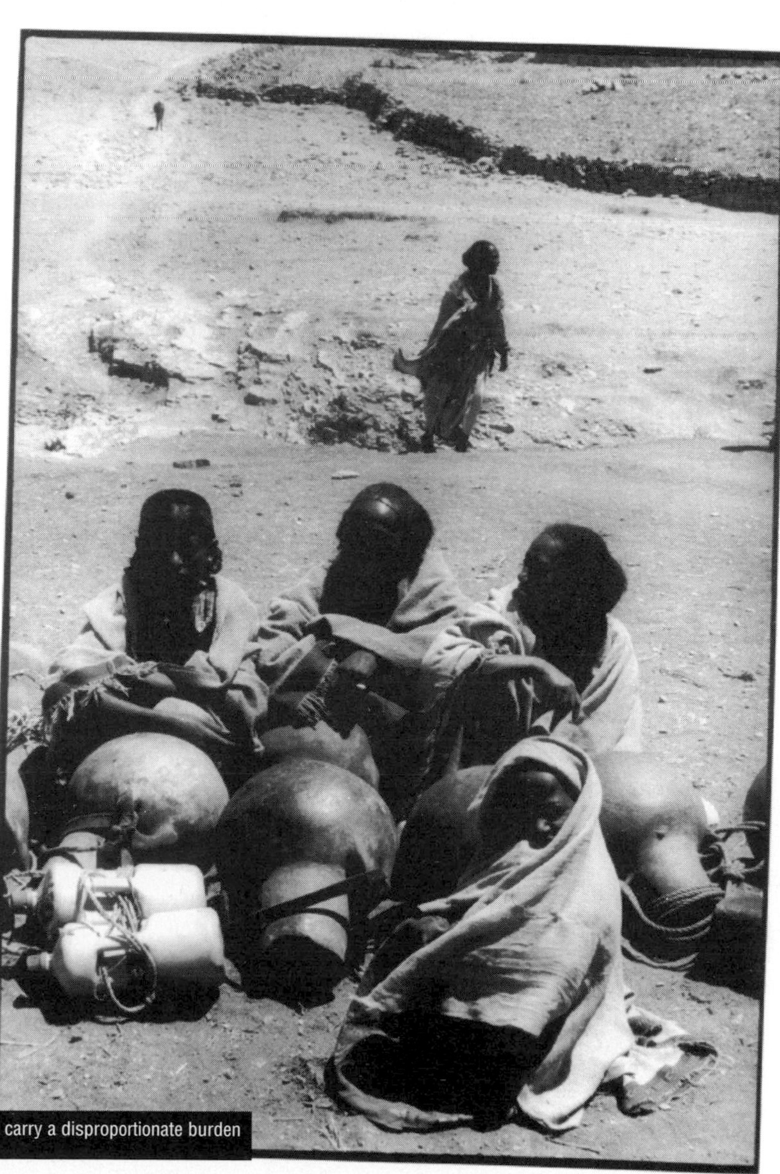

Women still carry a disproportionate burden

Debating Colonialism: The Old World Orders.

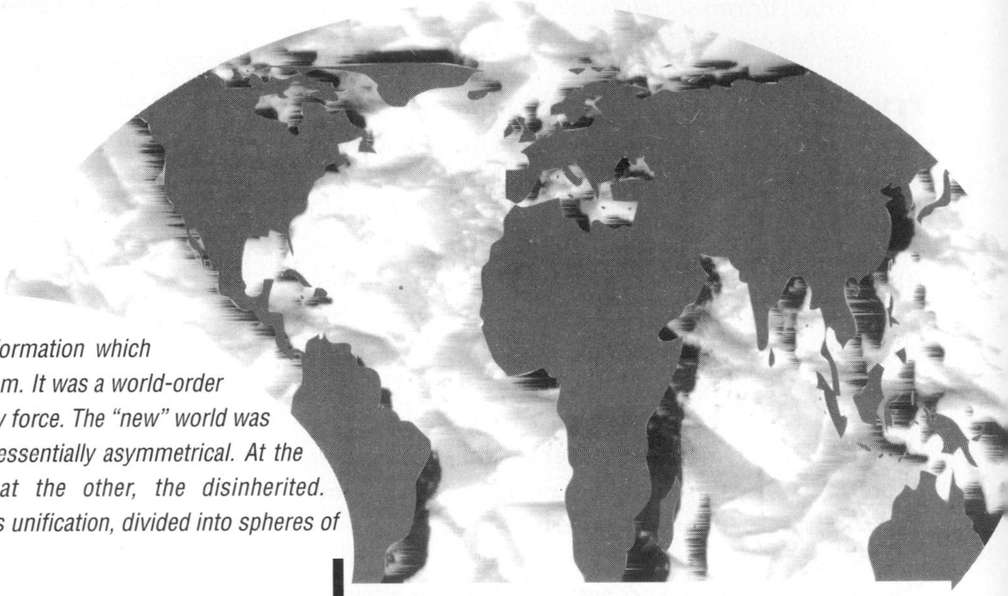

"Europe had accomplished a tranformation which created the world as a social system. It was a world-order founded on conquest and maintained by force. The "new" world was no egalitarian "family of nations": it was essentially asymmetrical. At the one pole stood industrialised Europe; at the other, the disinherited. Paradoxically, the world had been divided in its unification, divided into spheres of influence, and divided into rich and poor."

This was the view of sociologist Peter Worsley in his influential book ***The Third World*** published in 1964 (London, Weidenfeld and Nicholson), in which he examined in detail the impact of what he termed *"The European Interlude"* in the history of the Third World.

"This new contact with Europe brought gains to Africa as well as to Europe, especially in the exchange of goods and ideas. But it also brought the long and painful tragedy of the trans-Atlantic trade in Africans captured into slavery and sent to the Americas. This was very good for the development of the Americas, but very bad for the development of Africa. And the slave trade lasted more than 300 years.

Another challenge followed. By the middle of the nineteenth century the leading countries of Europe lost interest in exporting African labour to the Americas. Now they wanted to be able to use African labour in Africa itself. So Europe invaded Africa, took possession of Africa, and divided Africa into colonies of Europe."

Historian Basil Davidson (1983) ***Modern Africa: A Social and Political History,*** London, Longman.

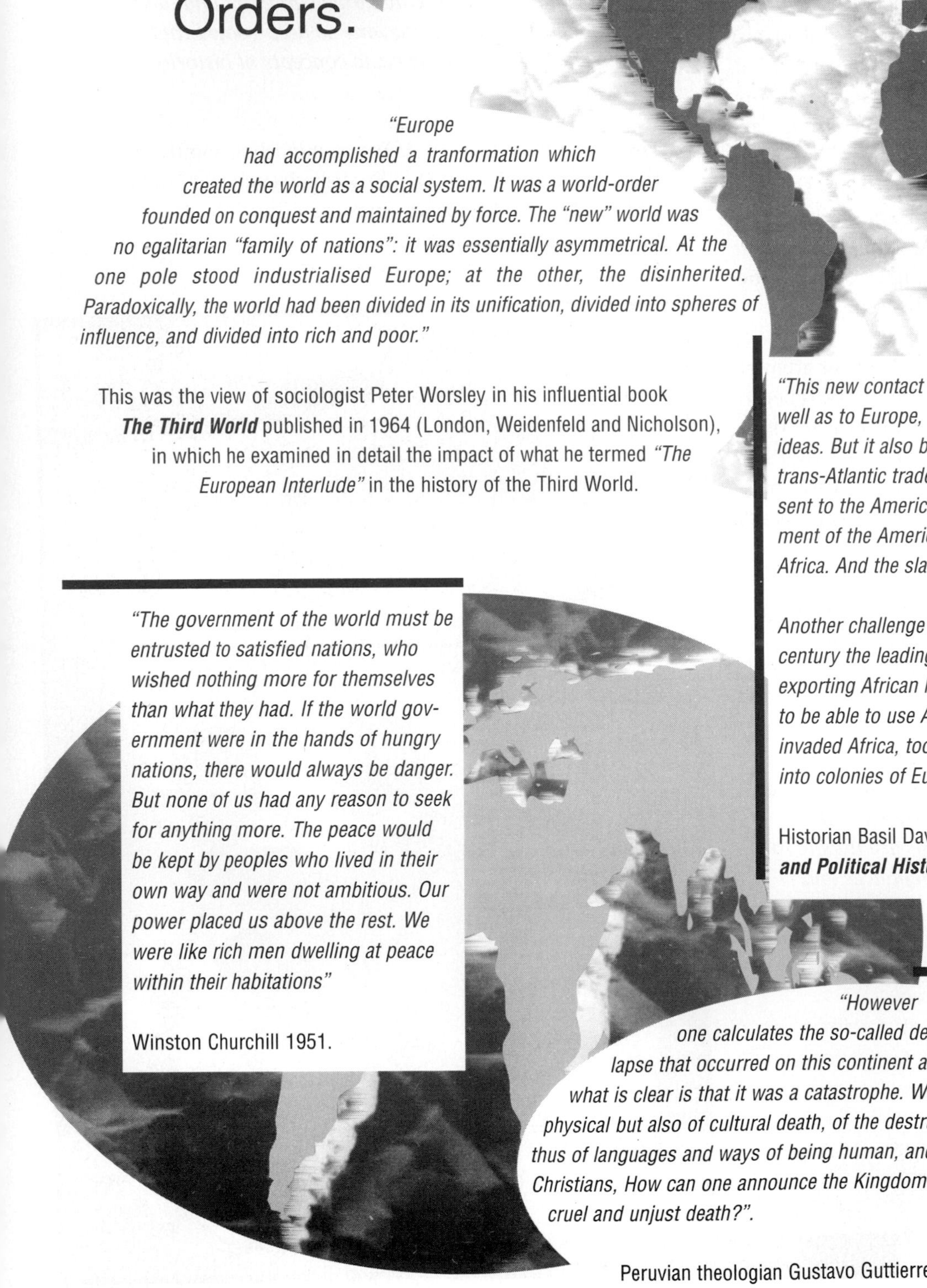

"The government of the world must be entrusted to satisfied nations, who wished nothing more for themselves than what they had. If the world government were in the hands of hungry nations, there would always be danger. But none of us had any reason to seek for anything more. The peace would be kept by peoples who lived in their own way and were not ambitious. Our power placed us above the rest. We were like rich men dwelling at peace within their habitations"

Winston Churchill 1951.

"However one calculates the so-called demographic collapse that occurred on this continent and specifically in Peru, what is clear is that it was a catastrophe. We are talking here not only of physical but also of cultural death, of the destruction of entire civilisations and thus of languages and ways of being human, and the question arises for us as Christians, How can one announce the Kingdom of Life in a situation marked by cruel and unjust death?".

Peruvian theologian Gustavo Guttierrez in ***Latin American Perspectives,*** Vol.19, No.3.

"In predominantly black countries, it was also true that the bulk of the social services went to whites. The southern part of Nigeria was one of the colonial areas that was supposed to have received the most from a benevolent "mother country". Ibadan, one of the most heavily settled cities in Africa, had only about 50 Europeans before the last war. For those chosen few, the British colonial government maintained a segregated hospital service of 11 beds in well-furnished surroundings. There were 34 beds for a half a million blacks. The situation was repeated in other areas, so that altogether the 4,000 Europeans in the country in the 1930s had 12 modern hospitals, while the African population of at least 40 million had 52 hospitals."

Guyanese writer Walter Rodney (1972) ***How Europe Underdeveloped Africa,*** London, Bogle-L'Overture.

"The Church was to play a central role in the Spanish Conquest of the New World. The conquest was spiritual as well as military...Spanish America was to be integrated into the European cosmos in accordance with the notion of Christendom, which unified the spiritual and temporal. Mass conversion of the indigenous population of Central America by the Spaniards was, in any case, as much a political as a spiritual necessity. The acceptance by the vanquished of the beliefs and values of the conquerors enormously facilitated control of their territories."

British writer Jenny Pearce (1992) ***Poverty and Power: Latin America after 500 Years,*** London, Cafod.

"You believe perhaps, gentlemen, that the production of coffee and sugar is the natural destiny of the West Indies. Two centuries ago, nature, which does not trouble herself about commerce, had planted neither sugarcane nor coffee trees there."

Karl Marx (1963) ***On the Poverty of Philosophy,*** New York, International Publishers.

"A close look at 'the global village' shows that all of the important spheres of life of mankind are under the control of from five to seven powerful nations. The system inaugurated by Columbus in 1492 is now, as it was 500 years ago, highly oligo polistic and antidemocratic.

In the economic sphere, it is the industrial nations of the Group of Seven that determine world economic policies. Although their decisions affect everyone on the planet, no democratic control or access to this elite club exists for any of the other states that form the world community.

In the political domain, it is the five veto-holding members of the United Nations Security Council that have the decisive leverage in political affairs that affect the world community. Again, there is no democratic control or legitimation of that body, whose composition represents the correlation of forces between capitalist and socialist victors at the end of World War Two. The only functioning world political institution that is at least formally democratic, the United Nations, has no real say in world political affairs"

Mexican Heinz Dieterich in ***Latin American Perspectives,*** Vol.19, No.3,1992.

"The president of my country is for the moment
named Colonel Fidel Sanchez Hernandez.
But the president of Nicaragua,
General Somoza, is also the president of my country.
And General Stroessner, the president of Paraguay,
is also, a little, the president of my country,
although less so than the president of Honduras.

And the president of the United States
is much more the president of my country
than the president of my country."

Salvadoran poet Roque Dalton

Sub-Saharan Africa in the 1980s

- Fourteen of the poorest 20 countries in the world are in Sub-Saharan Africa, many of which became poorer in the 1980s, with per capita GNPs below $300 in 1987. Meanwhile debt increased dramatically. In absolute terms, the region's total external debt rose from $6 billion in 1970 to $134 billion in 1988, an amount equal to sub-Saharan Africa's total GNP or to 3.5 times its total export earnings.
- Military spending increased between 1972 and 1987 almost in direct relation to cuts in social welfare spending. War was commonplace. From 1945 and 1989 there were more than 30 wars in the region.
- Many countries continue to rely on one agricultural commodity for more than 40% of export earnings. The real prices for these commodities dropped by more than 40% through the 1980s.
- Desertification of 650 million square kilometres in the last 30 years is said to have affected the livelihoods of 60 million people.

ECONOMIC DECLINE IN SUB-SAHARAN AFRICA 1980-1990

	1980	*1990*	*Change (%)*
Per capita output ($)	582	335	-42.5%
Per capita consumption ($)	465	279	-40.0%
Investment (% of GDP)	20.2	14.2	-29.7
Exports of goods ($ billions)	48.7	31.9	-34.5
Per capita food production ($)	107	94	-12.2
Total external debt ($ billions)	56.2	147	+162
Poverty (% below poverty line)	NA	62	—

Sources:
Tom Hewitt (1992) *"Developing Countries - 1945 to 1990"* in T.Allen and A.Thomas (eds.) **Poverty and Development in the 1990s,** Oxford University Press;
M. Todaro (1994) **Economic Development,** London, Longmans.

Figure 2.2

The Lost Decade in Latin America

"The Third World War has already started - the silent war, not for that reason any the less sinister. This war is tearing down Brazil, Latin America and practically all the Third World. Instead of soldiers dying there are children, instead of millions of wounded there are millions of unemployed; instead of destruction of bridges there is the tearing down of factories, schools, hospitals and entire economies"

This was the view of the impact of the "lost decade" in Brazil and Latin America outlined by Brazilian trade union leader and, later, Brazilian Presidential candidate, Luis Inacio da Silva - popularly known as Lula. In Latin America, countries whose economies had grown steadily since 1945 experienced decline and the impact of the IMF's adjustment strategies.
Throughout the region, factories closed, health and education services were seriously cut back, inflation became uncontrolled and money, virtually worthless. $198 billion left Latin America and the Caribbean in debt-servicing alone between 1982 and 1990.

- In Mexico real wages were halved and unemployment quadrupled between 1982 and 1987. According to writer Susan George, nearly three-quarters of poor Mexicans were forced to abandon rice, eggs, fruit, vegetables and milk - all of these became luxuries.
- Advances in health and nutrition were reversed; more Latin American children were malnourished or dying in the 1980s than 10 years earlier.
- In 1986, the Bolivian government, under pressure from the IMF, cut the national health budget by two-thirds at a time when over half the population was malnourished.
- In 1989, a week long "IMF riot", with an official death toll of 276, took place in normally peaceful Venezuela following the introduction of an IMF austerity package. Similar riots also took place in Brazil, Argentina and the Dominican Republic.
- The welcome rise of democracy in Latin America in the 1980s remains under threat as economic and social conditions deteriorate. Military regimes in Brazil, Argentina and Uruguay were replaced with civilian governments while changes of governments were achieved peacefully in another seven Latin American states from Bolivia to Venezuela. This situation has led The Economist to comment *"Much of Latin America is entering the 1990s in a race between economic deterioration and political progress".*

Sources: Duncan Green (1991) **Faces of Latin America,** London, Latin American Bureau;
Paul Kennedy (1993) **Preparing for the Twenty-First Century,** London, Harper;

Asia in the 1980s

"A Taiwanese child born in 1988 could expect to live seventy-four years, only a year less than an American or a West German, and fifteen years longer than a Taiwanese born in 1952; A South Korean born in 1988 could expect seventy years on earth, up from fifty-eight in 1965. In 1988 the Taiwanese took in 50% more calories each day than they had done thirty-five years earlier. They had two hundred times as many televisions, telephones and cars per household; in Korea the rise in the possession of these goods was even higher."

This was how The Economist magazine commented upon one important dimension of the succes enjoyed by many in Asia in the 1980s. If the people of sub-Saharan Africa were the greatest losers in the 1980s, then it is arguable that those who gained most were the populations of Asia's newly industrialising economies - where growth has been spectacular. Eastern Asian development has been spearheaded by Japan, followed by the 4 Asian "tigers" of Singapore, Hong Kong, Taiwan and South Korea; the larger states of Thailand, Malaysia and Indonesia and, to a lesser extent, Vietnam, Cambodia and North Korea. The western Pacific region's share of world trade has increased from about 9% in 1962 to 15% in 1982 and is expected to reach 25% by the year 2000.

Literacy means far more than just the ability to reading

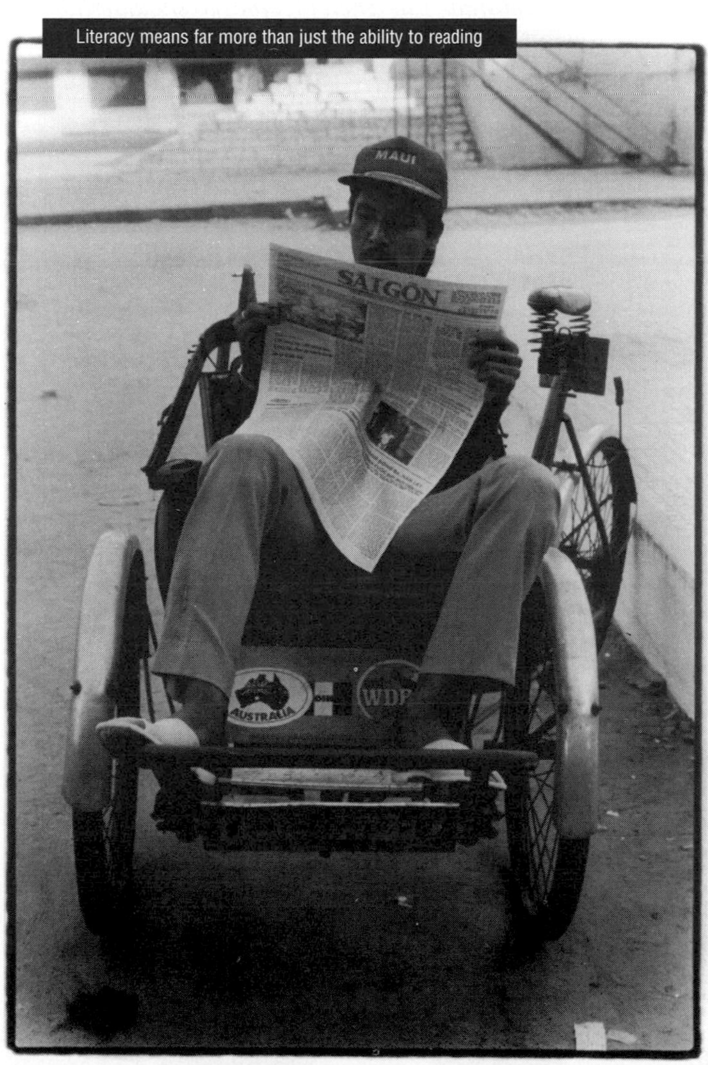

- This economic development has been translated into real social development in many states with basic social indicators moving upwards. The pattern, however, remains very uneven with huge percentages of the population of India, Bangladesh and, of course, China excluded from most of these benefits

- The impressive economic growth rates have not been without a downside - human rights restrictions, bans on trade union and labour agitation, poor and frequently dangerous working conditions (affecting women and children in some key industries such as garment making) and considerable environmental damage. Many Western observers argue that such restrictions were the inevitable price of the successes recorded and have argued that similar strategies should be pursued elsewhere.

- The export-led model of growth has depended heavily on access to US markets, an access which is no longer available for others; for some states (especially Taiwan and South Korea) the miracle was fuelled, to a significant extent by high levels of US aid and the area was stimulated extensively by the Vietnam war which "pump-primed" key sectors of the region's economy.

- Already, many of the companies which emerged during recent decades, are moving to other cheaper locations in the Caribbean and South-eastern Asia following recent increases in wage costs in the "tigers".

Sources: Paul Kennedy (1993) **Preparing for the Twenty-First Century,** London, Harper;
Walden Bello (1989) **Brave New Third World,** London, Earthscan.

The New World Order *Two Voices*

"Without the shadow of a doubt, freedom is always good news, for the East European states now enjoying it and for the entire world. But, at the same time, are the paeans to money and the virtues of the market place good news? The idolatry of the American way of life? The naive illusions of an invitation to membership in the International Club for the Rich? The bureaucracy, nimble only for the stepping into better positions, is rapidly adapting to the new situation and the old bureaucrats are beginning to transform themselves into a new bourgeoisie.

...For us, capitalism is not a dream to be made reality, but a nightmare come true. Our challenge lies not in privatising the state but in de-privatising it. Our states have been bought at bargain prices by the owners of the land, the banks and everything else. And for us, the market - the local market and the world market - is nothing more than a pirate ship - the greater its freedom, the worse its behaviour. The world market robs us with both arms. The commercial arm keeps charging us more and more for what it sells and paying less and less for what it buys from us. The financial arm that lends us our own money keeps paying us less and charging us more.

We live in a region where European prices and African wages prevail, where capitalism acts like the kind man who says "I'm so fond of poor people that it seems to me that there are never enough of them'."

Uruguayan Eduardo Galeano in Blackburn, R. (1991) **After the Fall,** London, Verso.

"...the new job...for the post-Cold War world...to help build and sustain a world order stable enough to allow the advanced economies of the world to function without constant interruption and threat from the Third World...(a task that will require) ...instant intervention from the advanced nations. (Britain is)... no match for Germany and Japan when it comes to wealth creation; or even for France and Italy. But when it comes to shouldering world responsibilities we are more than a match..."

Peregrine Worsthorne, editor **Sunday Telegraph,** September 16th, 1990.

The End of the Third World?

"The demise of communism placed the very term "Third World" in jeopardy. The countries behind the Iron Curtain were the second world to the West's first world. Now that the curtain has been pulled back, the old basis of the definition no longer exists.

We are left in a terminological chaos. The terms North and South are inaccurate. Australia and New Zealand are industrialised countries. So are Hong Kong, Singapore, Taiwan and South Korea. Developed and developing are no better. Though most international statistics are still divided up this way, the globe is no longer neatly polarised into haves and have-nots. There is a growing middle class.

What we now have is much more like a continuum. It ranged in 1990 - in terms of real purchasing power per person - from a low of $310 in Ethiopia right up to $21,690 in Switzerland. In between lie countries like Kenya and India on around $1,100 per person, Sri Lanka and Cameroon between $2,000 to $3,000, Thailand and Iran between $4,000 and $5,000. Next in line, probably, come the former communist countries of Eastern Europe and the Soviet Union. Countries like Korea, Greece and Ireland, on $7,000 to $9,000, provide the transition to the high income group on $10,000 plus. These now include the oil exporters of the Arabian Peninsula and Israel, Singapore and Hong Kong.

But the existence of a growing world middle class should not blind us to the existence of extremes. The poor of the earth still constitute the majority. In 1990, 53% of the world population lived in countries where average dollar incomes were less than $500. And the poor still live much as they did in the past... They are still mainly rural, still dependent on primary commodities, still hungry, ill in health, ill-housed and ill-educated. Women are still oppressed, and birth rates remain high.

The poor should not be confused with the booming Guangdongs (in China) and Malaysia, still less with the nouveaux riches like Singapore and Hong Kong. We still need a term that focuses world attention and concern on the poorest half of the human race. The term Third World should be retained to cover them." Paul Harrison (1993) **Inside the Third World**, London, Penguin.

"...Invented primarily as political and journalistic shorthand to describe an emerging coalition of newly independent states, the term (Third World) today is embedded in the discourse and diplomacy of international relations. Yet, as will become apparent, it is doubtful whether the term retains any convincing political or conceptual validity in the contemporary world, not least because of the demise of the Cold War which gave it its political currency. What is incontrovertible, however, is that from the late 50's through to the late 1970's, common economic problems, the desire to stand outside the East-West conflict, and the commitment to restructuring the global economic system provided the political motivation for these newly independent states to operate collectively as a bloc in the international arena." Anthony McGrew **"The Third World in the New Global Order"** in T.Allen and A.Thomas (eds.) **Poverty and Development in the 1990's,** Oxford University Press

"This discrepancy in performance between East Asia and Sub-Saharan Africa clearly makes redundant the term "Third World". However useful the expression might have been in the 1950's, when poor, non-aligned, and recently decolonized states were attempting to remain independent of the two super-power blocs, the rise of super rich oil producing countries a decade later already made it questionable. Now the prosperous East Asian societies posses higher per capita GNP's than Russia, Eastern Europe, and even Western European states like Portugal, the word seems less suitable than ever. With Taiwanese and Korean corporations establishing assembly plants in the Philippines and creating distribution networks within the European Community, we need to recognise the differences that exist among non-western economies." Paul Kennedy (1993) **Preparing for the Twenty-First Century,** London, Fontana.

"First World and Second World are meaningless terms in the post Cold-War era, since the rivalry they referred to does not exist any longer, but the concept of Third World refers to the everyday reality of two-thirds of humanity. The disparities are such that in more than one sense it is logical to talk of separate "worlds". But we all live on the same planet, and the present environmental crisis, with phenomena like global warming or depletion of genetic resources affects us all, rich and poor." Introduction **Third World Guide 1993/94,** Uruguay, Instituto del Tercer Mundo.

Challenging the Dominant World Order - The G-77

In the years following the Second World War, a significant number of international organisations which now shape world political and economic development were established - particularly those associated with the United Nations. Since then, many of these organisations have been the subject of intense debate and power politics as western powers have attempted to maintain control of them in the face of strong opposition from developing countries. The decades of the 1950s and 1960s were also a period of widespread de-colonisation and the emergence of the Third World as a political bloc. By 1960, the United Nations was dominated by states which did not even exist in 1947. The organisation which best expressed the interests of governments throughout the developing world, and which stood in opposition to the dominance of the OECD and the G-7, outlining an alternative set of international reforms to those of GATT, the World Bank and the IMF, was the Group of 77.

Prior to the setting up of the G-77, the interests of the newly independent Third World states were articulated by the Non-Aligned Movement of African and Asian states founded in Bandung in Indonesia in 1955. The Group of 77 emerged from the Non-Aligned Movement and throughout the period 1960 to the present (now consisting of over 130 developing countries) has frequently acted as a voting bloc at the United Nations. The G-77 sought to revise the trade regime established by GATT and to challenge the inbuilt inequalities of its system of regulation. The G-77 also succeeded in achieving the establishment of the United Nations Conference on Trade and Development (UNCTAD) and sought to use this forum to renegotiate import restrictions, reduce tariff barriers and agree trade regimes. In 1974, the G-77 persuaded the UN General Assembly to agree a Declaration on a New International Economic Order (NIEO) which sought to regulate trade, increase aid, control transnational corporations and reform international financial institutions. This latter issue was the subject of intense debate and opposition from the developed world.

The G-77 reached the pinnacle of its influence in the 1970s but had lost much of its impact by the mid 1980s as the cohesion of the Third World collapsed in the face of international recession, US opposition to mutilateral negotiations, the debt crisis and the success of states such the Newly Industrialising countries of Asia. There were also serious disagreements within the G-77 over issues such as "culture" and "genders"

Even today, the views of the G-77 are an important expression of the frustrations of Third World states in the face of declarations of the prospects within the "New World Order". In 1994, the then Chairperson of the G-77, Luis Jaramillo commented on the *"loss of economic and political standing"* of developing countries "*in the so-called New World Order...at the dawn of the 21st century"*. He argued that the strategy of the developed world is *"...clearly directed at strengthening more and more the economic institutions and agencies that operate outside the United Nations system"*, which, with all its serious flaws, remains *"the only multilateral mechanism in which the developing countries can have some say"*. In contrast, the structures set up by the Bretton Woods Agreement are being made *"the centre of gravity for the principal economic decisions that affect the developing countries"* and are marked by *"their undemocratic character, their lack of transparency, their dogmatic principles, their lack of pluralism in the debate of ideas and their impotence to influence the policies of the industrialised countries..."* (quoted in Noam Chomsky (1994) **World Orders, Old and New,** London, Pluto).

▼ References

T.Allen and A.Thomas (eds.) **Poverty and Development in the 1990's,** Oxford University Press

Noam Chomsky (1994) **World Orders, Old and New,** London, Pluto.

Fanon, F. (1963) **The Wretched of the Earth,** Harmondsworth, Penguin.

Galeano, E. (1973) **Open Veins of Latin America,** New York, Monthly Review Press.

Instituto del Tercer Mundo (1993/94) **Third World Guide,** Montevideo.

Ben Jackson (1990) **Poverty and the Planet,** London, Penguin.

Paul Kennedy (1993) **Preparing for the Twenty-First Century,** London, Harper;

Kitching, G. (1982) **Development and Underdevelopment in Historical Perspective,** London, Methuen.

Jenny Pearce (1992) **Poverty and Power: Latin America after 500 Years,** London, Cafod.

World Bank (1995) **World Development Report,** Oxford University Press.

A BALANCE SHEET OF HUMAN DEVELOPMENT

Colm Regan

"Just half a century ago, over 50 nations in Africa and Asia were ruled from London, Paris, Lisbon, Brussels or the Hague. Half a century ago, the National Party was about to introduce formal apartheid in South Africa. Half a century ago, communism....was establishing itself across Europe and beginning its advance into many areas of the developing world. Half a century ago, women in France and Japan did not have the right to vote. And half a century ago, across much of the United States, a black person could neither vote, nor serve on a jury, nor occupy a bus seat if a white person was standing...50 years ago, only a small proportion of the world's people had a voice or a vote in the selection of those who governed them; today, the proportion has risen to between half and three quarters."

UNICEF ***The State of the World's Children,*** (1995).

Introduction

In his *History of the Short Twentieth Century,* Eric Hobsbawm argues that the world's greatest political crisis at the end of the century is, not how to generate wealth (a major focus in the first half of the century) but, rather, how to improve its distribution. In this, he echoes the arguments of many others for whom the end of the century is characterised by fundamental contradictions and inequalities.

On the one hand, are the life protecting improvements referred to by UNICEF above (and outlined in some detail below) and the huge wealth which progress in this century has generated for potential human benefit. Against this, are the life threatening social inequalities in income, health and opportunities highlighted at various United Nations Summits towards the end of the century and the ever-widening global gap between rich and poor.

In practical terms, the contrast is graphically highlighted by the health, life expectancy and educational achievements of the past three decades and the threat posed to those achievements by debt adjustment strategies in the 1980s and 1990s. The contrast and the challenges are also illustrated by the gap between overall average social improvement and that experienced by women, especially in the Third World. The contrast is commented upon in the 1995 Human Development Report in the following terms

Figure 3.1

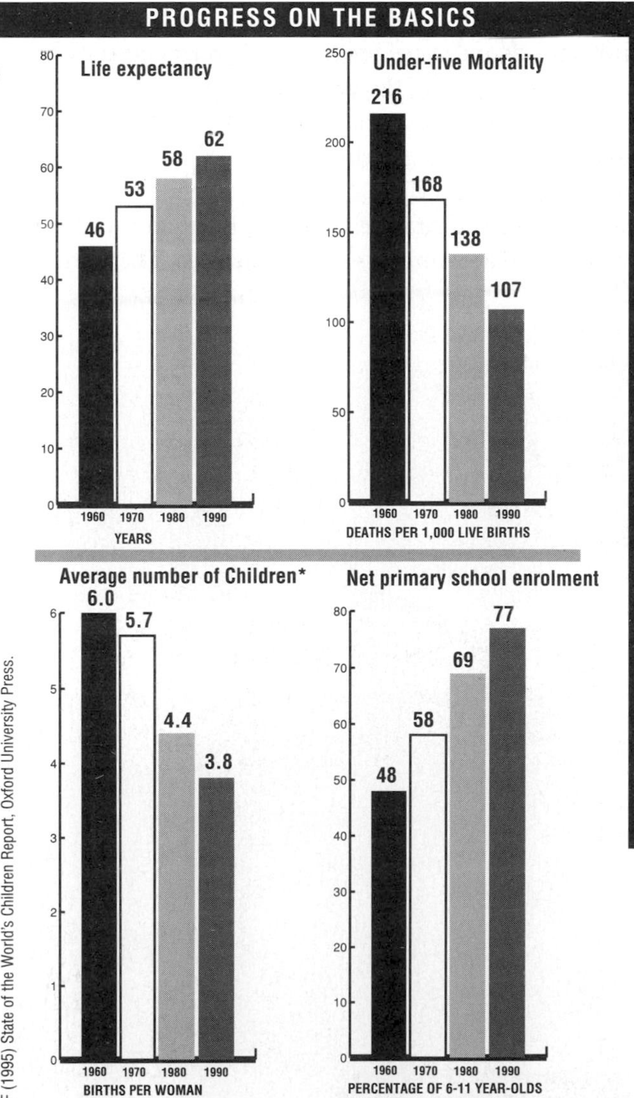

Source: UNICEF (1995) State of the World's Children Report, Oxford University Press.

*The figures given are for the total fertility rate — the number of children that would be born per woman if she were to live to the end of her child-bearing years and bear children at each age in accordance with prevailing age-specific fertility rates.

"the 1980s were...years when budgets were balanced at the cost of unbalancing people's lives. Human lives shrivelled in many regions, and among those most affected were women."

On the balance sheet of world human development, the past three decades have been marked by clear, unequivocal and impressive progress achieved through a partnership of the poor themselves, many local and national governments and international organisations, both voluntary and statutory. And this progress has been achieved at a minuscule cost. The past three decades have proven conclusively that real, life-enhancing progress can be achieved. But they have also shown that this progress is by no means guaranteed or automatic and can be heavily influenced (and even reversed) by economic trends.

Economic Growing and Social Progress

This major concern with the relationship between economic growth and social progress and greater equality has characterised much of the debate on development for the past three decades but it has been given greater urgency in recent years. The growing economic, environmental, political and human rights threats which gross inequality pose, and which characterise development in the 1990s, have given greater impetus to such debates. They formed a key element in the backdrop to the United Nations World Summits on Human Rights (held in Vienna in June 1994) and on Social Development (held in Copenhagen in March 1995). The Summits highlighted the often forgotten social and political aspects of development and the disagreements over the priority to be afforded these dimensions as against the more regularly reported and debated economic dimensions.

Huge advances have been made in the provision of food in large parts of Asia

At present, Third World governments spend an average of only 13% of their national budgets on basic human development - this is a function of both internal and external economic and political priorities. In many countries, public expenditure on human development has actually declined in recent years. For example, per capita spending on health in the Philippines is now lower as a direct result of 12 years of structural adjustment programmes administered by the IMF. Zimbabwe's spending on health and education was cut by one third in that country's structural adjustment programme. $10 billion is paid annually by Africans in repayment of multilateral debt and the IMF has received $2 billion more in repayments from Africa than it has handed out in loans since 1980. When allied to internal political decisions which downgrade human development investment priorities, the result is seriously damaging.

One of the proposals which was debated at the 1995 Social Summit was the creation of a 20:20 Compact for Human Development. Under this compact, developing country governments would have to devote 20% of their national budgets to human priority and, in turn, aid giving countries would increase their commitment to this area to 20% of aid budgets (currently, about 7% of aid goes to sectors such as basic education, health care, water supply etc.). Such a compact would increase spending in human development by nearly $40 billion per year. Such a budget would be used to achieve a very basic set of human development targets including:

- *Universal primary education*
- *A halving of adult illiteracy rates*
- *Primary health care for all*
- *The elimination of severe malnutrition*
- *Family planning for all willing couples*
- *Safe drinking water and sanitation for all*
- *Credit for all to encourage self-employment opportunities.*

Basic agreement on the Compact was forthcoming but the compact was made voluntary thus undermining its likely impact considerably.

The Human Face of Progress and Struggle

MUJERES EN LUCHA, SAN MIGUEL, MEXICO

"By day, San Miguel is a world of women and children. Men leave by the busload at dawn in search of a day's wage, and women are left to produce the miracle of survival, a task which has required collective action. For example, it was women, exasperated from washing babies, dishes and laundry on a barrel of water a week, who stood for hours outside city hall demanding access to city water.

Women's involvement in the (residents') association set off hundreds of household "revolutions", some negotiated, some violent, as women began to challenge their husbands' and in-laws' dictates and stepped into new roles. Although most of the work of the association was being carried out by women during the day, decisions were made during late-night assemblies. The few women who could be present at such hours rarely spoke.

In 1982 half a dozen activists came together to form the Grupo de Mujeres en Lucha (Group of Women in Struggle) as a committee of the association, to promote women's participation in leadership. The new group focused on issues of rape and battering. Arguing that domestic violence is not a private matter, but rather a crime against the community...Yet it was only after the economic crash of 1982, when Mujeres en Lucha began to focus on economic survival issues...that it began to grow beyond a handful of activists. For the first time, women not only filled the ranks of marches and sit-ins, but also negotiated demands with authorities and developed distribution systems for the resources they won...By integrating consciousness-raising workshops into their organising process, they worked to ensure that women who first dared step out of the house in search of cheaper tortillas stayed on to become an active part of the movement."

Elaine Burns (1989) ***Report on The Americas,*** *quoted in Duncan Green (1991)* ***Faces of Latin America,*** *London, Latin American Bureau.*

"AND SO HE SURVIVED..."

" So he survived. But malnutrition made him withdrawn and apathetic. His mother got no reward from playing with him, so he received little of the stimulation his brain needed to develop properly. As he grew older, infections grew less frequent, but by the time he went to school, aged eight, he was already a year behind normal physical development and two years behind mentally. The school, in any case, was a poor one, with only three classes, no equipment, and a poorly qualified teacher. As Francisco was continually worried as to whether and what he was going to eat that day, he was distracted, unable to concentrate, and seemed to show little interest in schoolwork. The teacher confirmed that he was a slow learner, and could not seem to get the hang of maths or reading and writing. As the family was poor, they did not want to keep him on at school...there seemed no point. He did a year...left...then did another year, then left for good, barely able to read or write more than a few letters.

He soon forgot what little he had learned. So, like his father, he began tramping round the local ranches, asking for work. And because so many were in the same boat, pay was low. When he was twenty two he married a local girl, Graciela, aged only fifteen. She too had been undernourished and was illiterate. She soon became pregnant...by the age of only twenty-five, Graciela had five children and had lost two. The children had every prospect of growing up much as Francisco and Graciela did...

Francisco's case illustrates perhaps the greatest tragedy of Third World poverty today...Poor people never reach their full human potential in physical strength, intelligence and well-being...They are trapped in a pattern of overlapping vicious circles..."

Paul Harrison (1993) ***Inside the Third World,*** *London, Penguin.*

DIMENSIONS OF HUMAN SOCIAL DEVELOPMENT

The remainder of this chapter examines some key dimensions of human social development - specifically, the nature and scale of world social progress and the challenges still remaining; progress in recent decades with regard to basic needs and the scale of world poverty. The chapter also briefly examines some key dimensions of poverty in these islands and its impact on the lives of the poor. Finally, the chapter outlines some of the current trends and issues in the world of work.

> *"Until the lions have their historians," declares an African proverb, "tales of hunting will always glorify the hunter." Likewise, the historians of the world's fortunate class - those billion-odd people who inhabit industrial lands - have already labelled the twentieth century a time of economic miracles.*
>
> *The history of the wealthy is impressive. Since 1900, the value of goods and services produced each year world-wide has grown twentyfold, the products of industry fiftyfold, and the average distance travelled by the well-to-do perhaps a thousandfold. As the century enters its final decade, commoners of the world's affluent nations live like the royalty of yesteryear, and elites literally live like gods.*
>
> *Yet the poor have a different tale to tell. The disparities in living standards that separate them from the rich verge on the grotesque. In 1989, the world had 157 billionaires, perhaps two million millionaires, and 100 million homeless. Americans spend $5 billion each year on special diets to lower their calorie consumption, while 400 million people around the world are malnourished, their bodies and minds are deteriorating. As water from a single spring in France is bottled and shipped to the prosperous around the globe, nearly 2 billion people drink and bathe in water contaminated with deadly parasites and pathogens."*

Alan B.Durning in "Ending Poverty" in L.Brown (ed.,1990) ***State of the World,*** New York, Norton.

A Charcoal wholesaler in Zambia

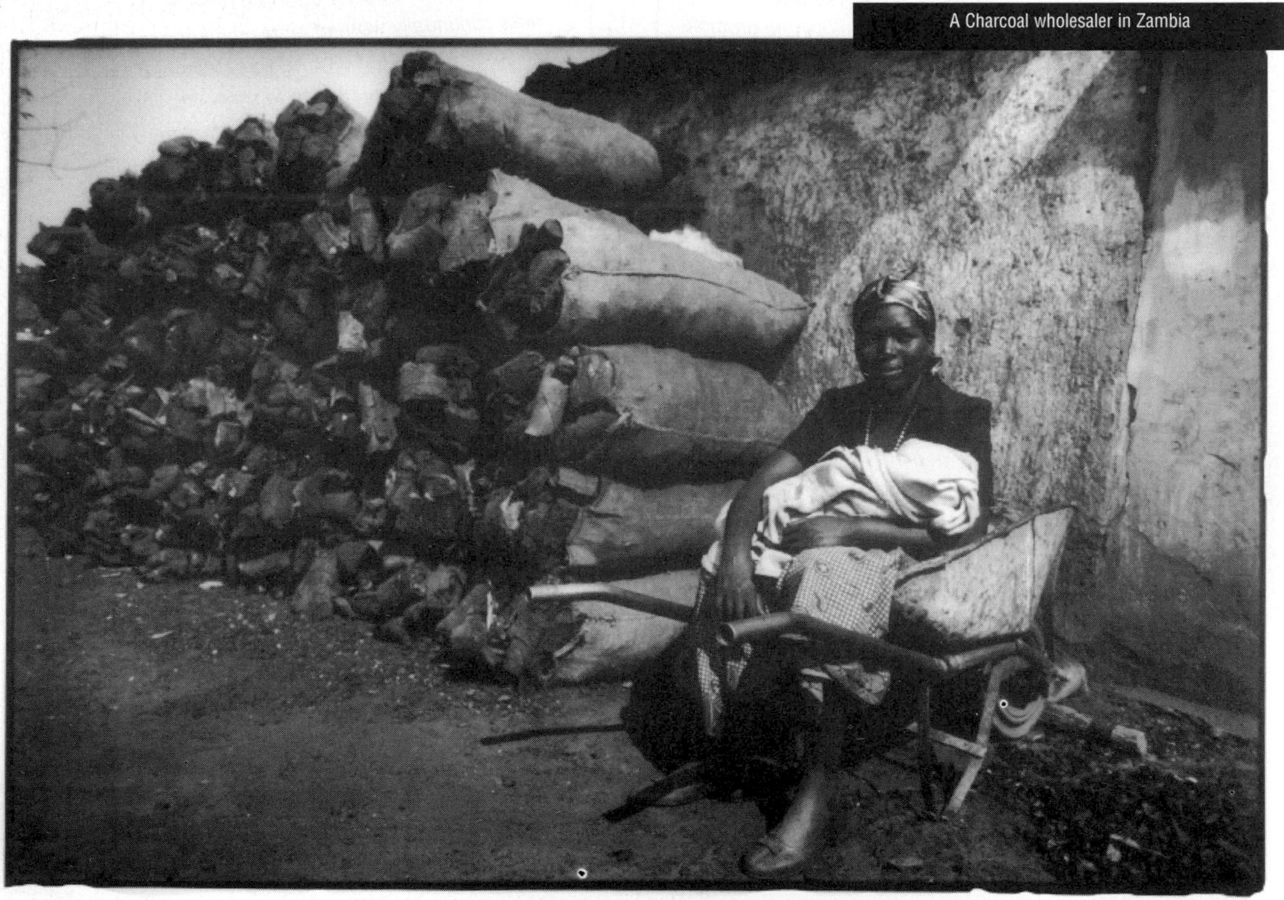

Profiles in Success

In 1995, UNICEF published a major report on the successes achieved in the area of human development in 11 developing countries as a result of their emphasis on three key areas - children, health and education. The countries were Malaysia, Costa Rica, Zimbabwe, Botswana, Mauritius, Sri Lanka, Barbados, Cuba, Mexico, the Republic of Korea and the state of Kerala in India.

According to the Report, the infant mortality rate in Malaysia dropped from 105 per 1,000 births in 1960 to 17 in 1993, while life expectancy has risen from 58.2 years in 1957 to 71 in 1993. Poverty has fallen significantly from 55% in 1973 to 15% in 1995. The male adult literacy rate in Botswana rose from 37% in 1970 to 84% in 1990 and from 44% to 65% for women in the same period. Life expectancy in Korea has risen by 20 years since 1960. Between 1959 and 1990, the infant mortality rate in Costa Rica dropped by 84%, illiteracy by 67% and malnutrition by over 71%. Cuba reduced its infant mortality rate from 39 per 1,000 births in 1960 to 9 in 1993 and, in that year, the number of doctors per 10,000 people was 46.7 as against 9.2 in 1958.

Statistics such as those above highlight the substantial social progress which has been achieved over the past few decades - progress which is most often measured in abstract figures but which has its real meaning in the transformation of the daily lives of those who have learnt to read, who can reasonably expect to live longer and more healthy lives and who can expect larger numbers of their children to survive and enjoy an improved quality of life. Stories such as these do not make the headlines and are consequently not popularly known even though they seriously challenge and mediate the unrelenting stories of unrelieved suffering which are the mainstay of reporting and fund-raising. They are an important reminder of what can and has been achieved - at an entirely affordable price and within a modest timeframe.

"Average life expectancy in the developing nations - that useful composite measure of improvements in incomes and nutrition, health care and education - has increased from approximately 40 years in 1950 to 62 years by 1990. Child death rates have fallen by two thirds, from around 300 to 100 per 1,000 births. Adult literacy rates have doubled to almost 70%. Smallpox, which killed approximately 5 million people a year in the early 1950s, has been eradicated. Polio, measles, malnutrition, micronutrient deficiencies, and diarrhoeal disease are being beaten. Overall, concluded the World Bank in 1993, "health conditions across the world have improved more in the past 40 years than in all of previous human history".

UNICEF (1995) **State of the World's Children,**
Oxford University Press.

Progress and Challenge
A Global Balance Sheet

Health

The average life expectancy in the Third World increased by over one-third between 1960 and 1990. It is now 65 years (85% that of the industrial world) while in Ireland it is 75 and in Britain 76.

But Still

10 million older children and young adults and 14 million young children die each year from easily and cheaply preventable diseases. In Sub-Saharan Africa, over 10 million people are now affected with the AIDS virus, while in South Asia, in countries such as Bangladesh and Nepal, female life expectancy is, uniquely, shorter than male life expectancy.

During the past 30 years, the death rate of infants under 5 years was halved - this is a very sensitive measure of human well-being.

But Still

Each day, 34,000 children die from easily preventable malnutrition and disease.

Security

Due to the ending of the Cold War and the reduction of superpower rivalry in the developing world, in 1990 alone, an estimated 380,000 refugees were able to return home.

But Still

War and internal conflicts now affect over 60 countries and 1 in every 115 people on earth is a refugee or a migrant with over 6 million refugees in Sub-Saharan Africa alone.

During the period 1974-93, 130 parliamentary elections were held in Latin America and the Caribbean, and, since 1980, 18 countries have made the transition from military dictatorships to democratic governments.

But Still

In 1992, Amnesty International reported human rights violations in 112 countries world-wide.

Literacy and Education

Throughout the developing world, adult literacy rates increased from 46% to 60% between 1970 and 1985.

But Still

Over 1 billion adults cannot read or write and this reality affects many aspects of their daily lives including their health, their wealth and their family's well-being. Southern Asia continues to have the lowest adult literacy rate.

The number of girls, in Third World countries, attending secondary school more than doubled in the past two decades.

But Still

Two-thirds of all women throughout the Third World are illiterate and in some rural areas the figure can be as high as 85%.

As a result of continuous effort in the 1960s and the 1970s, the number of children in developing countries completing 4 years of primary school had reached 50% or more.

But Still

As a result of the debt crisis in the 1980s and the interest repayments which developing countries were forced to pay, spending on primary schooling especially suffered and these gains are now under threat.

Women and Children

In the industrialised world, women now make up more than 40% of the labour force and hold about 28% of administrative and managerial positions and, in East Asia, the 19% female representation in parliaments is 1.6 times that of the industrial world.

But Still

Women comprise 66% of the world's illiterates and 70% of the world's poor; Asia alone has 374 million poor rural women, more than the population of Western Europe.

Between 1960 and 1992, the infant mortality rate more than halved in the developing world.

But Still

Children everywhere are vulnerable victims of violence - in Brazil, home to an estimated 200,000 street children, four youngsters a day are murdered while in Thailand, Sri Lanka and the Philippines, an estimated 500,000 children work as child prostitutes.

Water and Sanitation

The provision of clean, safe water throughout the Third World has increased by more than two-thirds over the past 20 years and nearly two-thirds of people there now have access to basic health services.

But Still

Another 1.5 billion people do not have access to health services or to clean water supplies and in Latin America, only 56% of the rural population have access to safe water as against 90% in urban areas.

Sources: UNDP (1990-95) ***Human Development Report,*** *Oxford University Press;*
UNICEF (1992-95) ***State of the World's Children Report,*** *Oxford University Press;*
World Bank (1990-95) ***World Development Report,*** *Oxford University Press;*
The World, A Third World Guide *(1993, 1995), Instituto del Tercer Mundo, Uruguay and Bread for the World Institute (1995)* ***State of World Hunger,*** *Silver Spring*

Food and Nutrition

Between 1965 and 1990, the number of developing countries that were able to meet the daily calorie needs of their people doubled - from about 25 to 50.

But Still

Approximately, 800 million people do not get enough to eat, 500 million remain chronically malnourished and, in 1990, over 100 million were affected by famine.

Population and Environment

In all continents of the globe, including Africa, population growth rates are declining.

But Still

Human population continues to increase by an average of 240,000 per day - the equivalent of another Switzerland every 30 days or a new China every 10 years with the greatest growth rates occurring in countries least able to support it.

Developing country emissions are less than one quarter that of industrialised countries, even though their population is 3.5 times larger.

But Still

About 200 million people are severely affected by desertification in the developing world while inhabitants of the industrialised world (one fifth of the world's population) consume nine times more commercial energy than people in the Third World.

Basic Needs 1950 - 1995

Life Expectancy

Since 1950, life expectancy for most developing countries has increased by over 50% - this has been achieved in 30 years as against the two centuries it required in the developed world. Life expectancy for all Third World countries increased from 43 years in 1950 to 65 years in 1993; Africa from 35 to 59, Latin America from 45 to 69 and Asia from 42 to 65. Despite the very real achievements, considerable variations continue to exist between a Third World highest of 76 in Cuba and Costa Rica and the lowest of 42. The countries of Sub-Saharan Africa remain at the bottom of the list overall.

Literacy

Nearly 66% of all adults in the Third World are now literate as against roughly 33% in 1950. The countries of Sub-Saharan Africa still display the highest rates of illiteracy (50% overall) with figures of 82% in Burkina Faso, 79% in Sierra Leone and 73% in the Gambia. Illiteracy rates for rural dwellers and for women remain significantly higher - female illiteracy is 91% in Burkina Faso, 89% in Sierra Leone and 84% in the Gambia. In contrast to this, female illiteracy rates in the Philippines are only 11% (10% overall), 1% in Jamaica (2% overall) and 4% in Uruguay (4% overall).

Infant Mortality Rates

UNICEF monitors the death rates of infants under 5 years (per 1,000 live births). Since 1950 the overall situation has improved greatly from 295 to 100 in 1992. As usual this overall average figure conceals huge variations - the figure for Sub-Saharan Africa is 160 while that for Afghanistan is 270, Sierra Leone 250 and 240 for Mozambique. However, some developing countries have made huge progress in this area - the corresponding figure for Cuba is 17, for Vietnam 50, for Jamaica 18 and for the Democratic Republic of Korea 28. Figures such as these help such developing countries to rise high up on the Human Development Index (see Chapter One).

Infant mortality rates for Britain and Ireland are 8 and 7 respectively. It is interesting to note that in 1960, the figures for Britain and Ireland were 27 and 36.

Inevitably the rates remain very high in those countries suffering war, drought, wide-spread illness and extreme poverty, e.g. Niger 320, Angola 292, Sierra Leone 284 and Somalia 211.

Food and Nutrition

In most areas of the Third World, with the notable exception of Sub-Saharan Africa, food production has outstripped population growth and, for many countries food availability has improved significantly. Average annual food availability, measured in calories per day, was 1,957 for the period 1961-1963; by 1991, this figure had increased to 2,480. But, again, such figures conceal huge variations. Today about 20% of the world's population remains undernourished while about 2 billion face vitamin and mineral deficiencies that pose serious health threats. In 1992, about 157 million or 3% of the world's population lived in countries affected by famine (the actual numbers directly affected was less). 70% of the world's chronically undernourished ("...people who, on average, during the course of a year did not consume enough food to maintain their weight and engage in light activity") lived in the Asia-Pacific region.

It is estimated that in 1969-71, 33% of the population of Sub-Saharan Africa was undernourished whereas the corresponding figure for 1990 was 37%; similar figures for Asia are 29% and 20% and for Latin America 19% and 13%. While the level of hunger in Asia and Latin America has decreased, that in the United States has increased.

Other Basic Needs Indicators

Improvements in other areas include the number of persons per doctor (from 8,300 in 1965 to 6,670 in 1990) although, again, serious extremes continue to exist (Africa changed from 33,840 to 35,680). Significant improvements have also been recorded in immunisation rates, attended births and in maternal mortality rates - with huge variations recorded once again. Another area where considerable progress has been achieved has been in the provision of access to safe water and sanitation. 66% of urban areas in developing countries had such access in 1970; this figure had increased to 80% by 1991. The improvement for rural areas was even better, from 13% to 54% although rural areas remain more seriously deprived.

Sources: Grindle, J. (1992) Bread and Freedom: Basic Needs and Human Rights, Dublin, Trocaire/Gill and Macmillan; UNDP (1993/94/95) Human Development Report, Oxford University Presss; UNICEF (1994/95) State of the World's Children Report, Oxford University Press and World Bank (1994/95) World Development Report, Oxford University Press.

World Poverty - the basic facts

Poverty is normally measured by the income or expenditure level that can sustain a bare minimum standard of living. But poverty is also a function of nutrition, life expectancy, access to safe water and sanitation, illness and literacy. Studies in countries such as Sri Lanka and India, the United States and England have shown that whether we use income or expenditure as the measurement, we tend to find, more or less, the same groups in the statistics of poverty.

In 1990, the World Bank published a major review of poverty world-wide. Some of its major findings were:

- Of the 5.6 billion people living on the planet more than a billion live in a state of absolute poverty (defined as having an income level of $370 or less per year) - this equals 1 in every 5 inhabitants. If present trends continue, the UN now estimates that a further 200 million absolutely poor people will be added to these figures by the year 2000.
- The poor are in virtually every country, but the overwhelming majority are in the developing world. The greatest concentrations of the poor are in the rural areas of Africa and Asia. In recent years, poverty has increased in Africa, Latin America and in the industrialised world while it has decreased in Asia.
- Numerically, the largest number of severely impoverished people live in South Asia, which is home to about 30% of the world's people. Africa has about 16% of world population, and half of all Africans are impoverished.
- Women suffer disproportionately representing 70% of all poverty stricken people, followed closely by the elderly. The poorest groups in the Third World live in households headed by women - for example, women head roughly 20% of poor households in India, 17% in Costa Rica and 40% in rural Kenya.
- Although urban poverty continues to grow, the rural poor still represent more than 80% of the total number of poor. 60% of Africa's rural population live in absolute poverty alongside 31% for Asia and 61% for Latin America and the Caribbean.
- In recent years, poverty in the developed world has also grown. For example, poverty in the United States affectes nearly 15% of the population.
- The extent of poverty varies greatly in different regions within countries - for example, the North-east of Brazil has more than 50% of the country's poor but only 27% of its population. Many of the poor are located in areas where land is scarce, agricultural productivity is low and drought, floods and environmental damage are common.
- According to UNICEF, *"...poverty has become more and more concentrated in marginal lands and in urban slums, two different destinations of which the common characteristic is that they are both environmentally vulnerable."*
- The poor of urban areas often experience certain aspects of poverty more seriously than rural dwellers - overcrowding, poor sanitation and infected water.
- The poor tend to have large families, few assets, are frequently landless or work marginal lands, have low levels of formal educational achievement and are usually illiterate. Poverty is often closely related to race and ethnic background and the poor are often separated by cultural barriers. They are therefore highly prone to being exploited and manipulated politically.

The World Summit For Social Development, was held in Copenhagen in March 1995. The Chairman of its Preparatory Conference, Chilean Juan Somavia, argued for an explicit commitment from each nation on the elimination of poverty - *"A political decision to eliminate-and yes, I mean eliminate - extreme poverty within a time frame distinctly specified by each nation would be a true achievement in which we could take legitimate pride".*

While the Summit failed to set a timeframe, it did, nonetheless achieve agreement on the goal of eradicating poverty.

Figure 3.2

Poverty in the Third World

Region	1985 Extremely Poor Number (millions)	1985 Extremely Poor Percentage of population	1985 Poor (including extremely poor) Number (millions)	1985 Poor (including extremely poor) Percentage of population	1990 Total Number (millions)	1990 Total Percentage of population
Sub-Saharan Africa	120	30.0	184	47.6	216	49.7
East Asia	120	9.0	182	13.2	169	11.3
South Asia	300	29.0	535	51.8	562	49.0
Middle East and North Africa	40	21.0	60	30.6	73	33.1
Latin America and the Caribbean	50	12.0	87	22.4	108	25.5
All Developing Countries	633	18.0	1,051	30.5	1,133	25.5

Source: Todaro, P. (1994) **Economic Development,** Harlow, Longman. p.146/147

"Nearly a quarter of a million New Yorkers - more than 3% of the city's population and more than 8% of its black children - have stayed in shelters over the past five years...London has about 400,000 registered homeless people. France has more than 500,000 - nearly 10,000 in Paris...In Calcutta, Dhaka and Mexico City, more than 25% of the people constitute what is sometimes called a floating population."

UNDP (1994) **Human Development Report,** Oxford University Press.

Figure 3.3

Population Below Poverty Line, Selected Countries, 1990.

	GNP per capita, 1990 ($US)	Population, 1992 (millions)	Percentage of Population in Poverty	Number of People in Poverty (millions)
Latin America (all countries)	2,170	453.0	35	158.5
Argentina	2,370	33.1	8	2.6
Brazil	2,680	150.8	43	64.8
Guatemala	900	9.7	73	7.1
Peru	1,160	22.5	59	13.3
Venezuela	2,560	18.9	37	7.0
Asia (all countries except Japan)	810	3,082.0	25	768.0
Bangladesh	200	111.4	86	95.8
India	350	882.6	48	423.6
Philippines	730	63.7	58	36.9
South Korea	5,400	44.3	16	7.1
Sri Lanka	470	17.6	10	1.8
Africa (all countries)	630	654.0	47	307.4
Ethiopia (including Eritrea)	120	54.3	64	34.8
Kenya	370	26.2	44	11.5
Nigeria	370	90.1	29	26.1
Sudan	260	26.5	85	22.5
Tanzania	120	27.4	46	12.6
Uganda	220	17.5	45	7.9

Poverty in these Islands

Britain

"For those at the top, these are the best of times. For those at the bottom, horizons are even narrower than they were a decade ago and the gap between rich and poor is greater than at any time since the 1930s."
Commission on Social Justice (1994) **Social Justice: Strategies for National Renewal,** London, Vintage.

▼ Between 1945 and 1980, the gap between rich and poor in Britain had gradually narrowed. Since then, this progress has been reversed with the gap between the earnings of the highest and lowest paid now greater than at any time since records began in 1886.

▼ Nearly two thirds of people live in households whose income is below the average.

▼ Between 1979 and 1991 – 92, the poorest 10% experienced a fall in income of 17% while the highest paid earners in the South-east increased their earnings by an average of £22,000 (1989-91) as 50% of earners took an average pay cut of £200 a year.

▼ When all taxes are taken into account ... the poorest one tenth of the population pay a higher proportion of their income in tax than the richest 10%, 43% as against 32%.

▼ In 1979, 1 in 10 children was living in a low-income family, today, poverty affects 1 in 3 (see diagram). It is estimated that about 20% of the British population is now living in poverty. The average family now has a debt of about 8 weeks wages - nearly double the 1980 figure.

▼ The UK has the second highest rate of homelessness in the EU after Germany while Ireland has the seventh highest.

▼ There is also a clear regional pattern to income inequality in the UK , income in the South-east is, on average, 25% above the national average and is also above average in East Anglia, the South-west and the East-midlands; in the North it is only 79% of the national average, in Wales 81%, in Scotland 87% while in Northern Ireland it is only 80%. These patterns do not change significantly when adjusted for housing costs.

▼ There is no official poverty line in Britain.

▼ During the 1980s, for the first time in ten years, the number of those living in poverty increased. The share of income received by the poorest 10% has fallen by half since 1979 from 4% to 2%, while the poorest 20% have lost more than one-third of their share. The bottom half of the population has seen its share of income decline by 20% while that of the top 50% has risen from just over two-thirds to three-quarters.

▼ The number of households accepted officially as homeless has tripled since 1978. It is estimated that poverty in the Northern region, in Wales, Scotland and Northern Ireland is almost twice what it is elsewhere.

▼ Poverty and social inequality in the UK also displays a number of other patterns along with greater levels of poverty likely among women and coloured groups.

"Individuals ...can be said to be in poverty when they lack the resources to obtain the types of diet, participate in the activities and have the living conditions and amenities which are customary ... in the societies to which they belong"
Peter Townsend (1993) **The International Analysis of Poverty,** London, Harvester.

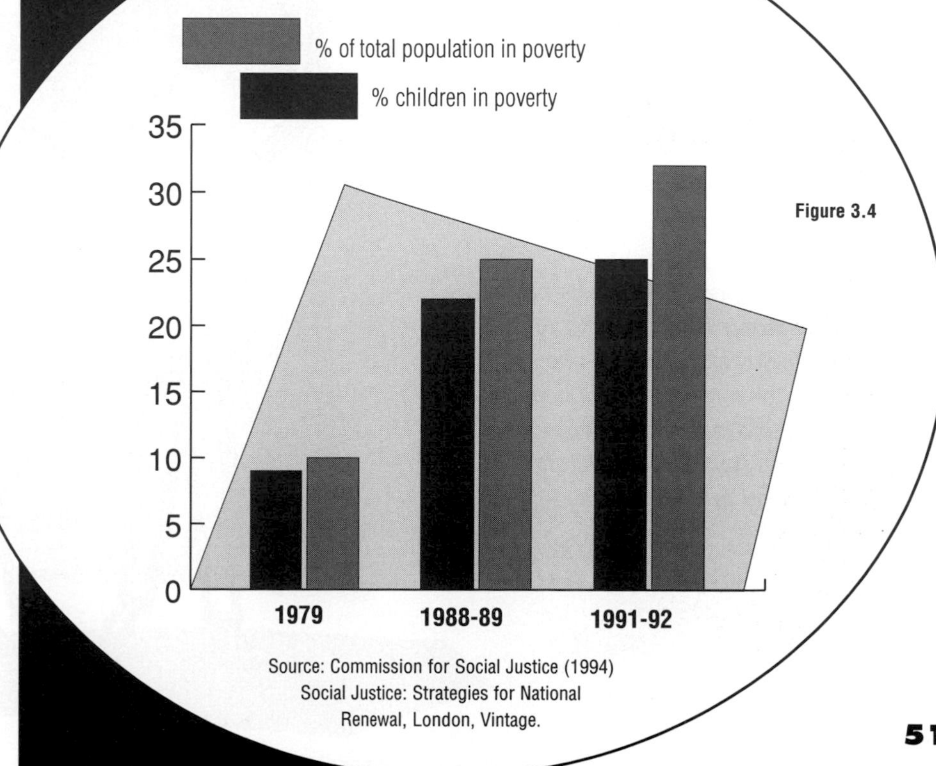

Figure 3.4

Scotland

According to a report published by Caledonian University and Save the Children:

▼ 1 in 3 children in Scotland are living in poverty and 25% of children under 16 in Scotland are living in households dependent on income support as is an estimated 17% of the total population.

▼ Those most likely to be at risk of poverty in Scotland include women on low pay, large families, lone parents, those with disability, young people and ethnic minorities.

▼ In 1979, the number of households with below 50% of the average income was 9%, by 1992, this figure had increased to 25%. In 1979, the main group in poverty were pensioners, by 1992, the main group were lone parents.

▼ Poverty and unemployment is higher amongst males and females within minority ethnic groups.

▼ Over the period 1980 to 1993, house repossessions, one very real measure of poverty, increased by 1500%.

"The statistics (proving Scottish poverty) are there. Unfortunately, they're not all that's there. For being poor is never statistical. It is specific and individual and sore..."

William McIlvanney (1983) **Being Poor**

"I hate being poor. I hate having to sit in the same room, having to save up for weeks on end to be able to go out for a night. I hate having to say no to the weans. They're too young, they just don't understand. I hate feeling inferior ... it's depressing."

A Parent in a Save the Children Project

Ireland

The latest detailed figures on poverty in Ireland come from a survey of households in 1987 (these figures are currently being updated and will be published by the Combat Poverty Agency, the Department of Social Welfare and the Economic and Social Research Institute).

▼ In 1987, 31.4% of the population was considered to be living in poverty (defined as having a household income of less than 60% of the national average). The figure was 8.2% when poverty was defined at less than 40% and 19.8% at less than 50%.

▼ In 1987, 26% of all children under the age of 14 were living in households with less than half the national average income.

▼ 53% of welfare recipients were women; lone parent families have a 29% risk of poverty and women head up 83% of one-parent families.

▼ In 1991, the top 1% of Irish people owned 10% of total wealth, the top 10% owned 42%, the bottom 70% owned 29%, while the bottom 50% owned 12%.

NORTHERN IRELAND

▼ In a major study of poverty in Britain and Northern Ireland in 1979, Peter Townsend discovered that 44.3% of households in the area were living in poverty.

▼ Northern Ireland remains the most disadvantaged area within the UK today. Apart altogether from the legacy of the "troubles", Northern Ireland continues to have lower wages, higher prices and the worst unemployment rate of any UK region.

▼ While historically Northern Ireland benefited considerably from its more complete integration into the industrial heartland of 19th century Britain than the rest of Ireland, it suffered very considerably after the Second World War. Shipbuilding, textiles and agriculture - the basic staple industries - experienced almost total collapse. This was further compounded by the recession from the mid 1970s. While the state has been successful to some degree in attracting foreign industry, the State continues to employ over one-third of the work force.

▼ As is the case in the Republic, recent research shows that the groups most at risk as a result of poverty are the elderly, low income families, those on low pay and, of course, single parent families.

▼ It is also clear from data collected in the past few years that the situation of Catholics is, in general, worse than that of Protestants. The census of 1991 indicated that Catholics accounted for two thirds of the unemployed despite the fact that they made up only one third of the population.

▼ A recent Save the Children report on poverty and children's health in Northern Ireland concluded *"Children's health is dependent on the conditions in which they live; - and the 'health divide' (between rich and poor) is a result of poverty - of low income, poor housing, unhealthy nutrition and lack of educational and employment opportunities. Save the Children believe it is a huge social injustice that children born into the most deprived communities in Northern Ireland have less chance of surviving, more illness, more disability and shorter lives than those who are more affluent"*

Sources: Caledonian University/Save the Children (1994) ***Child and Family Poverty in Scotland: The Facts;*** Combat Poverty Agency (1988) ***Poverty and the Social Welfare System in Ireland,*** Dublin; Commission for Social Justice (1994) ***Social Justice: Strategies for National Renewal,*** London, Vintage; Eileen Evason (1987) "Poverty in Northern Ireland Today" ***Shaping our Future: Work, Jobs and Unemployment: A Christian Response*** CMRS/NCPI; B. Nolan (1991) ***The Wealth of Irish Households,*** Combat Poverty Agency; Chris Philo (ed.,1995) ***Off the Map: The Social Geography of Poverty in the UK;*** Child Poverty Action Group, London; Save the Children (1995) ***Sick of Poverty,*** London and Peter Townsend (1993) ***The International Analysis of Poverty,*** London, Harvester.

WHAT IT MEANS TO BE POOR

In 1989 the Combat Poverty Agency in Ireland published a book entitled **Pictures of Poverty** - twelve accounts of life on low income which graphically describe the human face of poverty today. In its conclusion, the Agency outlined the most common characteristics of poverty as follows:

* Spending is confined to routine and basic items.
* Constant debt is due to the necessity for weekly and long-term borrowing from friends, family, moneylenders and financial institutions, and deferring payments for public services.
* Housing, health, education and legal services are experienced as inferior.
* Powerlessness and humiliation are common.
* People are isolated from family, community and society.
* Women carry a heavy burden as managers of the household, rearers of children and as financial dependants of men.
* Both adults and children see few opportunities to escape from a life of poverty.

It is clear from studies of poverty in Britain that these characteristics are repeated there.

Women and Poverty in Ireland

"Widespread poverty exists amidst plenty in this country today: Ireland is currently the 27th richest country in the world ... some people in Ireland are very wealthy with top salaries now exceeding £150,000 a year ... In January 1989 Irish Business magazine identified forty five of the most wealthy individuals in Ireland. Between them they had wealth in excess of £1 billion. None were women ...."

".... 274,000 adult women (compared with 244,000 adult men) live in households below a poverty line of £48 a week for an adult in 1987 ...."

".... Women in rural areas have a higher risk of poverty than women in urban areas. Age also affects women's risk of poverty ...."

"The following groups of women appear to be most at risk:

- *women rearing children on their own*
- *elderly women*
- *"minority" women, especially travellers and women who find themselves homeless*
- *women in low paying jobs*
- *some women working full-time in the "home"*

"In the 1986 census there were 81,087 households consisting solely of a lone parent with children .... 82% of these were headed by women .... 85,693 of mothers were not living with a man. The majority of these (64%) were widowed, 17% were married, 11% were separated and 7% were single. Between them these women had over 160,000 children ...."

".... 56% of all those over the age of 65 are women, but women are two-thirds of all those who reach 80 years of age. Although the ESRI research suggested that poverty among the elderly had declined between 1980 and 1987, the general consensus of research is that more women than men end their lives in poverty".

".... Traveller women are at a very high risk of poverty, not only because they are members of a community that is itself very vulnerable to poverty but also because of their lower status within that community".

"Women who find themselves homeless are among the poorest of all ...."

"Research .... based on information from 1979, estimated that almost half of all women workers then were low paid i.e. on wages of £65 a week or less ...."

"Women working in the home .... are the largest group of women in Ireland (nearly 700,000) .... Yet their economic and other circumstances are almost totally hidden from view ...."

"One group of women whose circumstances should be looked at closely is those caring for the elderly at home. 66,000 elderly people are estimated to be cared for in their homes .... 70% of the carers are women ...."

"So, a minimum of over a quarter of a million Irish women are living in financial poverty today. These women may be in different living situations but there are three characteristics that they share: motherhood, dependency status, and underpaid or unpaid work"

"The women represented in this book are survivors, not victims, exercising immense skill and creative ingenuity in balancing their family's finances and emotions, keeping their families going, working long and hard to shelter their husbands, children and other relatives from the worst excesses of poverty. But a survival existence on or just below the breadline is not a full life. And all women are entitled to that."

Excerpts from Daly, M (1989) **Women and Poverty,** Dublin, Attic Press.

The World of Work

"Duong is a Vietnamese peasant farmer who struggles to feed his family. He earns the equivalent of $10 a week for thirty eight hours of work in the rice fields, but he works full-time only six months of the year - during the off-season he can earn very little. His wife and four children work with him in the fields, but the family can afford to send only the two youngest to school. Duong's eleven year old daughter stays at home to help with housework, while his thirteen year old son works as a street trader in town. By any standard Duong's family is living in poverty. Workers like Duong, labouring on family farms in low- and middle- income countries, account for about 40% of the world's labour force."

"Hoa is a young Vietnamese city dweller experiencing relative affluence for the first time. In Ho Chi Minh City she earns the equivalent of £30 a week working forty-eight hours in a garment factory - a joint venture with a French firm. She works hard for her living and spends many hours looking after her three children as well; her husband works as a janitor. But Hoa's family has several times the living standard of Duong's and by Vietnamese standards, is relatively well off. There is every expectation that both she and her children will continue to have a vastly better standard of living than her parents had. Wage employees like Hoa, working in the formal sector in low- and middle-income countries, make up about 20% of the global labour force."

"Francoise is an immigrant in France of Vietnamese origin who works long hours as a waitress to make ends meet. She takes home the equivalent of $220 a week, after taxes and including tips, for fifty hours work. By French standards she is poor. Legally, Francoise is a casual worker and she has no job security, but she is much better off in France than she would have been in Vietnam. Her wage is almost eight times that earned by Hoa in Ho Chi Minh City. Francoise and other service sector workers in high income countries account for about 9% of the global labour force."

"Jean-Paul is a fifty-year-old Frenchman whose employment prospects look bleak. For ten years he has worked in a garment factory in Toulouse, taking home the equivalent of $400 a week - twelve times the average wage in Vietnam's garment industry. But next month he will lose his job when the factory closes. Unemployment benefits will partly shield him from the shock, but his chances of matching his old salary in a new job are slim. Frenchmen of Jean-Paul's age who lose their jobs are likely to stay unemployed for more than a year, and Jean-Paul is encouraging his son to work hard in school so he can go to college and learn computer programming. Workers in industry in high income countries, like Jean-Paul, make up just 4% of the world's labour force."

These four case studies illustrate vividly some of the key dimensions of work in today's global economy. They are taken from the ***World Development Report 1995*** published by the World Bank which examines the world of work.

- Of the 2.5 billion people working in productive activities world-wide, over 1.4 billion live in poor countries (defined, in 1993, as those with annual income per capita below $695). Another 660 million live in middle-income countries and the remainder, some 380 million, live in high-income countries (per capita income of $8,626).
- In poor countries, 61% of the labour force works in agriculture, mainly tending family farms; 22% work in the rural non-farm and urban informal sectors and 15% have wage labour, mainly in urban industrial and service employment.
- In middle-income countries, 29% of the labour force works on farms, 15% in rural and urban informal activities and 46% in wage labour in industry and services.
- In high-income countries, the bulk of workers have jobs in the formal sector with approximately 4% in agriculture, 27% in industry and 60% in services.
- Women's unpaid work world-wide is valued at $11 trillion while that of men is valued at $5 trillion and women earn, on average, only 75% of what men earn for the same industrial jobs (69.7% in Britain and 69% in Ireland).
- There are roughly 120 million unemployed people world-wide, although figures on unemployment in the developing world are usually seriously underestimated.
- Workers in low-income countries dominate the world's agricultural workforce but also account for roughly 50% of industrial workers and about one third of the unemployed.
- Although 90% of developing countries have some form of social security system, at best it covers only those in the formal sector, who make up only 15% of the labour force in low-income countries and 45% in middle-income countries.
- About 99% of the estimated 1 billion workers who are expected to join the world's labour force in the next 30 years will come from the low- and middle-income countries.

▼ References

Bread for the World Institute (1995) **State of World Hunger,** Silver Springs.

Caledonian University/Save the Children (1994) **Child and Family Poverty in Scotland: The Facts,** Glasgow.

Combat Poverty Agency (1988) **Poverty and the Social Welfare System in Ireland,** Dublin.

Commission on Social Justice (1994) **Social Justice: Strategies for National Renewal,** London, Vintage.

Mary Daly (l989) **Women and Poverty, Dublin,** Attic Press.

Eileen Evason (1987) **"Poverty in Northern Ireland Today" Shaping our Future: Work, jobs and unemployment: A Christian Response** CMRS/NCPI.

Duncan Green (1991) **Faces of Latin America,** London, Latin American Bureau.

Paul Harrison (1993) **Inside the Third World,** London, Penguin.

Chris Philo (ed.,1995) **Off the Map: The Social Geography of Poverty in the UK,** London, Child Poverty Action Group.

Save the Children (1995) **Sick of Poverty,** London.

Peter Townsend (1993) **The International Analysis of Poverty,** London, Harvester.

UNDP (1990-95) **Human Development Report,** Oxford University Press

UNICEF (1995) **The State of the World's Children,** Oxford University Press.

'...WEAVING THREADS OF HOPE AND LIGHT...'

People Making a Difference.

Colm Regan

INTRODUCTION

In 1992, Fr. Ricardo Rezende, parish priest of Rio Maria, a small town in the Amazonian state of Para, was presented with the Anti-Slavery medal by Anti-Slavery International for his fearless and unending work on behalf of the landless, many of whom had become modern day slaves because of their poverty. In his acceptance speech, Fr. Ricardo noted:

> *"...those who have hope and commitment and who suffer threats but who obstinately persevere with their task, at great danger to themselves. The prize is tribute to ...(the) martyrs of the land. It is a tribute to those who, in the depth of the night, weave threads of hope and light."*

Mention the poor, the unemployed or the homeless, especially those in the Third World and chances are that the instant popular image is one of hopelessness and pity and the corresponding response one of welfare and charity. Another image is of people who, by and large, have brought misfortune on themselves by being either lazy, unlucky or feckless or by having too many children or by being at the mercy of an unforgiving climate. The corresponding images are of aid/charity workers (in the case of the Third World Westerners) forever cast in the role of saviours either in the form of selfless volunteers or 'experts'. Overall the poor, homeless, hungry are usually presented as the 'objects' of development rather than its subjects. Seldom do we see the heroic efforts of the poor themselves to grapple with the problems they face - this is not the stuff of good television or of good advertising for fund-raising. There is a giving us and a deserving them.

NEGATIVE IMAGES AND THEIR CONSEQUENCES

The consequences of this approach have been graphically commented upon by many Third World observers, amongst them Bangladeshi photographer Shahidul Alam and Ethiopian researcher and writer Eshetu Chole. The former observes:

> *"Poorer countries have invariably been misrepresented by wealthier ones. The need to raise money has led to over-dramatised images of helplessness as being the only visual representation of nations with rich cultural heritages and enormous human potential. Floods, famines and disasters are coupled with stories of corruption and greed. The only exceptions to such views are shown by travel oriented agencies, which harp on mysticism, magic and natural beauty. In all cases, the ordinary people who go about their daily lives are forgotten for the exotic and the dramatic. The effects of imperialism on local customs is rarely analysed. Neither is the effectiveness of foreign aid questioned. A massive brain drain of home grown expertise to overseas countries combines with the effective purchase of well-trained professionals for non-decision making posts in foreign agencies, to leave the countries barren of much needed local expertise."*

In the context of media reporting of his country's famine in 1984/85, Eschetu Chole comments:

> *"...Ethiopians, over and above the damage inflicted on them by the famine, have also had, for a number of years now, to carry the heavy cross of the international beggar. The negative impact of this on the psychology of the people may never be accurately determined but is none the less real for that. To the shame of not being able to feed itself,*

Ethiopian society has had to live with the additional shame of living with international publicity - at times good natured and at others pernicious - that has cast Ethiopians as a people who owe their very survival to acts of international charity. This has made it impossible for this generation to raise its head; whether or not next generations will be spared this humiliation, only history will tell."

Apart altogether from the great dis-service which constant and overly negative images and analyses do to concepts such as partnership, human dignity and justice, they also portray a factually incorrect and dangerously partial view of the contribution of local groups and local organisations to their own development. Seldom do we hear, for example, of the over 23,000 women's groups actively involved in the development process in Kenya. Nor do we hear of the over 25,000 registered local groups in Tamil Nadu state in India or the 12,000 Bangladeshi groups or the 18,000 registered groups in the Philippines. The OECD estimates that there are as many as 50,000 major local organisations throughout the countries of the Third World - all of them actively involved in various dimensions of the development process.

In parallel to them are a host of non-governmental organisations, estimated to number over 4,000 in the OECD states alone. Recent research suggests that between them they disperse over $3 billion every year while working with over 20,000 Third World NGOs assisting up to 100 million people annually.

The work of such organisations has achieved considerable results and impact and we felt that some examples of their work should be included in 75:25. In the space available to us it would be impossible to do justice to the breadth and scope of their work. So inevitably we have had to choose a set of case studies which we believe exemplify what is best about this approach to development. Our central objective in presenting these case studies is to challenge those views which present the poor as helpless and hopeless and to indicate how many of them are active on a daily basis, often at great cost and risk to themselves, in the struggle for justice and development.

"Everyone reads life and the world like a book. Even the so-called "illiterate". But especially the "leaders" of our society, the most "responsible" non-dreamers: the politicians, the businessmen, the ones who make plans. Without the reading of the world as a book, there is no prediction, no planning, no taxes, no laws, no welfare, no war. Yet these leaders read the world in terms of rationality and averages, as if it were a textbook. The world actually writes itself with the many-levelled, unfixable intricacy and openness of a work of literature. If... we can ourselves learn and teach others to read the world in the "proper" risky way, and to act upon that lesson, perhaps we... would not forever be such helpless victims."

Gayatri Spivak, ***In Other Worlds,*** 1987.

CASE STUDY 1

'...weaving threads of hope and light...'

SLAVERY IN BRAZIL?

Slavery was officially abolished in Brazil in 1888 yet Associate Professor of Sociology in Sao Paulo University, Jose de Souza Martins, estimates that at least 90,000 people '...were at some time enslaved in Brazil's agricultural areas during the last 25 years'. This is the reality of the position of Brazil's landless peasants, driven ever further to the margins of life by poverty, exploitation and powerlessness in one of the world's richest countries endowed with massive resources and wealth. Since the abolition of slavery, reports continue to be published highlighting thousands of cases of people forced to work as slaves either through coercion or lack of alternative choice. Violence, inhuman conditions, torture and debt are commonplace. As Fr. Ricardo Rezende comments: *"Black slaves are no longer brought to Brazil from Africa; the modern badge of slavery is not colour, but poverty and unemployment."*

CHALLENGING SLAVERY

Fr. Ricardo is just one of the many activists working with the Pastoral Land Commission (CPT) of the Brazilian Catholic Church which was founded in 1975 by a group of bishops, priests and lay people in response to the needs of Brazil's peasants, rural workers and landless. The CPT links more than 2,000 parishes throughout Brazil. Its work, which symbolises the work of many parallel organisations and groups in Brazil, encompasses publicising and condemning abuses in rural areas; taking legal action in individual cases; campaigning against developments harmful to human rights and the environment and training grass-roots activists. Like so many other local organisations, it also offers legal, political and trade union advice as well as encouraging and linking with action internationally. CPT works alongside many other Brazilian organisations such as the CUT (National Trade Congress); the Rural Workers Union, the National Union of Rubber Tappers; the Rural Workers Federations of various states as well as a host of legal organisations.

According to CPT, of the 1,730 cases of killings of peasants, trade union leaders, indigenous people, church workers and lawyers in the context of land disputes between 1964 and 1992, only 30 had come to trial. In effect therefore only 2.8% of all these murders ever reached the courts. In June 1993, the Assistant Attorney General reported that, of the 173 cases of rural murders involving hired gunmen which were being investigated by his office, military policemen had participated directly in 72 of them, while 8 others involved members of the military police.

THE HUMAN FACE

One key dimension of their work is described in detail by Alison Sutton in her book **Slavery in Brazil: A link in the chain of modernisation:**

"In Caceres, Mato Grosso, the local human rights centre has been instrumental in denouncing many cases of slave labour in the state. In June 1991 they publicised the case of the Fazenda (large ranch) Continental ...in the north of Mato Grosso...Six workers out of 35 who had been taken in cattle trucks from Caceres in March 1991 had returned to the town after two and a half months without pay. Many of the workers had been affected by malaria and three had died.

...The human rights centre had enormous difficulty trying to get the authorities to respond. Federal police initially claimed that it was outside their jurisdiction. The local police also claimed lack of jurisdiction. The regional labour office maintained that it had no resources to visit the estate. After a great deal of pressure, the federal police took six testimonies and the civil police took three. The centre then forwarded the case to the State Legislative Assembly's Parliamentary Commission of Inquiry...

...For this and other work denouncing torture by the local police, the centre became the subject of death threats and attacks. In April 1992, members of the human rights centre received death threats by telephone, the secretary of the centre was forced into a car, threatened with rape and death, and the centre's offices were broken into and files stolen..."

In his book **Rio Maria: Song of the Earth,** Fr. Ricardo Rezende writes:

"Sometimes I feel embarrassed when someone marvels at our 'courage' and 'readiness to face difficulties'. We have not come here out of heroism or sacrifice. We have experienced pleasure in learning, teaching, sharing dreams, travelling through the forest, talking, celebrating, seeing a people who are constructing their history in spite of so much pain and sorrow. As Christians, we know that God will have the last word, not the lords of the world, of weapons, of land, of capital. People here have a saying: The devil creates the pot, God the lid."

Fr. Ricardo is one of eight people placed on a death list in 1984. He is one of only two on that list remaining alive.

Sources:
Ricardo Rezende (1994) **Rio Maria: Song of the Earth,** Dublin, Orbis, CIIR, Trocaire;
Alison Sutton (1994) **Slavery in Brazil: a link in the chain of modernisation,** London, Anti-Slavery Society.

CASE STUDY 2

Banking by and for the Poor

"I learned so many things, I started thinking this is the real university I missed out all my life...one woman's story led me to a series of events which finally culminated into a very special kind of bank. I came across a woman who earned only two pennies a day by making bamboo stools. I couldn't accept why anybody should work so hard and make only two pennies. She explained why she makes two pennies: she doesn't have the money to buy the bamboo which goes into the bamboo stool. So she had to borrow the money from a trader, the trader who buys the final product. He lends her the money to buy the bamboo. When he buys the final product, he offers her a price which barely covers the cost of the raw materials. Her labour comes almost free, she works almost like a slave. I said to myself, there is no reason why it should be this way. This can be solved very easily. It doesn't need big theories to solve this."

Professor Mohammud Yunus, Founder, Grameen Bank, Bangladesh.

GRAMEEN BANK

The world famous Grameen Bank began in the village of Jobra in Bangladesh in response to the needs of the poor woman (and the hundreds of thousands of others like her) described above. Today the Grameen Bank employs 14,000 staff; works in over 35,000 of Bangladesh's estimated 68,000 villages; lends out over half a billion dollars each year; has an education programme which reaches over 12 million of the world's poorest; has a clientele which is 94% women; has a loan repayment rate of 98%; has encouraged local savings to a total of over $94 million and has succeeded in taking countless hundreds of thousands of the poor out of poverty. Moreover, it is now assisting others to replicate the model in over 40 other countries from Malaysia to Vietnam to the Philippines and India. It now has a vision of reaching out to one-third of the world's poor by the year 2005 with its focus on providing credit for women to help make them economically self-sufficient. As journalist Shan Ali recently commented:

"A bank that exists to eliminate poverty is a rare beast, and one that claims to do so at little or no real cost to society is rarer still."

... IN VIETNAM.

The impact and the importance of schemes such as that of the Grameen Bank is well-illustrated by this brief excerpt from the story of Nguyen Thi Nguyet, a poor woman from Ho Chi Minh City in Vietnam who has benefited from a loan and savings scheme organised by CIDSE - a consortium of Catholic development agencies.

"After I finished paying back the first loan, although things did not dramatically improve, I felt happier and more confident. In the second loan cycle, I borrowed 500,000 dong (in early 1996, $1= just over 10,000 dong). The more profit I got, the more I saved for myself. I did not dare buy anything expensive or spend

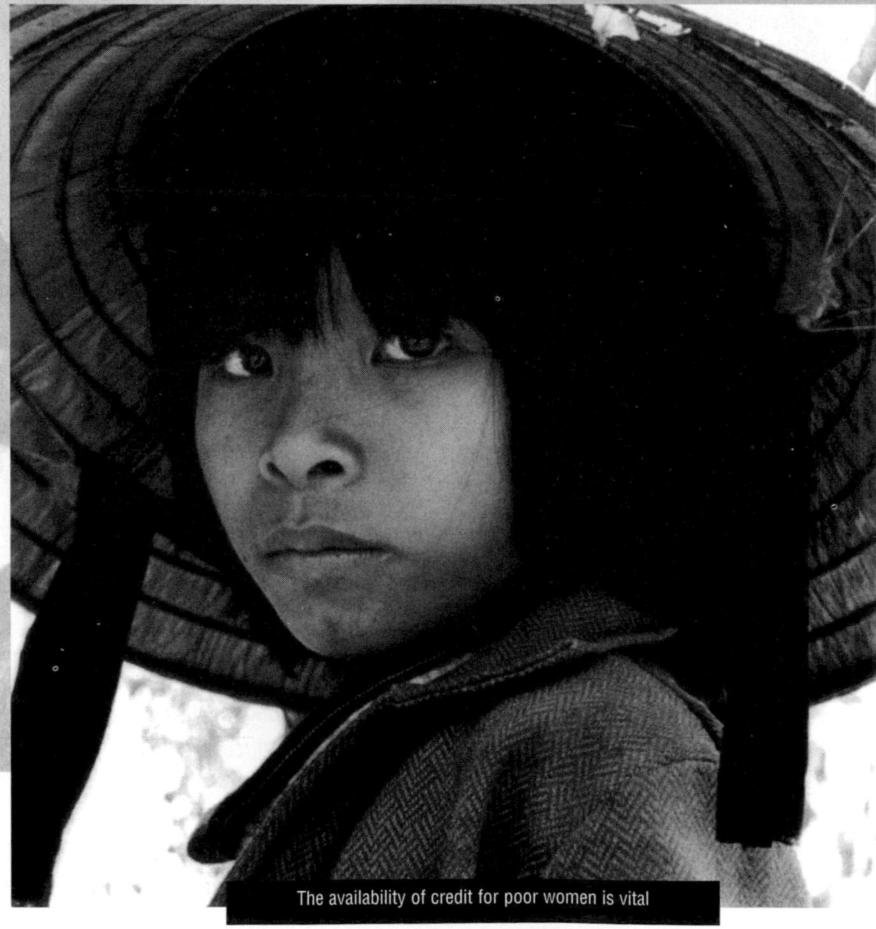

The availability of credit for poor women is vital

too much. The daily meals were now better and more nutritious. The other members of the family could bear less nutritious meals, but the eldest son (who was very ill) could not. I had to spend a little more money for buying tonic food for him.

I am now in my third loan cycle and have borrowed 600,000d. The repayment period is 6 months and my daily payment is only 4,000d. Aside from the fact that the daily payment has reduced, the loan has increased, I now feel more convinced and assured because of the stability and because meals are more nutritious and regular. Now I can turn my attention to my children's education."

The case of Nguyen Thi Nguyet illustrates well key dimensions of the benefits of a credit and savings scheme focused particularly on the needs of poor women and its impact not only on them but also on their families. Describing the impact of its programme, CIDSE has identified many of the direct and indirect results of such schemes. These are outlined below.

Sources:
New Internationalist, December 1995, CIDSE (1996) **"...armed with a confidence..."**, Vietnam and Belgium; personal research and notes.

"Never doubt that a small group of committed citizens can change the world. Indeed, it is the only thing that ever has"

Anthropologist Margaret Mead.

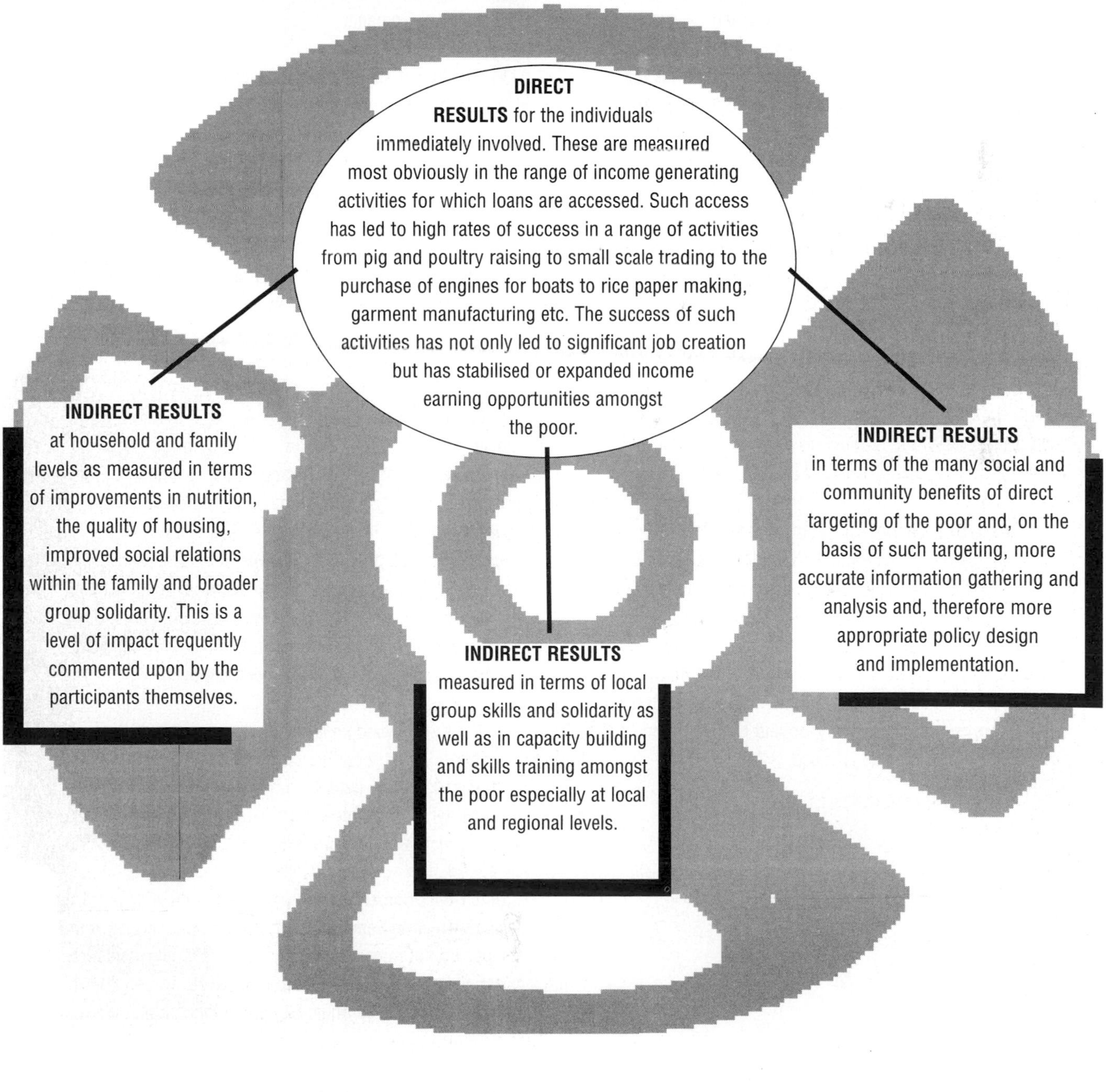

DIRECT RESULTS for the individuals immediately involved. These are measured most obviously in the range of income generating activities for which loans are accessed. Such access has led to high rates of success in a range of activities from pig and poultry raising to small scale trading to the purchase of engines for boats to rice paper making, garment manufacturing etc. The success of such activities has not only led to significant job creation but has stabilised or expanded income earning opportunities amongst the poor.

INDIRECT RESULTS at household and family levels as measured in terms of improvements in nutrition, the quality of housing, improved social relations within the family and broader group solidarity. This is a level of impact frequently commented upon by the participants themselves.

INDIRECT RESULTS measured in terms of local group skills and solidarity as well as in capacity building and skills training amongst the poor especially at local and regional levels.

INDIRECT RESULTS in terms of the many social and community benefits of direct targeting of the poor and, on the basis of such targeting, more accurate information gathering and analysis and, therefore more appropriate policy design and implementation.

Case Study 3

"...In my opinion the development of our country depends on this.'

Women in Agriculture

From the 1950s, agricultural policy in Kenya sought to 'stabilize' the African peasantry through the development of cash cropping, and 'land consolidation' - the transfer of lineage ownership of land to individual male heads of household. Legally, the output of the land thus became the property of the landowner, despite the fact that in many parts of Kenya men leave their farms to seek wage work elsewhere, and much of the cultivation is therefore carried out by women.

In practice, the distribution of the product of the farm is the result of negotiation between male 'owner' and female 'producer'. Against this background, the strong development of women's *mwethia,* or self-help, groups may be seen as a means of reasserting women's property rights. The groups may be saving clubs, with each member in turn receiving a lump sum payment which can be used to purchase 'capital' items, suchas livestock or tools, or they may be co-operative business ventures.

> *'...by channelling cash from crops into self-help organisations, they were preventing the appropriation of their product by their husbands,...*
> *secondly, they were attempting to accumulate capital as a means of protecting and enhancing.*

In Kenya's Machakos District, the women's *mwethia* have become well known for voluntarily hand-digging terraces on steeply sloping farmland. The terraces are a water-conservation measure which improves crop yields and stabilises drinking water supply. Their construction requires a large amount of labour (150-350 person-days per hectare) and the magnitude of the *mwethia* achievement is that from the mid-1980s 1000 km of terraces were constructed each year, and by 1990 some 70% of farmland in the district was terraced.

Maria Dem

"Mariam Dem's destiny as a young woman in Senegal was to marry, have children, take good care of her husband and children and in this way get to paradise. She comes from a traditional Senegalese family: her father came from a Marabout family of judges and educators, her mother's family were leading landowners, members of the Fulani tribe. Mariam was brought up by an uncle, who wanted Mariam to be a model Fulani woman...

...When she left school Mariam went to university and...joined the student movement. In the holidays the movement sent students out into the villages to enable them to understand the living conditions of rural people and to work with the farmers' organisations. This first-hand experience of poverty altered the course of her life...

> *'I began to come out of myself a bit, to see the world was larger than my home and school...I devote myself to development because I think that one of the monsters that women have to overthrow is under-development'*

...In the rural areas, although women work in farming and grow much of the food, they cannot own land. In the towns most women work in small-scale trading or in factories, and here, too, provide an important part of the family's income, although they have no authority in the household. Day to day survival has become increasingly difficult for the majority in Senegal. The government has embarked on a structural adjustment programme in an attempt to repay its external debts. Social investment in health, education and training has been cut, subsidies to poor farmers have been removed...

> *'The most striking effect is that women have become poorer...Enterprises are closed, men have lost their jobs, women have to work harder to get money to keep the family, or they become head of households when the men migrate or emigrate to look for work.'*

...Under-development and poverty are not the only problems facing women in Senegal. The Islamic religion places women in the position of minors in relation to male family members. As Islam allows men to have up to four wives, around 60% of marriages are polygamous. Mariam points out that the Koran

Women: the backbone of development

says that a man can only take four wives if he can look after all of them and treat them fairly. This qualification is usually forgotten...

...In the early 1970s Mariam became active in the emerging feminist movement...*'We realised we were not changing the existing conception, in terms of giving more power to women as a whole part of society'*...So they decided to create the first feminist movement, calling it Yewu Yewwi - Wake Up, Free Up...

...In Senegal there is a wide range of women's organisations concerned with trading, small-scale enterprises, health care and water supplies...Mariam's aim...is to help women to express themselves on topics that concern them, to speak about their own health problems, family planning, the land question and other injustices...Mariam wants to restore women's dignity...

> *'In the countryside, give her the land so that she can till it and feed her family. Give her the means to decide whether she wants to have children or not so that she can have them in the best conditions - so that she does not have to die after giving birth because the health facilities were ill-equipped. It is a long process. In my opinion the development of our country depends on this.'*

Sources:
Helen O'Connell (1993) **Dedicated Lives: Women Organising for a Fairer World,** Oxford, Oxfam;
UNDP (1995) **Human Development Report,** Oxford University Press.

Women Worldwide

The cases of Mariam Dem from Senegal and the mwethia of Machacos in Kenya represent but the tip of an enormous iceberg that is the women's movement world-wide - a movement which has touched every aspect of life especially that of development. As the ***Human Development Report*** for 1995 points out:

> *"The recognition of equal rights for women along with men, and the determination to combat discrimination on the basis of gender, are achievements equal in importance to the abolition of slavery, the elimination of colonialism and the establishment of equal rights for racial and ethnic minorities."*

The report goes on to point out that the issue of equality for women is not just about justice and human rights. It is also about economic and social development and about mobilising full human resources for the improvement of all. It is estimated, for example, that women's economic contributions are grossly undervalued to the order of $11 ***trillion*** each year. In 1979, the United Nations approved the Convention on the Elimination of All Forms of Discrimination Against Women but some 90 states still have reservations about its provisions to the point that they have not implemented it.

But throughout the world and especially throughout the Third World, women are on the move - organising and lobbying for profound change which will reap benefits for all. Change is taking place at a variety of levels from the most local (family, village and town), to the national (political structures, elections etc.) and the global (Conventions against Discrimination). Change is taking place in the economy through the recognition of women's role in agriculture and industry; in literacy and health; in politics; in the arts and in religion. Literally hundreds of millions of women have become far more politically mobilised and involved than before.

In her contribution to the 1995 ***Human Development Report,*** the Norwegian Prime Minister, Gro Harlem Brundtland, summarised the challenge in the following terms:

> *"It is about time that we all realise that investment in women is the single most important path to higher productivity for society as a whole - in industrial as well as in developing countries. The economic returns on investment in women's education are generally comparable to those for men, but the social returns in health and fertility regulation by far exceed what we achieve by educating men. Experience shows that women-oriented development projects are often highly successful in terms of social benefits.*
> *We are therefore clearly in need of a feminisation of our development policies."*

Case Study 4 'These are our trees'

"Rahela Khutan, a middle aged woman, sits in the shade of a 10 foot high tree, weaving a mat. In front of her a yellow flag flutters in the wind. 'These are our trees,' Rahela points proudly at the roadside trees. 'My samity (local self-help groups) planted 1,500 trees two years ago on a one-and-a-half kilometre stretch along the road'. Rahela is caretaker of these trees, her job symbolised by the yellow flag. She and two other women of the Mollapara Mahila Samity of Azimpur village in Singair (in Bangladesh) guard the trees so that no one can destroy them. In return, they receive five kilos of wheat a day from Proshika (one of Bangladesh's largest development NGO's).

The groups lease the 'khas' land (state-owned land) on condition that when the trees are sold for turning into furniture some 20 years later, the local government authorities will get half the money...The social forestry programme of the groups has stimulated another kind of activity in the villages. As demand for tree saplings has increased, the group members have set up their own nurseries...Ecological farming is also becoming popular. 'We now make our own natural fertiliser by decomposing (and mixing) cow dung, hay and water hyacinths,' says Nazan Banu of Madhya Chagram village, Singair. 'We don't use chemical fertiliser any more.' For pesticide, they make a kind of potion with leaves of the neem tree, tobacco and cow urine...'This is as good as any pesticide. It helps us in two ways - we don't have to spend money on chemicals and it doesn't harm our environment.'

Rahela Khutan and her colleagues are part of a huge range of community development and environment activists world-wide. In a recent article, Aaron Sachs identified a range of such activities world-wide. These are outlined below. He noted that *'...most environmentally sound development projects will probably come out of community-level initiatives that provide local people with relevant ecological information and empower them to take more control of their own fate. Policymakers could bring us all closer to sustainability by focusing on ways to give local people a stake in preserving their immediate environment".*

Sources: Inam Ahmed (1995) 'A Quiet Revolution' in **Let the Dawn Come: Social Development: Looking Behind the Cliches,** London, Panos and Aaron Sachs (1995) **Eco-Justice: Linking Human Rights and the Environment,** Worldwatch Paper No.127, Washington, Worldwatch Institute.

Sangam project, Deccan Development Society (DDS), Andhra Pradesh in India.

DDS helps organise sangams, communities of women, in Southern Indian villages, to work towards gender equity, establish credit programmes, cultivate and use medicinal herbs, incorporate organic farming techniques and multicropping systems into agricultural practices, and plant trees.

Yanesha Forestry Co-operative (COFYAL), Peruvian Amazon.

COFYAL is a sustainable forestry co-op run by the Yanesha Indians, who earn a living exporting forest products to Europe and the United States, while also protecting the rainforest from clear-cutting by ranchers and developers.

Kakadu National Park, Northern Australia.

Kakadu is co-managed by the Government's Park Service and the Aborigines who have inhabited the region for more than 50,000 years. Co-management has fostered effective nature conservation, a tourist industry that provides the Aborigines with a steady income, and the preservation of traditional communities.

Association for the Protection of the Environment (APE), Cairo, Egypt.

APE co-ordinates the efforts of Cairo's rubbish pickers, who earn a living by recycling paper, using organic wastes as fertiliser, and weaving rugs from discarded scraps of cotton.

InterTribal Sinkyone Wilderness Council (ITSWC), California, United States.

In early 1995, the 10 tribes of the ITSWC won back over 1,600 hectares of ancestral redwood rainforest from the state of California. Their plan is to create a wilderness park - complete with four traditional villages - that will serve as a model for sustainable land-use.

Annapurna Conservation Area Project (ACAP), Nepal.

ACAP has made local participation the cornerstone of its efforts to increase the direct benefits of tourism while decreasing its environmental impact - by improving local lodging services, using kerosene instead of trees for fuel and enforcing a Minimum Impact Code for trekkers.

CASE STUDY 5 Wrestling with Inequality

SUPERBARRIO

In July 1987 posters began to appear around Mexico City announcing the appearance of a new defender of the poor and the homeless against the power and wealth of the city's landowners. **Superbarrio,** as the masked wrestler became known, organised symbolic fights in a specially constructed wrestling ring against such evils as *"Catalino Creel"* ('the cruel landlord'), *"El Nucleosaurio"* (nuclear power) as well as AIDS and pollution. Superbarrio has led protests to block evictions and to lobby politicians and city administrators. His chief opponent is oppression of any kind.

Wrestling has long been popular in Mexico thus providing Superbarrio with his weapon to support the poor. Superbarrio is part of a popular community movement amongst Mexico City's poor - the Asamblea de Barrios. The movement began in 1985 after the earthquake which devastated the homes of the poor and now represents over 50,000 families in one of the world's largest cities with over 20 million people. Due to the power and influence of groups like the Asamblea, agreements have been reached with the City's authorities which have helped to provide thousands of simple new homes.

Marco Rascon, a member of the Council of the Asamblea describes Superbarrio as *"a collective citizen, representing the aspirations of thousands of ordinary citizens. He represents a sort of urban trinity - in the ring he is a wrestler, on the streets he is a social fighter, yet all the while he remains a tenant...humour is Superbarrio's strongest weapon. People in power hate to look ridiculous. They sit behind mahogany desks, surrounded by deep-pile carpets. And then they get a visit from Superbarrio!"*

IMAGES AND HOMELESS

Superbarrio is but one representative of the poor and homeless in a city such as Mexico City or indeed of similar cities throughout Latin America. Often our images of the poor and the homeless are of apathy and helplessness yet, in the vast majority of cases, nothing could be further from the truth. Throughout the barrios, favelas, pueblos jovenes of these cities, powerful and well-organised popular movements have appeared. Focused upon improving the economic, social and political life of slumdwellers, they have also become important political actors in their own right given that they often represent up to 20% of the urban population. One typical example is the Movimento do Favelado (MDF) in Sao Paulo, Brazil.

Overall, the MDF represents some 76,000 people in 41 slums and was set up in the late 1970s with the following objectives:

- ▼ to provide hope for those who seek work, food and shelter in the different favelas of the region.
- ▼ to promote and defend the interests and rights of favelados and those in similar situations.
- ▼ to demand and defend the rights and claims of favelados to sanitation, health, education, public services and to respect and dignity.
- ▼ to organise and support events which transform these objectives into realities.
- ▼ to assist favelados grow in their understanding of their situation as well as their rights.
- ▼ to celebrate the dream of a favelado community of hope, love and justice.

PAKISTAN

Urban social movements representing the poor are by no means limited to Latin America as is illustrated by Orangi, a suburb of Karachi in Pakistan. Orangi has over 700,000 people crowded into one of the city's poorest areas. Led by Aktar Hameed Khan, who had worked in community based projects in Bangladesh, the local community began to organise themselves to provide low cost sanitation and housing, women's work centres and education. Through their own efforts and with very little outside assistance, they have achieved significant results.

"The sanitation programme alone involves over 28,000 families who have constructed 430,000 feet of underground sewerage and built more than 28,000 latrines. More importantly, they have financed the work with their own savings to a total of 30 million rupees ($1.2 million). The average cost per household for providing sanitation was $66 - about one-quarter what it is estimated the cost would have been for the government."

Sources:
Chloe Sayer (1991) 'The Rise of Superbarrio' **Geographical Magazine,** February;
UNDP (1993) **Human Development Report,** Oxford University Press;
Alan Gilbert (1994) **The Latin American City,** London, Latin American Bureau;
Personal notes and research.

CASE STUDY 6

"...just as we would hope that they would help us in our hour of need..."

(The response of one campaigner on East Timor when asked what motivated his concern.)

Campaigning

Throughout the industrialised world, there are literally thousands of groups and organisations dedicated to campaigning for a more just world. Many are focused on local issues (unemployment, pollution, racism, equality), others on countries and issues in the Third World (hunger, debt, AIDS, East Timor, Nigeria) and others again on global issues (the arms trade, global warming, fair trade).

Such organisations have many roots and histories within the Churches, the trade union movement, within political parties, amongst groups of returned development workers, within the women's movement etc. They are part of what can be termed the global solidarity movement. Whilst there are many differences of origin, focus, philosophy and methodology amongst them, they, nonetheless, have a common perspective and goal at one level - human and planetary solidarity. It would be impossible to do justice to the full range of groups and actions, so we have chosen the following three examples for illustrative purposes.

> *"In April 1987, after working for British Aerospace Military Aircraft Division for over 12 years, I resigned. My reasons for resignation were quite simple - my letter said, "I have for many years found it increasingly difficult to bring the work I do at BAe within my Christian faith. I have now reached the point where that is impossible, and so I must respond to God and leave BAe ".*
>
> *Aircraft have, and always will fascinate me. I was good at engineering and grew up near Heathrow , so it was natural to study Aeronautics at University and, at the end, to go into the military field, for that is where the greater demand was - both technically and in numbers of people employed .*
>
> *I enjoyed my job. But throughout the '80s that moral concern grew. The debate over nuclear arms was at its height, the Falklands and Thatcher's Britain all played their part, as did the proposed export of aircraft to some not very nice places. I grew more and more unhappy about the part I was playing - a small cog, but I was still a cog !*
>
> *So I set myself targets, firstly, to actively prepare for the job that I thought God was calling me to, and secondly, to think of leaving BAe in two years time. Six months later I knew (or thought I did) what God wanted me to do. To leave BAe, inevitably becoming unemployed, and to trust in him.*
>
> *But that night he gave me faith to do precisely that, and so I wrote that resignation letter "*

David Wheeler, an Anglican Vicar living in Manchester.

World Development Movement

> ***"Isn't it time we tackled the causes of Third World Poverty and not just the symptoms? Don't take pity, take action!"***

So proclaims a brochure published by the World Development Movement - an independent British organisation, supported by many of Britain's voluntary development agencies, which campaigns for policy changes which directly benefit the poor of the world. It has campaigned on issues such as the quality and targeting of government aid, the scandal of government support and the use of taxpayers money to subsidise the arms trade, unjust trade barriers against Third World Producers and the continuing debt crisis.

Chris Patten, British Minister for Overseas Development from 1986 to 1989 commented on the approach of WDM:

> *"WDM has taught me a great deal. As a result of the strength of their intellectual arguments they have convinced me to change my mind on at least two specific matters of policy."*

Currently, the WDM is campaigning against the arms trade and in support of a European Code of Conduct on arms sales. It points out that in 1994, the British Government cut aid to Africa while increasing the financial backing for arms exports fivefold - *"up to £4 million a day. The government uses this money as an insurance for arms sales - even to repressive regimes. If a country does not repay the arms company or the bank financing the deal, then you, the taxpayer, foot the bill.*

And the risks are high. Taxpayers are footing a £652 million bill since Saddam Hussein stopped paying for British goods including military supplies. Britain, as the world's second largest arms seller, has a duty - and the power - to set the pace for global arms controls. We can make a difference - and we must start now."

Amnesty International

"When the first two hundred letters came , the guards gave me back my clothes. Then the next two hundred came and the prison director got in touch with his superior. The letters kept coming and coming; they still kept coming and the President called the prison and told them to let me go. The President called me to his office and said to me: 'How is it that a trade union leader like you has so many friends all over the world'. He showed me an enormous box full of letters he had received and when we parted, he gave them to me. I still have them."

This is how one Dominican Republic trade unionist described the results of the work of one of the world's most popular and effective human rights organisations, Amnesty International. One of its most effective methods of putting pressure on governments to release prisoners of conscience (those who have been detained for their beliefs, colour, sex, ethnic origin, language or religion who have not used or advocated violence) is through encouraging its members to send letters of protest to prison authorities, Ministries of Justice, Presidents and Military Authorities. Amnesty also campaigns against the death penalty and torture and for the promotion and protection of human rights world-wide. Amnesty has more than 700,000 members in over 150 countries- it has 3,800 local groups in Africa, the Americas, Europe and the Middle East. The symbol of Amnesty International is the lighted candle, which, according to founder Peter Benenson *"...burns not for us, but for all t hose whom we failed to rescue from prison, who were shot on the way to prison, who were tortured, who were kidnapped, who 'disappeared'."*

Sources:
Campaign Against the Arms Trade News, Feb.'95;
World Development Movement (1995)
Gunrunners Gold: how the public's money finances arms sales, London;
Amnesty International News (various editions).

Campaigning against the abuse of human rights is an integral part of the development process

Case Study 7

"...a critical awareness..."

Young People's Views

The views listed to the right are but a tiny sample of some of the views and responses of young people in a recent survey (1994) of nearly 400 students in the south-west of England. Throughout the survey, the young people interviewed expressed high levels of interest in local and global development, justice and environmental matters. A large proportion of those interviewed expressed dissatisfaction with the notion that a future world would mirror the present one. They expressed fears about a wide range of issues including unemployment, loneliness, pollution, racism, poverty and conflict. They did not express great faith in the ability of adults to create a better future and had doubts about their own ability to create real change. They also highlighted the influence of television in shaping their views; the fact that they don't get too many chances to go into important issues in detail and, as one girl put it, "I really don't know what to expect in the future at all." There was, however, evidence that these young people were not only interested in becoming active on these issues but were already active.

The views of these English students are paralleled in many important respects by those of their Irish counterparts surveyed recently by the Development Education for Youth Project. In 1994, using a market research company they surveyed the views of a representative sample of young people and discovered very high levels of interest in and involvement with development, environmental and justice issues. Once again, the dominance of television as a source of information and analysis was highlighted as were issues such as unemployment, war, famine, drugs and poverty. As was the case with the English survey, young people expressed themselves to be not only strongly interested in these issues but also concerned to do something about them.

Education and Action

These surveys highlight another important force for global change - education and action here in the Industrialised World, especially amongst young people. Over the past thirty years, a wide range of groups have sought to bring the global, justice and environmental perspectives to bear on the educational processes within our society. At the root of this approach is the knowledge that charity and welfare, while they may address many of the symptoms of underdevelopment and inequality, will never overcome them unless there is a recognition of the underlying processes and structures which create the problems in the first place. Action to change those processes and structures is urgently needed and must be based upon a knowledge of the issues.

Development education and its allied areas of human rights, environmental, multicultural, anti-racist and futures education has sought to provide a creative forum for people here in Europe for both information, discussion and debate as well as action on such issues. This has meant a variety of projects and programmes with teachers, educationalists, students, youth organisations, the women's movement, trade unions and trades councils, town twinning groups, community organisations etc.

"At the rate we're going...if there's more unemployment there will be more violence...\they're dead bored and they have no jobs...If there's a bad environment and natural resources are dropping, people will have to pay more for water and they'll have less money, so there'll be more fighting" (11 year old)

"It (violence) will get worse because I think other people from other countries will come over and there'll be lots of fighting...There's a lot of crime in America and they might come over here" (11 year old)

"There may be nuclear war if all the countries disagree. There's just one button...they could blow up England with one button...That's quite scary." (18 year old)

"I'd have thought poorer countries, they want to recycle, because they can't afford to make things. They're not doing much to pollute the atmosphere, but rich countries, they think 'what the heck', they can't be bothered to recycle...like acid rain; it doesn't affect us. We make it and it just goes up to Norway." (18 year old).

"There will be more poverty...a bigger gap between North and South and between developing and non-developing countries."

"I disagree - I think the Northern countries will realise the Southern countries need help." (18 year olds)

Development Education

According to the United Nations:

"The objective of development education is to enable people to participate in the development of their community, their nation and the world as a whole. Such participation implies a critical awareness of local, national and international situations based on an understanding of the social, economic and political processes."

In less formal language the same objectives were expressed by two development activists - the first, an Australian Aboriginal woman, speaking at an international conference on Environment and Development in Manila who commented:

"If you have come to help me you can go home again. But if you see my struggle as part of your own survival then perhaps we can work together."

The second was Bishop Dom Helder Camara of Brazil who commented:

"When I feed the poor, they call me a saint. When I ask why the poor are hungry, they call me a communist."

In his book **Getting to the 21st Century: Voluntary Action and the Global Agenda,** American writer and activist D.C. Korten has tried to graphically summarise the various 'generations' of development oriented groups and the various types of work they undertake. The approaches outlined in the seven case studies above may be viewed in the light of his framework.

STRATEGIES OF DEVELOPMENT - ORIENTED NGOS: FOUR GENERATIONS

	FIRST *Relief and Welfare*	**SECOND** *Community Development*	**THIRD** *Sustainable System Development*	**FOURTH** *People's Movements*
Problem Definition	Shortage	Local inertia	Institutional and Policy Constraints	Inadequate Mobilizing Vision
Time Frame	Immediate	Project Life	Ten to Twenty Years	Indefinite Future
Scope	Individual or Family	Neighborhood or Village	Region or Nation	National or Global
Chief Actors	NGO	NGO plus Community	All Relevant Public and Private Institutions	Loosely Defined Networks of People & Organisations
NGO Role	Doer	Mobilizer	Catalyst	Activist / Educator
Management Orientation	Logistics Management	Project Management	Strategic Management	Coalescing and Energizing Self-Management Networks
Development Education	Starving Children	Community Self-Help	Constraining Policies and Institutions	Spaceship Earth

▼ References

CIDSE (1996) **"...armed with a confidence...Selected Case Studies from CIDSE's Credit and Savings Programme"**, Vietnam and Belgium.

Fabiana Frayssinet et al (1995) **'A Quiet Revolution'** in **Let the Dawn Come: Social Development: Looking Behind the Cliches**, London, Panos.

Alan Gilbert (1994) **The Latin American City**, London, Latin American Bureau.

David Hicks and Charles Townley (1982) **Teaching World Studies: an introduction to global perspectives in the curriculum**, London, Longman.

K.C. Korten (1990) **Getting to the 21st Century: Voluntary Action and the Global Agenda**, Connecticut, Kumerian Press.

Helen O'Connell (1993) **Dedicated Lives: Women Organising for a Fairer World**, Oxford, Oxfam.

Ricardo Rezende (1994) **Rio Maria: Song of the Earth**, Dublin, Orbis, CIIR, Trocaire;

Alison Sutton (1994) **Slavery in Brazil: a link in the chain of modernisation**, London, Anti-Slavery Society.

UNDP (1995) **Human Development Report**, Oxford University Press.

World Development Movement (1995) **Gunrunners Gold: how the public's money finances arms sales**, London

Women: the backbone of development

IMPOVERISHING PEOPLE AND DESPOILING THE EARTH

Environment and Development

Sean McDonagh

A Contemporary Parable

A group of people were invited to attend a banquet in a beautiful medieval castle situated in a magnificent courtyard. It was a splendid feast with a profusion of sumptuous dishes, a delicious range of wines and other drinks, superb service and an excellent orchestra to entertain the guests as they ate. The food was so sumptuous and the drink so delicious that the guests simply couldn't get enough. They continued to gorge themselves long after the point of satiation. As the night wore on, instead of ending the meal, relaxing and going home, the revellers became more and more intent on securing additional helpings of the mouth-watering food.

Their demands became so voracious that all the food was consumed. The Master of the house, in order to avoid being embarrassed in front of his guests, sent out his servants, backed by the militia, to collect more food from the poor inhabitants in the surrounding countryside. Fuel also ran out. So the cooks ordered some servants to begin chipping away at the timber pillars that supported the roof in order to get fire wood to continue cooking. After a while some pillars began to sag a little and cracks appeared in the ceiling. But the banqueters were so absorbed in the meal that they were completely unaware of the long-term implications of what was happening. Neither they nor those who were cutting strips off the beams understood that unless they stopped hacking at the supporting pillars, the ceiling would eventually come crashing down on their heads. Needless to say not a thought was given to the fact that hundreds of servants living in the castle compound would also perish if the castle collapsed.

The din, buzz and activity in the kitchen and dining hall was electrifying. People were milling around the cooking stoves, shouting orders for more food and eating with relish. Yet not everyone was caught up in the frenzy. A small number of protestors stood by the doors with neither plates nor glasses in their hands. Some of the protestors who were members of human rights and justice groups denounced the diners. They pointed out that the heavy cost of the meal was being borne by the poor in the surrounding countryside. Other protestors, sensitive to the ecological implications of what was happening, were conscious that the beams were already sagging and that a tragedy was imminent. They implored the diners to end the meal and thus avert the disaster. A few of those eating would occasionally stop to listen to their heartfelt pleas, they might even cast a fleeting glance towards the ceiling, but as soon as a waiter with food came close, they would lose interest and join in the scramble for more. The majority of those who were celebrating, however, didn't take any notice at all. They were simply so engrossed in the meal that nothing else really mattered.

Introduction

The above parable *(which I wrote after reading a sentence by Fazlun M. Khalid, in the preface to Islam and Ecology, 1992, Chapman, London)* captures some aspects of the development and ecological crisis which I will explore in this chapter. The parable also highlights the inability of many people, especially those in leadership roles in institutions like industry, politics, economics, education and religion, to deal in an effective way with either crisis.

I make no bones about the fact that I am writing from the perspective of a missionary who lived in the Philippines between 1969 and 1989. For much of that time I lived among a Tribal community called the T'boli on the island of Mindanao. While in the Philippines I witnessed two trends operating both at the national and international level. The first was the increasing gap between the rich and the poor in the Philippines and between rich and poor nations world-wide. The second was the impact of the modern technological, industrial, consumer, throw-away society on the fabric of life on earth. Already the human impact on the planet is breaching the capacity of important ecosystems like rainforests to regenerate themselves and, at the same time, we are going beyond the ability of the biosphere to absorb human-generated pollution.

Impoverishing the Poor

Everyone will admit that the modern, industrial, throw-away society which is usually associated with the notion of development and economic growth has benefited a number of individuals and groups. It has brought huge profits and a growing control of world production and markets to multinational corporations and financial institutions. It has delivered innumerable comforts and incredible possibilities for consumer choices to the rich and middle classes in Northern countries and to the elite in the Third World. All these groups taken together add up to about one billion people which is less than one in five of all the people living today. The down-side of this international economy is that two-thirds of the world's population has not been served by it and a significant percentage, especially those living in the South, have been impoverished by its operations.

One simple way of judging the success of any economic system is to look at how it provides for the basic needs of people. Every person needs an adequate intake of nutritious food, adequate clothing, a decent place to live and access to basic education and health care. The present economic system fails to deliver most of the above to the majority of the world's population. And the situation is deteriorating. In the early 1980s, the World Bank and UN Food and Agriculture Organisation (FAO) estimated that between 700 million and 1 billion people lived in absolute poverty. Robert McNamara, a former President of the World Bank, described absolute poverty as a condition of life so limited by malnutrition, illiteracy, disease, squalid surroundings, high infant mortality, and low life expectancy as to be beneath any reasonable definition of human dignity.

McNamara was concerned about the world situation in the late 1970s. Yet in 1996 most indicators suggest that poverty has increased dramatically in Sub-Saharan Africa, and to a lesser extent in most of Latin America and significant areas of South Asia and South East Asia. The number living in absolute poverty in 1992 stood at 1.2 billion. This included millions of rural women and children living in situations where a woman is the sole parent. What is more alarming is that, while the percentage of the world's population who are in this category dropped steadily between the 1950s and 1970s, it began to climb again during the 1980s. In the 1980s, for example, the percentage of the world's population living in absolute poverty increased from 22.3% to 23.4%. This increase has taken place, despite all the talk about three decades of development and international aid apparently focused on reducing world poverty.

Rich get Richer

Modern development theory and practice assumes that economic improvement will take place if the volume of economic activity is increased. In general it subscribes to neo-liberal economic policies with its formula of minimal government restrictions on market forces, the sanctity of private property, private management of the economy and unfettered competition. It accepts that in the initial states of 'development' there will probably be a concentration of wealth in the hands of the rich. However, it claims that, when the benefits of capital accumulation and growth have reached a certain threshold, significant economic benefits will 'trickle down' and enhance the lives of the poor.

Unfortunately, this is not the way things operate in the real world where politics, economics and ecology meet. What, in fact, happens is that the gap between the rich and poor, on a national and world wide stage, increases as income distribution becomes more lopsided. It is important to emphasise that this yawning gap has not always existed. According to the Swiss economist Paul Bairoch the per capita gross national product for 'developed' and 'underdeveloped' countries in 1750 was more or less similar. In 1930, it had grown to a ratio of 4 to 1 and by 1990, 8 to 1. The tragedy of recent decades is that, despite the fine rhetoric from politicians and multilateral lending agencies about promoting poverty reduction the gap is growing.

During the 1980s, the neo-liberal economic policies championed by Britain's Margaret Thatcher and the US's Ronald Reagan were thrust upon the Third World by both the World Bank and the International Monetary Fund (IMF). As a result the share of global wealth enjoyed by the Third World fell from 22 percent to 18 percent. In 1990 the top 20 per cent Northern majority enjoyed 82.7 percent of the world's gross national product, 81.9 percent of world trade; 94.6 percent of all commercial lending; 80.6 percent of all domestic savings and 94 percent of all research and development. The situation has reached crisis point as a result of the adjustment programmes which have been forced upon the poor as a result of the debt crisis.

What's the difference between Tanzania and Goldman Sachs?

Every now and then a report, or a statistic, or a particularly graphic photo captures the obscenity of the immense difference between the standard of living of the rich and that of the poor. **The Guardian** (10 December, 1993), achieved this with a simple question, What's the difference between Tanzania and Goldman Sachs?

The answer to the question is that one is an African country that makes $2.2 billion per annum and shares it among 25 million people. The other is an investment Bank that made $2.6 billion profit in 1992 and shares that with 161 people.

An Ethiopian Market

The Earth's Resources are Limited

The opening parable also illustrates that our present economic system is causing extensive ecological destruction by promoting activity which breaches the ability of local and global ecosystems to regenerate themselves. Conventional economic theories insist that high levels of economic growth are essential for development, especially in the Third World. But this begs the question of whether humans can continue to promote ever increasing levels of economic growth on a finite planet without doing ever increasing damage to the fabric of life on Earth?

The debate about the possible upper limits to the earth's capacity to cope with human activity was first addressed in a serious way in the Club of Rome's **Limits of Growth** published in 1972. The book was an instant best-seller, topping the 10 million copies mark. It gave rise to many controversies about the methodology used and the inaccuracy of some of the predictions.

Critics argued that the authors did not take human ingenuity sufficiently into account and thus they under-estimated the capability of technology to find substitutes for the projected scarcities. It was predicted, for example, that the supply of copper would soon run out given its rising demand in the field of telecommunications. The invention of fibre optics changed all that by revolutionising telecommunications. This took the pressure off a metal like copper. In fact the subsequent price fall had a devastating impact on the economies of copper producing countries like Bolivia and Zambia.

Supporters of the **Limits of Growth** perspective counter such criticism by pointing out that although technological innovation can reduce both raw material and energy use, this may be offset by a sizeable increase in quantity of a given item. For example, in the aftermath of the hike in oil prices between 1973 and 1988 there was a marked increase in the energy efficiency of cars. Consumption per kilometre fell by 29 per cent. This gain, however, was quickly offset by a 58 percent increase in the number of cars during the same period. In fact, despite the introduction of energy efficient cars, petrol consumption increased by 17 percent.

While there were quibbles here and there with some of the predictions made in **Limits of Growth,** the main significance of the book was that it focused people's attention on the fact that the Earth is a finite planet and that it cannot sustain continuous, expanding demands on its resources. Furthermore, the 'limits to growth' perspective torpedoed one of the main assumptions of the present development theory that the 5.5 billion people on earth in the mid 1990s - and the projected population of 11 billion by year 2050 - can aspire to the present affluent standards of living enjoyed by many Northern middle class people and the elite in the Southern countries. In reality the present demands which humans

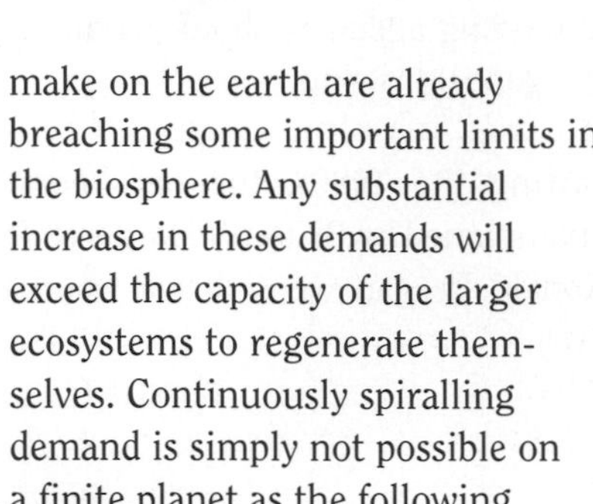

make on the earth are already breaching some important limits in the biosphere. Any substantial increase in these demands will exceed the capacity of the larger ecosystems to regenerate themselves. Continuously spiralling demand is simply not possible on a finite planet as the following examples illustrate all too clearly.

Limits on Food Production - as Agricultural and Fisheries Output Falls

It would seem today that humans are already coming up against limits in many crucial areas of life. Like other organisms, human beings need an adequate intake of nutritious food to survive and thrive. Because of widespread poverty in much of the South many people there do not have a nutritionally adequate diet at the moment. In fact the average person among the 4 billion people there consumes almost a thousand calories per day less than their counterpart in Western Europe or the US

Unfortunately it is predicted that this situation will further deteriorate as the human population continues to grow. It would appear that, in the not too distant future, there will be a conflict between human beings' demand for food and the physical capacity of the earth to meet those needs. For example, between 1950 and 1984 the production of grain, the staple crop of millions of people, expanded at around three per cent per annum. This meant that it edged ahead of population growth and, thus, per capita consumption rose. Since 1984, however, despite improved technology, irrigation and petrochemicals, grain production has only expanded by one per cent per annum.

The rangelands of the world, which support flocks that provide humans with animal protein, are also under stress. In the four decades between 1950 and 1990, beef and mutton production increased 2.6 fold. Once again this resulted in a 26% per capita increase. Now, however, because of the destruction of rangelands it is not expected to rise even as the population continues to increase.

Water Pollution

Though we call our planet Earth, almost three quarters of the surface of the planet is, in fact, water. From space our planet has a blue-green hue coloured by the 66 oceans and seas which are found right around the globe. All life began in the womb of the oceans and even those forms of life that now make their home on dry land depend on water, recycled by rain for their survival.

Today human activity is polluting the oceans, rivers, lakes and aquifers of the world in an unprecedented way. In the cover story in **Time**, November 5, 1990, the authors surveyed the condition of the waters of the world. They concluded that *"population growth and development have depleted and polluted the world's water supply, raising the risks of starvation, epidemics and even war"*. Right around the world some of the most fertile areas of the oceans, close to continental shelves have been contaminated by human, agricultural, industrial and radio-active waste. The havoc wrecked on the Aral Sea by decades of inappropriate irrigation and chemical pollutants boggles the imagination. This once fertile sea, supported a thriving fishing industry. Now what remains is a toxic, saline wasteland. The surface area has shrunk by two-thirds in the past 30 years.

A World Bank report in the Summer of 1995 warns that the gap between the demand for water for industry and agriculture and the present sources of supply is growing at a dangerous rate. In recent times world-wide demand has doubled every 21 years. The study predicts that in the next decade the supply of water per person will fall by 30 percent in Egypt, 40 percent in Nigeria and 50 percent in Kenya with similar drops in other parts of the world. Many fear that the resource wars of the 21st century will be fought about water and not about land or oil. In the Middle East and the Indian Sub-continent, two areas where wars have been fought in recent decades, water rights are hotly disputed.

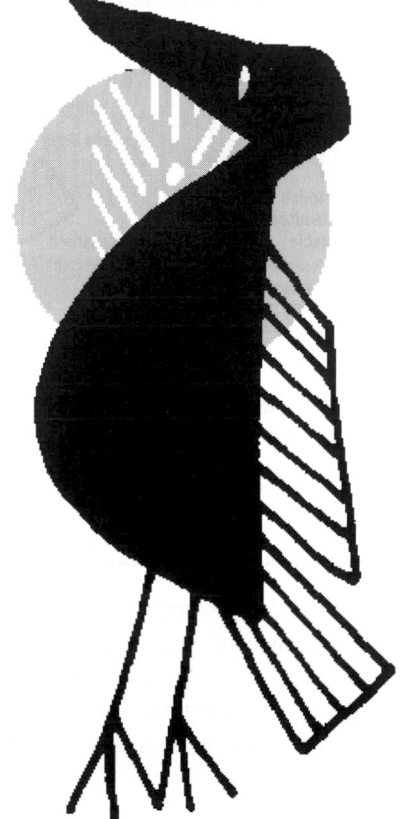

Once again the poor have unequal access to this simple but vital resource. In 1990 the World Resources Institute estimated that two-thirds of the world's population had to get by with one-seventh the amount of water used by the average US citizen. In 1995 a World Bank study calculated that 40 percent of the world's population does not have access to clean water or sanitation.

Despite the short drought in the summer of 1995, Ireland is well-known for its ample supply of rainfall. This might lead one to believe that the threats to water, evident in so many other parts of the world, are not present in Ireland. Unfortunately this is not so - rivers, lakes and seas around Ireland are being contaminated by human sewage, agricultural effluent and industrial waste.

Dwindling Fish Stocks and...too much Fishing

World-wide, fish provides more than half the animal protein consumed by human beings. The proportion is even higher in many countries of the South.

Waste and the Disposable Society

The unsustainability and vulnerability of our present day industrial and commercial society is also very evident when one looks at it from the other end - the ever-increasing mound of waste which is created by our throw-away culture. **Newsweek** (27, November, 1989) portrayed the industrial world being "buried alive" in garbage. The statistics are astounding: each consumer in the industrial world accumulates 3.5 pounds of garbage every day. Where to put it is becoming a major problem. It is now cluttering up landfills in towns and cities around the world. Many communities are simply running out of space.

The US with its affluence and disposable mentality is by far the worst offender. Each year Americans throw away 16 billion disposable diapers, 1.6 billion pens, 2 billion razors and blades and 220 million tyres. They discard enough aluminium to rebuild the entire US commercial airline fleet every three months.

But space to dump things in is fast running out. In the US, 80 percent of solid waste is now dumped into 6,000 landfills. In the past 10 years, however, almost 5,000 have been filled and shut down. More than two thirds of the landfills in the US have been closed since the late 1970s.

PEPSI'S PLASTICS

Under Pepsi's two-part scheme, plastic for single use bottles will be manufactured in India and exported to the United States and Europe, while the toxic by-products of the plastic production process will stay in India. Used plastic bottles will then be returned from these countries to India. Activists first learned of Pepsi's waste exports to India through US Customs Department data. The records indicated that all of the waste exports were destined for Madras.

Much of the waste was dumped at the site of a factory owned by Futura Industries in Tiruvallur, outside Madras. "As we came over the hill in our auto-rickshaw, we saw a mountain of plastic waste", recounts Madras environmentalist Satish Vangal. "Piles and piles of used soda bottles stacked behind a wall. As we got closer to the factory, we found many bottles and plastic scrap along the road and blowing in the wind. Every bottle we saw said 'California Redemption Value'. They were all from California's recycling programme and now they are sitting in a pile in India! We have enough problems dealing with our own plastics waste; why should we import other people's rubbish?".

The senior manager at the Futura Plant estimated that 60 to 70 percent of the waste can be processed at his factory, but the rest is either too contaminated, or is the wrong type of plastic. He refused to disclose the fate of the waste which is not recycled.

Greenpeace researcher Ann Leonard,
Multinational Monitor, *Sept. 1994.*

DRUGS AND MEDICINES

About twice as much money is spent by pharmaceutical companies on promoting and marketing their drugs as on researching them. Drug multinationals restricted by law in the West have a field day handing out free samples and "sweeteners" in countries with more lenient legislation. Marketing the product can lead to blatant and dangerous misinformation: The Office of Technology Assessment (OTA) of the US Congress found that the label and package inserts for at least half of a sample of products sold by US-based companies in Brazil, Kenya, Panama and Thailand failed to provide sufficient information. The OTA concluded that reliance on the information could lead to "serious or life-threatening medical problems or, at best, ineffective treatment."

Health writer Andrew Chetley, **The New Internationalist,**
No 272, Oct. 1995

Palm it off on Poor Communities in the Third World

Many see the Third World as a ideal dump for First World waste. With growth in the not-in-my-back-yard (NIMBY) mentality communities would like to move the garbage elsewhere. Trains and trucks loaded with garbage criss-cross the US and, of course, the Two-Thirds World is a soft-option for dumping toxic waste. **Time** (2, January, 1989) carried an account of the voyage of the Pelicano. For two years it sailed around the world seeking a port that would accept its 14,000 ton cargo of toxic ash. In October 1989 the Pelicano illegally dumped some of its cargo off Haiti and probably dumped the rest overboard on the high seas. The Pelicano was a clear symbol of the final twist in the saga of the First World's exploitation of the Third World. After centuries of abuse of their resources and human labour, the First World is now completing the circle of exploitation by dumping its toxic waste on unsuspecting Third World people.

Toxic Waste for Bangladeshi Farmers

In late 1991, three South Carolina corporations concocted an elaborate scheme to export hazardous waste, known as baghouse dust, captured in the smokestack filters of the metal smelting furnaces of the Gaston Copper Recycling Corporation. A hazardous waste broker, Hy-Tex Marketing Inc., transported the waste to Stroller Chemical Corporation. Stroller then secretly mixed the hazardous waste with other materials to make fertiliser and illegally shipped the toxic brew to Bangladesh. The alternative to adding waste to fertiliser would be to spend $200 a tonne to put it in a dump, or send it to a waste treatment facility for $150 a tonne.

The US Embassy notified the Bangladeshi government about the consignment, but before the presence of dangerous quantities of lead and cadmium was diagnosed much of the fertiliser was distributed from Chittagong into the marketing system. 3,000 tonnes were sold, mainly in Chittagong and Khulna, no one knows at what cost to the health of the purchasers.

Ann Leonard, ***Multinational Monitor,*** *April 1993*

Figure 5:3

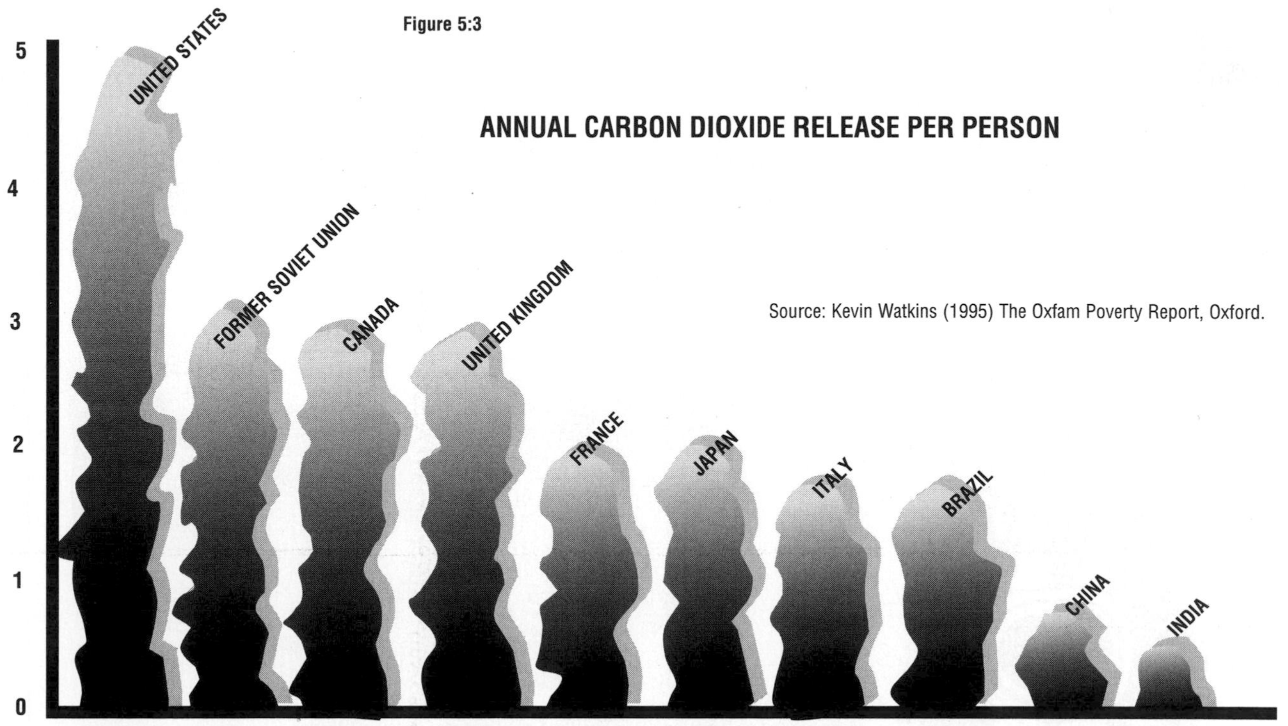

Photosynthesis Places Limits on Human Exploitation of Nature

The final element in the argument in favour of sustainability comes from considering the mechanism of photosynthesis. Like other plants and animals humans need food and energy in order to sustain life. If the human species is to continue to reproduce and survive, humans must meet their food and energy needs in a way that does not destroy the world. They must operate within the limits of the natural world, living, as it were, on the interest which nature provides without drawing down the ecological capital.

All plants obtain their energy from the Sun. Through the complex biochemistry of photosynthesis plants transform solar energy into usable energy in the form of sugars. This energy, in turn, becomes available for other creatures, the herbivores and carnivores. Plants, however, are more efficient users of the Sun's energy. It takes vast quantities of plants to feed herbivores and, still larger amounts in order to feed carnivores. When the number and demands of a carnivorous species, like humans, increase dramatically, this can put enormous pressure on other species within the biosphere. This is particularly true in recent decades since humans have developed the technology to exploit and even destroy the habitat of other creatures.

In Summary

The argument throughout this chapter is that our contemporary industrial culture is interfering in a massive way with the functioning of the biosphere. Any single ingredient in the argument from global warming to the poisoning of water is a most serious issue in itself. All of the above and numerous others like acid rain, the destruction of the tropical forests and the threat of chemical or radioactive poisoning are interlocking problems which feed, as it were, on each other. Taken together they constitute the most serious challenge which has ever faced humankind or the earth itself.

In the final analysis unlimited economic growth which is a basic assumption in much of the contemporary business and economic literature is simply impossible on a finite planet. The treadmill of sustained growth which Our Common Future says is essential to fuel economic growth is not sustainable. If the 2% annual growth rate in industrial production which was achieved between 1970 and 1990 was to continue indefinitely industrial production would double every 25 years. This would jump to a sixteenfold increase each century, a 250 fold increase in two centuries and a 4,000 fold increase in three centuries. Given the havoc that the present industrial climate wreaks on the planet, it is clear that the biosphere could not sustain much more doubling without major ecological collapse.

The environmental movement is constantly trying to highlight the importance of developing ways of living which do not destroy ecological capital. Needless to say, this perspective is not universally shared and is often attacked by those who are benefiting from the unjust way the world's resources are currently distributed.

Figure 5:4

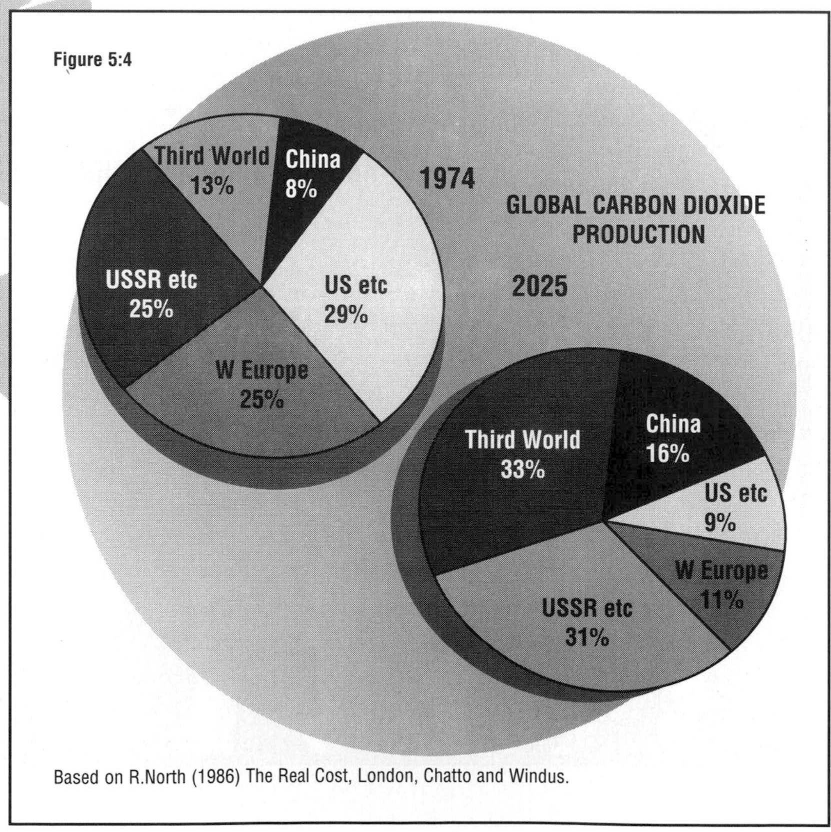

Based on R.North (1986) The Real Cost, London, Chatto and Windus.

Tackling soil erosion and its impact is one of the key jobs of African environmentalists

What Needs to be Done

The first thing that needs to be done is to critique the assumptions and record of modern development, especially in the Third World. That, however, is only the first step. It will be necessary to design an economic system that promotes and enhances human community and, at the same time, is sustainable. Many people, among them economists, have been attempting to do this during the past decade. One of the most successful in my opinion is called **For the Common Good.** It is co-authored by John Cobb, a theologian, and Herman Daly, an economist. They argue that economic policies which put economic growth and industrialisation ahead of the needs of people, human communities and the well-being of the environment, need to be radically changed.

David Kortens, another US commentator, argues that sustainability means taking seriously the carrying capacity of the environment while at the same time allocating available resources to meet the basic needs of community members. In order to promote the real development of human communities and the environment, it is crucial to develop economic policies which promote economic diversification at all levels of the economy. This will also mean allocating local resources to the production of goods and services to meet the basic needs of the local population. These policies contrast sharply with the prevailing free-trade ideology which sees the earth as a single quarry of resources to be mined and distributed at the global supermarket. In Kortens' view the national, and even international, economies should be comprised of interlinked, self-reliant economic communities that can insulate themselves from the shocks of the national and international economic system and at the same time conserve local environmental resources.

On the agricultural front it will be necessary to design policies which will help to move communities away from the large mono-crop, petrochemically addicted agribusiness approach where animals are produced in

SOCIAL FORESTRY IN INDIA

In India social forestry programmes have been started by several state governments in order to provide fuelwood, fodder, small timber, and minor forest produce to the rural people. Social forestry in India has three aspects: (1) farm forestry, where the farmers are supplied with free or subsidised seedlings in order to encourage them to plant more trees on their land, (2) community woodlots, where village communities are encouraged to plant trees on common lands to be equally shared, and (3) forestry woodlots, where trees are planted for the community by the government forestry department on public lands such as along the roads or banks of canals. In general, it looks like a successful project in many areas, but there are three areas where criticism has been levelled at the system. First, the programme, which is expected to use short rotation trees as cash crop, tends to benefit prosperous farmers more than the poorer section of the community; second, the community woodlot part of the programme is not progressing successfully; and third, the extensive use of eucalyptus as a cash crop undoubtedly provides fuelwood but by lowering the water table it depletes the soil of nutrients and in general degrades the area ecologically. The advantage of social forestry is that it involves the society and government at various levels in preservation of the vegetative cover, which is the most successful way to attempt afforestation. In Gujarat a phenomenally successful afforestation programme has been carried out by providing the schoolchildren with the seeds of the subabul tree, and encouraging them to look after their trees, which in turn supply the community with fuel and fodder. The effect of social forestry programmes in India has been discussed in detail by Agarwal and Narain in their edited volume. **The State of India's Environment 1984-85.**

a cruel way. He would like to see a return to policies which promote small scale family farms which use bio-intensive and environmentally friendly technologies.

Machines Replace People

Present day industrial economies, fuelled by a growth ideology, promote energy-intensive and capital-intensive technologies. It economises on labour costs as more and more sophisticated machines replace people in the work place. According to Kortens, industry would be much less destructive if it was concentrated on small or intermediate scale production and used environmentally sound, resource-conserving, labour-using technologies designed to add value to local resources and products. It should also primarily serve and enhance competitive efficiency within domestic markets rather than beginning with the global market.

In many communities a tension often arises today between those who wish to protect the environment and those who, because of pressing unemployment, want jobs at all cost. Trade unions have often shied away from this dilemma because of the fear that tougher environmental standards might lead to job losses. This is why the "Jobs and the Environment" seminar prepared by the New York Public Health Institute in conjunction with the Labour Institute (1994) is such an important new department.

This workshop which involves eight different activities explores the environmental, economic and social dimension of many of the issues in the jobs versus environment dilemma. Dialogue and sharing information are central to the process; those who devised the seminar recognise that unless accurate and relevant information is made available the participants will not be able to make an informed judgement about whether a particular factory or an industry is either appropriate or sustainable. One interesting statistic from the US Department of Labour states that unemployment is higher in States within extensive toxic-related industries.

At the end of the seminar the participants can begin to weigh up the real cost, for example, of the chemical industry. The participants are encouraged to ask questions like, Are toxic industries really worth it? Do the losses outweigh the gains? Are there realistic, non-toxic alternatives?

On the broader employment front some of the data presented during the seminar presents statistics on the size and power of large corporations. For example, the top 500 companies in the US own 76 percent of all US industrial assets. It is legitimate to ask whether it is good for democracy that such a small group of people, who are answerable to no one except the shareholders

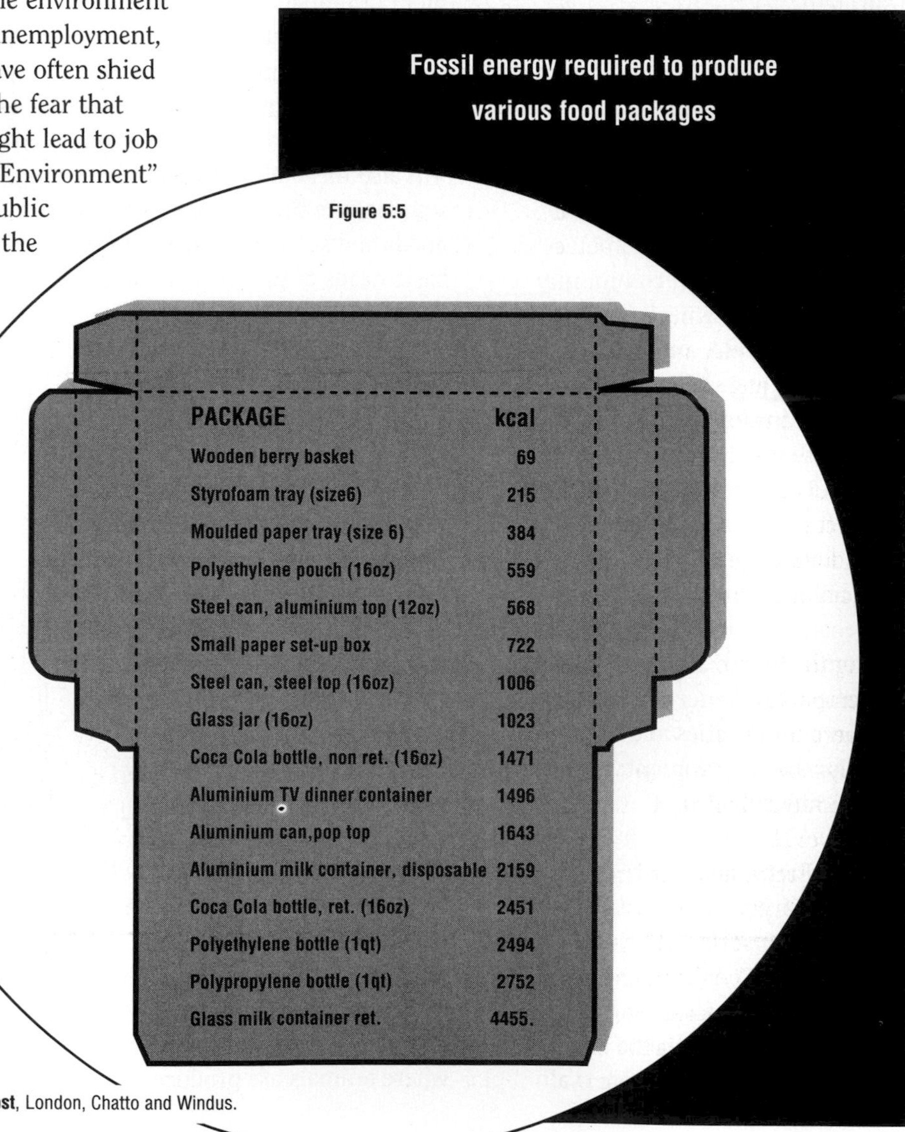

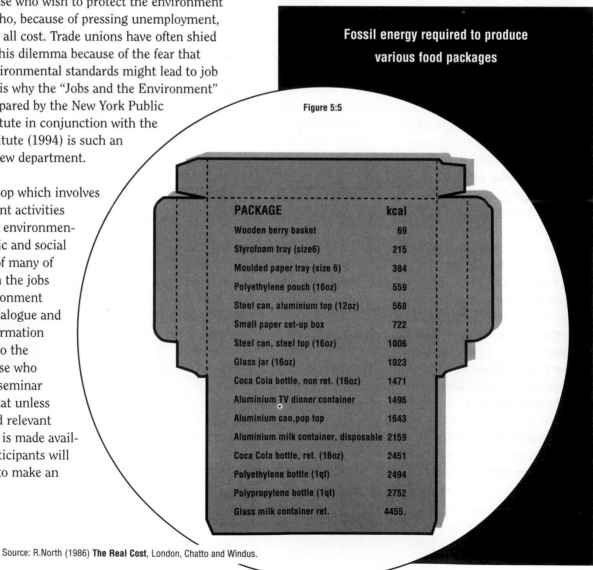

Fossil energy required to produce various food packages

Figure 5:5

PACKAGE	kcal
Wooden berry basket	69
Styrofoam tray (size6)	215
Moulded paper tray (size 6)	384
Polyethylene pouch (16oz)	559
Steel can, aluminium top (12oz)	568
Small paper set-up box	722
Steel can, steel top (16oz)	1006
Glass jar (16oz)	1023
Coca Cola bottle, non ret. (16oz)	1471
Aluminium TV dinner container	1496
Aluminium can,pop top	1643
Aluminium milk container, disposable	2159
Coca Cola bottle, ret. (16oz)	2451
Polyethylene bottle (1qt)	2494
Polypropylene bottle (1qt)	2752
Glass milk container ret.	4455.

Source: R.North (1986) **The Real Cost**, London, Chatto and Windus.

of their respective companies, should have such a hold over the US economy? Given this kind of stranglehold on the economy is it really possible for local entrepreneurs to generate sustainable jobs in local communities?

Jobs and the Environment

The kind of debate involved in the Jobs and the Environment question presupposes a relevant education system which equips ordinary people with information and values to empower them to take control of their lives, their work place and their environment. Unfortunately, formal education programmes in most countries fail to do this. In fact they have actively promoted the development ideology and thus have not succeeded in addressing the environmental crisis in a serious and comprehensive way. If this crisis is to be understood in its proper magnitude and urgency it will be necessary to thoroughly overhaul educational systems in many countries. On a very broad level this will mean giving priority to the land, culture and people in the local community and giving priority to their needs. Such an educational system will also attempt to pass to people the appropriate values and skills which will help them to shape their own lives and chart the destiny of their local community.

Major changes will also be called for in the political arena. These must include a truly participative, accountable and well-financed system of local government. Such reforms would give local people a strong voice in the shape of their own future. At the present time crucial decisions about locating a factory in a particular place or protecting the environment are often dictated by distant politicians, bureaucrats or financial institutions.

Taking the environment seriously will also challenge all contemporary religious traditions. Many religious believers today are too centred on the spiritual, other-worldly aspect of their particular tradition. This must change radically if religion is to remain a credible force in the world. Contemporary religious teaching must take the Earth, and particularly the massive destruction of the Earth, much more seriously. In future, religions must devote a lot more energy to halting the destruction that is taking place and healing the damage which already has been done. Many of the major religions of the world, like Christianity and Islam, have much to learn from the wisdom of primal religions which are much more sensitive to the presence of the Divine in the natural world. Early Irish Saints like Columba and Columban successfully married a deep experience of the Christian faith with a sense of God's presence in nature. Their example ought to guide Irish Christians in pursuing the Christian vocation today which ought to involve working for justice, peace and the integrity of Creation.

Only in this way will it be possible to build institutions which will ensure equity, sustainability and inclusiveness. The stakes are high - nothing less than the survival of humankind, many other species and almost every eco-system on earth. At the moment these policies and programmes only exist on the fringe of international consciousness and in small, fairly powerless groups. The sooner they become the norm and move to centre stage the better for all concerned.

Each of us is challenged to do what we can at the individual and institutional level to promote this new vision. It will mean living as far as possible by the light of the 3 Rs -Reduce, Reuse and Recycle. Many people rightly fear that unless this generation calls off its massive attack on the planet Earth, future generations, if they survive at all, will be forced to live, not merely amid the ruins of an industrial society, but amid the ruins of the natural world itself.

▼ References

Some of this material is presented in my writings, **To care for the Earth** (1995, Chapman, London); **The Greening of the Church** (1990, Chapman, London) and **Passion for the Earth** (Chapman 1994).

Thomas Berry, and Brian Swimme (1992), **The Universe Story,** HarperCollins, New York.

Lester Brown (1995) **The State of the World,** W.W. Norton and Company, London.

Fritjof Capra (1983), **The Turning Point,** Bantam Books, New York.

Herman Daly and John B. Cobb Jr (1989), **For the Common Good,** Green Print, London.

Richard Douthwaithe (1992) **The Growth Illusion,** The Lilliput Press, Ireland.

Susan George (1992), **The Debt Boomerang,** Pluto Press, London.

Paul Hawken (1994), **The Ecology of Commerce,** HarperCollins, New York.

The World Commission on Environment and Development (1987) **Our Common Future**, Oxford University Press, London.

Bruce Rich (1994), **Mortgaging the Earth,** Beacon Press, Boston.

E.F Schumacher (1973), **Small is Beautiful,** Harper and Row, New York.

Ted Trainer (1989), **Developed to Death,** Green Print, London.

Tim Lang and Colin Hines (1993), **The New Protectionism: Protecting the Future against Free Trade,** Earthscan Publications Ltd, London.

UNDP (1992), **Human Development Report** New York, Oxford University Press.

"...THE VERY VOICES IT HAD SILENCED..."
Women and Development

Pauline Eccles

INTRODUCTION

Twenty years have now passed since the first World Conference on Women was held in Mexico. Three further World Conferences on Women have been held, and a United Nations Decade for Women (from 1975 to 1985) focused specifically on dealing with the problems of inequality and poverty which women face world-wide. A number of other important UN Conferences have also taken place during the period, particularly in the last five years:

- the Rio de Janeiro Conference on the Environment in 1992
- the Vienna Human Rights Conference in 1993
- the Cairo Conference on Population in 1994
- the Copenhagen Conference on Social Development in 1995
- the Beijing Conference on Women in 1995.

All of these have placed gender issues at the heart of their debates.

In the broader arena, major geo-political and economic events have occurred during the last twenty years. To name but four -

- the Berlin Wall fell, marking the fall of communist regimes throughout Eastern Europe and the Soviet Union and the ending of the Cold War
- Third World debt became increasingly insupportable and the adjustment programmes have increased poverty, especially amongst women
- with the notable, and recent, exception of Ireland, official aid has stagnated or decreased during the period and there are few signs of a reversal of the trend
- there is major and growing insecurity due to famine, ethnic conflicts and other catastrophes which have affected areas such as Sub-Saharan Africa and the former Yugoslavia.

Eighty years ago, when James Connolly, in an essay entitled *"Woman"*, described women workers in Ireland as the slaves of slaves, the parallels with women in the Third World today were even more apparent. Women workers in Ireland at that time were *"compelled to bear all the worst burdens...and yet be denied even the few political rights enjoyed by the male portion of their fellow sufferers"*. And like women in the rural areas of the Third World today, women in Connolly's Ireland also *"toiled on the farms from earliest childhood, attaining usually to the age of ripe womanhood without ever being vouchsafed the right to claim...a single penny of the money earned by her labour and knowing that all her toil and privation could not earn her that right to the farm..."*

All of these events have had significant gender implications. Bearing these events and initiatives in mind, what is the situation of women today? Are women now better or worse off than they were in 1975?

BETTER OR WORSE?

Statistics and evidence on the ground show that in some ways, the situation of women has improved. The 1995 **Human Development Report** indicates that women and girls are better educated than ever before and that the Arab States have led the way in closing the gender gap in education and health, more than doubling female literacy between 1970 and 1990.

Women live longer and health risks incurred in bearing children have declined. In relation to some indicators, women's gains have even been faster than men's, e.g. female life expectancy has increased 20% faster than male life expectancy over the past twenty years; and female rates of adult literacy and combined school enrolment in the developing world increased twice as fast as male rates between 1970 and 1990.

On the other hand, as the 1995 **Human Development Report** notes, *"..in no society do women enjoy the same opportunities as men"*. Women outnumber men two to one in illiteracy while 60% of children without access to primary school are girls. Most serious of all is the growing feminisation of poverty over the past decade. 70% of the 1.3 billion people living in poverty world-wide are women.

Women's poverty is specifically linked to gender issues, as well as to class, race and age as is the case for men also. For women, subordination within the family, lower pay than men and more insecure employment are combined with even greater lack of access to capital, land, technology and other economic resources than poor men. Poverty among women is particularly bad when they are forced to raise their families alone. Then, the combination of the burden of children and inadequate support from absent men makes for a serious situation for around 30% of the world's families.

It is now finally conceded by the international community, as the Declaration agreed in September 1995 at the Fourth World Conference on Women affirms, that such intransigent poverty has its origins *"in both the national and international domain"*. and is exacerbated in particular by *"unfavourable international political, economic and social forces..."*. This statement reflects a more realistic understanding of global poverty and inequality and an encouraging trend in the way we look at women's issues.

100
90
80
70
60
50
40
30
20
10

In the past, because of the lack of recognition of women's contributions to society - politics, economics, and the public arena in general ignored women. Today, this kind of gender blindness is rapidly becoming obsolete and issues of gender equality are moving to the top of the global agenda.

A Platform for Action

Because of this, the Platform for Action of the 1995 Fourth World Conference on Women conceded the necessity for macro-economic policies to be rethought from a gender perspective. To put this in simple terms, it means that governments and NGOs are called upon when planning their budgets, policies and programmes to take account of the equal but often different needs and interests of women and men. The growing awareness, at all levels, of gender issues has not just happened in a vacuum. It has been brought about by the massive efforts of women world-wide and their allies within the global women's movement, among NGOs concerned with justice and human rights, at the academic and research level, and as a result of national governments' political commitments to equality.

Some of the key factors involved in this change of consciousness are:-

- the mobilisation of women at local, national, regional and international level;
- increased resources for gender-related research and statistics, e.g. into the level and value of women's unpaid work, and the inequalities between men and women, girls and boys in relation to health, education, access to resources and participation in decision-making, etc.;
- more emphasis on gender - men and women's often unequal relationship - than on women as a category;
- alliances between women from the developed countries and the Third World.

Figure 6:1

Out of 1.3 billion people living in absolute poverty, over 70% are women

Source:
Human Development Report 1995, UNDP.

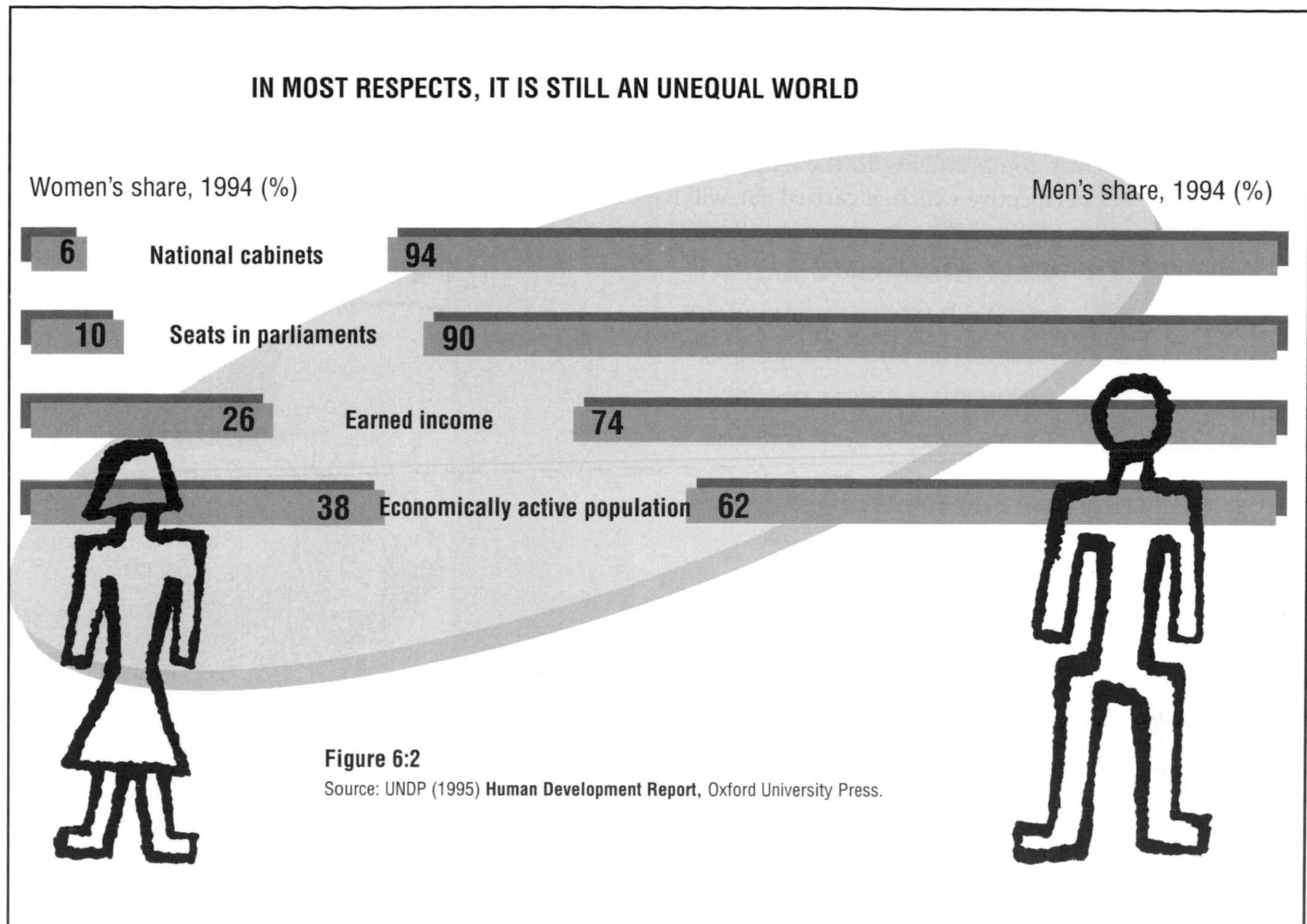

Figure 6:2

Source: UNDP (1995) **Human Development Report,** Oxford University Press.

Apart from the fact that women make up over fifty per cent of the population, earn only ten per cent of the world's wages and own only 1% of the world's property, there has been a growing acceptance of the fact that women contribute hugely to the world's economy and well-being through their unpaid work in the home, their participation in the paid labour market and as voluntary community managers and workers.

The most encouraging sign is that we are no longer looking at women in isolation, but rather recognising that we cannot talk about women's needs and interests without discussing their relationship in a variety of ways, both privately and in society, with the other half of the human race, men. The new awareness takes in the fact that these relationships are often unequal and also that women and men have very often different needs and interests. In that new awareness, we are now talking more about gender than about women per se. Men as a group are beginning to slowly work with women towards gender equality in their own interests.

In addition, issues related to the wider world are now acknowledged to have gender implications and therefore solutions to problems related to armed conflict, debt, trade, and other so-called 'macro' issues have to involve analysis of both women's and men's needs and interests.

Beijing 1995

To try and come to grips with these and other related questions, the United Nations, regional blocks like the European Union, and individual countries, met in Beijing, China in September 1995 for two weeks of intense negotiations. Their central goal was to assess the gains made since the Third World Conference on Women, held in Nairobi in 1985 and to set new targets for women's needs and interests to the end of the millennium.

"An ever more important role..."

In the mid 1970s, at international level, a general awareness began to grow that women world-wide were discriminated against in terms of their equality with men and in respect of economic and social roles and status. In particular, it was becoming apparent that in the Third World, women were performing massive productive work with virtually no reward and, at the same time, were being given no support from the development community for their productive roles. A growing consensus at the UN on these issues resulted in a major impetus in the mid-seventies to put the situation of women on the map.

In 1975 the first UN Conference on the situation of women world-wide took place in Mexico. A Decade of Women was decided. In 1980, the Second Conference on Women took place in Copenhagen to review progress. And in 1985, in Nairobi, the Third World Conference took place marking the end of the decade.

In Nairobi, the Forward Looking Strategies for the Advancement of Women to the Year 2000 were agreed and there was fresh impetus for UN member states to ratify the UN Convention Against All Forms of Discrimination Against Women.

The achievement of the 1985 Nairobi Conference and the Decade for Women was to highlight and make visible the role of women and their situation world-wide. Since then, two additional steps forward have been taken: better methods of research and statistics gathering have helped to make women more visible e.g. breaking down indicators such as life expectancy, infant mortality, literacy and so on into their gender dimensions. This has highlighted some very distinct issues of women's subordination and hardship both globally and regionally.

For instance, although women generally live longer than men, in some regions of the world, particularly India and Bangladesh, as well as in certain Islamic states, women actually die before men as well as being more malnourished. And, in general, women get less food and medical services than men.

Women today are much more empowered than in 1985 in terms of lobbying, networking and taking joint action at national and international levels. For instance, there are now world coalitions of women in relation to the environment, reproductive rights, human rights and women in development which have played a role at international negotiations unlike before. This has happened at NGDO level through workshops, petitions, the lobbying of national governments etc. and also at official levels, the so-called Women's Caucus is playing an ever more important role.

1995 - The Fourth World Conference on Women

In September 1995, the largest ever gathering at a United Nations event took place in Beijing, China. Around 35,000 women and some men travelled to the NGO Women's Forum held in Huairou outside the capital from the 30th of August to the 8th of September. Another 15,000 official delegates, journalists and representatives of non-governmental organisations attended the official Fourth World Conference on Women from September 4th to September 15th.

The main negotiating document was the draft Platform for Action (PFA). As the conference got under way, 40% of the PFA was still not agreed in spite of three preparatory committee meetings and a week of informal consultations a month previously.

The PFA consists of six chapters and a Declaration dealing with issues related to women's rights, needs and interests and practical strategies for their fulfilment. The main focus of the PFA is on strategic objectives around critical areas of concern including:

- women in poverty
- education
- health care
- violence against women
- the effects of conflict on women
- power-sharing and decision making
- mechanisms to promote the advancement of women
- human rights
- the mass media
- women's management of natural resources and the environment
- the girl child.

Women and Poverty

- over 70% of people living in poverty are women
- around 30% of all families are headed by women on their own - these are amongst the poorest groups in society
- there is a key link between land and poverty - women rarely own land.

Literacy and Education

- educated women are the key to development
- 64% of the world's illiterates are women
- the primary school enrolment rate for girls now equals that for boys in Africa and Asia, but more girls than boys still drop out at secondary school level in the Third World.

Women's Health

- life expectancy for women and men has increased nearly everywhere, but 500,000 women are still dying from pregnancy and childbirth related causes each year
- an African woman's risk of dying from pregnancy and childbirth causes is 1 in 23, compared with 1 in 4,000 for women in the North
- the maternal mortality rate is twice as high in Eastern Europe than in Western Europe
- 43% of all women suffer from anaemia. In India, over 70% are now being treated during pregnancy with iron tablets.

Women in the Global Economy

- women will make up more than half of the formal labour force by the year 2000
- most women still earn only 50 - 80% of men's wages
- women still hold only 10% of managerial positions
- in 144 countries, no women hold positions in economic ministries
- in most countries, women work twice as much unpaid time as men (usually in the household)
- the UN estimates that the value of women's unpaid household work amounts to 10-35% of global GDP.

Violence Against Women

- in most countries, violence by family members is a leading cause of injury to women
- an EU finding estimated that 20,000 women were raped in Bosnia in the first months of the war there. Mass rape has been documented recently in Cambodia, Liberia, Peru, Somalia and Uganda
- an estimated 2 million girls suffer genital mutilation each year in Africa and Asia
- World Bank analysis says that rape and domestic violence are significant causes of disability and death amongst women world-wide.

Human Rights

- until 1989, a woman in Ecuador could be forced to live with her husband, and laws in Chile and Guatemala still exonerate a man if he agrees to marry a woman he has raped
- in a number of countries, only a husband can obtain a divorce on grounds of adultery

Politics and Decision-making

- only 24 women have been elected heads of government or heads of state this century
- under 6% of cabinet ministers are women, an increase of nearly double since 1987
- one-third of ministers in Denmark, Finland, the Netherlands, Norway, the Seychelles and Sweden are women
- at the UN, 20% of delegates to the General Assembly are women, but the number of women in senior management is only 13%.

The Girl Child

- girls are at higher risk of dying before the age of 5 than boys
- more boys are immunised and treated in hospital than girls
- the estimated loss in girls because of son preference is between 60 million and 100 million world-wide
- at least 2 million girls between the ages of 4 and 8 undergo genital mutilation each year
- the work burden of girls is much heavier than that of boys in many countries world-wide
- genetic testing for sex selection has been banned in India and in China since 1995.

After two weeks of intense negotiations on what were often disputed issues, consensus was reached on the Platform for Action. It was agreed by most that the document exceeded expectations. So what were the main steps forward which were agreed?

- the commitments made at previous UN conferences on the Environment, Human Rights, Population and Social Development were integrated from a gender perspective into the PFA and at times even went beyond what had previously been agreed to. For instance, the call to protect human rights activists is new. And systematic rape during armed conflict has been declared to be a war crime and, in some cases, a crime against humanity. Children's rights to enjoy privacy, respect and access to counselling in relation to sexual and reproductive health was also recognised
- the Conference became a 'Conference of Commitments' in which individual governments pledged undertakings in line with the PFA
- between Nairobi and Beijing, the women's agenda has become a gender agenda. The links between women's lives and the wider arena of macro-economic issues, politics and war was firmly agreed in Beijing often with a new emphasis on women's human rights
- member states are committed to a follow up process of implementation which is to involve non-governmental organisations and to set plans for this in motion before the end of 1995.

Women and Development: Two Views

"Peasant women are the most affected by the economic situation because they do not have the financial means to study...As far as peasant women are concerned nothing has changed in the last 30 years. They don't have a hospital, for example, or a health post. They have no light, water, farming tools, none of that. They still do everything by hand, with ploughs pulled by oxen. Their lack of education holds them back, they can't make any progress. The little that they earn from what they sow and harvest buys a little sugar and rice to subsist on. They badly need education so as to see to their children's health and learn the value of different foods...Many housewives cannot afford to buy meat for themselves anymore...The crisis affects women because the wages are very low. Of course, there's plenty of food, you can get it anywhere. But there is not any money, the wages are not enough to buy anything. Households have seven, ten, twelve, fifteen members. Women have to devote more energy to finding money whenever they can. Women have to support their homes on their own when their husband is not working. They sell a few potatoes or onions. They make their small children join in, too. They send them to polish shoes or sell newspapers or sweets while they are selling somewhere else...Women here in Bolivia try to meet their needs in the crisis as best they can, in desperation. But the government doesn't realise, that we women are forgetting our culture, neglecting education and knowledge...".

The views of Ester on three decades of 'development' and the impact of the debt crisis on the lives on women.

"Recovering the feminine principle as respect for life in nature and society appears to be the only way forward, for men as well as women, in the North as well as in the South...(the) dominant mode of organising the world today is being challenged by the very voices it had silenced. These voices, muted through subjugation, are now quietly but firmly suggesting that the Western male has produced only one culture, and that there are other ways of structuring the world. Women's struggles for survival through the protection of nature are ...challenging the belief of the dominant world view that nature and women are worthless and waste, that they are obstacles to progress and must be sacrificed.

The two central shifts in thinking that are being induced by women's ecological struggles relate to economic and intellectual worth. The shift relates to our understanding of what constitutes knowledge, and who the knowers and producers of intellectual value are. The second involves concepts of wealth and economic value and who the producers of wealth and economic value are. Women producing survival are showing us that nature is the very basis and matrix for economic life through its function in life support and livelihood...They are challenging concepts of waste, rubbish and dispensability as the modern West has defined them. They are showing that production of sustenance is basic to survival itself and cannot be deleted from economic calculations: if production of life cannot be reckoned with in money terms, then it is economic models, and not women's work in producing sustenance and life, that must be sacrificed...By elbowing out 'life' from being the central concern in organising human society, the dominant paradigm of knowledge has become a threat to life itself. Third World women are bringing the concern with living and survival back to the centre-stage of human history."

Indian activist Vandana Shiva

Source: Julia Cleves Mosse (1993) **Half the World, Half a Chance: An Introduction to Gender and Development,** Oxford, Oxfam.

'WOMAN OF THE WORLD'

In 1989, Professor Wangari Maathai was awarded Women's Aid's 'Woman of the World' award in recognition of her work in setting up the Green Belt Movement in Kenya. In her work over 14 years, she had persuaded communities throughout Kenya to plant more than 10 million trees and, in response to her success, another 35 African countries have adopted the scheme.

She started the movement despite opposition from 'experts' who argued that all Kenya needed was greater production of cash crops for export and more fertiliser to increase production. Professor Maathai realised that Kenya had already been substantially denuded of trees and that more cash crops would only increase the problem. In most parts of the country there was little firewood left to gather and soil erosion and land degradation had increased. Rural Kenyans were being forced by such circumstances to depend on less nutritious food and on dried dung for cooking as well as on expensive processed foods.

Thousands of rural dwellers were also being forced to move into the slums of Kenya's cities. Professor Maathai argued that these slums were simply a symptom of the degradation of the land and the neglect of environmental issues. *"Economic investment was the god when the problem was really one of simple things like firewood, food and topsoil".* Thousand of green belts have now been planted and many hundreds of community based tree nurseries established. Women have also pioneered the collection of seeds from local trees and have developed nurseries based upon them. Such actions as well as the many others promoted by the Green Belt Movement have helped tackle key environmental issues.

Source: John Vidal (1989) "Root causes, root answers" **Guardian Newspaper**

"...so-called 'women's issues' have come out of the attic into the clear light of day...and are finally recognised as central and integral to the progress and prosperity of human society"

Ms. Joan Burton TD., Minister of State at the Department of Foreign Affairs Ireland, Informal Forum on Development Co-operation, 7.10.95

Women in Ireland facts and figures

EMPLOYMENT

- In 1992 34% of Irish women of working age were in the labour force, in comparison to 70% of men
- Ireland had the lowest rate of female unemployment in the EU
- In 1993, women earned only 61.30% of average gross male earnings
- 85% of low paid part-time workers and 53% of social welfare recipients are women.
- In 1994, in excess of 60,000 women were in receipt of social welfare payments because they were rearing children alone.

EDUCATION

- 45% of all second level teachers are women, only 10% of principals are women
- Only 16% of secondary school inspectors are women
- In 1993-94, 26% of university lectureships and 3.8% of professorships were women
- Women make up 70% of those in adult education but only 13% of the membership of Vocational Education Committees themselves.

HEALTH

- The maternal death rate has fallen from 31 in 1970 to 2 in 1992, per 100,000 births
- Married women have worse mental health than either single or married men, with single women experiencing the least psychological distress of all
- Traveller women live, on average, 12 years less than settled women.

VIOLENCE

- There are no national statistics on violence against women in Ireland
- Women's Aid national helpline received 17,510 calls between 1992 and 1995
- In a four month period the special domestic violence and sexual assault unit set up by the gardai in Dublin received 5,000 calls
- There are only 14 family spaces in refuges in Dublin and 79 in the whole of the Republic.

DECISION-MAKING

- 2 cabinet members out of 15 are women and a further 4 are Ministers of State
- 4 out of 15 MEPs are women
- 12.4% of TDs are women - 22 out of 166
- 12% of the Seanad, or Upper House of Parliament, are women
- In the civil service - women comprise 45% of the work-force, only one is a Departmental Secretary, 5 are Assistant Secretaries, 3% are at Principal Officer level and 84% are clerical assistants
- The quota of women on state boards is 40% but only 20.9% are actually women
- The equivalent figure in the private sector is only 3.5%.

Source: National Women's Council of Ireland (1995) **Independent Report to the 4th UN World Conference on Women, "Beijing and Beyond"**.

"We argue that men, at least a significant number of men in every community, are willing to support - rather than inhibit - women's empowerment...'Improving the status of women is not a women's issue, it is a human issue. It is time, therefore, to call men to action in this area...

We also know that many programmes that seek to bring women into the mainstream are most effective if, in the early stages, they build on the strengths of women as a separate group...

In countless development programmes women have successfully taken the lead and men have found it in their interest to follow. More often than not, the results of women's educational and economic empowerment, whether they be improved health and nutrition or higher incomes, benefit families and the community as a whole."

Nick Danforth (1995) "Let's Not Forget About the Men", **Choices,** New York, UNDP.

Women in the UK facts and figures

Women's Economic Activity 1991

SECTOR	NUMBER
Economically active in the 'formal' economy	11,437,000
Students	833,000
Retired	4,775,000
Permanently 'sick'	759,000
Others - at home, informal work etc.	5,132,000

	Women	Men
Full Time Employees	5,985,000	11,566,000
Part Time Employees	3,839,000	472,000

Pay and Hours 1994

FULL-TIME EMPLOYMENT - MEDIAN PAY AND HOURS

	Pay		Hours
	Per Week	Hour	
All Women	£229	£6.02	38
All Men	£313	£7.39	42
Manual Women	£165	£4.20	40
Manual Men	£262	£5.95	45
Non-manual women	£247	£6.25	38
Non-manual men	£376	£9.67	37

Women's Work 1994

Women represent:
80% of clerical workers; 97% of secretaries; 3% of senior managers; 9% of management; 4% of board members of major UK companies; 9% of members of Parliament and 2% of science professors.

Women and Success in Education

SCHOOL LEAVERS 1992/93	MALE	FEMALE
With good GCSE's	42,000	52,000
With good A Levels	75,000	82,000
UNIVERSITIES		
1992/93 new full-time students	68,667	61,970
1992 first degrees	46,888	38,005
1992 higher degrees	24,929	14,034
1991/92 Lecturers	25,000	5,000

In the United Kingdom, Women's Affairs are the responsibility of the Secretary of State, Department of Education and Employment.

Sources: **Annual Abstract of Statistics,** Margaret L. Flanders (1994) **Breakthrough,** London, Paul Chapman and **Guardian Education,** 30.5.95.
Roger Robinson, DEC.

Women's work extends beyond the economy into the household and the community - Sugar workers on Negros Island, the Philippines.

▼ REFERENCES

Convention on the Elimination of All Forms of Discrimination Against Women, (CEDAW), United Nations, Dept. of Public Information, UN, New York.

Mandy Macdonald (ed. 1995) **Living and Working - An Illustration of the Feminisation of Poverty in Europe,** WIDE, Belgium.

W. Harcourt, L.Woestman and L.Grogan (1995) **Towards Alternative Economics from a European Perspective,** WIDE, Belgium.

Dublin Stationery Office (1994) **National Report of Ireland, United Nations Fourth World Conference on Women,** Dublin.

National Women's Council of Ireland (1995) **Women, Beijing and Beyond, Achieving an Effective Platform for Action,** An Independent Report to the 4th UN World Conference ,Dublin.

Development Research Unit, Irish Commission for Justice and Peace (1995) **"The Girl Child",** Gender and Justice Issues, Briefing Paper No. 1., Dublin.

Development Research Unit, Irish Commission for Justice and Peace (1995) **"Violation Against Women- A Violation of Human Rights",** Gender and Justice Issues, Briefing Paper No. 2., Dublin.

Marilee Karl (1995) **Women and Empowerment, Participation & Decision Making,** London, Zed Books.

J. Cleves Mosse (1993) **Half the World, Half a Chance: An Introduction to Gender and Development,** Oxford, Oxfam.

J. Henshall Momsen (1991) **Women and Development in the Third World,** London, Routledge.

UNDP (1995) **Human Development Report,** London, Oxford University Press.

"...THEY DIE VERY QUIETLY": HUNGER TODAY

Colm Regan and Sinéad Tynan

"Two decades ago, the 1974 World Food Conference in Rome expressed alarm at the prospect of long-term food shortages and massive starvation in developing countries. However, every year since then, the world has had more than adequate food supplies for everyone to enjoy a minimally adequate diet (2,350 calories per person per day). Since 1974, the number and proportion of chronically undernourished people (i.e., people who do not consume enough protein and calories) in the developing world has fallen significantly."
Fifth Annual Report on the State of World Hunger (1995)

"The era in which we live has the odious distinction of being the period when more people will die of famine than in any previous century"
K. Cahill (ed.) (1982) **Famine,** New York, Orbis.

Introduction

The reality of hunger in the world today is, quite simply, a major scandal. It is so because at least 800 million people (20% of the Third World's people) are still undernourished while some 2 billion face vitamin and mineral deficiencies which seriously undermine the quality of their lives. It is also a scandal because the world continues to have more than enough food to adequately feed all and the technical capacity to do so, but lacks the political will to achieve this objective - so frequently and solemnly stated at international conferences. It is also a scandal because the cost of eliminating the scourge of hunger is so small by comparison with world resources and because most of the major causes of hunger could be swiftly and effectively addressed. The simple fact is that in today's world, hunger does not just happen, it is created - by human action and inaction.

"It's been called the invisible killer, the silent emergency. It is not famine and it does not make the headlines. It is the grinding poverty which, day in day out, deprives millions of people across the globe of the essentials of a decent life. In particular, they are deprived of an adequate diet. This 'normal hunger' will kill their children in the first year, destroy their health in adulthood, and take them to an early grave. More than one thousand million people are chronically hungry. Every 24 hours, 35 thousand of them die as a result...They die very quietly. They are the brothers and sisters of Alberto, who died aged six months from malnutrition and infection, because his father, a cocoa worker in Brazil, does not earn enough to buy sufficient food, let alone medicine. They are the cousins of Hassan, who died aged three months from malnutrition and TB in a hospital ward in Sudan, long after the famine had ended."

Chris Bryer in **The Hunger**

Ideology and Hunger -

Analysing the causes of world hunger has been a matter of intense debate and disagreement - these relate not just to hunger but to broader issues of development in general and poverty in particular. Recent writers have identified a variety of viewpoints related to the issue of hunger. According to John Warnock in his 1987 book, **The Politics of Hunger,** it is possible to identify five approaches:

The Neo-Malthusians - they argue that the central problem is the unchecked growth of population and the inability of food production rates to keep up with that growth. They accept that there are serious inequalities in income and power within society but issues of distribution and social justice remain of secondary interest to them. Examples of this approach include the Worldwatch Institute in Washington and The Global 2000 Report commissioned by US President Jimmy Carter in 1978.

The "Steady State" Ecology Approach

This approach emphasises the need to move away from debates about the quantity of goods and people on the earth to a focus on the quality of life and the need to slow energy consumption. This school views the earth as a closed energy system which cannot continue to grow without limits. There is a need to reduce population growth and energy use. This school of thought provides much support for the neo-malthusian approach noted above. Examples of this approach can be seen in the work of ecologists such as Eugene Odum or economists such as Kenneth Boulding.

The Marxist Approach

This approach contrasts strongly with that of the neo-malthusians in arguing that there is plenty of food available to feed the world but that its distribution under capitalism is so unequal that hunger inevitably follows. Marxists believe that society is capable of increasing food production to match increased population growth. Within Marxism there are a variety of views, many of which increasingly accept the need for population planning but stress that this must be voluntary and is not the primary issue for action. Examples of this approach include the work of Marx himself, Michael Redclift and many economists in the former Soviet Union.

Orthodox Economics

This approach has many common elements with the Marxist approach, emphasising the need for continued growth and the removal of restrictions on the greater production of resources. The larger economic pie will help to allow the poor to escape both their poverty and their hunger. Again, there are a great variety of approaches and emphases within orthodox economics with some placing the primary emphasis on the need to free the market in order to increase production while others stress the need for regulating markets to insure against inequality. Examples of this approach include that of the World Bank.

Distributive Justice

The emphasis within this school is on freedom from hunger as an inalienable human right. There is acceptance that the world is currently producing enough food to feed all adequately but that the key issue is distribution. This approach rejects the neo-malthusian view that population growth is the issue and the Marxist approach which argues that it is not an issue. In this approach there is a heavy emphasis on the ethical dimensions of hunger and on the need for free choice on the issue of family planning. Examples of this approach are to be seen in the work of Liberation Theologists or more popular writers such as Susan George.

In essence the debates on world hunger and its relationship to population growth and poverty are between a technocratic approach which believes society can and will overcome resource shortages and difficulties and which sees the issue of population numbers as secondary and an ecological approach which emphasises the need to take the environment and its limitations into account and thus sees growing population numbers as a major threat.

Figure 7:1

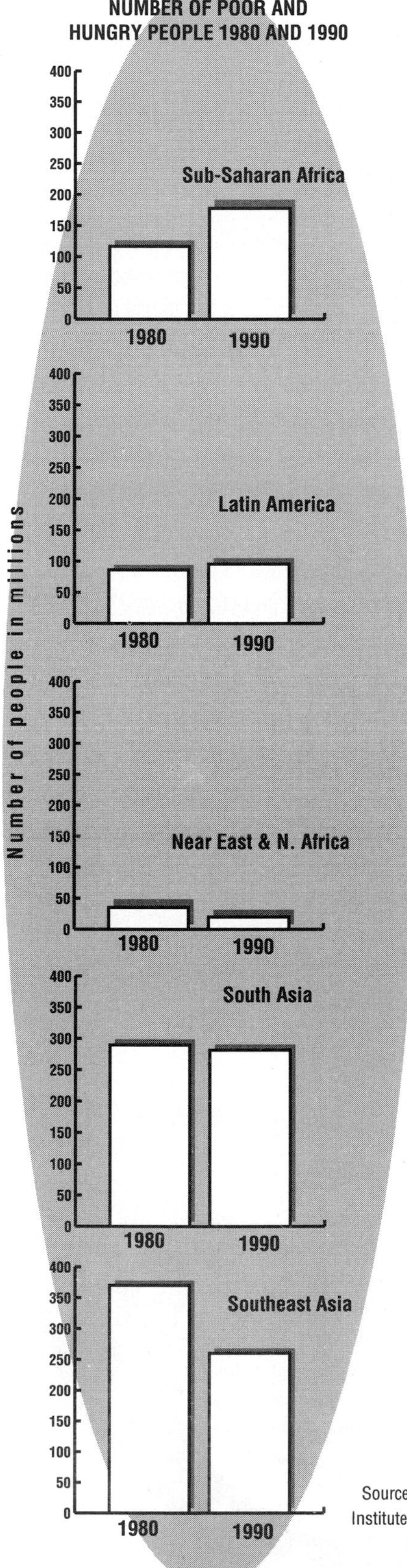

Source: Bread for the World Institute (1995) **Hunger 1995**, Silver Springs.

Defining terms

Strange as it might seem the issue of defining what precisely a famine is and when does hunger become famine has been the subject of considerable discussion and research. Governments and local political leaders and merchants are slow to accept that famine exists as it has obvious major political, economic and logistical consequences. Governments have traditionally been reluctant to admit the existence of famine because it reflects badly on their policies and strategies, or because it relates to conflict situations within the country or region or because it will threaten their power base and perhaps provide support to opposition groups.

One of the better definitions of famine is given by Cox who refers to"*...the regional failure of food production or distribution systems, leading to sharply increased mortality due to starvation and associated disease."* Another definition which lays stress on the roots of famine is provided by Field who argues that *"...famine is the endpoint of a lengthy process...typically covering two or more crop seasons."* Tynan, in summarising the issue of definition concludes:

"In summary then, famine is a regional phenomenon which is characterised by both disease and starvation. As the final stage of a lengthy process it can also involve a significant change in the levels of food supply and demand (relative to the norm), economic recession, and societal disintegration. Finally, and perhaps most importantly, famine is not an uncontrollable tragedy, but is rather a largely preventable human occurrence"

Figure 7:2

CRONICALLY UNDERNOURISHED DEVELOPING COUNTRIES

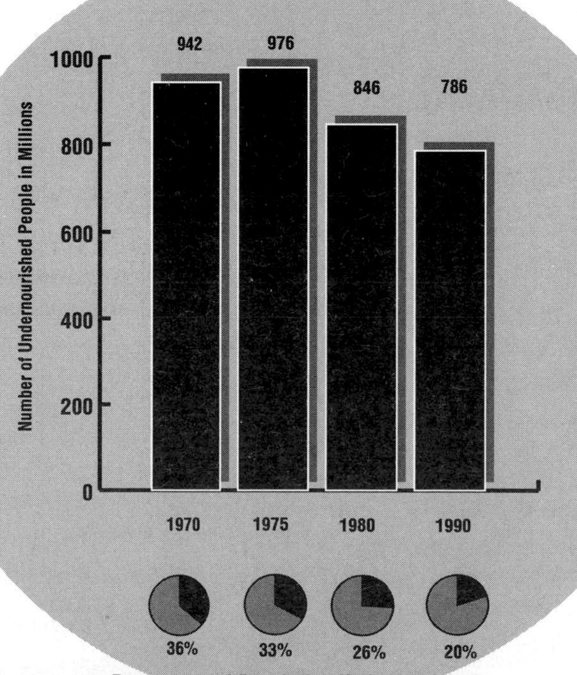

Famine and its effects

FAMINE AND THE INDIVIDUAL

▼ famine first affects the old, the young and the sick - those least able to defend themselves; children are affected by stunted growth, body wasting and reduced mental development. Lack of food inhibits adults' ability to work; it increases greatly vulnerability to disease (measles, diarrhoea, cholera, dysentery etc.).

FAMINE AND THE FAMILY

▼ hardship felt most severely at this level. Discrimination with regard to access to food within the family occurs but not as much as often thought. In Asia, in particular, there may be discrimination on the basis of gender. Males often leave the family in search of employment in order to increase income or to increase individual intake by reducing numbers or to abandon other members of the family. Sometimes entire families will migrate but usually only as a final option.

FAMINE AT THE LOCAL LEVEL

▼ Drought, flooding or war can destroy whole crops regionally and can trigger price fluctuations; a drop in prices affects farmers badly whereas a rise in prices affects pastoralists. Negative consequences for one group will spread to others locally who depend on that group. This can affect not just merchants and shopkeepers but also local small scale producers. Crime tends to increase sharply and local customs of sharing can also suffer.

FAMINE AT NATIONAL LEVEL

▼ Countries which experience famine will already be suffering economically and politically long before its people begin to starve. Famine makes that situation even worse. Violent responses to famine conditions are a regular occurrence, especially in non-democratic and non-open states (see Starving in Silence below). Food shortages necessitate food imports which can reduce the foreign reserves of poor States even further. Distribution of food aid will also increase distribution costs while States take considerable time to overcome the local shortages of food production and so remain vulnerable long after an actual famine situation ends.

"The word 'hunger' is emotive and imprecise. The over-used expression 'world hunger' conjures up images of starvation, shrunken limbs, staring eyes and begging-bowls. But the truth is that though malnutrition is almost everywhere among the poor, the traveller in the Third World rarely sees people who are nothing but skin and bone. Only in extreme situations, in Biafra, Bangladesh or the Sahel, do these occur in large numbers. The everyday reality of malnutrition in the Third World is less dramatic. It is adults scraping through, physically and mentally fatigued and vulnerable to illness. It is children - often dying, not so frequently of hunger alone, as of hunger working hand in hand with sickness; but more often surviving impaired for life."

Paul Harrison (1993) ***Inside the Third World,***

Debating the causes of famine

There is no clear consensus as to the causes of famine although there is now widespread agreement that geo-physical events such as drought or floods or hurricanes etc. cannot and do not, in themselves , cause famine. Most critics accept that famine is a human creation although there is little agreement as to where to pinpoint blame. This is indicated quite well by the range of quotes below which emphasise a variety of factors. For the purposes of identifying some of the major factors which contribute to causing particular famines, we have chosen the three case studies which follow - Ireland, Ethiopia and Somalia.

"...the United Nations must share the blame. In the past quarter century, the UN has made the economic development of Africa's newly independent nations a major priority. Between 1980 and 1984 alone, the UN spent some $16 billion on development and humanitarian aid to Africa. Much of this money tragically has been spent on programmes that undermine agricultural output. Thus instead of assisting African nations to achieve economic growth, the UN has contributed to the deterioration of Africa's agriculture-based economies by promoting and sustaining a philosophy of economic development that encourages government interference in the rural economy and discourages the individual farmer from working hard and taking risks."
Roger Brooks (1986) "Africa is starving and the United Nations shares the blame" **Backgrounder,** Heritage Foundation.

"Most food aid is given at highly concessional prices to governments in the Third World. The food is not even intended to feed the poor and hungry. Rather it is meant to be a form of budgetary support for governments; a very different matter. Governments receive the food, sell it on the market to those with money to buy it, and keep the money to supplement their incomes. Those who benefit, apart from the government, are people in towns and cities who can afford to buy the food. Obviously, this generally misses out the poor."
Tony Jackson "Food Aid: a poisonous gift" **Links** No.20.

"If African leaders wish to end the recurrent famines they would do well to...abandon their socialist policies and permit the free market to operate."
David Osterfield (1985) "African famine: the Harvest of Socialist Agriculture" **The Freeman.**

"The forces that have institutionalised hunger in Africa are made up of African elites, multinational corporations, western governments and international agencies. Together they form an 'anti-farmer' coalition whose lifestyle and interests are very different from those of Africa's rural majority."
Kevin Danaher (1985) "How the US and Europe caused Africa's famine" **Food First News.**

"Perhaps no other continent's destiny has been so shaped by population growth as has Africa's in the late twentieth century. Not only is its population growth the fastest of any continent in history, but in country after country, demands of escalating human numbers are exceeding the sustainable yield of local life-support systems - croplands, grasslands, and forests. Each year Africa's farmers attempt to feed 16 million additional people, roughly 10 times the annual addition of North America or Europe."
Lester Brown and Edward Wolf (1985) "Reversing Africa's Decline" **Worldwatch Paper** No. 65.

"People are to blame...the spreading of the Sahara and Kalahari deserts can be linked directly to overgrazing and overuse of land. Even shortages of rain, foresters speculate, are caused not by natural fluctuations in climate but by the rapid clearing of rainforests. Blaming the weather, moaning over acts of God and accusing poor farmers are superficial responses to a complex problem. It is more revealing to examine the policies which starve the poor, pressure the land and make entire countries vulnerable to drought."
Tony Jackson and Paula Park (1984) "Nature Pleads Not Guilty" **New Internationalist.**

"War has been the single most important factor in the starvation deaths of more than 10,000 people since 1983."
Nicholas Motten (1986) "War and Famine" **Maryknoll Magazine.**

"There are doubtless many, many more causes and contributing factors to world hunger, but these should be more than enough to deter us from simplistic shibboleths and to invite us to serious reflection on the interconnectedness of reality, life, values, economies, etc. There are no simple solutions to such complex reality, no 'quick fixes'".
Simon Smith (1985) "Complex Causes of Hunger" **Maryknoll Magazine.**

Famine in Somalia 1992

SOME OF THE KEY CAUSES

REFUGEES

Since 1974, Somalia received over 1 million refugees from Ethiopia (escaping war and famine there). This placed huge financial, political and physical burdens on a very poor country. The influx of refugees also helped to destabilise Somalia.

POVERTY

Somalians are amongst the world's very poorest people and the poverty of development in general in Somalia was a major contributor to the crisis.

AID

Because of superpower involvement in Somalia, aid had been sporadic and related primarily, not to the needs of poor Somalians, but to those of superpower interests. Aid for health, education and basic services such as water and sanitation was tiny. Aid for the development of infrastructure such as key roads, ports and for the military was huge.

ENVIRONMENTAL DAMAGE

Recurring drought and environmental damage such as deforestation have been important contributors to the trigger mechanisms for the crisis which affected Somalia.

HISTORY

Somalia experienced considerable outside interference by Ethiopia, Britain, Italy, France and most recently the United States and the former Soviet Union. This contributed much to poverty and conflict.

POLITICS

Superpower interference and clan rivalry destabilised Somalia and blocked the normal development of political life. Western and Soviet support for undemocratic leaders and regimes allowed systematic and widespread abuse of human rights and a lack of basic respect for human life.

WAR

Violence, conflict and war have been important factors in Somalia in the past and also today. Colonialism, clan rivalry, territorial aggression and the arms industry all contributed to the crisis. All of the world's major superpowers in the last two centuries used Somalia as a pawn in their global strategies.

Starving in Silence?

Another factor in the build up to famine and in the response to it is the often neglected issue of information, its accuracy, availability and impact. In a study published in 1990, the human rights organisation Article 19 noted that while there had been growing acceptance of the importance of economic and political processes in the build up to famine, there had not been as much recognition of the issue of information flow. The report argued *"...if timely information can be collected and if it is then made freely available to governments and donors, widespread damage and loss of life can be mitigated".*

The report examined three case studies, the Great Famine in China between 1959-61 *(...the truth was deliberately veiled and millions died as a result...")* and Ethiopia and Sudan in the 1980s *(...information on the impending famines was available, but it was in the political interests of the governments, as well as the international donor countries, to suppress and ignore warnings until the need to act became overwhelming, and too late to save the lives of many thousands...").*

The report goes on to argue *"...Underdevelopment, which is the root cause of famine, is a political as well as an economic issue. It cannot be resolved in the absence of freedom of information and freedom of expression. This is not a momentous discovery...the peculiar significance of 'censorship' in famine is not a connection frequently made by development agencies. This is partly because censorship is all too often thought of as the banning of newspapers or of radio and TV programmes or the imprisonment of journalists and writers. It is, of course, all these things, but it is also a far more pervasive and insidious abuse involving the suppression of legitimate cries for help and of calls for the more equal distribution of wealth."*

On the basis of the case studies in the report, its authors conclude that the governments of China, Ethiopia and Sudan must accept responsibility for the suppression of vital information and for distorting much of the available information on regional famines which led directly to the death of thousands of their citizens prematurely.

Starvation amid Plenty

Famines are commonly thought of as Nature's revenge on hapless humanity. Although Nature can certainly create food shortages, human beings turn those shortages into widespread famines. People go hungry not because food is unavailable - but because they cannot afford it.

The Bengal Famine of 1943 shows why. Between two million and three million lives were lost, even though there was no overall shortage of food. In fact, the per capita supply of foodgrains in 1943 was 9% higher than in 1940.

The famine was partly a product of an economic boom. Sudden increases in war-related activities exerted powerful inflationary pressures on the economy and caused food prices to rise. In the urban areas, those with work could pay these prices. But in the rural areas, agricultural labourers and other workers found they could no longer afford to eat, and thousands headed for the cities, particularly Calcutta, in the hope of survival. Prices were then driven even higher by speculation and panic buying.

The famine could probably have been averted by timely government action. But the colonial government did nothing to stop hoarding by producers, traders and consumers. The general policy was 'wait and see'. Relief work was totally inadequate, and the distribution of foodgrains to the rural districts was inefficient. Even in October 1942, with 100,000 sick and destitute people on the streets of Calcutta, the government continued to deny the existence of a famine.

The result was one of the largest man-made catastrophies of our time.

Source: UNDP (1994) **Human Development Report**, Oxford University Press.

"Protein is distributed just as unevenly. An adult man on a typical Western diet rich in animal proteins, which are well balanced and easily assimilated, needs only around forty grams per day. But only two of thirty-four developed countries were getting less than eighty grams per day in the mid-seventies. The great beefsteak for breakfast carnivores were New Zealand (107 grams per day); the USA and Russia (105 grams); Icelanders (114 grams). In the developing world the typical diet of the poor is of staple cereals, in which protein is not so well balanced; under such a diet, sixty-two grams of protein would be needed for the average man. Twenty-seven out of 128 developing countries got an average of less than fifty grams. And since there was a deficit of calories everywhere, much of the protein would be burned up for energy."

Paul Harrison (1993) ***Inside the Third World****, Penguin*

"Yet even if these forget, I will never forget you"

(Isaiah 49:15)

Extracts from a pastoral letter of the Catholic Bishops of Ireland on Famine Remembrance Sunday, September 24th, 1995.

"We must remember our past, including its more painful chapters, so that we may move forward to a new future. This is why the commemoration of the Irish Famine, which begins this year and to which this Sunday is devoted, is of such significance... The pain of the past must not be forgotten but it must be redeemed...We play our part in redeeming the pain of the memory of the Irish Famine by opening our yes and making ourselves aware of the reality of famine in our world today. This is the best form of remembering - to see the past in the present and the present in the past. As we become more aware, we see clearly that famine in not exclusively a natural event. Rather it is due to a combination of factors such as crop failure or war and unjust social, political and economic structures. This was the case in the 1840s and it still holds true today...

...Nothing in our various acts of remembering should obscure or deny the devastation experienced by such a large proportion of the population of Ireland at that time...

...Advanced technology makes it possible to predict climatic changes, crop failures and, therefore, areas of likely food scarcity. Where famine happens, it does so largely as a result of human action - and inaction. Famine and its dreadful consequences are not natural...Remembering that poverty is the single greatest factor in vulnerability to hunger and hunger-related disease, we condemn political and economic systems which reduce so much of the world's population to an impoverished state. In the words of Pope John Paul: 'One must denounce the existence of economic, financial and social mechanisms which accentuate the situation of wealth for some and poverty for the rest' (Sollicitudo Rei Socialis n.16)...We condemn also the pernicious influence of the arms industry which fuels the conflicts which ravage so many of the world's poorest regions...Equally to be condemned is the wholesale destruction of the environment which serves the short-term economic interest of a priviledged few while increasing the vulnerability to famine and hunger of a great many...

...We must reject as fundamentally unchristian any individualist approach to the problem of world hunger which attempts to suggest that it is not our business to provide for others. We must equally reject any attempt to downplay the political dimensions of the crisis...

...Action is needed today on a number of key issues. The burden of debt repayments...must be denounced unequivocally...In the aftermath of famine, we cannot confine ourselves to short-term relief but must also commit ourselves to the long-term rehabilitation of local communities which will be the best defence against a recurrence of disaster...At this time of remembrance of our own famine, Ireland has a great opportunity to be a prophetic voice on such matters. If we speak with courage on behalf of the hungry of today's world, then we will be truly remembering our own famine dead...

...Justice groups could re-awaken our ancient tradition of fasting which is so embedded in our language that weekdays are named after various fasts: Dé Céadaoin (the first fast), Deardaoin (the day between the two fasts), Dé hAoine (the fast). To fast in this way is to fly in the face of the individualistic consumerism which is so characteristic of our times...

The Lord 'raises the poor from the dust and lifts the needy from the ash heap to make them sit with princes' (Ps.113:7). The Lord God does not forget those who end up on the "ash heap" of life. It is we who forget and we who need to remember..."

Poverty and Hunger

"Sharifa laughs, exposing her red stained gums. 'Without betel nut I wouldn't survive. Whenever I feel hunger, I chew it and it helps the pain in my stomach. I can go on for days without eating - it's only worrying about my children that makes me thin.' She looks at her daughter asleep on the bed. 'Do you know what it's like when your children are hungry? They cry because you can't feed them...

If I'd been a different woman, I would have left my husband and children and fled to a different place. But I stay here with him - it's my fate and I accept it.'

She brushes a strand of hair from her forehead. 'Why do you sit there listening to our troubles?' she asks. 'You should hear happier stories. When people in this country are happy and their bellies are full, they won't listen to stories of sorrow. They say, 'Why are you telling me this? I don't want to hear.'

Abu nods, and adds, 'Allah says a rich man should care for a poor man. He should ask him if he has eaten. But in this country a rich man won't even look at a poor man.'

Source: B.Hartmann and J.Boyce (1983) **A Quiet Violence: Views from a Bangladesh Village,** London, Zed.

Mina and Hasna: Gender and Hunger

Mina

"In 1984, Mina, a Hindu widow aged about forty, lived with her son aged twelve and her three daughters aged ten, seven and two. All except the son were severely malnourished. Mina herself weighed only 25 kilogrammes and suffered from a chronic 'gastric ulcer' for which she was unable to afford treatment or relief. There were two income earners for three dependants. Mina worked twenty one hours a week as a domestic servant and water carrier, and her son thirty five hours a week as a piece-rate bread seller. Household income in cash and kind was around 400 taka per month which placed it in the poorest 10% of households in the slum. Mina owned no productive assets and minimal household assets...

...Mina's husband contracted TB and two years later died. Mina then became totally dependent on the patronage of her employer/landlord. He arranged for her husband's funeral, and for the marriage of an elder daughter just before her husband's death, and occasionally donated food to the family when the children were hungry. Mina's relationship with her patron was deferential. Without his charity she might not have survived at all, but she realised that he paid her less than 50% of the going rate for domestic servants...

...In December 1986, Mina reported that support from her patron had diminished. She still worked for him for the same wages as two years earlier. Her son had managed to secure an apprenticeship with a Hindu workshop owner through the charity of another neighbour. The three meals a day he received as payment in kind ensured that his nutritional condition remained adequate for his height. The three unmarried daughters, however, were forced to beg together in the market-place. Their nutritional condition remained critical and all three had contracted TB. Significantly, Mina had refused an offer of free medical treatment for them, saying that their fate was in the hands of the gods. Neighbours, however, felt that Mina's own ill-health and severe malnutrition, together with the economic pressure of maintaining and marrying the daughters, were important factors contributing to her decision."

Hasna

"In 1984, Hasna was thirty-two and lived with her husband, aged about fifty, their four daughters aged fifteen, twelve, seven and twenty-one months and their niece aged seventeen. Hasna and the youngest daughter were severely malnourished. The household was under great economic strain. Abdullah who worked as a fisherman was chronically ill with various complaints and could not work regularly. The twelve year old daughter worked as a servant in the main market. Income in cash and in kind was around 600 taka per month (among the poorest 25% of households in the slum)...

...at the age of twenty-seven or twenty-eight Abdullah married Hasna who was about ten years old. Two daughters were born. In 1968 Abdullah became partially paralysed and they went to Khulna in hope of treatment. They lived in a squatter settlement and survived for the first year by Hasna begging in the market with her young sister who subsequently died...

...Since then the family have been struggling to survive...In 1984, Hasna went into the black market in Indian saris which despite its risks was becoming increasingly common among women in the slum...Hasna started as a small trader by borrowing 1,000 taka from three women in the slum at an interest rate of 10% per month. She went to the Indian border three to four times weekly and bought three to four saris at a time...the economic situation (of the family) had clearly improved but Hasna understood the risks of illegal marketing. Four of her women friends had been imprisoned; Hasna herself had been severely beaten...New legislation ...made it not only illegal to smuggle saris over the border but also to sell them within Bangladesh... All the family were malnourished and Hasna was pregnant for the ninth time, clearly not by her husband, and she did not want to talk about it. Her women friends told us that the tighter border controls had resulted in greater sexual harassment. Whether Hasna had been forced into sexual favours to protect her income, had been raped, or had entered prostitution (increasingly linked to the sari trade) was not clear."

Source: Naila Kabeer (1990) "Poverty, Purdah and Women's Survival Strategies in Rural Bangladesh" in H.Bernstein, B.Crow, M.MacKintosh and C.Martin (eds.) **The Food Question: Profits Versus People?**, London, Earthscan.

Reporting Famine

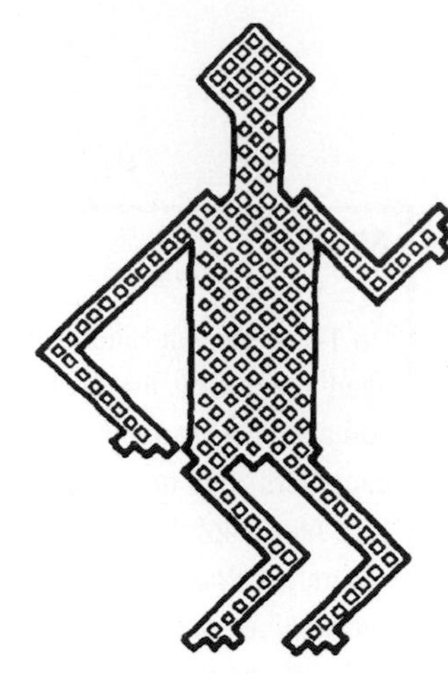

"As we drove south it began to look as though Fintan (Fintan Farrelly, Field Director with the Irish Agency, Concern) had exaggerated. The countryside around us was still green, and there were no obvious signs of drought or famine. All seemed well. There was poverty, as there is in most African rural areas, but no sign of starvation and death. Until we met Claire Chamberlain, the Dublin nurse who watched children die every day in her feeding centre. What she showed us took our complacency away...

...The first impression was of the tremendous smell of humanity, like the warm smell of a cowshed, yet somehow different. The sounds were the coughs, cries, whines and moans of humans in various states of distress, disease, malnutrition and death. The sight was a wretched mass of destitution, human frames that barely contained lives, and had no fight left in them. There in the windowless gloom the inhabitants of the shelter looked like they were being forced by starvation to pose for some awesome painting of the degradation of man..."

Paul Harrison in Paul Harrison and Robin Palmer (1986) ***News Out of Africa: Biafra to Band Aid,*** *London, Hilary Shipman.*

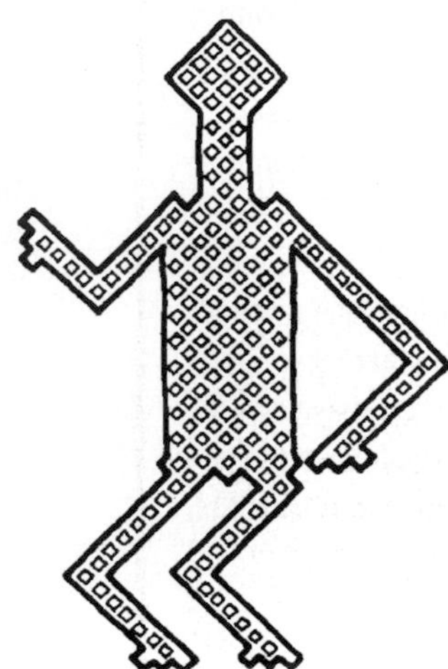

"We drove through the 'town' of Makelle, and there was this sort of bank which went down, slightly wooded, little bit of a church, and there were something like 50,000 people there. It was quite extraordinary. The curious thing - it came out in the first film that we did - is the biblical business. People looked like those depicted in the colour illustrations in my old school Bible. Sort of sackcloth colour and a certain nobility of features. I think it's a factor that the Ethiopians' distress did engage people's sympathy precisely because they're such a fine looking people...

...Then we went down to this place where they had these huge sheds and went in and everybody was just dying in front of us. There was a sepulchral feeling about the whole place...There they were, packed into sheds. A few people crying. People dying...

...The curious thing was that I'd been in the job for quite a long time and one tends to have quite a detached and professional attitude about it. I sometimes think to myself, particularly in South Africa, 'bloody hell, this is a good story, somebody's been burned to death!' You feel this dreadful divergence between 'gosh, this is a really good story' and 'Christ, this is absolutely tragic'. But I didn't feel that about Ethiopia at all. In fact I got quite overwhelmed, and so did Mohammed Amin, whose experience of this sort of thing was much greater than mine."

Michael Buerk quoted in Paul Harrison and Robin Palmer (1986) ***News Out of Africa: Biafra to Band Aid,*** *London, Hilary Shipman.*

"Dawn, and as the sun breaks through the piercing chill of night on the plain outside Korem, it lights up a biblical famine, now, in the 20th century. This place, say workers here, is the closest thing to hell on earth. Thousands of wasted people are coming here for help. Many find only death. They flood in every day from villages hundreds of miles away, felled by hunger, driven beyond the point of desperation. Death is all around. A child or an adult dies every 20 minutes. Korem, an insignificant town, has become a place of grief."

Michael Buerk, ***BBC News,*** *October 24th 1984.*

▼ References

Bread for the World Institute (1994) **Fifth Annual Report on the State of World Hunger**, Silver Spring.

K. Cahill (ed.) (1982) **Famine,** New York, Orbis.

Paul Harrison (1993) **Inside the Third World,** Penguin

B.Hartmann and J.Boyce (1983) **A Quiet Violence: Views from a Bangladesh Village**, London, Zed.

Paul Harrison and Robin Palmer (1986) **News Out of Africa: Biafra to Band Aid,** London, Hilary Shipman.

H.Bernstein, B.Crow, M.MacKintosh and C.Martin (eds.) **The Food Question: Profits Versus People?,** London, Earthscan.

Susan George (1976) **How the Other Half Dies,** London, Penguin.

Sinead Tynan (1995) **Famine: Causes, Prevention and Relief,** Dublin, Trocaire.

Johnathan Bell et al (1995) **Remembering our Past...Remembering our Future...?,** Dublin, Ulster Folk and Transport Museum, National Famine Museum, Trocaire.

Article 19 (1990) **Starving in Silence: A Report on Famine and Censorship,** London.

John Warnock (1987) **The Politics of Hunger,** London, Methuen.

LINKING HUMAN RIGHTS AND DEVELOPMENT: THE RIGHT WAY TO GO

Peadar Cremin

Case Study:

Who killed Iqbal Masih?

No one shall be held in slavery or servitude; slavery and the slave trade shall be prohibited in all their forms.

The United Nations Universal Declaration of Human Rights, Article 4.

Iqbal Masih lived in the village of Muridke in Pakistan. His family was extremely poor and lived in a two-roomed hut. When Iqbal was four years old, his family was given a loan of 800 rupees (about £16.00) in return for putting Iqbal to work in the village carpet factory. 500,000 children aged between 4 and 14 work in carpet factories in Pakistan. They are considered good workers. They work for fourteen hours a day. Their small hands are good for tying the knots of expensive hand-knotted carpets.

These child workers receive no formal education. They are not allowed to speak during working time in case they make mistakes in the patterns. They have one thirty minute lunch break per day and often are forced to work overtime without extra pay. Complaints result in beatings, having their fingers plunged into boiling water or other punishments.

Iqbal was extremely unhappy at the carpet factory but his parents could not afford to have him set free. One day, in 1992, Iqbal heard the founder of the Bonded Labour Liberation Front (BLLF) speak about their work in freeing bonded labourers and about new laws which forbade child labour. Iqbal asked how he could be set free. He knew that the factory owner claimed that his parents now owed 16,000 rupees. He was afraid that his entire life would be spent repaying the debt. He wanted to have a childhood like other children.

When Iqbal returned to the factory, he told the owner of his rights under the law and stated that he would no longer work as a slave. The carpet-master was furious and punished him severely, but still the child refused to work. Iqbal said "I am not afraid of the carpet-master. He should be afraid of me". The factory owner demanded his worker or his money. The family could not convince Iqbal to work and so the factory owner threatened them. The family had to flee from their village. Iqbal was taken by the BLLF to a school which they had in Lahore. He was ten years of age and he worked very hard, quickly learning to read and write. He hoped that one day he could become a lawyer helping to free child labourers.

In 1993, when he was eleven, Iqbal began to work with the BLLF. He sneaked into factories to see where the child labourers were kept. He began to make speeches at the factory gates telling the workers of their rights. As a result 3000 child labourers broke away from their masters and thousands of adults began to demand improved working conditions. In 1993 and 1994, people in the West learned about Iqbal's work. They began to ask questions about carpet production in Pakistan. Carpet exports fell for the first time in three decades. The manufacturers and exporters blamed Iqbal Masih for the problems in their industry. In 1994, Iqbal was given a number of human rights awards and invitations to visit a number of Western countries. Doctors in Sweden found that he was the size of a child half his age. He suffered from tuberculosis, and various vascular and pulmonary problems. His spine was curved, his fingers bent by arthritis. Malnutrition and abuse had left him physically maimed.

On his return from his triumphant visit to the West, Iqbal found that the BLLF was in trouble. Threats of violence had been made against the BLLF's workers and teachers. The government was involved in investigating BLLF's staff. The carpet factory owners were planning to challenge the work of the organisation.

In April 1995, Iqbal went on a visit to Muridke to see some members of his family. As he travelled with a cousin through fields near the village, a shot rang out and Iqbal Masih fell dead. A poor labourer called Muhammad Ashraf at first confessed to the killing but later withdrew his confession. International pressure has failed to get any satisfactory answer as to why Iqbal Masih, aged 13, died.

Introduction

The hope of establishing freedom, justice and peace throughout the world is entirely dependant on the extension to every human being of a range of human rights. It is also dependant on the action of individuals in claiming their own rights and in supporting the rights of others to whom they may, at a particular time, be denied. The notion that there are fundamental human rights to which every human being has an entitlement is a relatively recent one. Winning these rights has involved the efforts of many individuals and groups down through the centuries. In the struggle to establish the rights which are now considered "fundamental" many individuals have made the supreme sacrifice of their own lives. Others have been vilified in their own societies as they sought to extend these rights to less fortunate individuals or minority groups.

Even today, there is a global need to continue this struggle and to bring support and solidarity to the many groups and individuals who suffer from a denial of many of these basic rights. It is similarly important to ensure that all individuals in every society are literate in regard to their own rights and those of others. Finally, it is important that in a society where the cult of individualism is powerful, stress be placed on the obligations which arise from living in a human community and on the idea that there is an obligation on every individual and most especially on those in positions of power to show care and concern for those who are weak and vulnerable. The idea that the broader community is prepared to protect those who cannot always protect themselves is a key idea in any notion of human rights.

Debating Rights

The following short list identifies some of those rights which are matters of debate in society today. The list is not presented as an exhaustive list and may easily be extended.

- *The right to life (right of the unborn)*
- *The right to life (abolition of the death penalty)*
- *The right to sustenance*
- *The right to health and health services*
- *The rights of the child*
- *The right to education*
- *The right to work*
- *The rights of women (to vote, to equal treatment in the workplace etc.)*
- *The rights of all people to equal treatment under the law*
- *The rights of ethnic minorities (travellers or gypsies, minority language groups etc.) to cultural identity and equal treatment in society*

Rights and Responsibilities

This idea leads to the notion of obligations which arise from one's commitment to the fundamental human rights. These obligations may be said to include:

- the obligation to support those whose human rights are under threat;
- the obligation to respect the views of minorities;
- the obligation to contribute to improving the situation of those who are disadvantaged.

Developing Rights

The work of identifying and establishing human rights is an ongoing work. While various international agreements have identified a range of rights which the ratifying states have agreed upon, there is the problem of ensuring that these rights are actually applied. This requires the work of various international bodies, such as the **International Court of Justice** or the **European Court of Human Rights**, or of voluntary organisations, such as **Amnesty International**. At the same time, citizens of various states are involved in identifying how their internal laws and arrangements need to be changed so as to bring about a society in which there is greater justice and equity for all citizens. Securing equality in social, cultural and economic rights may involve painful decisions and may represent a significant challenge to the status quo. In theory, such rights as the right to education, to work or to health and health services, may seem perfectly acceptable as ideals. When, however, the delivery of these ideals becomes a threat to those powerful sectors of society whose well-being and wealth, at least in part, derives from the fact that they have cornered the market in these areas, it quickly becomes apparent that there can be large gaps between the rhetoric and the fulfilment of human rights.

New understandings of the human condition lead to new ideas about fundamental human rights. For example, the threat of pollution and destruction of the planet, has formented a great debate on such issues as the right to a clean environment, both now and in the future. The idea that this generation should not profit from pillaging the planet to such an extent as might threaten our life support system in the future has led to the notion of "intergenerational equity". This has also led to an increasing recognition of the extent to which human rights may be interlinked with the rights of other species to a sustainable future. Long-term considerations of care and concern for the quality of all life on the planet are leading to new debate about protecting the global future as well as to a dawning recognition of the rights of the earth's future citizens. A more short term and practical example of how this principle may be applied can be found in such items as international action to protect fish stocks. In the mid-1990s, the European Union cut the permitted fishing quotas on various stocks of fish in response to the advice of scientists and in spite of the protests of the fishing community who, in the short term, would suffer losses from such a policy.

The Rights of Nations?

One of the most cherished rights of nations is that to liberty and self-determination. Yet throughout the world, certain peoples have for centuries struggled for their right to express the distinct identity of their nations. The post-colonial period in Africa, the liberation of Eastern Europe and of some former Soviet states in Asia, the deep ethnic tensions of the Balkans all point to the heritage of mistrust and suspicion which is the result of the denial of such rights over long periods.

In many parts of the world, there is evidence of deliberate campaigns to wipe out subjugated peoples and to abolish traces of their separate identities. The plight of the Kurdish people, the East Timorese, the Tibetans, just as much as that of indigenous peoples in North or South America, in Australia or elsewhere all evoke a sympathetic response in those whose historical experiences have given them a taste of the power struggles that seem to be a constant element in the human condition. The adage that "the end justifies the means" has sometimes been used as an element in justifying

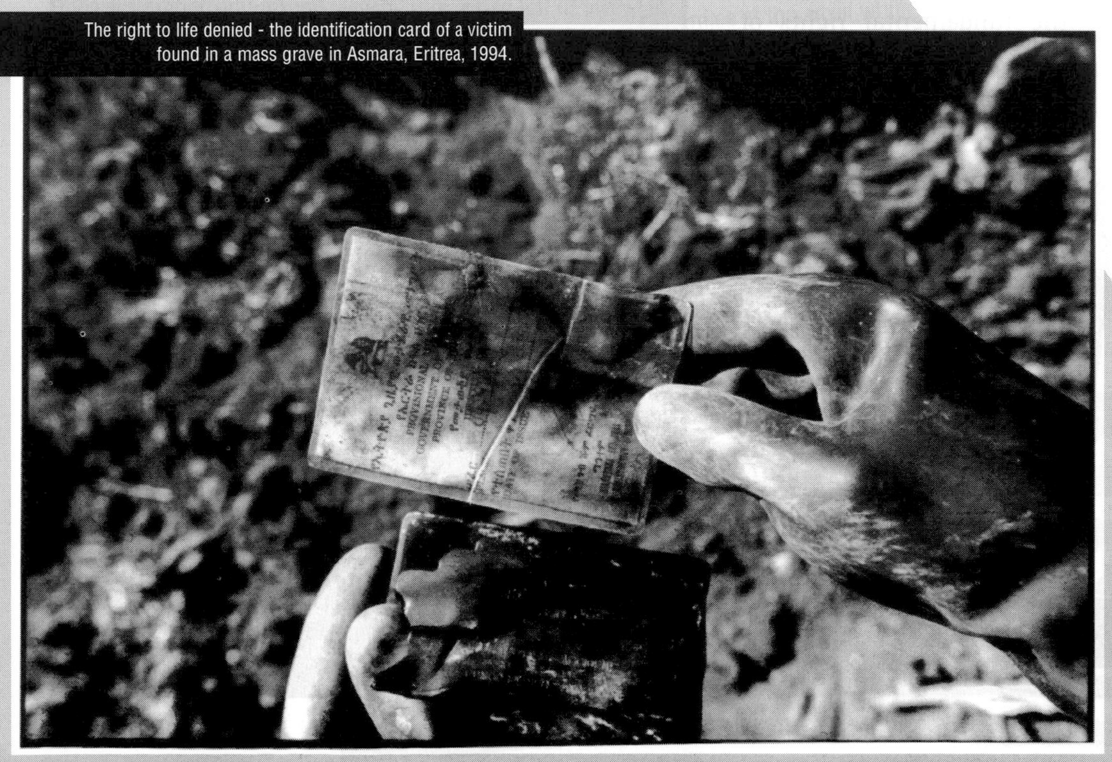

The right to life denied - the identification card of a victim found in a mass grave in Asmara, Eritrea, 1994.

A Short History of Capital Punishment

The Code of Hammurabi (1750 B.C.) is the oldest record of the sanctioned use of the death penalty.

The Bible prescribed death as the appropriate punishment for a range of crimes including murder and some sexual crimes.

By 1800, English law listed over 200 capital crimes and as a result more than 1000 people annually were sentenced to death, although Royal pardons might be extended to those so sentenced.

From the end of the eighteenth century, the Society of Friends (Quakers) have led campaigns to abolish the death penalty in the English-speaking world.

The first countries to entirely abolish the death penalty were Costa Rica (1877), San Marino (1865) and Venezuela (1853). Other countries such as Portugal had abolished the death sentence for ordinary crimes as long ago as 1867 but did not commit themselves to total abolition of the death penalty until 1976.

Michigan, in 1847, became the first US state to entirely abolish the death penalty.

Following a ten-year moratorium, the state of Utah became the first American state to reapply the death penalty when convicted murderer, Gary Gilmore, was executed by firing squad in 1977. Also in 1977, the states of Oklahoma and Texas became the first jurisdictions in the world to adopt the administration of lethal injections as a form of execution.

In 1981, the World Medical Association declared "that it is unethical for physicians to participate in capital punishment, although this does not preclude physicians certifying death".

The Case of Rickey Ray Rector

"Rickey Ray Rector died by lethal injection at Cummins Unit at 10:09p.m. Friday, in an execution that took medical staff more than 50 minutes to find veins in his arms.' (Arkansas Democrat-Gazette, Sat. 25-Jan 1992)

Rickey Ray Rector was convicted in 1982 of the murder in November 1981 of Bob Martin, a white police officer who was investigating Rector's involvement in another homicide. After shooting Bob Martin, Rector who was black, attempted to take his own life by shooting himself in the head. The bullet wound, and subsequent surgery to remove a bullet from his head resulted in a frontal lobotomy (the loss of a three-inch section of his brain), leaving him mentally impaired. He suffered memory loss and medical examinations revealed him to be severely limited in his mental capacity He was found to be unable to recognise or communicate facts and thus unable to assist his attorneys in his defence. According to one doctor who testified for the defence, *"he was like a child with the mind of a six year old - no emotions, no awareness, nothing".*

Rector's execution, by lethal injection, took place in the middle of the US Presidential campaign. The note telling him of the execution was signed by Bill Clinton, who as the then governor of Arkansas had the final decision on whether he would live or die. On the 24th of January, Governor Clinton took time off from his election campaign in New Hampshire to return for the execution.

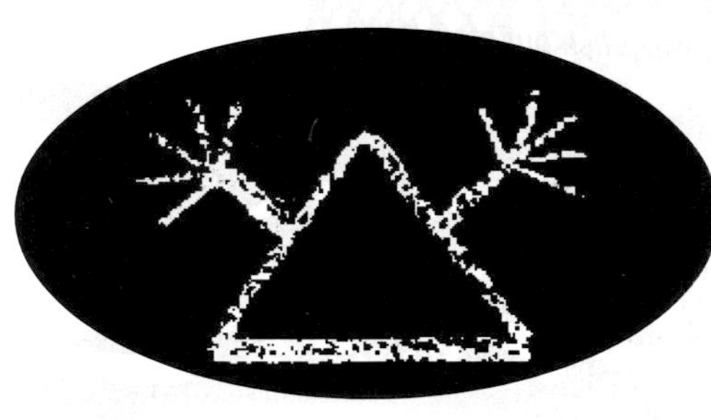

The execution itself was carried out in an extremely disturbing manner. Witnesses to the execution reported hearing moans or outbursts coming from the execution chamber as technicians searched for almost an hour to find suitable veins in which to inject the chemicals. Rickey Ray Rector was apparently aware of the problem and helped the execution team in their task. In a newspaper article, on Jan 26th 1992, the, administrator of medical and dental services for the Arkansas Department of Correction said. *"We weren't just sticking him every minute. We were looking for a new vein. We kept thinking the next one would be it. We thought we had it, but we didn't, that's unusual, but it happens. He had spindly veins that collapsed easily. We searched. We were lucky to find a vein at all.'*

Arguments for Capital Punishment	Arguments against Capital Punishment
The fact that the death sentence is a more severe sentence than any other means that it is a better deterrent than any other.	States which have reintroduced the death penalty do not show any significant change in the murder rate.
Well developed legal systems, the requirements of high standards of proof and the availability of the right to appeal all ensure that the risk of executing an innocent person is minimal.	Miscarriages of justice have led to innocent people being incarcerated for years, even decades. Had such persons been subjected to the death sentence, there would be no way for society to undo such wrongs.
The death sentence is essential for the protection of the State and so should be applied to traitors, terrorists and those who kill officers of the State including police and soldiers.	States which use the death sentence tend to have marginally more murders than States where the death sentence does not apply.
Capital punishment is a "final solution". Where it has been replaced by "life imprisonment", those punished have often been released in their lifetime and may kill again. In the UK, 75 murders have been committed by persons paroled from a life sentence since 1965.	Adjacent States, where the death sentence has been abolished in one but not in the other have remarkably similar rates of capital crimes.
Abolition of capital punishment leads to an increasing number of murders. For example, in the year when the UK abolished capital punishment (1965), there were 296 murders but in 1994, there were 638.	The present view among those who study crime is that the death sentence is not a greater deterrent to crime than a life sentence. Many of those who commit crimes punishable by death are under the influence of drugs or alcohol, are mentally unstable or under great emotional stress at the time of the crime and do not think of the legal consequences.
The Bible justifies capital punishment when it says that "He who sheds man's blood, shall have his blood shed by man" (Genesis 9.6) and again "Anyone who strikes a man and so causes his death, must die... but should a man dare to kill his fellow by treacherous intent, you must take him even from my altar to be put to death" (Exodus 21.12-17).	The Bible forbids all killing in the commandment that "You shall not kill" (Exodus 20.13)

Resources used in this section include: **"When the State Kills ...... The death penalty v. human rights"** published by Amnesty International in 1989 which gives a comprehensive account of the application of the death penalty in the preceding decade, including a valuable country-by-country profile of the use of the death penalty in various states; **Encarta '95; New Internationalist,** June 1993; **Irish Times,** January 27th, 1996.

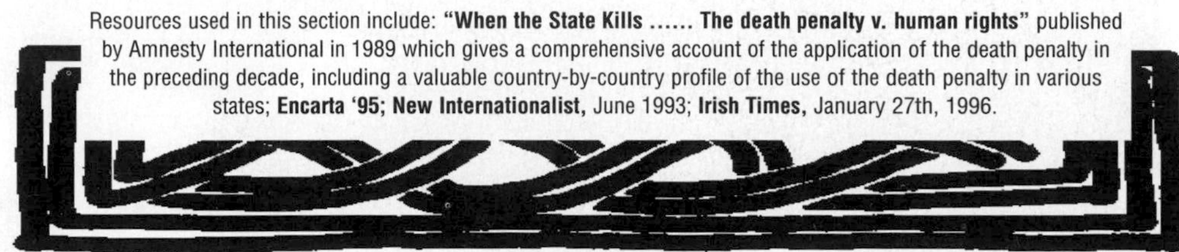

Human Rights: A Reality?

During the past three decades, there have been consistent improvements in the delivery of the basic human rights to food, education and health, but there remains an immense gulf between the haves and the have-nots (see Chapter Two). The data presented in these pages goes some way towards indicating that so many rights, agreed in principle, continue to be denied in fact. Some issues, such as the individual's right to life or the state's right to use its money for armaments rather than on housing, health or education remain matters of controversy across and within societies.

Safely Home?

Everyone has the right to life, liberty and security of person.

The United Nations Universal Declaration of Human Rights, Article 3.

The United Nations High Commission for refugees defines as refugees those who have fled their countries for fear of political, religious or ethnic persecution or of war. They have been called the "human barometer of political stability, of justice and order". The number of refugees has risen almost every year since the mid-1970s, with some 19 million asylum seekers in the world now. By the end of 1991, 5,000,000 children were in refugee camps as a result of war while a further 12,000,000 had lost their homes. While homelessness is an immense problem throughout the Third World, it also effects richer states. Germany has between 25,000 and 30,000 people living on the streets. In the winter of 1992/'93, 29 cases of people freezing to death on park benches, in bus shelters or on streets were recorded.

Born Equal?

All human beings are born free and equal in dignity and rights.

The United Nations Universal Declaration of Human Rights, Article 1.

While the world looks back in horror at the extermination of Jews and gypsies in Nazi Germany, racial discrimination remains a fact of life. In 1992, when there was a growth in the number of right-wing organisations, 80 Jewish cemeteries were desecrated in Germany. In an 18 month period to November 1993, 24 people lost their lives in anti-Semitic and xenophobic attacks in Germany. Between 6 April and 15 July 1994, up to one million Tutsis and moderate Hutus were killed in massacres in Rwanda. Following the Rwandan massacres of 1994, more than 2,000,000 Hutus fled to neighbouring states.

A Right to Work?

Everyone has the right to work, to free choice of employment, to just and favourable conditions of work and to protection against unemployment.

The United Nations Universal Declaration of Human Rights, Article 23.

Globally, the UN estimates that 120 million people want and need work which they cannot find and that a further 700 million are under-employed (many working long hours but still not earning enough for their own needs and those of their dependants. By January 1993, the number of unemployed people

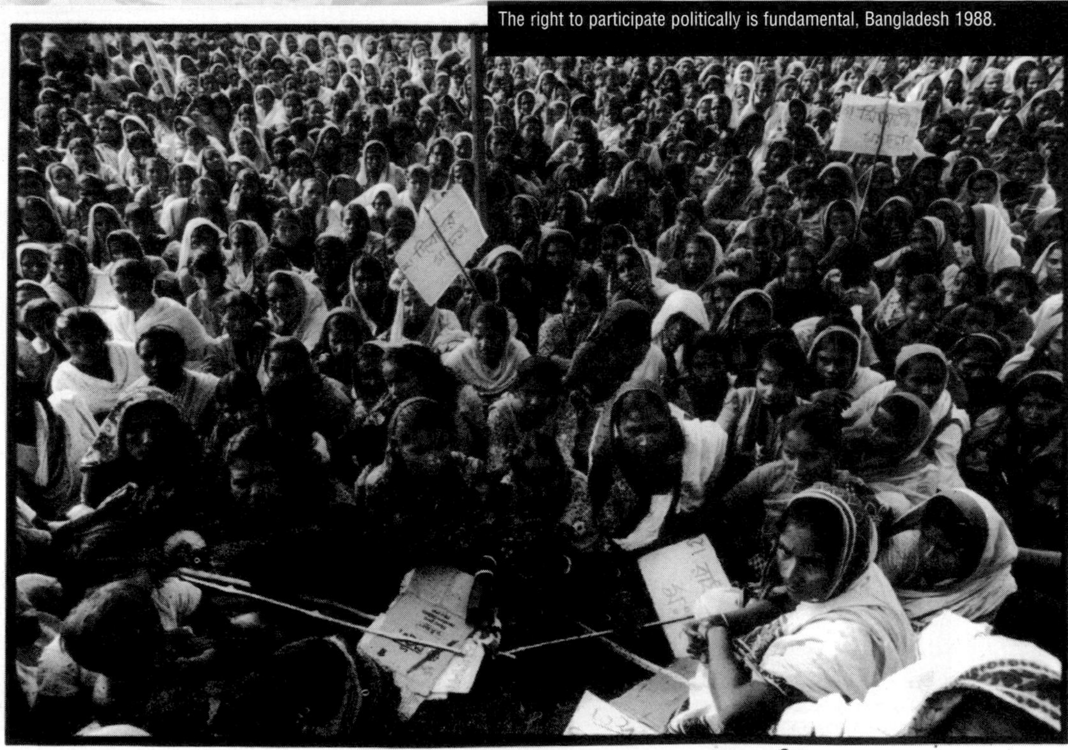

The right to participate politically is fundamental, Bangladesh 1988.

on the live register in Ireland stood at 302,200 the highest level in the history of the state, up to that time. Unemployment in the EU was also steadily rising with 10.4% of the Community's workforce out of work in August 1993 and an expected 17,000,000 unemployed by the end of 1993. In August 1993, Ireland's unemployment rate (18.2%) was the second highest in the EU (Spain having a rate of 21.2%). Unemployment for the under-25 age-group was even higher at 26.5% in Ireland (as opposed to Spain's 36.2%).

Of Ireland's unemployed at the beginning of 1995, 135,000 were unemployed for more than one year, 92,000 for more than two years and 64,000 for more than three years, giving Ireland the worst long-term unemployment record in Europe. In Northern Ireland, there was an unemployment rate of 11.6% by July 1996, with some 88,000 people out of work. In Northern Ireland, 43% of Catholic men were out of work in 1991 as opposed to 26% of non-Catholic men.

In July 1995, the official unemployment rate for the United Kingdom was 9.4% (amounting to 2,314 million) - the rate in Wales was 9.3%, in Scotland 9.2%, in Northern Ireland 12.9% and 9.3% in England. In January 1995, the unemployment rate for men as a percentage of the male labour force was 12.9% while that for women was 4.9%.

A Right to Life?

Every child has the inherent right to life, and the State has an obligation to ensure the child's survival and development.

The Convention on the Rights of the Child, Article 6

The International Planned Parenthood Federation says that between 36,000,000 and 53,000,000 abortions are performed around the world each year. This gives a rate of between 32 and 46 per 1,000 women which is equivalent to each woman having one abortion in her lifetime. The American Constitution was amended in 1973 to permit abortion. Abortion was legalised in France on 17 January 1975. France only permits abortion up to the twelfth week, but yet France has between 160,000 and 180,000 abortions annually, the majority being conducted on single women aged between 20 and 30. Some 5,000 French women go to Britain or the Netherlands annually for abortions, having gone beyond the 12-week limit. The Netherlands has 5 abortions per 1,000 women as opposed to a Western European average of 14 per 1,000. In Latin America, where abortions are almost completely illegal, the rate is estimated to be between 30 and 60 per 1,000 women. In Kenya, complications resulting from illegal abortions lead to more than 50% of all gynaecological admissions and more than 25% of all hospital admissions.

Although Irish people have consistently rejected legalising abortion, during 1991, 4,154 women who gave Irish addresses had abortions in Britain. Counsellors in Ireland and Britain suggest that the true total is more likely to be between 6,000 and 8,000. The official figure for 1992 was 4,254. This figure increased to 4,399 in 1993.

"The titanic effort that has brought liberation to South Africa and ensured the total liberation of Africa constitutes an act of redemption for the black people of the world. It is a gift of emancipation to those who, because they were white, imposed on themselves the heavy burden of assuming the mantle of rulers of all humanity. It says to all who will listen that, by ending the apartheid barbarity that was the off spring of European colonisation, Africa has, once more, contributed to the advance of human civilisation and expanded the frontiers of liberty everywhere....

...Rwanda stands as a stern and severe rebuke to all of us for having failed to address these matters. As a result a terrible slaughter of the innocent is taking place in front of our very eyes. Thus do we give reason to the peoples of the world to say of Africa that she will never know stability and peace, that she will forever experience poverty and dehumanisation and that we shall be forever knocking on somebody's door pleading for a slice of bread. We know that we have it in ourselves, as Africans, to change all this. We must assert our will to do so. We must say that there is no obstacle big enough to stop us from bringing about an African renaissance."

Nelson Mandela speaking to the Organisation of African Unity, June 1994 quoted in **Africa (1994)**, London, Granta.

SILENT CLASSROOMS

Mention Tuol Sleng to anyone and few will even know what you're talking about. Mention Auswhitz or the Warsaw Ghetto and you'll probably register some flicker of recognition. Extermination is the all embracing word we use to describe what happened at these camps, genocide is the other term we end up using when we realise the extent of what happened there. It's in the history books, school children study it as part of their history course. Mention Tuol Sleng and they'll be none the wiser. Personally, I had never of it, but on the 22nd of April this year (1993), I actually visited Tuol Sleng.

Tuol Sleng is now the Genocidal Museum in Phnom Penh, the capital of Cambodia. Before the 17th of April 1975, Tuol Sleng was a normal high school in a residential area. On that day, however, Khmer Rouge forces triumphantly occupied Phnom Penh and declared the People's Republic of Democratic Kampuchea. Cambodia was no more. Life for the people of Cambodia would never be the same again. Tuol Sleng was to become an interrogation and detention centre for the next four years.

...It is unclear why Tuol Sleng was chosen. In my city I have seen schools turned into military installations without explanation or apology. Ours is not to question the wisdom of the military. To do so in Democratic Kampuchea was to risk inevitable if not instant death...The Khmer Rouge are accused of the death of at least 1.5 million of their fellow countryfolk. They died by murder, famine and exhaustion...

However, Tuol Sleng fulfilled a specialist function, essentially political and systematically organised. Tuol Sleng's ordinariness is disarming. There are no turrets nor sentry boxes nor railway sidings, just an ordinary school with ominous barbed wire fences of the compound variety and that's the only clue. The strands of barbed wire and the configuration of the fence are not the usual school perimeter...There isn't the least sign of so much as a search light. Tuol Sleng is very ordinary in appearance except for what you initially discern and sense in your understanding of these things...Tuol Sleng is ordinary, no big deal.

...Tuol Sleng is an ordinary derelict school like the one I used to teach in - closed up - an empty capsule of memories for the times that are gone and the people that made them...The commentary by the guide triggered off a landslide of other memories for me, "interrogation", "prisoners", "confessions" ...To have been a prisoner alone in interrogation, photographed and frightened, dehumanised by an alien process is an experience which is not lost on me but to stand in a torture chamber in South East Asia in "Pol Pot time" is to travel a million miles into the worst nightmare imaginable...to travel the repetoire of vocabulary from brutality to inhumanity and barbarity...To linger in the rooms where our brothers and sisters were tortured to the point of death to satisfy pure political fanaticism ...To inspect the crude implements of torture...to observe the blood stains of the last victims...

It is unbelievable and it's easy to become detached from the reality that this is not a film set or a museum exhibit and yet, nonetheless a classroom like the one I used to teach in, but so totally and absolutely different...I left the room and passed on to the next and the next and ...my God, my God why did you forsake these people?

...In another block are the thousands of photographs of victims and the chair which they sat in for the photograph. Men, women, children and babies. Tuol Sleng is by no means ordinary. What happened in Tuol Sleng must have been awful but what happened in Tuol Sleng was literally what happened in Cambodia...In the same block are photographs of the Khmer Rouge leadership of the 1970s: Pol Pot, Khieu Samphan, Ta Mok...all of them are still alive and well and met recently in Chong Baranae near the Thai border (29/4/93) plotting their return to power...

Our schools are empty now for the summer. Their emptiness shares in common with the emptiness of Tuol Sleng. Tuol Sleng is silent now the nightmare is over. Luckily its walls can't talk. They don't need to.

Excerpts from an article written by Frank McGuinness of Belfast after visiting Tuol Sleng. Before becoming a member of staff with the Irish development agency Trócaire, he was a school teacher.

A Happy Childhood?

Everyone has the right to life, liberty and security of person.

The United Nations Universal Declaration of Human Rights, Article 3.

Child killing is most remarkable as a phenomenon in Brazil. Between 1988 and 1991, 5,644 Brazilian children in the age range 5 to 17 suffered violent deaths. In 1991, 674 street children and adolescents were killed in São Paulo alone. A further 390 were killed in the first six months of 1992. Similar killings are conducted in other areas of Brazil. The death squads often include off-duty police and security guards in their membership. Few of these have ever been accused, much less convicted for their crimes. In 1994, the Brazilian newspaper **Hot List** carried an advertisement advising people to *"Kill a Child Criminal"*.

Freedom from Hunger?

Everyone has the right to a standard of living adequate for health and well-being for himself and of his family, including food, clothing, housing and medical care and necessary social services ......

The United Nations Universal Declaration of Human Rights, Article 25 (1).

The World Bank estimates that in the year 2000, a billion people world-wide will suffer from hunger. The UN estimates that about 1.3 billion of the world's people live in absolute poverty. Those earning less than $370 per annum per capita are classed as poor while those earning less than $275 are classed as chronically poor. More than 35% (140 million) of Africa's population suffer from hunger on a daily basis. Between 30 and 40 million Africans [mostly in Ethiopia (2 ml.), Somalia (3.5 ml.), Sudan (8 ml.), Zimbabwe (4.5 ml.), and Mozambique (3 ml.)] are in danger of starving to death. About 10 million children per annum die of hunger and poverty related illnesses. This is equivalent to about 70 Jumbo jets of children crashing per day! In Africa alone, about 10,000 children die every day from malnutrition and lack of health care.

A Right to an Equal or Fair Share of Resources?

Every child has the right to a standard of living adequate to his or her physical, mental, spiritual, moral and social development....

The Convention on the Rights of the Child, Article 27

The Third World's external debt rose in 1990 to 1,350,000,000,000 US dollars, of which Africa owes 270,000,000,000 US dollars. In 1993, the indebtedness of the world's developing countries reached 1.77 trillion US dollars. Between 1982 and 1990, there was a net transfer of $418 billion in debt repayments alone from the South to the North. At the end of this period, the countries of the South were 61% more indebted to the North than they had been at the beginning. Debt servicing takes more than four times as much from the budgets of developing countries than health care and almost twice as much as education. In a world which spends £28 billion annually on golf and £200 billion on smoking, a mere £3 billion would provide access to primary education for all those children who currently do not receive it.

The Right to Peace and Real Security?

Only 5% of the casualties of the First World War were civilians. In the Second World War, 50% of deaths were of civilians. By the end of the century, this figure has risen to 80% civilian deaths, most being women and children. During the 1980s, more than 1,500,000 children were killed in wars. More than 4,000,000 children were physically disabled - limbs amputated, brains damaged, eyesight or hearing lost - through bombing, land mines, firearms or torture. In the period from January to August 1991, in the wake of the Second Gulf War, infant mortality (under five's) jumped from 28 out of every thousand to 104. This meant that over one out of every ten Iraqi children under the age of five died in the war or its aftermath. Wars in Angola, Bosnia and Rwanda have similarly affected children. In the ten years to 1995, more innocent children than armed soldiers were killed or disabled by wars. During the decade, according to UNICEF statistics, some two million children have died in wars, five million have been disabled and twelve million have been made homeless.

The amount spent on arms annually is over a trillion dollars (over one million million). Three quarters of global arms flow went to developing countries during the 1970s and 1980s. Developing countries which can ill afford this cost, spend an estimated 200 billion dollars on their armed forces, with most of their arms being supplied by the USA. In 1990, the USA had 18.5 billion dollars of arms sales. The United States is now the world's principal arms supplier, being responsible for about 60% of sales to the Third World in 1992. In the aftermath of the Second Gulf War, there has been intense arms selling in the Middle East with sales clocking up to between £18 and £24 billion by mid-1992.

One of the great threats to people's rights and futures rests in the size of the world's nuclear arsenal. It has been estimated that the world's nuclear arsenal peaked in 1986 when there were 69,480 nuclear warheads. The START-II Treaty, signed by the USA and Russia in January 1993, set a ceiling of 3,500 nuclear warheads on both of these countries by 2003 at the latest. In 1993, the number of nuclear warheads world-wide declined from 52,875 to 49,910. France's resumption of nuclear testing in the Pacific in September of 1995 led to unprecedented world-wide protests.

The Political and Legal Instruments for Promoting Human Rights

Historical Instruments

1215 Magna Carta: Attempt to control the King and his taxes; prisoners had the right to be judged by their equals.

1679 Habeus Corpus Act: Allowed Court to test legality of detention; curtailed arbitrary detention.

1689 English Bill of Rights: Right to trial by jury, to liberty, property and the pursuit of happiness but not for women.

1789 American Bill of Rights: Rights to life, liberty, property and the pursuit of happiness except for women, Indians and Negroes.

1776 American Declaration of Independence: End of English rule; asserted democracy, the precedence of human rights over the rights of property and the power of a written constitution.

1833 Laws abolishing Slavery in the British Empire.

Instruments Related to Labour

1958 International Labour Organisation (ILO) Convention (No.111) Concerning Discrimination in Respect of Employment and Occupation (1960)

1964 ILO Convention (No.122) Concerning Employment Policy

1964 ILO Convention (No.141) Concerning Organisations of Rural Workers and their Role in Economic and Social Development (1977)

1981 ILO Convention (No.156) Concerning Equal Opportunities and Equal Treatment for Men and Women Workers: Workers with Family Responsibilities (1983)

These lists of instruments are derived from the work of Sinead Tynan in Maura Ward PBVM (1995) **Yes, You Do Count**, Dublin, Irish Commission for Justice and Peace and the Irish Council of Churches.

United Nations Instruments

1944 Founding of the United Nations: First attempt to draw up a universal code of fundamental rights

1948 Universal Declaration of Human Rights: Basic international statement on basic human rights but without legal effect

1948 Convention on the Prevention and Punishment of the Crime of Genocide

1952 Convention on the Political Rights of Women

1960 UNESCO Convention Against Discrimination in Education

1962 Convention on Consent to Marriage, Minimum Age for Marriage and Registration of Marriages (1964)

1951 Convention Related to the Status of Refugees

1956 Supplementary Convention on the Abolition of Slavery, the Slave Trade and Institutions and Practices of Slavery

1966 International Convention on the Elimination of All Forms of Racial Discrimination

1976 International Bill of Rights: made up of **The International Covenant on Economic, Social and Cultural Rights** (1976); **The International Covenant on Civil and Political Rights** (1976) and **First Optional Protocol to the Convention Dealing with Civil and Political Rights** which give legal effect to human rights

Additional UN Instruments

1971 UN Declaration on the Rights of Mentally Retarded Persons

1973 International Convention on the Suppression and Punishment of the Crime of Apartheid

1975 UN Declaration on the Rights of Disabled Persons

1980 Convention on the Elimination of All Forms of Discrimination Against Women

1981 Convention on the Protection of Individuals with Regard to the Processing of Personal Data (1985)

1984 UN Convention Against Torture and other Cruel, Inhuman or Degrading Treatment or Punishment (1987)

1989 Revised Convention (No.169) Concerning Indigenous and Tribal People in Independent Countries

1989 Second Optional Protocol to the Convention dealing with Civil and Political Rights (1991)

1989 Convention on the Rights of the Child

1991 UN Draft Declaration on the Rights of Minorities

European Instruments

1949 Establishment of the Council of Europe

1950 The European Convention for the Protection of Human Rights and Fundamental Freedoms (1953)

1961 European Social Charter

1983 Protocol No.6 to the European Convention concerning the abolition of the death penalty

1987 The European Convention for the Prevention of Torture and Degrading Treatment of Prisoners

Organisation of American States

1948 Charter of the Organisation of American States (1951)

1967 Protocol of Buenos Aires created Inter American Commission on Human Rights

1969 American Convention on Human Rights

1985 Inter American Convention to Prevent and Punish Torture (1987)

1988 Additional Protocol to the American Convention on Human Rights in the Area of Economic, Social and Cultural Rights (1990)

Organisation of African Unity

1963 Establishment of the Organisation of African Unity

1981 African Charter on Human and People's Rights or the Banjul Charter

Notes

Many of the instruments listed have two dates: the first denotes the year in which it was adopted; the second, in brackets, denotes the year in which it entered into force after receiving the number of ratifications specified.

▼ References

Amnesty International (1989) **When the State Kills ...... The death penalty v. human rights,** London.

Francine Best (1992) **Human Rights Education: Summary essay on the work of the Council of Europe,** Strasbourg, Council for Cultural Co-operation.

M. Bridle et al. (1989) **40 Years On - Ideas and Resources for learning about human rights,** Dublin, Trócaire and Birmingham Development Education Centre.

Human Rights Watch (1993) **Human Rights Watch World Report 1994: Events of 1993,** New York, Human Rights.

Swedish NGO Child Convention Group (1989) **My Rights:** Part 1 (5-8 years); Part 2 (9-12 years); Part 3 (13-18 years), Goteborg, BARNkonventionsgruppen.

Charles Humana (1992-3rd ed.) **World Human Rights Guide,** Oxford University Press.

Hugh Starkey (1991) **The Challenges of Human Rights Education,** London, Cassell.

PROGRESS DESPITE EVERYTHING: Population and Health

Colm Regan

"It cannot be said too often that flesh and blood is the last resort of the poor who, in their poverty, create the only resource they have - the hope of a new generation."

Jeremy Seabrook, ***The World: A Third World Guide,*** *1995.*

Eva's Story

Reporter Susanna Rance outlines Eva's story from Bolivia:

"The sky is a piercing blue, the air is fresh and clean. Tacahira is a farming community at an altitude of 12,000 feet on the Bolivian altiplano. Low mud-brick 'adobe' houses are scattered over the plain. A flat treeless expanse of farmland stretches towards the purplish-brown Andean ranges on the horizon.

'I practically gave birth on my own, squatting on the bed in our room' says Martha Sanchez. 'Only my husband Bonifacio was with me. When my little girl was born she cried right away, my husband cut the cord and bathed her and wrapped her up.'

The Sanchez family lives in one of four adjoining rooms around a mud yard. Bonifacio's two brothers each has one of the other rooms and the fourth serves as a kitchen. The house has no running water, electricity or sanitation. A low wall around the yard opens out directly onto their farmland and you can see the cows and the pecking chickens.

'When my daughters grow up I want them to study and live in the city', says Martha. 'Here the young people don't care about studying, they just think about the animals.'

Eva's early years will be spent largely in the family's room and the adjoining yard. She will sleep with her mother until she has been weaned from the breast at around 15 months. For her first year she will be carried constantly on her mother's back, swaddled so tightly that she will not be able to move arms or legs. Later she will be bound more loosely and will be able to peer out and play with her mother's braided hair. When Martha goes off to sell milk, Eva will go too, jogging against her mother's back as she visits each of her regular customers.

'When we got married,' says Bonifacio, 'we thought we'd have just three or four children. I've seen families have lots of kids and they suffer because the parents don't earn enough to support them, for their education, to buy them clothes, their school materials.

They can't be bothered to study. Their minds aren't equipped for it because they are malnourished. If a child isn't well nourished it won't want to go to school and pay attention.'

Bonifacio works voluntarily at the local health centre. He has acquired some knowledge of the rhythm method of family planning. Martha is unclear how it works. They have attempted using this method since being married but have had three children in four years. Eva's arrival was unplanned and Martha says they did not 'take care' the month she was conceived.

Eva is fortunate living in a community where they are organising to improve standards of health. They have their own form of health insurance, whereby each family contributes 100 pounds of potatoes yearly to the local parish hospital and in turn has the right to preventative care and medical treatment.

Bolivia has a very low population density - six people per square kilometre. Government policy neither encourages nor prohibits family planning. Only 24% of adults use any form of contraception - mostly natural methods such as rhythm, abstinence or breast-feeding. However the country has one of the lowest standards of living in Latin America and a high infant mortality rate. So the challenge to provide health and other services to a population which will increase by 50% by the year 2000 is a considerable one.

'Really, we wanted the baby to be a boy', says Martha. 'My husband was sad, he wanted a son to keep him company. But I don't want to have any more children. We've got no money and life is so expensive."

Eva's story captures many of the realities of population issues within the Third World as viewed from the perspective of poor women. There are few issues which generate as much debate and disagreement as that of population growth and its impact on development, gender and the environment. On one side are the arguments which emphasise the implications of unchecked population growth on the future well-being of the planet and the need for controls on population expansion especially in the Third World. Against this are those arguments which see Western concerns about population growth amongst the world's poor as a thinly disguised argument in favour of maintaining Western over-consumption by placing the blame for the depletion of world resources on the poor who in reality consume least. In between are a host of additional viewpoints which highlight the gender, religious, cultural and environmental dimensions of the debate.

On the opposite page, we include some of the viewpoints and arguments around this issue. They need to be reviewed within the overall context of the various conflicting theories of population growth and its relationship to development.

Theories of Population Growth

- *Demographic Transformation Theory* - this approach emphasises four stages of population growth. Stage 1 is an agrarian society with high birth and death rates thus creating a stable or slow population growth rate. In stage 2, while the birth rate remains high, the death rate reduces due to better sanitation, medical treatment and greater productivity (usually associated with industrialisation). This leads to rapid population growth. A great many countries remained in stage 1 until the

Children, "...the hope of a new generation", Ethiopia, 1992

Arguing over Population

"Human population has exploded five-fold in the past century and a half. For the past hundred years this explosion did not impose irreversible pressures on the biosphere. Over the past fifty, however, the inexorable growth of human population and increasingly numerous industrial off-shoots have come to threaten the health of the planet."

British Medical Journal **The Lancet,** 1990.

"It is depressing to monitor the increasingly obscure and technical discussions about population (and how the 'explosion' is to be 'controlled'), when the only known pathway to limiting the birth-rate is clear and simple; not by ever more ingenious forms of contraception, not by 'educating' the poor so that they will produce fewer children, not even by rhetoric about 'giving' women control over their own fertility; but by the provision of an assured and adequate social security to all people. The existence of a level of subsistence and health care below which no human being will be allowed to fall is the surest way of confounding the apocalyptic forecasts of population disaster."

Jeremy Seabrook, **The World: A Third World Guide,** 1995.

"The number of hungry people in the world has increased dramatically during the eighties. Reversing the spread of hunger will depend on a massive effort to cut the world rate of population growth and restore the health of the planet. We can no longer separate our health from that of our home. If the health of the planet continues to deteriorate, so will that of its inhabitants."

Lester Brown, **State of the World,** 1990.

"While...recognition of the links between women's autonomy over their lives and fertility control is to be lauded, multilateral agencies and national governments continue to treat women in an instrumental manner with respect to population programmes. For example, there is little understanding among policy makers of the mixed responses to family planning programmes by Third World women themselves. While there can be little doubt of the unmet need for birth control among women, the methods actually available are all highly unsatisfactory. Many international pharmaceutical companies treat Third World women as guinea pigs for new methods...control over reproduction is a basic need and a basic right for all women....Women know that child bearing is a social, not purely a personal, phenomenon; nor do we deny that world population trends are likely to exert considerable pressure on resources and institutions by the end of this century. But our bodies have become a pawn in the struggles among states, religions, male heads of households, and private corporations..."

Gita Sen and Caren Grown, **Development Crises and Alternative Visions,** 1987.

"Present rates of population growth cannot continue. They already compromise many governments' abilities to provide education, care, and food security for people, much less their abilities to raise living standards...Yet the population issue is not solely about numbers...People are the ultimate resource. Improvements in education, health, and nutrition allow them to better use the resources they command, to stretch them further. In addition, threats to the sustainable use of resources come as much from inequalities in people's access to resources and from the ways in which they use them as from the sheer numbers of people. Thus concern over the 'population problem' also calls forth concern for human progress and human equality."

World Commission on Environment and Development, 1987.

"Who is right? It's not easy to see clearly. Population has become a battleground on which everybody wields their favourite sword. For free-market conservatives free markets are the answer. Social justice is the solution for egalitarian socialists. More gentle technology and stronger pollution controls for the critics of modern technology. And there are other armies on the field. Third World nationalists still see concern with population problems as a smokescreen for Western fears of increasing Southern strength...Minority groups cry genocide when there is talk of 'population control'...Religious groups have weighed into the melee...sexual politics enter the fray...Unlikely allies fight side by side against family planning: socialists and conservatives, fundamentalist Moslems and Catholics, male chauvinists and feminists horrified by stories of compulsion in China or Bangladesh...The battlefield has been stamped into a morass..."

Paul Harrison, **The Third Revolution,** 1992.

"The population problem is serious, certainly, but neither because of 'the proportion between the natural increase of population and food' nor because of some impending apocalypse. There are reasons for worry about the long-term effects of population growth on the environment; and there are strong reasons for concern about the adverse effects of high birth rates on the quality of life, especially of women. With greater opportunities for education (especially female education), reduction of mortality rates (especially of children), improvement of economic security (especially in old age), and greater participation of women in employment and in political action, fast reductions in birth rates can be expected to result through the decisions of those whose lives depend on them."

Amartya Sen, **New York Review,** September, 1994.

end of World War Two and some African countries have only reached stage 2 in recent decades. Stage 3 is characterised by continued urbanisation and industrialisation. The birth rate begins to drop, smaller families become the norm and the population growth rate declines considerably. Stage 4 finds the population growth rate stable or increasing very slowly. Most of the countries of the industrialised world are now in stage 4 while countries such as Argentina and Chile are in stage 2. Debates abound as to where the countries of the Third World are located in the model. Some critics argue that the model is based upon European experiences and values and is of little use in other cultural areas. Some argue that the model proves that population will follow this trend throughout the world while yet others argue that the resources of the earth cannot sustain the population growth rates anticipated by the model in coming decades as world population moves towards stage 4 overall.

- *Malthusian Theory* - this view was first put by an Englishman, Thomas Malthus, in 1798. It is based upon two basic premises (1) that human numbers increase geometrically while (2) our capacity to produce food and fiber expands only arithmetically. Thus there is an inevitable and inherent tension in population growth unless war, disease and famine intervene to check and limit growth. The predictions of Thomas Malthus about a population crisis appeared to have been overstated in the context of the huge productive increases associated with the Industrial Revolution in Europe which produced enough to feed all. However, in recent decades, Neo-Malthusians have been arguing that the inevitable crisis was simply postponed and that disaster may yet strike.

- *Marxist Theory* - directly challenges that of Malthus in that Marx viewed increasing population as an incentive to greater prosperity if resources and productivity are adequately developed and distributed. Alongside others such as Ester Boserup, this view argues that increased population will fuel demand and thus lead to change in both attitudes and productivity.

- *Radical Feminist Theory* - in recent years a strong critique of many of the dominant models of demography has been developed by many feminist writers. Starting from the view that much traditional theory ignored the views, needs and realities of women and was designed to protect and bolster traditional patriarchy, these writers have emphasised the rights of women to have control over their own bodies and, in particular, over reproduction.

The basic facts and figures of modern global demography are outlined below and despite the huge variations in population structures and growth rates internationally, population growth rates are now slowing down in every continent including Africa but yet population numbers will continue to grow considerably for the next 50 years at least, as is illustrated in the diagrams opposite.

"Fears of Being Engulfed..."

"...It is easy to understand the fears of relatively well-off people at the thought of being surrounded by a fast growing and increasingly impoverished Southern population...the thesis of growing impoverishment does not stand up to much scrutiny; but it is important to address the psychologically tense issue of racial balance in the world (even though racial composition as a consideration has only as much importance as we choose to give it). Here it is worth recollecting that the Third World is right now going through the same kind of demographic shift - a rapid expansion of population for a temporary but long stretch - that Europe and North America experienced during their industrial revolution. In 1650 the share of Asia and Africa in world population is estimated to have been 78.4%, and it stayed around there even in 1750. With the Industrial Revolution, the share of Asia and Africa diminished because of the rapid rise of population in Europe and North America; for example, during the nineteenth century while the inhabitants of Asia and Africa grew by about 4% per decade or less, the population of 'the area of European settlement' grew by around 10% every decade.

Even now the combined share of Asia and Africa (71.2%) is considerably below what its share was in 1650 or 1750. If the United Nations prediction that this share will rise to 78.5% by 2050 comes true, then the Asians and the Africans would return to being proportionately almost exactly as numerous as they were before the European industrial revolution. There is, of course, nothing sacrosanct about the distributions of populations in the past; but the sense of 'the growing imbalance' in the world, based only on recent trends, ignores history and implicitly presumes that the expansion of Europeans earlier on was natural, whereas the same process happening now to other populations unnaturally disturbs the 'balance'."

Amartya Sen, ***New York Review,*** *September 1994.*

World Population - The Facts and Figures

- ***According to the United Nations, total world population reached 5,501 billion by mid-1993 and is projected to reach 6.3 billion by the year 2000 and 10 billion by 2025, if present trends continue. The world's six-billionth inhabitant will be born sometime during 1998.***

- ***About 79% of world population now lives in the Third World. This contrasts with about 70% in 1950, 75% in 1980 and a projected figure of 84% by 2025. In contrast, the corresponding figures for Europe, North America and the former Soviet Union are 30% in 1950 and an estimated 15% in 2025.***

- ***About 90% of population growth is now taking place in the Third World. The population growth rate is highest in Africa (3.1% over the past decade but now down to 2.6% per year) followed by Latin America (2.1% per year), Asia (1.9%), North America (0.7%) and Europe (0.3%).***

- ***The greatest absolute increases in numbers are taking place in Asia, where 517 million people have been added in the past decade (146 million in China and 166 million in India). If current trends continue, Asia's estimated population in 2025 will be over 400% bigger than it was in 1950.***

- ***The world's 15 largest countries account for over 70% of all population growth (China, India, Former USSR, United States, Indonesia, Brazil, Japan, Nigeria, Bangladesh, Pakistan, Mexico, Vietnam, Philippines, Germany and Italy).***

- ***Before 1650, it took nearly 35,000 years for world population to double; today, it takes just 43 years.***

- ***Population growth is due, significantly, to the fact that death rates in Africa, Latin America and Asia have fallen by as much as 50% within the last 30 to 40 years (largely as a result of improvements in medicine and sanitation), whereas birth rates have only more recently begun to decline.***

- ***Today, about 48% of world population is urbanised (it was about 30% in 1950) and urban populations are now increasing more rapidly than rural. It is estimated that about 60% of the population of the Third World will be urbanised by the year 2025. Such increases are occurring in circumstances of widespread poverty.***

- ***There is now a major global demographic faultline between, on the one hand, the poor, fast growing, youthful, poorly resourced and un-educated societies and the rich, technically advanced yet ageing and demographically declining societies.***

- ***Today, population growth rates are decreasing in all continents and it is estimated that world population will stabilise at a total figure of 11 billion by the year 2100.***

Sources:
Population Reference Bureau (1990) ***World Population Data Sheet,*** *Washington, DC.*
Lean, G. and D. Hinrichsen (1992) ***Atlas of The Environment,*** *Oxford, Helicon Publishing.*
World Bank (1995) ***World Development Report 1995,*** *Oxford University Press.*

FIGURE 9:1
Source: Population Reference Burea (1990) **World Ppopulation Data Sheet,** Washington D.C.

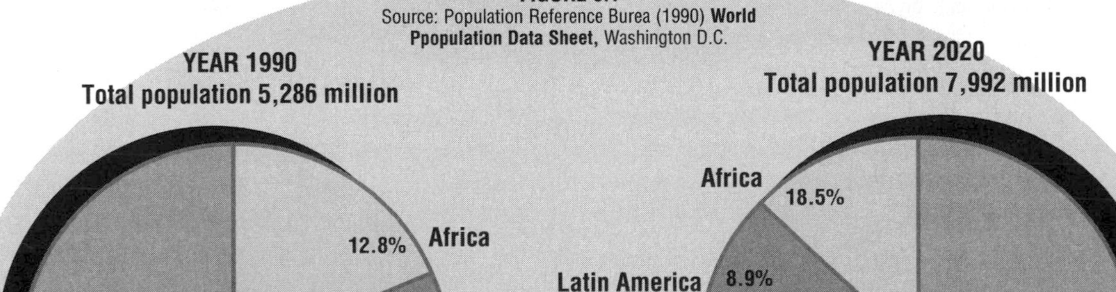
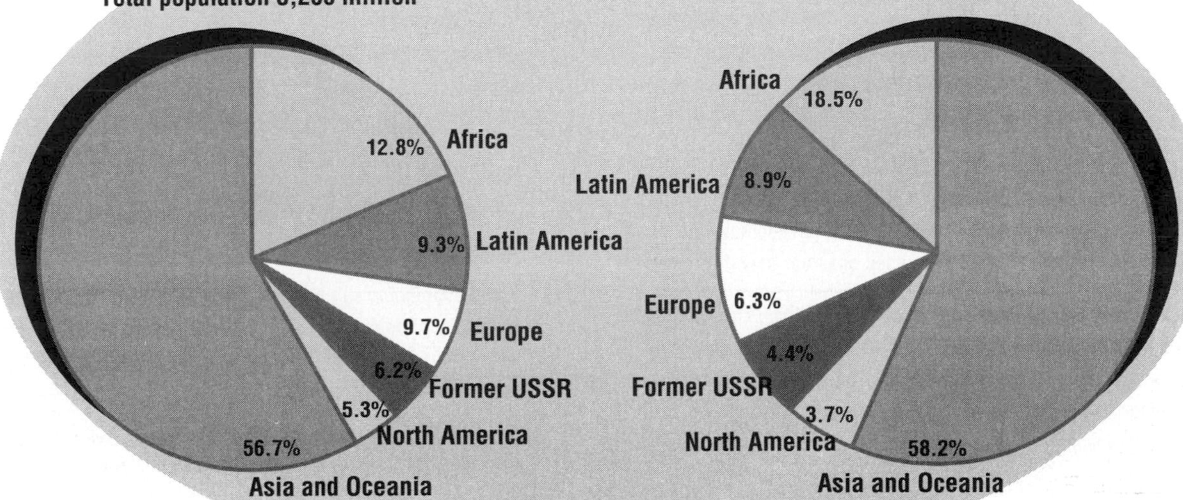

Why do Poor People have Large Families?

It is almost impossible today to have a discussion on any Third World topic without the issue of population and 'overpopulation' arising. This issue is amongst the most frequently cited 'reasons' as to why the poor of the Third World stay poor - there are just too many people for the available resources and population growth rates are just too high. Behind these ideas are others which are less frequently expressed - Third World people cannot control their sexuality, they do not understand fertility and how to control it and their educational levels prevent them from understanding. Such reasoning has often led to plans for involuntary 'control' of population growth - strategies which have not only led to serious abuses of human rights and to some of the worst expressions of Western imperialism but have also been ineffective because they ignore the reality of why poor people have large families.

One of the best discussions of this issue which is readily available is by Paul Harrison in ***Inside the Third World*** cited above - much of the following argument is extracted from his work.

Harrison refers to surveys carried out in the developed world in the 1960s and 70s on people's preferred family size - nowhere did the proportion of women wanting five or more children exceed 9%. In Third World countries, ideal family sizes ranged from a low of 3.8 in Thailand, between 4 and 5 in Chile, Indonesia, Korea and the Philippines, 5.7 in Nigeria to 7.5 in rural Ghana to 9.4 in one Kenyan survey. Highest ideal family sizes were consistently recorded in Sub-Saharan Africa. Harrison concludes that the reason birth rates have not declined in Africa, Southern Asia and the Middle East is that people there actually want large families and believe that it is in their interests to have them. *"These people are planning their families and they are planning large ones...".*

There are many logical and rational reasons behind their decision - reasons which, until very recently, also existed in many parts of Europe. These include:

ECONOMIC REASONS

Children are seen throughout the Third World as a source of labour, they can carry out simple domestic chores such as collecting water and fuelwood, they can mind younger children or animals; they can undertake agricultural work on the family land or for another farmer or work in the local town (income from such work could also help buy more land). It is estimated that the cost of feeding one son is only 1/4 that of feeding an outside agricultural worker. Sons, in particular, are valued because they are literally 'muscle power' and not just in work terms - they are important in conflicts over land and local politics.

SOCIO-POLITICAL REASONS

In many developing countries, the extended family is an important political and social unit, it is often through that structure that the needs and aspirations of its members are met. For example, in traditional African society, a man with many sons will receive extra farming land and the surplus he then creates will allow him to take other wives thus increasing his wealth further. This, it can be argued, is a 'logical growth strategy'. Large families are also positive in that they allow alliances through marriage to be forged with other families thus strengthening political and social power further.

SURVIVAL REASONS

So long as infant mortality rates remain high, poor people will continue to have large numbers of children to ensure they survive beyond youth. This is crucial for parents in their old age. One study in Gujarat state in India found that couples planned their families so that at least two sons survived to support the parents in old age. Class has a lot to do with this - one study across Asia discovered that while middle class families would not depend on their children for financial help in old age, between 62% and 90% of poor urban and rural families would do so.

CULTURAL REASONS

Despite changing attitudes, sons are still seen in many cultures as more important than daughters. In the Hindu religion, only a son can perform the funeral rights for the father's soul; in Asia, sons attract dowries and, everywhere, men earn more than women. Many women's groups throughout the Third World are now challenging many of these cultural practices but until they are replaced, they form part of the logic of large families.

Harrison concludes by commenting:
"Clearly these people who insist on producing children in vast numbers are not insane, nor are they fools. They are acting according to what they themselves see as their best interests in the competitive society they live in. But these individual interests are in conflict with the interests of the society as a whole."

Among the social costs of continued population growth in the broader society are land erosion, fragmentation of holdings, unemployment etc. but, as Harrison points out, the family itself does not bear the costs:

"It exports them, dumps them on the village or the national doorstep, or the future. The land fragmentation problem will hit your children - let them worry about it when you're dead. They can always head for the village. In the last resort the whole village can export its population problem."

The parallels with the way people in the industrialised world think about environmental problems is striking! So too are the parallels with how the poor have often been presented in our own history particularly in the context of the Great Famine (see, for example, the essays by Peter Gray and Christine Kinealy in Cathal Poirteir (ed.1995) ***The Great Irish Famine,*** Cork, Mercier Press/RTE).
Looking to the future in the context of the above arguments, another commentator, Michael Todaro, notes:

"All of the foregoing can be summarised as saying that the effect of social and economic progress in lowering fertility in developing countries will be the greatest when the majority of the population and especially the very poor share in its benefits"

Sources: Paul Harrison (1993) **Inside the Third World,** London, Penguin and M. Todaro (1994) **Economic Development,** London, Longman.

Health and Development

In 1977, the World Health Organisation set a goal of "Health for All" by the year 2000. This goal will not now be met despite the very significant and real progress which has been achieved. Despite effective and targeted health programmes involving international organisations, local governments and local communities, many groups remain vulnerable to basic diseases and death, new diseases are emerging and some old diseases are returning with a vengeance. For example, AIDS has become a major threat to the health of many communities while tuberculosis is, once again, on the increase and malaria is now killing as many as it did before. The disastrous economic conditions of the poorest countries and the impact of the debt crisis make effective responses to this situation all the more difficult.

Progress but...

Overall, life expectancy in the Third World has increased dramatically since 1950 to over 63 years in 1992 as against 50 in 1950. Infant mortality has dropped from an average of 280 to 106 per 1000 births in the same period. Life expectancy has improved because of the success in containing infectious diseases especially those which strike during pregnancy and early life. Significant progress in vaccination (against diphtheria, tetanus, whooping cough and measles) has been recorded even in Sub-Saharan Africa where 57% of the total population has now been covered. Progress has also been recorded in the provision of safe water and sanitation, mother and child health care and the provision of rural health services. as well as in the campaign to eliminate leprosy and malaria completely.

However, there are also growing concerns that this progress will not be sustained to agreed targets and may even be reversed and that those who have not benefited as much as others will simply fall further and further behind in the world health stakes. Concern is highest in relation to the poor of Sub-Saharan Africa and the widening gap between their welfare and that of others in Latin America and Asia. Specific groups of the poor throughout the Third World have also fallen through the health net - those in rural areas and in recently settled slum areas of expanding cities. Progress on non-infectious diseases such as cardiac and respiratory ailments has also been very slow and the drive on vaccinations has slowed significantly. Tuberculosis remains the world's biggest killer (4 million annually - more than AIDS, diarrhoea, leprosy, malaria and all other tropical diseases combined!). Dirty water is responsible for 4/5ths of all sickness and 1 of every 3 deaths in the world today.

Inequality in Spending

International spending on the provision of health also displays considerable inequality as well as highlighting the need for urgent action. World spending on health care (both public and private) amounted to a total of $1700 billion in 1990. Richer countries consumed 90% of this with an average per capita spending of $1500 with the United States alone accounting for 41% of the global budget. Third World countries spent a total of $170 billion or an average of $41 per person - less than 1/30th of that of industrialised countries. Other key inequalities in the map of global healthcare are illustrated in the table on the next page.

One of the issues which many commentators have drawn attention to in recent years has been the growing inequality in the provision of health-care in the industrialised world. There has been a significant return of traditional diseases of poverty - in France for example, infectious, parasitic and respiratory diseases caused more than 24,000 deaths in 1990, twice the number for 1980. The incidence of these diseases began to reduce at the beginning of the century due to reduced over-crowding and improved nutrition, social conditions, sanitation and health care. According to many epidemiologists, the resurgence of infectious diseases in the 1990s appears to be linked to growing poverty and deprivation in many North American and European cities. Over half the people who have TB are black and the risk of getting the disease is 35 times higher in predominantly black Harlem than in predominantly white neighbourhoods. The chances of a New York child contracting TB increased 300% between 1987 and 1991. While AIDS contributed significantly to this increase, poverty and social deprivation played a key role also.

Poverty not only increases the likelihood of disease, it also adversely affects the provision of health care. About 15% of the population of the United States has no medical insurance. In France, a 1993 research study showed that one person in five (21.7%) went without some form of basic health care, including medical consultations and X-rays, due to lack of money. Unqualified workers (27.9%) were twice as likely as top executives (15.3%) to restrict their use of health services and 32.8% of the unemployed went without care for financial reasons.

Excerpts from the World Health Organisation's World Health Report 1995

"Poverty is the world's deadliest disease. It wields its destructive influence at every stage of human life. While life expectancy is increasing in most developing countries, it is actually shrinking in some of the poorest... For many of us, improvements in the quality of lives are almost taken for granted. But at the same time, vast numbers of people of all ages are suffering and dying for want of safe water, adequate sanitation and basic health care. This in the last years of the twentieth century is totally unacceptable...

...Growing inequality is literally a matter of life and death for millions of people since the poor pay the price of social inequality with their health...Poverty reduction need not be a long-term process. Many developing countries have demonstrated that the worst forms of poverty can be rapidly reduced or eliminated in a relatively short time with determined, well designed and effectively implemented strategies..."

The World Health Organisation's target between now and the year 2000 include the global eradication of polio and guinea-worm disease; the elimination of leprosy as a public health problem; the elimination of neonatal tetanus and measles as well as nutrient deficiencies of vitamin A and iodine; a 50% reduction in maternal mortality rates and improved access to local basic health care for many millions of the world's poorest.

"The means exist; what are lacking are the commitment and resources to apply them so that these goals can be achieved."

HEALTH INDICATORS FOR SELECTED COUNTRIES

Country	Life Expectancy at birth (years) 1993	% Population with access to: Health Services 1985-93	Safe Water 1988-93	Sanitation 1988-93
Costa Rica	76.3	80	93	97
Chile	73.8	97	86	83
United Arab Emirates	73.8	99	95	77
Brazil	66.3	na	87	72
Cuba	75.3	98	98	92
Philippines	66.3	76	82	69
China	68.5	90	69	16
Cameroon	56.0	41	50	74
India	60.4	85	79	27
Nigeria	50.4	66	36	35
Cambodia	51.6	53	36	14
Angola	46.5	30	41	19
Ethiopia	47.5	46	25	19
Sierra Leone	39.0	38	37	58

Source: UNDP ***Human Development Report 1995****, Oxford University Press.*

Figure 9:2

Breast is Still the Best

In 1981, in response to continued campaigning on the issue, the World Health Assembly adopted the International Code of Marketing of Breastmilk Substitutes to protect mothers and babies from the aggressive and dubious marketing practices of the infant formula industry. The main points of the international voluntary code are:

- No advertising of breastmilk substitutes
- No free samples or supplies
- No promotion of products through healthcare facilities
- No contact between company marketing officials and mothers
- No gifts or personal supplies to health workers
- No idealisation of artificial feeding on product labels
- Only scientific and factual information to health workers
- All labels should outline the value of breastfeeding and the dangers of the misuse of artificial feeding
- No marketing of unsuitable baby products

This code was developed and promoted by the World Health Organisation and UNICEF but neither organisation has any legal powers to enforce it and the monitoring of its use has been very weak. A watered down version of the Code was also adopted by the European Union in 1991 and in 1992 the EU also adopted an Export Directive which sought to control the marketing practices of European companies abroad. All of these codes were introduced or adopted after intense lobbying and pressure by voluntary groups and organisations. Claims that the infant formula companies were breaking the code has led in recent years to calls for a boycott of their products. The companies claim that they are observing the code and that any breaches of it are immediately noted and acted upon. The organisation which monitors the actions of the companies - The International Baby Food Action Network (IBFAN) strongly disagrees and the debate continues today.

Breastfeeding is the most natural and effective means of feeding babies and has many obvious advantages over artificial feeding. The view of the vast bulk of health workers is that artificial feeding should only be necessary in a minority of cases. However, in recent times artificial feeding has grown significantly as a result of bad practice in anti-natal care, ignorance, changes in work habits and the actions of the infant formula industry. This is a particularly worrying trend especially in the context of poverty and poor health and sanitation conditions in many Third World countries. About one-third of the world's population has no access to safe water - a vital ingredient in the preparation and proper use of infant formula. In 23 countries world-wide, over 75% of women cannot read which contributes to widespread errors in the preparation of formula and the sterilisation of bottles etc. Poverty is also an issue as studies have shown that baby milk can consume as much as 50% of household income thus encouraging mothers to dilute it further.

A recent report from the Catholic Institute for International Relations noted:

> *"Breastfeeding declined rapidly in the 1960s. In Mexico in 1960 almost 100% of six-month old babies were breastfed, in 1966, it was only 40%; in Chile in 1960 over 90% of 13 month-old babies were breastfed, in 1968 only 5%; in Singapore in 1951 over 80% of 3 month-old babies were breastfed, by 1971 it was only 5%. By 1979 the infant formula market was valued at an estimated US$2,000 million world-wide, of which the developing country share had changed from one-third to one half during the decade."*

Due to the promotional efforts of health workers and a growing realisation of the benefits of breastfeeding, this situation is once again changing to the disadvantage of the baby milk industry. Many of those opposed to the marketing practices of the producing companies argue that the companies keep attempting to devalue breastfeeding and promote artificial feeding instead. Many companies are involved in the production and sale of infant formula including Cow and Gate, Wyeth, Milupa and Nestle. Such companies deny the claims that they regularly and routinely breach the Code of Conduct and have, in some cases hired marketing companies to challenge their critics.
But organisations such as IBFAN remain unconvinced and continue to campaign for the vigorous enforcement of the Code and against the practices of many of the companies.

> *"There is an inherent conflict between the aim of the Code and the goals of the baby milk industry. Companies promote their products in order to sell more, but when marketing channels are restricted, sales will fall. Companies should stop looking at the baby feeding market as a large money maker. Instead, they should make their products available for those who need to buy them, without setting aside a promotional budget for increasing sales."*

International Baby Food Action Network, 1994.

> *"Ill-conceived and unprofessional monitoring by activist groups acting as self-appointed prosecutor, judge, and jury, as reflected in "Breaking the Rules", will do nothing to resolve these problems (monitoring and reporting alleged violations) nor will they promote improved infant nutrition, which has always been the aim of the International Code of Marketing of Breast-milk Substitutes."*

Nestle, 1994.

Sources: Catholic Institute for International Relations (1993) **Baby Milk: Destruction of a World Resource**, London; IBFAN (1994) **Breaking the Rules** 1994, Cambridge; Nestle (1994) **Marketing of Infant Formula: Nestle Response to 'Breaking the Rules'**, Dublin.

AIDS and its Impact

AIDS (Acquired Immune Deficiency Syndrome) is the name given to the disease that results from long-term infection with HIV (Human Immunodeficiency Virus). HIV damages the body's natural protection system and therefore reduces the body's ability to protect itself. Death is not caused by HIV but by the infections which cannot be resisted. For those dealing with this disease the real problem is not AIDS but HIV which is now described as a pandemic (a disease prevalent all over the world). The HIV pandemic is important not only because of its immediate effect on those infected but also because of its broader and longer-term consequences for economic and social development.

In terms of numbers dying from the infection, HIV is not a major killer - it kills only 100,000 world-wide each year compared with 1 million from malaria, 3 million from TB and 12 million from heart disease. But HIV/AIDS is important for a number of reasons - medical science has so far proved ineffective against it; AIDS is showing an extraordinary ability for growth unlike any other disease; the long gap between infection and disease (up to 10 years) makes it hard to convince people and governments of its importance and AIDS attacks people in their 20s, 30s and 40s - the most productive sectors of society.

The World Health Organisation (WHO) estimates that world-wide over 1.7 million adults had developed or died from AIDS by mid-1992. It is estimated that over 12 million adults (over 6 million men and 5 million women) are infected with HIV. This is equal to 1 in every 250 of the world's adult population. Over 80% of all cases are in the Third World with infection rates in some countries of 1 in 10 adults. Contrary to ill-informed popular opinion, HIV is predominantly a heterosexual disease with 70-75% of infections occurring as a result of heterosexual intercourse, between 5 and 10% from homosexual intercourse, blood products accounting for 3-5%, sharing injection equipment 5-10% and mother to child transmissions 5-10%.

Figure 9:3

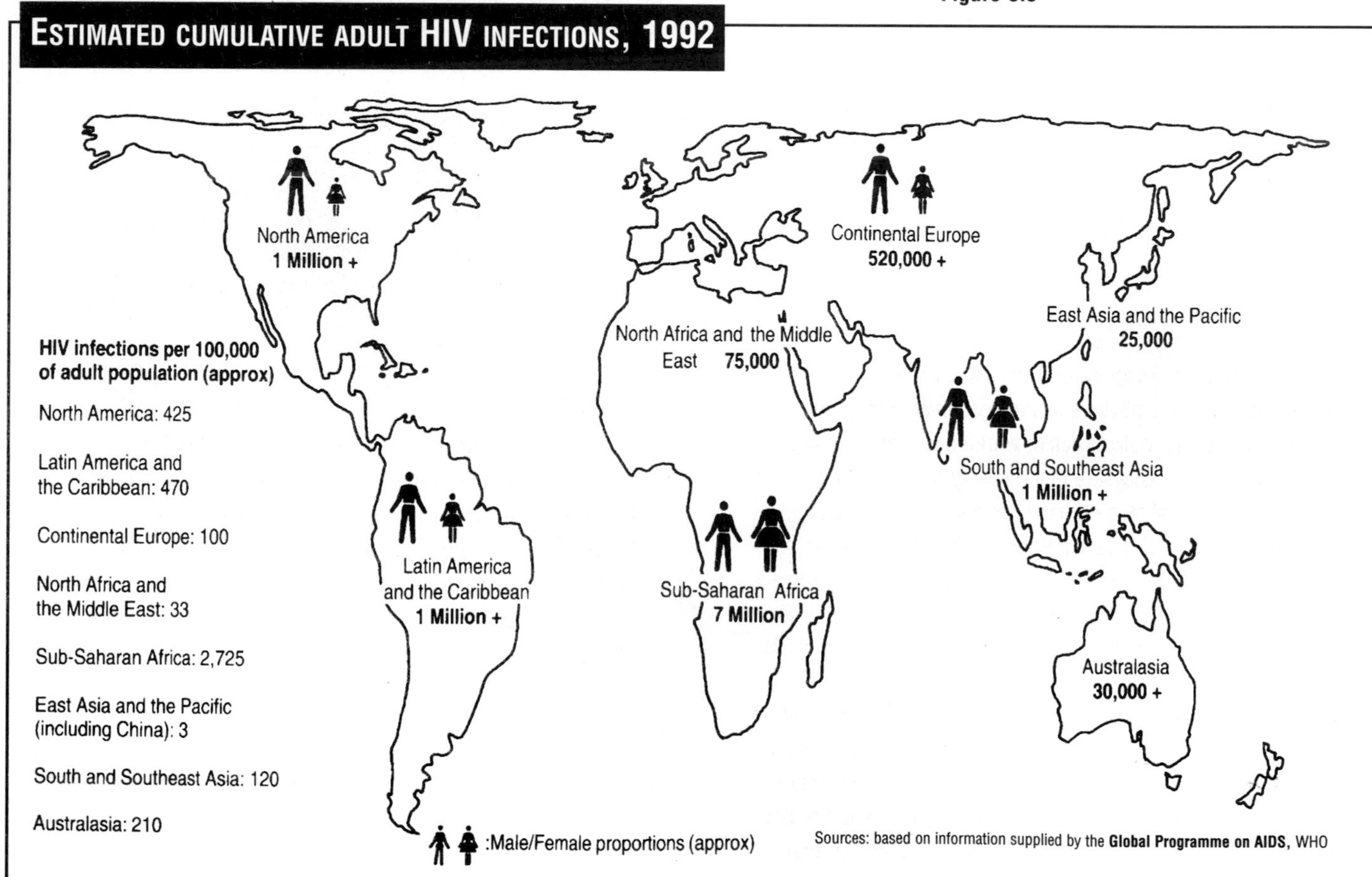

Impact in Different Areas

Apart from the direct impact and costs of HIV/AIDS, there are also a series of important indirect costs and impacts which affect development overall. Initially there is the obvious ***Demographic Impact*** in both the immediate context and in the future. It is estimated that as many as 40 million people could be affected by the virus by the year 2000 with about 10 million having AIDS or having died from it (90% in the Third World). In many Third World countries the number of young and old who depend for their survival on those in their 20s, 30s and 40s is very high. These are precisely the groups the virus attacks thus affecting the demographic structures of households and communities. It is also feared that AIDS will wipe out the progress made in recent decades in the area of child mortality - where there is a high incidence of HIV amongst women, child mortality rates have been found to be as much as 30% higher than normal. The WHO is unclear as to the long-term impact of HIV/AIDS on fertility rates but it is estimated that it will reduce the overall proportion of children in the population in many areas.

There are also serious ***Health Impacts.*** In 1990 the cost of AIDS treatment amounted to between $2.6 and $3.5 billion but only 2% of this was spent in Africa where 50% of all cases are located. The direct cost of AIDS arises from the need to provide medical care for those affected and its indirect costs arise from diverting resources from other diseases. These costs can be potentially huge in some of the world's poorest countries. For example, it is estimated that if Tanzania were to pay the direct health costs of treating those with HIV/AIDS it would consume over 40% of the country's total health budget.

The ***Social Costs*** are also enormous as HIV/AIDS moves beyond being an individual/family problem into a community issue. The disease attacks both birth-givers and breadwinners thus affecting the community at large. AIDS is actually known as the "family disease" in Africa. Apart from the cost of medicines, there is also the cost of social welfare for those affected; the family and community costs of special food for those affected; the loss of income to families when breadwinners become ill; the costs of funerals and of loss of labour to look after the sick; the impact on education as young people are taken out of school to work or look after those affected; and the cost of caring for orphans etc.

The *Economic Impact* is potentially massive as HIV/AIDS tends to initially attack society's most productive and capable age groups and those with higher levels of skills development and education. Many Third World countries are already short of adequate numbers of skilled people in key sectors and the disease makes this situation worse. The economic costs of the disease are felt throughout all sectors of the economy from agriculture to industry, from local industries to multinational companies. The disease also impacts on ***Food Security*** especially in rural areas when the family's most productive and able workers become infected. HIV/AIDS also contributes to growing inequality as some farmers expand and grow at the expense of those families affected. Many of the overall costs of the disease are summarised in the diagram on the following pages.

Another less publicised impact of AIDS is in the perception of the disease in the West and the ***prejudice*** and even ***racism*** which such (mis)perceptions generate. Despite all available evidence, many groups blame the emergence of AIDS on Africans or black people, or homosexuals or drug addicts or students or prostitutes etc. As the Panos Institute has recently commented *"The United States has blamed homosexual men and Haitians; Europeans and Indians have blamed Africans; Africans have blamed Europeans; Asians have blamed American seamen; others have blamed students, or foreigners or prostitutes, or ethnic minorities, or capitalists or unbelievers..."*

Policies for containing and tackling HIV/AIDS focus heavily on education in prevention as well as in encouraging changes in the sexual habits of those most at risk. Condoms are heavily promoted as a means of preventing infection and the spread of the disease. Considerable resources are also invested in developing community-based support structures for those individuals and families affected. Medical research also inevitably forms a crucial part of the overall response. The importance of women as a group at high levels of risk in many countries has also been emphasised especially in the context of the impact of female infection on children and their important role in the community overall.

Sources: Panos Institute (1992) **The Hidden Cost of Aids** and **Blaming Others: Prejudice, Race and World-Wide AIDS** (1988) London and Washington.

The Globa

DEVELOPING COUNTRIES

- ***About 17 million people die each year from infectious and parasitic diseases such as malaria, diarrhoea and tuberculosis***
- ***More than 90% of the 17 million HIV-infected people live in developing countries***
- ***Nearly 800 million people do not get enough food and about 500 million are chronically malnourished***
- ***Maternal mortality in the Third World, at 350 per 100,000 live births, is about nine times higher than in OECD countries***
- ***The under-five mortality rate, at 100 per thousand live births, is still nearly seven times higher than in industrial countries***

INDUSTRIAL COUNTRIES

- ***More than 1.5 million people are infected with HIV***
- ***More than 5 million are homeless***
- ***Nearly 130,000 rapes are reported annually in the age group 15-59 years***
- ***The direct and indirect costs of HIV infections was $210 billion in the 1980s***
- ***The average homicide rate is 4 per 100,000***
- ***1 in every 3 adults smoke.***

Rich Country, Poor Children

According to **The State of America's Children 1991** published by the Children's Defence Fund in Washington:

- Children aged under 5 living in the poorest families are one-third less likely than children in more affluent families to be in excellent health
- Poor 5-17 year olds are about half as likely to be in excellent health as their more affluent counterparts
- The poorest 5-17 year olds lose 1.5 times more schooling because of acute or chronic health conditions
- Poor children are twice as likely to have physical or mental health conditions that impair daily activity
- In Los Angeles, 23% of homeless parents interviewed said that their children were often or always hungry
- 375,000 children are born drug-exposed each year
- 12% of all US children under 18 in 1989 experienced emotional disorders.

LATIN AMERICA AND THE CARIBBEAN

- ***Only 56% of the rural population have access to safe water as against 90% for urban areas***
- ***Two million people have been infected with HIV***
- ***In some of the major cities, more than 100,000 children live on the streets***
- ***At the end of 1993, nearly 150,000 people were refugees.***

"The typical Third World doctor is an intriguing piece of very inappropriate technology. He is about as helpful in improving his countrymen's health as a tiny fleet of Rolls-Royces might be in providing transport for the masses. Until the last few years he was modelled in almost every detail on his Western counterpart. Usually he is trained in dealing with acute medical problems using surgery or drugs, and his training is grotesquely expensive.
For example, in 1965, when it cost $19,630 (£10,000 st.) to produce one medical graduate in the USA, the cost in Guatemala was $19,000; in Jamaica and Kenya $24,000; in Colombia $29,000 and in Senegal $84,000.

Paul Harrison in **Inside the Third World** (1993) Penguin.

Health Agenda

ARAB STATES

- *Less than three fifths of the rural population have access to safe water and only half have access to basic sanitation facilities*
- *At 83 per 1,000 live births, the under five mortality rate is more than five times higher than in industrial countries*
- *With less than 1,000 cubic metres of water per capita available each year, about 55% experience serious water scarcity affecting overall health*
- *At the end of 1983, more than 1 million people were refugees.*

SOUTH ASIA

- *South Asia is the only region in the world where in countries such as Bangladesh, Maldives and Nepal, female life expectancy is shorter than that of males*
- *About 280 million people lack access to safe water and 800 million to basic sanitation*
- *About 300 million do not have enough to eat*
- *About 80% of pregnant women suffer from anaemia - the highest rate in the world*
- *About 1/3rd of new-born babies are underweight*
- *At the end of 1993, nearly 5 million people were refugees*

SUB-SAHARAN AFRICA

- *There is only one doctor for every 18,000 people compared with one for every 7,000 in the Third World overall and one for every 390 people in industrial countries*
- *More than 10 million people have been infected with HIV (2/3rds of those affected world-wide and there are 6 HIV infected women for every 4 infected men)*
- *About 170 million do not get enough to eat*
- *Sub-Saharan Africa has the world's highest maternal mortality rate at 600 per 100,000 live births (as against 10 in the industrialised world)*
- *About 26 million children are malnourished and 15% of new-born babies are underweight*
- *At the end of 1993, more than 6 million people were refugees.*

EAST/SOUTH-EAST ASIA AND THE PACIFIC

- *More than 2 million people have been infected with HIV*
- *In South-east Asia and the Pacific, rural access to safe water at 47%, and to basic sanitation at 38%, are only wo-thirds of urban access*
- *The maternal mortality rate in South-east Asia and the Pacific, at 295 per 100,000 live births is more than three times higher than that of East Asia, at 92 per 100,000 live births*
- *More than one-third of children under five are malnourished*
- *At the end of 1993, more than 1/2 million people were refugees.*

Source: UNDP (1993 and 1995) **Human Development Report,** Oxford University Press.

The health dimensions of the Gulf War have been constantly underestimated - Kurdish refugees, Iran 1991.

▼ References

Instituto Del Tercer Mundo (1995) **The World: A Third World Guide 1995/96,** Montevideo.

World Commission on Environment and Development (1987) **Our Common Future,** Oxford University Press.

Paul Harrison (1992) **The Third Revolution,** London, Penguin.

Paul Harrison (1993) **Inside the Third World,** London, Penguin.

Population Reference Bureau (1990) **World Population Data Sheet,** Washington.

G. Lean and D. Hinrichsen (1992) **Atlas of the Environment,** Oxford, Helicon Publishing.

World Bank (1995) **World Development Report 1995,** Oxford University Press.

Cathal Poirteir (ed.1995) **The Great Irish Famine,** Cork, Mercier Press/RTE.

Kevin Watkins (1995) **The Oxfam Poverty Report,** Oxford, Oxfam.

UNDP **Human Development Report 1995,** Oxford University Press.

Panos Institute (1992) **The Hidden Cost of Aids and Blaming Others: Prejudice, Race and World-Wide AIDS** (1988) London and Washington.

M. Todaro (1994-5th ed.) **Economic Development,** London, Longman.

OUR NAME IS TODAY: CHILDREN, YOUTH AND DEVELOPMENT

Anne Leahy and Liam Wegimont

Introduction

99 per cent of the world's children now live in countries whose governments have committed themselves to the United Nations Convention on the Rights of the Child. Over 185 countries have ratified the Convention and aspire to give children a better future. It is now universally acknowledged that children's lives should be ones *"of joy and peace, of playing and learning and growing, their future shaped in harmony and co-operation"*.

For millions of children the reality is shockingly different. Many suffer immensely as casualties of war, as victims of aggression, violence, racial discrimination, as refugees and displaced children, as victims of neglect or cruelty or exploitation.

But children aren't just victims. They are also creative agents for change. It is no longer acceptable to understand children as anything less than citizens in their own right. By the year 2000 the majority of the world's population will be under 18 years. Children and youth are not only the future of the world; they are also the present, dispossessed, owners of today. Development that excludes the voices of children and youth is redundant; the ultimate in unsustainability.

This chapter highlights the gap between the rhetoric of children's rights - almost universally agreed - and the reality of children's lives. It examines our understandings of childhood; it explores the life situations of children in extremely difficult situations - street children, child labourers, children in war zones etc. Closer to home, it outlines the continuum between physical violence against children (e.g. physical punishment) and the causes of war. Finally, it looks at movements and networks of children's and youths' participation and mobilisation as signs of hope for today and tomorrow.

Children's Rights and Global Wrongs

"For the sake of both individual and global development, children round the world need to understand the concept of rights, to know what rights they are entitled to, to empathise with those whose rights have been denied, and to be empowered to take action on behalf of their own rights and those of others".

Susan Fountain (1993) ***It's Only Right: A Practical Guide to Learning about the Convention on the Rights of the Child,*** *UNICEF.*

There is almost universal agreement, that children's rights are paramount. International Convenants and benchmarks include:

<u>1924 -</u> League of Nations - World Child Welfare Charter adopted;
<u>1959 -</u> UN General Assembly - Declaration on the Rights of the Child;
<u>1979 -</u> UN International Year of the Child;
<u>1989 -</u> UN Convention on the Rights of the Child;
<u>1990 -</u> World Summit for Children. Joint Declaration and Plan of Action.

These international agreements are crucial to securing a better world for children in spite of criticism regarding their limitations or lack of implementation. They set benchmarks against which governments can be, and are, judged.

While the Convention on the Rights of the Child is a comprehensive statement of the rights of the child, it can be summarised in Ten Basic Rights illustrated overleaf

Taking a tour of the world and keeping in mind the agreement of most States to the Convention on the Rights of the Child, it becomes obvious that the gap between rhetoric and reality is huge.

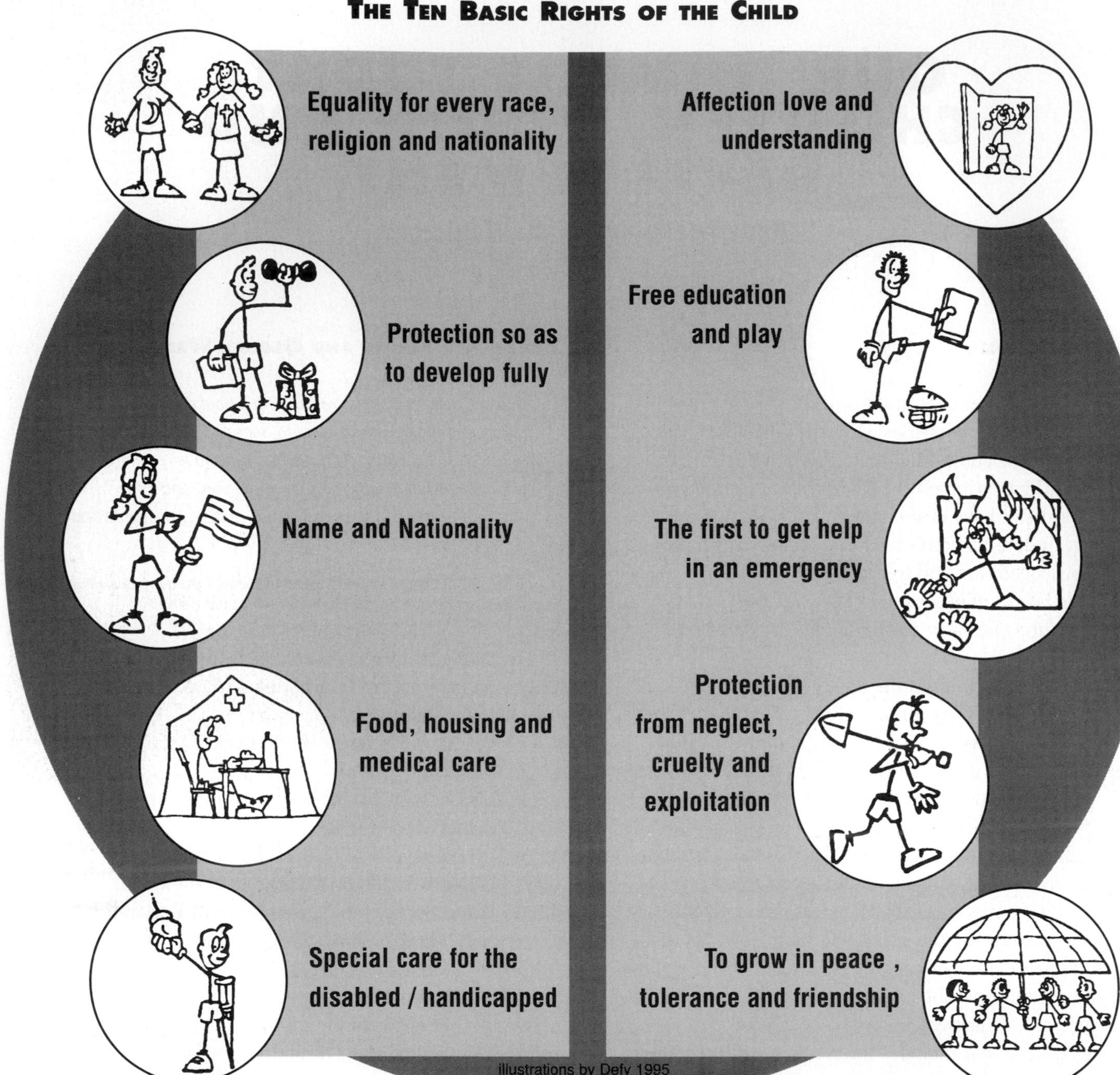
THE TEN BASIC RIGHTS OF THE CHILD
Equality for every race, religion and nationality
Affection love and understanding
Protection so as to develop fully
Free education and play
Name and Nationality
The first to get help in an emergency
Food, housing and medical care
Protection from neglect, cruelty and exploitation
Special care for the disabled / handicapped
To grow in peace , tolerance and friendship
illustrations by Defy 1995

Violation of Children's Rights

- Approximately 13 million children die every year in the developing world, often due to lack of immunisation. Every week 250,000 children die as victims of malnutrition and illness.
- Diarrhoeal dehydration, which after pneumonia and other respiratory infections, is the greatest killer of children in the developing world, claims the lives of nearly 3 million children each year. This is closely linked to poor sanitation. In the developing world, some 1.3 billion people have no access to safe drinking water and 1.9 billion lack adequate sanitation facilities.
- Acute respiratory infections claim the lives of 3.6 million children every year.
- Measles kills over a million children each year.

- In 1989, around 1 million confirmed cases of dracunculiasis, known as guinea worm disease and contracted by drinking infected water, were reported in 16 African nations and in parts of India and Pakistan.

- By the year 2000, an estimated 10 million children will have been infected with the AIDS virus, and in Africa alone 9 million will have been orphaned by the disease.

- In 1993, 130 million school-age children (6 - 11 years) were not in school. Over 90% of the developing world's children start school, many drop out after first grade and at present only 68% reach fifth grade.

- The total number of children under 15 engaged in child labour is in excess of 100 million. These children are exploited and often work in hazardous conditions.

- The nature of wars in the last decade has resulted in more children than soldiers being killed and disabled. Over that period approximately 2 million children have died in wars, between 4 and 5 million have been physically disabled, more than 5 million forced into refugee camps and more than 12 million left homeless. An estimated 10 million children are victims of psychological trauma.

- There is one landmine for every 20 children around the world. 2,000 people are killed or maimed weekly due to the explosive force or spewing of metal fragments from landmines. 80% of the victims are children.

- In the refugee populations living in camps, the proportion of under 18s is regularly more than 50%.

- Every year 120,000 children are born with severe mental and physical retardation and some 30,000 foetuses are still-born because their mothers were iodine deficient during pregnancy. About 50 million children are unable to take full advantage of primary schooling because of iodine deficiency disorders.

Children's Rights and Children's Realities - Brazil

Reports show worsening conditions of children.

Two reports were published on December 11, 1995 giving detailed information of the living conditions being experienced by Brazilian children. The Brazilian Institute of Geography and Economics (IBGE) published a report entitled "Children and Adolescents - Social Indicators" and UNICEF published its annual report on children.

The IBGE study shows that the number of children and adolescents under 17 years of age living in families earning up to half a minimum salary each month (US $50) has increased. For example in the North-east, 26.4% of all children and adolescents live in such families as compared to 10.6% in 1980. When rural areas of the North-east are examined the situation has grown worse at an alarming rate during the same period. In 1980, 23.6% of rural children and adolescents lived in families earning up to half a minimum salary. The figure for 1991 was 50.8%.

However, the more prosperous South-east has shown a marked decline when similar statistics are compared. In 1980 in this region 7.9% of rural children and adolescents were members of families earning up to half a minimum salary. By 1991 this figure had increased to 25.2%. Illiteracy amongst children and adolescents dropped in this 11 year period. In 1980, 20.6% of children between 11 and 14 years were illiterate. The 1991 figure stands at 16.1%.

The UNICEF report shows that the death rate of children in Brazil between 0 and 5 years is 61 per 1000. This compares with war-torn Bosnia where the death rate for the same age group is 17 per 1000. According to the UNICEF representative in Brazil, Agop Kayayan, considering the degree of economic development in Brazil this figure is extremely high. He estimated that it should stand somewhere between 15 and 20 per 1000.

- There are over 2 million under 18s involved in prostitution, 1 million in Asia alone and 300,000 in the United States.

At the same time, children are not just passive victims. More and more there is a recognition among NGOs, educators, children's rights activists, even governments, that children must participate in their own development. Development that is not engendered is mal-development; it is also true that development without children's voices is development which excludes the majority and the future.

While it is true that the rights of children are grossly violated world-wide, that children continue to be brutalised, denied equal rights with adults, rendered invisible and abused physically and through imagery, this is not the complete picture. There have been signs of progress in the last 50 years:

- In Sub-Saharan Africa, the number of children in primary school has quadrupled since 1960.

Nevertheless, only half of the eligible children are enrolled and the gender gap remains wide.

- In South Asia, where one quarter of all children in the world live, survival prospects have doubled: in 1960, 1 in 4 children died by age 5; in 1993, it was 1 in 8. Nevertheless, this compares with an under-five mortality rate in Ireland and the UK of 7%, 1 in 14.

- In Latin America, in 1981 only 45% of children were immunised against vaccine preventable disease; by 1993, the rate of immunisation had increased to 80%.

- In East Asia and the Pacific, life expectancy has increased from 41 to 67 years over the last 50 years. Nevertheless, malnutrition is still rampant, with 1 child in 4 suffering from stunting as a result of under-nourishment, in 1990.

... by involving children in development planning and addressing their needs, emphasis is being placed on the importance of integrating child focused analysis and the gender perspective within the overall analysis of any given society.

Listening to smaller voices ...means....greater empowerment for children. Listening to smaller voices, by which children are brought into the process of planning, implementation and evaluation of endeavours undertaken in the interests of the whole community, means embracing the interlinked concepts of gender and generation.

Robert Dodd (1995) **Listening to Smaller Voices,** Action Aid.

Understanding Children

In Ireland, 43.74% of the population are under 25 years. In many developing countries, children make up the majority of the population. Children are the only future society has, so the quality of that future very much depends on the quality of life those children experience. Yet there is a tendency to understand childhood, not as a reality in itself, but as a journey from infancy to adulthood. For children, childhood is a life space, not only a journey. It is here and now. Children are our present, not just our future. Children are human **beings,** not **becomings** or **belongings.** As child development expert Penelope Leech puts it *"We must see children as junior selves rather than as potential others."*

In order to operationalise the UN Charter of Children's Rights and make them effective for all children, children need to be recognised as having rights like any adult, the right to participation, the right to be listened to, the right to a decent life. Understandings of childhood which associate children with innocence, naturalism, truth, dependence, are, to a large extent, modern Western constructions. While children have universally represented the sacred, they have done so in far more active ways in other civilisations.

If it is true that understandings of childhood function to define for the world the meaning of adulthood, it is also true that there is a complex relationship between images of childhood and Western understandings of the South - particularly in situations of disaster.

Figure 10:1
Source: UNICEF (1995) **State of the World's Children Report,** Oxford University Press..

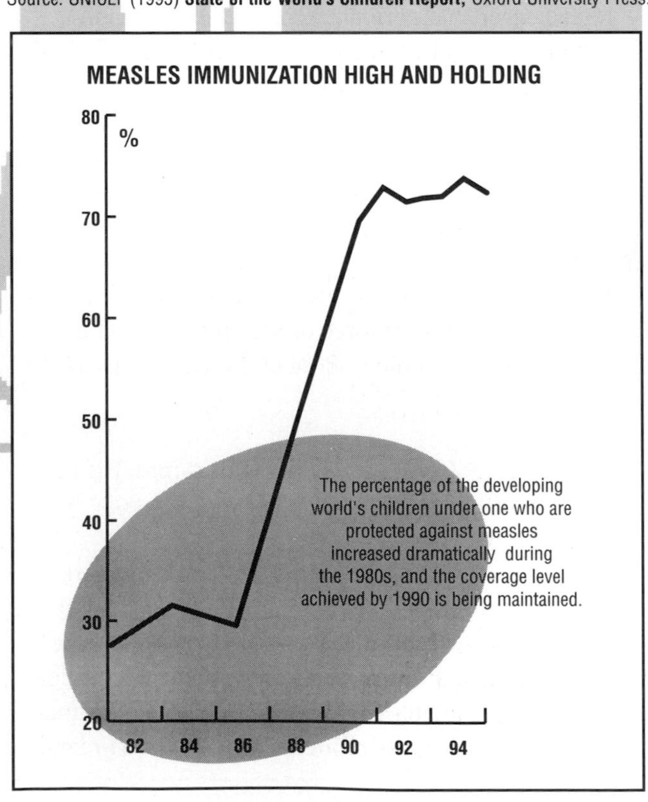
MEASLES IMMUNIZATION HIGH AND HOLDING
%
80
70
60
50
40
30
20
82
84
86
88
90
92
94
The percentage of the developing world's children under one who are protected against measles increased dramatically during the 1980s, and the coverage level achieved by 1990 is being maintained.

Education, a key to young people's future.

Figure 10:2

Source: UNICEF (1995) **State of the World's Children Report,** Oxford University Press..

Figure 10:3

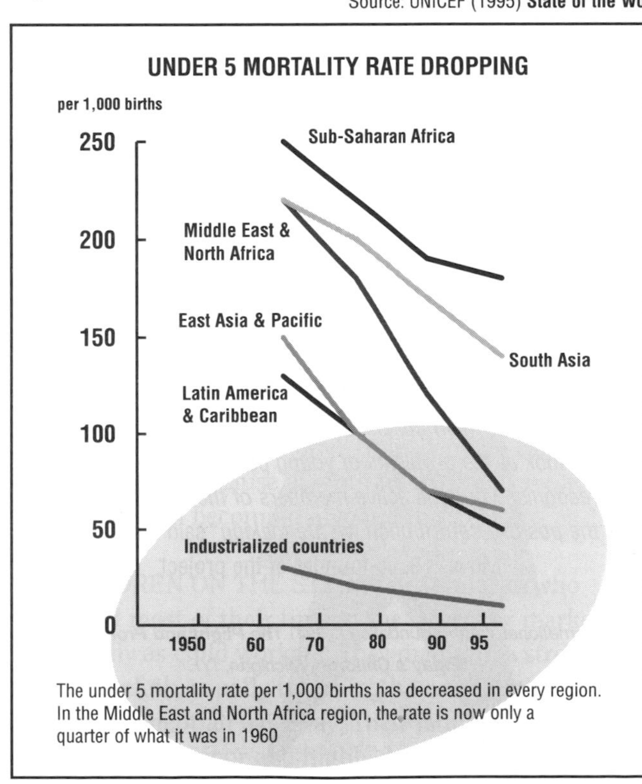

The under 5 mortality rate per 1,000 births has decreased in every region. In the Middle East and North Africa region, the rate is now only a quarter of what it was in 1960

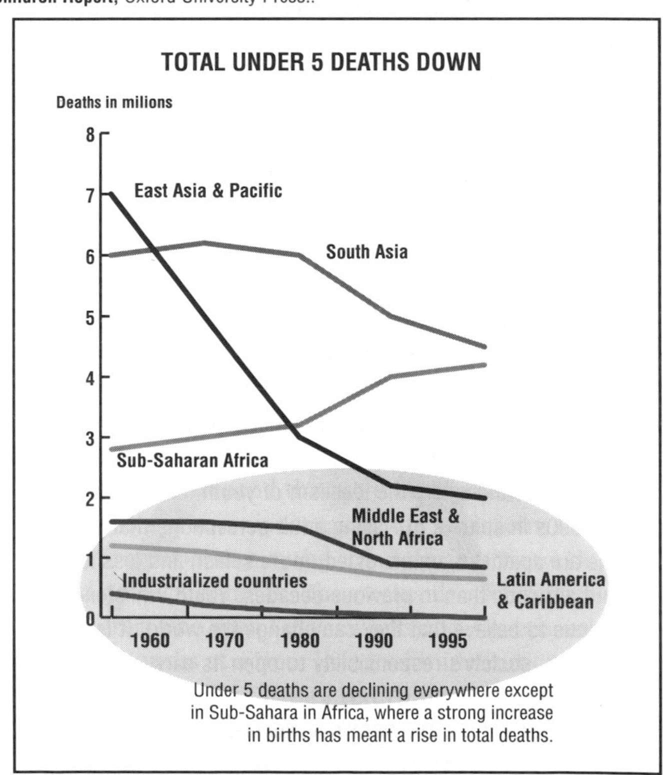

Under 5 deaths are declining everywhere except in Sub-Sahara in Africa, where a strong increase in births has meant a rise in total deaths.

- Children who may spend weeks or months off the street with their families or close relatives in an attempt to re-establish themselves, or they may live with somebody else who takes temporary charge of them out of compassion or for some other reason;
- Children who may develop a business partnership with persons who use them for their purposes, in return for food and a place to sleep.

LIFE ON THE STREET IS NOT EASY

Street children are exposed to violence, abuse, massacre and exploitation. In Brazil, there are an estimated seven to ten million street children, many of whom experience severe torture. The Candeleria massacre in Rio de Janeiro saw eight young children gunned down as they slept near the local church. In the suburb of Nova Iguacu, in Rio, an average of four children are killed every day on the streets.

In other Latin American countries similar circumstances prevail. For example, there are estimates of 200,000 children (5-18 years) on the streets of Mexico and another 5,000 in Guatemala. Abuse and murder of street children is a reality, the prime violators have been the Government and its security force. The elimination of children is often at the hands of death squads (vigilantes) as the children are often perceived as a public scandal which has adverse effects on tourism.

In Asia, and more specifically in countries such as India, Indonesia, Thailand, Sri Lanka, the Philippines and Malaysia, street life, child sexual abuse and prostitution are major problemss with severe and damaging consequences. For example, of the 1.2 million street children in the Philippines, 33% are sexually abused. In Thailand, it is estimated that there are 80,000 child prostitutes under 16 years of age. In Indonesia, over 2.7 million children (10-14 years) are forced into harsh working conditions. In Malaysia, many children are sold in the trafficking of children; others are abandoned. This is also a feature in Nepal, where children are airlifted into brothels in Calcutta.

In all of the major cities in India i.e. Calcutta, Delhi, Bombay, Madras, Bangalore, there are large populations of street children (100-200,000). The key issues for them, as for many street children globally, are:

- Acute poverty, malnutrition, ill health, lack of shelter, lack of possessions;
- Lack of socialisation;
- Exploitation and abuse within the family and in the street context.

In South Africa there are over one million street children. The causes of their plight are rooted in apartheid. Prior to 1994, widespread black unemployment, the

The Convention on the Rights of the Child and Child Labour.

Two articles of the Convention on the Rights of the Child are especially applicable to the circumstances of street and working children': Article 19: The right to protection from violence, abuse and neglect states:

- 1. Parties shall take all appropriate legislative, administrative, social and educational measures to protect the child from all forms of physical or mental violence, injury or abuse, neglect or negligent treatment, maltreatment or exploitation, including sexual abuse, while in the care of parent(s), legal guardian(s) or any other person who has the care of the child.
- 2. Such protective measures should, as appropriate, include effective procedures for the establishment of social programmes to provide necessary support for the child and for those who have the care of the child, as well as for other forms of prevention and for identification, reporting, referral, investigation, treatment and follow-up of instances of child maltreatment described heretofore, and, as appropriate, for judicial involvement.

Article 32: The right to protection from economic exploitation states:

- 1. Parties recognise the right of the child to be protected from economic exploitation and from performing any work that is likely to be hazardous or to interfere with the child's education, or to be harmful to the child's health or physical, mental, spiritual, moral or social development.
- 2. Parties shall take legislative, administrative, social and educational measures to ensure the implementation of the present article. To this end, and having regard to the relevant provision of other international instruments, Parties shall in particular:
- (a) Provide for a minimum age or minimum ages for admission to employment;
- (b) Provide for appropriate regulation of the hours and conditions of employment;
- (c) Provide for appropriate penalties or other sanctions to ensure the effective enforcement of the present article.

Sources: UNICEF **State of the World's Children 1995**, 1996; **The Courier**, no. 143. Jan/Feb 1994; **A World That Works:** DEFY 1994.

migrant labour system and the Group Areas Act relegated black children and their families to live in bare and impoverished 'homelands' which contributed to the number of children living and working in the streets. In Ethiopia, there are over one million people living in squalid conditions, up to 500,000 are children and the majority are forced onto the streets and engage in work.

Street children are seen as a menace, their behaviour is regarded as a danger to the public. Street children represent deviations from the 'normal view' that the child should grow up with natal parents or that the child should be protected by a responsible adult or group of adults. Again, street children offend our image of children as innocent and dependent.

Literature on street children illustrates that the majority spend their time on the street as workers yet maintain strong family links. It is important to note that even though most street children are working children in some form or other, not all working children are street children.

Child Labour

In terms of the size of the population involved, child labour is probably the issue that involves the largest number of children world wide. The International Labour Organisation estimates that the total global workforce of children under 15 is about 100 million. Of that, 95% live in developing countries. Half are in Asia, the most highly populated region in the world; but the highest proportion of working children - one in three - is in Africa.

COUNTRY	POPULATION UNDER 16	UNDER 16 ENGAGED I N CHILD LABOUR
Indonesia	69 million	2.7 million
Pakistan	62 million	19.0 million
Brazil	55 million	7.0 million
Nigeria	50 million	12.0 million
Bangladesh	49 million	15.0 million
Mexico	35 million	11.0 million
Philippines	27 million	5.0 million
Egypt	25 million	1.4 million
India	340 million	100 million

Source: ILO 1995: Bureau of International Affairs: UNHCR.

Figure 10:4

Child Labour in Brazil

Approximately 3.5 million children under 14 years of age work in Brazil. More than 70% of them earn only US $50 per month. Other children and adolescents work in semi-slave conditions receiving no salary and often working as many as 12 hours per day.

Many work in unhealthy conditions and help to supply raw materials for large and well known industries. Examples include :

- the furnaces which provide charcoal for the steel industry which in turn supplies parts for the car industry;
- the harvesting of sugar cane - many children cut up to two tons daily which is used in the production of alcohol by the national petroleum company, Petrobras;
- the shoe industries where they come in contact with highly poisonous glues;
- harvesting oranges which are used by multinational companies to produce juice for export.

In most cases such children do not go to school. Many suffer health problems as a consequence of their work; an example is the youth and children picking oranges who are forced to carry hundreds of kilos of fruit each day - very soon they suffer from back problems. Some companies do not know the conditions in which their raw material is produced and are scarcely interested in this information. Others simply close their eyes to what is happening.

News from Brazil, Servicio Brasiliero de Justica e Paz, Jan 11, 1996.

DEBATING CHILD LABOUR : NO SIMPLE SOLUTIONS.

"Any form of work is detrimental to a child's development. Childhood should be a free space for education and play".

"Child labour takes adult jobs, which creates general poverty. To break the cycle, do away with child labour".

"Child labour creates necessary income for families and communities. Take it away and it is the children who will suffer most".

"The Western concern with child labour is exporting Western models of childhood".

"Safe child work is o.k.; the focus should be on eliminating hazardous child labour".

"Poverty causes child labour - tackle the causes".

"In some cases children don't need to work; it's a free choice".

"There is a difference between work (domestic/unpaid) and labour (paid). Focus on labour".

"That difference has been oversimplified. Child work can be even more exploitative. Re-focus on work".

"Child labour needs to be tackled in the broader context of community development which is child centred".

Child labour is the major global children's rights issue. Through ILO conventions, the Convention on the Rights of the Child, and reiteration of international support for the eradication of child labour through fora such as the World Summit for Social Development, governments claim to be committed to the reduction of the suffering of children under cruel and exploitative working and labour conditions. Public opinion in Western countries has also forced major companies to review their links with suppliers or sub-contractors who exploit children. Atrocities against children's rights activists and child labour union organisers are the focus of Western media attention.

At the same time, Western abhorrence of child labour, which has at times been effectively mobilised on behalf of children's rights, can sometimes lead to oversimplified solutions to what are complex situations. Take, for example, the prevalent image of a child worker : urban, factory based, in clothing or textiles. The reality is that most child labour is rural based and agricultural. Immediate bans on imports involving child labour have, in some cases, caused greater poverty in the lives of the children they most wished to assist.

War Children

The 1996 UNICEF State of the World's Children Report sets out an anti-war agenda because, as it explains: Wars and civil conflicts are taking a massive toll on children. The numbers, though imprecise, are devastating...in the past decades approximately

- ▼ 2 million children killed;
- ▼ 4 - 5 million disabled;
- ▼ 12 million uprooted from their homes;
- ▼ Countless others died from disease and malnutrition caused by war;
- ▼ 10 million psychologically traumatised.

Child Soldiers - why?

"Over the past decade, government forces in El Salvador, Ethiopia, Guatemala, Myanmar, among others, have all conscripted children...opposition movements in many countries have also seized children, as in Angola, Mozambique, Sri Lanka and Sudan..."

The question why Child Soldiers must be asked. There are a number of reason soffered:

- ▼ It's nothing new. The term 'infantry' suggests that historically, foot soldiers were youngsters.
- ▼ The increase in the use of light weaponry (AK47s or M-16s) makes children more useful as soldiers.
- ▼ Children are easier to brainwash and intimidate, and cheaper as no salaries are required.
- ▼ Many wars last for generations - half of the wars ongoing in 1993 had lasted more than a decade. In these situations war is all children know - it is normality for them.
- ▼ For abandoned children, an army unit can act as a surrogate family unit.
- ▼ For many children in war situations, it is the only way to survive.
- ▼ Children may want to fight - against injustice, for revenge, or to gain peer esteem.

Source: UNICEF **State of the World's Children** 1996

Lobbying for Change : Raising the Age Limit for Recruitment into Armed Forces

When the UN Convention on the Rights of the Child was drafted, one of the most contentious issues was the minimum age for recruitment into armed forces and participation in hostilities. Under the Additional Protocols to the 1949 Geneva Conventions, the minimum age is 15 years. Much effort was put into trying to raise this to 18 years in the Convention on the Rights of the Child - in line with the general age of majority set by that Convention. Those efforts failed - at least overtly because of opposition by the USA - and article 38 of the Convention endorses 15 years as the minimum legal age.

However, the non-governmental organisations enlisted the interest of the expert committee created by the Convention, the Committee on the Rights of the Child. This Committee decided to devote its very first day of discussion (October 5, 1992) to the topic of "Children in Armed Conflict". Two of the recommendations which arose from that discussion were: first, that there should be an optional protocol to the Convention on the Rights of the Child raising the minimum age for recruitment and participation in hostilities to 18 years; second, that the UN Secretary-General should be requested to appoint an expert to undertake a study on the impact of armed conflict on children. Both these recommendations have been taken up.

Why18?

A common reaction in the developed world is what is wrong with 15 or 16 year olds entering the armed forces as long as they volunteer? This raises a number of issues. First, most countries in the world set the age of political majority at 18 years, and many restrict entry to hazardous occupations, to pornographic films and to the purchase of alcohol to adults. There is nothing inherently illogical in extending these protective restrictions to service in the armed forces. In particular, the emerging evidence of the greater impact of injuries on those who have not reached physical maturity, as well as the psychological impact on the young, reinforces the merits of precluding even genuine volunteers under the age of 18. However, there is also the problem of what constitutes voluntary participation. In many circumstances, pressure is exerted - economic, social, ideological and so - which are not necessarily obvious and call into question the degree of real choice available.

Draft Optional Protocol:

The first session of the Working Group to draft the optional protocol took place in October 1994 and the second in January 1996. Considerable progress was made although many problems remain. NGOs are very actively involved in the Working Group, in particular reminding the governments drafting the protocol of the realities on the ground, and that the purpose is not to produce an agreement which will not require them to change their law or practice, but a text which improves the protection for children around the world.

The key provisions:

There was general agreement that no-one under the age of 18 years should take part in hostilities. However, Pakistan, South Korea and the USA sought a limit of 17 years rather than 18, and the USA wanted the prohibition in less than absolute terms so that only taking "a direct part" in hostilities would be covered.

There was agreement that no-one under the age of 18 years should be subject to compulsory recruitment (conscription) into governmental armed forces. No agreement could be reached on the situation with regard to volunteers because Australia, Canada, Denmark, the UK, Netherlands and New Zealand supported by the USA, take volunteers from 16 years and are not prepared to change their practice in this respect.
A related unresolved problem is the possibility of an exception of volunteers below the age of 18 for military education or training purposes only.

There was general agreement on a total prohibition on recruitment of under-18s into non-governmental (opposition) armed groups and their use in hostilities. Most other issues have been resolved. Progress on the protocol would be greatly assisted if governments were made aware that this is seen as an important issue and representations were made about the specific problems being caused by some governmental positions, in particular those recruiting 16 year olds and those wishing to send 17 year olds into combat.

World Council of Churches **Ecumenical Refugee and Migration News** 1996 No. 2.

▼ References

Susan Fountain (1993) **It's Only Right: A Practical Guide to Learning about the Convention on the Rights of the Child,** UNICEF.

Victoria Johnson et al (1995) **Listening to Smaller Voices, Children in an Environment of Change,** London,Actionaid.

DEFY/IMS (1995) **The DEFY Development Education for Youth Survey,** Dublin.

UNICEF (1996) **State of the World's Children Report,** Oxford University Press.

R. Carney et al (l994) **The Cost of a Child,** Dublin, Combat Poverty Agency.

Annie Allsebrook and Anthony Swift (1989) **Broken Promises: The World of Endangered Children,** London, Hodder and Stoughton.

Christian Aid (1994) **Give Children a Childhood: Worship Ideas for Secondary Schools,** Dublin and London.

Anne Leahy (1994) **An Analysis of Street Childrens Problems in Calcutta,** Unpublished Dissertation, available from DEFY.

International Youth Foundation (1994) **The Plight and Promise of Today's Children,** Michigan, I.Y.F.

A. James and A. Proust (1990) **Constructing and Reconstructing Childhood:** Contemporary Issues in the Sociological Study of Childhood, Hampshire: Falmer Press.J.

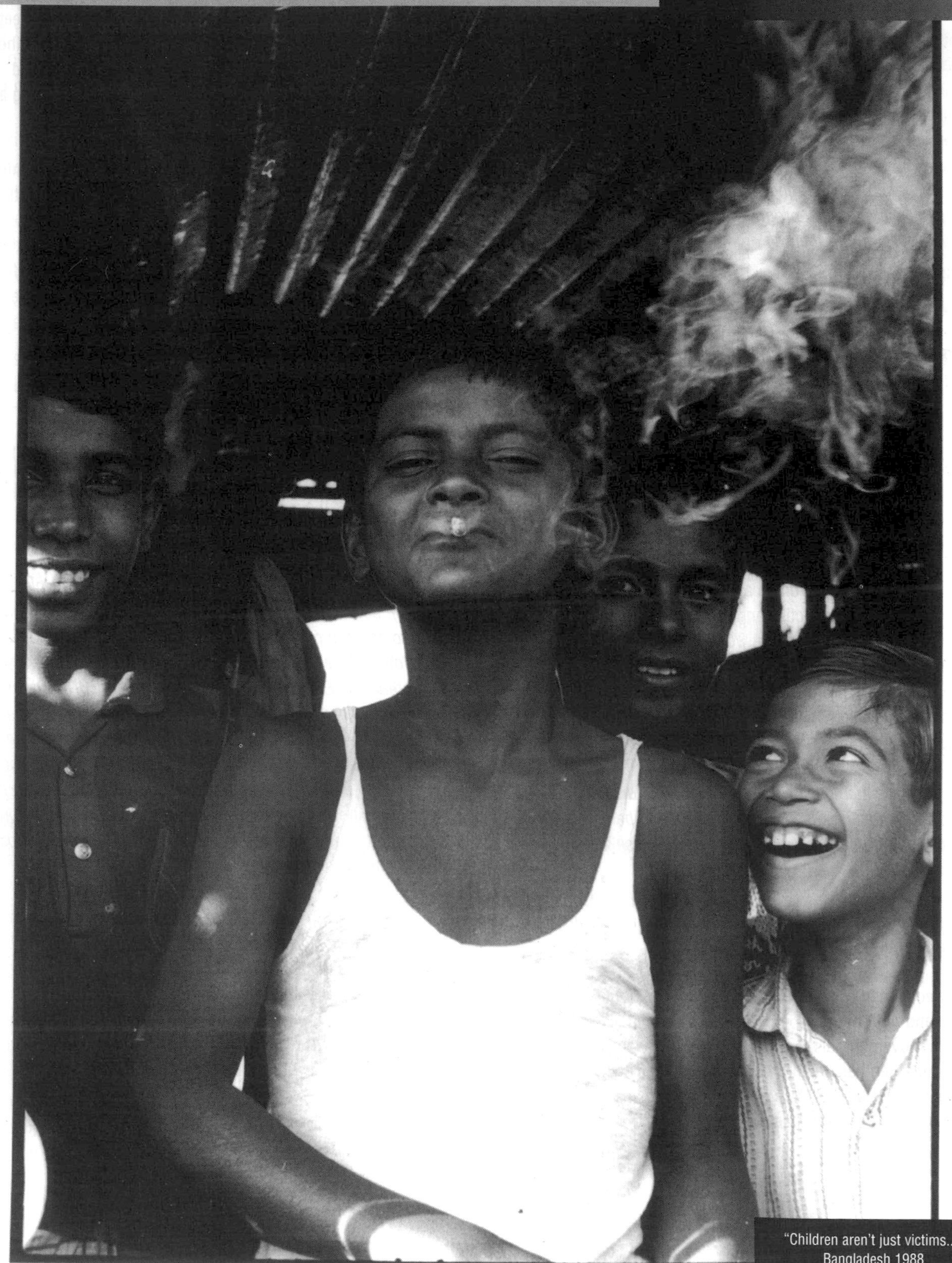

"Children aren't just victims...", Bangladesh 1988.

GOING BEYOND CHARITY?

Colm Regan

" ...the relevant virtue for fighting hunger...is justice, because charity can never be more than a stop-gap - it does not and cannot change unjust structures. Injustice and inequalities are structural, and have firm foundations."

Susan George (1987) in John Bennett **The Hunger Machine,** Cambridge, Polity Press.

Introduction

Ask the average person in Britain or Ireland about the financial links between the developed world and the Third World and chances are that most believe the flow of income is from the rich to the poor. This was, in fact the truth of the matter in the early 1980s - in 1981, for example, there was a net inflow of funds to developing countries of approximately $46 billion. But for many people throughout the developing world, the 1980s became a "lost decade" as the world was turned upside down and the flow of resources was reversed.

Between 1985 and 1988 the average outflow, from the world's poor to rich, was $11 billion each year. The total amount transferred between 1984 and 1989 was $46 billion or $12 out of the pocket of each poor person. Today, the United Nations Development Programme estimates that while total aid, from both governments and voluntary organisations, amounts to about $55 billion each year, global economic structures and processes cost the Third World $500 billion each year. In short, for every $1 given in aid, approximately $9 is taken back.

In Ireland and Britain and throughout much of the rest of Europe, public support for aid to the Third World remains high and there is a strong belief that the majority of this aid is "poverty focused". While this may be true for specific projects and countries, it cannot be said to be true for government aid in general as is indicated below. Like so many other dimensions of relations between the North and South, aid, its uses and its distribution, have become highly contentious and politicised, especially for the world's biggest donor countries. Official aid is routinely used to support "friendly" governments, former colonies, businesses at home; to secure trade or arms deals; to extend cultural or political control and to challenge trends or movements deemed by the donor government to be politically "negative".

Against this, much excellent and life saving humanitarian aid has been expended in countries such as Ethiopia (1984/85), Somalia (1992/93) and Rwanda (1994) - even if it has frequently arrived late and in quantities much smaller than needed. Individuals, families and communities who have received much needed assistance will clearly and correctly argue for continuing and increasing volumes of official aid. Others concerned about the misuses of aid will argue differently - their conflicting views are outlined below. One issue at least is clear - aid is not simple, straightforward and free from controversy.

Aid Patterns Since 1945

Since 1945 it is possible to identify at least five major periods in the emergence of aid or as it is officially called Official Development Assistance (ODA).

(1) The 1950s and 1960s witnessed the rapid development of ODA. Then the United States accounted for about a half of all aid; France for about 30% and Britain for 10%. US aid was concentrated amongst a group of countries from Greece to South Korea along the periphery of what was then described as the Sino-Soviet bloc. French and British aid was concentrated in former colonies.

(2) ***The mid 1960s and early 1970s*** witnessed the establishment of many new international aid institutions and the setting up of aid ministries in many countries. The US continued to donate approximately 1/3rd of all ODA while French and British aid declined. These declines were partly offset by the rise of a new group of donors - the Nordic countries. The expanding world economy and the continuing development crisis in many parts of the Third World led to substantial increases in ODA. The General Assembly of the United Nations agreed to a target of 0.7% of GNP for ODA but by 1985 the record of achieving this was poor.

(3) ***The mid 1970s to mid 1980s*** was characterised by international recession, oil crises and increased needs in the Third World. United States aid continued to decline to 1/5th of total ODA and their aid became more concentrated in the Caribbean and Middle East. Overall, aid continued to grow by about 2% per annum. By 1983/84 Sub-Saharan Africa replaced Asia as the focus of most aid. In some country, aid programmes (particularly amongst Nordic donors) became increasingly focused on the poorest sectors of the Third World and on basic needs such as food, shelter, etc.

(4) ***From the mid 1980s to the early 90s*** - the continuing impact of international recession, depressed oil prices, widespread domestic problems and the diversion of aid to regions formerly part of the USSR, all affected aid. ODA levels stagnated and, in many cases, substantially declined. Serious cutbacks in aid occurred in the US, in Italy, in Germany, in Australia, in Britain, in the Arab States and in Ireland. As against this, some countries - Norway, the Netherlands, Denmark, Sweden, Finland and Spain instituted increases.

(5) ***The present situation*** - recent aid volumes have experienced a sharp drop from $61 billion in 1992 to $56 billion in 1993 with little likelihood of an overall increase in the immediate future (17 of the 21 DAC members have cut their aid). Measured in percent of GNP terms, aid is now at its lowest point for 20 years. In volume terms, Japan is the biggest donor followed by the United States and France but only Denmark, Sweden, Norway and the Netherlands have reached the agreed UN target of 0.7% of GNP. This situation has led the **Reality of Aid Report 1995** to comment:

"The era of gradually growing assistance for the poor seems to have come to an end. NGOs are concerned, not only by the sharp cut in aid, but also by the fact that most donors have made no commitment to avoid further cuts. Donor governments are frequently guilty of double-talk when it comes to the relationship between aid spending and economic growth. Many fail to move towards the UN 0.7% target during times of economic growth, often using the excuse that it is difficult to make progress when the target itself is growing.

Then during periods of recession when the target is becoming easier to reach, governments excuse aid cuts on the grounds that public expenditure must be kept down."

The Uses Of Aid

The term 'aid' can, in fact, be quite misleading as some 60% of all capital transfers to developing countries involves private transactions in the form of bank loans and direct private investment by individuals or companies on straight commercial terms. Official Development Assistance, on the other hand, tends to be non-commercial in nature and is most often provided in the form of loans, usually at lower than world average interest rates, in debt relief or as straight grants for projects and is divided between multilateral aid and bi-lateral aid.

The Organisation for Economic Co-operation and Development surveyed the major uses of aid between 1960 and 1985 and identified the following pattern

	1960 - 1985 % OF TOTAL
Social Infrastructure and Services	**19.3**
Education	8.8
Health	3.6
Water/Sanitation/Public Administration	6.9
Economic Infrastructure and Services	**26.8**
Transport and Communications	12.0
Energy	14.8
Production Sectors	**31.7**
Agriculture	17.1
River Development	4.4
Industry	10.2
Non-Project Assistance	**17.3**
Financial Assistance	10.7
Debt Relief	0.5
Food Aid	6.1
Aid Via Non-Governmental Organisations	**2.9**

While most developing country governments are anxious to receive aid and while most international development reports and aid agencies call for an increase in ODA, aid itself is an issue of intense debate. There is little doubt that if properly planned and administered, aid programmes and projects can have considerable impact in critical areas, such as humanitarian assistance in times of emergency, health care, agricultural development and education - particularly where it is geared towards the needs and interests of the poorest people. However, aid today continues to be heavily influenced by political and economic considerations and it is precisely within this context that most of the debate has taken place.

Critics of aid come from all perspectives and political persuasions - from the right who argue that aid distorts the market, undermines enterprise, subsidises inefficiency, etc. and from the left who argue that aid creates dependency, subsidises the middle class and the elite, puts recipients at a disadvantage vis-à-vis donors and undermines self-sufficiency. Critics of aid also refer to many huge aid projects which clear peasants or indigenous people off their land (for dams for example); which promote inappropriate development strategies (industrialisation at the expense of agriculture for example); and which do not address the needs of the poor, women or the environment. They also criticise aid which bypasses those for whom it is intended (no dialogue, consultations, etc.). These criticisms relate as much to aid within Europe as to that between Europe and the Third World.

Perhaps the most serious criticisms of many official aid programmes are that they often do not suit the needs and circumstances of developing countries or their poorest people; that they frequently respond more directly to donor country needs and interests and that they are still too "tied" to the purchase of goods or services in the donor country and often simply reflect and re-inforce ethnocentrism.

"(In the 1980s) Aid continued to be distributed on political grounds, not according to need. South Asia, with the world's biggest concentration of absolute poor and the lowest average incomes, got only $5 per person in 1989-90. Latin America, with average incomes four times higher, got twice as much per person. Arab states, with four times the income, got nearly nine times as much per capita. The UN Development Programme calculated that in 1989 the countries with the richest 40% of developing country populations got 2.2 times as much aid per person as those with the poorest 40%."

Paul Harrison **Inside the Third World** (1993).

Debating Aid

The Case For and Against Aid

Some commentators argue that:

- When properly administered and used, aid can help those most in need by providing emergency assistance as well as help with long-term development. Thus, aid can help save lives today and prevent them being lost in the future.
- Aid can help developing country governments to provide vital development infrastructure and planning e.g. roads, water and sanitation, planning services and education. In this way, aid can act as a "pump-primer" in getting development underway. Aid can help overcome "bottlenecks" to economic development in a country where local savings are small or where there is a lack of foreign exchange.
- Aid acts as an expression of humanitarian concern and provides people in the developed world with a channel through which to direct that concern.
- Aid acts as a limited but effective means of redistributing global wealth.
- Aid can help establish practical links between countries and thus foster international understanding and, ultimately, peace.
- Aid is a mechanism where by the experience and expertise of the better off parts of the world are made available to the poorer sections.
- Aid is a means through which countries and governments can pursue their own interests (both as donors and recipients), thus giving practical expression to the term "interdependence".

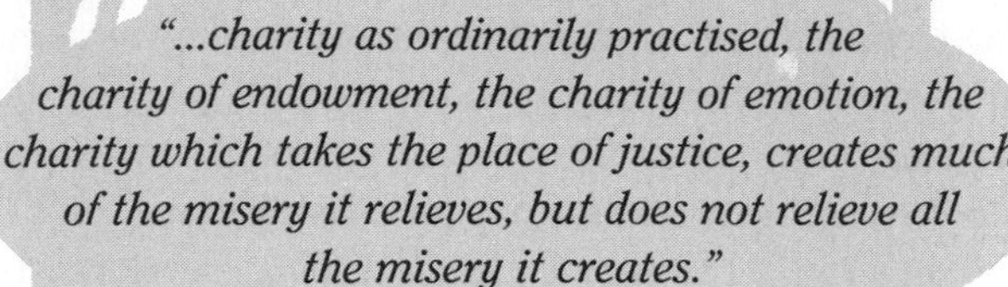

"...charity as ordinarily practised, the charity of endowment, the charity of emotion, the charity which takes the place of justice, creates much of the misery it relieves, but does not relieve all the misery it creates."

Joseph Rowntree, 1865.

Other commentators argue that:

- Aid from government to government only favours the rich of the world and has little effect on the poor. Aid has been used by authoritarian governments to consolidate their power.
- Aid creates dependency by making weaker governments / countries dependent on stronger ones, thus putting them at a disadvantage in economic or political discussions.
- Aid is frequently "tied" - its terms dictate that recipients buy goods or services from the donor country; it is thus a hidden subsidy to the professions in the developed world.
- Aid distorts the free market which is the most important engine of growth as has been shown in the past history of the now developed world.
- Aid is used to divert attention from other more important areas e.g. trade, where major structural changes would have vastly more beneficial results. We should not waste time arguing about aid when trade is the real issue.
- Since we are the givers and they are the receivers, aid can promote attitudes of superiority and can re-inforce those of racism. Aid re-inforces stereotypical images.
- Aid is currently used for economic, political and strategic reasons and is thus aimed at maintaining the current character of world inequality, rather than challenging it.

Multilateral Aid consists of (a) contributions (forming part of Official Development Assistance, ODA) made to an international institution for use in or on behalf of a developing country (b) financial aid and technical co-operation provided by an international institution to developing countries. In 1987 Ireland contributed 54% of its total ODA to multilateral aid while Britain's equivalent figure was 45%.

Bilateral Aid is ODA provided on a country to country basis. Ireland's Bilateral Aid Programme is concentrated on Lesotho, Tanzania, Zambia, Ethiopia, Mozambique and Sudan. In 1987 it amounted to 46% of total ODA. Britain's Bilateral Aid amounted to 55%.

"Protecting the poorest from the worst of the cuts is not enough to prevent increasing poverty in Africa. Half the continent's population is expected to be living below the poverty line by the year 2000. At a conservative estimate, this means that between 1990 and 2000, the number of people surviving on the equivalent of less than $1 a day will have risen by 75 million in Sub-Saharan Africa.

Reduced aid to Africa is likely to mean further environmental degradation, increased disease, conflict and refugee flows. The human cost will be terrible, and the long term financial cost is likely to far outweigh the price of an effective strategy to assist Africa now."

Actionaid (1995) **The Reality of Aid,** Earthscan, London

EUROPEAN UNION AID

European Union aid declined significantly between 1992 and 1993 largely due to the ending of the Gulf Crisis and reductions in trade related aid (a decline of 15%).

EU ODA figures, 1984 -93 (in $US million)

1984	1987	1989	1991	1993
1,287	1,747	2,420	3,478	3,637

EU aid falls into two parts:

1) Aid to 70 African, Caribbean and Pacific countries which have a special relationship with the European Union. In 1993 this amounted to 1,354 million ECUs.
2) Aid equalling 1,810 million ECUs spent directly on food aid (23%), projects in Asia, Latin America and Africa (20%), projects in Mediterranean countries (19%), direct humanitarian relief (19%), other [including environment and tourism projects (11%) and projects in partnership with Non-Governmental Organisations (7%)].

Aid Trends - The Facts and Figures 1993

Figure 11:1

Top 10 aid donors (DAC countries) and selected others

Country	$millions	% of GNP 1993 (1992)
Denmark	1,340	1.03 (1.02)
Norway	1,014	1.01 (1.16)
Sweden	1,769	0.98 (1.03)
Netherlands	2,525	0.82 (0.86)
France	7,915	0.63 (0.63)
Finland	355	0.45 (0.64)
Canada	2,373	0.45 (0.46)
Belgium	808	0.39 (0.39)
Germany	6,954	0.37 (0.39)
Australia	953	0.35 (0.37)
United Kingdom	2,908	0.31 (0.31)
Ireland	81	0.20 (0.16)
United States	9,721	0.15 (0.20)
Saudi Arabia	539	0.43 (0.65)
Kuwait	381	1.30 (0.87)
China	110 (1992 est.)	0.03 est.
India	34	0.03 est.
Korea	85	0.03 (0.02)

Top 10 aid receivers

Country	ODA as % of GNP (1991)	$ per capita (1993)
Oman	9.2	538
Sierra Leone	164.0	269
Israel	1.8	242
Mauritania	34.9	153
Namibia	6.2	105
Gabon	1.9	100
Zambia	23.6	97
Guinea Bissau	40.3	95
Botswana	3.3	90
Gambia	25.5	88
Rwanda	24.1	48
Egypt	5.9	41
Tanzania	40.0	34
Ethiopia	16.5	21
Bangladesh	5.8	12

> *"Eliminating poverty, minimising inequality, promoting environmentally sustainable development, and raising levels of living for the masses of less developed country people may turn out to be in the most fundamental self-interest of developed nations. This is not because of any humanitarian ideals (though we would hope that these are present) but simply because in the long run there can be no two futures for humankind, one for the very rich, another for the very poor, without the proliferation of global or regional conflict. Enlightened self-interest may therefore be the only peg on which to hang the hope for a "new international economic order", one in which both foreign assistance and private investment can begin to make a real and lasting contribution to Third World development"*
>
> Michael P. Todaro **Economic Development** (1994).

Profiling the Aid Givers

THE UNITED STATES

In 1993, total US aid amounted to $9,721 million (0.15% of GNP and 0.91% of government spending and equal to $38 per person). About 17% of US aid is tied formally. The major recipients of US aid in 1992/93 were Israel, Egypt, El Salvador, Somalia and the Philippines. Multilateral aid equals 26.6% of the total.

Drastic budget reductions are now being proposed and there is considerable fear that poverty focused programmes will suffer badly. Recent surveys have indicated strong public support for such programmes although surveys show that Americans believe their government is giving more in aid than is, in reality, the case.

THE UNITED KINGDOM

Total UK aid in 1994/95 was £2,349 million - a fall of £51 million fro 1993/94 representing 0.31% of GNP and £40 per person. 35.5% of aid is formally tied. Major aid recipients were India, Bangladesh, Zambia, Tanzania, the states of the former Yugoslavia and Ghana. As we go to press, indications are that the British Government will cut aid substantially in 1996.

Recent debates around the UK aid budget have focused upon aid reductions and the Pergau Dam affair in which the High Court found the government guilty of misusing aid money. A large majority of the public indicate strong support for increases in aid.

IRELAND

Total Irish aid amounted to £70.3 million in 1994 equalling 0.24% of GNP and £19 per person - representing a significant increase after many years of almost no growth or actual cuts. The government has indicated its commitment to continuing aid increases. Major recipient countries were Tanzania, Lesotho, Zambia, Sudan, Somalia and the states of the former Yugoslavia. Indications are that Irish aid will continue to increase (to an expected figure of £106 million in 1996).

Aid from Irish voluntary organisations amounted to about £17 million in 1993. There is strong public support for aid but concern amongst voluntary agencies that the government's commitment may not be shared by other political parties.

JAPAN

Japanese aid amounted to $11.3 billion in 1994, the highest amongst DAC countries although this represented a decline of 12% on the previous year. This figure equals 0.26% of GNP and about £60 per person. Major recipients were Indonesia, China, the Philippines, Egypt and Thailand.Debate on Japanese aid indicates that it will most likely decline in the future and that public support is also weak and declining. Japanese aid is estimated to be approximately 12.5% tied.

SAUDI ARABIA

In the 1980s, aid from countries such as Saudi Arabia frequently amounted to 3/4% of GNP but this figure has been declining since to a total of $539 million in 1993 (0.43% of GNP). Major recipients of this aid continue to be other Arab countries with some aid going to countries such as Sudan and Egypt.

KOREA

Precise figures for Korean aid are not yet available but it is estimated to amount to $85 million (0.02% of GNP).

Sources used in the compilation of these pages: Actionaid (1995) **The Reality of Aid,** Earthscan, London; Organisation for Economic Co-operation and Development (1994) **Development Co-operation: Development Assistance Committee Report,** Paris; World Bank (1995) **World Development Report,** Oxford University Press.

From Aid to Solidarity?

The Role of Voluntary Aid Agencies

While official or government aid remains by far the largest source of assistance, there are literally thousands of large and small voluntary aid agencies world-wide. They exist in both the developed and underdeveloped worlds and provide a host of services and support ranging from humanitarian assistance to the funding of a variety of projects to volunteers to campaigning and education. They can vary in scale from the multinational aid agencies with hundreds of millions of dollars to tiny local community groups with perhaps one or two projects. Many are motivated by church teaching, others by political philosophies or by human concern; some focus on relief and welfare, others on development and human rights while others concentrate on campaigning and education work in the developed world. Despite their different emphases and philosophies they have become a major force in the overall development and justice debate and they have managed to generate high levels of public support.

It is difficult to accurately measure the total amount of aid provided by the voluntary sector but the Organisation for Economic Co-operation and Development concluded that voluntary agency aid amounted to $2.89 billion in 1985. In addition to this about 5% of government aid was channelled through voluntary agencies or non-government organisations (NGOs). It is estimated that in 1993, the percentage of individual country aid which was provided by the NGO sector ranged from 19.5% in Ireland, 13% in New Zealand and 11% in Norway to 5% in the UK and Canada to 1% in Finland and 0.07% in Luxembourg. NGOs in Britain and Ireland channelled a total of £302 million and £17IR million respectively in 1993.

Overall NGOs have developed a good reputation in Third World support work as was evidenced in the public responses to agency appeals for the crises in Ethiopia in 1984/85, Somalia in 1992 and Rwanda in 1994. Most multilateral aid agencies and most governments now accept NGOs as important partners in the aid and development process and they are frequently in receipt of substantial government funding - an issue which is a matter of considerable debate.

As with any sector there are differences in philosophy and approach amongst NGOs reflecting, ultimately, differences in origins and understandings of the Third World or world development debate. At least four broad

Official Aid is often distributed on the basis of politics rather than need. This was often the case in the build-up to the Ethiopian crisis of 1984/85.

approaches can be identified:

- **The Welfare Approach** - This is characterised by the provision of welfare and relief work usually without direct reference to the politics of development. It is a pragmatic, often effective way of delivering relief without confronting the institutional or political causes of poverty. There is often a heavy emphasis on volunteers or "experts". NGOs have been increasingly successful in attracting support for this approach which appeals to both governments and the public alike.

- **The Developmental Approach** - This invalues the provision of support to local groups (either independently or via "experts") within the Third World who are involved in self-help development projects. The bulk of NGOs fall into this category and provide aid for health, housing, agricultural, educational projects, etc. This approach can involve volunteers or "experts" but often simply supports local groups directly. Many voluntary agencies combine both the "welfare" and "development" approaches.

- **The Empowerment Approach** - This approach is usually more explicitly political and radical than the two previous approaches. It defines development as a process of empowering local people to claim their rights, to challenge inequality and injustice and to challenge international inequality. Usually this approach does not involve volunteers or "experts" since those suffering oppression or injustice are the experts. This approach is more problematic as it raises many political questions which frequently challenge dominant groups within countries or internationally and often draws public scepticism

- **The Educational/Campaigning Approach -** Some NGOs recognise that tackling the world economic and political systems of inequality is crucial to real human development. Thus, they concentrate on educational programmes to raise public consciousness of injustice and thence to campaign for its elimination. Many NGOs mix this approach with some or all of those described above but the proportion of time and resources devoted to education and campaigning remains severely restricted overall. Education and campaigning remain very weak within the NGO sector.

Clearly the above approaches are not mutually exclusive and some NGOs are involved in all while others overlap between two or more approaches. Yet it cannot be denied that there are also many important and serious differences between the approaches and how they mediate relations with international institutions, governments and local Third World partners. The approaches range from simple direct "aid" to what is often called "solidarity" and can be seen to operate amongst Irish and British NGOs.

In terms of practical development on the ground these approaches mean that voluntary agencies are involved in:

- the provision of relief and humanitarian assistance - food aid, medical assistance, refugee support, transport, emergency shelter etc.
- short and long term financial and personnel support for rehabilitation projects in education, health, agriculture, medicine, housing, literacy, etc. which help people overcome the immediate consequences of disasters or crises.
- short and long term support for projects training local leaders, defending human rights, encouraging real participation, challenging injustice, racism, etc. This is frequently called "local capacity building" and is usually pursued through hundreds of small scale, cost effective, projects run by local organisations.
- the promotion of educational projects here in the developed world aimed at highlighting the causes of poverty and inequality and our responsibilities vis-à-vis world injustices.

Projects can vary in size from those involving hundreds of pounds, funded by one agency to those involving hundreds of thousands of pounds funded by a consortium of agencies and governments.

"How long will the West continue to believe itself involved in an act of charity towards the Third World? First, it was to "civilise" it and then the Third World was despoiled of its precious metals and its sovereignty, then it was to "develop" it and the Third World was dispossessed of its raw materials, then to "modernise" it and the Third World was drained of its financial reserves whilst the North got rid of its industrial surplus and got back three dollars for every dollar lent, and now it is to "feed" it. What price will have to be paid this time for Western charity? Those in the majority in the Third World, the peasants, are already suffering the consequences. Enough of the hypocrisy! The countries of the South ask only for their freedom and respect for their sovereignty. The process of decolonisation is not yet complete. Under such conditions, how can the North speak of co-operation, of aid...?

A Latin American commentator, quoted in T.Verhelst (1987).

European Aid to Britain and Ireland

Since accession to the European Community in 1973, Ireland has been a net recipient of aid amounting to £8,034 million (end 1988). In 1994, Ireland received a total of IR£1,956 million while contributing IR£543 million to the EU. The overwhelming majority of the aid received went into the price guarantee mechanisms of agriculture. The results of this aid are to be seen everywhere throughout the country - in farming, industry, roads, etc. The purposes for which this EU aid is used are a matter of intense debate within Ireland and within the EU, especially the heavy percentage which goes to price support in agriculture. Most recently there has been considerable debate and controversy over the lack of community involvement in the design of Irish government plans for EU aid for community development.

In 1994, the United Kingdom contributed £6,300 million to the European Union and received a total of £4,800 in aid thus leaving the UK as a net contributor to the EU - a pattern which has existed since Britain joined the European Community. As is the case with Ireland, the sector receiving the greatest amounts of this aid was agriculture (and within that, the price support structures) followed by aid from the Social Fund and the Regional Fund.

There are a number of important characteristics of NGOs which often distinguish them and highlight the differences between the approach of the voluntary and state sectors:

- They frequently bypass governments and can thus get more directly in touch with local people and their needs. This fact is particularly important where governments are not representative or in conflict situations.
- Because NGOs are usually small scale, large extensive and, often inappropriate, projects can be avoided. Large scale projects (huge dams, specialised hospitals, irrigation, etc.) have often hindered rather than helped human development.
- NGOs can often have more direct and ongoing contact with representative groups thus helping to ensure that their assistance is geared directly to local needs.
- NGOs can work in areas where, because of international politics or local conflicts, governments could not.
- NGOs can work for political change in the developed world - they can frequently and openly challenge injustice and inequality - the root cause of poverty.

Despite such advantages there are also disadvantages to the approach of NGOs:

- The scale of their work is tiny by comparison with the scale of the problems.
- Often they are based on a "do-gooder" philosophy alone and can thus be ineffective or unprofessional and can fail to address the real issues.
- Often they are representative of and driven by the needs and views of people in the developed rather than the underdeveloped worlds.
- In recent years intense competition between agencies has placed considerable emphasis on fund-raising or on publicity often to the neglect of the issues themselves. Sometimes NGOs have been so successful in publicising themselves that they create the impression that they can solve the issue of global poverty and inequality when clearly their size and impact remains severely restricted.
- Some NGOs still believe that the "starving baby" image of the Third World is the most effective fund-raising image even if it distorts the reality and creates an, at best, distorted understanding of the reality. Other methods of fund-raising have also been the subject of controversy, for example, there has been considerable debate within NGOs on the issue of child sponsorship.
- NGOs have been increasingly funded by governments and this can place constraints on what they can or are prepared to do and say for fear of the loss of support.
- As NGOs become bigger and more "professional", they, like all large organisations, run the risk of becoming bureaucracies, more concerned with their own survival than the issues at stake.
- As development and justice issues become more complex and interrelated, NGOs find it difficult to effectively respond to problems such as debt, hunger, etc. which involve multinational institutions and powerful interest groups and states.

In the past two decades, NGOs have become a vibrant and progressive part of the world development agenda here in these islands. They have succeeded in raising important issues and challenging serious injustices and they have managed to capture the public imagination to a very considerable degree. For some observers, NGOs are now facing important questions and challenges as attitudes change in the developed world and as the realities of continuing injustice and poverty deepen in many parts and amongst many groups in the Third World. As the editors of a recent collection of essays on the NGO experience have commented:

"The NGO of the future may look very different from the NGO of the present, but in all cases a fundamental requirement will be how to retain a sense of humility while celebrating and building on what has been successful. NGOs need to be careful that the increasing resources and attention they are receiving from the international community do not lure them into a sense of complacency or self-delusion, when their real impact on world poverty still remains very limited."

Michael Edwards and David Hulme (eds.1992).

The Images Debate

Within the development movement today there is a vigorous debate underway around the issue of how best to portray the often horrible and tragic realities of widespread poverty and hunger. Frequently this debate focuses on images of the Third World - often those of the hungry and emaciated, sometimes on the verge of death. Such images are very powerful and can generate tremendous actions of human compassion, especially when children are involved. Sometimes they are used to express the anger and outrage of so many that hunger remains widespread today; sometimes they are used to embarrass governments into action; other times they are used simply as an effective f und-raising strategy.

However, such images can also be very negative and can have an effect opposite to that intended. On the one hand they can be a true and accurate expression of the suffering of those depicted - portraying the pain and suffering experienced in the extreme by many people. Against this they can also be false - denying the dignity, achievements, history, culture and hopes of so many others. They can also be false because they can imply that the limited picture presented is, by implication, the full picture. If people in the developed world see only the negative side of life in the Third World, then their overall image of its people can be negative. What may have begun as a simple fund-raising strategy may therefore become something much more - especially if these are the only images used or if they are used to imply that extreme distress and suffering are the norm.

> *"Wide angle, black and white shots, grainy, high contrast images characterise the typical Third World helpless victim. Huge billboards with a dying malnourished child in a corner with outstretched arms. A clear message in polished bold font in the top left corner cleverly left blank. The message reads 'We shall always be*

The best aid is built upon the dignity, creativity and resourefulness of local people.

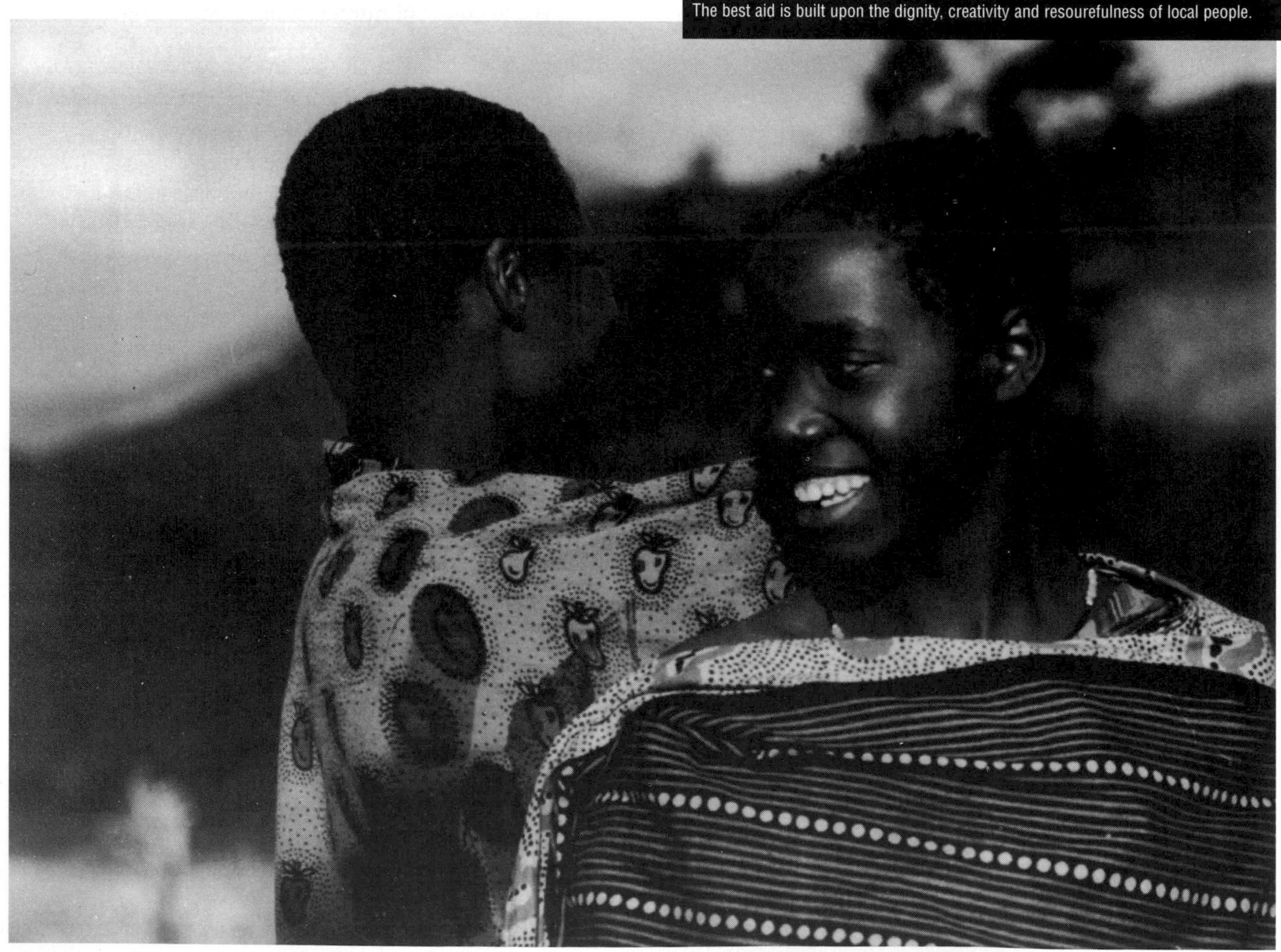

there'. A reality constructed for and by those who want us to forget the implications."

Bangladeshi photographer Shahidul Alam.

Many people from the Third World become angry when such images are used without sensitivity, thus denying those portrayed their dignity (even in death). They feel such images portray Third World peoples as helpless and pathetic, dependent on, and the objects of, Western aid when, in many cases, it is the injustice of the world system which has generated many of the difficulties. When such images also focus exclusively on Western aid workers and agencies they also perpetrate the notion that local people are doing little to either help themselves or their neighbours. Such images can also fuel attitudes of superiority and, sometimes, racism.

"NGOs take pains to inform their respective publics about the harsh reality of the Third World. Some have no hesitation, to shock the minds and open wallets, in showing photographs of starving children, stomachs swollen, skeletal hands outstretched towards generous donors. Inside the Third World, such highly offensive images arouse strong reactions. Some people speak of development pornography, the reduction of human suffering to an object used to make money. Luckily, most NGOs have long since given up this style of presentation. And the most clear-headed of them have denounced the economic mechanisms that cause and explain (at least to a certain degree) the situation of the countries of the South."

Thierry Verhelst (1987).

Images are important in shaping our attitudes to life especially as lived in distant places. Images can be liberating or debilitating depending on the context and content of their use - especially when they are used in education and, even more especially, when used with young children. This is an issue we need to be particularly sensitive to as regards images of the Third World and the messages they put out and the understandings or misunderstandings they help to create.

In 1989 to help overcome these problems, the European NGO-EU Liaison Committee (which represents European NGOs in their relations with the Commission of the European Union) agreed a voluntary code for advertising. The Code seeks to be a guide for the way in which the people of the Third World are projected in the work of the NGOs. It calls on NGOs to:

- avoid catastrophic or idyllic images which appeal to charity and lead to a clear conscience rather than a consideration of the root problems
- present people as human beings in a manner which respects their cultural identity and human dignity
- allow Third World people to speak for themselves rather than through a third party
- illustrate that Third World people do take responsibility for themselves
- avoid generalisations
- explain all the causes of disaster or crisis - both internal and external
- emphasise interdependence and joint responsibility
- explain the causes of poverty
- avoid all forms of discrimination
- consult local Third World partners in the design of the messages
- ensure others observe the code.

▼ References

Actionaid (1995) **The Reality of Aid,** Earthscan, London.

Organisation for Economic Co-operation and Development (1994) **Development Co-operation: Development Assistance Committee Report,** Paris.

World Bank (1995) **World Development Report,** Oxford University Press.

Michael P. Todaro (1994) **Economic Development,** London, Longman.

Michael Edwards and David Hulme (eds.1992) **Making a Difference: NGOs and Development in a Changing World,** London, Earthscan.

Ian Smillie (1995) **The Alms Bazaar: Altruism under Fire - Non-Profit Organisations and International Development,** London, Intermediate Technology Publications.

Anne Winter (1995) **Is Anyone Listening? Communicating Development in Donor Countries,** Geneva, UN Non-Governmental Liaison Service.

Colm Regan (1996) **Images and Impact: Media and Voluntary Agency Images, Messages and their Impact,** Cork, Comhlamh Action Network.

D.C. Korten (1990) **Getting to the 21st Century: Voluntary Action and the Global Agenda,** Connecticut, Kumarian Press.

Liaison Committee of Development NGOs to the European Communities (1989) **Code of Conduct: Images and Messages Relating to the Third World,** Brussels.

Joanna Macrae and Anthony Zwi (eds. 1994) **War and Hunger: Rethinking International Responses to Complex Emergencies,** London, Zed Press with Save the Children Fund.

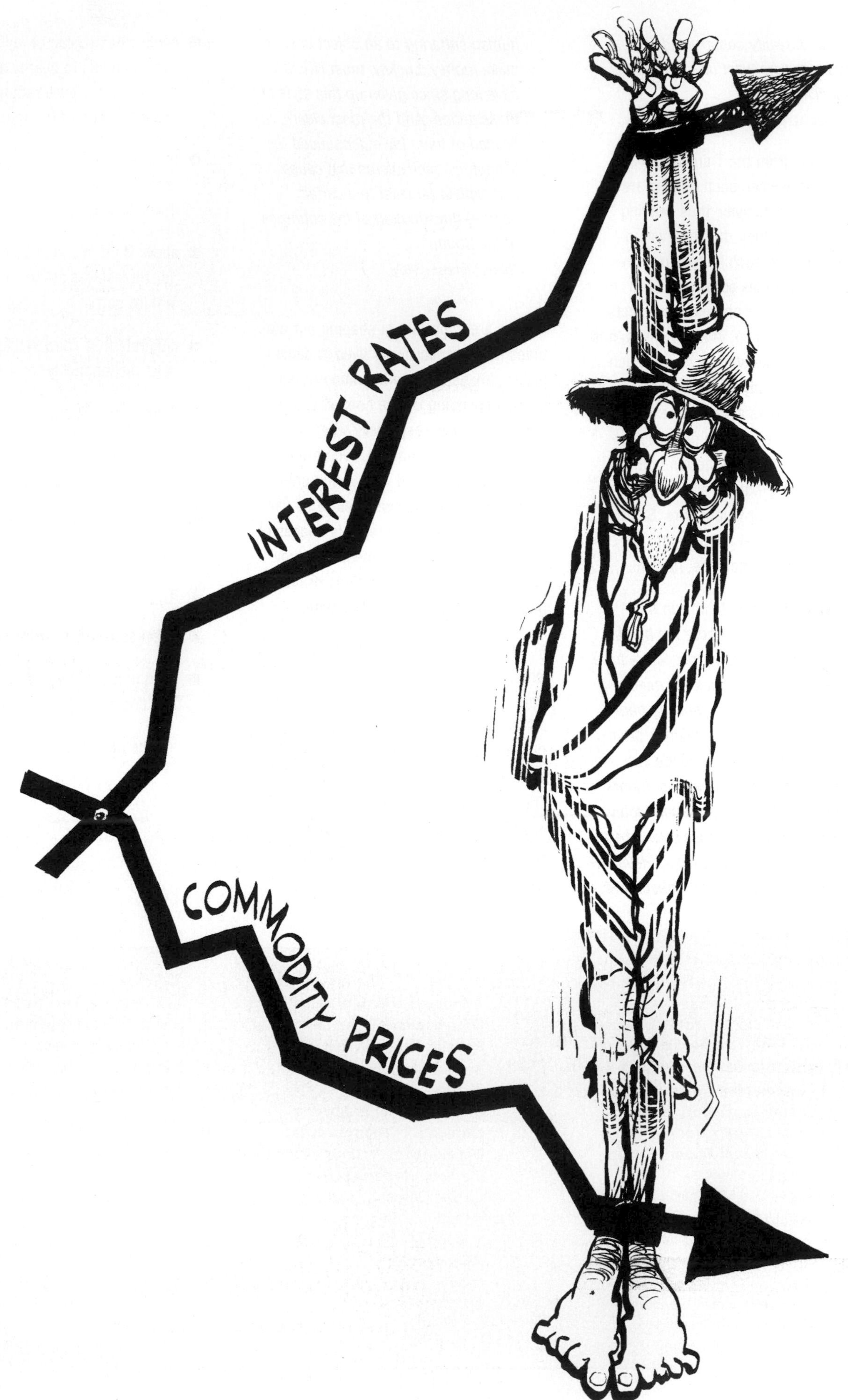
INTEREST RATES
COMMODITY PRICES

Is Debt the New Colonialism?

DEBT: THE NEW COLONIALISM

Jean Somers

"Were I a Third World leader in the dock, accused of getting my country hopelessly ensnared in debt, my defence would be that money was too cheap in the 1970s not to take advantage of the windfall... How was I, a debtor government, to foresee - much less control - the unprecedented upward swing of interest rates, due largely to demented military spending by the capitalist world super-power? I would further tell the jury: 'Every single Western expert who ever came to our country, especially those from the development banks, told us that to develop we had to industrialise. Was our country to remain for ever in peonage, exporting raw materials North so that others could transform them into finished goods and make all the money? Where were we supposed to get the capital for energy and for industrialisation if not by borrowing?'"

Susan George (1988) ***A Fate Worse Than Debt***, Pelican.

Introduction

Debt continues to be a major burden for developing countries a decade and a half after the start of the debt crisis. The continued existence of Third World debt challenges the accepted view of North-South relationships, particularly that of a generous North providing significant resources for Southern development. On the contrary, developing countries pay four times more in debt repayments than they receive in official aid. Debt repayments rise while aid levels drop. This raises the stark question, who is aiding whom?

It can be argued, however, that the debt problem, isn't ultimately about money although this has reached colossal levels. It is about the power relationships between North and South and about who benefits from the continued existence of the debt treadmill. Under the old colonial system, the colonisers extracted raw materials from their colonies for their own development, whereas now wealth is extracted in the form of debt repayments.

Third World Debt: The Scale of the Problem

According to the World Bank Third World debt now stands at the astronomical level of $1.9 trillion. As with individual debt, the immediate problem isn't necessarily the amount owed but the ability to make the repayments due. Poor countries are paying Northern governments, banks and financial institutions $16.5 billion per month or $542 million per day in debt repayments. This represents a huge outflow of desperately needed resources from developing countries. They are, in fact, paying their debts with the health, welfare and even, in extreme cases, the lives of their people.

Getting into Debt

Countries have always borrowed - to sort out temporary difficulties paying their import bills or to provide investment for major projects. Debt in itself isn't a problem when loans have been used productively and the borrower is able to repay. The immediate question is how did these countries get so deeply into debt? Why are they unable to repay the loans? Underlying this question is a more fundamental one - who is responsible for the debt problem?

The immediate roots of the crisis are to be found in the quadrupling of oil prices in 1973 . This generated billions of surplus dollars for the oil producing countries, much of which they deposited in Western banks. These became known as petrodollaras. The banks were anxious to lend these dollars so they would be earning interest. They were encouraged in this by Northern governments who wished to avoid a serious recession in the industrialised world by ensuring that developing countries were able to continue to import from the North. They were supported in this by the International Monetary Fund.

Developing countries themselves were desperate for loans - to cover their increased oil costs and also for development. The needs of the banks and those of developing countries appeared neatly matched. Interest rates were low, money was plentiful. Banks were so anxious to lend that they poured out loans without taking normal banking precautions, e.g. checking the viability of the projects for which they were lending. To quote Angel Gurria, head of Mexico's Office of Public Credit: *'The Banks were hot to get in. All the banks in the US and Europe and Japan stepped forward. They showed no foresight. They didn't do any credit analysis. It was wild.'* They were particularly interested in large scale projects because they wanted to shift big sums of money. Banks operated on the principle that as they were lending to governments and governments can't go bankrupt, their loans were safe.

How was the money spent?

In the first instance borrowed money was used to cover increased energy bills following the oil price rises - and this accounted for a quarter of the debt accumulated. Significant amounts of the money were spent unproductively or disappeared through corruption. This was partly due to the undemocratic nature of most of the borrowing governments. Most Latin American countries, where the bulk of the loans went, were run by military dictatorships during the '70s. A further important factor was the prevailing model of development shared by borrowers and lenders alike. Northern style modernisation was seen as the key goal to be pursued by Southern governments. This involved large scale infrastructural projects - building roads, airports, hydroelectric schemes - to promote rapid industrialisation, leaving agriculture, the source of income for the majority of people in many countries, seriously neglected.

> *Large scale projects:* These were preferred by the banks who wanted to shift large sums of money as quickly as possible. Military governments also preferred giant projects many of which had a devastating effect on the environment. Big projects were seen as prestigious but were often accompanied by waste and corruption. In the Philippines, the Bataan Nuclear power plant planned in 1976 was sited in the middle of the Pacific earthquake zone at the foot of a volcano. It cost $2.1 billion and according to the New York Times, President Marcos received $80 million commission from the company contracted to build the plant. Bolivia borrowed for an oil refinery with a capacity way beyond its needs.
>
> *Capital flight:* Some of the loans never made it into the borrowing country's economy. Massive sums were siphoned off and returned to bank accounts in the USA. Susan George estimates that $55 billion escaped back into US banks in capital flight between 1977 and 1983.
>
> *Military spending:* Given that many borrowing countries were run by military dictators, it isn't surprising that military spending rocketed between 1972 and 1981 from $2.5 billion to $29 billion.

Who was responsible?

Clearly a bonanza of irresponsible borrowing and lending took place. Unaccountable military dictators were supported by loans from equally unaccountable bankers. Northern governments and the IMF also carry a share of the blame, their main concern being to protect the industrialised world against recession. The people of Third World countries who neither authorised nor benefited from the loans are now shouldering the debt burden. Dominga de Velasques, speaking on behalf of Amas de Casa (Housewives) of La Paz Bolivia expresses this reality well:

> *"And we, the housewives, ask ourselves: What have we done to incur this foreign debt? Is it possible that our children have eaten too much? Is it possible that they have studied in the best colleges? Have our wages become too great? Together we say: No, no , we have not eaten too much. No, we have not dressed any better. We do not have better medical assistance. Then to whom have the benefits gone? Why are we the ones who have to pay for this debt?"*

An insider's view comes from Jorge Sol, former IMF executive director for Central America:

> *"The Third World elites who borrowed the money came from the same class as those who lent it and those who managed it at the IMF. They went to the same schools, belonged to the same clubs. They all profited from the debt"*

The bubble bursts

A number of developments towards the end of the '70s brought the lending and spending spree to a halt. The cost of repaying loans from the banks shot up as interest rates rose sharply. The increase was a knock on effect from a rise in US interest rates aimed at attracting investment to the US in order to tackle their huge deficit

WHO ARE THE INTERNATIONAL MONETARY FUND AND WORLD BANK?

The International Monetary Fund and World Bank were set up by the Allies towards the end of the Second World War at Bretton Woods in the USA. They are sometimes referred to as the Bretton Woods Institutions (BWIs). The Allies saw a need for international institutions which could support post war rehabilitation and promote international trade which had ground to a halt during the war. There was strong feeling about the need to prevent the conditions which contributed to World War II recurring. These were seen as protectionist policies whereby countries undercut each other, the collapse of commodity prices, stock exchange collapse and most importantly mass unemployment which was seen as a significant contributory factor to the rise of fascism.

The role of the IMF would be to support an orderly international monetary system. This would help facilitate international trade. It now has 179 member countries. Each member state enters into an agreement to allow its currency to be exchanged for other currencies with a minimum of restrictions, to inform the IMF about its monetary and financial policies, and to adjust these policies to accommodate the needs of other members. Countries with balance of payment problems can borrow from the Fund. In return they must implement economic policies laid down by the IMF. The Fund's Articles of Agreement specify that these policies must be implemented "without resorting to measures destructive of national or international prosperity".

The World Bank is the IMF's sister institution. Although its initial role was to help rebuild Europe after the war, its primary focus since then has been to provide longer term loans to developing countries to support their development. It has funded dams, roads and electrification schemes, etc.

In recent years, the distinction between the roles of the IMF and World Bank have become somewhat blurred. Together they have been providing adjustment loans to heavily indebted countries to enable them to pay off their creditors, especially the commercial banks. These loans are given in exchange for the adoption of structural adjustment programmes.

Unlike the UN where the principle of one country one vote largely prevails, voting power in the IMF and World Bank is related to the size of the financial contribution countries make. Inevitably these institutions are dominated by the views of the richest and most powerful states. The US holds by far the greater share of voting power.

which was run up to finance the US's largest ever peacetime military build up. Commodity prices also fell dramatically. Developing countries depend on export of primary goods - coffee, cotton, copper - to earn the foreign exchange needed to repay their debts. External debt must be paid in foreign exchange (one of the major world currencies, e.g., dollars or yen). Indebted countries were now faced with a situation where the cost of their loans had rocketed while their ability to repay had declined.. On top of this oil prices rose steeply once more.

The interest rate and oil price rises coupled with commodity price drops highlight the fact that even if all the loans had been well spent, developing countries would still have found themselves deeply in debt. The debt crisis cannot be explained within the popular stereotype of corrupt, inefficient Southern governments mis-managing their economies. Clearly the needs of the USA, and the unequal trading relationship between North and South were core factors. A further factor was the willingness to do business with oppressive military regimes. The IMF, for example, made a loan to General Somoza, the Nicaraguan dictator, just before he was routed by the Sandinista guerrillas. It was clear to the world Somoza was about to be deposed. The General emptied the coffers before he fled the country.

The debt crisis was recognised as such only when it was perceived as a threat to the international banking system. In August 1982, Mexico, one of the biggest debtors, announced that they could not continue to repay their debt. The threat of a default sent shudders throughout the international community.

Divide and Rule: Creditors' Cartels

Fearing the collapse of their banks, Northern governments moved swiftly to contain the crisis. The priority was to ensure that indebted countries continued to pay as a default could undermine confidence in major banks. The banks had to be protected at all costs from the consequences of their irresponsibility. The crisis was defined as a problem of individual countries which had borrowed too much rather than also being a result of how the international community had handled the oil crisis.

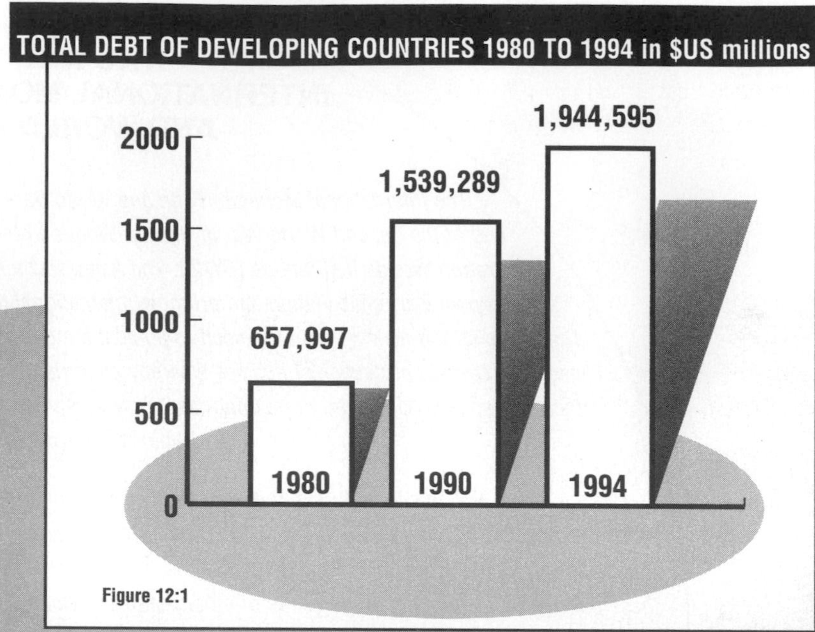

Figure 12:1

A major concern was to prevent developing countries uniting in a debtors' cartel which could speak from a position of strength, dictating terms, e.g. setting limits to how much they could or would repay. It was made clear to debtors what the consequences of default would be. R. T. MacNamara, then Deputy Secretary of the USA Treasury spelt this out in a speech to the US Chamber of Commerce in October 1983

> *'.. the foreign assets of a country that repudiated its debt would be attacked by creditors throughout the world; its exports seized by creditors at each dock where they landed; its national airlines unable to operate; and its sources of desperately needed capital goods and spare parts virtually eliminated. In many countries, even food imports would be curtailed. Hardly a pleasant scenario.'*

In 1984 Argentina, one of the biggest debtors found itself isolated when its government tried to stop paying interest. Newly elected President Alan Garcia in Peru announced in his inaugural speech in 1985 that he would limit debt payments to 10% of export earnings. The IMF retaliated by declaring Peru ineligible for all loans. Peru was boycotted by all lenders, commercial banks and the World Bank. Starved of resources conditions in Peru deteriorated.

While ensuring debtors were isolated, the creditors came together, themselves, in cartels to deal with developing countries on a case by case basis. Debt was owed to three groups of creditors: to commercial banks (commercial debt), to individual governments (bilateral debt) and to international financial institutions like the IMF and World Bank (multilateral debt). The banks were seen as the priority creditors at the start of the crisis. Individual indebted countries were forced to negotiate with all of its commercial creditors together. Government to government debt is dealt with in the Paris Club - another creditors' cartel which developing countries must approach individually.

Setting the Debt Treadmill in Motion

The first step in tackling the crisis was to raise the necessary loans for developing countries to ensure they maintained their repayments until new arrangements could be reached on debt payments. As a result of this approach the debt crisis is still with us a decade and a half later. Debts mounted as countries used new loans to repay old debts, leading to greater interest payments due and so the debt reached its current colossal levels. Debtor countries are only able to repay part of what is owing and unpaid debts also swell the size of the total outstanding debt.

The main tool used to deal with the crisis was debt rescheduling. By

COUNTRY	DEBT PER CAPITA	GNP PER CAPITA
Mozambique	$319	$ 60
Ethiopia	$ 86	$110
Tanzania	$290	$110
Uganda	$175	$170
Zambia	$818	$352
Nicaragua	$2,678	$340
Honduras	$715	$580

postponing repayment dates, the immediate pressure was eased. There have been endless reschedulings over the past decade and a half with different creditors - the commercial banks and individual governments. This has placed a huge drain on the policy, planning and financial expertise of debtor governments. It is estimated that during the '80s African governments participated in over 8,000 debt meetings only to receive tiny amounts of debt reductions. While some debts have been written off, these have not alleviated the problem as only a small portion of what countries are unable to repay has been dealt with. In fact, for ever dollar of the debt of the lowest income indebted countries (mainly Africa) that has been forgiven since 1989 another three have been added to the debt burden. It is estimated that the lowest income countries will need debt reduction in the region of 80-100% in order to escape the debt treadmill, that is to bring their debt burden to a level where they will no longer need continual rescheduling or new borrowing to cover old loans. There have been a plethora of debt relief plans.

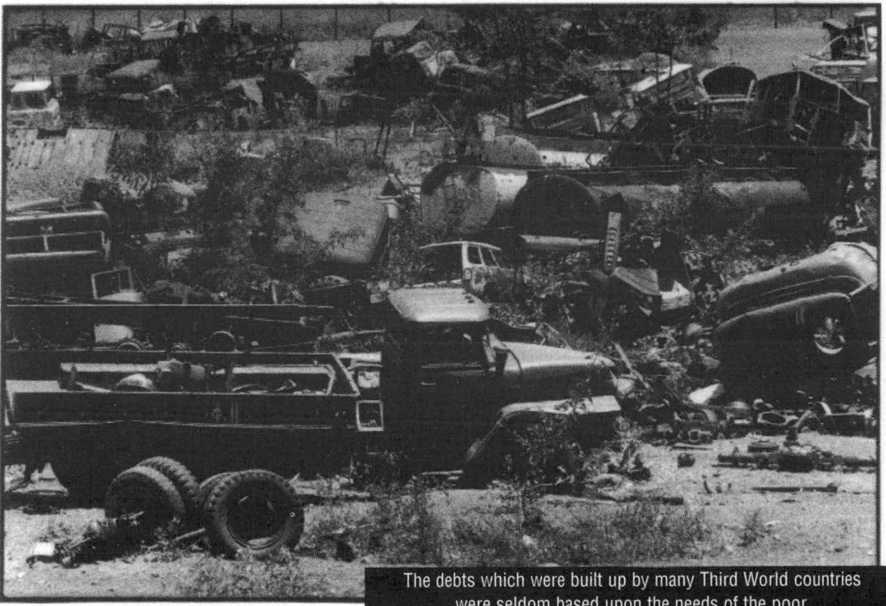

The debts which were built up by many Third World countries were seldom based upon the needs of the poor.

It is frustrating that all the technical expertise has been applied to developing debt plans which just keep the treadmill operating rather than going to the heart of the problem which is the need for debt cancellation.

Policing the Debt Crisis: Enter The International Monetary Fund and World Bank

The IMF and World Bank play a dual role in the debt crisis:

a) As major creditors:

While the debt crisis started as a problem between Banks and developing countries, the biggest burden for the poorest countries, is now multilateral debt, owed mainly to the IMF and World Bank. Debt to multilateral creditors increased form $98 billion to $304 billion between 1982 and 1992 and now 50% of the debt repayments of the poorest countries goes to international bodies, mainly the IMF and World Bank. This debt is particularly onerous as it can neither be rescheduled nor cancelled. These bodies are adamant that their debts must be repaid at whatever the cost even though the price paid is the lives and welfare of the poorest people. Uganda pays 4 times more in debt repayments than it does on health - the bulk of its repayments goes to the IMF. The IMF will argue that as it is a lender of last resort, its debts must be repaid. The World Bank argues that if it cancels debts its credibility with the financial markets will be damaged and so they will have to pay a higher interest on the money they borrow to lend developing countries.

There is a growing recognition that these arguments are spurious. The amount of debt owed by the lowest income countries, while a huge burden on their small economies, is a drop in the ocean in terms of the international money markets. Further, both of these institutions have considerable reserves which could be used for debt cancellation. Part of the reason for a financial institution to build up reserves, in the first place, is against the possibility of borrowers defaulting on their debts.

b) As managers of the debt repayment process:

The IMF was given the role of reforming developing countries' economies so they would be in a position to repay their debts from their own foreign exchange earnings. This was done by imposing 'adjustment programmes' on indebted countries with the support of the World Bank. While 'adjustment' suggests minor changes, these programmes operate as ideological battering rams, forcing root and branch changes which open Southern economies to Northern trade and investment. It can be argued that while the debt is a burden to developing countries, it has proved an opportunity for the North to tighten its stranglehold on the South.

Adjustment programmes are a set of 'free market' economic policies whose stated aims are: - to attract foreign investment by removing controls on investment and eliminating barriers to trade; to boost foreign exchange earnings by promoting exports and to reduce government deficits by cuts in public spending.

While adjustment programmes may vary slightly from country to country, typical policies include: currency devaluation, the removal of trade tariffs, cutting social spending, e.g. on health, education and food subsidies; privatising government enterprises; cutting wages; restricting credit and increasing interest rates.

Why did developing countries introduce policies which were inevitably going to be unpopular with their people? The incentive to cooperate is that an IMF agreed programme is a pre-requisite for access to money from any source - governments, commercial banks, the IMF or World Bank. Once the principle of a case by case approach to the debt crisis was established in the early '80s, the second step of ongoing intervention in individual country's economies became a possibility. Tanzania demonstrates clearly how the process works. For the first half of the 80s Tanzania, under President Nyerere, refused to implement IMF conditions. As a result aid to Tanzania plummeted from $147 million in 1980 to $20 million in 1985. President Nyerere resigned enabling a new president more willing to do business with the IMF to take over and Tanzania is now undertaking its third adjustment programme.

The impact of structural adjustment

The emphasis of adjustment is on broad macroeconomic policies, covering fiscal policy, trade policy and interest rates. There is no recognition that a well educated, healthy population is a key element in promoting sustainable development. There is no mention of how adjustment policies will affect people on the ground. The assumption is that these policies will generate economic growth from which all will benefit. No consideration is given as to how any wealth generated will be distributed, the unfounded assumption being that the benefits of adjustment will trickle down to all sectors of society. As it was always believed that adjustment would be a short term process, no provision was necessary for safety nets to protect the poorest people from the long term effects of harsh economic policies.

Adjustment had and continues to have a devastating effect mainly on poor people but also on sections of the middle class in indebted countries.

Cuts in Government Expenditure

Public expenditure cuts have been savage with health and education heavily affected, widespread redundancies among public employees and the removal of food subsidies. The costs of these cuts are carried disproportionately by people in poverty. The price is not just a one off payment but will have an impact way into the future as is recognised by UNICEF:

> *"Hundreds of thousands of the developing world's children have given their lives to pay their countries' debts, and many millions more are still paying the interest with their malnourished minds and bodies"*

The effects of government cuts are well documented in many Southern countries:

- In Africa real spending per head on education dropped by one third. Schools have been left without books. Teachers' morale has been sapped by wage cuts and lack of teaching materials. Increasingly, local communities have been called on to fill the gap left by the withdrawal of state support by paying to maintain schools and finance salaries. It has been estimated that in Zambia parents pay 80% of the costs of primary education .

- In Latin America average State spending on primary education fell from $164 a head at the beginning of the 1980s to $118 at the end.

- In Tanzania primary school enrolment dropped from 100% in 1979 to 63% in 1990. As in other developing countries, evidence shows that there is a disproportionately higher drop out rate among girls.

- In Nicaragua overall budget spending on health is now less than half the level in the early '80s. Infant mortality rates are increasing after declining steadily for more than a decade

- Cholera returned to South America for the first time in 60 years in 1991 following the deterioration of sewage and water systems . TB and malaria are also on the rise.

The removal of food subsidies is often the first adjustment shock for ordinary people. In Tanzania the price of maizemeal, the main staple food, shot up 450% when the subsidy was removed. The removal of food subsidies hurts poor people most. The household diet changes, less is eaten per meal and less meals per day are eaten. Malnutrition, particularly in children, increases, with irreversible future consequences.

Because of the emphasis put on increasing exports to earn the dollars needed to repay debts, the most fertile land is often used to grow cash crops for export. Crops like tobacco, cotton, soya and sugar cane are given priority in the allocation of land, credit and technical support while beans, cassava and other crops which form the staple diet are unsupported. The bias towards export crops favours large commercial farms and increases inequality in landownership as small holders are forced off their land and become landless labourers or swell the numbers in the shanty towns in the large urban centres.

Jamaica: After two decades of adjustment

Jamaica was one of the first developing countries to implement a structural adjustment programme. The IMF's role has been controversial from the start. Its first programme conflicted directly with the social programme of an elected government. The opportunity to negotiate further funds from the IMF became a major issue for political parties during the 1980 election.

The debt burden continues to drain much needed resources while poverty remains high. Between 1988 and 1992 the government cut its expenditure on everything except debt repayments by a quarter. In 1992/93, total debt servicing was over 7 times the health budget. In 1995/96 debt servicing was expected to take 41% of the government's total budget. Yet in 1995, 30% of the population was living in poverty .

Budget cuts have taken a heavy toll in the education sector. Expenditure on primary education declined in real terms by about 30% between 1977 and 1987. Teachers' salaries have been outstripped by inflation and many teachers now have to take on two jobs in order to live. There has been an exodus from Jamaica of qualified teachers. In 1976 over 60% of high school teachers had university degrees. By 1989, after 13 years of adjustment, less than 30% had degrees.

. Even the World Bank was forced to acknowledge the consequences of debt and adjustment on Jamaica

'In 1991/92 half of tax revenues went to service external debt, while roads deteriorated for lack of maintenance, schoolchildren were short of books, and hospitals were short of medicines. The indirect effects compound the problem by slowing growth. The high debt burden makes business reluctant to invest in Jamaica and encourages young people to move abroad if they have acquired enough education and skills to achieve access to the international labour market'

Source: Christian Aid **Sacrificing the Future: Structural Adjustment in Jamaica,**

The Debt Boomerangs Back on the North

While the major burden of the debt crisis lies on the people of the South of the globe, the North has not escaped unaffected. There are a number of ways in which the debt crisis is indirectly impacting on the North:

- environmentally: because we live in one world, the effects of environmental destruction are felt across the globe. One of the most significant ways the debt boomerangs back on the North is through the global problems arising from deforestation. Forest destruction accounts directly for roughly one-fifth of greenhouse gas emissions which contribute to unpredictable climate change, including global warming. While two-thirds of the emissions are produced by cars and industry in the North which must be curtailed, the effects of deforestation are causing widespread concern.
- drugs: the drugs trade is being protected by many governments because it is one of the few sources of foreign exchange needed to pay off their debts. This alarming connection between drugs and debt is illustrated clearly in Bolivia, Peru and Columbia, the three countries most deeply involved in the cocaine trade in Latin America. Bolivia has the most drug dependent economy in the region and is saddled with massive debts. It is estimated that one job out of every three or four is provided by drug related activities. Without this drug economy, the Bolivian government could not generate enough revenue to meet payments on its massive debt.
- unemployment: the contraction of Southern economies, in particular the severe cut back on imports, has had a direct impact on Northern economies relying on Southern, particularly Latin American markets, to sell their goods. This has resulted in the loss of millions of manufacturing and agricultural jobs. The USA was particularly affected because of their closeness to the Latin American markets. It is estimated that by 1985 nearly 1.4 million jobs had been lost due to the recession in the South. In the case of Europe, it is estimated that about half a million jobs or potential jobs were lost each year as a result of the debt crisis in the '80s.

Source: Susan George (1992) **The Debt Boomerang: How the Third World Debt Harms Us All,** London, Pluto Press.

Women as the shock absorbers of adjustment

Research into how women in a low income community in Ecuador were affected by adjustment, found they were typically working in excess of 18 hours per day and sacrificing time with their children in order to generate income outside the home. The study concluded that 30% were coping; 55% were barely getting by, mortgaging the future of their children, and especially their daughters to survive; and another 15% were exhausted, their families disintegrating and children dropping out of school.

In Zambia a study of Chawama, a low income settlement in Lusaka, showed that the number of women working outside the home tripled during the 1980s. Most of this employment expansion has taken place in the informal economy, where female labour is typically concentrated in sectors with the lowest economic returns and where long hours of work are required to generate small amount of income.

A Zimbabwean woman living in a low income settlement in Harare highlighted the dilemmas facing women:

'My daughter is sick, but what am I supposed to do? If I take her to the clinic, I cannot afford to pay for treatment - so what is the point? If I stay at home to care for her, how will we buy the food we need to stay alive?

Source: Kevin Watkins (1995) **The Oxfam Poverty Report,** Oxfam.

Why Luis and Dorcelli are hungry

Luis and Dorcelli have lived in the southernmost state of Brazil all their lives. Luis inherited a small plot of land from his father, on which they grew beans and maize for themselves and their five children. They usually had enough over to sell in the local market to cover their other needs. For the months following harvest all was well but as the year advanced they had to borrow to tide themselves over between sowing and reaping. This used not to be too much of a worry, as the government made cheap credits available to small farmers. It was they, after all, who grew most of the food for the Brazilian population.

However, when the debt crisis broke in 1982 things began to change. Commercial banks were unwilling to continue lending money to the Brazilian government, afraid that it would not pay it back. They insisted first on an agreement between Brazil and the International Monetary Fund to 'restructure' the economy. Government expenditure was to be cut. There would be no more room for lending to peasant farmers at low interest rates. Incentives would be given instead to large farmers who were planting crops for export rather than home consumption.

Luis and Dorcelli thus had to turn to another source of finance when they money ran out at sowing time. They borrowed money from their local bank which charged them interest at 24% a month. Their debt soared. Harvest came. They sold their entire crop, leaving nothing for themselves to eat but still they could not pay back the loan.

Now Luis and Dorcelli live in a small wooden shack in a poor area of the town of Sapiranga. They have no land, no stable income and are often hungry. Dorcelli and the children use the daylight hours to sew shoes at home for a pitiful wage from a local shoe factory. Luis takes jobs where he can. They had to sell their land to the bank to repay their loan. Now it has been taken over by a large landowner who is growing soya beans to feed European cows.

Source: Clive Robinson (1989) **Hungry Farmers,** Christian Aid

Raiding natural resources

Adjustment has lead to intensified exploitation of natural resources. Yet the IMF and World Bank have not counted the environmental costs of their programmes. Natural resources are taken as a free gift to the market. Increased emphasis on export-led growth has played a key part in environmental degradation. In Africa and Asia, the emphasis has been on increased logging for timber exports. In Brazil, providing land for cattle ranching to provide meat for the North American market has been the motivating force for clearing large swathes of the Amazonian forest. Small holders pushed off their farms by the expansion of commercial farming also moved to the Amazonian area where they burned part of the forest in order to clear land to produce subsistence crops.

As pointed out already, an inevitable result of all developing countries struggling to produce more of the same few commodities will be a glut on the market and a drop in prices. To counter this the World Bank has been encouraging countries to diversify into non-traditional products e.g. luxury foods and flowers for Northern markets. In many cases this has resulted in massive use of agrochemicals so that products which are mainly non-indigenous can reach the high standards demanded by Northern consumers. Ethiopia, Kenya and Columbia are supplying cut flowers to the Western market. According to Miala Majaraj, a Dutch freelance researcher writing in the *Guardian* Newspaper on 7 November 1994: '*commercial flower-growing is the most polluting form of agriculture known. Nobody will buy a bloom that has been half-eaten by bugs. So every hectare must be fed 10 tons of fertilisers and pesticides every year: the soil must be biologically dead.*'

Arguing about the effects of Adjustment Programmes

Adjustment frees up the market and reduces government intervention in the economy through:

- ***reducing import controls:*** competition from cheap imports forces producers to become more efficient is the argument of the IMF and the World Bank while that of their critics is that such competition puts local factories and farms out of work.
- ***reducing government subsidies and price controls:*** in this way only efficient producers survive and government spending is reduced argues the IMF and the World Bank while others claim that this leads to an increase in the price of important basic goods (e.g. fertiliser), people become worse off and can afford less food, education, health care etc.
- ***privatising industry and services:*** through this inefficient government systems are closed down and opportunities for corruption are reduced, argues the IMF and the World Bank but critics claim that, as a result, remote and rural areas lose essential services because it is not profitable for private industry to supply them.
- ***devaluing local currencies:*** exports become cheaper for foreign buyers so more are sold while imports become more expensive and so fewer are bought, argues the World Bank and the IMF. Critics disagree arguing that as a result land needed for food is frequently used to grow cash crops while the price of many important and vital imports such as medicine and equipment goes up.

Adjustment tackles inflation and reduces the government deficit through:

- ***promoting high interest rates:*** the supply of money is controlled and people reduce spending argues the IMF and the World Bank while others argue that this means both companies and farmers cannot afford to borrow and so go out of business or reduce production.
- ***reducing government spending:*** this reduces the government's deficit argues the World Bank and the IMF. Critics argue that this leads to the cuts being felt hardest by those often in most need.

Adjustment often introduces social safety nets, for example, food for work or income support for the poor:

- this protects the poorest while adjustment programmes are given a chance to work argues the World Bank and the IMF while critics argue that many people are left out of these schemes and the economy often does not 'restart' because of a lack of funds.

Based on J. Madeley, D. Sullivan and J. Woodroffe (1994) **Who Runs the World?**, London, Christian Aid.

Unemployment grows

The World Bank states that a key element in their strategy to reduce poverty is increased employment. Problems arise when the actual policies implemented through IMF / World Bank structural adjustment programmes are examined. Cuts in government expenditure have inevitably led to huge job losses. UNICEF estimate that 300,000 health workers left Africa during the 1980s. In Nicaragua, unemployment has doubled and industrial employment had fallen by nearly a third by

1993. According to the International Labour Organisation, real wages in Africa have fallen by between 50% and 60% since the early '80s in most countries. In Argentina and Venezuela real wages dropped by 53% and 23% respectively between 1980 and 1990. Trade Union rights have been curtailed in Ghana, Zimbabwe, Mexico and the Philippines. Unemployment has been made worse by the abrupt removal of protective tariffs which has damaged local industry unable to compete with the flood of cheap imports. In Zambia more than 75% of textile factories closed in 1994 leading to mass unemployment.

Assessing adjustment

While the IMF and World Bank will claim that their policies are working where governments implement them rigorously, adjustment has failed to achieve its stated aim of creating an economic climate where indebted countries are able to service their debts. Indeed, over a decade of adjustment, the debt has risen as 'adjustment loans' piled up on the already enormous debt. What has been achieved is that commercial banks have continued to receive payment and so have been bailed out of the debt crisis. This has allowed the international financial community to claim that the debt crisis is now over. Yes, the crisis may be over for the banks but it continues to be a crisis for the people of indebted countries.

The IMF and World Bank will point to decreases in levels of inflation and to some economic growth. Certainly inflation has decreased from the astronomical levels it reached in the '80s and there has been some economic growth particularly in Latin America.

According to the World Bank African governments who followed closely the World Bank and IMF's policies succeeded in cutting their budget deficits by a third by the end of the 80s. These cuts, however, were mainly achieved through reduced spending rather than increased revenue, the axe falling particularly sharply on social investment. A significant feature of adjustment programmes is a drop in investment which has serious consequences for future growth, for employment and poverty reduction. Between 1980 and 1990 countries following intensive adjustment programmes suffered a drop in investment from 25% of gross domestic product to 15%.

In claiming success, the IMF and World Bank have focused on economic indicators - reducing inflation and budget deficits, interest rates, economic growth. They have not even tried to measure the effects on the distribution of resources within societies or on levels of poverty. In its 1994 report, ***Adjustment in Africa: reforms, results, and the road ahead,*** the World Bank is extremely tentative in its analysis of the impact of adjustment on poor people. They admit that they haven't got the necessary information to make a realistic assessment: *'It is a sorry state of affairs when we know least about poverty in the region where poverty is most a problem'.* All they can conclude is that *"Adjustment led growth has probably helped the poor".*

Poverty obviously predates the debt crisis and adjustment. These have, however, led to a seriously worsened situation. One of the most negative effects has been the reversal of gains in human development achieved over the previous two decades. In Latin America the 1980s started hopefully with a return to democracy across the continent as in one country after the other the military retreated to their barracks leaving government in civilian hands.

Social Safety Nets

An obvious question which arises is, were the IMF and World Bank not aware of the effects of their adjustment programmes? Their initial approach was to claim that adjustment involved short term pain for long term gain. As adjustment proved not to bring about a rapid economic recovery, growing concern was expressed at the unacceptable social costs. The 1987 UNICEF Report, ***Adjustment with a Human Face,*** marked a turning point. This Report highlighted the serious deterioration in child welfare in the '80s, particularly in nutrition and education. Adjustment policies were identified as an important contributory factor.

This led to some modification of adjustment programmes to integrate what became known as social safety nets with the aim of protecting the most vulnerable sectors from the harshest effects of adjustment. These have taken various forms, employment generation schemes like public works, nutrition supplements or exemption from health and education costs on a means tested basis. These are funded mainly through external aid.

While some schemes have been more effective than others, it is clear that overall they have been inadequate in the face of the harsh reality of adjustment. They have been badly targeted or badly designed, often not reaching those hardest hit by adjustment. A particular criticism has been the under-representation of women on employment schemes. In Bolivia, only 1% of those employed under the social fund were women; in Honduras, 75% of the jobs created went to men and only 16% of the participants on India's rural employment programme are women.

It seems clear that while safety nets are a recognition that poor people carry a disproportionate share of the burden of adjustment, they are not the answer to the social costs of adjustment. What is needed is a recognition that poverty alleviation should be a central focus of any reform programme rather than bolting on limited safety nets with the hope of mopping up the worst effects of adjustment

The Debt Crisis in Europe: an Irish example

How do the debt crises of European countries relate to those in the Third World? Ireland, for example, has an enormous debt, one of the highest debts per capita in the world. While there are some similarities between the causes and the impact of the debt there are also significant differences.

By 1994, Ireland's debt had reached almost £30 billion and absorbed almost a fifth of government expenditure. While Irish debt reached levels comparable to that of poor countries, it posed a less serious problem as far as international creditors were concerned because serious doubt was not cast on Ireland's ability to repay. This was due to Ireland's strong export performance and the fact that the country was perceived as being politically stable as a result of membership of the European Union.

The Irish government eventually brought the debt burden under control by a version of structural adjustment practised in developing countries. In 1987 health spending was cut by 6%, education by 7%, spending on roads and houses by 11%. Apart from the loss of services, the spiralling rate of unemployment can also be partly attributed to debt induced cuts. Ireland introduced and carried out its adjustment voluntarily without the intervention of the IMF.

Conclusion

The debt crisis has proved to be far more than a short sharp shock but instead is a long drawn out painful process and the end is still not in sight. This is largely because the political will doesn't exist to tackle the problem effectively. This is because the debt has proved a useful tool to force open developing countries economies to Northern financial interests - governments and transnational corporations. The IMF and World Bank are the agents for Northern interests coercing developing countries into a global economy in which they can only participate unequally. If they weren't trapped by debt, developing countries could not have been brought into line with such speed and apparent ease by the IMF and World Bank.

The debt crisis represents a huge transfer of resources from developing countries but it also represents a loss of autonomy and democracy as power moves from national governments to remote faceless financial institutions. While all countries North and South are being propelled forward towards greater globalisation, the pace and lack of room to manoeuvre to protect their own interest is far greater in developing countries.

This loss of ownership and control has derailed the development process. Resources and ownership are important features of an autonomous development process. Colonialism, the old and the new, is about imposing systems which operate in the interests of the powerful. Resolving the debt problem will open the way for more equitable North-South relations and for developing countries to prioritise the needs of their own people.

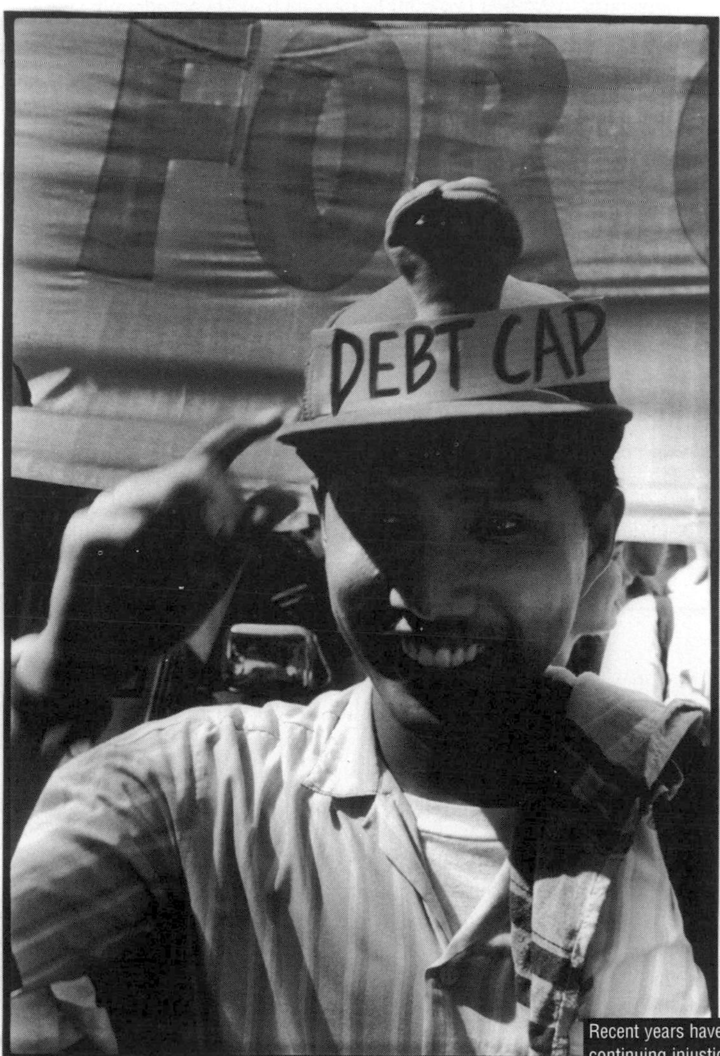

Recent years have seen the emergence of local organisations campaigning against the continuing injustice of debt and debt repayments as here in the Philippines in 1991.

Resisting Debt

Initial resistance took the form of strikes, demonstrations and what were called Èwhen the first price rises for basic goods followed adjustment. These took place from Argentina to Zambia. One of the most bloody IMF riots took place in l984 in the Dominican Republic when the price of basic foodstuff doubled and the price of medicines went up 200% . Four days of rioting left 112 dead and 500 wounded. Riots in Caracas, Venezuela broke out following the adoption of an adjustment programme in l989 which caused wages to collapse to less than half their l980 level and prices to shoot up as subsidies were cut. Hundreds died (estimates vary widely from 300 to 1,500). Demonstrations, strikes and riots have continued intermittently across various countries, highlighting the divisive and destabilising effects of these policies.

As debt and adjustment has continued a more co-ordinated people's response has emerged. Campaigning groups have formed in debtor countries and regions to raise awareness of how debt and structural adjustment underpin many of the economic and social problems people are facing. These groups campaign for debt cancellation, for radical changes in structural adjustment programmes, and the involvement of local organisations in dialogue on these policies.

"Better to forgive than to receive.
Stop the aid to the First World"
Philippine Freedom from Debt Coalition

Launched in l987, the Philippine Freedom from Debt Coalition (FDC) is the longest established and most visible Third World campaign. Backed by over 250 trade unions, grass roots organisations, political parties and academics, the campaign focuses on calling for a just solution to the country's debt which now stands at $34.4 billion. The FDC proposes that debt servicing be limited to 10% of their export earnings. It also focuses on budgetary issues. Almost 50% of the government budget is eaten up in debt servicing. The FDC points out that debt payments between l986 and l992 amounted to $23 billion while new money coming into the country only amounted to $14 billion. This left them with a deficit of $9 billion to find through budget cuts.

The title of their Newsletter, ***PAID*** (People against Immoral Debt), highlights one of their major campaigning points, opposing repayment of fraudulent debts. There was a substantial amount of corruption involved in the debt run up under President Marcos. They also call for a democratisation of the decision making on debt; the elected Philippines Congress was recently bypassed by the government who signed debt deals which accepted responsibility for some of the blatantly fraudulent loans run up by Marcos.

In their *"Campaign for a People Oriented Budget"*, they are calling for increased spending on health and education and other basic services and the reform of the tax system

Groups have also been formed in Africa (African Network on Debt and Development: AFRODAD) and Asia. Women's groups are also tackling structural adjustment and debt. The Philippine Freedom from Debt Coalition has a strong women's committee which works with women's groups. A number of women's networks developed in East Africa in the early '90s. Maude Mugisha from the Ugandan women's network which brings together over 20 women's groups visited Europe in l995. She outlined the purpose of the network - to ensure that women understand how debt and structural adjustment underpins many of the problems they are facing and to develop ways to influence the government, the IMF and World Bank. Women's networks have also been set up in Kenya and Tanzania.

Campaigning groups in the South are supported by campaign groups across the North. Campaigns in Europe group together in the European Network on Debt and Development. In the USA, the 50 Years is Enough Campaign (set up in l994 which marked the 50th anniversary of the IMF and World Bank) has led the demand for fundamental change in the way these institutions work.

References

Susan George (1988) **A Fate Worse Than Debt,** Pelican.

Christian Aid (1993) **Sacrificing the Future: Structural Adjustment in Jamaica,** London.

Susan George (l992) **The Debt Boomerang: How the Third World Debt Harms Us All,** London, Pluto Press.

Clive Robinson (l989) **Hungry Farmers,** London, Christian Aid.

Kevin Watkins (1995) **The Oxfam Poverty Report,** Oxford, Oxfam.

J. Madeley, D. Sullivan and J. Woodroffe (1994) **Who Runs the World?,** London, Christian Aid.

Mary McCarthy and Thomas McCarthy (1993) **Towards an Equitable Solution,** Dublin, Trocaire and Gill and Macmillan.

WHERE IT REALLY COUNTS: Trade and Transnationals

Colm Regan

"International trade conjures up images of giant cartels, impenetrable and seemingly endless rounds of GATT negotiations, disputes between the major economic powers, and frenetic activity on the floors of commodity markets. Such images partially reflect reality. But international trade is also to do with people's livelihoods and their most basic social and economic rights. For millions of the world's poorest people trade is part of daily life, and a crucial determinant of welfare...Trade has the power to create opportunities and support livelihoods; and it has the power to destroy them."

Kevin Watkins (1995) ***The Oxfam Poverty Report****, Oxford, Oxfam.*

Introduction

This is how journalist Paul Vallely outlined the connections between the international market and the price of cocoa and the poverty and vulnerability of hundreds of thousands of Brazil's poor:

"Her name was Maria, let us call her that, for she was anxious not to be identified. She thought I was a buyer from one of the multinational cocoa-processing firms which are the influential middle-men in the international chocolate industry. 'Raise the minimum wage. We work hard here, but we do not get enough to live off. We get some wage rises but the price rises are always more and faster..."

Wages in the cocoa plantations have fallen in recent years. At the time of my visit workers earned, on average, only two-thirds of what the Brazilian government decreed to be the national minimum wage which is itself, in real terms, worth less now than at any time since it was introduced in 1940. Working conditions had deteriorated too. Employers now routinely denied workers a national insurance card (to avoid the employer's contribution); they refused to pay the holiday pay or the annual bonus which was legally compulsory. Many routinely sacked all the workers after eighty-nine days, and then re-employed them after a few days gap, because certain statutory rights applied after ninety days. Others imposed new conditions on workers, only taking on women who could produce a doctor's certificate to show they had been sterilised or requiring all employees to sign an undated resignation letter so that they could be dismissed without payment or complications whenever the estate required. The alternative was all too clear - 225,000 of the area's 350,000 cocoa workers were currently unemployed.

The cause of all this is a fall in the international price of cocoa which has put sixty-five percent of the region's 350,000 cocoa workers out of a job as the plantation owners try to maintain their profit-margins. Cocoa is today only a third of the price it was on the international market in 1985..."

We are all vaguely aware of some connection between the price of the goods we buy or consume - our bar of chocolate or cup of coffee or tea - and the producers of the raw materials which go into such products, thousands of miles away.

Global Interdependence

In the 'global economy' of today, nothing better exemplifies the interconnectedness between us all than commodities - electrical goods, clothes, beverages, sugar, minerals etc. And nothing illustrates better the unequal nature and structure of that interconnectedness than those same products as we struggle to keep their end price to us as low as possible while those on the other end often struggle for the most basic of conditions, wages and dignity. And we all do this in a world which is increasingly dominated by a smaller and smaller group of larger and larger powerful corporations and countries who continue to 're-structure' the world's economy to suit their interests.

In today's global market the statistics of international trade and commerce are staggering. As the diagram below clearly illustrates, the richest 20% of the world's people control 84% of all world trade, while the poorest 20% control just 0.9% and as each year goes by their percentage declines further. The cost of current global markets to the Third World is graphically illustrated by the United Nations Development Programme diagram below.

Throughout the 1960s and 1970s, the total volume of world trade continued to grow, but throughout the 1980s this trend was reversed and is only now showing an upward direction once again. The causes of the decline include the impact of world recession in 1980-1983; fluctuations in the value of the US $; continuing decline in the value of Third World commodity prices; increased protectionism in the industrialised countries and the continuing debt crisis. The international trade slowdown has affected everyone but none more so than those in the Third World who have borne the brunt of its impact. In 1990, the Third World earned US$ 951 million from the export of goods and services - representing approximately 17.8% of world exports. This figure represented a serious decrease from 27.9% in 1980.

However within these figures there are huge variations. Four Asian countries - Hong Kong, Korea, Taiwan and Singapore - account for over one-third of all such exports. As economist Michael Todaro points out:

"...some exporters have prospered - notably the newly-industrialising countries (NICs), South Korea, Hong Kong, Singapore, and Taiwan and the Persian Gulf oil producers - while most others have stagnated or even declined in real terms (particularly those in sub-Saharan Africa and parts of Latin America). Thus while the four Asian exporters of manufactured products have more than doubled their share of total Third World manufactured exports by more than 250%, from 30.8% in 1965 to 82.8% in 1990, the non-oil producing, non-NIC, less developed countries have seen their shares steadily drop, especially during the difficult times of the 1980s."

For many of the world's poorest nations and peoples, especially in sub-Saharan Africa and Latin America, the situation has been disastrous with international trade statistics and trends spelling increased poverty and vulnerability at one end of the spectrum and incredible versatility and ingenuity at the other end (see Barefoot Businessmen and Women below).

Figure 13:1

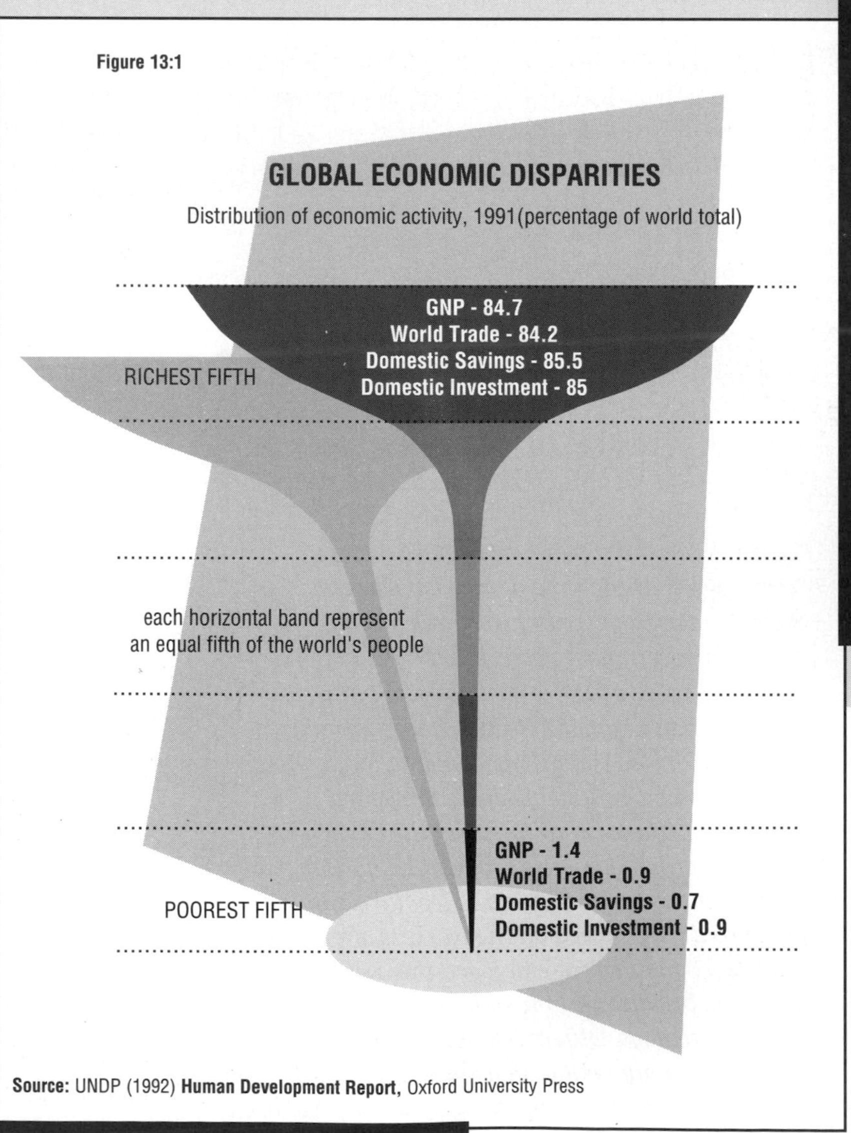

Source: UNDP (1992) **Human Development Report,** Oxford University Press

Nimble Fingers and Ruined Eyesight

It has become customary for many business people and governments to refer to the increased threat of the newly industrialising countries of Asia in world trade and manufacturing. The ability of companies (many of them multinationals) to produce goods for sale on the world market at much lower cost in such locations has often been used as a way to reduce wages and lower working standards in the industrialised world and to set workers from one part of the world in opposition to workers in other parts. Many industries have simply closed down manufacturing in the West in favour of production in low wage economies. However, from the point of view of human development it is worth considering the human cost of much of the economic miracle of what are often referred to as the 'Asian Tigers'. The following case study, from John Madeley's book ***Trade and the Poor,*** illustrates one important dimension of the miracle often forgotten in discussion.

One of the great 'success stories' from South-East Asia has been the electronics industry which has developed in the 'Export-processing Zones' of countries like South Korea. In this region, nine out of every ten workers are women aged between 16 and 23. *"Nimble fingers are a great asset in assembling tiny chips, but the process puts an unbearable strain on the eyes. In the process of assembling and testing electronics components, a silicon wafer about 2-4 inches (5-10 cm) in diameter might be sliced into about 500 separate chips. Each individual chip is bonded with wire lead; this is a labour intensive procedure in which each assembler, peering through a microscope or highly-powered magnifying lens, attaches a variety of minuscule wires, each the size of a human hair, to a chip using fine soldering equipment."*

According to an International Labour Office study: *"...After several years, it deteriorates to the point that the workers cannot continue."* John Madeley also points out that female microchip workers are also exposed to toxic chemicals and suspected carcinogens that can damage their health in the future. He cites the case of Elfreda Castellano who worked in the firm Dynetics Inc. in the Philippines and was confined to hospital after one year's work: she was diagnosed as having cancer of the lymph nodes caused by her work.

Other critics of the Asian model of economic development point to many other negative dimensions such as the lack of basic trade union rights in many industries (in some cases, unions are officially banned by the government); dangerous and hazardous working conditions; extensive environmental damage and increased loss of local control and sovereignty.

Sources: John Madeley (1992) ***Trade and the Poor,*** *London, Intermediate Technology.*
Walden Bello (1990) ***Brave New Third World****, London, Earthscan.*
David C. Korten (1995) ***When Corporations Rule the World,*** *London, Earthscan.*

Primary Commodity Dependence

For the vast majority of Third World countries primary commodities, (unprocessed or minimally processed raw materials) make up the major part of their exports. Excluding oil, 51 Third World countries depend on exports of three or fewer primary commodities for over 70% of their export earnings. Another 15 countries, 11 of them in Africa, depend on the export of three or fewer commodities for over 85% of their earnings and, despite arguments to the contrary, their dependence is growing. Such dependence might be acceptable if the international trade was stable and 'free' but this is not the case. International trade in such primary commodities is dominated, in most cases, by powerful multinational firms which influence prices dramatically; by severe restrictions in industrialised States on the import of anything but unprocessed products (making a mockery of the frequently quoted concept of the 'free market') and by massive fluctuations in prices and by serious terms of trade problems.

A brief review of the trends with regard to the most important primary commodities upon which many Third World countries depend for precious foreign earnings with which to fund development and repay their debt reveals, almost without exception, that price trends have been downwards and that they have fluctuated wildly making planning for development all the more difficult.

Figure 13:3

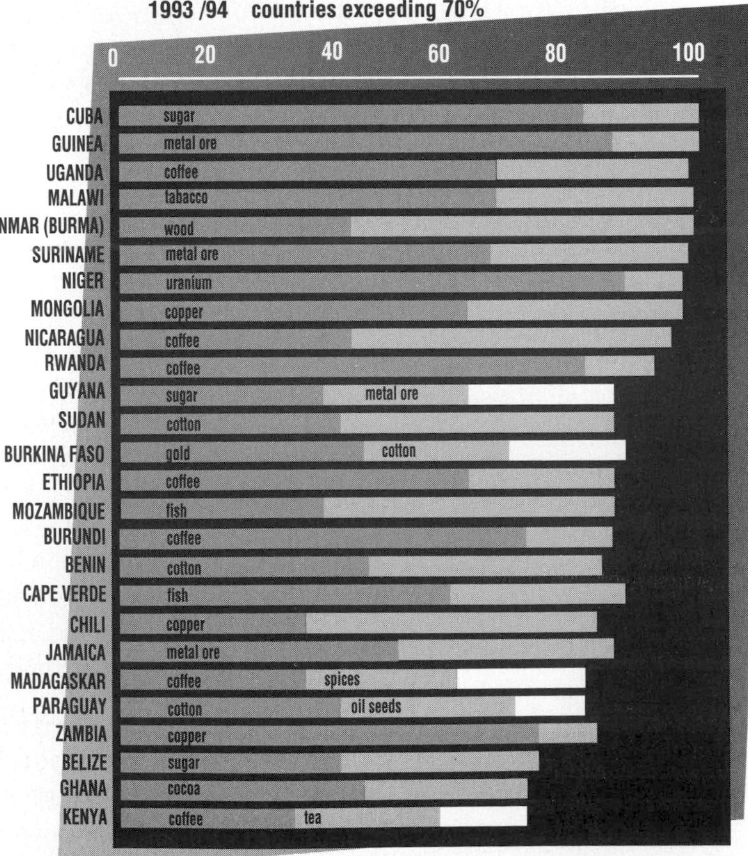

Source:
UNCTAD (1993) **Handbook of International Trade and Development Statistics**, Geneva

Figure 13:2

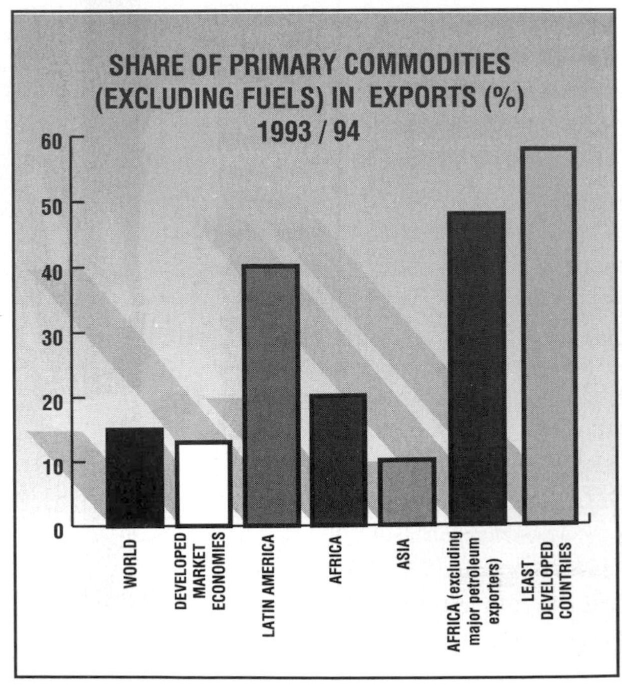

- In the case of tea, world prices have fallen steeply and according to the Food and Agriculture Organisation (FAO) "...tea prices are expected to remain depressed.";
- In the case of coffee, no other agricultural commodity has experienced a steeper fall in price, there is still massive overproduction and the price trend remains downwards;
- While cocoa prices rose by 50% between 1960 and 1990, this equalled a fall in real terms and UNCTAD foresaw, in a recent report "...increasing over supply and consequent persistent low prices in the coming years.";
- In March 1992, the price of sugar, a commodity in which almost every country is both producer and consumer, was below the cost of production with the long term prospects not good;
- While the price of cotton doubled between 1960 and 1990, it has not kept pace with inflation and prices are expected to remain depressed especially with rapidly increased production in China
- In the case of many other important primary commodity earners - tropical timber, palm oil, tobacco etc., the situation is much the same.

The tables on these page indicate the share of primary commodities in the exports of many regions and individual Third World states as well as price fluctuations for two key commodities - cocoa and coffee. In summary the export dependence of Third World countries on a limited number of primary commodities whose prices fluctuate considerably and which are controlled to a significant extent by transnational companies makes the development strategies of their governments highly uncertain.

Figure 13:4

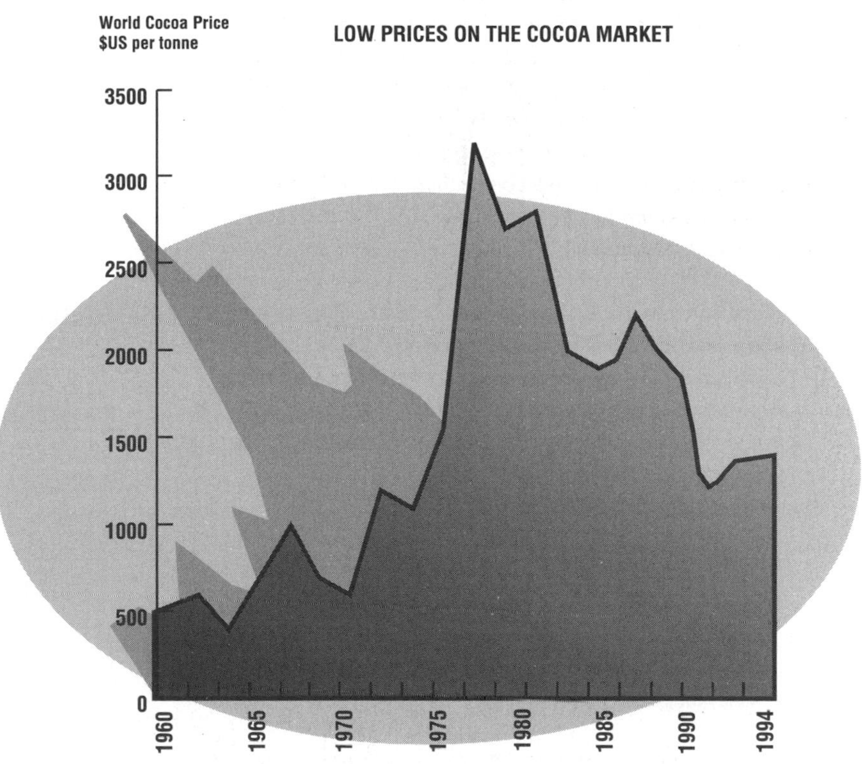

Source:
European Fair Trade Association (1995)
Fair Trade Year Book 2995, Maastricht

Figure 13:5

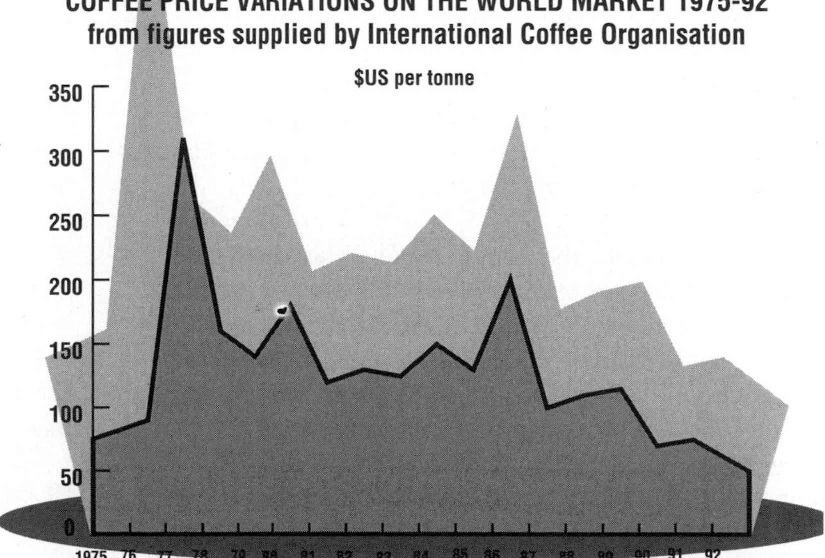

The Cost of Global Markets

"We grow food to fill our stomachs and as insurance against hard times. But it is the income we get from coffee that clothes us, pays for school fees, and buys seed and implements. In the old days we got a very bad price for our coffee crop. The traders got most of the profit. Now we get a better price because we have formed a co-operative and we control the marketing. But we don't control the world market, where prices are too low.

Coffee Farmer, Dominican Republic

"They say free trade is good for our country. They say it will bring new opportunities and more wealth. But where is our opportunity? We cannot compete with this American maize. How can they produce it so cheap? What are we to do? This free trade will be the end of us. Our only opportunity is to leave our land and move to the city.

Smallholder maize farmer, Mexico

"In the old days, there were enough fish to support all of our villages. Today, there are fewer and fewer fish. There are giant ships from Japan which come to our shores and take too many fish. We can't survive if it goes on like this.

Fisherman, Philippines

The alternative to exporting primary commodities is the development of manufactured goods and the export of them onto global markets. The value of manufactured goods as a proportion of overall exports by Third World countries increased from 10% in 1965 to 40% in 1975 to 55% in 1990. This positive picture is modified however by two important trends - one, it reflects the decreasing value of primary commodity exports (which artificially inflates the apparent value of manufactured goods) and, two, most of the exports of manufactured goods are coming from a very small number of countries. In addition to these trends, industrialised countries have increasingly resorted to creating barriers to the import of goods from the Third World. The World Bank estimates that trade barriers cost Third World countries between $50 billion and $100 billion each year.

Trade barriers take the form of ***tariffs*** (a tax levied on a product at the port of entry); ***quotas*** (a quantity restriction) or, increasingly, ***health or environmental restrictions.*** Madeley comments that the purpose of such trade restrictions *"...have traditionally been the first line of protection, keeping out goods from the importing country by artificially raising their price, making them uncompetitive."* The net impact of such restrictions, is obvious for Third World manufacturers as well as having negative consequences for consumers in the industrialised world. For example, restrictions on the import of textiles is estimated to cost British shoppers an average of £18 per person per year. Third World countries are regularly asked to *"voluntarily"* restrict their exports but such agreements are seldom voluntary in any real sense of the word as enforcement or penalties follow if agreement is not reached. The table below indicates a range of tariffs on certain products.

Figure 13:6

TARIFFS ON TROPICAL PRODUCTS BY DEGREE OF PROCESSING (%)

Product Group	EU	Japan	USA
Coffee			
Raw	9.0	0.0	0
Roasted, ground	16.5	20.0	0
Extracts	18.0	20.5	0
Tea			
In bulk	0	12.5	0
For retail sale	5.0	20.0	0
Extracts, essences		12.0	17.3
Cocoa			
Beans	3.0	0.0	0
Paste	15.0	15.0	0
Butter	12.0	2.5	0
Powder	16.0	21.5	0.4
Chocolate		26.7	1.9
Tobacco			
Unmanufactured	30.0	0.0	15.9
Manufactured	81.0	68.9	16.8
Bananas			
Fresh, dried	20.0	18.0	0.4
Flour, prepared	17.0	25.0	3.5
Jute			
Raw	0.0	0.0	0.0
Processed			0.0
Yarns	5.3	8.0	4.1
Woven fabric	8.7	16.0	1.8
Made-up articles	7.7	9.3	3.8

Source: Belinda Coote (1992) **The Trade Trap,** Oxford, Oxfam

Another major problem faced by Third World countries is the relationship between the price of goods exported and those which are imported - this relationship is known as the Terms of Trade. If the price of goods exported tends to fall, then the exporting country will have to export more in order to earn the same income. This situation is made all the worse when the cost of imported goods is rising. Historically, the price of primary commodities has tended to decline relative to that of manufactured goods. As a result the terms of trade have tended to deteriorate for Third World countries while they have improved for industrialised countries. According to Todaro, *"One estimate has placed the extra costs of deteriorating terms of trade for the LDCs at over $2.5 billion per year during the past decade. As a result Third World merchandise trade balances steadily worsened during the 1980s from $55.8 billion in 1981 to $1.9 billion in 1991."* The tables below indicate the terms of trade for non-oil exporting Third World countries between 1965 and 1992 and the total cost of global markets to those countries.

Figure 13:7

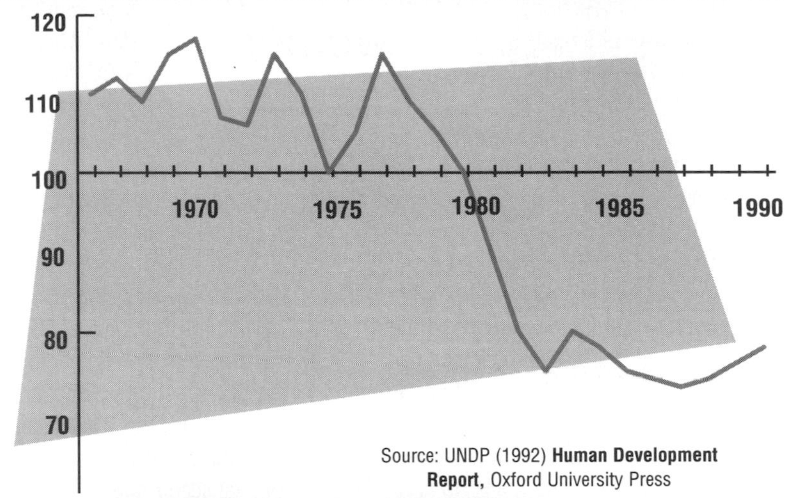

Source: UNDP (1992) **Human Development Report,** Oxford University Press

Terms of Trade Indices (1980 = 100)

	1980	1984	1988	1990
Developing Countries	100	98	71	75
Africa	100	96	59	68
Asia	100	103	71	76
Latin America	100	93	74	74

Source: United Nations Conference on Trade and Development (1991) **Handbook of International Trade and Development Statistics,** Geneva.

"By encouraging a large number of producers to export a small number of commodities into already saturated markets the IMF and World Bank contributed to the deep depression in world prices. Cocoa provides a clear example. Between l980 and l992, West Africa cocoa producers increased their production from 1.6 million to 2.3 million tons. Because these countries are major suppliers to the world market, the resulting increase in exports contributed to the collapse of world prices, which fell by more than half over the same period. As a result, countries, such as Ghana, doubled their exports but earned less foreign exchange."

Kevin Watkins (1995) ***The Oxfam Poverty Report,*** *Oxford, Oxfam*

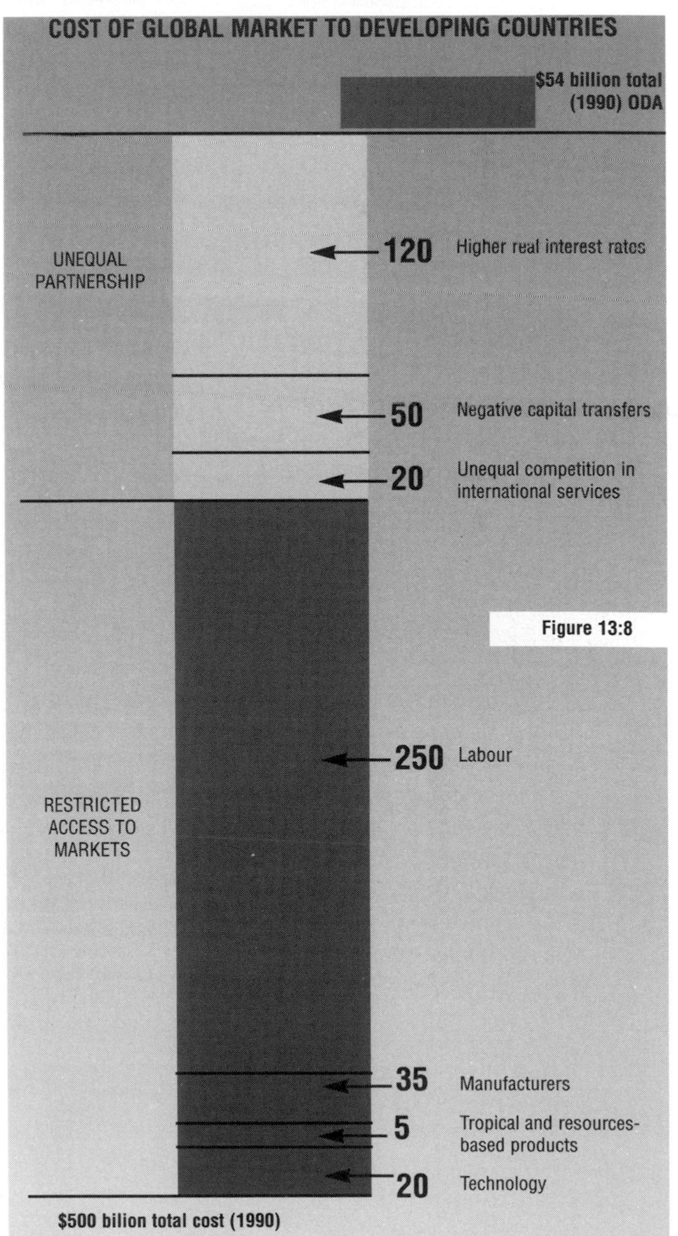

Figure 13:8

Barefoot Businessmen/women

Current Western ideas of a businessman or woman abound with images of sharp suits, mobile phones, office buildings, the stock-exchange and magical phrases such as the 'Dow Jones index', 'financial markets' and 'the city'. As an image of one segment of the world's business sector - admittedly one of the most powerful sectors - this image has some validity. But as an image of the majority of the world's entrepreneurs and business people, it is wholly inaccurate. Like so many other dimensions of current thinking, this Western image of the quintessential business person has become the norm by which all are judged. Yet a visit to any of the world's large cities - Mexico City or Sao Paulo - or to any of the world's up and coming cities - Ho Chi Minh City or Calcutta, will highlight an entirely different image of the modern business person. The image is of what Paul Harrison has called the 'barefoot businessman'. These are the millions and millions of people who work outside the official economy in what is often called the 'informal sector' supplying a limitless range of services and goods.

> *"The bustling market of Bouake, second biggest city in the Ivory Coast, hums with activity. Diviners sit cross-legged on collapsed boxes...traditional medicine men sell...while over a boy tailor dreaming at his treadle sewing machine, a sign proclaims: 'Pop fashions here, dress yourself at Mr. O Dao's'. Meanwhile King Hairdresser invites you in for a crop - take your pick of the exotically named but uninviting convict-style profiles painted on the door: Mirano, 75 style, Afro, Hercules, Casino, Ghana style, Santiago, Cockroach or the two-penny all off, Ordinary..."*

The list of the many enterprises in the informal sector is endless - tailors, weavers, taxis, rickshaw pullers, sellers of all kinds, repairers, carpenters and joiners, blacksmiths, hairdressers, cooks, photographers, typists, prostitutes, cleaners, shoe-shiners etc. This sector continues to grow faster than the official sector and represents the means whereby poor people (and the not-so-poor) 'make out' in the modern town and city. The traditional conception of those working in this sector was that they were outside capitalism but as one recent commentator has noted: *"...those in the informal sector have not escaped capitalism, they are merely in another part of it."* The importance of this sector means that many of the official statistics of work and wealth constantly underestimate the work and the versatility of those in this sector. It is a particularly valuable and productive sector for a variety of reasons including: ease of entry, the use of local inputs and resources, its frequent base in the family, its small scale, its labour intensity, its ability to adapt technology and the fact that it is usually unregulated. It is thus a perfectly suited model of economic activity for the bulk of the local population whose other options are severely restricted.

Sources: Paul Harrison (1993) **Inside the Third World,** Penguin; Alan Gilbert (1994) **The Latin American City,** London, Latin American Bureau and D. Drakakis-Smith (1987) **The Third World City,** London, Methuen.

Transnationals and Development: Debating the Issues

Few issues have become as controversial and politicised as the role of transnational companies in development especially, but by no means exclusively, in the Third World. It is estimated that they employ over 70 million people worldwide and have come to control many of the most important sectors of the global economy. Transnationals increased their investments outside their home countries by 29% per year between 1983 and 1989, with the major companies coming from the United States, Japan and Europe. Because of their power and influence and their ability to create jobs and to stimulate the local economy they are welcomed by most Third World countries and also fiercely criticised by local groups and communities who live with the many economic, social, cultural and environmental consequences of their activities.

Some of the principal arguments in favour of investment by transnationals and those against such investment are outlined on the next page.

Figure 13:9

COMPARISON OF TOP TEN TRANSNATIONAL CORPORATIONSAND SELECTED COUNTRIES BY GDP, 1990.

Rank	Country or Company (HQ)	GDP or Gross Sales ($ billions)
1.	General Motors (USA)	125.1
	Indonesia	107.3
2.	Royal Dutch/Shell (UK/Netherlands)	107.2
3.	Exxon (USA)	105.9
	Norway	105.8
4.	Ford Motor (USA)	98.3
	Turkey	96.5
	Argentina	93.6
	Thailand	80.1
5.	IBM (USA)	69.0
6.	Toyota (Japan)	64.5
7.	IRI (Italy)	61.4
8.	British Petroleum (UK)	59.5
9.	Mobil (USA)	58.8
10.	General Electric (USA)	58.4
	Portugal	56.8
	Venezuela	48.3
	Philippines	43.8
	Malaysia	42.4
	Nigeria	34.7
	Egypt	33.2
	Bangladesh	22.8
	Kenya	7.5

Source: M. Todaro (1994) **Economic Development**, London, Longman, P.529.

THE PROS

- ▼ Foreign companies make up for weak local financial markets (both private and public) by providing crucial investment. In this way they can help stimulate local investment and development.
- ▼ Foreign companies provide jobs, often at higher than normal wages and are seen by local governments and groups to make up for local deficiencies in job creation.
- ▼ Foreign investment often provides management skills which are usually under developed in Third World countries.
- ▼ Foreign companies make available research and development capacity which would otherwise be unavailable for local and national development.
- ▼ Foreign companies have vast international linkages which can provide preferential access which might not be available to local companies.
- ▼ Foreign companies often enter into alliances with local companies or the state thus, ultimately, strengthening local development capacity.

THE CONS

- ▼ Foreign companies may actually adversely affect local savings and investment because they frequently seek exclusive agreements which hinder local initiatives. They regularly export their profits thus "draining" local wealth.
- ▼ Because of their international linkages, foreign companies frequently import their inputs rather than having them manufactured locally - hence, their "downstream" linkages in a local economy may be quite weak.
- ▼ While foreign companies do provide much needed jobs, they tend to be at the bottom end of the industry with the more valuable and skills building jobs being retained in the industrialised world.
- ▼ Foreign companies are notoriously mobile, especially in recent years, and frequently leave as other more attractive locations arise.
- ▼ Foreign companies, because of their profile and power, have interfered in local political processes, often opposed trade union activity (playing workers in one location off against others elsewhere) and sometimes negatively affect employment standards in the host country.
- ▼ In the case of some industries, foreign companies can seriously damage the local resource base and the environment. Regulatory legislation is often very difficult to enforce.

Barefoot Businessmen and women make up the majority of traders in most Third World Countries.

Large Tea Corporations and the Price of the Cuppa

The price of tea is largely determined by supple and demand. But large tea corporations such as Brooke-Bond Lipton Ltd. (Unilever), Lyons Tetley and Premier Brands have a considerable influence on supply and demand and thus on the price-fixing process. Market concentration is extremely high: 90% of Western trade is in the hands of 7 transnational companies and 85% of world production is sold by multinationals. Their market power is a main determinant at all tea auctions. With their buying policy these corporations strongly influence both price movements and the demand for certain qualities of tea. Their ownership of both plantations and processing factories is called horizontal integration, but there is vertical integration as well (in that they also control transport companies, shipping agencies etc.). This concentration of power, with corporations sometimes controlling the entire production process from tea shrub to tea bag, offers ample scope for manipulation.

This happened, for instance, in the mid 1980s, when Indian tea prices rose considerably because the former Soviet Union bought up large quantities of tea, while consumption of tea in India was increasing as well. The transnational companies decided to bring down the high price by temporarily refraining from buying Indian tea, which gradually depressed the price. During that period, the Indian Government attempted twice to get a grip on the market by imposing export restrictions, thus trying to avoid shortages on the local market. At the same time, it set a minimum export price with the aim of keeping prices at a profitable level. The large tea corporations then decided to withdraw collectively from the Indian market, with the result that nothing could be exported at all. The Indian government had no choice but to lift the measures again. Transnational corporations can afford such actions thanks to their high degree of flexibility, their buffer stocks and their speculative transactions. The flexibility of companies is enhanced by deliberately reducing differences in quality. With the exception of a few quality- conscious consumer countries, a constant degeneration and adaptation of tea qualities goes on all over the world. Many tea qualities have become exchangeable and are bought where they are cheapest.

Sources: European Fair Trade Association (1995) **European Fair Trade Yearbook**, EFTA

Figure 13:10

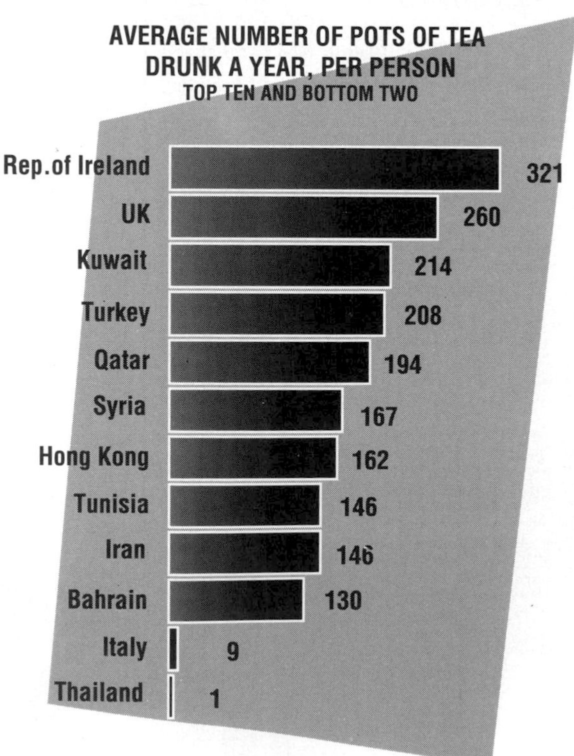

How much do we owe the Third World?

In chapter 12, we examined the debt crisis and the amount 'owed' by the Third World to international banks and financial institutions. Seldom do we see attempts to calculate the amount owed by the industrialised world to the Third World as a result of the inherent inequalities and injustices of the international economy, both in the past and the present. There can be little doubt that the plunder of the Third World in the past contributed significantly to the development process of the colonial powers. Land, resources, control of trade routes and commodities, slavery, taxation etc. all contributed to the wealth of Europe. It would be impossible to come up with an accurate calculation of the cost of colonialism to the peoples of the Third World.

The contemporary international market also costs these very same people. The UNDP estimates that the operations of the international market cost the Third World approximately $500 billion each year. In his book, ***Inside the Third World,*** Paul Harrison, using the work of a range of commentators, attempts to calculate some of what we owe to the Third World.

He quotes the French economist Paul Bairoch who calculates that declining terms of trade cost the Third World between $3.5 billion and $11 billion in 1962 and anything from $5 billion upwards in 1970. He estimates that between 1953 and 1973, the total cost to the Third World was from $70 billion upwards and interestingly adds: *"...Repayment of this at prevailing interest rates might cost $7 billion a year."*

Harrison points out that currently, multinational companies are taking out about $7 billion annually more than they are putting in. The 'brain drain' is estimated to be costing at least $5 billion per year while service payments on debts averaged around $16 billion per year between 1971 and 1976. Harrison goes on to pose the following 'taster':

"...recall the calculations made by the Chilean government of Salvador Allende when deciding on compensation for nationalising the copper multinationals. The Chileans estimated that the companies had made excess profits of $774 millions and that far from having a right to any compensation, the companies actually owed Chile $378 millions."

Harrison concludes his discussion with the following, interesting proposition:

"Leaving aside the question of reparations, the total cost of the inequities in the prevailing economic order appears to be at least $35 billion a year, on the most conservative estimates. This figure is, of course, only the crudest of guesses, but it gives some idea of the order of aid necessary simply to restore the balance, let alone really qualify for the name of aid. This is two and a half times the amount given by the Western nations in 1977, or about 0.75% of their GNP. Paul Bairoch has calculated - arguing from needs rather than entitlements - that Western countries should be giving 2 percent of their national incomes as aid, if Third World countries are to be helped to achieve more rapid rates of growth..."

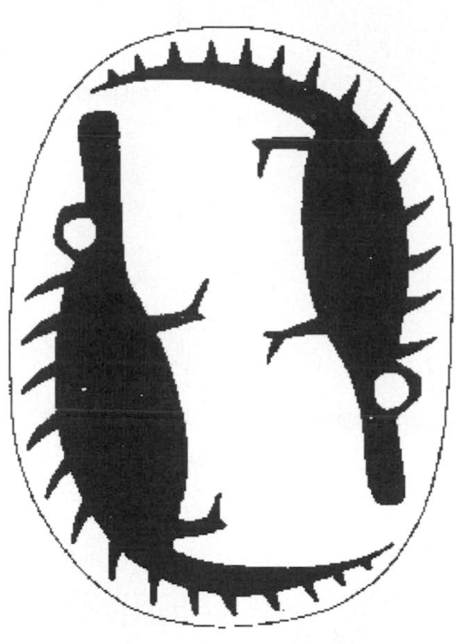

An Alternative - Fair Trade

Fair Trade Organisations

In 1959, the Fair Trade Organisation was founded by a number of youth members of a Catholic political party in the Dutch town of Kerkade. The Foundation's first focus was on the provision of milk-powder for Sicily and it became involved in fund-raising and providing financial support for projects in 'underdeveloped regions'. The Foundation's overall objective was to help people to support themselves and thus a major emphasis was on vocational training and on workshops. However, it soon became clear that the selling of products manufactured was a major problem. This situation led the Fair Trade Organisation to buy products from producer groups in developing countries and sell them in Europe.

The first products imported were wood-carvings from producers in the slums of Port-au-Prince in Haiti. During these early years, only craft products - the majority from missionary projects - were imported. Cactus pots, plant hangers, bamboo ashtrays and shell-decorated products from the Philippines, earthenware products from Mexico and

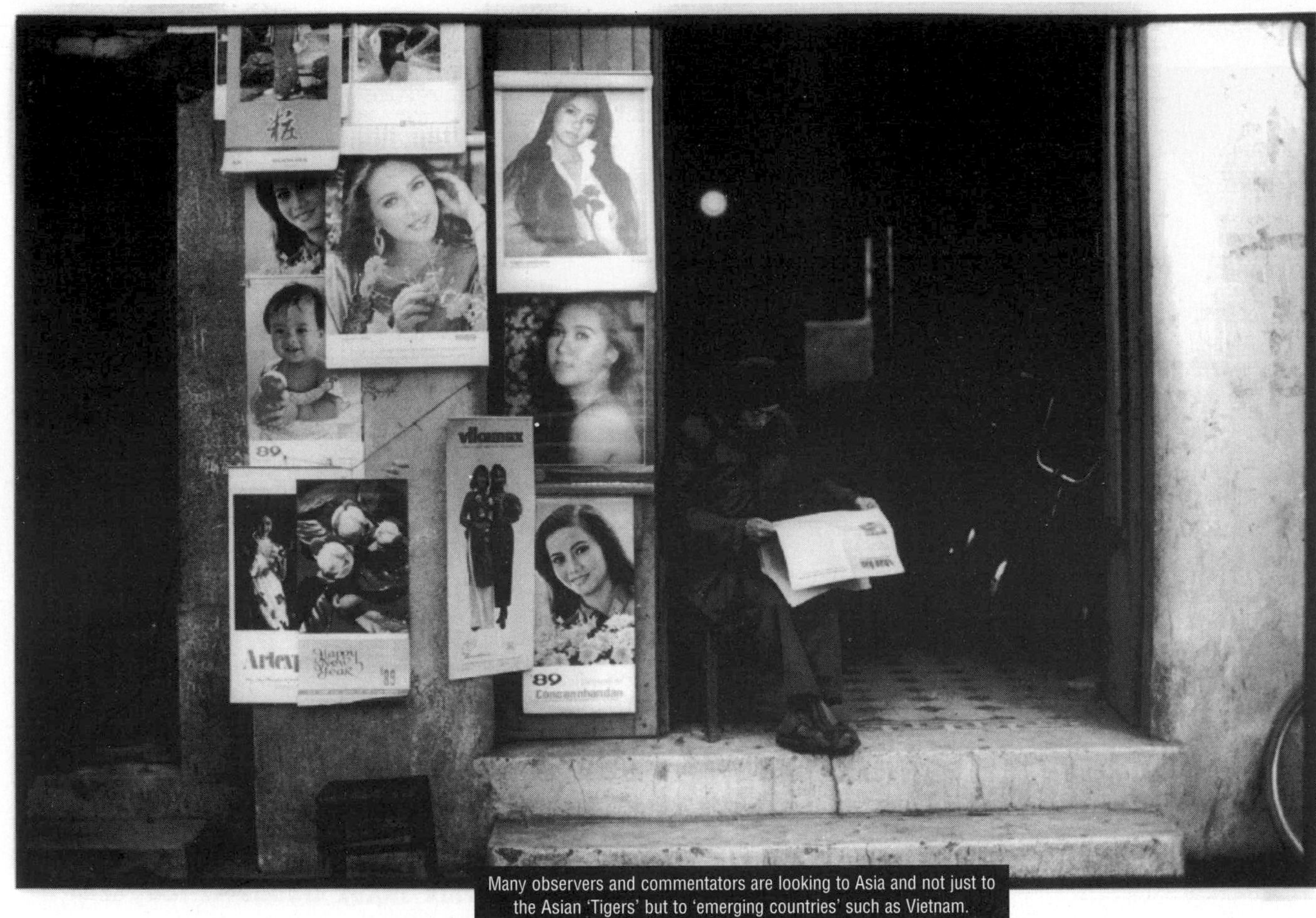

Many observers and commentators are looking to Asia and not just to the Asian 'Tigers' but to 'emerging countries' such as Vietnam.

sandals from India were just some of the imports. The products were sold through Third World groups, missionary exhibitions and mail order.

In 1973, fair trade coffee was added to the list with the first beans coming from Fedecocagua, an association of coffee producers in Guatemala. Within a very short period of time, coffee sales exceeded those of the other products. From the early 1970s onwards, the fair trade approach was adopted in many European countries and since then over 65 organisations have been established throughout Europe. In 1990, 11 of them came together and formed EFTA (European Fair Trade Association). *"EFTA seeks to stimulate practical co-operation between its members, develop common policies and offer joint support to producers and strives for the adoption of fair trade principles in commercial trading in Europe."*

World Shops

The slogan 'Trade not aid' became a popular rallying cry after the 1968 United Nations Conference on Trade and Development but little practical action was taken to achieve this goal. The response of some Third World groups revolved around the sale of cane sugar, much of it from Cuba - the view was that by buying cane sugar *"...you increase the pressure on the governments of the rich countries...to give the poor countries also a place in the sun."* These cane sugar groups then developed into 'World Shops' which also began to import handicrafts. The first world shop was established in the Dutch town of Breukelen in 1969 and within two years there were over 120 such shops in seven European states. Today, there are over 3,000 such shops organised into 15 organisations in Europe represented by the group NEWS (The Network of European World Shops). These shops combine the sale of crafts and other products with education and advocacy work around trade issues.

Fair Trade Labels

Yet another dimension of the fair trade movement has involved the use of Fair Trade labelling building on increased consumer interest in buying fairly traded products. In 1986, a national coffee campaign was organised by the Dutch NGDO Solidaridad who introduced the label Max Havelaar (now used in Belgium, Switzerland, Denmark and France also). Other similar initiatives were established in other countries and today there are two other fair trade labels - Transfer (in Germany, Luxembourg and Austria) and the Fair Trade Mark (in the UK and Ireland). These labels now market coffee, cocoa, chocolate, honey, sugar and tea. Such products are now sold in over 13,000 shops and supermarkets and account for 200 million ecu in retail sales.

Together these fair trade initiatives support over 600 producer groups throughout the Third World and seek to provide the public in Europe with the opportunity to purchase products which have been fairly traded and to provide a new dimension to the concept of consumer power. They also act in close collaboration with each other to organise campaigns to promote the cause of fair trade. As EFTA has pointed out *"...markets don't only function on the basis of prices, but also - increasingly so - on the basis of products' characteristics: its features, its quality, its design/appearance, and - a crucial characteristic for fair trade - its non-material aspects. In other words, fair traders can afford to pay producers a higher price and keep earning a healthy profit because consumers are willing to pay more for the higher ethical value of a fair trade product."*

What is Fair Trade?

Fair Trade means:

- prices which enable producers and their families to earn an adequate living - this implies a fair price, advance payments when needed and a long-term relationship;
- a fair working environment - one that does not harm producers either physically, psychologically or socially;
- production which is both economically and ecologically sustainable - one which meets the needs of this generation without damaging the needs of future generations;
- uses efficient methods to get products from producers to consumers and which bypasses speculators and unnecessary intermediaries;
- preference for local production, medium sized enterprises and equal distribution of the income generated;
- raising awareness in Europe about fair trade issues;
- campaigning against unfair trading practices.

Sources: European Fair Trade Association (1995) **European Fair Trade Yearbook**, EFTA (1995) **Fair Trade in Europe**, and EFTA (1994) **Joining Fair Trade Forces in Europe**, Maastricht.

References

Kevin Watkins (1995) **The Oxfam Poverty Report**, Oxford, Oxfam.

David C. Korten (1995) **When Corporations Rule the World**, London, Earthscan.

John Madeley (1992) **Trade and the Poor**, London, Intermediate Technology.

Walden Bello (1990) **Brave New Third World**, London, Earthscan.

Belinda Coote (1992) **The Trade Trap**, Oxford, Oxfam.

United Nations Conference on Trade and Development (1991) **Handbook of International Trade and Development Statistics**, Geneva.

Paul Harrison (1993) **Inside the Third World**, Penguin.

Alan Gilbert (1994) **The Latin American City**, London, Latin American Bureau.

D. Drakakis-Smith (1987) **The Third World City**, London, Methuen.

M. Todaro (1994) **Economic Development**, London, Longman.

John Madeley (1992) **Trade and the Poor**, London, IT Publications.

European Fair Trade Association (1995) **European Fair Trade Yearbook**, EFTA.

Paul Harrison; **Inside the Third World.**

EFTA (1994) **Joining Fair Trade Forces in Europe**, Maastricht.

THE ULTIMATE
THE ULTIMATE
NOTHING PERSONAL...
IT'S JUST BUSINESS...
ARMS TRADE

ARMING OURSELVES TO DEATH

Colm Regan

"One of the most useful indicators of political insecurity in a country is the priority the government accords military strength - since governments sometimes use armies to repress their own people. If a government is more concerned about its military establishment than its people, this imbalance shows up in the ratio of military to social spending. The two nations with the highest ratio of military spending to education and health spending in 1980 were Iraq (8 to 1) and Somalia (5 to 1). Is it any surprise that these two nations ran into serious trouble during the 1980s and that the same powers that supplied them arms a decade ago are now struggling to disarm them?

United Nations Development Programme (1994) **Human Development Report,** Oxford University Press.

Introduction

A few days into the 1991 Gulf War, United States President George Bush announced, *"We've kicked the Vietnam syndrome once and for all"*. In this he was referring to the perception of many Americans that aggressive military actions in the Gulf and their victorious consequences had overcome the legacy of the earlier defeat of the US at the hands of the Vietnamese. The Gulf War was good not only for the American psyche but also, of course, for the American economy. Its army, its leadership role and its victories in the Gulf said a lot about America's place in the world and, coming so quickly after the collapse of communism, about capitalism as well. It assured Americans and others throughout the world that security could really only be guaranteed against dictators and aggressors through the ultimate sanction of arms.

Not so much was said about the civilian casualties of the war - about the estimated 250,000 plus Iraqis who died (over 50% of them children), many of them victims of "smart-bombs" which located them in their air-raid shelters and annihilated them. Little was said about the massive damage to the basics of life in Iraq, about the long-term damage to the economy, the society, the health and the environment of the Iraqi people. And little was said about those Western powers who were amongst those who had promoted and armed Saddam Hussein and backed him in the earlier Iran-Iraq war.

Equally little was said about the losses to Third World countries from the war or about the poor of the region and other regions who will remain hungry, homeless and poor because the war used up such vast amounts of resources. Ultimately, little was said in official circles about the sheer cost of it all and how the Gulf War was such a microcosm of the world's second largest industry - the arms trade. The Gulf War was presented, especially on television, as epitomising the new high-tech, sophisticated arms industry at work - clinical, effective, exciting.

"When arms and armies take precedence over basic needs, when economic progress leaves behind millions of marginalised individuals who are desperate, there is no security, and more weapons will not produce it ...on the other hand development based on equality and justice has a healthy multiplier effect and people become sources of wealth and security themselves".

Researcher and Writer Ruth Leger Sivard

We are used to hearing of the trillions and billions and unimaginable quantities of money which disappear into the military "blackhole" each year. We read about the high-tech equipment, the smart bombs, the highly professional armies and leaders, the sophisticated strategies and the sheer excitement of it all. In a different context, we also hear a lot about hunger and poverty and about the Third World and of so much need and so few resources and we wonder about the connections to the arms trade - they can't afford basic health care or food for all but they seem to be able to afford weapons; who supplies them and how are they paid for?

The earth is still scarred,
mutilated with the scars of wars.
Now killing has become an art
when once it was merely a trade.
From all those thousands of borders
we have lost only the human one -
the border between good and evil.

Russian Poet Yevgeny Yevtushenko

The Arms Industry and Its Effects - in facts and figures

▼ Global military spending since 1945 has amounted to a colossal $30 - $35 trillion. The world now has over 26,000,000 regular soldiers, another estimated 40,000,000 in military reserves of one kind or another, a stockpile of over 50,000 nuclear weapons, 66 countries known to be in the business of pushing arms, 64 countries under some form of military government and, in 1993, 34 wars underway (the highest number in any one year to date).

▼ Each year we spend on arms an average of $180 for every woman, man and child on this planet.

▼ The weapons industry is the world's number two industry after oil. Roughly 70% of its investment comes from the industrialised world but the Third World share is growing fast. Military spending in the Third World doubled between 1974 and 1984.

▼ Industrialised countries devote over $500 billion annually to the military but only approximately $50 billion to development aid.

▼ Military spending in 1992 ($815 billion) equalled the combined income of 49% of the world's people.

▼ Despite the fact that military spending has been reduced, today military budgets remain as high as they were in the late 1970s. Between 1987 and 1994, the cumulative reduction in military spending amounted to approximately $935 billion - the equivalent to one year's spending.

▼ In 1994, the world's governments spent roughly $16 billion on demilitarisation and peace building, or about 2% of global military expenditures.

▼ While global military budgets have decreased over the past eight years (from their peak in 1987) due in large measure to the ending of the Cold War, the amount of resources devoted to military research and development has increased and this sector now employs one-fifth of the world's research scientists and engineers.

▼ Despite having over 800 million people living in absolute poverty, South Asia and Sub-Saharan Africa continue to spend heavily on arms ($19 billion and $8 billion respectively per annum).

▼ Today developing countries have eight times as many soldiers as doctors.

▼ Despite the ending of the Cold War, the world is now less secure than before. In the 1950s the average number of outbreaks of war was 9 per year. In the 1980s, the number had increased to an average of 16.

▼ During 1993, 42 countries in the world had 52 major conflicts and another 37 had political violence. Of these 79 countries, 65 were in the Third World.

▼ The nature of conflict is also changing. Of the 82 conflicts between 1989 and 1992, only three were between States, the remainder were conflicts within States.

▼ Often, it is safer to be a soldier in battle than a civilian on the sidelines. Of the estimated 22 million people killed in war since 1945 the majority have been civilians; around three-quarters of them killed in the wars of the 1980s.

▼ Between 1989 and 1992, more than a thousand people were dying each year in 8 countries - Afghanistan, Angola, India, Peru, the Philippines, Somalia, Sri Lanka and Sudan.

▼ In the last 20 years, the number of war refugees has increased from 3 million to 15 million.

▼ The world's armed forces are the single biggest polluters on earth - in the US they produce more toxic waste than the top five chemical companies combined.

▼ The nuclear threat remains. Despite the reductions proposed in recent treaties (START 1 and 2), not a single warhead has yet been dismantled.

▼ In addition to the 5 acknowledged nuclear powers (China, France, Russia, the UK and the US), nuclear weapons are also controlled by Belarus, Kazakhstan and Ukraine. India, Israel and Pakistan are presumed to have nuclear weapons while Algeria, The Democratic Republic of Korea, Iran and Iraq have advanced nuclear development programmes. Against this, Argentina, Brazil and South Africa appear to have halted nuclear weapons development.

▼ The nuclear payload carried by one single nuclear Trident submarine is equivalent to 8 times the total firepower expended during World War Two - enough firepower to destroy all the major cities of the Northern hemisphere and equivalent to the firepower of one million Hiroshimas.

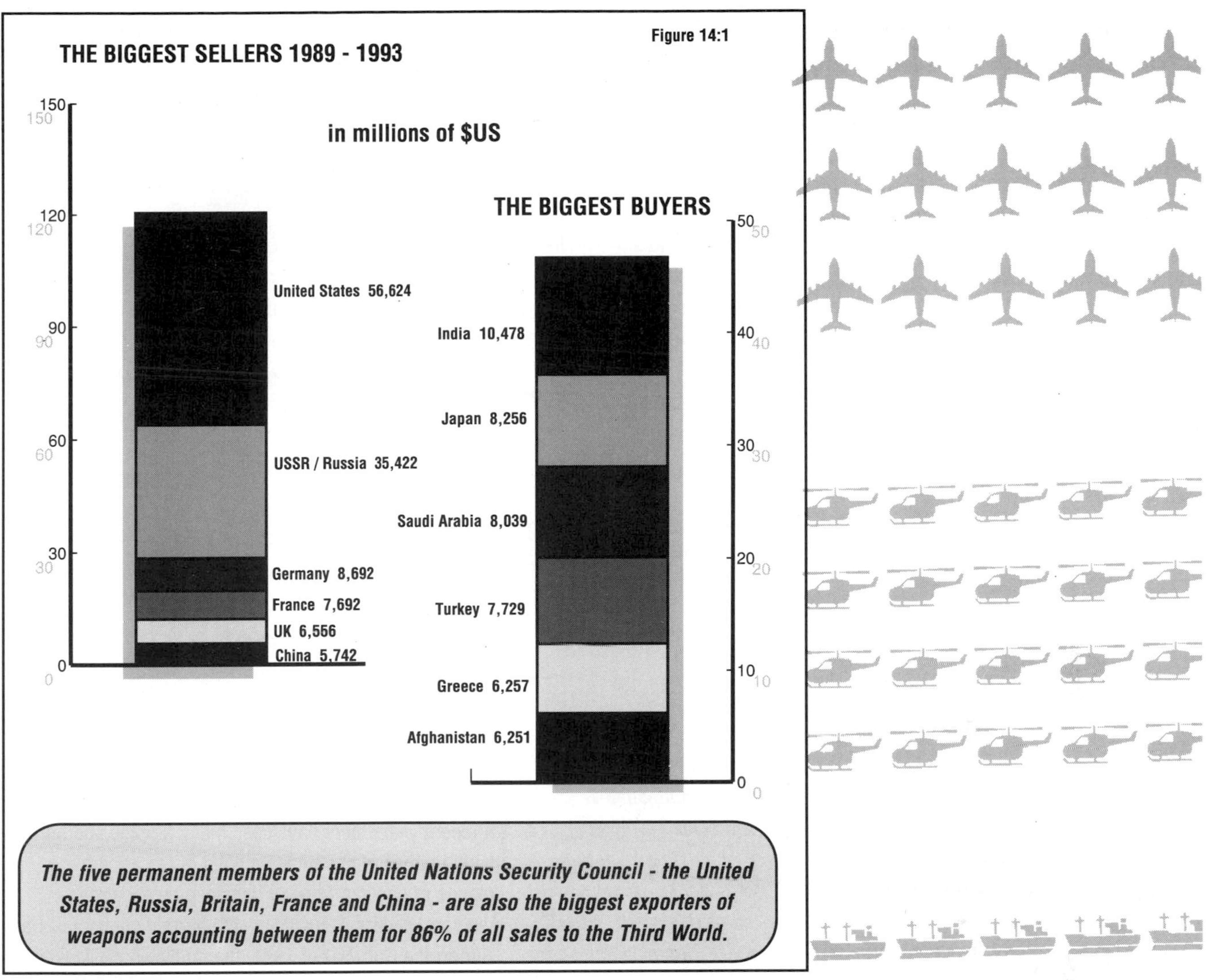

Who is the Arms Business?

"Beware of Imitations", "Proven, Clearly More Effective", "Combat Without Casualties", "Born of Necessity, Tested Under Fire"

These are just some of the "arms-speak" headlines used by the arms industry in the process of marketing its products. The arms industry is a notoriously murky business, characterised by intense secrecy and often protected from public scrutiny by government and a media aversion to this issue. Only when major stories break, such as the Pergau Dam affair in Britain, does the industry receive widespread publicity.

And yet, many of the world's well known companies are directly involved in the production of arms. Included are McDonnell Douglas and Boeing, General Electric Company, Vickers Shipbuilding, Ford, BP, Philips, Thorn EMI, Toshiba, Rolls Royce, Lucas, British Aerospace, Agnelli (FIAT), ICL, PYE, Westinghouse, Dassault, Shorts, Harland and Wolf, to name but a small few plus a huge assortment of companies in computers and communications and countless smaller companies involved in providing inputs and components for the industry.

Because of secrecy and the frequently quoted need for "national security" it is impossible to get a complete picture of the scale of the arms industry in Europe.

According to the British Ministry of Defence, it is estimated that, in 1990, over 570,000 people were involved directly and indirectly in the arms industry. £1,506 million worth of orders left Britain in 1992 and additional orders worth £5,000 million were signed. The European countries most heavily involved in the arms trade include France, Britain, Belgium, Germany, the Netherlands, Italy, Spain, Sweden, The Czech Republic and, of course, Russia.

Britain remains one of Europe's major arms manufacturers - with the ninth largest economy in the world, Britain has its third largest arms industry. The industry remains heavily dependent on government support and promotion. The Ministry of Defence, via its Defence Export Services Organisation, organises major arms exhibitions which attract representatives from over 100 countries each year - many of them amongst the world's most repressive regimes. And yet, European governments claim that one of the criteria for the granting of arms export licences is the human rights record of the recipient regime.

It is not just military equipment which is sold but also training and personnel. Between 1979 and 1990, the British Government provided training for armies in 110 different countries while over 25,000 trainees from 99 countries attended military establishments in the UK. In 1991, an electronic torture chamber was sold to the United Arab Emirates by a British firm while a UK building firm (Laing), provided three 12 foot high gallows to Sheikh Zayed of Abu Dhabi. In 1990, Asia Watch and Physicians for Human Rights accused the SAS of training soldiers for both sides in the conflict in Cambodia. This training included training in the use of landmines and explosives. Most notorious in recent years has been the British Government's active promotion of major arms sales to Indonesia - particularly, the provision of Britain's largest arms company British Aerospace Hawk jet fighters and 80 light tanks - despite Indonesia's invasion of East Timor in 1975 and the subsequent killing of over 200,000 East Timorese and its continuing refusal to recognise even the most basic of East Timorese human rights.

THE UNITED NATIONS ACTS TO CONTROL ARMS SALES

In 1992, the Secretary General of the United Nations published for the first time a register of conventional armaments. In it, 80 countries including all the major suppliers provided detail of the weapons transferred. The categories included battle tanks, armoured combat vehicles, large-calibre artillery systems, combat aircraft, attack helicopters, warships and missiles and missile launchers. Not included were bombs, small arms and ground-to-air missiles.

Almost all exporters provided information but over 60% of importers failed to do so. While weaknesses currently undermine the effectiveness of the Register, it nonetheless represents a significant move forward - activists against the arms trade hope that it will be strengthened in coming years with real sanctions being introduced to effect change in current practice.

"We see several possibilities such as the sale of Hawk fighter jets and scorpion light tanks and other equipment...it is not for me to get involved in the politics of another country. Quite clearly it is an issue which concerns some but what I am concerned with is the working relationship between the armed forces of Britain and Indonesia"

British Chief of Defence Staff, Field Marshall Peter Inge, following a 1994 meeting with President Suharto of Indonesia.

The Social Cost of the Arms Trade

The Immediate Human Impact

In recent years there have been many graphic and horrifying images of the human impact of the arms trade - images of children horribly damaged by napalm in Vietnam, civilian casualties in the air raid shelters of Iraq during the Gulf War of 1991, the mutilated civilians in Cambodian clinics suffering landmine wounds etc. An immediate consequence of the arms industry and the wars and conflicts which it helps to create and sustain can be seen in the casualty figures. A total of 21 million people have died from war since 1945, overwhelmingly in the Third World.

In 1900 there were a total of 10 civil and 6 international wars. By 1940 there were 13 civil and 6 international wars and by 1980/89, there were 29 and 6 respectively. The number of deaths were as follows:

- 1900-1909 - 243,000 - 95% civilian
- 1940-1949 - 39,285,000 - 52% civilian
- 1980-1989 - 1,733,000 - 40% civilian

The total number of deaths from war between 1900 and 1989 was 69,229,000 of which 55% were civilian (if one excludes the Second World War then the deaths are overwhelmingly civilian).

Arms sales to Indonesia defended

Reuter in London

THE British government said yesterday it had approved the sale of fighter aircraft to Indonesia after concluding they would probably not be used against opponents of the Jakarta government.

The Trade Minister, Anthony Nelson, said he had authorised the issue of licences to British Aerospace for a contract it signed in 1993 to sell 24 Hawk trainers and ground-attack fighters worth £500 million.

Mr Nelson said in a written parliamentary answer he had given the go-ahead after consulting the Ministry of Defence and the Foreign Office. He said the sale was in line with internationally agreed criteria for arms exports.

"In accordance with government policy, a thorough assessment of the likelihood of these aircraft being used for internal repression in Indonesia or East Timor has been undertaken. This assessment has concluded that it is not likely that these aircraft will so be used," he said.

"The Indonesian government has given assurances that these aircraft will not be used for internal security or against civilians in any part of Indonesia or East Timor."

A senior Indonesian air force officer said earlier this year that 16 of the fighters would be stationed at Pekanbaru, capital of Riau province in eastern Sumatra, to strengthen air defences. Human rights groups have fiercely criticised Britain for its arms sales to Jakarta.

Mr Nelson said he was making an exception to the government's rule of not disclosing details of export licences because the public interest in this case outweighed the need for confidentiality.

GUARDIAN 20TH DEC. 1995

All but 11,000 war deaths since 1949 (excluding the conflict over the former Yugoslavia) occurred in the Third World. Asia has led the way with 6 million civilian dead and 3.4 million military dead. African figures are 4 million civilian and 1.4 million military; South Asia 2.5 million and 0.6 million respectively; the Middle East 0.7 million and 1.3 million; and Latin America with 0.4 million and 0.2 million respectively.

Parallel figures for those injured or mutilated in war do not exist but it is clear that the medical, social, psychological and economic costs are extremely high. For example, US research suggests that the medical and pension costs for wounded soldiers alone tend to be three times the original cost of the war itself. No such equivalent civilian figures exist.

War and conflict cause direct and immediate consequences at a number of levels. Economic activity is usually severely affected as crops, agriculture, industry, transport and communications are disrupted. The cost of the 1980-1988 Iran/Iraq war is estimated at over $600 billion which amounted to more than the combined income of the two States since the export of petroleum began. The war against the Iraqi occupation of Kuwait cost $676 billion - excluding the environmental damage caused.

Other immediate social and economic consequences of arms and wars can be measured in the number of war refugees. For example, the budget of the United Nations High Commission for Refugees has increased from approximately $12 million in the early 1970s to $1.1 billion in 1993 reflecting the dramatic increase in refugee numbers significantly as a result of conflict.

The Cost in Human Development Terms

Human security is not simply a function of the absence of conflict or war. It is characterised by the need for security in economic, food, health, environmental, personal, community and political levels. The international arms industry fundamentally undermines human security as it diverts priority attention, and therefore resources, away from human needs. This is particularly the case in the developing world where basic human needs are greatest and yet where so much of the arms industry's exports are targeted.

The ratio of military to social spending (combined spending on education and health) is one of the crucial measures of the social cost of the arms industry. A small sample of country ratios, for 1990/91, illustrates clearly the social cost - in Syria, the ratio is 373%, in Iraq 271%, in Angola 208%, in Somalia 200%, in Ethiopia 190% and in Jordan 138%.

Current military spending in the developing world amounts to approximately $125 billion. Just 12% of this could provide the additional cost of primary health care for all including immunisation of all children, the reduction, by 50%, of moderate malnutrition and the provision of safe drinking water for all. Just 4% represents the additional cost of reducing adult illiteracy by 50%, providing universal primary education and educating women to the same level as men. All of this represents crucial lost opportunities in the struggle against poverty and acute human suffering. It is estimated that the cost of arms purchases by developing country governments wipes out all perceived benefits of the aid programmes focused upon those countries.

Manufacturing Insecurity

Military spending reached a peak in 1987 and has been falling each year since then. It is often argued that such military spending secures peace and yet the number of conflicts per year have significantly increased. By 1993 they were at their highest level at a total of 34. The two nations with the highest ratios of military to social spending in 1980 were Iraq and Somalia contributing to, rather than reducing, conflict in subsequent years. This stands in stark contrast to the relatively peaceful experiences of Botswana, Costa Rica and Mauritius, where the ratio is infinitely lower. Human security is not bought by arms but by a fundamental respect for basic human rights at all levels.

Additionally, it is argued that the purchase of weapons by developing country governments is for the protection of its citizens from foreign aggression. Yet, according to the United Nations, the chances of dying from social neglect (from malnutrition and preventable diseases) in developing countries, are 33 times greater than the chances of dying in a war from external aggression. The fact remains that developing countries have fought very few international wars while many have used their armies and weaponry to repress their own people.

Huge levels of military spending in the nuclear arms industry has also contributed towards human insecurity. Despite the recent welcome reduction in the world's nuclear stockpile by 10%, this arsenal still constitutes a massive threat to humanity with an explosive force equivalent to 1,600 times the firepower released in 3 major wars (World War Two, Korea and Vietnam) - wars which killed 44 million people. Fears are now also growing regarding nuclear proliferation, smuggling in plutonium and the environmental dangers of nuclear weapons and installations as well as biological and chemical weapons.

Wasting Resources and Human Ingenuity

World-wide public investment in military research and development is $100 billion per year exceeding research into health care, new sources of energy, education and other social needs. Military related research and development work employs one-fifth of the world's research scientists and engineers (of the 2.25 million scientists world-wide, about 500,000 work on military research with over 50% working exclusively on weapons research). Thus, military needs absorb scientific and technological capabilities that are ten times greater than those available to all developing countries and deflect such human creativity away from life-saving research into what is frequently life-taking research.

Today's military activity uses up significant amounts of the world's limited resources consuming, for example, as much aluminium, copper, nickel, and platinum as the peoples of the developing world. Military activity also contributes greatly to world pollution. The world's armed forces are the single biggest polluters on earth - in the US they produce more toxic waste than the top five chemical companies combined. Armies are also major users of land, not just for bases but also for training grounds, firing and testing ranges etc. and often these tend to be located in environmentally sensitive areas. According to a 1982 United Nations survey, during World War Two an armoured infantry battalion in the United States, made up of approximately 600 soldiers, required less than 16 square kilometres. A similar unit today requires 20 times as much.

Militarism can also affect the availability and use of other limited resources such as public expenditure - in effect using public finances to subsidise the production of arms. For example, in the US an estimated one-third of exports are paid for not by the governments buying the arms but by the US taxpayer. Hidden subsidies take the form of loans for sales or the wiping out of previous military debts such as the $7 billion "forgiven" Egypt for its support of the allies during the Gulf War. In 1989, the British government gave export credits worth $9.75 million to Iraq for machine tools to be used in the Iraqi chemical weapons industry which had produced the goods so effectively used against groups such as the Kurds.

The annual report on World Military and Social Expenditure shows a high correlation between high military expenditure and low social well-being in industrialised countries such as the United States, Russia, France, the UK etc. The 1991 report concluded: *"The neglect of human capital translates into the*

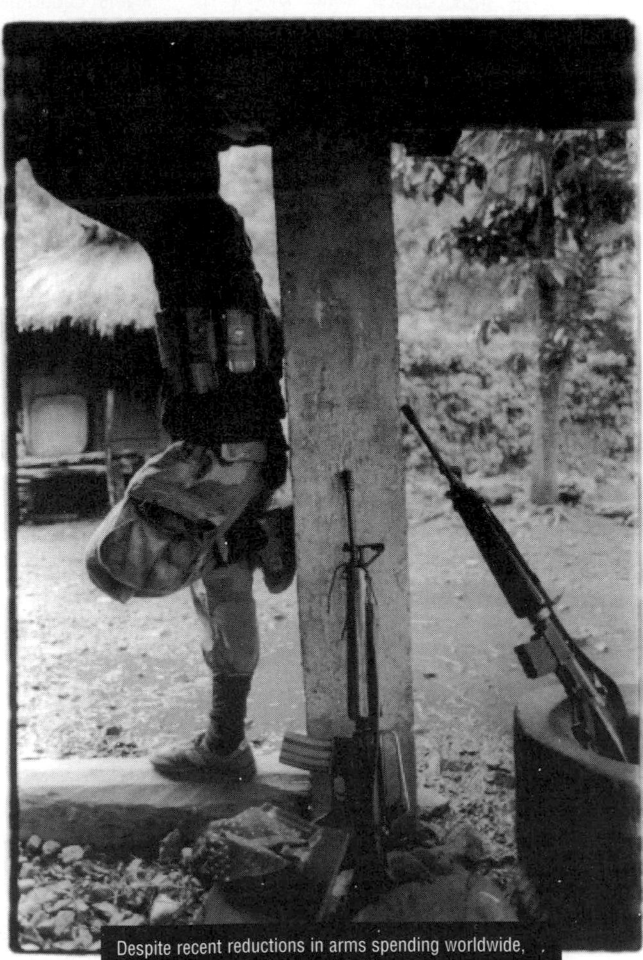

Despite recent reductions in arms spending worldwide, arms sales to the Third World continue to grow.

neglect of economic development, because it is on the human factor that society's growth ultimately depends..."

The Environmental Impact

As has already been noted, military activities often have serious environmental consequences not just for this generation which must deal with the results of today's actions but also for future generations which will have to deal with the legacy of those actions. Vast areas of Vietnam's forests and crops were destroyed by herbicides, which led to massive soil erosion with both short and medium term consequences. During the 1991 Gulf War, there was a massive oil spill off the coast of Kuwait, and 613 oil wells were ignited in the fighting, burning between 4 and 8 million barrels of oil per day. It is estimated that in Kuwait the cost of rehabilitation will be $70 billion while in Iraq it is estimated at $200 billion.

The Canadian organisation Science for Peace calculates that the world's armed forces account for 10% of all emissions of greenhouse gases, and two-thirds of all emissions of gases which do most damage to the ozone layer. Military accidents have left at least 50 nuclear warheads and 11 nuclear reactors on the ocean floor, while NATO manoeuvres in the former Federal Republic of Germany generated an estimated $100 million environmental damage. And, as many commentators note, this represents the damage during peacetime!.

A Legacy For the Future

The United Nations Commission on Environment and Development commented that *"...We borrow environmental capital from future generations with no intention or prospect of repaying. They may damn us for our spendthrift ways, but they can never collect our debt to them"*. This sentiment applies with equal relevance to the legacy of militarism which we will pass on to future generations. Our short-sightedness with regard to profits and greed today with all its human, social, environmental and security dimensions takes no account of future generations. We continue to run the risk of leaving our planet less secure, more twisted in its development, more at risk of nuclear and environmental damage and, ultimately, more unjust than many previous generations.

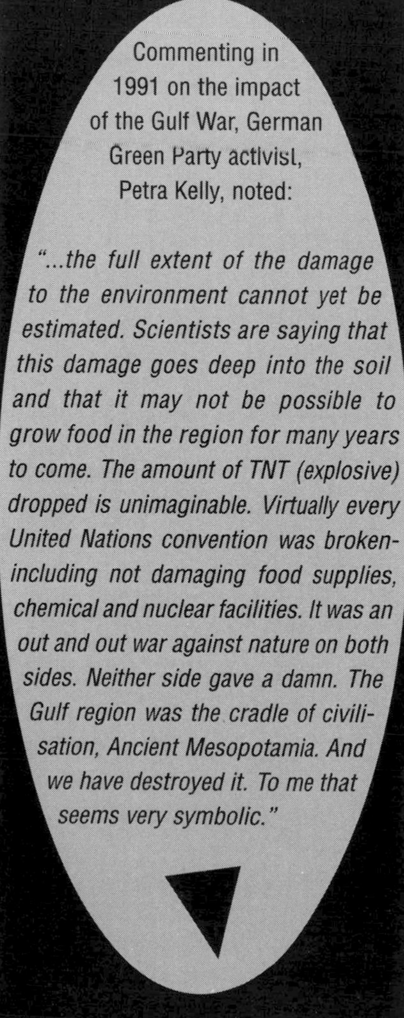

Commenting in 1991 on the impact of the Gulf War, German Green Party activist, Petra Kelly, noted:

"...the full extent of the damage to the environment cannot yet be estimated. Scientists are saying that this damage goes deep into the soil and that it may not be possible to grow food in the region for many years to come. The amount of TNT (explosive) dropped is unimaginable. Virtually every United Nations convention was broken- including not damaging food supplies, chemical and nuclear facilities. It was an out and out war against nature on both sides. Neither side gave a damn. The Gulf region was the cradle of civilisation, Ancient Mesopotamia. And we have destroyed it. To me that seems very symbolic."

Getting rid of the accumulated arsenals is a huge cost, so also the cost of decontaminating and rehabilitating land and facilities used to produce and test weapons. One American researcher, Michael Renner, has tried to list many of the future consequences of today's arms race, the overall costs of which are astronomical and unquantifiable at this stage - but they will clearly be the legacy we leave to future generations. He lists some of the immediate legacies of war:

- reconstruction, landmine and other unexploded ordinance removal, environmental cleanup, refugee repatriation, demobilisation of armies and the social reintegration of ex-combatants. He then cites a second generation of consequences:

- decommissioning and dismantling of arms, bans and restrictions on arms production and trade, treaty verification, military base closures, conversion of military facilities and resources.

Finally, he lists the positive structures and processes which must be put in place to begin to secure peace:

- peacekeeping, conflict early warning systems, conflict resolution and mediation, strengthened international legal systems, peace research and peace education.

The vast bulk of the cost of such actions will not be borne by today's arms industry or even by today's taxpayers. The legacy of damage and destruction represents a real subsidy by future generations to today's arms manufacturers - a subsidy they neither recognise or consider.

"...Everybody tries to cheat..."

"...all governments are hypocritical about the arms trade. They keep business out of the public eye whilst selling as much as they possibly can. Controls like the UN Conventional Arms Register could work, but only if governments were willing to admit what they have been selling. There will always be a breach in the system as it relies on honesty - and in the arms trade everybody tries to cheat. Also many buyers want to keep their purchases secret and suppliers have to agree or they may lose their contracts."

A Geneva based international weapons dealer quoted in **The New Internationalist** November 1994.

World Military Spending and its Alternatives

Figure 14:2

Total Chart = Total Annual World Military Expenditures $1 trillion

One-tenth of One Percent of Annual World Military Expenditure= $1 billion

Source:
Instituto del Tercar Mundo (1992) **Third World Guide,** Uruguay

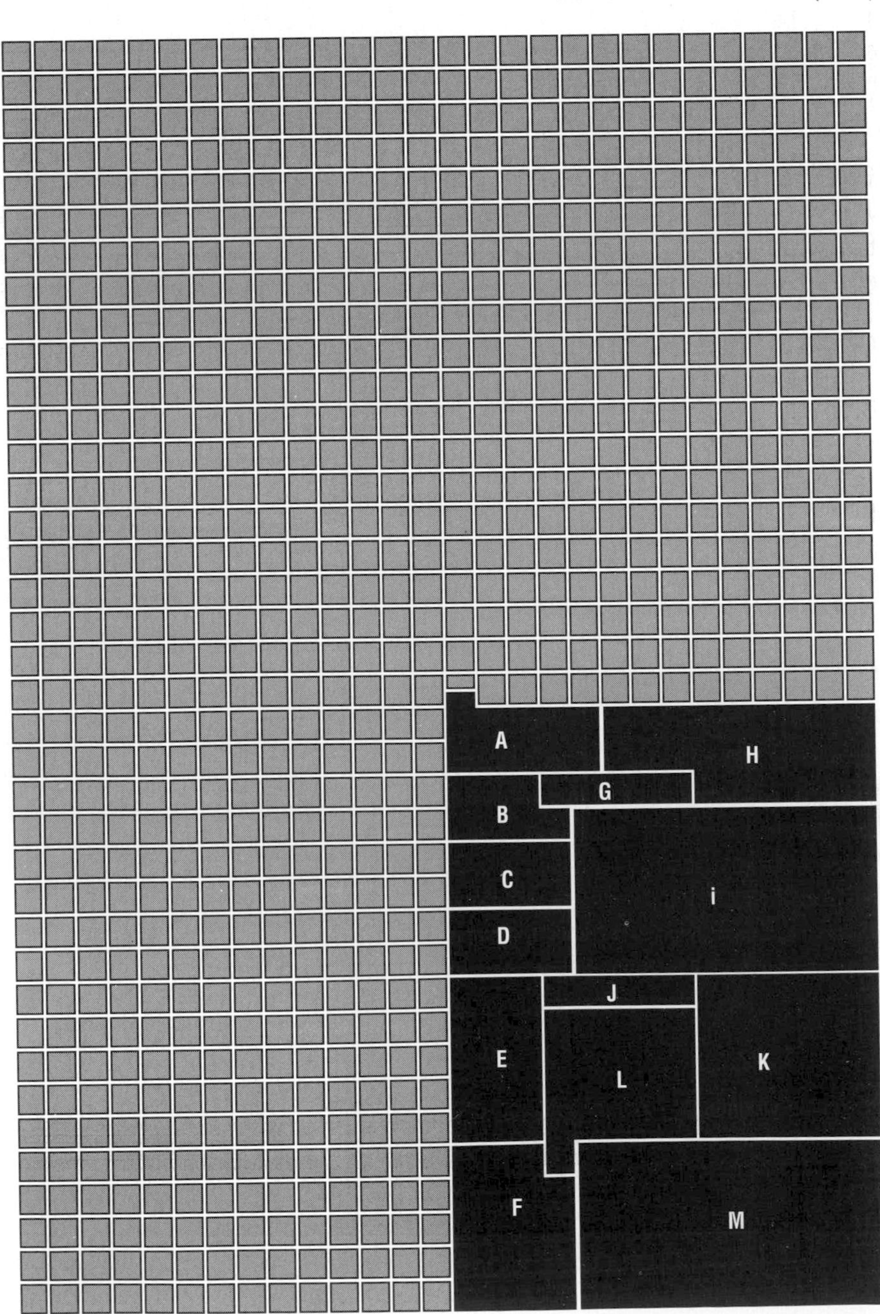

A) STABILIZE POPULATION *$10.5 billion*

B) STOP DEFORESTATION *$7 billion*

C) PREVENT GLOBAL WARMING *$8 billion*

D) PREVENT ACID RAIN *$8 billion*

E) PROVIDE HEALTH CARE *$15 billion*

F) ELIMINATE STARVATION AND MALNOURISHMENT *$19 billion*

G) STOP OZONE DEPLETION *$5 billion*

H) PREVENT SOIL EROSION *$24 billion*

i) PROVIDE CLEAN, SAFE ENERGY
Renewable Energy *$17 billion*
Energy Efficiency *$33 billion*

J) ELIMINATE ILLITTERACY *$5 billion*

K) END DEVELOPING NATIONS' DEBTS *$30 billion*

L) PROVIDE SHELTER *$21 billion*

M) PROVIDE SAFE CLEAN WATER *$50 billion*

"...and in a moment they were gone..."

"August the 6th 1945, 8.15a.m. The streets are full of people; people going to work, people going to school. It is a lovely summer morning: sunshine and blue sky. Blue sky stands for happiness in Japan. The air raid sirens sound. No one pays attention. There's only a single enemy aircraft in the sky.

The aircraft flies across the city. Above the centre something falls, It's hard to see - the bomb is very small; two kilograms in weight, a little larger than a tennis ball in size.

It falls for 10 or 15 seconds, it falls and falls. Then there is a sudden searing flash of light, brighter than a thousand suns. Those who were looking directly at it had their eyes burnt directly in their sockets. They never looked again on people or things.

In the street below there was a business man walking to his work; a lady, as elegant as she was beautiful; a brilliant student, leader of the class; a little girl, laughing as she ran.

And in a moment they were gone. They vanished from the earth. They were utterly consumed by the furnace of the flash. There were no ashes even on the pavement, nothing but their thousand black shadows on the stones. Scores of thousands more, sheltered by walls or buildings from the flash, were driven mad by an intolerable thirst that followed from the heat. They ran in frenzied hordes towards the seven rivers of the deltas upon which Hiroshima is built.

They fought like maniacs to reach the water. If they succeeded, they stopped to drink the poisoned stream, and in a month they, too, were dead.

The Human Development Cost of Arms Imports - Some Case Studies

In the context of the international arms trade, human development priorities often take second place. This is particularly the case in the developing world as the following examples, from 1992, illustrate:

- **CHINA** *bought 6 combat aircraft from Russian a deal which cost the equivalent of providing clean and safe water to 140 million of the 200 million Chinese who currently do not have access to safe water.*
- **INDIA** - *Providing basic education to all of the 15 million Indian girls who do not currently attend school would have cost the equivalent of the 20 MIG.29 jet fighters bought from Russia.*
- **IRAN** *bought two submarines from Russia at a cost that could have provided basic medicines to the country many times over at a time when 13% of the population have no access to health services.*
- **THE REPUBLIC OF KOREA** *ordered 28 missiles from the United States for a cost equivalent to that of immunising 120,000 children and providing safe water, for 3 years, to the 3.5 million Koreans now without it.*
- **MALAYSIA** *bought two warships from the UK at a cost equivalent to providing water for 1/4 of the 5 million Malaysians currently without it.*
- **NIGERIA** *chose to purchase 80 battle tanks from the UK instead of immunising over 2 million unimmunised children.*
- **PAKISTAN** *ordered 40 Mirage jet fighters from France at a cost equivalent to providing safe water for 55 million, family planning services for 20 million, essential medicines for 13 million and health care for 12 million children.*

Widows '95

Widows '95 is the political operating system which frees the world from the drudgery of negotiating, accommodating other opinions, and letting people get on with their lives. It is easy to install, makes millions for arms dealers and manufacturers and is currently available in hundreds of countries around the world*

See the system operate at these major outlets; Bosnia-Herzegovina, Rwanda, Burundi, Zaire, Chechnya, China, and many other parts of Africa, Asia, the Americas and Europe. See the U.N. for details

*Not presently functioning in Northern Ireland

Then came the blast, thousands of miles an hour. Buildings in all directions for kilometres, flattened to the ground. Lorries, cars, milk-carts, human beings, babies' prams, picked up and hurled like lethal projectiles hundreds of metres through the air.

Then the fireball touched the earth, and scores of conflagrations, fanned by hurricane winds, joined in a firestorm. And many thousands more, trapped by walls of flame that leaped higher than the highest tower in the town, in swift or in longer agony, were burnt to death. Then all went black as night.

The mushroom cloud rose 12,000 metres. It blotted out the sun. It dropped its poisoned dust, its fallout, on everything that still remained not lethal in Hiroshima. And death by radio active sickness from the fallout was the fate of those who had survived the flash, the river, the blast, the fire-storm."

Philip Noel-Baker, one of those responsible for the drawing up of the United Nations Charter.

"They don't know the war is over..."

Nayan Chanda, Deputy Editor of the **Far Eastern Economic Review**, writes on the human dimensions of the landmines issue in Cambodia.

"It is nine in the morning. The sun shines brightly through the dusty blinds of Phnom Penh's Preah Ket Meales military hospital. But Hem Sin's face is dark as he waves away the persistent flies buzzing over the dark patch on his bandaged stump. He gathers his crutches and struggles onto his one leg, to confront another day of nightmare since he stepped on a landmine. He stares at the ground below, his 35-year-old face wrinkled like an old man's, and says softly: 'I don't know what I'll do.' Today, his wife and three of his eight children are with him, sharing his hospital food. But tomorrow?

For Cambodia's 30,000 landmine victims - who, like Hem Sin, have lost limbs and livelihoods - tomorrow looks bleak. As if 25 years of warfare, B-52 bombings and mass murder by the Khmer Rouge were not enough, a silent war rages on in Cambodia's countryside, killing or maiming an average of 10 people every day.

This time the enemy is the 10 million landmines, laid by armies of all stripes, that await unsuspecting victims.

'The landmines are very efficient. They do their jobs,' Russell Bedford notes wryly.

The former British-army sergeant is one of four expatriate members of a private voluntary agency, known as the Mine Advisory Group, that was set up in 1992 by Ray McGrath, another British-army officer. MAG's mandate is to rid Cambodia of these silent agents of death. Says Bedford: 'They don't discriminate between friend or foe; they don't know that the war is over".

"Fancy thinking like that..."

"They used near nuclear weapons. Fuel air explosives....They send out a cloud of propane and then they explode the propane gas and the explosion is so great that it sucks the oxygen out of the people's lungs and they suffocate. Great weapon. Then they use cluster bombs. That's one bomb breaking down into little bomblets that also explode. Some of them are made of plastic so that if shrapnel gets into a human you can't see it by x-ray. You can't find where the thing is. It's hard enough to find a bullet in the body, if you're a surgeon. It's pretty difficult. But to find a piece of plastic that you can't see on an x-ray is impossible. That foreign body stays in the patient. It becomes infected and abscessed and the patient dies. Fancy thinking like that to kill people..."

Australian Paediatrician, Helen Caldicott, first President of Physicians for Social Responsibility.

Landmines cheap and profitable to make - expensive and dangerous to remove

Landmines - a case study of the Immorality of Arms

According to the International Committee of the Red Cross:
"Mines may be described as fighters that never miss, strike blindly, and go on killing long after hostilities have ended. In short, mines are the greatest violators of international humanitarian law. They are the most ruthless of terrorists".

International Red Cross statistics on landmines indicate that:

- World-wide, at least 800 people die each month from mine explosions, especially women, children and agricultural workers - the majority from Third World countries. Africa is the most severely affected with an estimated 30 million mines strewn in 18 countries.
- Angola, Afghanistan and Cambodia are the countries worst hit, with an estimated 9 million mines in Angola spread over 33% of the countryside.
- Some 3.5 million refugees are afraid to return to Afghanistan because mountain roads and fields are infested with mines - there are an estimated 9-10 million landmines left in the ground. 8 out of every 10 landmine victims are dead before reaching hospital.
- In Cambodia, there are 30,000 amputees (one for every 236 citizens) - 25 years of conflict have left between 4 and 7 million mines.
- In Mozambique, 18 years of civil war have left a legacy of 2 million landmines affecting all major roads.
- Experts believe that over 3 million mines have been laid in the former Yugoslavia.

In recent years landmines have come to personify so much of the human suffering associated with the arms trade. Today landmines litter the globe, causing death, mutilation, fear as well as agricultural and economic damage. They are located on communications routes, around abandoned military bases, scattered randomly in fields and woods. According to the US State Department, the scale of the problem is huge with over 110 million mines in 62 countries. Landmines come in two types - anti-personnel mines triggered by human beings and designed to maim and kill and anti-tank mines aimed at tanks and military vehicles. The latter are often fitted with anti-handling devices which thus make them anti-personnel mines as well. The increased use of landmines reflects the changes in modern conflicts. Many wars are now long-drawn out, low-intensity conflicts in which one of the objectives is to destabilise and demoralise the opposing army and surrounding civilians. Originally designed for use in war situations, landmines have become, in effect, a development problem because of their social, medical and economic impact. Their impact on those affected by them has become truly horrendous.

Landmines are a particularly lucrative part of the arms trade with at least 340 types of mine in production. Over 48 countries now produce them and at least 29 are known to export them. China, Italy, Romania and the United States are amongst the world's leading exporters.

Clearing away landmines is both expensive and dangerous. The cost of de-commissioning is between \$300 and \$1,000 per mine whereas the original cost of production can be as little as \$3. Thus the total cost of removing current mines will amount to over \$300 billion - and even as governments struggle to remove 80,000 mines per year, another 2 million are put in place.

The Convention on Inhuman Weapons

In 1980, the United Nations adopted a Convention commonly known as the Convention on Inhumane Weapons to which some 36 countries have become signatories. This is one positive sign of progress but until there is a full prohibition on the manufacture and export of landmines and related weapons, civilian populations will remain under serious threat. In 1992, an international campaign for the banning of landmines was launched which calls for an international ban, the establishment of an international fund to promote mine awareness and clearance and for all countries responsible for the production of landmines to contribute to the fund. There are now over 350 organisations involved in the international campaign.

The Irish Government was an original signatory to the UN Inhumane Weapons Convention and ratified it in March 1995 and has consistently called for an international ban on the production of landmines. To date all European States with the exception of Luxembourg and Portugal have ratified the Convention

Discussing Alternatives - The Debate on Conversion

"During 1987-94, the industrial nations appear to have cumulatively saved some $810 billion, and the developing nations $125 billion, producing a sizeable peace dividend of $935 billion. But it is difficult to track where these funds went. Most of the savings appear to have been committed to budget deficit reductions, rather than to social development or to environmental improvements. It is frustrating that, just as social and human agendas were pushed aside at a time of rising military budgets, they continue to be neglected even when military expenditures are being reduced."

Human Development Report 1994, UNDP.

For many decades peace activists and campaigners have argued that a vigorous and creative programme of conversion from military to civilian production was vital for a number of reasons. These reasons include the immorality of the arms industry itself and its destructive capacity; the dangers of ever growing and proliferating arms dealing; the inability of the industry to police itself and the use to which its products would be put; the inherent wastefulness of the industry and its scandalous misuse of resources and human brain power and the potential which conversion would unleash. While most governments and companies paid scant attention to such arguments in the past, they have been given a fresh currency by the reality of reductions in arms spending since the late 1980s.

Instead of seizing the opportunities which reduced military spending has provided, governments have chosen to simply reduce spending overall. Thus the anticipated *"peace dividend"* which the ending of the Cold War promised has not materialised. Instead it has, in the words of researcher Michael Renner, *"...disappeared into a gigantic fiscal Bermuda Triangle"*. Renner stresses three key areas in the overall conversion strategy - assisting countries to overcome the devastation of warfare and the legacies which it leaves behind; to reduce significantly the arsenals of weapons which have accumulated over time and the need to build peacemaking institutions. He stresses the greatly reduced costs of making peace rather than war and argues that a relatively modest budget of perhaps $20-$30 billion per year could make a huge and real difference.

Such conversion expenditure needs to be budgeted for as increasing numbers of military personnel are now being demobilised. Of the approximately 32 million soldiers world-wide in 1990, some 2.2 million were demobilised in 1990/92 and similar reductions are anticipated for subsequent years. Such demobilisations need to be also placed alongside the civilian consequences of reductions in spending. Most of the major powers are currently involved in large scale reductions - in the case of the US, some 895 base closures are planned along with the bringing home of approximately 174,000 troops. In Europe it is estimated that due to the reductions in military spending world-wide, over 1/2 million jobs could be lost in the industry in Europe between 1990 and 1996. In order to deal with such realities, conversion must be firmly placed on the agenda. As against this and contrary to the view that conversion will have negative consequences, the IMF suggests that an internationally co-ordinated 20% cut in defence spending would actually boost world trade. The positive benefits of conversion are also frequently overlooked. According to researcher Mary Kaldor writing on the arms trade in India, it costs $13,500 to create one job in the arms industry, $3,800 in civilian industry, $90 in road construction, $80 in agriculture and $9 in trade and commerce.

However, other studies point out that the conversion programmes implemented in most States to date have been "small or unimportant". There appears to be little will to tackle the reality in any systematic and sustained manner. States such as Germany, Spain and the UK have not created conversion budgets at all while those of Italy, France, China and Eastern Europe are tiny. The situation in Russia is extremely difficult due to political uncertainty and to economic crisis. Until public opinion forces governments to tackle the issue forcefully, the grounds for optimism on the realising of the *peace dividend* remain weak.

Proposing a Global Demilitarisation Fund

In 1994, Nobel Peace Prize laureate, Oscar Arias, proposed that industrial countries set aside one-fifth of their peace dividend, and that developing countries set aside one-tenth, to establish a Global Demilitarisation Fund. Under such a mechanism the Fund could reach as much as $126 billion for the period 1995-2000. The Fund would assist countries overcome the legacy of war; fund weapons dismantlement and conversion and help build a global peace system. To date the proposal has fallen on deaf ears.

Laser Weapons

Weapons for the specific purpose of inflicting permanent blindness are expected to become operational within the next five years. Laser rifles are capable of inflicting permanent blindness at a range of up to one kilometre via a silent, invisible laser beam which burns the retina and causes haemorrhaging.

Blindness is a particularly severe form of permanent injury. Their use would have widespread implications for civilians as well as military. Intentional blinding as a method of warfare causes long-term damage and suffering and should be abhorrent to all right thinking people.

For further information on these weapons and on what you can do about them, contact Pax Christi in either Dublin or London (see addresses).

Undergoing Change and Conversion - Case Studies

SCOTLAND

When General Electric bought the Edinburgh factory of the Ferranti Corporation in 1990, the non-military sector was not included in the deal, leaving the factory 100% dependent on military contracts. With falling military budgets, the Manufacturing, Science and Finance Union launched a campaign to save jobs through converting away from military to civilian contracts. There was considerable public support for the initiative and by the end of 1992, a separately funded civilian department was set up. This department then won a major contract worth £4 million for a communications system for the Channel Tunnel overnight rolling stock. Just one year after the practical application of a conversion strategy, 5% of the turnover of the plant has been diversified away from military production. Developing this further will no doubt be extremely difficult, but this start bodes well.

RUSSIA

In 1993, the Russian Federation sponsored the "Conversion 93" conference and exhibition in Birmingham with a view to winning contracts for the civil products produced by over 200 previously military factories in Russia. One company, Almaz, previously built ships for the Russian Navy but is now producing vessels for environmental protection use while another, Vesta, which used to make electronic products for the military, is now successfully manufacturing washing machines since 1989. Overall the former USSR has undergone the most dramatic conversion programme - with 778 establishments and 347 research organisations converted since the Cold War ended. There were major job losses, but two-thirds of the 887,000 defence workers affected were rehired on civil work.

ENGLAND

In England, defence company Dowty Aerospace (UK) has diversified into civil production, making landing gear for the Airbus. A GEC-Marconi subsidiary has successfully moved into making TV satellite dishes.

Source: **Fire and Forget,** An Information Pack 1994, Commonweal, Scotland.

The human consequences of arms dealing are horrific - a Kurdish refugee 1991.

▼ REFERENCES

Commonweal (1994) **Fire and Forget: An Information Pack on the World Arms Trade,** Edinburgh.

Pax Christi (1990) **Arms for the Poor** and (1992) **On the Arms Trade,** Antwerp.

Colm Regan (1995) **The Business of Blood,** Dublin, Calypso Productions.

Ruth Sivard (1991-93) **World Military and Social Expenditures,** World Priorities, Washington.

UNICEF (1996) **State of the World's Children Report,** Oxford University Press.

UNDP (1992 and 1995) **Human Development Report,** Oxford University Press.

Worldwatch Institute (1995) **State of the World Report,** Washington.

World Development Movement (1995) **Gunrunners Gold: how the public's money finances arms sales,** London.

Note: This chapter was originally written as an information pack on arms commissioned by Calypso Theatre Company to support its production of the play Business of Blood by Donal O'Kelly and Kenny Kenneth. Thanks to Calypso for permission to reproduce it here.

BRITAIN, THE RICH WORLD for whom?

Roger Robinson

"The British are increasingly at risk. The chances of their jobs disappearing, of their incomes falling, of their homes being repossessed or being impossible to sell, of their families breaking up, of their networks of friendships disintegrating, have not been higher since the war."

Economist Will Hutton, **The Guardian** 30.10.95

Introduction

Will Hutton obviously believes that the development process in Britain leaves a lot to be desired. Of course injustice and inequality are less extreme within Britain than at a global scale. You might say that given our inability, or reluctance, to commit resources to ameliorate dreadful situations of global absolute poverty and mal-distribution of resources, what hope is there for us to rise to the challenge of the less obvious relative poverty and injustice at home? On the other hand you might suggest that if we could at least cope with our own situation we would learn something and transfer attention to the global issues.

Poverty and Relative Poverty

Relative poverty is a serious issue in Britain, with the situation for some people approaching absolute poverty. The lack of basic needs has increasingly been used as an indication of poverty.

> *"Basic needs are those things that an individual must have in order to survive as a human being. Essentially , these are clean (unpolluted) air and water, adequate and balanced food, physical and emotional security, physical and mental rest, and culturally and climatically appropriate clothing and shelter."*

Development economist Stan Burkey, **People First**, Zed Books, London, 1993.

No-one would argue with these obvious needs, and if they are not being met for people they are in a condition of **absolute poverty.** But individuals do not exist in a vacuum, and there are other basic needs.

> *"It is necessary to expand the list of basic individual needs to include those of a community. These might be defined as sexual regeneration, a system of communication (language), a belief and educational system for cultural continuity, physical and cultural security, a political system defining leadership and decision making, and systems of health and recreation for maintaining well-being among sufficient numbers to maintain the community."*

Stan Burkey, **People First.**

The detail of this list can be debated, but the general thrust cannot be denied. Though it is not in itself a statement of morality it does form the basis for a moral agenda for development.

Relative poverty is less easy to measure but can be the cause of great mental and physical pain and suffering. Relative poverty is a condition in which basic needs are met, but where there is an inability to meet additional perceived needs and desires. In Britain such needs could include a personal living space, access to TV, radio, more than one set of clothes relatively new, a variety of diet, access to transport and so on - many of which can be essential to a person's well-being in British urban society.

Serious poverty is by and large spatially confined in Britain to people living in certain areas of Inner Cities and in peripheral parts of Britain with specific employment problems. While 10 million people enjoy a use of resources averaging nearly £400 per week, and 20 million use £200, there are 10 million people using only an average of £70 each. The poorest one million include people like Felicia in William Trevor's novel.

Felicia has come from Ireland to a town in the Midlands of England in search of her boy friend, by whom she is pregnant. Most of her money is gone.

That evening the hostel is full when she arrives. In a Spud-U-Like she spends some of her money on a cup of tea and asks the people whose table she shares if the bus station remains open all night. It's not something they'd know, they say. On the street again she is accosted by two men loitering outside a pool-hall. They want to know her name and when she tells them they want to know where she's from. They say they can fix her up, but she doesn't understand. She feels frightened and hurries on. When she arrives at the bus station she settles herself on a seat, but an hour later is told that no further buses are due either to arrive or depart, and she is asked to go. She finds the railway station, and lies on a wooden seat in the waiting room, but from there, too, she is eventually moved on.

....

She wanders on eventually, resting sometimes on a pavement seat, moving again when it becomes too cold. At a stall beneath a bridge where taxi drivers stand about she buys a sausage roll that is reduced to fourpence because it's stale. The air is dank with mist.

Already, hours ago, the homeless of this town have found their night-time resting places - in doorways, and underground passages left open in error, in abandoned vehicles, in the derelict gardens of demolished houses. As maggots make their way into cracks in masonry, so the people of the streets have crept into one-night homes in graveyards and on building sites, in alleyways and courtyards, making walls of dustbins pulled close together, and roofs of whatever lies nearby. Some have crawled up scaffolding to find a corner beneath the tarpaulin that protects an untiled expanse. Others have settled down in cardboard cartons that once contained dishwashers or refrigerators.

Hidden away, the people of the streets drift into sleep induced by alcohol or agitated by despair, into dreams that carry them back to lives that were once theirs.

Novelist William Trevor, ***Felicia's Journey****, Penguin 1995.*

Spatial and Social Segregation

The spatial segregation of social groups means that the wealthy and so-called middle classes, who make up at least 3/5 of Britain's population, are seldom brought face to face with the realities of deprivation even in the cities in which they live and work. Homelessness did become a live issue largely because suburban residents arriving at Waterloo Station in Central London had to walk through a "Cardboard City" to get to their offices each day. Suddenly it became a political priority to get the homeless off the streets. Out of sight is out of mind - would something happen if the middle classes were continuously brought face to face with inner city deprivation and the reality of 40% male unemployment and hopelessness? I expect we would suffer from reality fatigue.

The situation described in Manor estate on the following page is not unique, life like this exists in cities all over Britain in spite of continuous efforts for improvements. Monsal estate in Manchester has had £14 million of national and local government money spent on it in the last five years. In the short term things are better - no boarded up houses, water and power connected, burglaries are down and drug dealers no longer control the streets, and most important perceptions have changed. But in the longer term what will happen? The grants are finished, unemployment is still 25%, the drug dealers are still there underground.

Britain's major development issue must be "how do we manage to spend so much money, both as individuals and as a State, without improving the quality of life for so many people?" Britain has for each person as much money as Ghana or India have for 20 people, or Brazil has for 5 people. But most people in those countries have their individual basic needs, and many are very comfortable. Yet the amount two people in the UK spend each year on Alcohol and Tobacco is equivalent to one average person's total use of resources in India for the year.

The average UK resident used about £6,000 on consumer spending in 1993, the GDP per person was over £9,000. This doesn't mean there was a lot of saving, but rather

TO THE MANOR BORN

Mick and Shane portray the emptiness of life on the estate where 'society is breaking down'

It was only 11am but the two-litre plastic bottle of cider was already half empty.

Mick, 23, and Shane, 22, took a swig each and examined the remains of a bonfire from the night before in the cehtre of Sheffield's Manor estate.

"It's not us causing trouble. It's the babbies - the kids," said Mick, a "Manorite", born and raised on this sprawling high-crime, post-industrial council estate overlooking Sheffield's city centre.

"The kids smash windows. All we do is light the bonfires. You spend all day supping 'cos there's nowt else to do. Then you gather here at night for the buzz and you have a laugh and build a fire to keep warm."

Sometimes between 40 and 50 youths and their girlfriends will leave their crumbling 1920s council homes and walk up the road to this patch of waste land behind St. Swithun's Church and a development of smart new council homes, to gather round these fires.

There is, they say, nothing else to do. They take drugs, drink beer and cider and have sex - local residents are forever finding discarded condoms.

The bonfires are a problem. Barely a wooden fence remains standing in this pocket of the estate because they have been ripped up and burned along with the large wooden sleepers that Sheffield council had innovatively used to surround once neat flowerbeds.

....

Resources have been ploughed into Manor estate, which has views out across the disused pits and rusty steelworks.

Nevertheless there is a sense of slow moral and physical decay. New brickwork bears graffiti. Smashed windows in houses not even completed tell a stark story of wanton vandalism.

"There is intimidation rather than violence. We've not got gun-toting gangs. What we have got is the drip, drip, drip effect."

Road after road on the estate contains boarded-up houses where residents have simply left and no-one has been willing to replace them.

"There are many elderly people here and we've all been abandoned"

Ronnie, 82, a retired miner, has had six different neighbours in the last 12 months that he has lived in his council bungsalow.

"One lot were burned out the first night and left the next day. The yobs started a fire in their garden," he said. "They run across the roofs, you know. You can hear their feet on the slates at 3 am sometimes. It's a terrible racket.

Not a day goes by without someone swearing at me, threatening me, stealing wood for fires, throwing bricks at the door and windows."

There are initiatives. "It's not all bad," says Ernest a 50-year-old former cutlery worker. "I have a vision of all the good things happening, the new building works, the way most people look out for each other, it keeps me going."

*Journalist Caroline Davies, **The Daily Telegraph** p4 26.10.95*

Wards are small administrative areas - more wards had concentrated poverty in 1991 than in 1981, and the troubles pile up in the same areas.

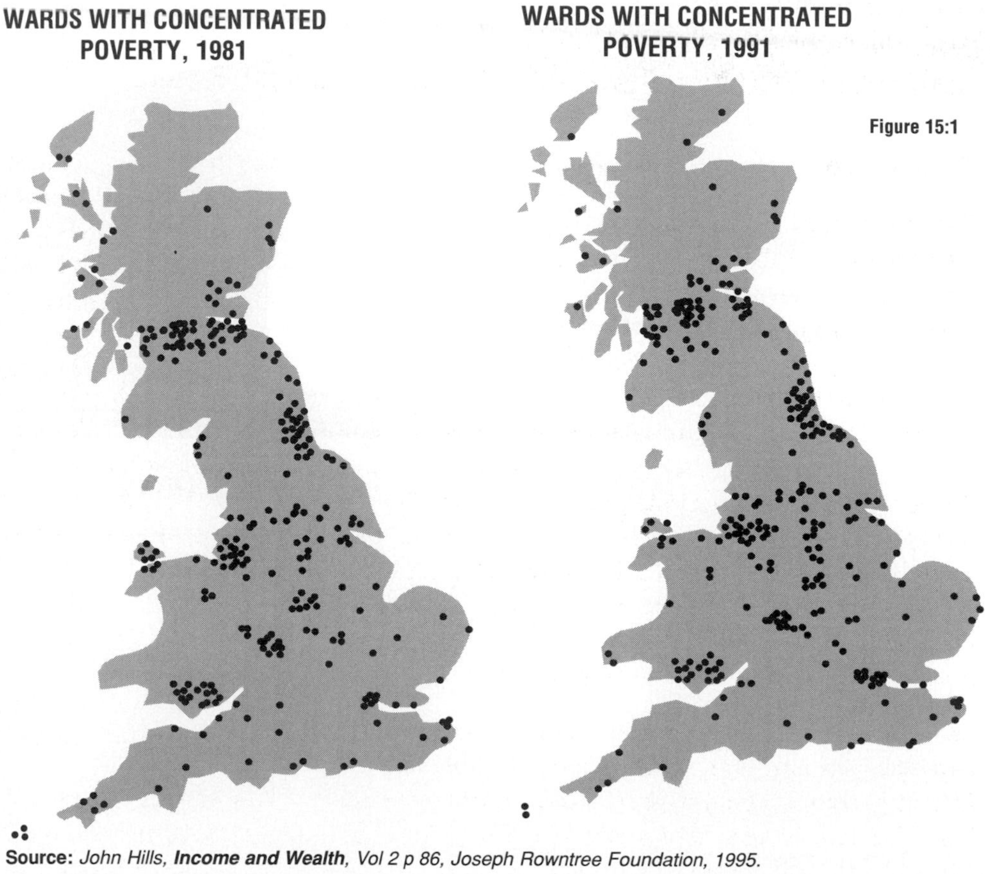

Figure 15:1

Source: *John Hills, **Income and Wealth**, Vol 2 p 86, Joseph Rowntree Foundation, 1995.*

that taxes and National Insurance are high and government spend about £3,000 per person.

This spending is not spread evenly across society.

The table of UK spending shows that basic items like housing, food and fuel are very expensive - an average Third World income would not go very far in these terms. But any comparison with the Third World must take into account exchange rates (which often do not reflect the purchasing power of the money in its own country) and prices. On average you would get about five times as much for each £ in a Third World country as you would in Britain. However, people in the UK do spend a lot on "extras" like tobacco, alcohol and leisure. The table below shows some regional variations in spending - less in Wales and Northern Ireland than in Scotland and England, and it does show how the larger population of England dominates the UK economic scene.

Britain has created an economy and expectations that demand an ever increasing production and flow of money to ensure that the rich get richer, which might be acceptable if the poor received an increasing share of improvements. But the reverse is true and the poor are being left behind and their numbers are increasing. Between 1971 and 1992 the proportion of people receiving below half the average national income increased from 11% to 21%.

From 1979 to 1992 the proportion of the national income going to the poorest 20% of the population dropped from 10% to 7%. The real income of the poorest tenth dropped by 15%. Is this "development"?

The growth in the gap between rich and poor is widening in Britain but this generalisation covers a complex situation. Each income bracket includes a wide variety of families, the extract from "The Parade" in the Rowntree Foundation's *Inquiry into Income and Wealth* shows just a couple of families from each fifth of the income distribution.

Figure 15:2

COMPOSITON OF HOUSEHOLD INCOME 1992

	POOREST TENTH £	%	RICHEST TENTH £	%
Wages and salaries	700	13	32700	69
+Self-employment	300	6	6400	4
+Occupational pensions	100	2	2200	5
+Other market income	300	6	4700	10
=TOTAL MARKET INCOME	**1500**	**28**	**46000**	**98**
+Retirement pensions	1100	21	500	1
+Means-tested benefits	1800	34	100	0
+Other cash benefits	900	17	400	1
=GROSS INCOME	**5300**	**100**	**47000**	**100**
-Direct Taxes	800	15	10700	23
-Indirect taxes	1700	32	5200	11
=POST-TAX INCOME	**2800**	**53**	**31100**	**66**

People with the least income pay a greater proportion of it out in taxes!

John Hills, **Income and Wealth**, Vol 2 p 16, Joseph Rowntree Trust, 1995.

Figure 15:3

UK SPENDING PER HOUSEHOLD IN 1993 *£ per week*

	Housing	Fuel	Food	Alc&Tob	Clothes	Household & services	Motor & fares	Leisure	Misc	Total	Per person	No of HH
UK	45	13	50	18	17	39	43	39	13	277	111.7	23,430
England	47	13	50	17	17	39	44	40	13	280	113.4	19,620
Wales	39	14	49	18	18	34	38	31	10	250	99.7	1,148
Scotland	35	14	50	20	19	34	41	38	14	265	107.7	2,089
N.I.	25	16	54	18	18	34	47	30	12	254	89.0	573

Source: **Social Trends**, HMSO, 1995.

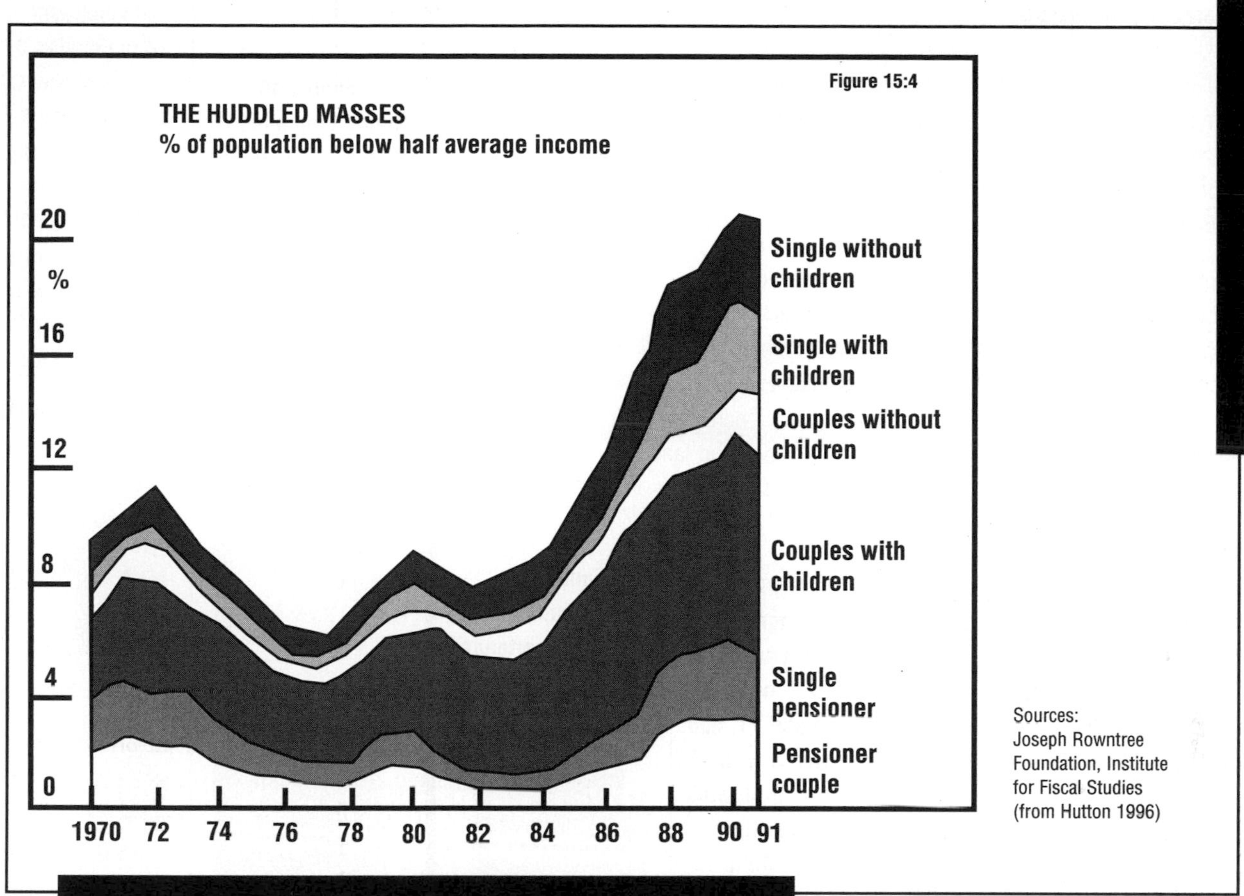

Sources:
Joseph Rowntree Foundation, Institute for Fiscal Studies (from Hutton 1996)

The UK Income Parade

The Parade ranks families into fifths by their net incomes (after tax, National Insurance etc has been deducted), adjusted to allow for the relative size of households. Incomes are at April 1993 prices. The full Parade contained 50 families. For visual comparison the "height" of each person is given assuming the average income height is 5 feet.

A new element in the pattern seems to be a large group of people in the middle of the income spread who experience the uncertainty of insecurity. Whilst some forms of uncertainty can lead to creativity and excitement for some individuals, the kind of uncertaintity associated with lack of tenure at work, forces insisting on continuously increasing productivity, high levels of financial commitments for housing and family needs, and low savings, is debilitating and eventually disintegrating for individuals, friends and family.

Britain's economy since 1979 is an example of the implementation of a "successful" Structural Adjustment Policy (SAP), a model of the IMF policy demanded of so many countries in the South before assistence funds are made available.

Family 3
Couple aged 52 (woman) and 60 (man) with son 13, living in housing association accommodation. He is unemployed. Receive Child Benefit, Income Support and local tax benefit. Equivalent income £66.

Family 9
Couple both aged 40 with daughter, 12, and son, 9, with private landlord. Both work full-time (one is more or less self-employed). They also receive Family Credit, Child Benefit and local tax benefit. Equivalent income £102.

Family 23
Couple aged 36 (woman) and 41 (man) with two sons aged 14 and 11, and daughter, 3, with a mortgage. Both work full-time. They receive Child Benefit. Equivalent income £196.

Family 27
Single woman aged 53 with a mortgage and in full-time work. Equivalent income £239.

Family 40
Single man aged 26 with a mortgage and working full-time in self-employment. Equivalent income £344.

Family 48
Couple aged 62 (woman) and 66 (man) owning their own home outright. He works full-time in self-employment; she works part-time. They receive the state pension. Equivalent income £617.

THE BOTTOM FIFTH | THE MIDDLE FIFTH | THE TOP FIFTH

Figure 15:5 **Source**: Profiles of 10 families from John Hills, **Income and Wealth** Vol 2, Rowntree Foundation, 1995

Figure 15:6

PERCENTAGE OF ALL ADULTS AGED 16 TO RETIREMENT

THE ADVANTAGED 40%
Those in full time employment for 2 years or more and on more than 50% of median earnings
Those in full time self employment for 2 years or more
Those in part time employment for 5 years or more
THE NEWLY INSECURE 30%
Those in full time employment for less than 2 years and those on less than 50% median earnings
Those in part time employment for less than 2 years
Those in temporary employment
THE DISADVANTAGED 30%
The unemployed
The so-called economically "inactive", which includes unpaid work - child-rearing, housework, shopping, learning and so on!

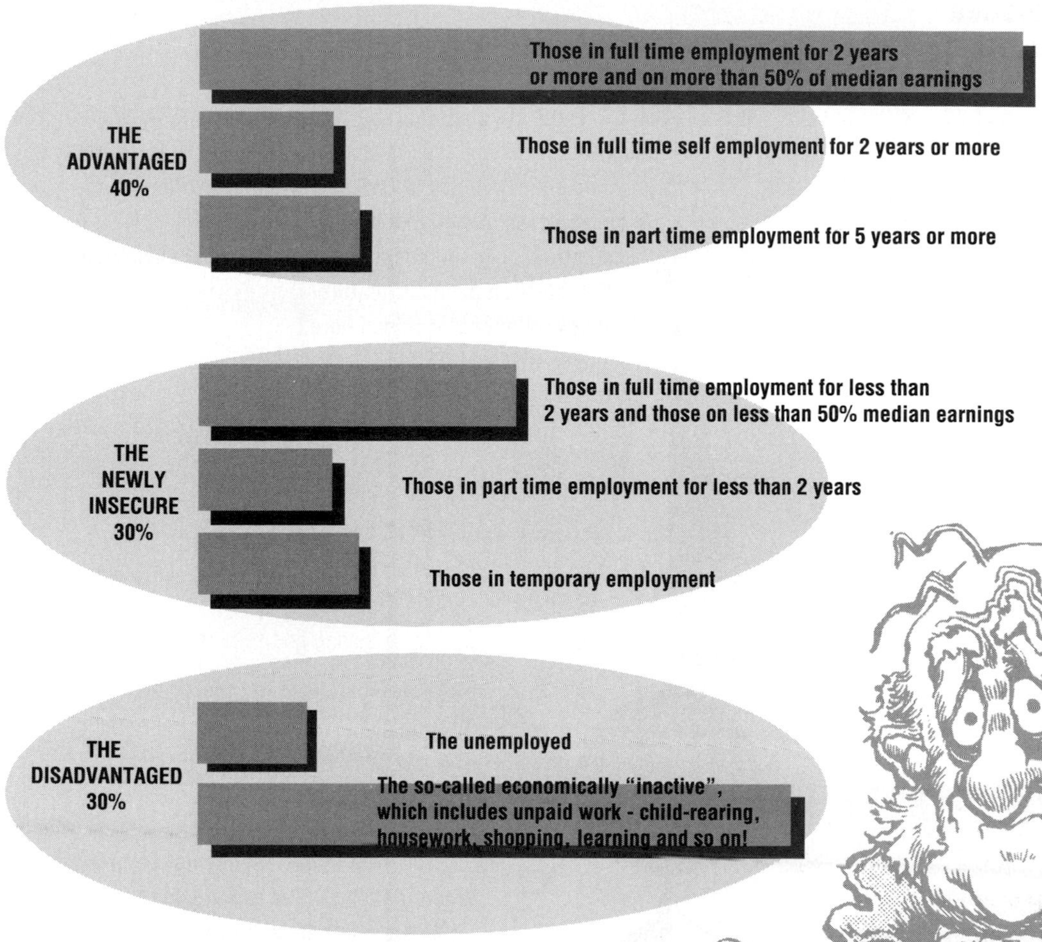

There is a new source of inequality abroad. On top of the long standing concerns about the growing gap between rich and poor, there is an increasing awareness of a new range of risks that are bringing fresh patterns of social distress and exclusion. Unemployment and low pay are no longer the sole measures of inequity and lack of social well-being; with the rise of new forms of casualised, temporary and contract forms of employment, even those on average incomes and above can become the victims of pressures beyond their control. They too can be left partially or completely excluded from their social networks.

Economist Will Hutton **Guardian 30.10.95**

Development issues in Britain

Development issues can be very complex. The Development Compass Rose helps to feature the major dimensions of development and the way in which they combine in specific situations.

NATURAL: These are questions about the environment - energy, air, water, soil, living things and their relationships to each other. These questions are about the built as well as the 'natural' environment.

What reserves of coal remain?
What effect does the mining have on the local environment?
What effect on people's health?
What kind of coal is mined here?

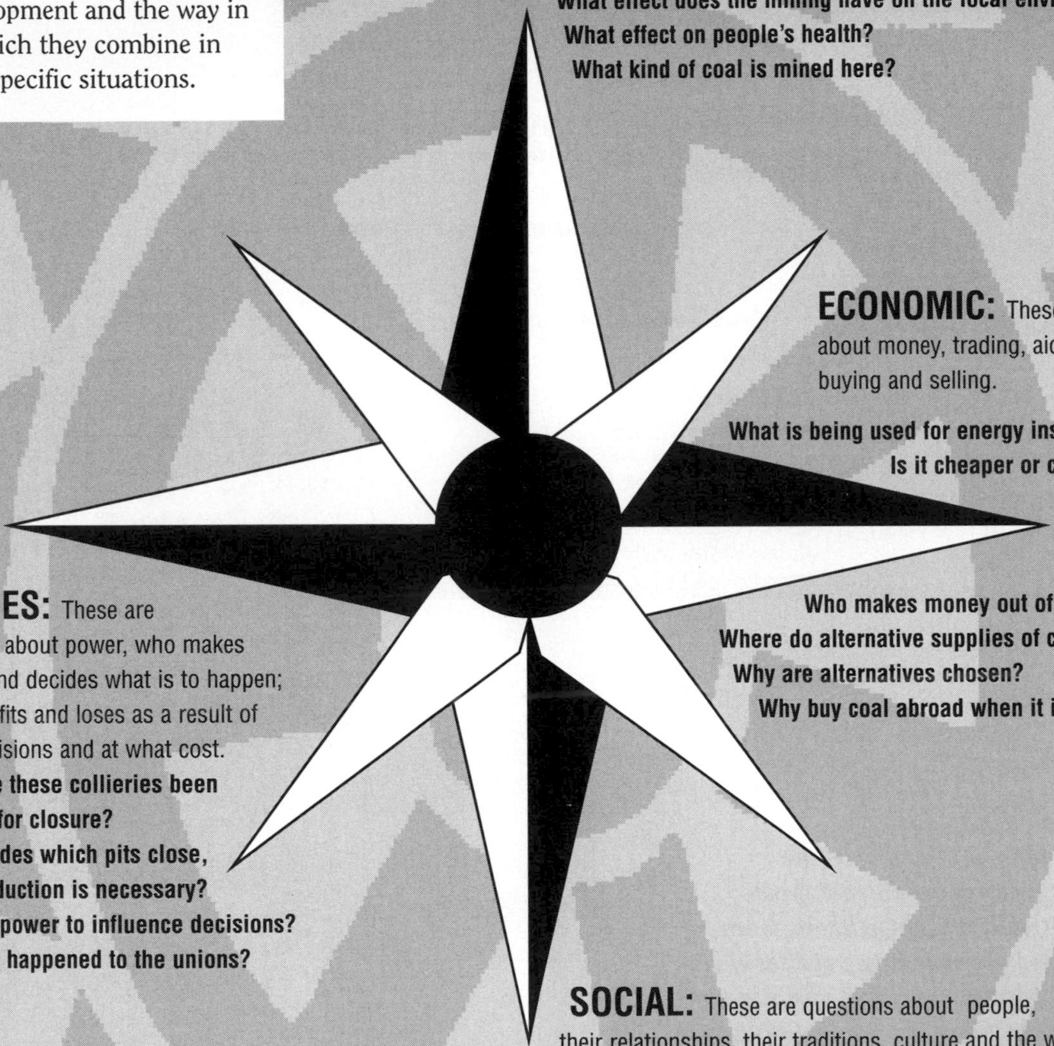

ECONOMIC: These are questions about money, trading, aid, ownership, buying and selling.

What is being used for energy instead of coal?
Is it cheaper or cleaner?

Who makes money out of the enterprise?
Where do alternative supplies of coal come from?
Why are alternatives chosen?
Why buy coal abroad when it is available here?

WHO DECIDES: These are questions about power, who makes choices and decides what is to happen; who benefits and loses as a result of these decisions and at what cost.

Why have these collieries been selected for closure?
Who decides which pits close, what production is necessary?
Who has power to influence decisions?
What has happened to the unions?

SOCIAL: These are questions about people, their relationships, their traditions, culture and the way they live. They include questions about how, for example, gender, race, disability, class and age affect social relationships.

How much do the local communities rely on coal mining?
What will happen in mining villages with closure?
What will redundant miners do?
What effect will closure have on their families and children, and on their self-esteem?

The example of change in the South Staffordshire coal mining industry refers to events in a particular locality. But these events have ramifications and are influenced by events and processes at regional, national and global scales as well.

Figure 15:7

Sources: Tide (1995) **Development Compass Rose: A Consultation Pack,** Birmingham, DEC

Democracy - is it working?

Britain's first past the post election system has its drawbacks. Since 1979 for instance, with a Conservative government virtually unchallenged, the majority of the electorate who didn't vote Conservative have been powerless in the face of radical right policies. The same thing could happen to non-Labour voters in South East England for the next 20 years! The situation in Scotland points up weaknesses in the system even more dramatically, where national identity and political preferance combine. Conservatives would not be in power in any National Assembly for Scotland, and the Scottish people have been virtually disenfranchised by English dominance.

Both major parties are afraid of losing power if any alternative system were introduced and so proposals for reform are constantly marginalised. But the question of democratic representation and the balance of power between local and national authorities are issues at the centre of future development in the UK.

The natural disenchantment in Scotland, and in many other parts of Britian (especially Wales), with Westminster and the further centralisation of power, must lead to a re-assessment of the democratic processes.

Democracy at work

(In 1995 more than 1,000 phosphorous devices were washed up on the shores of South-West Scotland; Dounreay is a nuclear fuel reprocessing plant on the far north coast of Scotland; Brent Spar is a North Sea oil rig.)

House of Commons 24 October 1995
Opposition Day
3.45 pm
Ms Roseanna Cunningham (Perth and Kinross): I beg to move,
"That this House recognises the depth of public concern in Scotland and beyond at HM Government's failure to provide proper stewardship of Scotland's environment; notes the triple threat posed by plans to increase the number of reprocessing contracts at Dounreay, the disclosure of the munitions dump at Beaufort Dyke and continuing uncertainty over Shell's plans to decommission the Brent Spar;
....
...................and rejects the contemptuous treatment which fleeces Scotland of its natural resources while imposing unacceptable environmental dangers upon the Scottish population, threatening industries such as fishiing, farming, food processing, whisky and tourism which depend critically on Scotland's perception as a country with a clean environment."
In choosing this topic for debate, my colleagues and I in the Scottish National Party seek to highlight what we consider to be the real concerns that are uppermost in the minds of the Scottish people. We have chosen to focus on three specific issues. First, I refer to the disclosure by the Ministry of Defence in June of this year that more than 1 million tonnes of conventional munitions had been dumped at Beaufort Dyke off the South-West coast of Scotland over 50 years, between the 1920s and the 1970s. Secondly, there is a prospect of up to 15,000 spent nuclear fuel rods of United States origin making their way to Dounreay for reprocessing, with all the risks that that will inevitably entail, both at Dounreay and in the course of transportation. Thirdly, I want to mention the continuing uncertainty over the disposal of Brent Spar, with the Government refusing to rule out the idea that it could yet be dumped at sea. Each of these issues is of vital importance to every man, woman and child in Scotland, because of their impact on the perception of Scotland as a clean country .... Each issue is different, but they all have one thing in common: they raise questions about the safety of people's lives, the security of their jobs and the sustainability of their communities.
They also have something else in common - an apparent view of Scotland as some kind of convenient waste disposal unit. That certainly makes a change from the Thatcher years, when Scotland appeared to be regarded as a testing ground, but I do not think the people of Scotland will regard it as a change for the better.

4.16 pm
After debate dominated by concerned Scottish MPs:
The Parliamentary Under-Secretary of State for Scotland (Mr. Raymond S. Robertson): I beg to move, to leave out from "House" to the end of the Question, and add instead thereof:
"congratulates Her Majesty's Government on their environmental achievements in Scotland and applauds their continues commitment to the further protection and enhancement of the environment, notably through the creation of the Scottish Environment Protection Agency; ...."
...... Scotland has an international reputation as an environmental beacon. I fear that the only problem is that the perenniel parochialism of the SNP creates an extreme distortion of the current healthy situation.

7.02 pm
After further debate ranging widely around the issues the motion was put to the vote and the Question negatived by 26 to 159 votes. The Question was then amended and passed as proposed by Mr. Robertson.
***Hansard** 24.11.95*

Long term development of Britain

Britain's development has historically been dominated by the arrival of waves of colonists, conquerors and settlers. Since 8000 BC during the Middle Stone Age, the British Isles have been physically separated from the continent and invaders have arrived by sea, mostly landing in the South and East and working their way Westwards. Giving development processes an historical perspective provides a basis for a better understanding of what is going on now.

The Norman invasion and successful occupation and settlement of England from 1066 concluded the series of migrations from Europe that peopled Britain.

After a vivid account in a History lesson of the Norman invasion and conquest of Britain, Luke, an 11 year-old British Afro-Caribbean boy, put up his hand and asked "Well, where are all the Normans now?" Any answers?

Each succeeding group had a technology that enabled them to subdue the existing settlers, and develop an economic and political system based on their own needs and priorities. Eventually each invader either melded with or expelled the existing groups. The exception was the Roman interlude when few Romans actually settled and the occupation came to an end when the Roman Empire crumbled. Since the establishment of Norman control, development seems much more complicated yet continuous threads can be seen. By 1200 AD Britain was already a truly multi-cultural country with Celts, Picts, Vikings, Saxons, Normans and Belgae (as well as descendants of earlier peoples) living together. By the 18th century, England, Wales and Scotland had became a united country (Great Britain), largely by the expansion of English/Norman political power, but without large scale immigrant settlement.

The scale and speed of activities changed rapidly from 1400, so that global movements and expansions by rich nations became the norm, with British ships sailing for trade and conquest to Africa, the East and then to the Americas and Australia. Little concern was shown for the inhabitants of those places, just as invaders of Britain had only wished to subdue and use the inhabitants they found.

Before the industrial revolution some British had moved with other Europeans to settle in the Americas and Africa, but it was the new technologies of the late 18th and early 19th centuries, the increasing population in Europe, and the huge resource demands of the increased production, that made it possible (and seen as a necessity) for people to migrate from Britain and Europe in large numbers to America, Australia and Africa.

So the waves of people with superior technology continued to advance towards what were seen as the edges of the known and settled world, still with scant regard for those already there.
In the same way that England had become independent from the

Early Development in Britain
Invaders, migrants and settlers

3500 BC *New Stone Age invaders from France and the Low Countries to South-east England; from Western France, Spain and Portugal to the West coasts of Britain and Ireland. Megaliths, long barrows and farming.*

1900 BC *Bronze Age "Beaker Folk" landing on the South and East coasts from central Europe and the Steppes of Asia.*
Henges, round barrows and more productive sedentary agriculture.

900 BC *Waves of immigrant Celts landing in the South and East and some via Western seas into Ireland and Scotland. First surviving languages: Gaelic, Scots, Irish, Welsh and Cornish.*

300 BC *Pictic Celts in Northern Scotland, British Celts in Southern Scotland, refugees from the Roman Empire including the Belgae from the Lower Rhine settling in Britain.*

43 AD to 200 AD *Roman conquest. All of England occupied and controlled by the Romans, Wales subdued, Hadrian's Wall marked the eventual limit of Roman control.*
The pattern of Roman towns, roads and villas can still be seen today.

400 AD *Roman withdrawal. Scots Celts from Northern Ireland settle in and Christianise Scotland.*

600 AD *Anglo-Saxon invasions in South and East push many Celts into Wales and Scotland. Saxons develop lowland farming and reinforce pattern of towns as market centres. Scandinavians (especially Vikings) invade the North and Northeast, many settle.*

1066 AD *Norman invasion and settlement, manorial system established. The Kingdom of England was united and stabilised. England, Wales and Scotland became a single nation state in the 18th century.*

Normans in France, so the British settlers took independence from Britain. As the Roman occupation ended in Britain, so did British rule in the Indian sub-continent, Africa and the Caribbean.

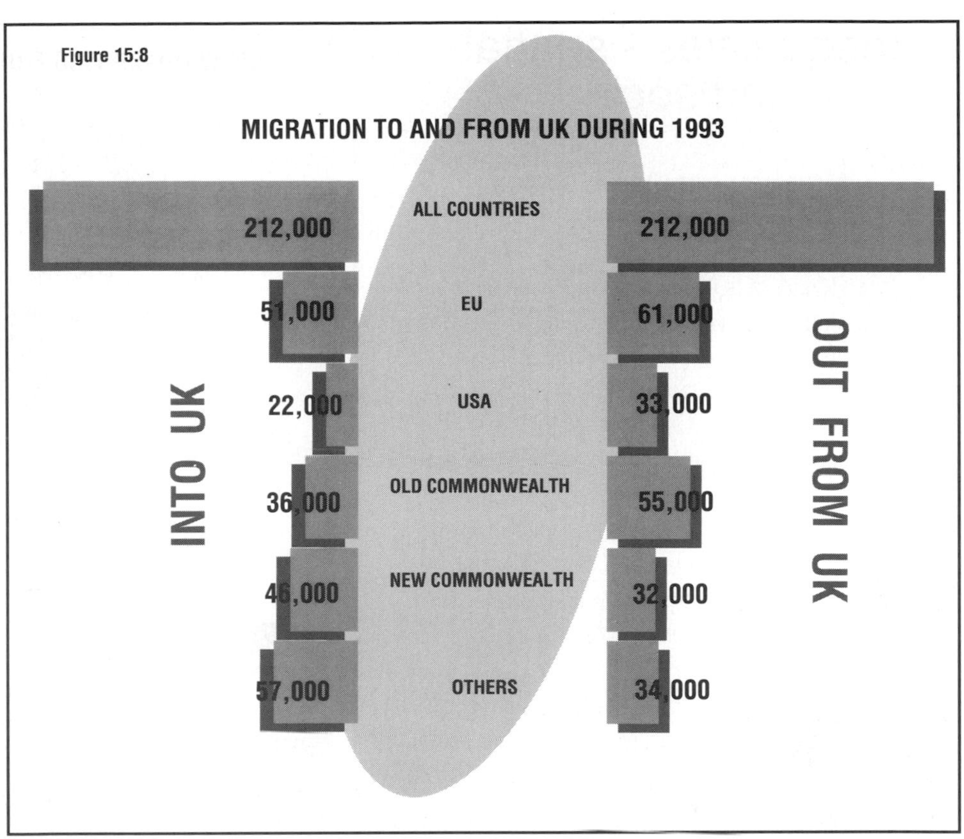

Since the 19th century the waves of migration have been less likely to be powerful peoples seeking new space - the world seems "full" - but more often peoples who have been dispossessed in their own land or who are simply looking for a new and better life. So Irish and Southern European people continued to migrate to the "New World" in large numbers during the 20th century. In the early and mid 20th century, Germany, Russia and Japan tried to expand their boundaries, Russia creating a huge "empire" of USSR and then Eastern Europe which has broken up only recently. Germany and Japan both for a few years controlled huge areas but were eventually thwarted by defeat in the Second World War. Britain's peripheral location and the allied power of the USA and USSR saved Britain from another wave of invaders in 1939.

Since 1950 Britain has become even more multi-cultural than in the Middle Ages, with large numbers of settlers attracted from the Indian sub-continent and the Caribbean to work in the large cities. But in recent years a balance has been struck between emigration and immigration.

Political and economic conquest and control still goes on apace. First the European nations, then the USA and now Japan and the Pacific Rim countries are colonising the rest of the economic world, Britain included.
Since 1950 Britain has been become less and less the centre from which waves emanate (generally to the benefit of the emanators), and has resumed its historical position. Not only do international financial organisations like the IMF influence British policy, but more and more of the country's economy is controlled by foreign multinationals. Recently investment from Germany, USA, Japan, South Korea has been welcomed. In 1993 investment from abroad totalled £20,000 million.

With Britain now seen as an excellent entry point into the EU the rulers of the global economy are keen to invest. But even so Britain is in danger of being treated as a low labour cost location, only to be used by the global economy whilst it is "competitive".

Modern communications - bringing us closer together or further apart?

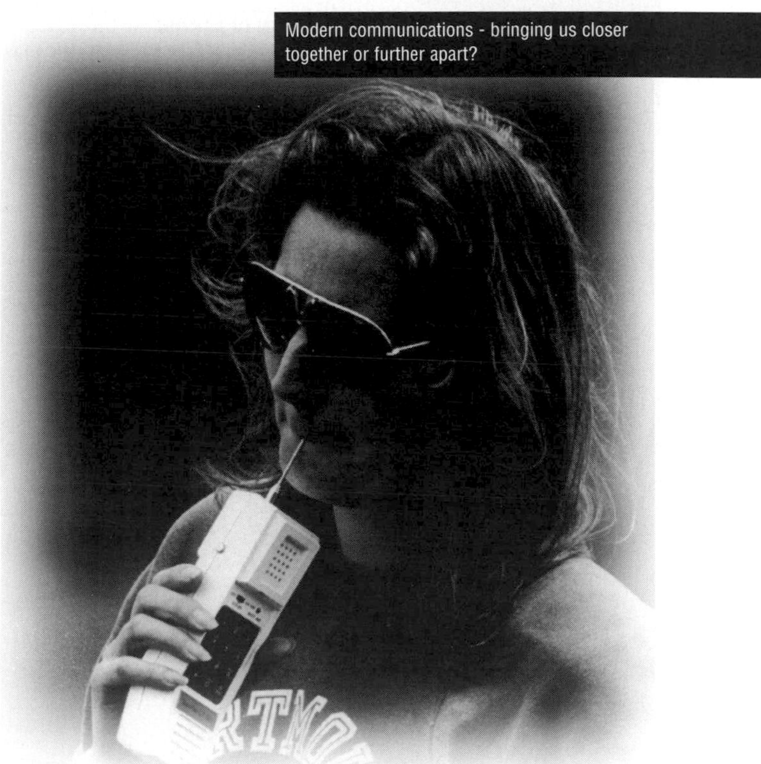

Inequalities - spatial and social

National, regional and local variations

The United Kingdom is far from homogenous in terms of the distribution of wealth and employment. England seems to be better off by most economic measures, with Wales and Northern Ireland trailing. Within each country there are areas of high and low income, and locally there are pockets of deep poverty and patches of high affluence. In Glasgow for instance unemployment is concentrated in some wards, especially near the centre and in council estates on the outskirts. Here unemployment runs at over 20%, which means over 30% male unemployment.

Attempts have been made to reduce these inequalities by investment and subsidy, especially from European funds. In fact the UK pays some billion pounds more to the EU than it receives in funding, but at least the system does encourage the government to redistribute wealth to the poorer regions. EU Structural Funds are just part of the aid.

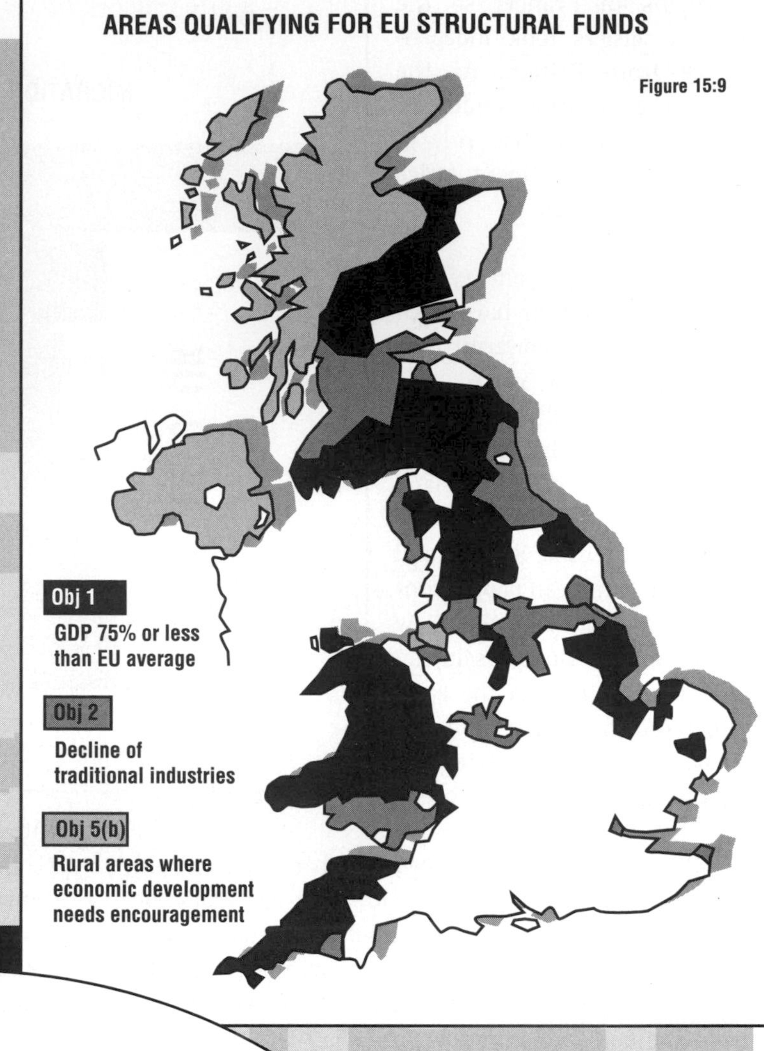

Figure 15:9

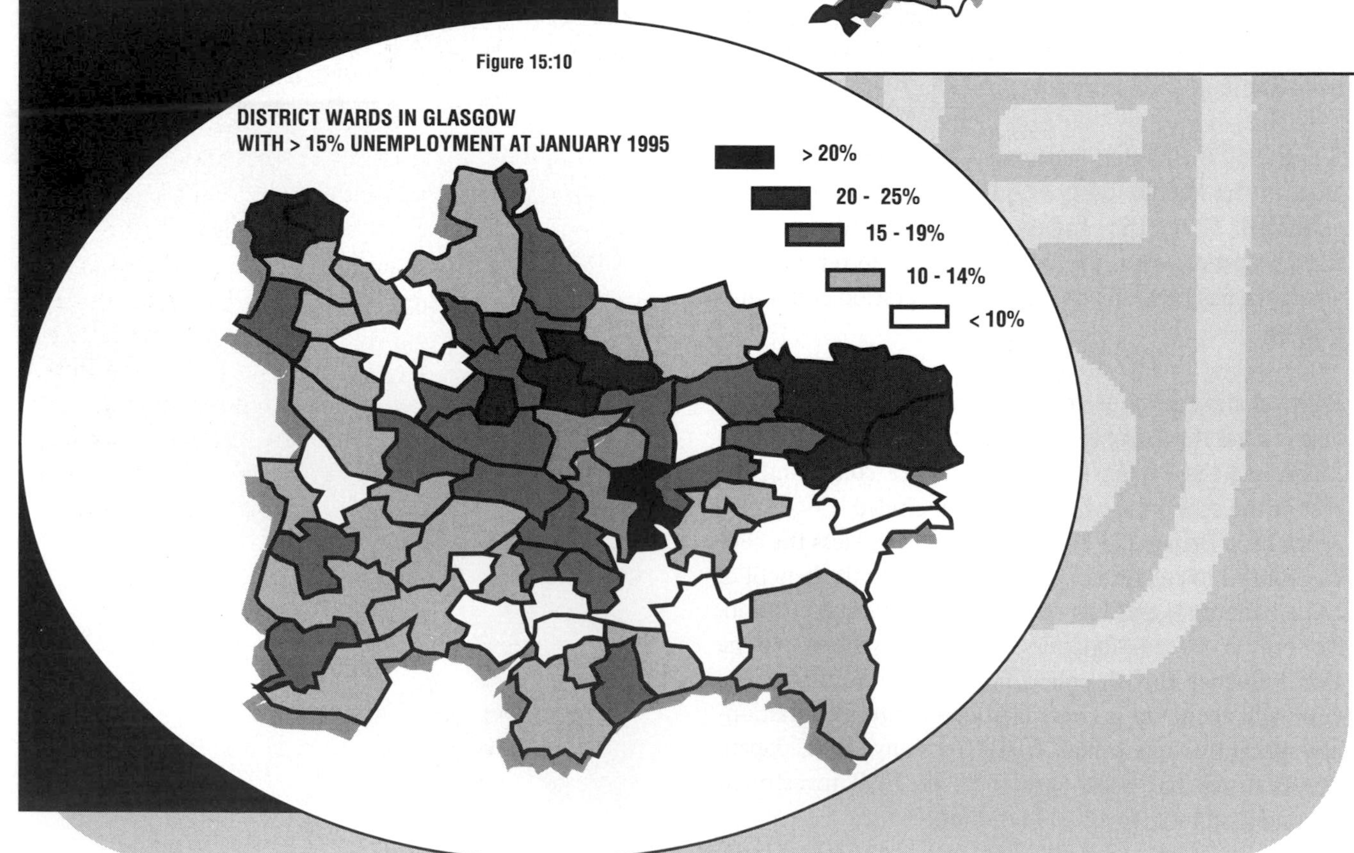

Figure 15:10

Economic change in Scotland

Changes in the structure of the economy in Scotland over the past 20 years reflect a pattern common to most of the UK. Decline in traditional heavy industries has been accompanied by increases in light manufacturing and the service industries. An extra and relieving element for Scotland has been the continued production of oil and gas off-shore. Generally this process has meant relative prosperity for the Aberdeen area, and deep recession for Clydeside and much of West Central Scotland. But no situation in a modern economy is static. Two industries represent opposite sides of the story of change.

The Steel Industry

The post-war Scottish steel industry was located to the East of Glasgow. In 1972 a new integrated plant was built at Ravenscraig, a decision based on social rather than geographical or economic grounds. The loss of major markets with the failure of the Scottish motor industry (highlighted by the closure of the Linwood car plant in 1981), and the retrenchment of the shipbuilding industry on the Clyde, were hammer blows that undermined the economic rationale of Scottish steel. In 1991 the closure of several steel mills and blast furnaces, including part of Ravenscraig, led to the loss of over 3,000 jobs in an area already suffering high unemployment. The final nail in the coffin was the closure of the remainder of Ravenscraig in 1992. With 15,000 jobs dependent directly or indirectly on the steel industry the impact on the local economy was profound.

The electronics industry

The growth of the electronics industry is one of the success stories of Scotland's recent economic development. By 1991 the industry accounted for 21% of Scottish manufacturing output and 13% of manufacturing employment. 60% of this employment is provided by foreign-owned plants, with US-owned companies controlling 45% of electronics jobs. Most of this development is concentrated in the central belt (Silicon Glen), with a substantial presence in the five New Towns.

The 3 ,000 job project at Mossend in Lanarkshire by the Taiwanese computer and television tube manufacturers Chungwha Picture Tubes (90% owned by Tatung who already have a factory in Telford) cost the Scottish Development Agency an estimated £80 million pounds, and the UK government spends on tax deals and other incentives.

In 1991 only 12% of the components used in the Scottish electronics industry were purchased locally, the rest came mainly from other parts of the UK (30%), Asia (30%) and the EU (19%). There has been little technology-based linking with local firms, and most Research and development is taking place outside Scotland. Scotland is thus in a Third World situation, with restricted technology transfer and at the mercy of the efects of corporate restructuring and rationalisation at times of difficulty in the industry.

Figure 15:11

THE NEW STRUCTURE: CHANGES SINCE 1979

Percentage share in total GDP

	Agriculture	Manufacturing	Services	Energy	Construction & water
1979	3.35	28.53	54.6	5.55	7.99
1988	2.69	21.93	62.7	5.09	7.57

Source: Geographer Michael Pacione, **Geography,** No 347,Vol 80, Part 2, April 1995.

The reliance on an extractive industry for some prosperity clearly has some dangers; the oil and gas supplies are not inexhaustible, the industry is at the mercy of global prices and is very responsive to recession when sales can rapidly decline. But the heavy reliance on foreign-owned manufacturing also has its drawbacks. There has been a high price to pay to attract the companies.

Ethnic discrimination and inequality

In spite of work by so many groups, black and white, racism is still a potent force in the UK and still leads to social and economic discrimination. Statistics for employment and income by ethnic group demonstrate this .

In June 1995 The Runnymede Bulletin gave a succinct account of the situation.

The ethnic minority population

Around 1,999,000 or 5.9% of the population of working age are of ethnic minority origin. Of these, 560,000 are of Indian origin, 530,000 are black, 444,000 are of Pakistani/Bangladeshi origin, while the remainder are of Chinese, mixed or other origins. Ethnic minorities are more concentrated in the younger age groups. 9% of young people aged 16 and under and 7% of those aged 16-19 are of ethnic minority origin, compared with 6% of the total working population and less than 2% of those over State retirement age.

Country of Birth and Nationality

Nearly 46% of all people of ethnic minority origin living in Britain were born here. Only 14% of those under 16 were born abroad, compared with almsot three quarters of the working age population. Virtually all people over the age of 35 were born abroad.

Young people

A higher proportion of young people from ethnic minority groups stay in full time education than their white counterparts, 48% compared to 31%. The only exception is Pakistani/Bangladeshi young women (28% compared with 31% of young white women). More black young women (52%) were in full time education than men (36%). Among other ethnic groups more young men than women were in education.

Patterns of employment

White people are more likely to be private sector employees (62%) than those from ethnic minorities (57%). There is a greater concentration of both black men and women in the public sector while Indian, Pakistani and Bangladeshi men and women are more likely to be self-employed.

A higher percentage of black women work in the public sector (51%) compared to 13% for all women and 19% of Asian women are self-employed.
For men, 32% of Afro-Caribbean men are in the public sector compared with 18% of both white and Indian men. 23% of Indian men and 26% of Pakistani / Bangladeshi men are self-employed compared to 17% of white men.

Average earnings

The average hourly earnings of ethnic minority employees working full time were about 92% of those of white employees. Most of the difference is due to the difference between the earnings of white and ethnic minority men. The latter earn 89% of what white men earn. While white women's earnings are about 80% of men's earnings, ethnic minority women were estimated to earn around 88% of men's earnings.

From **The Runnymede Bulletin,** June 1995.

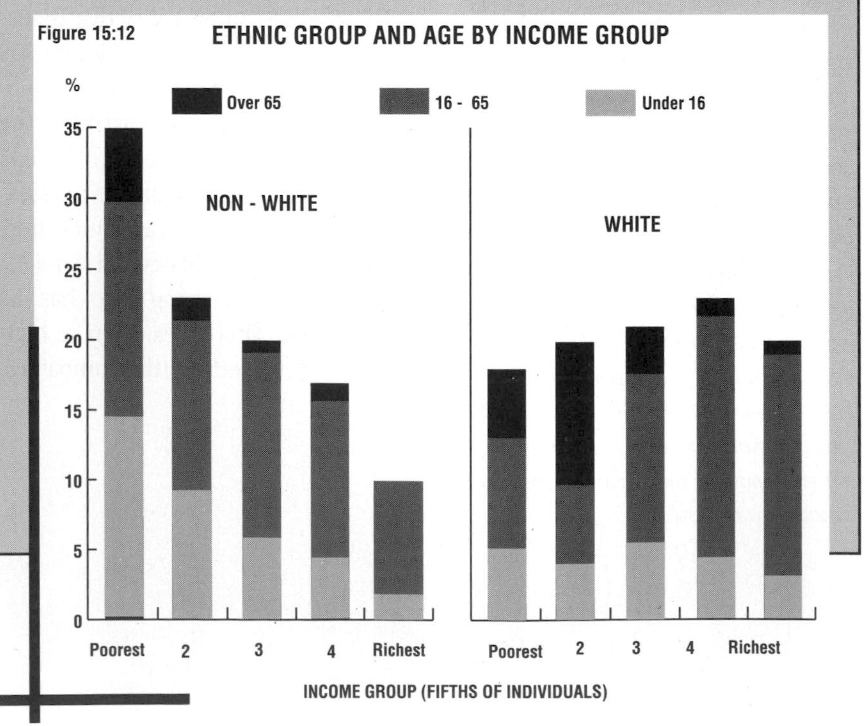

There are other manifestations of race prejudice in Britain besides employment patterns, for example, in education, inspite of the Swann Report in 1985 which clarified the nature of institutional racism and which led to subsequent positive efforts.

> *"Institutional racism has changed since 1985, but it still exists - in school and in wider society. There are many questions and few satisfactory answers about the number of exclusions of black pupils. New laws on Immigration are on the agenda of the Conservative Party. So, what has changed?*
> *In terms of education in the narrow sense, the 1988 Education Reform Act and the coming of Local Management of Schools and the National Curriculum has been largely responsible for the ending of the active quest for a genuinely equal opportunity, a fairer system for all.*
> *Opportunities are there, but they have become marginalised and risky to implement. Schools which used to take pride in their ability to offer a "broad and balanced curriculum", truly relevant for all their pupils in a multi-ethnic community have become more traditionally conventional and more anglo-centric in their approach."*

Susan Murray, Secretary of NAME, **Arena,** No 39, Winter 1995.

STOP AND SEARCH FIGURES, METROPOLITAN POLICE, WEST MIDLANDS, HUMBERSIDE AND LEICESTERSHIRE

Police Force Area	Searches made of: White persons	Ethnic minorities	% of searches ethnic minorities	% of total pop. ethnic minorities
Metropolitan Police	132,565	95,751	41.9	20.0
West Midlands	4,098	1,927	32.0	14.6
Humberside	1,063	26	2.4	1.0

Source: **The Runnymede Bulletin** March 1995.

Figure 15:13

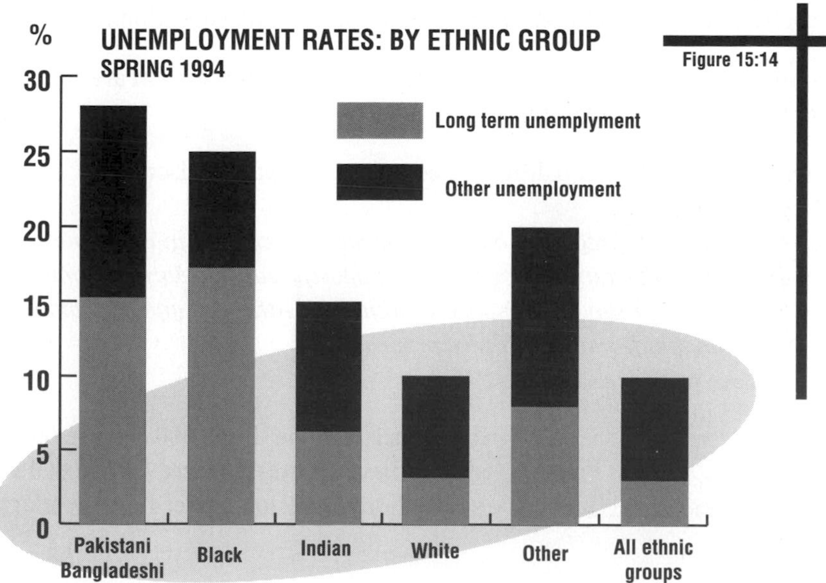

Figure 15:14

Out on the streets questions have also to be asked. Racial violence is regularly reported, but Stop and Search figures suggest that police are still more likely to stop ethnic minority people than white. At the same time there is evidence of the criminalisation of Black women. 36% of the female prison population is black.

Ethnic minority young women often have to deal with traditional restrictions and sexism within their communities, as well as racism and sexism in the wider community.

> *"Nonetheless, Black young women are not allowing either their colour or their sex to prevent them from doing what they can to empower themselves. An example of this is the Jagoroni Project set up by young Bangladeshi women who felt that there was no provision for them in mainstream youth services. The main aim of Jagoroni (meaning Awakening) is to enhance the active participation of young Bangladeshi women in society. The group has already become involved in lobbying and giving public speeches. Jagoroni breaks the stereotype of Asian women being passive and housebound. Today, the work done by young Black women in Britain already shows how their vital contribution in combating racism and oppression cannot be underplayed."*

Black to Black, No 4, March 1995, The 1990 Trust.

WHITENESS
Tina Tansho

Whiteness
Whatever that may be,
tried to impose
its "supremacy"
on an African child
born in the mild,
though hostile climes
of post war England.

Schooling
fifteen years denied,
her natural sense of
racial pride,
to be of "Mixed race"
was a form of disgrace,
in the hostile climes
of post war England.

Adolescence
brought growing pain,
and a desperate need
to feel whole again,
One personality
split into three,
in the hostile climes
of post war England.

Womanhood
whatever that may be,
yet another struggle
for liberty,
She saw through the lies
and learned to DESPISE,
the hostile climes
of post war England.

Black on Black,
No 4, March 1995.

Gender and inequality

"Government policies in the 1980s have exacerbated women's vulnerability to poverty. Deregulation of the labour market, the shifting boundaries between public and private provision and the emphasis on family obligations and responsibilities have all resulted in substantially greater disadvantages for women. For example, labour market policies have done little to improve the low earning of millions of women employees but have instead led to a worsening of job security and employment conditions. Reductions in social welfare services have generally resulted in more work - largely unpaid - for women in the private domain, as the care of children, sick and frail elderly people increasingly falls to them."

Caroline Gendinning, **Women and poverty in Britain,** Harvester Wheatsheaf, 1992

In spite of these worsening background conditions women have improved their position in the world of paid work. More married women are working, many part-time, and in 1994 46% of women with children under the age of 5 were in employment compared with 24% in 1983. Women make up 45% of the labour force.

How has this come about? Women are certainly changing their role in society, influenced by the Women's Movement. There has been a change in the nature of the family with people marrying later, having fewer children, liviing longer, and divorcing more frequently. Opportunities for employment have increased with more part-time jobs and the expansion of the service industries - many traditionally employers of women.

However this increase in formal economic activity has not led to any rapid improvement in women's remuneration or opportunities for promotion. 40% of part-time women employees are in low status, low skill jobs which have poor promotion prospects. Women are still penalized for breaks in employment (which average only 3 years) and on return are often down-skilled. Their contribution is concentrated in only a few occupations - catering, cleaning and selling part-time; clerical and education full time.

Women's pay is catching up, but oh so slowly. It is still only on average about three-quarters of men's pay.

The reasons for these inequalities are complex. Marilyn Davidson and Cary Cooper include:

"sex-stereotyping, job segregation based on gender, deficiences in education, vocational guidance and training; poor union support; weak legislation; home/work conflicts; discrimination within organisations; prejudiced attitudes and behaviour towards working women; inadequate childcare provision."

M.J.Davidson and C.L.Cooper, **Shattering the glass ceiling,** PCP, 1992.

The UK has the worst childcare and maternity provisions in Europe: 1 in 5,000 can use nurseries provided by employers; only 1.5% of under 5 year olds have a nursery place; 1 in 20,000 gets a childcare allowance from her firm; 1 in 50 organisations have job-share, home-working or school term deals.

Representation in the high pay, high status sectors of employment and public life also improved during the 1980s but has slowed down again. Only 11% of managerial staff are women, and mainly in catering and retail trades. 3% of company directors are women. The UK is well down the European list for women MPs (6%), cabinet ministers (5%) and MEPs (15%).

But progress even in these fields can be speeded up. A new organisation, **Opportunity 2000** encourages its members to promote gender equality. A third of the managers in the 293 member companies are women, and from 1994 to 1995 the proportion of directors doubled to 16%.

Homeworking

Women continuously battle to improve their economic prospects. Homeworking often means very low pay and poor employment conditions, but as the extract below demonstrates it is possible to take combined action to improve things.

Homeworking can be isolated, stressful and poorly paid. In 1989, for example, out of 21 women questioned in Kirklees, Yorkshire, 11 were earning less than 50 pence per hour. Employers can pressurise workers, and they have no security of tenure. Garment making is probably the most common kind of homework found in Britain, but engineering assembly work, packing, painting and many other labour-intensive tasks are widespread. Now of course more and more clerical and secretarial work is carried out at home.

In the 1970s and '80s women began to organise cooperation in Britain, especially with the Leicester Outwork Campaign involving women of the Gujarati community. Since then homeworkers have linked nationally and internationally to improve conditions.

> *"In West Yorkshire the homeworking campaign has been built round an alliance of homeworkers, women working in voluntary organisations, members of church and community organisations, local authority officers and others, with the support of the trade unions. Asian women's groups and advice or law centres have provided and maintained contacts.*
>
> *There still remains a major problem of women's invisibility or women's representation in major international bodies. "*

Jane Tate

> *"Against all odds, utilising predominantly their everyday skills and resources, poor women in many parts of the world can be observed shifting organisational structures and ways of seeing. Dignity and daily bread are very basic demands."*

Sheila Rowbotham and Swasti Mitter, **Dignity and Daily Bread**, Routledge,1994.

Conclusion

The redistribution of wealth is a painful process. The only people worse off after the 1995 Budget were the poorest and already disadvantaged. The Budget continued a 15 year process of extending the differences between the rich and the poor. In Britain, as in much of the world, the poor and disadvantaged are most often blamed by the rich for their own misfortunes. When the National Lottery extended its funding to Charities as well as sport and culture, the mass media response was predictable:

ANGER AT LOTTERY CASH FOR ADDICTS

Drug addicts, refugees, single mothers, alcoholics and ethnic groups are to get National Lottery grants totalling hundreds of thousands of pounds.

Large national charities like Help the Aged, NSPCC and Barnardo's are expected to lose out as 600 local community-based projects benefit.

Peter Hooley, front page headline, **Sunday Express**, 22.10.95.

But, later in the same article a Lottery Charities Board spokesman is quoted:

"There is going to be help for drug addicts and battered women and that sort of group because the people who support them have put in good quality bids and there is no way we are going to run away from that."

The headline seeking to pre-empt the reader's judgement of the text represents the kind of journalism that doesn't help our understanding of development issues. Maybe the likeliest way forward lies with education for democracy that includes media criticism and political literacy. It may then be possible that justice and equality become top of the national agenda.

▼ REFERENCES

Stan Burley (1993) **People First,** London, Zed Books.

Commission on Social Justice (1994) **Social Justice: Strategies for National Renewal,** London, Vintage.

M.J. Davidson and C.L. Cooper (1992) **Shattering the Glass Ceiling,** London PCP.

DEC (1995) **The Development Compass Rose: a consultation pack,** Birmingham.

Caroline Glendinning (1992) **Women and Poverty in Britain,** London, Harvester Wheatsheaf.

John Hills (1995) **Income and Wealth,** London, Joseph Rowntree Foundation.

Will Hutton (1996) **The State We're In,** London, Vintage.

HMSO (Annually) **Social Trends.**

HMSO (Annually) **Regional Trends.**

Sheila Rowbotham and Swasti Mitter (1994) **Dignity and Daily Bread,** London, Routledge.

OUR OWN DOORSTEP: Dimensions of Development in Ireland Today

Stephen McCloskey, Colm Regan, Roland Tormey

"True solidarity is not a one-way process. Is it not arrogant to wish to resolve single-handedly the development problems of the South when our own society is itself suffering from widespread development problems."

(In 1989, the General Assembly of the Liaison Committee of Development NGOs to the European Communities adopted a Code of Conduct on Images and Messages Relating to the Third World. This Code was adopted by the General Assembly of Irish Development NGOs in 1995.)

Introduction

It is a truism to say that some Irish commentators and analysts can be quite radical in their prescriptions for development and justice in the Third World while being simultaneously conservative on similar issues at home. In this they are frequently recognising the complexity of issues at home while often denying similar complexity in situations overseas. Equally, commentators often object to parallels being drawn between development and justice issues here in Ireland and those within the Third World.

Frequently we separate development at home from that abroad, not recognising that all peoples and places are constantly developing or underdeveloping and that there are many interesting and challenging lessons and analyses to be explored through a comparative approach. Development in the Third World is regularly presented as being essentially a technical issue (a matter of the right inputs - aid, experts, methods, technology, etc.) whereas development in Ireland and Britain is presented as a highly complex political process involving a great many actors, perspectives, value decisions and judgements. Development *"here"* is presented as a highly complex issue whereas development *"there"* is essentially simple - a matter of controlling population growth, learning proper or modern agricultural methods, adopting Western democratic models etc.

There is much to be learned about the development process through a comparative approach. A *"local/global"* perspective is essential to understanding world economic, political, social and cultural processes today. Many recent analysts of Irish development have drawn attention to similarities and dissimilarities with other European countries and those beyond and have pointed to the benefits of such a comparative approach. Some key dimensions of this approach are discussed in this chapter alongside some of the key justice dimensions of recent years. The chapter is by no means comprehensive and simply seeks to introduce such dimensions.

"The evident failure of Ireland's economy must be viewed in the context of Third World Underdevelopment. Ireland, though geographically part of the West, alone of European countries shares the profound historical experience of having had superimposed on its own indigenous, tribal pastoralism, an alien, individualistic capitalism. And alone of European countries it underdevelops: and does so in company with every one of the 138 or so countries that were colonies of the capitalist system".

Economist Raymond Crotty (1986) **Ireland in Crisis: a study in capitalist colonial development,** Dingle, Brandon Books.

Competing Images

There are many competing and often contradictory images of Ireland today:

- Ireland is an ultra-modern society of sophisticated financial, industrial and communications centres; a country on the European periphery which expe-

"Comparative perspective can illuminate our understanding of the Irish condition. Yet there is no wholly comparable case. Many distinctive features of the Irish experience might be listed...The South achieved a degree of political stability rare for a new State. Northern Ireland...failed to acquire legitimacy in the eyes of a sufficient number of its inhabitants to prevent itself from being torn apart...The South has succeeded in maintaining military neutrality, but it has succumbed ever more to cultural dependence. It has a unique demographic history, and a most unusual economic history, with the slowest rate of growth of gross national product of any European country in the twentieth century. The North, too, in a rather different way, counts among the striking economic failures of the century. Even this cursory catalogue suffices to remind us that recent Irish historical experience cannot be encompassed within conventional categories of either European or Third World historiography."

Historian Joe Lee (1989) **Ireland 1912-1985: Politics and Society,** Cambridge, University Press.

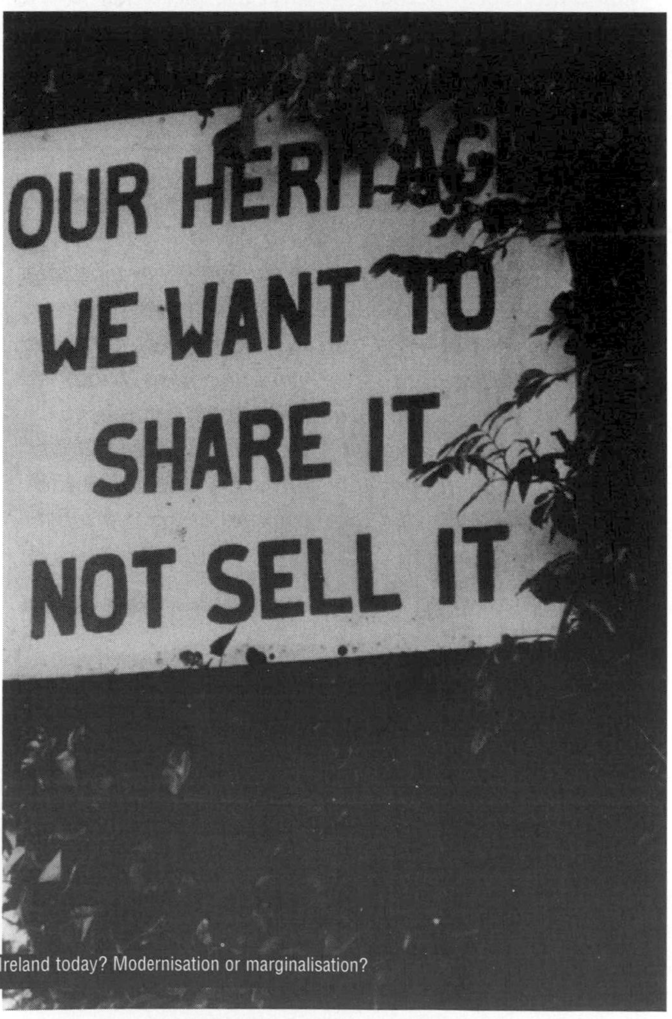

Ireland today? Modernisation or marginalisation?

rienced rapid, albeit late, industrialisation; a country with a growing number of millionaires (by no means exclusively urban) and a property boom and with its own class of highly paid and influential bureaucrats and businessmen and women. Ireland is a country emerging from its traditional, poor, conservative and, of course, colonial past to become an energetic and progressive member of the European Union. Ireland is best represented in the advertising line of Ireland's Industrial Development Agency which boldly proclaims at Dublin Airport *"Ireland - the home of the young Europeans"*.

- Ireland is a country of the poor and the marginalised. Those who inhabit this Ireland are easy to identify - the long-term unemployed, the single parent family, the Travellers, the small farmer and the old - a growing "underclass". Ireland is the land of the emigrant - they may well be better off than those emigrating before them but most of them are still economic refugees - forced to leave, prompting one observer to dub Ireland "the emigrant nursery". Ireland is well represented by the squalor of the majority of Traveller halting sites, the despair and alienation of many sub-urban housing estates and the welcomes and farewells of Irish airports at holiday times.

- Ireland is a middle class country - reasonably well off, employed - with at least some sense of security, and provided with a basic, if somewhat limited, health, welfare and educational service. Historically this middle class is conservative, unsure about the future, wary of jeopardising its position and yet, to an increasing degree, volatile enough (especially amongst the young) not to be taken for granted as recent elections and referenda have demonstrated. Ireland is well represented, for example, in the phenomenal growth of restaurants specialising in international food and the emergence of specialist interior design shops.

And then there is Northern Ireland, until recently fitfully enjoying a tentative cease-fire with the hope of lasting peace and the reality of ongoing violence:

- Northern Ireland remains a bulwark of traditional British values and beliefs. Since the 1960s, Northern Ireland has undergone profound change (brought about by a combination of internal and external pressure). Despite the continuing legacy of violence and division, there is also the Northern

Ireland of razor sharp wit, indomitable spirit and considerable community resilience.

- Northern Ireland is a divided society, unstable as a result of being Britain's last colony. Injustice remains a reality in the structure of every day society for many people.

And so we are left with a number of divergent images and realities of Ireland. On the one hand the modern, increasingly wealthy and progressive member of the European Union - the world's 23rd richest state, clearly a member of the First World. As against this, the relatively poor, ex-colonial state still dominated by structural underdevelopment and poverty - a state with much in common with the Third World.

"I'll admit that an unemployed man in El Salvador might suffer a thousand times more physically because he doesn't have the dole that cushions the unemployed here in Ireland. But a sensitive human being in this country, condemned to a life of unemployment, can suffer just as much psychologically, mentally and spiritually as any Salvadorean."

Quoted in Peadar Kirby **Has Ireland a Future?,** 1988 Cork, Mercier Press.

"The suggestion that Ireland should be compared to Third World countries is often met with a combination of derision and indignation. What! Are we not white? And European? and, compared with the countries of the Third World, wealthy? And educated?

These objections are all true, but none of them negate our history and the political heritage it has left us, which has profound implications for the permanence and stability of our institutions and their capacity to permit major reform".

Carol Coulter (1990) **Ireland: Between First and Third Worlds,** Attic Press, Dublin.

Ireland - First or Third?

For many observers then, Ireland can be said to have much in common with Third World countries. They point to:

- Ireland's large workforce in agriculture and its weak industrial base.
- High levels of dependence on transnational companies.
- A huge national debt.
- The openness of our economy.
- High levels of unemployment and emigration.
- An ongoing national question, itself the result of our colonial past.
- A political culture which has much in common with that of Third World societies.

Other observers argue that Ireland cannot be equated with the majority of Third World countries because the scale and depth of hunger, poverty, ill-health, homelessness, etc. as well as the existence of a social welfare system makes comparison impossible. They argue that, the Free State and, later, the Republic have done remarkably well. Considerable wealth has been created (stimulated by huge State investment), a basic health, welfare and education system is in place, infrastructure has been developed and the political system remains stable despite considerable pressure from time to time.

Irish incomes have doubled within the past three decades; Ireland ranks well on the Human Development Index recently designed by the United Nations Development Programme (19th on the list of 174 countries); the educational achievements of the Irish State in the past 70 years have been very considerable; health standards are now well up to European norms and, despite the conflict in Northern Ireland, the Irish State has experienced stability since its foundation. By world standards the average quality of life in Ireland remains good and a recent study concluded that children growing up in Ireland were amongst some of the world's safest and healthiest.

While few would underestimate the very real transformation through which Ireland has passed especially in the past three and a half decades, nonetheless fundamental and persistent problems and questions remain. Behind the average indices of success lie the alternative downside of failure and neglect. Whereas it was estimated that in 1971, the poor numbered 20% of the population, the latest figures (hotly contested by politicians and some academics) suggest that 1 in 3 are poor today. Ireland continues to have one of the highest rates of unemployment within the EU and one of its most unequal income distribution patterns.

The statistician and economist Raymond Crotty accepts that Ireland's colonial experience fits into the general pattern of capitalist colonialism but argues that it diverged in many important respects. It was the only European country to be colonised; it was the only colony in which most of the land was confiscated and it was one of the rare cases where, in one part of the land - Ulster - the indigenous farmers were replaced by settler farmers. *"It was, finally, the only capitalist colony where the colonisers were distinguished from the colonised by religion rather than race."*

"No more than half those born in Ireland (26 counties) since 1821 and surviving childhood have got a living here. For the first 30 years of this 160-year period, before the channels of emigration were open and clear, very many of those who failed to get a living in Ireland starved to death. Many did so during the chronic famine conditions of the 1820s and 1830s. A million people, or one-eighth of the island's total population, perished by famine or famine-related diseases in the 1840's. With the opening up of the channels of emigration, few Irish remained to starve after 1851. Almost half those born and surviving childhood have emigrated from Ireland since 1871, when registration of births and deaths became compulsory. The rate at which people have emigrated has hardly changed since the country became independent in 1922. Net emigration between 1911, the last pre-independence census year, and 1961 was 45% of the number of births registered.

A comparison of the workforces now and in the past, in Ireland and in neighbouring Britain, provides another measure of Ireland's failure. The country's workforce was 38% of Britain's in 1841. It has since declined by more than half while Britain's has more than trebled, so that the Republic's workforce is now only 7% of its neighbours. The number at work in the Republic has continued to decline since 1911, while that of Northern Ireland has increased. The 26 counties' share of the number getting a livelihood in Ireland has declined from 77% in 1841 to 66% now. It is, in effect, less than at any time during the past 250 years. This is at a period during which the world's population has increased sixfold.

Responsibility for this loss could be attributed to the colonial British power for 100 of the last 160-odd years. But Ireland has been politically independent for over 60 years and...the failure of people to secure a livelihood has been almost as pronounced in post-independence as in pre-independence years."

Economist Raymond Crotty (1986) **Ireland in Crisis: a study in capitalist colonial development**, Dingle, Brandon Books.

"...it may be claimed that the political parties have in many respects served the Southern State rather well. However close run a thing it was, the manner in which the supremacy of parliament was achieved consolidated the democratic tradition in Irish nationalism.

The State that was moulded in the bitter crucible of the civil war proved highly creative in party political terms. Many observers felt that the Irish could not create a coherent party political order, particularly in the context of an electoral system based on the potentially destabilising principle of proportional representation with the single transferable vote in multi-member constituencies. That the nexus of ideals and interests out of which political movements are fashioned has hitherto sufficed to provide so striking a degree of governmental stability testifies to the professional skill with which the politicians responded to the challenge..."

Historian Joe Lee (1989) **Ireland 1912-1985: Politics and Society,** Cambridge University Press.

Ireland - Success of Modernisation Theory?

Ireland, like most Third World countries, has sought to find a way of industrialising after independence. Of the two models discussed in chapter one, Ireland chose the modernisation approach. This involved removal of tarrif barriers, stimulation of free enterprise and industrialisation by the invitation to Ireland of transnational companies. It was assumed that the expansion of the economy would lead to a "trickling down" of the benefits to all. Just as this view has been proven to be erroneous in the Third World, so too has it been the case in Ireland. The hoped for and expected result of a "rising tide raising all boats" (as stated by Taoiseach Sean Lemass) has not been realised.

Modernising Ireland?

Extensive arguments exist also about the model of industrial development adopted by the Irish Government through its Industrial Development Authority/Agency. At present there is intense competition between Ireland, Scotland, England and Wales to attract international investment particularly from Japan and South East Asia and the United States and there is just as intense debate about the value and impact of such investment. Proponents of unfettered foreign investment argue that without it, Ireland's economic development would not be nearly so impressive, that job creation would have suffered even more and that emigration would have been even higher. They also point to the fact that indigenous Irish capital has never been capable of generating national economic development.

Underdeveloping Ireland?

Opponents of this view argue that Ireland has simply become a dependent economy where the search for suitable foreign companies to invest replaces the need to develop indigenous industry and effort whether it be in the private or public sector. They argue that the focus on 'economic fundamentals' like inflation and GNP per capita hides the degree of inequality created by our economic system. The processes which cause this inequality are, they argue, the same as the processes which cause a higher degree of inequality in Third World countries. They argue that while jobs are created, they are seldom, if ever in the numbers promised in the context of the grants provided; that foreign corporations constantly repatriate huge amounts of their profits rather than invest them in Ireland; that the long-term stability of the economy is overwhelmingly dependent on outside decisions and trends; and that many of the industries are increasingly damaging the Irish environment. They point out, for example, that despite their weakness Irish companies spend some 79% of earnings in Ireland, foreign companies spend only 44%. Between 1980 and 1985, the repatriation of profits, dividends and royalties rose five-fold from £258 million to £1,321 million. In 1987 alone it is estimated that £1.4 billion left the country in the form of profits, royalties and dividends. This was referred to by many observers as the 'black hole' through which profits flowed outwards in the 1980s. It is estimated that profit repatriations make up as much as 11 - 13% of Irish GDP.

However, the central problem of the economic development model remains its inability, even in times of impressive growth (Ireland has generally performed well - indeed often better then most - in times of economic upsurge within the EU), to turn economic growth into sustained job creation. This means that apart from the national question, Ireland's most enduring problems are the twin issues of unemployment - especially long-term unemployment, and emigration.

An additional issue in recent years has been Ireland's debt. In order to meet continued public spending (state spending on jobs and services equalled 60% of GNP in 1987), consecutive governments were forced to borrow internationally to the point where the national debt stood at £24,611 million at the end of 1988. Recent years have witnessed severe cutbacks in public spending in health, welfare and education.

"Ireland proved itself over this period to be immensely attractive to multinational capital. Currently it is believed there are over 850 subsidiaries of foreign multinationals in Ireland. Of these 325 are American-based, 177 are British, 122 are German and 230 are from other European countries."

Robert Allen and Tara Jones (1990) **Guests of the Nation**, London, Earthscan.

"Ireland's historically weak employment performance is closely bound up with long-standing inadequacies in its rate and pattern of economic development. Never for any sustained period did it create enough jobs to absorb the potential increase in the labour force, so that it always had a problem of labour surplus even when full employment was the norm elsewhere. Traditionally this surplus was relieved chiefly through emigration..."

Kieran Kennedy (1993) **Facing the Unemployment Crisis in Ireland**, Undercurrents Series, Cork University Press.

"...despite its volume and social class composition, conventional wisdom today tends to individualise emigration by treating emigrants as enterprising individuals rather than social groups victimised as a result of structural changes in Irish society, including structural changes in the relationship between Ireland and overseas labour markets. There is also a tendency today to treat young emigrants as individuals set apart from their predecessors by their superior skills, and from their peers by their spirit of adventure."

"Revisionism has so thoroughly pervaded our most crucial assumptions about Irish society that its effects have often gone unnoticed. This is particularly apparent in the case of Irish attitudes to emigration. Political leaders, and the general public, increasingly regard Europe and the United States as acceptable hosts to Ireland's surplus labour. In so doing, they de-nationalise the causes of Irish emigration and externalise its solutions."

Jim McLaughlin (1994) **Ireland: The Emigrant Nursery and the World Economy**, Undercurrents, Cork University Press.

Ireland and the Unemployment Issue

"Here . . . you're very unlikely to meet a man who is able to say to you, come and marry me and I'll take you off the welfare?

Ah janey, that's a dream. Around here it's a dream. Nearly all the fellahs around here use drugs. There's nothing else for them to do. They just go out and steal for their habit . . .

Are you very unlikely to meet a man who is working here in Ballymun?

Not around here anyway. You can't go out to other places to meet people. You're just stuck here, like. You have your kids. This is your life. You can't go anywhere"

- Susan, Ballymun flats, in Paddy O'Gorman's (1994) ***Queuing for a Living***

One of the most intractable problems which has continually affected the Irish State then, has been unemployment - Ireland has experienced its own variant of the Brazilian problem of the economy doing well while the people do not. There are difficulties in estimating how many people are unemployed in Ireland at any one time. The most widely used figure in Ireland is the 'Live Register' figure, available at the end of each month. This does not reflect the real state of unemployment as some people who are unemployed do not qualify to register. Other measures, like the annual Labour Force Survey use different criteria. Because of this there is often argument about how high unemployment actually is.

In 1978 the then Taoiseach said that a figure of 100,000 people unemployed should cause the government to loose power. By 1984, only six years later, unemployment was double that at 204,000. By 1986, the figure was up to one quarter of a million people. In January 1993 there was, once more, considerable debate and comment about unemployment which was by now about to reach the new crisis figure of 300,000. As the figures rose, the definition of when unemployment would become a crisis rose. As each new crisis came and went, those in power realised that it wasn't a crisis for them, and therefore wasn't a crisis.

In January 1996, there were 287,880 on the 'live register' (one measure of unemployment). The number of people who had been unemployed for one year or more was 133,742. These people are known as 'long term' unemployed. The longer a person is unemployed the smaller the chance of them gaining employment again. This means that we have gone a long way towards creating a situation where a sizeable proportion of the Irish population do not work and may never work again. In urban areas they are collected together in huge estates of joblessness. They then raise their children in a situation where there is no hope of work.

Why unemployment?

There are any number of reasons advanced by many commentators as to why unemployment remains such a huge problem:

▼ Our peculiar situation in being a 'developed' country on the periphery without natural resources and with a small population means that Irish people want high wages without having the physical or social means to sustain high numbers of jobs. *"No matter what policies had been pursued, unemployment in Ireland would in any event today have been at a high level"* -

Dr. Garret FitzGerald, former Taoiseach.

▼ The Irish State has been an 'interventionist' State. It has instituted laws and a social welfare system which have interfered with the proper working of the market and prevented people taking jobs at their proper market value. *"In this present crisis, government is not the solution, it is the problem"* -

Ronald Reagan, former US President, speaking about the USA.

▼ Unemployment is at the current high level because Ireland, as a former colony, is really a Third World country. We are blind to this fact because we are white and European. Because we are being run by proponents of modernisation theory we are obsessed with a desire for 'sound economic fundamentals' which our new European masters tell us we need to be part of their club. *"The chips are down. An ass-and-cart economy, which is the product of a colonial past and provides a livelihood for only half the people, with the end of emigration is now required to support all of the people. . . Stripped of the expedients of the past, Ireland's political leaders are reduced to infantile exercises like the Culliton Report, which are comparable to fussily re-arranging the deck furniture while the Lusitania sinks. Various members of an economics establishment that has disgraced itself morally and intellectually, by condoning for decades policies that were clearly headed for disaster, now peep over the parapet and sound off about the need to adjust down to ass-and-cart living standards".*-

Raymond Crotty, statistician and economist.

Effects of Unemployment

Poverty - A survey by the Economic and Social Research Institute in 1987 found that while unemployed households were only 10% of those surveyed, they constituted 34% of those living in poverty. 6 out of 10 unemployed households were living in poverty. Employee headed households on the other hand made up almost 40% of the sample and only 10% of those living in poverty. Only 4% of employed households were living in poverty. They concluded that "the most important cause of poverty in Ireland today is unemployment".

Children - Unemployment particularly affects those who have never had a choice. The same survey found that "over half the children in households below the [poverty line] in 1987 were in households with and unemployed head; unemployment is central to the high risk of poverty facing children and to the very substantial rise in that risk over the 1970s and 1980s".

Psychological Distress - In a survey in 1991 it was found that "the unemployed are five times more likely than employees to be above the GHQ [General Health Questionnaire] threshold [of psychological disturbance] ".

Source: Nolan, B. and Callan, T. **Poverty and Policy in Ireland,** 1994; Whelan, C.T. et al. **Unemployment Poverty and Psychological Distress,** 1991.

▼ The reason that unemployment is so high in Ireland is that those in power don't really care. Most of the Irish electorate have never experienced unemployment. In a survey in 1987, 62% of Irish households had never experienced unemployment. We are all more worried about pay, tax and mortgage interest than about the effects of unemployment. The Professor of Economics in Harvard University, J.K. Galbraith, calls this 'The Culture of Contentment'. *"In Ireland selfishness and short-term self-interest have become elevated to the level of high principle. Newspapers which in their marketing strategies target themselves at the contented . . . make demands for 'rationalisation' of 'unviable' public services, like railways and post offices, usually in places where their readers are not conspicuous. So-called 'economic experts', who are themselves comfortable as a result of pouncing off the economics of contentment, are trotted on to radio and television programmes to provide supposedly objective scientific analyses to back up the conventional wisdom".* -
John Waters, Irish Times Columnist and Author.

▼ Since the nature of the world economy has changed we can no longer expect full employment in the market place. Therefore the notion of unemployment is an old one we should do away with. We only keep it because it serves the needs of employers to treat those not formally employed as 'doing nothing', thereby having a lower status. This encourages people to take lowly paid jobs.

When the government fails . . .

When it becomes clear that government is uninterested, or feels itself unable, to do anything about unemployment, people do it for themselves. Among those in power this causes suspicion and alarm. When the European Commission offered Ireland eight million pounds the Irish government turned it down because the money had to be administered through community groups.

One such community group is the **Ballymun Community Coalition.** BCC was set up in September 1984 as a response to the fact that services, such as banks, were leaving Ballymun because an area with 60% unemployment could not provide them with profits. In the summer of 1985 the community coalition took advantage of the local government elections to highlight the lack of support for those who were trying to find or make employment in Ballymun. In the autumn of that year a Job Centre Steering Group was set up and in January 1987 the Ballymun Job Centre, a community co-operative, began to provide services to the people of Ballymun.

The job centre has a register of local unemployed people seeking work and an outreach programme informing private business of its work. It has a good record in job placement. By 1992 it had 3,843 people on the register and had placed 773 people in full time work and 429 in part time work.

The centre also provides help for those who wish to set up their own business, undertaking feasibility studies etc. Between 1987 and 1989 18 such projects were supported. Such projects are often made possible by local people working on an unpaid basis. There are a great deal of demands made on such people. Working as the treasurer in a credit union, for example, takes 35 hours a week on an unpaid basis, but there are benefits too, as one activist points out:

" For some people, unpaid work is meeting the need we all have to work, feel safe, have status. In areas of high unemployment, the status of having a job, or a certain kind of job, has become increasingly irrelevant. Instead, for those involved in unpaid work, the status comes from what you are doing in the community".

These benefits do not, however, feed a family. The programme is also beset by other problems. The enterprise development scheme has had a high failure rate, and the job placement scheme cannot get skilled work for unskilled people.

Source: Kelleher, P. and Whelan, M.(1992) **Dublin Communities in Action**

Racism and Intolerance in Ireland Today?

The Case of the Travellers

"The Constitution is the rights of the people written down in a document for all times. It can be used by Travellers, because if someone has a grudge of any kind against Travellers, just because he is a Traveller, he has his human right to be treated equally to anybody else, so is stated in the Constitution and they can take him to court" - Eddie McCarthy.

"The word 'tinker' should not be used now. Travellers didn't mind the word tinker one time, but now they don't like it when settled people say 'tinkers'. They don't mean it as a trade. They mean it as dirt and the lowest class of people" - Willie Sherlock.

"They will always see Travellers as tinkers. They will always keep calling names. People will always say we are all the same" - David Keenan.

"One day when my cousin went down town, she met a few town boys and they started laughing and calling names like tinker and they said:

> *"Don't walk the same side of the street as the tinker".*

She told me that they called her more names. I don't know why they called Travellers bad names. Maybe it's because they don't like them" - Nellie McDonald.

Facing the Facts?

Writing in the ***Sunday Independent*** in February 1995, Journalist Patricia Redlitch argued:

"The truth is that Irish society does not want the intellectual discomfort of facing the facts when it comes to dealing with our travelling community. We do not want to baldly state what we really feel, namely that we disapprove of much of what happens in the context of the travelling lifestyle, from their migrant behaviour, halting sites close to settled communities, perceived lack of respect for law and order, and roadside trading. Instead we package those feelings in pious statements about respecting their different culture and neatly pass the buck by arguing that the authorities should find the appropriate solution."

There are few issues in Ireland which spark as much controversy and frequent bitterness, outright prejudice and, sadly, violence as that of the Travellers. As Irish society becomes more 'developed' and as the Travellers fit less and less easily into the dominant ethos of that development, tension and conflict have increased. Disagreement is not simply about housing, halting sites, rubbish and accusations of petty crime - although all of these represent real and important flashpoints - it is also, and perhaps more importantly, about who the Travellers are, what they represent and what the nature of tolerance and intolerance is in Ireland today. Recent years have witnessed an important shift in the debate as the issue of Travellers 'welfare' has ceased to be the concern of charitable groups and individuals predominantly and is now directly championed by Traveller organisations and individuals who have become more articulate and forceful about their rights and dignity and about the political context of the issues.

In a recent review of the literature and arguments around the origins of the Travelling Community, UCC political geographer Jim Mac Laughlin has argued that clear distinctions between the 'settled' and Traveller population is complicated in a *'peripheral society'* like Ireland for three reasons. First, colonial conquest in Ireland meant that there was a considerable 'shake-out' within the indigenous population as colonial settlers arrived. This led to an increase among nomadic and traditional vagrant groups. *" This meant that, from a purely materialist perspective at least, there was often a very thin divide separating 'settlers' from the 'dispossessed' and 'Travellers' in colonial Ireland."* Secondly, large sections of the population in nineteenth and early twentieth century Ireland were extremely mobile especially in rural areas. This led many young Irish people to move to Britain, the United States, Canada, Australia and South Africa. Thirdly, large numbers of Irish moved regularly and seasonally between Ireland and England and Scotland and were often indistinguishable from conventional Travellers. In such circumstances, 'travelling' was an effective survival strategy which united rather than divided large sections of the Irish population.

Mac Laughlin surveys the evolution and situation of travelling groups and nomads throughout the world and traces the evolution of discrimination and suspicion towards them as part of the transition from feudalism to capitalism, the rise of religion and the decline of traditional belief systems and the rise of urbanism. He argues that the emergence of serious discrimination against Travellers occurred later in Ireland and was associated with the decline of plebeian agrarian society, the growth of bourgeois Irish nationalism and clericalism after the Famine. *"Thus in Ireland, as elsewhere in nineteenth century Europe, discrimination and suspicion followed Travellers and 'tinkers', but unlike most European countries where gypsies were considered 'outsiders', in Ireland discrimination was practised by the settled Irish on the travelling Irish."*

At the level of Irish people's perception of themselves and of the modern Irish State after independence and 'modernisation' in the late 1950s and throughout the 1960s, there was a strong move to leave behind Ireland's past and those who did not fit this new image of the State. Travellers were one such group. This period witnessed the 'pathologisation' of the Travellers and their history was seen as *"...an endless and monotonous cycle of hardship and poverty. As in other European nations, Travellers' interests in Ireland were deemed an intellectual diversion. Their problems were judged a social annoyance, their history was considered an anomaly and their very presence was considered inessential at best, and at worst, a threat to the well-being and interests of settled society."*

The situation of increased tension between the settled community and the Travellers was made all the more difficult by the significant growth in the numbers of Travellers between 1960 and 1980; by the economic and social problems thrown up by that growth; and by the urbanisation of Travellers and the collapse of their traditional means of livelihood. Prejudice was fuelled by the depiction of Travellers as 'spongers', as health risks, as the perpetrators of petty crime and by the growth of large, but by no means disproportionate, Traveller encampments around major cities.

YEAR	NO. OF FAMILIES	NO. OF PERSONS
1960	1198	6591
1971	1302	7778
1980	2342	14821
1995 (est.)	3100	22000

It is further estimated that there are approximately 15,000 Irish Travellers in Britain and some 10,000 in the United States.

There is considerable difference between the age composition of the Traveller community and the Irish population at large. Nearly 40% of all Travellers are under 10 years and well over half under 15 years as compared with 20% and 30% respectively in the settled population. Other important differences should also be noted. The proportion of Traveller women aged 55 and over is only one fifth that of women in the general population. This is true of men also although to a less extreme extent. The percentage of young children (under 5) is also higher among roadside Travellers (excludes those with housing). Infant and child mortality among Travellers is extremely high - in 1981 it was 14.2% for age under 1 year (as against a national figure of 2.3%), 25% under 5 (2.8%), 31.8% under 10 (3.1%) and 35.2% under 15 (3.4%).

The Travellers' distinctive age structure is such that the proportion of women of child bearing age is quite high so that population growth will almost certainly continue to be rapid for the foreseeable future.

An Economic and Social Research Institute report of 1986 pointed out that little reliable evidence exists as to the health problems of Travellers - the necessary studies have not been done. One 1981 study, by Dr. James Kiely concluded: *".... Travellers' children suffer unmeasurably greater as a result of the deprivation and disadvantage associated with their lives."*

The ESRI study of Travellers concluded that Irish Travellers have deplorable living conditions. Evidence points to a high death rate, notably amongst infants and children, and a short life expectancy at birth. Mothers have very large families by Irish standards, and see many of their children die. Half of Irish Travellers live their lives along the roadside, almost all of them in trailers and caravans, on unapproved and unserviced sites. Most Travellers have no access to piped water, hot water tap, fixed bath or shower, toilet facilities, or electrical supply. It is clear that Irish Travellers today live in conditions based on standards of provision and availability that date back to the 1940s or earlier....

The ESRI concluded *"The central conclusion of this study is an inescapable one: the circumstances of the Irish Travelling people are intolerable. No humane and decent society, once made aware of such circumstances, could permit them to exist...."* While the exact details of the status and living conditions of Travellers may not be known to the settled population at large, there can be little doubt that there is widespread knowledge within Irish society that their condition is far from acceptable.

This situation has led ***Irish Times*** journalist Fintan O'Toole to compare their situation not to that of nomads but rather to those of refugees. He argues:

> *"These conditions in and of themselves produce anger, disorder and disorder with settled people. In some parts of Dublin, local officials will only visit these sites with expensively hired security guards in tow. And herded into these dirty, ugly, isolated and unhappy squatter camps, the Travellers themselves become easy targets for self-appointed vigilantes. The herding together of Travellers of different families is itself creating hysteria..."*

Many people argue that Travellers bring the conditions upon themselves as they do not accept housing when offered, insisting on facilities which suit their lifestyle. "If they cared about their children, they'd move into houses. If they won't help themselves what can we do?", the arguement goes. This arguement takes the facilities available to those who live in houses for granted, as if running water and adequate sanitation were natural things. It does not recognise that these things have to be built into houses and could just as easily be made available to the Travelling community. It works from the mistaken understanding that living in one place is a normal situation. It says in effect that we will recognise their rights if they act as other Irish people do. It is, in essence, an attempt to undercut the Travellers' right to be different.

In recent years, Travellers have organised themselves into a growing number of groups variously labelled as 'visibility', 'education and development', 'solidarity' groups. They have refused to continue to accept their sub-ordinate status within Irish society and have begun to effectively lobby for their rights, for respect, for their identity and culture and for effective legal and political instruments to promote and defend them. In particular Travellers not only want effective legislation but also a tribunal to ensure its implementation. Yet, prejudice against the Travellers is rife and there has yet to be a parallel movement within the settled community.

In concluding his study, Mac Laughlin observes:

> *"In valorising Traveller culture this new leadership (*within the Travelling community*) has also been struggling against the internalisation of racial inferiority. In so doing, it has ... politicised and radicalised Traveller issues..."*

Sources: Jim Mac Laughlin (1995) **Travellers and Ireland: Whose Country, Whose History,** Undercurrents, Cork University Press; D. Rottman, A.Tussing and M.Wiley (1986) **The Population Structure and Living Circumstances of Irish Travellers:** Results from the 1981 Census of Traveller Families, Dublin; Economic And Social Research Institute, **Paper No. 131;** M. McDonagh et al (1988), **Pride and Prejudice: The Case of the Travellers,** Navan Travellers Committee.

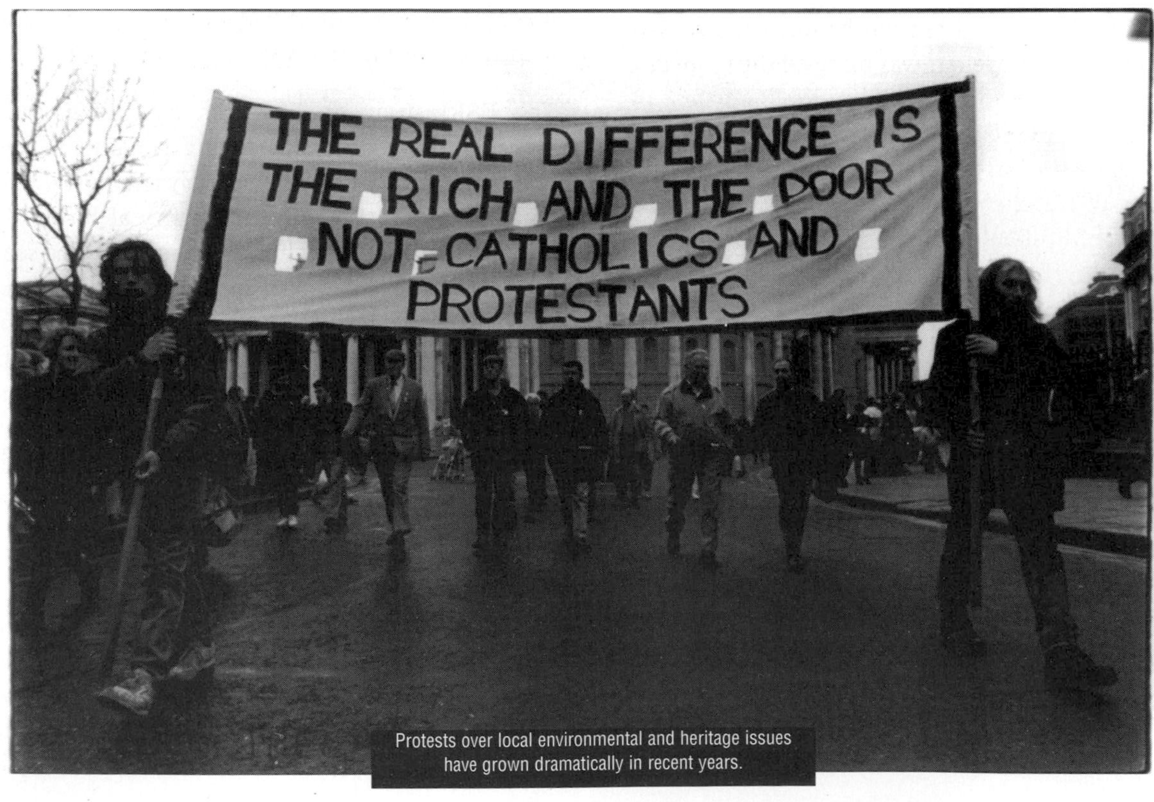

Protests over local environmental and heritage issues have grown dramatically in recent years.

Ireland in the Wider World - A case of double standards?

IRELAND AND THE THIRD WORLD - SOME QUESTIONS FOR DISCUSSION

In a special supplement on *"The Developing World"* in the Irish Times on November 22nd, 1995 (published in association with the National Committee for Development Education), Michael Holmes of University College Dublin reviewed the evolution of Ireland's links with the Third World. He cited the traditional image of Ireland's links as essentially beneficial and positive but added:

> *"...a glance over the development of Ireland's policy towards the Third World reveals some paradoxes. While there are positive aspects that must be acknowledged, there were also some less glorious moments".*

In relation to the latter point, Holmes cites:

- the involvement of many Irish people in the maintenance of the British Empire;
- the reluctance of the newly independent Irish state to become too closely involved in the wider world;
- the more recent ongoing debates about the levels of Irish aid;
- Ireland's ongoing support for the Common Agricultural Policy of the EU;
- Irish acquiescence over events such as France's interventions in Zaire and Rwanda;
- our lack of willingness to challenge the creation of an effective external European border.

On the positive side, Holmes refers to:

- the growth of close bi-lateral relations between Ireland and many African states;
- the role of Irish non-Governmental development agencies;
- Ireland's role in international peace-keeping;
- recent stances by the Government on East Timor;
- the general positive and progressive tone of Ireland's policies towards the Third World.

In this context it may be worth considering and debating some additional points regarding Ireland's past and current relations with the Third World.

While recognising the huge contribution which Irish missionaries have made and continue to make to the well-being of some of the world's poorest and most oppressed (a contribution which has heavily moulded Ireland's overall response), we should recognise many of the negative dimensions which often accompanied that contribution - the neglect of local religions and cultures, the imposition of alien practices and beliefs, the attitudes to other faiths and the dominance of western values which accompanied Irish missionaries (see Chapter 17).

The overdominance of the *"charitable imperative"* in Irish relations, was a dominant attitude which continues to this day. This approach regularly emphasises the giving of charity at the expense of or to the neglect of justice. Frequently it diverts attention away from the structural causes of underdevelopment and injustice and the ordinary Irish person's part in that underdevelopment and injustice through our part in the Western world's trade, political and economic policies. and can also contribute significantly to ill-informed comment and to the promotion of stereotypical images of the peoples of the Third World.

This charity fixation, which has once again become overwhelmingly dominant since the Somalian and Rwandan crises of 1992 and 1994, has much of its roots in Ireland's past and present religious links and in the weight of the NGDO sector in Ireland's overall response. This dominant charity framework which mediates so much of Ireland's overall development co-operation role not only distorts people's understanding of the issues involved, it also helps avoid many of the uncomfortable questions which a consideration of underlying structures and processes creating and sustaining underdevelopment would pose and it militates against more radical involvement in favour of the safe charitable response.

The fact that, apart from charitable giving, concern for and involvement with issues of world development and justice remain the preserve and concern of a very small groups of Irish people raises serious questions about Ireland's overall response to Third World and to local justice issues. While the Irish Aid programme and the Irish NGDO sector continue to operate effective yet limited programmes, Ireland's growing commercial and trading links appear to be no different than those of other European or Western interests. We seldom challenge EU trade, investment or debt policy, nor indeed the actions of those companies we invite to invest in Ireland. As has often been said, Ireland can afford to be positive and progressive when our own interests are not challenged but when we might have to choose between our own self-interest and that of the poor, our progressiveness has distinct limitations.

In 1977 the Irish Commission for Justice and Peace published a list of "fundamental principles" which, it argued, should guide Irish involvement in development co-operation. These were:

- The aim of "development" is to achieve some sort of world order. This must mean accepting the consequences of applying globally the principles of social justice now taken for granted domestically.
- Ireland is part of an interdependent world. Interdependence is irreversible and growing; it must be regulated for the common good.
- Irish domestic politics are, therefore, to an important extent, international foreign politics and her international politics are by and large development politics.
- Development co-operation is about human rights, their meaning and irreversibility.
- No coherent development co-operation "philosophy" is possible without relating it to development problems in Ireland.
- A partial approach to development may be more dangerous than none at all. Partial approaches foster a misleading idea of the nature of world development issues, as well as permitting unnecessary and costly inconsistencies in development programmes.
- Involvement in development co-operation will have to be, for Ireland at least, a struggle to liberate herself intellectually, conceptually, culturally from a cherished and deep-rooted mind set.

Few would doubt the value and impact of Irish non-governmental agencies in their responses to both crisis situations and to the longer-term dimensions of underdevelopment. Irish NGDOs have been to the forefront in the delivery of emergency humanitarian assistance, rehabilitation programmes designed to help people overcome such emergencies, and project aid in all key areas such as health, education, rural development, literacy etc. Irish volunteers and aid workers are known and respected worldwide. But in recent years competition in fund-raising between NGDOs has led to what many believe is an overstatement of the impact of their work. No matter how hard NGDOs work and no matter how effective their work, their impact remains extremely limited in terms of the scale of the problems they address. Another criticism which many voice is that NGDOs have overemphasised the contribution of Irish/British aid workers/volunteers to the neglect of local Third World workers who are often in the majority. Other criticisms which are often cited include the advertising images used by many NGDOs which portray the people of the Third World as passive and helpless victims, and the continuing lack of effective support for development education throughout the NGDO sector in both Britain and Ireland.

For a more extended review of the evolution of Ireland's foreign policy in relation to the Third World see Michael Holmes, Nicholas Rees and Bernadette Whelan (1993) ***The Poor Relation: Irish Foreign Policy and the Third World,*** Dublin, Trocaire and Gill and Macmillan.

"But neither our personal compassion nor our actions as a country prevail against world-wide poverty. The movement towards, for example, free trade - facilitated, ironically, by an Irishman [Peter Sutherland, Chairman of the GATT talks] - is leaving the powerless of the world still more powerless.

The Asian 'economic miracle' depends on making things as cheaply as possible, and that means using child labour and exploited labour and prison and slave labour and finally unpaid labour, such as I saw in Subic Bay in the Philippines.

Capitalism has no conscience. We are called by the media, to feel for human suffering and to understand the world-wide system of which that suffering is part.

And we're further called to the bitter realisation that understanding it does nothing to change it."

Nuala O'Faolain, **Irish Times** 29.1.96

Northern Ireland

This section introduces various dimensions of the current situation in Northern Ireland. It focuses on underlying issues and questions which will remain part of the legacy of the conflict regardless of what political solution may be agreed. As we noted at the beginning of this chaper it is often more difficult for people to address issues which are closer to home because they have a vested interest in them. Nowhere is this more true than in discussions about Northern Ireland.

A Profile of Northern Ireland

The population of Northern Ireland is 1,577,836, of which 50.6% are Protestant, and 38.4% are Catholic (11% of the population have no or no stated religion). The population of the Republic of Ireland, is 3,523,401, of which 95.0% are Catholic, 3.4% Protestant (1.6% other or no stated religion).

The all-Ireland population therefore is 5,101,237, of which 77.0% are nominally Catholic, 18.4% nominally Protestant, and 4.6% other or no stated religion.

> *"The majority of people in Northern Ireland define themselves as Protestants, though the proportion of Catholics has significantly increased since the State was created in 1920. Catholics' higher (though declining) birthrate has led to speculation that they will become a majority around 2025 but there would be a time lag before this majority was reflected in the population of voting age."*

(**New Internationalist,** May 1994).

The economy of the North is largely sustained by the transfer of capital from Britain in conjunction with EU structural funding and US financial support in the form of the International Fund for Ireland. Consequently, the North has developed an uncompetitive economic system which is unlikely to expand. After the cease-fire announcements in 1994 the EU established a Special Support Programme for Peace and Reconciliation, largely aimed at community organisations to imbed the peace process, and involving the dissemination of 240 million ECU in grants over a three year period.

> *"Northern Ireland is locked into a downward economic spiral. It has not only all the problems of a peripheral region, but is a region of a wider British economy, itself in trouble. It neither controls its own affairs, nor does it benefit from a wider set of economic institutions which generates growth and employment."*

(Economist Will Hutton quoted in *Fortnight,* November, 1994).

National Income per capita 1990

	GNP $	UK=100%	GDP $	UK=100%
UK	12,555	100	12,511	100
South	7,731	61.6	8,898	71.1
North	9,543	76.00	9,543	76.3

Sources: CSO, UK National Accounts 1993; NI Annual Abstract of Statistics, 1992; National Income and Expenditure 1991, CSO Dublin.

Annual Average Growth Rates (1965 - 1991)

Aggregate Growth Measures (%)

	UK	South	North	EC
real GDP	2.3	3.9	2.6	3.1
real GNP	2.1	3.1	-	-
employment	0.1	0.3	0.4	0.4

> *"The enterprise culture in Northern Ireland gets an input of £300 million per year while community development, in the very broadest sense, receives approximately £36 million."*

(Community Development Review Group, **Community Development in Northern Ireland,** Belfast: WEA, 1991, p.18).

> *"Northern Ireland is massively subsidised by the rest of the UK. In 1992-93 the subvention - public spending in the province not covered by tax raised there - amounted to £3.3 billion ($4.8 billion)."*

(**New Internationalist,** May 1994).

In the Republic, high unemployment, and in the North the 'Troubles', have led - some would say compelled - around a million people to migrate from Ireland, North and South since the mid-1960s. On 14 April 1994, the total number of unemployed in the North was 98,383 (13.3%); 76,999 (17.7%) were men and 21,384 (6.9%) were women. ***(Belfast Telegraph,** 18 May 1994).*

In Northern Ireland, *"Unemployment is persistently above the UK average: at its lowest point, in October 1990, it was 94,000 - 13.7 per cent of the labour force, compared with Britain's post-war peak of 11.5 per cent."* (**Red Pepper,** August 1994, p.7).

> *"It has often been remarked that such unemployment represents a massive loss of potential output and a waste of people's lives. It is considered also to be a threat to the social fabric, which is particularly poignant in the circumstances of Northern Ireland."* (Victor Hewitt, 'Comparisons from the North', **Studies,** Spring 1993, p.24).

"Northern Ireland is the poorest of the UK's regions, its GDP per capita being 74% of the European Union average. Even this position for Northern Ireland is misleading - its economy is kept afloat by vast subsidies from Britain. What was once the economic power-house of the Irish island has suffered from deindustrialisation with a vengeance while the Irish Republic has an economy with much greater underlying strength."

(**New Internationalist,** May 1994).

Employment in Manufacturing, North and South of Ireland, 1960-1993

	1960	1993
Republic	175,000	232,000
N. Ireland	184,000	110,000

In Northern Ireland *"poverty is something which affects 38% of householders, 42% of individuals and 33% of families in Northern Ireland. A typical group in Northern Ireland living in poverty was a family of two adults with children."* (Community Development Review Group, **Community Development in Northern Ireland,** Belfast: WEA, 1991, p.18).

"Everywhere in Northern Ireland where it is good to stand at the bottom, Northern Ireland is at the top (highest infant mortality, highest housing unfitness rate, highest unemployment). Everywhere it is good to be at the top, Northern Ireland is at the bottom (lowest amount of consumer durables, lowest economic activity rates, smallest proportion of job vacancies)."

(Monica McWilliams, **Fortnight,** October 1985).

"The effects of poverty on children in Northern Ireland can begin at birth. Northern Ireland has the highest incidences of prenatal mortality, infant mortality and still births than any other region in the United Kingdom." (Northern Ireland Poverty Lobby, **A Life of Poverty,** p.25).

"The last twenty-five years of conflict (in Northern Ireland) have led to an unprecedented expansion of State expenditures, and with it State employment. Superficially, the North is an island of Keynesianism in a UK free market sea." (M. Tomlinson, **25 Years On,** p.14).

"The economic subsidy is much more of a drain than the cost of keeping the army there. The total cost of the military presence was £405.6 million ($592.2 million) in 1993 - just 1.7% of the total UK defence budget." (**New Internationalist,** May 1994, p.19).

Dimensions of Recent History

Ireland's industrial revolution was largely confined to the North-east region, what is now Northern Ireland. Here a huge linen industry developed in the eighteenth and nineteenth centuries. Then came the thriving ship-building and engineering industries towards the end of the nineteenth century. The area around Belfast had, by 1900, become one of the most industrialised areas in the world. By 1911, a half of all industrial jobs in Ireland were located in its North-eastern corner, while one in five were in Belfast alone. Some argue that it was the economic prosperity of North-eastern Ireland, together with political pressure exerted by Ulster Unionists, which determined British government support for an artificial Northern Ireland state, and partition similar to the model later adopted in leaving other colonies.

Others argue that Northern Ireland was a distinct and separate entity which made a logical State. Even in the last centuries BC, Ulster's inhabitants had erected a great earthwork wall from Bundoran in Donegal to South Armagh. The people who were brought from Scotland by the plantations were in fact descendents of the pre-Celtic Irish who had been driven out by the Celtic invaders. They were comparable to the Israelites who returned to their homeland after 1,848 years. In the twentieth century, the different type and rate of development in different parts of the island, combined with different histories and different religions to make two natural States on the island.

> *"It was in Ulster that Ireland's only succesful manufacturing industries, shipbuilding and linen, were to be found . . . These enterprises were Protestant controlled, with a skilled workforce overwhelmingly (93%) Protestant, and dependent on export markets and sources of raw material in the extensive free trade area of the British Empire. It was believed that the nationalist demands for tariff autonomy under Home Rule (to say nothing of independence) would spell ruin since it would condemn them to a protectionist regime that would expose them to retaliatory discrimination in the world outside, offering them as recompense only the impoverished agrarian Irish hinterland"*

Professor Antony Alcock, **Understanding Ulster,** Ulster Society, 1994.

The Northern Ireland State was administered by a parliament controlled by the Ulster Unionist party. In the 1930s Lord Craigavon - formerly Sir James Craig -

boasted of having created a "Protestant parliament and a Protestant State". The Northern parliament excluded the Nationalist minority from the institutions of government. The Unionist administration abolished proportional representation in local government elections and gave itself the power to redraw electoral boundaries thereby minimising the electoral influence of Nationalist voters. The franchise was restricted to ratepayers, their wives and tenants, thereby disen-franchising one quarter of the electorate. Furthermore, control of local government facilitated discrimination in other areas such as in the allocation of jobs and housing.

"…. some 2,300 have died. Between 1971 and 1982, there were over 28,500 shooting incidents in Northern Ireland, over 7,200 bomb explosions and another 3,100 plus bombs neutralised, over 9,600 armed robberies, and over 17,000 civilian injuries - an injury or death in one out of every twenty households. Which means that in the tight knit community that is Northern Ireland there is hardly a family that does not personally know at least one other family that has sustained at least an injury as a result of the violence of the last decade. And behind every injury there is a personal story - of random victims, luckless scapegoats, and innocent pawns caught in the vice of the extreme.

You get an idea of the scale of the violence if you multiply the figures by a factor of 150 to arrive at comparable figures for the US population. Thus, the number of dead would stand at 345,000 - almost as many as the number of people who died in the American Civil War - and the number of civilians injured at 2,550,000."

Padraig O Malley (1983), **The Uncivil Wars**, Belfast, Blackstaff Press.

Northern Ireland was policed by a 3,000 strong Royal Ulster Constabulary (RUC), and an exclusively Protestant armed militia with 12,000 members knows as the B Specials. Emergency legislation (the Special Powers Act) was introduced by the Northern Ireland parliament in 1922 and gave almost limitless powers to the Northern Ireland Minister of Home Affairs. The majority of Nationalists in Northern Ireland refused to recognise the Northern State because of their opposition to partition and the discriminatory nature of the Unionist administration.

Deaths caused by conflict

In 25 years of violence in Northern Ireland, a total of 3,163 people have died with another 36,603 injured, many maimed for life. (**Irish News**, 8 August 1994). Civilians killed by:

Loyalist paramilitaries	871 (95.7% of victims were civilians)
Republican paramilitaries	829 (43.1% of victims were civilians)
British Security Forces	203 (56.9% of victims were civilians)

Civil Rights

In the late 1960s, a student civil rights movement took to the streets of Northern Ireland under the banner 'one man - one vote', inspired by black civil rights protesters in the United States and other parts of the world. Peaceful protests dissolved into sectarian bitterness and conflict, and the British government introduced British troops on to the streets of Belfast and Derry in 1969.

Republic of Ireland

Following partition, Unionists in Northern Ireland have reacted strongly to the dominant influence of the Catholic Church on secular life in the Republic of Ireland. They consider that the Irish Constitution places limitations on civil liberties, particularly resented by non catholic and this accounts for their fear of being absorbed into an all-Ireland state. The 1937 constitution, for example, prohibited divorce (legalised in November 1995), abortion and even conferred on Catholicism a unique status within the Constitution. Although this article was also later amended, many North and South still feel that the 1937 Constitution reflects Catholic teaching.

Many Unionists regard the Constitution as a failure by both the church and State in the Republic to recognise and acknowledge the religious and political affiliations of the majority in Northern Ireland. In particular, Unionists have long regarded articles 2 and 3 of the Constitution as a threat to the sovereign status in Northern Ireland. Article 2 defines *"the national territory"* as *"the whole island of Ireland"*, while article 3 suggests that the laws of the State *"pending the re-integration of the national territory"* shall have jurisdiction over the whole of the national territory including Northern Ireland. Unionists have vigorously urged the Irish government to drop or amend Articles 2 and 3 from the Constitution in order to improve the prospects for peace in Northern Ireland.

Direct Rule

In March 1972, as violence escalated on the streets of Northern Ireland, the Northern parliament at Stormont was dismissed and Direct Rule from Westminster introduced. Direct Rule was expected to be a temporary arrangement but the period since 1972 has been marked by a range of unsuccessful efforts to restore devolved government to Northern Ireland, or indeed find any formula for a lasting settlement.

A Peace Process?

On 31st August 1994, the Irish Republican Army (IRA) announced "a complete cessation of military operations" and so embarked on a 17 month cease-fire "in order to enhance the democratic peace process." (**Irish Times,** 10 February 1996). Within weeks, loyalist paramilitaries followed the IRA's lead and announced their own cease-fire.

The origins of the peace process and events leading up to the IRA's announcement go back many years and have involved both public and private talks between party leaders and 'go-betweens' in Northern Ireland and in the Republic, between the British Government and all parties in Northern Ireland (including, and in many cases, secretly, Sinn Fein), between the Irish and British Governments with strong involvement from the US Government and also, to a more limited extent the European Parliament and Commission.

On Friday February 9th, 1996, the IRA cease-fire was abruptly ended with the bombing of Canary Wharf in London, thus seriously threatening current peace process.

Northern Ireland: Managing Difference

In 1995, the Minority Rights Group published an important and useful report entitled *Northern Ireland: Managing Difference.* Its author was Professor John Darby of INCORE (Initiative on Conflict Resolution and Ethnicity - a United Nations University Initiative) at the University of Ulster. The report provides a brief overview of key dimensions of the conflict in Northern Ireland and highlights, in particular, four key dimensions which have major implications for the future whatever form that may take. Here we present some excerpts from the MRG Report.

"The Northern Ireland conflict has been described as an ethnic conflict. The term 'ethnic' is used in its broad sense to include allegiances which are based on race, religion, language or other cultural manifestations. It is recognised that there is another definition of 'ethnic' which takes a more precise view of the term, but the broader definition allows a more comprehensive analysis of the issue. In relation to Northern Ireland, the 'ethnic' definition is more suitable than other definitions which view it exclusively as a constitutional or religious conflict, or one based on economic, social or cultural inequalities. All of these are part of the problem, but none can claim exclusive rights to define it...

So history has bequeathed a varied inheritance. The common view that the Irish conflict is intractable because it is unchanging is demonstrably untrue. Since the Norman invasion by Henry! of England in the twelfth century, it is possible to discern significant shifts in the Irish problem. Until 1921 the political dispute focused on Ireland's attempt to maintain or secure independence from Britain. From 1921 the emphasis shifted to relationships within the island of Ireland, between what later became the 26 counties of the Republic of Ireland and NI's six counties. Finally since the outbreak of the current violence in 1969, relationships between Catholics and Protestants within the province have played a much more dominant role in defining the Irish conflict..."

The historian ATQ Stewart:

"Most people, if asked to define the chief symptoms of the Northern Ireland troubles, would say it is that the two communities cannot live together. The very essence of the Ulster question, however, is that they do live together and have done for centuries. They

share the same homeland and, like it or not, the two diametrically opposed wills must co-exist on the same narrow ground."

Professor Darby adds:

"They must co-exist in a struggling economy. NI has few natural resources, and has suffered severely since the 1960s for its dependency on traditional industries, especially ship-building and textiles...

In some ways the people who have benefited most from public subsidy are NI's middle-classes, not the poor. Catholics have been under-represented in the workforce since 1921, and discrimination was one of the main triggers for the Troubles...Catholic unemployment rates, however, remain stubbornly and significantly higher than for Protestants. In 1995 Catholic men were still almost twice as likely to be unemployed, although the differential was diminishing slowly. For women the differential was 1:1.5..."

Darby then goes on to describe the Northern Ireland problem as *"a multi-layered problem."*

"Protestants are more likely to see the conflict in constitutional and security terms, and are primarily concerned about preserving the union with Britain and resisting the threat of a united Ireland. Catholic views fall generally into two broad categories. The first perceives the issue as a nationalist struggle for self-determination, looking back to what they regard as the historical integrity of the island and the gerrymander of partition; for many the problem cannot be resolved by any measures short of British withdrawal and Irish unity. The second approach it as a problem of corruption or unfair practices which, if removed, would create a society in which both Catholics and Protestants could live together peacefully...There is some common ground between Protestant and Catholic analyses. Opinion polls indicate that they are equally opposed to the use of violence...The situation is further complicated by an increasingly disinterested view towards the province in both Britain and the Irish Republic..."

Professor Darby then goes on to identify 4 intractable problems which need to be addressed if any real and lasting progress is to be made - politics, inequality, violence and justice, and community relations.

Politics

"Every election since the formation of the state has demonstrated that the centre has been decimated by sectarian politics...The main problem for unionist and nationalist parties has been to ensure that they do not lose support to more extreme opponents from their own tradition...

Since the dissolution of the Northern Ireland Parliament and the introduction of Direct Rule from Westminster in 1972, movement towards a political settlement has been frustrated by two disputes - about the constitutional context in which Northern Ireland should function, and the political arrangements which should govern executive power...For unionists, Northern Ireland was the context which provided them with majority status. For Catholics the context was the island of Ireland. The demand by nationalists that the Irish Republic should have a role in the governance of NI, and the refusal of unionists to allow any Dublin involvement, was the first block to political settlement...

The other block concerned the political arrangements which would govern the province internally. For unionists, NI should have the same political system which operates in the rest of the UK. Governments should be formed by a majority of members, elected in a first past the post election. For nationalists this approach would ensure permanent exclusion from power..."

Inequality

"For most nationalists the Northern Ireland state was an area artificially carved out of the island of Ireland to create and maintain a Protestant majority...For the unionist majority the new arrangements and the union itself could be maintained only by constant vigilance...local government electoral boundaries were openly gerrymandered, a device also used by nationalists where they were able to do so. A system of economic discrimination was introduced against the Catholic minority in NI...In 1964 the Northern Ireland Civil Rights Association was formed to demand internal reforms, including the removal of discrimination in the allocation of jobs and houses, permanent emergency legislation and electoral abuses...

There have been a number of policy initiatives aimed at addressing minority grievances... Paradoxically, the removal of democracy (after the introduction of Direct Rule in 1972) led to the first systematic removal of minority inequalities. Any attempt to remove minority grievances in a more democratic local setting would have been severely hampered by the sectarianism which is a feature of all ethnic politics...

Nevertheless, on virtually every indicator of socio-economic disadvantage, Catholics still experience higher levels of need or disadvantage than Protestants..."

VIOLENCE AND JUSTICE

"The conflict in NI has been exceptionally persistent. No generation since the plantation has escaped its heritage of violence...This constant antagonism has primarily been between two internal hostile neighbours rather than between hostile neighbouring countries. The distinction between internal conflicts and international wars needs to be emphasised...

During the early 1970s many observers believed that the upsurge of violence in NI could lead to only two outcomes; either the belligerents would be shocked into an internal accommodation, or they would be propelled into genocidal massacre. Neither occurred. The initial rioting between Catholics and Protestants was soon replaced by more structured violence after the arrival of the British army and its confrontations with the Catholic community. The emergence of the Provisional IRA, strengthened by the introduction of Internment in 1991, converted the violence to more organised confrontation between the IRA and the British army, with interventions from loyalist paramilitary organisations...

All three actors were both perpetrators and victims of violence. Between 1969 and the declaration of the cease-fires by republican and loyalist paramilitary organisations in 1994, the Troubles had claimed 3,173 deaths in NI, and a total of 235 in Britain, the Irish Republic and the rest of Europe...25 years of violence raised tensions between the two communities and obstructed the search for political accommodation..."

COMMUNITY RELATIONS

"People in NI are born into communities which have often been structurally and sometimes residentially divided since the Plantation of Ulster. The divisions are ratified and reinforced by different social patterns and mutual suspicion. Therefore, it is surprising that contact between Protestants and Catholics has continued at a number of levels within society. Cross community contact takes place regularly in most districts of NI, in many workplaces, in higher education, and in social and leisure activities. It is true that relationships are rarely made in ignorance of religious affiliation, but they are often made despite this...

Perhaps more surprising is that most people are in favour of increased contact. The obstacles frustrating natural relationships across the religious divide are important. A society cannot hope to function fairly and peacefully if there is a central split about its very nature...Psychological factors, including real and imagined fears, are serious barriers to conciliation..."

▼ REFERENCES

Therese Caherty et al (eds.1992) **Is Ireland a Third World Country?**, Belfast, Centre for Research and Documentation.

Carol Coulter (1990) **Ireland: Between First and Third Worlds**, Attic Press, Dublin.

Raymond Crotty (1986) **Ireland in Crisis: a study in capitalist colonial development**, Dingle, Brandon Books.

John Darby (1995) **Northern Ireland: Managing Difference**, London, Minority Rights Group.

Michael Holmes, Nicholas Rees and Bernadette Whelan (1993) **The Poor Relation: Irish Foreign Policy and the Third World**, Dublin, Trocaire and Gill and Macmillan.

Kieran Kennedy (1993) **Facing the Unemployment Crisis in Ireland**, Undercurrents Series, Cork University Press.

Peadar Kirby (1992) **Ireland and Latin America, Links and Lessons**, Dublin, Trocaire and Gill and Macmillan.

Joe Lee (1989) **Ireland 1912-1985: Politics and Society**, Cambridge University Press.

Gerard McCann et al (1994) **A Guide To Ireland In a Developing World**, Belfast, One World Centre.

M. McDonagh et al (1988), **Pride and Prejudice: The Case of the Travellers**, Navan Travellers Committee.

Jim McLaughlin (1994) **Ireland: The Emigrant Nursery and the World Economy**, Undercurrents, Cork University Press.

Jim Mac Laughlin (1995) **Travellers and Ireland: Whose Country, Whose History**, Undercurrents, Cork University Press.

Padraig O'Malley (1983), **The Uncivil Wars**, Belfast, Blackstaff Press.

D. Rottman, A.Tussing and M.Wiley (1986) **The Population Structure and Living Circumstances of Irish Travellers:** Results from the 1981 Census of Traveller Families, Dublin, Economic And Social Research Institute, Paper No. 131.

Bob Rowthorn and Naiomi Wayne (1988) **Northern Ireland, The Political Economy of Northern Ireland**, Polity Press, Cambridge.

RELIGION AND DEVELOPMENT

Liam Wegimont

"Much of the best and worst of human history has been created in the name of its gods, and religious traditions continue to provide both an ethical critique of, as well as a justification for, much bloodletting. The... study of religion has important insights into the central issues of how we can live together in our multicultural global village as well as helpful tools for investigating the problems created by our newly created common life with its diverse norms and values.... The world's religions will be an integral part of the process..."

Kurtz, Lester (1995) **Gods in the Global Village,** Pine Forge Press, London

Introduction

This chapter examines the complex relationship between religion and development. It explores the negative effects of religion through colonialism, and the oppression of women. It travels through the liberating traditions of religion: surveying the world religions and their commitment to justice. It also examines the history of mission.

The chapter also reviews the manner in which the very notion of development itself has functioned as a religious idea, and how faith in the Western model of development functions as a religion - and a soul-less religion at that. The chapter argues that alternatives to this particular 'faith' can be found in the search for a new global ethic, being embarked upon by religious people today.

Religion and Development

The relationship between religion and development is a varied one. Christianity, the religion of the majority of the world, has been associated, in its various forms, with the Crusades, the Inquisition, witch-burning, colonisation, the rise of Capitalism, the subjugation of nature and the oppression of women. It has also been at the forefront of movements against oppression - participating in new understandings of the relationship between capital and labour, creating space for social protest in the face of dictatorship as well as mobilising national movements for change. Islam, so often caricatured by the media as simply fundamentalist and fanatical, is at core a call to live more justly towards others. Through the third pillar of its belief system, Zakat, Islam insists that the redistribution of wealth is a prerequisite for holiness and that there is a social responsibility attached to all material wealth. Against this that same religious tradition clings jealously to the notion of a very particular role for women (seen by many to be the subordination of women) as a fundamental tenet of religious and family life.

Other examples of the complex and contradictory nature of the relationship between religion and development abound. Simply stated, a tour of the history of the world will reveal that religions are to blame for much of what has led to oppression. An examination of personal experience of religious institutions might, in some instances, say the same. That is not the full story, however. Religion has also been at the forefront of radical change and has been, literally, the cry of the oppressed. As world religions recognise, and repent for, their own culpability, their traditions of justice, equality, communitarian vision need also to be rediscovered and acknowledged.

Two American sociologists of religions, Rodney Stark and William Bainbridge have argued that *"Most sociological discussion of the political role of religion is not merely misleading, but pernicious. The standard view, enshrined in dozens of textbooks, is that religion sustains the political status quo - that religion serves as a conservative, even reactionary force in human society. Clearly, such claims apply at best only to some religions and only in some special social circumstances. Unfortunately, too many sociologists have paid attention to only a few notable instances in recent Western history. Many have mistated the case because of their particular theoretical commitments (to say nothing of their personal antagonism towards religion) ..".*

The following pages attempt to look at the story from both sides.

Religion and Oppression - Colonialism

"80% of the world's goods are in the hands of a small minority of the world's people and the gap between rich and poor nations grows constantly wider. This is the consequence of colonialism. If for the most part the colonial empires have disappeared, the economic shackles forged are not so easily broken. Most of the new nations remain producers of raw materials, subject to the vicissitudes of a world market of which the terms of trade are not in their favour, and are blocked by the restrictive tariff policies of the powerful industrialised nations from developing export industries of their own.

What should be the attitude of religion in the face of these realities? Its first posture should be one of repentance for having remained singularly indifferent to the idolatry of riches and the perversion of their use. Especially called to repentance is the Christian world inasmuch as, with some exceptions, the part of the world where wealth is concentrated is - or is called - Christian. Contrary to the Spirit of Christ, social injustice was protected by the paradoxical attitude of many Christians who looked upon the accumulated wealth as a reward for virtue and the burden of poverty as a punishment for sin or a cross to be borne in expectation of liberation in the next world. Religions other than Christian are, however, not to be entirely absolved of blame. For, by excessive emphasis upon the relative unimportance of the material, they weakened the forces opposed to its hegemony. "

World Conference on Religion and Peace, Kyoto, 1970

If colonialism is indeed responsible for the vast inequalities that exist in the world today, then Christians have to repent for the atrocious history of Christian involvement in the colonial enterprise. Historically, the Roman Catholic church was at the forefront of the initial colonisation of Latin America. It provided much of the ideological framework which made it acceptable to plunder and to pillage. Its theology was based on assumptions of Christian superiority. In this way of thinking, anyone not Christian was not quite human. The Churches association with Catholic states, particularly Spain and Portugal, meant it acted as a broker between rival colonial powers.

Closer to home, three and a half centuries earlier, the papal bull "Laudabiliter", issued by the English Pope, Adrian IV, in December 1154 granted rights to the English monarch, Henry II, to get his hands on the island of Ireland, on the basis that he was far more

trustworthy as a loyal Roman Catholic than the Irish, with their particular brand of monastic independence from Rome, might ever prove to be. Indeed, as many historians have pointed out, with tongue in cheek, Henry II was given authority by a succession of popes to invade Ireland and even to gather taxes for Rome.

Roman Catholicism gave the blessings of God to Latin American colonisation, the Conquistadores headed West in search of gold, and with them went the church in search of converts. Catholicism also supported the enslavement of the Indians as the quest for gold turned into a process of extraction of abundant commodities using slave labour. It was alright to enslave the indigenous population so long as there was the possibility that they could be brought into the fold and converted to Christianity. Debate raged over whether or not it was permitted to convert indigenous peoples through force. Christianity provided not only the rationale, but also the symbolism for abuse; on Hispaniola, not only did the invaders cut off the limbs of the native Arawaks and feed them to their dogs (to give them a taste for Indian flesh), they also hanged recaptured escapees in groups of 13, signifying Christ and the Apostles.

On the other hand, Catholic priests, particularly some Dominicans, Franciscans and Jesuits were at the forefront of criticism. Men like Antonio de Montesinos threatened the Spanish conquerors with eternal damnation if they treated the indigenous population in any way other than as equals. Bartolome de Las Casas, a champion of indigenous peoples, denounced his fellow Spaniards and came to the defence of the Indians. Denunciation did not limit itself to individual condemnation or theological treatise, but also resulted in the setting up of alternatives to colonialism such as the Reductions, which attempted to resist the slave trade.

The greatest injustice perpetrated on the indigenous population by the Church was not through its association with the secular authorities, but more directly through the process of evangelization. It was through the attempts to Christianise the indigenous populations of the Americas that cultures were killed, religious traditions discredited and demeaned and the heart torn out of ancient peoples.

The role of the Roman Catholic Church in the colonisation of the body and spirit of Latin America was paralleled by other denominations in Africa, and is equally

..HE WENT BACK TO SPAIN AND THEN RETURNED WITH 17 SHIPS FULL OF ARMED SOLDIERS.....
TO 3,4,5,6,7,8,9, 10,11,12,13,14,15,16,17...
2
1

REDUCTIONS

The Reductions excluded non-Indians and were clearly focused on community development and on the protection of the Indians from capture and enslavement by the Spanish. The programmes associated with the Reductions reflected a remarkable sensitivity to the Guarani Indian ways and values.

The thirty cities that comprised the system had a combined population of about 140,000. Although the first to organise a Reduction was the Franciscan Luis de Buanos, it was the Jesuits, especially men like Father Ruiz de Montoya, who made the Reductions the remarkable settlements that they were. These cities formed safe havens against Spanish exploitation, especially against the enslavement of Indians.

Although the pope had condemned the enslavement of Indians in 1537, in one year alone no less than 30,000 Indians are said to have been killed or captured. Ruiz de Montoya obtained permission from the Crown to set up a military defence system especially to combat slavery, a serious evil that had made 300,000 freedom-loving Indians into slaves. In 1604 the pope declared Paraguay a Jesuit province. The area extended well beyond what is known today as Paraguay . The first Reduction was founded six years later.

Reductions were well-organised, semi-autonomous communities that owed allegiance to the Crown and paid taxes. They had collective farms and herds, and they stressed community development and both religious and practical education. Evaluations of the endeavour will vary. Some find fault with the barrack-like life, which was very un-Guaranian. The system however, was definitely functional, culturally sensitive, and socially conscious. While the Reductions may have been monastic and their living conditions were indeed barrack-like, their communities formed an excellent self-defence. They were also an example of community development and of a serious attempt at guided acculturation and adjustment to the inescapable effects of colonialism.

Source: Louis J. Luzbetak (1988) **The Church and Cultures: New Perspectives in Missiological Anthropology,** New York, Orbis.

HE ALSO SOLD THE IDEA OF CONVERTING THE INDIANS TO CHRISTIANITY AND PLANTED CROSSES WHEREVER HE WENT.....
Ye Treasure Map
...WHICH PROVED USEFUL TO THOSE WHO FOLLOWED LOOKING FOR GOLD...

true of other Protestant Western Christian denominations. Protestant Christianity developed missionary endeavour only in later centuries. As early as the sixteenth and seventeenth centuries, however, the effect of the relationship between Protestant Christian mission and colonial power was being experienced in Europe and elsewhere. The Irish experienced it at the hands of Cromwell - whose military activities were informed by religious fervour, and included plans to set up a Protestant Mission Congregation. The Lapps experienced it at the hands of the Swedish King, Gustav Vasa, who held with the principle 'cuius regio eius religio' the ruler of the domain decides its religion.

Just as Spain and Portugal's invasion of Latin America in the 15th and 16th centuries brought with it Roman Catholicism, in the 17th Century the profit pursuit and colonial enterprise of England, Denmark and the Netherlands was accompanied by Protestant missionary zeal.

Max Weber, the German sociologist, in his influential 'Protestant Ethic and the Spirit of Capitalism', analysed the relationship between Protestantism and the rise of belief in profit and progress. He argued that the Reformation, pulling the rug as it did from under Western certainty and institutional access to truth and salvation, led people to look for new signs of salvation. If people are called by God, God must show signs of election in other ways than through pope or priest. If believers work hard to participate in salvation, the signs will be evident. Economic success came to be seen as a sign of salvation or election. This idea, as an idea that had an elective affinity or congruence with social movements at the time, paved the way for the rise of capitalism.

Western missionaries attacked the cultural and religious symbols that gave meaning to the lives of African peoples -rituals, music, dance and divine images were destroyed, condemned or appropriated. In some instances, the first generation of African converts did even more damage to traditional religion and culture in zealous attempts to become more Western than the Christians themselves. The Kenyan writer Ngugi wa Thiong'o tells us that:

> *"In Kenya, while the European settler robbed the people of their land and the products of their sweat, the missionary robbed people of their souls.'*

Religion and Opression against Women

The work of feminist theologians over the past 30 years has drawn our attention to the way in which Christianity has functioned to sub-ordinate women. There are a number of ways in which this has happened:

- Religious Texts: The Hebrew Bible, for example, was told, written, re-told, edited, for specific times and places in the history of the Israelite and Jewish people. In the process - dominated by men - women were written out of the stroy. Feminist theologians now return to the Bible to uncover the other side of the story - stories of women's experiences of countering oppression and domination. Others believe that the biblical texts are irretrivable, and discover alternative, women-centred texts. Many do both.
- God dess: How we imagine God is the very basis for religious people's value systems. For many religious, God is more than humans can fully imagine. For this reason, religions such as Judaism, Islam and Christianity have a prohibition against idolatry - idolatry being imagining that one particular image or picture of God is God. Feminist theologians point out that for many, the traditional image of God is God as male, God the Father. The fatherhood of God - calling God Abba - Daddy - is central to Christianity. Feminist theology points out that when masculine images of God are the only ones available, they stop being images and start becoming idols. If we can only think about God in male terms, then it is not God we are thinking about. And, as American philosopher, Mary Daly puts it *'if God is male, then the male is God'.*

Limiting God to maleness has been the ultimate sanction for the subordination of women. Feminist theologians try to change this stiuation in various ways. Some complement male images with female images of God. God is described in the Bible as a mother, a midwife, a woman lover, a sister, a mother hen. Her qualities are loving, wisdom, tenderness, kindness, justice - qualities that are lacking in patriarchal structures dominated by men. These qualities are re-discovered by feminist theologians. Others argue that it is necessary to journey to Goddess - to break the stronghold that maleness has on God by praying to Goddess who loves us.

- **Structures of Male Domination within Religion:** Many women find it difficult to accept calls by the Roman Catholic Church for equality between the sexes, in all structures and institutions, except the Roman Catholic Church itself. The issue of ordination of women often takes second place to the issue of the sub-ordination of women. The phenomenon is, however, to be found globally, as Mary Daly points out in her classic analysis of misogynistic practices worldwide. In this brilliantly researched analysis, Daly examines Hindu sutee (the practice of burning child brides with their recently deceased husbands); Chinese foot-binding (the torture of Chinese girl-children, so that their feet grow stubbed and mis-shaped); African genital mutilation: (the widespread practice in some African and Middle Eastern countries of female circumcision); American gynecology (developed, as it was, from practices learnt through the death-camps of Nazi Germany) and European witch-burning (the crazes which used religion to exterminate powerful women).

The participation of religion in the history of oppression is not limited to colonialism or patriarchy. Biblical texts have also been interpreted in an ethnocentric and triumphalist manner, to give divine ligitimisation to imperialism and the eradication of different cultures; they have been interpreted in a literalist fashion to give sanction to racism and apartheid; they have been interpreted in a heterosexist or homophobic manner to give divine (and ecclesial) backing to discrimination against homosexual men and women; they have been interpreted in an acosmological manner to give divine sanction to the plunder and pillage of the Earth in the name of progress and the subjugation of nature; they have also been interpreted in a militaristic manner to obtain divine sanction for war, military spending and nuclearism.

The social teaching of the churches lays emphasis on human development not material development

Religious Traditions and Human Liberation.

"The basic values of the ancient religious traditions are in no way opposed to development On the contrary. However, over the long centuries, customs and traditions, many of which have been impediments to human progress, have like barnacles attached themselves to all religions without exception....What is imperative...is not the total rejection of traditional values but an honest and critical examination to separate the essential from the accretions of time. The former which can serve to further the development of ...[humanity]... should be preserved, renewed, strengthened. The latter, which stand in the way, must be courageously removed"...

If religious traditions have at times been implicated in the history of oppression, providing Divine sanction and ideological impetus for enslavement and domination, it is also true, if not truer, that world religions, as well as less populous traditions, are essentially about justice. Religions have been at the forefront of social change, providing ultimate sanction for revolt against injustice and oppression.

Did you know that the Hebrew tradition began with the revolt of slaves against oppression? The original hero and heroine of Judaism - Abraham and Sarah - were refugees? Christianity was founded by an itinerant preacher who turned the contemporary Jewish notion of the Kingdom of God into a potent symbol of a world free from injustice and oppression, while his mother believed in a God who favours poor over rich, powerless over powerful, hungry over full. Islam was founded by the Prophet who grew disenchanted with a life of luxury and commerce and set bout reforming Mecca, only to be hounded by the religious and politically powerful of his time. Guatama Buddha, born in 563 B.C.E. the son of a king, also rejected power and luxury after experiencing at first hand the realities of poverty, illness and death. And while some adherents of Hinduism claim that it had no beginning, since its earliest times there has been a consistent belief that there are many and different paths to truth.

World religions provide meaning for the peoples of the world. And within these meanings, social justice, tolerance, peace, equlaity, harmony with nature, and belief in a better world loom large.

Islam

"The Islamic faith is one of the fastest growing and most misunderstood religions in the world today. Approximately one out of seven people, many living in some of the most politically sensitive parts of the world, call themselves Muslims" - Lester Kurtz

Islam as a faith is much misunderstood by non-Muslim Westerners, for a number of reasons. Firstly, the charge of "fundamentalism" is used widely by an ethno-centric media in reference to all varieties of Islam. This ensures that non-Muslims can avoid an analysis of the causes of Islamic revival, and also serves to fuel European anti-Islamic racism. While the reality of Islamic "revival" or Islamic traditionalism is one which is complex in its relations to Western values and systems, not all Muslims ascribe to such revival. The Dutch Christian theologian and middle-Eastern scholar, Anton Wessels, sums up the situation well when he writes:

"In our time there is much talk about...Islamic revival. In part this "revival" has to be interpreted as a largely legitimate form of resistance to foreign - especially Western - economic domination. To many, Islam serves as a symbol of such resistance. But most often the term...is used of an Islamic manifestation of a rightest fundamentaliest phenomenon that is not restricted to Islam... ...examples show, however, that one cannot simply say that the entire Islamic world is fundamentalistic. Fundamentalism and Islam cannot be equated. It is primarily Muslims themselves who are the victims of...fundamentalism."

Muslim have also been oppressed in the Western world because of a history of *"the other"*. Since the Crusades, Islam has been to Christianity a handy symbol for *"the enemy"*. This has its contemporary manifestation in modern Britain. Robbie McVeigh, the Northern Irish activist and student of sectarianism, points to this second excuse for discounting Islam:

"Religious stereotyping is sometimes a function of the decline of unproblematic racialisation. This is certainly true of the rise in anti-Islamic prejudice in Britain. As the obvious otherness of first generation Black immigrants was replaced by a more confusing interface with second generation Black Britishness, the importance of "Islam" as a signifier of difference increased, so that Hindus, Sikhs and Christians of Asian origin all became "Muslim" as a post-Rushdie pejorative shorthand for "British Asian"."

Robbie Mc Veigh, 1995.

A study of Islam, however, uncovers a religion which has profound insights into the importance of social justice, peace, harmony and the re-distribution of wealth: ZAKAT, one of the five "pillars" of Islam - is a tax of wealth. It is based on the notion of radical hospitality, and the requirement that wealth be re-distributed so that social needs are met. Social justice is given priority, through Zakat, even over private property. The requirement on all Muslims to share a portion of their wealth, while often interpreted in charitable terms, is based on the prophet Muhammed's dream of a society of justice for all. It includes an inherent critique of unbridled materialism. Through the ritual associated with Zakat, the sharing of wealth is made sacred. "Zaket" literally means purification: wealth that is not shared defiles humanity before Allah.

Islam is a religion of the Book, the Qu'ran, revealed to the prophet Muhammed. The Qu'ran contains numerous references to the establishment of universal peace, justice and harmony. It refers to God's reasons for giving humanity such revelation *"Indeed, we sent the Book and the Balance, so that humanity may establish justice"*. Qu'ran 57:25.

Women in Islam

"...it is ironic that the most outstanding contradiction regarding the inequities suffered by Muslim women is that Mohammad, the founder of Islam, was among the world's greatest reformers on behalf of women. He abolished such sex-discriminating practices as female infanticide, slavery, and levirate (marriage between a man and his brother's widow), while introducing concepts guaranteeing women the right to inherit and bequeath property, and the right to exercise full possession and control over their own wealth. Islam, in fact, may be the only religion that formally specified women's rights and sought to protect them. Today's Islamic spokesmen frequently extol the Prophet's revolutionary innovations, but usually fail to note that they are rarely honoured in reality...

"Muslims, the First Feminists" Jan Goodwin (1995) **Honour: Muslim Women Lift the Veil of Silence on the Islamic World** London: Warner Books.

An example of crime against women that goes virtually ignored by the country's legal and religious authorities is what is known in Pakistan as dowry burnings. Newlywed young women whose dowries are considered insufficient despite prenuptial agreements are burned to death by their husbands or his relatives when the bride's family is unable to contribute more. In a ten-month period in 1991, two thousand women under twenty-five died in such cases; others may have gone unreported. Explained the relative of one such woman to hospital authorities, *"We didn't report it to the police because we didn't want to create a scandal; and anyway, if she survives, she will have to go back to her husband. It will be bad enough for her as it is."*

Christianity

Christianity is based on the teachings of Jesus of Nazereth, an itinerant preacher who, 2,000 years ago, re-interpreted a contemporary Jewish symbol - "the Kingdom of God". His preaching focuses on this symbol, which represents a belief that a radically transformed political, social and ecological life is in the process of becoming, was present with Jesus himself, and continues to be sacred.

Jesus himself was murdered by the political and religious authorities of his day because his message threatened the political status quo. He articulated the core of his message, when, in the first address of his public ministry, he said:

"The Spirit of the Lord is upon me,
because he has annointed me
to preach good news to the poor.
He has sent me to proclaim release to the captives
and recovery of sight to the blind,
to set at liberty those who are oppressed
to proclaim the acceptable year of the Lord."

Luke 4: 18-19.

Some central tenets of Christian belief which have sustained struggles for justice include: ***Incarnation:*** the belief that in Jesus, the divine became human, so that, in the words of St. John Chrysostom, the human might become divine. This teaching provides the basis for the belief that all human life is sacred and that any systems or structures that impede full human life are evil; ***Eucharist:*** while different Christian Churches give greater or lesser predominence to sacraments - sacred symbols and celebration of the divine in the everyday - the Eucharist, is typically central. Eucharist - based on the Last Supper of Jesus - recognises God's presence in the sharing of bread. It symbolizes the sacredness of community, solidarity and freedom from hunger.

Any study of Catholic Church teaching, however, makes it clear that there is a richness and radicalism in providing alternative analyses to contemporary reality, as well as the call of Paul VI and the US Bishops "...we urge you all to be part of the rebirth of utopias". To ignore Roman Catholic social teaching is a serious omission for anyone interested in justice aand development issues.

Catholics and Social Justice

Roman Catholic social teaching over the past 100 years has provided Catholics with what one edition has named *"our best kept secret"*. Many non-Catholics think that Roman Catholicism places more importance on sexual morality than on social justice. This is simply incorrect, and, as some Latin American theologians point out, serves the ideological function of maintaining the status quo. In Catholic Church teaching the notion of a "hierarchy of truths" suggests, simply, that some things are more important than others. While sexual morality is undoubtedly important in a world of commodification - Catholic church teaching on social teaching is less well advertised.

Donal Dorr, in his monumental work on Catholic social teaching ***Option for the Poor*** (1983) points to some of the strengths and weaknesses of Catholic social teaching.

Some Strengths

- Catholic social teaching is humanistic.
- It focuses on two key values - participation and solidarity.
- It is compatible with pluralism and applicable to different contexts (it doesn't offer readymade solutions).
- It is based on social analysis - working at the level of causes and structures.
- It is biblical, which means that it is open to ecumenical dialogue.
- It is prophetic - radically challenging.

Some Weaknesses

- It is lacking in ecological grounding.
- It does not fully acknowledge the Western bias of the cultural values it proposes as universal.
- It has yet to provide serious alternatives to the present model of development.
- It fails to provide an adequate treatment of the issue of justice for women.
- The question of confrontation and conflict is under-developed.
- The question of justice within the Church itself is not tackled.

Other World Religions

Other World Religions support the establishment of justice, peace and harmony with nature. Buddhism, particularly engaged Buddhism, seeks to bring Buddhist principles to bear on global problems: Ken Jones, a British Buddhist, states:

> *"The task of Buddhists in both East and West in the twenty first century is to demonstrate its acute and urgent relevance for the ills of...society."*

Hinduism, also, has seeds of liberation, as the Thai Hindu author Sulak Sivaraksa, explains:

> *"Hinduism has been often criticised for its overemphasis on the individual's salvation. Under the pressure of casteism and the dualistic doctrine of some of the spiritual leaders of Hinduism, the social dimension of religious experience was, to a great extent, underplayed. But, as the Hindu reformers of the last two centuries have testified through their writings and their radical commitment to social change, there is an undercurrent of social concern in the Hindu scriptures and spiritual traditions."*

As well as majority religions, minority religions provide visions of alternative relationships between humanity and nature which are symbiotic rather than destructive.

Cultural as well as religious commentators increasingly describe 'development' itself as a religion, especially in the West.

Mission Past, Present and Future

Robert Schieter outlines 3 phases in the history of Christian mission and its understanding.

1492 - 1945: Mission as Expansion

In this phase of Christian missionary involvement with non-Christian peoples and indigenous cultures, mission was set in the context of expansion. The promotion of Christianity was also the promotion of European culture as universally normative. Christianity came to indigneous cultures through the cultural trappings of Europe, with elements of European identity attached. True Christians were European - to become Christian, indigenous peoples had also, in the words of Paulo Freire, to internalise the oppressors' culture. The theological hope of missionaries was to create a world mission, where Eurocentric expansion would lead to the salvation of souls. Indigenous cultural practices and rituals were dismissed as anti-Christian; at best, assimilated, at worst, annihilated. Mission was understood as *"plantatio ecclesia"*, the plantation of European models of church onto indigenous populations.

More culturally sensitive dialogue or enculturation of Christianity with indigenous cultures were often attempted during this period. The liberative message contained in Christianity could not be totally stifled by its association with cultural imperialism. Serious attempts at adapting Christianity to conform to and respect existing cultures were undertaken. Those efforts were not limited to the exertions of individual missionaries. The establishment of the Sacred Congregation de Propaganda Fide made efforts which included instructions for the distancing of missionary activity from colonialism, promoted explicit policies to safeguard against Eurocentricity, and promoted respect for indigenous culture.

This heritage is not to be dismissed as past aberration or the understandable barbarity of the "men of their age". It must be faced squarely and recognised for what it is: past atrocity with present fall-out. The U.S. National Conference of Catholic Bishops recognised the present legacy of Christianity's predominant model of mission when, in 1991, its Ad Hoc Committee for the Observance of the Fifth Centenary of the Evangelization of the Americas wrote:

> *"The history of Europe's "discovery" and colonisation of the Americas and of the missionaries who accompanied these forays is full of pride and greed and lust...assumptions of European superiority over native and African*

cultures, contempt for all those who seem different from ourselves; invasion of other people's lands and greed for other people's goods, a barbaric slave trade...the sins may be of the past, but the atmosphere and attitudes they spawned and nourished continue to poison our minds and to maim our common lives."

1945 - 1989 Mission in the Context of Development

A second phase of missionary activity took place from 1945 - 1989. It took place in a very different global context - the context of "development". Gustavo Esteva and Vandana Seva, among others, point out that "development" and "under-development" were invented in the 1940s. Oppression had been around for a long time - what was new was the understanding of progress whereby the "under-developed" or "economically backward regions" would become equal to the developed regions. An essential optimism, coupled with equally ethnocentric notions of neo-colonial superiority, came into play.

In this renewed context, missionary activity, and the understanding of mission, took on a new face. The predominant image of the world and Europe's place in it became one of development. So for missionary activity, the predominant form of universality changed from one of Europeanisation and "civilisation" of native cultures and religions, and was replaced with a hope in progress, an optimism that all nations would follow where Europe had gone.

At the same time, movements from within the missionary societies were radicalising the meaning of mission. Missionary association had been set up since the late nineteenth century with the specific brief of material aid. The theological hope of saving souls was replaced with the more human, immediate and, ultimately, more theological hope of saving lives and ensuring that people's "might have life, and have it to the full". Christian mission became an activity of enculturation - adaptation to and understanding of native cultures - and mission activity became more and more to be understood in terms of solidarity. As Catholic and mainstream Protestant missionaries took up the call to side with the oppressed, the experience of working with the poor radicalised understandings of mission.

While Catholic theology of mission was radically altered by the opening up of the Catholic Church as a result of the Second Vatican Council, it was most altered towards radicality by the advent of liberation theology. The term development has synthesized the aspirations of poor peoples during the last few decades. Recently, however, it has become the object of severe criticism due both to the deficiencies of the development policies proposed to the poor countries to lead them out of their underdevelopment and also to the lack of concrete achievements of the interested governments.

"Development must attack the root causes of the problems and among them the deepest is economic, social, political and cultural dependence of some countries upon others - an expression of the domination of some social classes over others. Attempts to bring about changes within the existing order have proven futile. Only a radical break from the status quo, that is, a profound transformation of the private property system, access to power of the exploited class, and a social revolution that would break this dependence would allow for the change to a new society, a socialist society - or at least allow that such a society might be possible. In this light, to speak about the process of liberation begins to appear more appropraite and richer in human content. Liberation in fact expresses the inescapable moment of radical change which is foreign to the ordinary use of the term development. Only in the context of such a process can a policy of development be effectively implemeted, have any real meaning, and avoid misleading formulations.

Gustavo Gutierrez

This second phase of missionary activity which Schieter outlines is one in which invasion is replaced by mutuality, with Christianity becoming radically re-interpreted in the light of the experiences of the developing world. Whether it is the minjung theology of Asia, Black theology in Africa, or liberation theologies of Latin America, Christianity from 1945 - 1989 began to achieve mission in reverse. As European Christianity diminishes in global terms and Christianity becomes a predominantly Third World religion, new models of mission become possible. Reverse mission in the sense of the radicalisation of European Christianity, becomes a reality.

1989 - Future Mission Post-modern

Schrieter suggests that there is a third era or phase of mission in the making. The context of mission has now changed radically, as the predominant image for our understanding of the world becomes not development, but global capitalism. In this context, cultural issues become more complex. We have ceased living in a world where one culture can invade another. As global hyperculture gives rise to new modes of universality - local expression of diversity and difference become crucial to a new understanding of mission.

Trends in mission theology and practice today suggest that mission for the twenty-first century: - will be necessarily ecumenical as lines are drawn not between churches or religions, but between radical, liberal or conservative relationships between religion and politics; - will be truly local rather than falsely universal; going beyond dialogue with cultures to mutual hospitality and critique; - will be catholic - in the sense of true universality.

C.O.R.I, the Conference of Religious of Ireland has, through its justice commitment, provided the most radical and consistent critique of the values underlying Ireland's social and economic situation. This is informed by a commitment to justice influenced by Roman Catholic social teaching, and also by the experience of missionary orders.

C.O.R.I. asks radical questions of Irish government budget strategies: "How will resources be allocated? Which areas will get priority? Will resources be used to eliminate poverty? tackle unemployment?" etc.

They also adderss the B.I.G. question - the question of a "Basic Income Guarantee for every woman, man and child in Ireland".

And, keeping global, national and local policy on the agenda, they propose that the government put sustainable development at the centre of its socioeconomic framework.

Sources: C.O.R.I. **Tackling Poverty, Unemployment and Exclusion,** 1994

Irish Missions Past, Present and Future.

Irish perceptions of the developing world have, it is often claimed, been formed by the images presented by Irish missionaries, for good or ill. The "box for the black babies" is often cited to exemplify the demeaning imagery of Africans promoted by returned missionaries and their congregations, while on the other hand the incredible per capita generosity of the Irish population to aid agencies can be explained in terms of Ireland's strong missionary roots. These varying interpretations at least evidence the ambiguous nature of missionary involvement.

Here is the testimony of one Irish Missionary in Peru:

"Many missionaries go to Latin America. They are stripped of language, culture and identity itself. The landscape is entirely new. This is the first pain. But later, if we are honest, a far deeper pain is to realise that we carry within us prisons of prejudice, reams of racism, and the most well disguised of all diseases, goodwill - that desire to fix up everything and everyone - recreating all in sight into our own myopic image..."

IRISH CATHOLIC MISSIONARIES OVERSEAS IN 1994 — **Figure 17:1**

Continent	Priests	Sisters	Brothers	Laity	Total
Africa	935	1352	125	61	2,473
Asia-Oceania	465	285	91	51	892
Latin America Caribbean	345	228	41	15	629
Middle East	1	15	-	16	32
Totals	**1746**	**1880**	**257**	**143**	**4026**

IRISH MISSIONARIES FROM OTHER CHRISTIAN CHURCHES AND PERSONNEL FROM DEVELOPMENT AND RELIEF AGENCIES

Continent	Christian Churches			Development/Relief Agencies			Total	
	1992	1994	% Diff.	1992	1994	% Diff.	1992	1994
Africa	74	90	+21.6%	290	287	-1.03%	351	377
Asia/Oceania	67	90	+16.4%	98	130	+32.65%	165	208
Latin America Caribbean	1	25	+2400%	13	3	-23%	27	28
Middle East	5	-	-	-	-	-	5	-
Totals	**147**	**193**	**+31.28%**	**401**	**420**	**+4.7%**	**548**	**613**

Source: Irish Missionary Union

*"December 1991 saw a world premiere, with the potential to rock the Irish missionary in Latin America, or indeed in any part of the globe. On the walls of a clinic in Trojillo, Northern Peru, was written the accusation **Irlandeses Imperialistas**, Irish "imperialists". Laughable, isn't it? Or is it?...*

I have always been proud of my nationality as Irlandesa, while living in Latin America. It allows me to relate to the experience of a colonised people: the planters estate linking with the hacienda, famine and work-houses giving one an inherited familiarity with cholera and typhoid... Sometimes, however, this identification with another oppressed people can blind us to our having learnt best from the oppressor - how to oppress others ourselves.

When caught in a hand-out syndrome, when making decisions "for" rather than "with", when organising what we perceive as chaos into what we consider order,... when rushing in for efficiency's sake rather than waiting for God's sake, the praxis of the missionary in Latin America can still look good to the admiring eye, but be lacking in cultural sensitivity and long-term development plans...

Suzanne Ryder "The Prayer, The Poetry, The Praxis: A Missionary in Latin America" in Enda McDonagh (ed.1994) **A Second Book of Mayo Theology** Dublin: Columba Press. 1994.

Figure 17:2

Totals for all Missionary Societies & Development Agencies:

	1992	1994
Africa	2989	2849
Asia-Oceania	971	1100
Latin America/ Caribbean	644	657
Middle East	31	16
Totals	**4635**	**4622**

Development as Religion

Religious traditions have been at the forefront of the critique of the development paradigm. As far back as 1968, in an address to Latin American priests in Medellin, Gustavo Gutierrez, the father of Latin American Liberation theology, summed up the disillusion that many Third World commentators had with the prevalent model of development. Development was seen to be synonymous with reformism, maintained by hegemonic interests, and maintaining of the status quo. The model of development was under fire.

Since then, there has been a growing radical critique of the power and performance of "development" as a concept, movement and destructive force in our world. This critique comes from many sources, among them, religiously motivated people working for change. An interesting aspect of this growing critique is the analysis of the way in which the idea of development has functioned as a religious creed - some would say the predominant religious creed of the past five decades.

The radical critique is eloquently articulated below by various thinkers such as Vandana Shiva:

"The disappearance of local knowledge through its interaction with the dominant Western knowledge takes place at many levels, through many steps...Western systems of knowledge have generally been viewed as universal. However, the dominant system is also a local system, with its social basis in a particular culture, class and gender. It is not universal in an epistemological sense. It is merely the globalized version of a very local and parochial tradition. Emerging from a dominating and colonising culture, modern knowledge systems are themselves colonising.

"Modern Western knowledge is a particular cultural system with a particular relationship to power. It has, however, been projected as above and beyond culture and politics. Its relationship without the project of economic development has been invisible; and therefore it has become a more effective legitimise for the homogenisation of the world and the erosion of its ecological and cultural richness."

As Shiva suggests "development" has the characteristics formerly projected onto religion - it is universal truth which is beyond question, above culture, and powerful as God. The Irish academic and socialist, Desmond Fennell, also attests to this blind faith in "development", which has functioned like an "imagio Dei", an image of the divine - but an idolatrous one. He suggests that we need to lose faith in this image of development:

"Identifying the real world will start, necessarily, by rejecting - losing faith in - the prevalent image of contemporary reality, and by identifying how things are and came to be that way. The established view of the world, the world image which is presented to us and by which we largely see the world, is, needless to say, the tranquillising propaganda image disseminated by London and New York. Its purpose is to represent the Western World - both as it is and as it impinges on the rest of the world, - as benign, natural, normal and inevitable. Regardless of how you and I personally regard this system of power and control, the fact is that it depends for its existence, not on nuclear bombs or standing armies or accumulated wealth, but on the faith of hundreds of millions - including four million Irish - in that imperial world image and its message"

Reading between the lines it becomes clear that these radical critiques of development suggest that belief in development has functioned as a religion. Like a dys-functional religion, development is..:

Development is unquestionable.

Development is all powerful.

Development operates at the level of imagination.

Development provides a frame of reference above and beyond culture, science, life.

Development promises heaven.

Development has saints and martyrs.

Development has power over life and death.

Development is all pervasive.

Development is invisible.

Development is used to oppress.

Globalisation and Religion

"The study of development, or indeed the study of human life in general, necessitates the study of shared values of all kinds, and the examination of their multifaceted transformations. Religion and kinship are just as significant as economic transactions and the political life of nation states, and in fact these things are not really seperable or comparable. They do not exist in isolation from one another."

Tim Allen and Alan Thomas (1992)
Poverty and Development in the 1990s
Oxford, O.U.P.

The revival of Islam, the rise of fundamentalist Christianity in the Americas, religious Zionism in Israel, liberation theological movements, alternative religious movements: all these phenomena have sociologists of religion thinking: something is up in the world of religions. Many begin to analyse these phenomena in terms of globalisation. It is argued that the process of globalisation - the world becoming one - has effects on religious adherence. How people behave religiously is effected by the world becoming one. We can look to globalisation theory to understand this phenomenon. At the same time, religions have been struggling with the issues of one world: human, ecological, local and global, peace, justice and harmony for thousands of years. Globalisation can give us hints to understand religion in the context of "global village"; religion can point us towards alternatives to predominant, oppressive or dictational views of that one world.

Peter Beyer, in ***Religion and Globalisation*** points out that globalisation theory - theory which *"takes as its primary point of social analysis the entire globe, [and] treats it as a single social system"* - ise very recent. He outlines four schools of globalisation theory:

- Theories of Global Economy, focus on the world system as an economy.
- Theories of Global Polity, add political dimensions to economic models analysing the world in terms of political relationships between nation states, in the context of global norms and pressures.
- Theories of Globalisation from the Perspective of Culture, emphasise the movement towards a global culture, and the effects that such a culture has on other, less globally powerful cultures.
- Theories of Global Society, stress the importance of global communication and modernisation as causes of globalisation. They emphasise the way in which the world functioning as a society may effect the functioning of smaller units.

In attempting to understand religion in the context of

globalisation, it becomes clear that particular identities and religious affiliations are undermined by globalisation, by the process of a world becoming one. This undermining is a mixed blessing from the point of view of justice, harmony and world peace. On the one hand, it leads to the reassertion of particular, usually traditional identities in the face of globalisation.

On the other hand, globalisation can lead to a radically ecumenical involvement in the political arena. As different religions are faced with similar socially oppressive situations, and are similarily excluded from the predominant global discourse, they develop common strategies for social protest. Indeed, religions that provide radical critiques of prevalent social structures tend to engender greater commitment than those who support the status quo. As the limitations of the present model of development are becoming widely recognised, religion, ethics and spirituality are being called upon. There is a dawning realisation that science and development don't provide the answers. In this global context - where can we go?

The answer - to learn from what is liberating in the religion of the world.

"The spiritual/political split is a problem of white people. The dominant culture can afford to cast power purely in terms of power-over, for it has at its disposal the backing of that power...The resistance to questions of the spirit among radicals is itself born of the white culture...But the dispossessed, to survive, to have power at all, must seek another source. They know that power of common bonds of culture, of song, of ritual, of drum and dance, of healing to sustain hope and strength to resist oppression...Spirituality was a powerful force in the black civil rights movement...In the movement for justice for native Americans and indigenous peoples, religion plays a central role...In Nicaragua what the people read in the Gospels becomes the concrete practice of revolution: to serve the poor, to work for justice, to share what people have".

Starhawk. **Truth or Dare.**

▼ References

K.C.Abrahams (1990) **Third World Theologies: Commonalities and Differences,** Ney York, Maryknoll.

Peter Beyer (1994) **Religion and Globalisation,** London, Sage.

Mary Condren (1989) **The Serpent and the Goddesss: Women, Religion and Power in Celtic Ireland,** San Francisco, Harper and Row.

Donal Dorr (1992 revised ed.) **Option for the Poor,** Dublin, Gill and Macmillan.

Lester Kurtz (1995) **Gods in the Global Village: The World's Religions in Sociological Perspective,** California, Pine Forge Press.

Sean McDonagh (1994) **Passion for the Earth,** London, Chapman.

Allen Moore (1989) **Religious Education as Social Transformation,** Birmingham, Alabama, Religious Education Press.

Wolfgang Sachs (1992) **The Development Dictionary,** London, Zed Books.

Starhawk (1987) **Truth or Dare: Encounters with Power, Authority and Mystery,** San Francisco, Harper.

F.J.Verstraelen (1995) **Missiolgy, An Ecumenical Introduction: Texts and Contexts of Global Christianity,** Michigan, Eerdmans.

Michael Walsh and Brian Davies (eds.), (1984) **Proclaiming Justice and Peace,** London, CAFOD and Collins.

EXODUS: Migrants, Refugees and Development

Roland Tormey

"... the upheavals in the former Soviet Bloc; the Gulf War; the Infada in occupied Palestine; the crumbling of Apartheid in South Africa; wars, famines and crises throughout Africa; rapid growth and development in Asia; a shift from dictatorships to unstable and debt-plagued democracies in Latin America; and growing economic and political integration in Western Europe. All these developments have one thing in common: they have been linked in various ways with mass population movements. It therefore seems fitting to predict that the last decade of the twentieth century and the first of the twenty first will be the age of migration."

Castles, S & Miller, M. **The Age of Migration** Macmillan, 1993.

Why Worry?

Why should the world be worried about refugees and migrants? There are a number of reasons:

RESPECT FOR HUMAN RIGHTS: Providing asylum for refugees has nothing to do with charity, it is simply about respect for human rights. Refugees are fleeing from persecution and everyone has a right not to be persecuted. If we turn away refugees we are saying that life and liberty are privileges, not rights. In saying that, we say that we have no right to these things.

INTERNATIONAL SECURITY: Refugee crises and mass movements are often caused by conflict, but they can also cause or perpetuate conflict. The civil war in Rwanda started when the RPF, mostly refugees from conflict in the 1950s, re-entered the country in 1990. The UN intervened after the Gulf War to protect Kurdish refugees which were fleeing northern Iraq into Turkey, as they posed a risk to the stability of the area. Throughout the 1980s the United States armed the Contras (made up of Nicaraguan refugees) in Honduras and Costa Rica, in the hope they would return to Nicaragua and fight the socialist government there.

ENVIRONMENTAL REASONS: In July 1994 10,000 people per day crossed the Rwandan border into the Goma area of Zaire. There were few resources in place to deal with the influx. An area which had supported a small population was now swamped with hundreds of thousands of people requiring water, food, fuel and shelter. When this happens, it takes only a short period for the ecosystem of the area to be devastated.

DEVELOPMENTAL REASONS: The great majority of the world's refugees seek asylum in the world's poorer countries. Among the 20 African countries listed by the UN in 1988 as critically affected by famine, 13 were hosting a substantial number of refugees. Zaire and Tanzania received the bulk of refugees from Rwanda. The 1995 Human Development Index gives Zaire a score of 0.384. Tanzania has an even lower score, at 0.364. Both are listed as 'poorly developed'. This compares to an Irish score of 0.915 and a UK score of 0.916. In other words, those least able to afford refugee crises end up paying.

Introduction

It is common to think about societies as naturally settled. We think of each country being made up of people who are born, live and die there. In other words, we think of people as sedentary. The importance of movements of people in the past, the present and the future is something of a blind spot. It is something we only notice when it is labelled a crisis, either because it is felt that too many people are leaving (the Irish experience) or because some feel that too many people are arriving (the British experience).

Despite our general reluctance to recognise the importance of migration the facts are staggering.

- There are an estimated 100 million people living outside the country of their birth today.
- Of these an estimated 20 million are refugees. There are a further 26 million people living in 'refugee-like-situations' inside their own countries.
- In Ireland during the 1980s between 6% and 8% of the Irish population emigrated.

- It is estimated that $67 billion was sent from migrants to their country of origin in each year of the early 1990s. This makes the movement of people one of the biggest trades in the world. For many countries it provides their only means of balancing their national accounts. It is more than the total of all aid given by the First World to the Third each year.

It is hardly surprising then that Castles and Miller have dubbed the 1990s the beginning of the Age of Migration.

The Irish Experience

Large scale movements of population are nothing new to Ireland or Britain. In this section we will look at the movements of people in these countries and the links to the rest of the world.

"Emigration is at the centre of the Irish experience of being modern. It has been the safety valve that has enabled Ireland to cope successfully with the problems of transition from a traditional rural society to a modern industrial one. The transition has been made possible by the simple expedient of Ireland offering a modern way of life to 75% of its population. The remaining 25% have had, for a long time past, a choice of unemployment at home or migration abroad; they have always generously chosen to promote the welfare of the 75% at home by opting for the latter alternative. Consequently, to discuss Irish emigration in the twentieth century is virtually the same as to discuss Ireland . . ."

Liam Ryan, **Migrations**, R.Kearney, (ed.1990).

The famine which hit Ireland between 1845 and 1850 did not start emigration. In fact, between 1815 and 1844 an estimated 800,000 to 1,000,000 people left Ireland to settle in North America. What the famine did was turn emigration from an infection into an epidemic.

Had there been no famine it is estimated that by 1851 the population of Ireland would have stood at 9 million people. It actually stood at 6.5 million, some two million less than the population in 1845. About half of the missing two million people had died. The rest had left. Between 1845 and 1855 a total of about two million people left Ireland. The vast bulk of this depopulation happened in rural areas.

The movement was not simply away from the island. Within the island there was considerable movement, particularly towards Dublin, Belfast and Derry. The urban population, which had accounted for about one-eighth of the population in 1841, accounted for one third by 1911.

By the 1930s people in the Southern State found themselves in a familiar position. The post-independence economy had failed to take off and was rapidly going nowhere. In 1931 the average income per head in Ireland was only 61% of that in Britain. By 1939 it was down to 49%. Emigration once more picked up. The Second World War and the prospect of work in Britain, made the exodus even quicker. This time the exodus was from the towns as well as the countryside.

Figure 18:1

NET EMIGRATION FROM IRELAND, 1926 TO 1986

Period	Net Emigration
1926-36	166,751
1936-46	187,111
1946-56	316,304
1956-66	292,608
1966-71	53,906
1971-81	-103,889
1981-86	75,300

Notes: Minus Figure indicates immigration
Source: Breen et al, **Understanding Contemporary Ireland** (1990)

Figure 18:2

ASYLUM APPLICATIONS TO IRELAND, 1987 - '94

Year	Number of Asylum Applications
1987	50
1988	49
1989	36
1990	62
1991	31
1992	39
1993	91
1994	355

Source: **Irish Refugee Council**, (1995)

While there was a period of net immigration during the 1970s, the trend reasserted itself in the 1980s. In the 1980s alone between 6% and 8% of the population of Ireland (the official figure was 216,000 people) left.

If Ireland was busily exporting those who may have prompted a radical rethink of her policies, her relative isolation from the non-Western world meant that refugees and those seeking political asylum rarely landed on Ireland's shores. On occasion, during a specific refugee crisis, the Irish government offered asylum to a number of invited refugees. Apart from those who were specifically invited the numbers of those arriving at Irish ports seeking asylum were limited. The fact that there was little access to Ireland except through Europe or the US was undoubtedly a factor in this.

The Effects on Ireland

- According to the historian F.S.L. Lyons, the famine established a *"practical, if unpalatable alternative to dumb acquiescence in extreme poverty and insecurity at home"*. The fact that emigration was seen as practical is important in explaining why it happened.
- *Remittances,* money sent home from those who had left, became an important part of how people survived. In 1848 remittances accounted for £460,000. By 1852 they accounted for £1.4 million.
- F.S.L. Lyons also notes, *"The political consequences of this unending exodus of a permanently antagonised population were literally incalculable, but the most fundamental effect is plain to be seen. With the establishment of strong Irish settlements in the United States, Canada, Australia and New Zealand, as well as in Britain herself, the Irish question became and remained an international question".*
- However, at a later date emigration served to prevent a radical political alternative. When opinion makers claimed there was nothing to be done to save the ailing economy, those who could have forced a radical rethink were catching the boat to Holyhead. As one commentator said in outlining his reservations to the ***Reports of the Commission on Emigration,*** *"High emigration, granted a population excess, releases social tensions which would otherwise explode and makes possible a stability of manners and customs which would otherwise be the subject of radical change".* In short, many opinion makers had come to think that emigration was not a problem as it helped maintain the status quo. In fact, it could be said to be an outright benefit to those who benefited from the status quo. The Tanaiste (Deputy Prime Minister) and Minister for Foreign Affairs Brian Lenihan was, therefore, able to say in October 1987 that emigration was not a defeat for the Government. *"After all"*, he said, *"we can't all live on a small island".*

The British Experience

The British experience of migration is quite different. Historically, most of the migration involving Britain has been internal.

This migration had a number of notable effects. Huge, crowded, working class slums were created. These became associated with high mortality rates. In 1842 in Manchester, the average age of death was eighteen. By comparison in Bath, a town without slums, the average age of death was thirty one. This migration was strongly influenced by a number of factors. Knowledge of the intended destination through already existing social links (such as family or friends) was important. Increased job opportunities because of industrialisation, and better wages were also a factor.

These same reasons influenced the growth of emigration after 1850. Up to the 1890s the most attractive destination was the USA. Between 1905 and 1914, the countries of the Empire, Australia, Canada and New Zealand were the most attractive. In the peak period of the 1880s and 1890s, gross emigration accounted for 4 million people. Throughout this period more migrants left Britain than arrived.

At the same time, Britain had a proud record of providing asylum for refugees. In 1853 **The Times of London** wrote: *"Every civilised person on the face of the earth must be fully aware that this country is the asylum of nations, and that it will defend the asylum to the last ounce of its treasure, and the last drop of its blood. There is no point whatever on which we are prouder and more resolute".*

The most notable groups of refugees during this period were Irish fleeing the Great Famine and Jews fleeing persecution in Eastern Europe. Between 1880 and 1914 about 120,000 Eastern European Jews settled in Britain. Despite the fact that Britain was busily shipping its sons and daughters to other countries, the years 1900 to 1915 saw an anti-immigration campaign develop in England, led by a Major General Evans Gordon. As a result of this campaign an Aliens Act was enacted in 1905 which regulated entrance to Britain. Among other things, it excluded the immigrant who was sick and those who might not be able to support themselves.

Net emigration continued at quite high levels until the 1920s, but was replaced by a net inflow in the following decade, mostly people returning from Britain's colonies. Despite common assumptions, most of the period since the Second World War has seen net emigration. While the late 1950s saw a net inflow, immigration restrictions sharply reduced this inflow after 1961.

The huge growth in world refugee numbers in the 1980s saw a growth in asylum applications to Britain reaching a peak in 1991. This figure started to fall again in 1992 *(see Table below).*

Despite this growth in application numbers Britain still received less applications per head of population than most of her European neighbours. The Applicant: Population ratio for Britain in 1991 stood at 1: 1,277, in Sweden it was 1:314, in Germany it was 1: 303 and in Switzerland it was 1:158.

A number of different factors have since come into play. The first is the 1993 Asylum and Immigration (Appeals) Act. The refusal rate has risen since the Act came into effect. For example, before the Act, 98% of Sri Lankan applicants were granted Asylum or Leave to Remain. Since the Act, this figure has fallen to 16%. Other factors operate to stop people reaching a place of safety. These include fines on airlines who carry people that have forged documents, (this is called Carrier Sanctions). Since many refugees are forced to flee without the luxury of proper documentation, carrier sanctions mean that asylum seekers may be prevented reaching a place of refuge by untrained airline officials and returned to danger or death. The British Government is currently working on new asylum legislation which many feel will make it even more difficult for those fleeing persecution to find sanctuary.

The British Experience of Migration

- Movement of populations can have a huge political importance for the sending and the receiving country. Britain has seen racist anti-immigration movements, and fears of an influx of migrants have brought about legislation to make it increasingly difficult for immigrants and asylum seekers. There have been some allegations that political parties play 'the race card' as a means of seeking political power.
- Urbanisation played a part in the industrialisation of Britain, providing labour for the industrial revolution. International labour migration also provided labour in times of shortage, such as the Second world War.
- In social terms, urbanisation caused the growth of slums which had poor health services and high mortality rates. British emigration overseas created social links with other countries which facilitated further emigration.

The failure of modernisation theory (see chapter 1) has shown us that trying to explain what is happening in other countries based on what happened in the West is often a dangerous and unprofitable exercise. However, there are some lessons we can learn from the British and Irish experiences.

Figure 18:3

SIZE OF BRITISH URBAN POPULATION 1750 - 1901
(000's).

Town	1750	1801	1851	1901
Birmingham	24	71	265	760
Glasgow	—	77	375	762
Greater London	—	1,117	2,685	6,586
Manchester	43*	75	338	645
% Population urban in England and Wales	—	30%	50%	77%

Notes: '*' indicates data from 1788
Source: Moore, C. **The Industrial Age** (1989)

Figure 18:4

ASYLUM APPLICATIONS TO BRITAIN, 1984 - '91

Year	Number of Asylum Applications
1984	2,905
1985	4,389
1986	4,266
1987	4,256
1988	3,998
1989	11,635
1990	22,005
1991	44,845

Source: **Refugee Council**, (1992)

Understanding Population Movements

In this section we will look at the theories of population movement, and see what they can tell us about the good and the bad of population movements.

Population Movement Models

As with all other theories in the field of development, theories of population movement have changed across the years. The early theories of development, modernisation theories, were based largely on the west's experience. They sought to be scientific, building mathematical models of an economy's 'take-off'. The early theories of migration were similar. They sought only to explain the reasons why people move from one area to another. An example of this kind of model is Samuel Stouffer's *'Intervening Opportunities'* model. In a very good example of the mathematical style language adopted by such theorists, he claimed that, *"the number of persons going a given distance is directly proportional to the number of opportunities at that distance and inversely proportional to the number of intervening opportunities"*.

Following on from this kind of theory was the *push/pull* model of migration. This looks at the economic and political factors which 'cause' people to move from one place to another. According to this theory, Irish people going to work in Britain during the Second World War were going to a place where there was high wages and a labour shortage. These two factors were 'pull' factors. Irish people going to Britain in the 1840s went because landlords, unable or unwilling to pay rates on land they got no money from during the famine, evicted them. Evictions and famine were 'push' factors.

Some theorists suggested that these movements were in some ways a natural, if unpleasant, thing a society had to go through as it developed, something like growing pains. The clearing of people off the land was, according to this model, an important part of modernising Irish agriculture, and emigration to industrial cities provided a labour supply which allowed economic growth.
There were clear problems with this model however.

Difficulties with Models

- ▼ It cannot explain why urbanisation happens in the Third World at a time when urban unemployment continues to rise. Surely high unemployment should be a 'push' factor, not a 'pull' factor?
- ▼ It cannot properly explain why people choose one destination over another.
- ▼ It leaves out any mention of the *dynamic aspects* of migration. In other words it does not try to say anything about the effects of migration on the society which sends people, or on the society which receives them.

... putting the pieces together ...

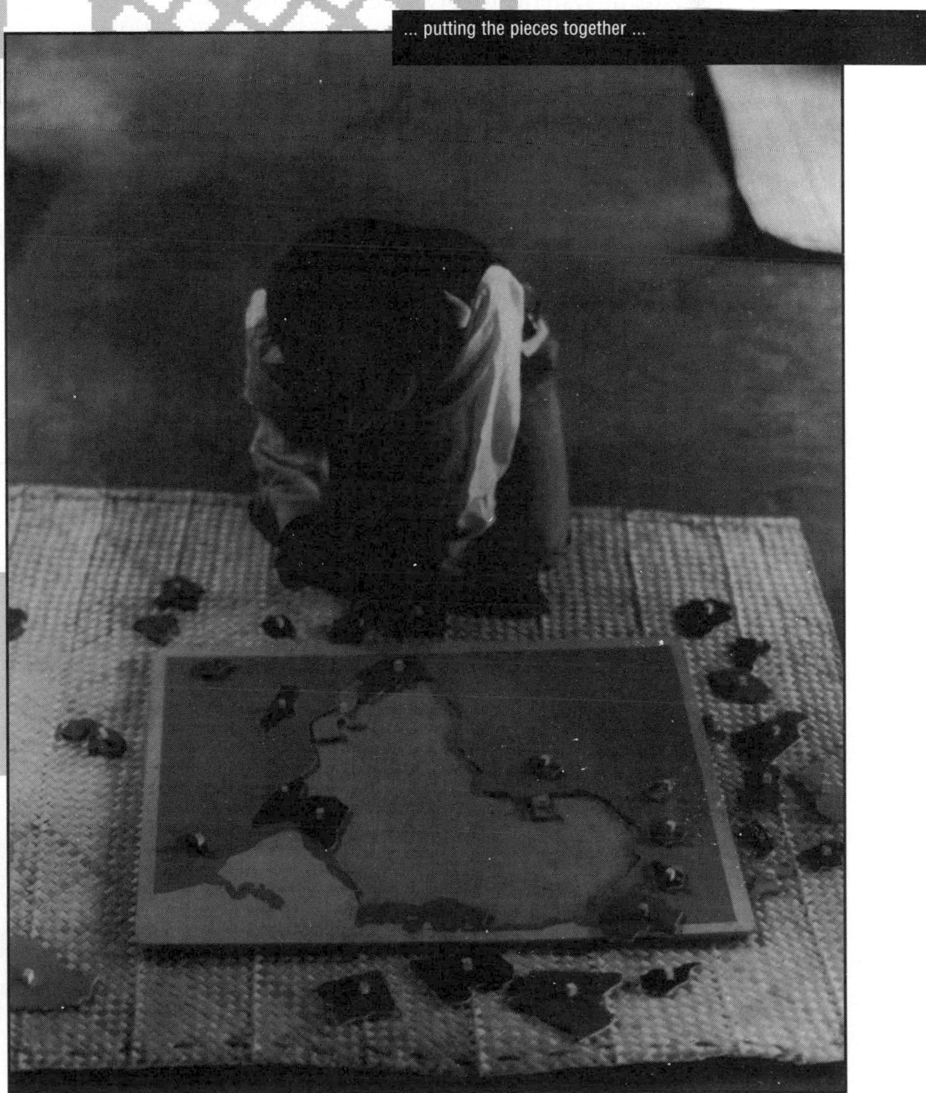

Some people, like the economist Michael Todaro, still try to use more complex forms of this sort of model to understand migration. However, at about the same time as dependency theory was becoming more important in development studies as a whole, a related set of theories, which I will call *systems theory,* was becoming more popular in understanding migration. In the same way that dependency theory looked at the historical links which existed between countries, systems theory saw migration as happening within systems which had been set up in history and which changed across time and with the process of migration. For example, Algerian migrants went to France because France was the coloniser of Algeria. This meant that there were special legal arrangements (before 1962 people from Algeria were French citizens), it meant they shared a language and that the migrants knew something about the people who lived in France.

In this example, a network had been established linking the two countries: politically; economically; and socially. Some proponents of systems theory focused on the economic links of the international capitalist economy. People in peripheral countries were seen as an extra labour supply to be used as necessary by the core (colonising) countries and sent back when no longer needed. In turn, the exploitation of the peripheral country by the core country meant that people were forced to move. In this sense, the international capitalist economy both encouraged and facilitated migration. For example, the *guestworker* scheme in Germany was based on inviting 'guests' from peripheral countries to come and work as long as they were needed. The plan was to send them back when they were no longer needed. This is not what happened.

Social and Economic Factors

In fact, there were social as well as economic factors which came into effect. Workers were invited for economic reasons, but stayed because they had made a home, or because this was the place their children had grown up in. As a whole the economistic theories tend to underestimate the role of social and political factors.

While the systems approach provides a better framework for understanding population movements than the modernisation approach, it is only fully satisfactory when it incorporates economic, political and social aspects. In this form, it can provide an explanation for the movement of people, internally as well as internationally.

Rural - Urban Migration in the Third World

The process of Urbanisation in the Third World is creating enormous cities which have, as a consequence, enormous problems. In 1950 there were under 1 billion people living in urban areas. Almost two thirds were in the First World. By 1990 there were nearly 2.5 billion people living in urban areas, with only two fifths living in the First World. By the year 2000 there will be an estimated 3.2 billion urban dwellers, with over two thirds living in the Third World. The table. on the opposite page illustrates the growth of the world's major urban areas.

During the nineteenth century in the West, urbanisation was an integral part of the industrialisation process. Modernisation theorists argued that the same would have to happen in the Third World. As was noted above, their arguments no longer stand up.

▼ The fastest rate of urbanisation achieved by any European city in the nineteenth century was 2.1% per year. Rates of urbanisation in the Third World have been significantly higher. Between 1957 and 1967 the population of Dar-Es-Salam in Tanzania increased by 8% per year. Between 1950 and 1963 the population of Lagos in Nigeria grew by over 9% per year.

▼ In the West, urbanisation contributed to economic growth. This has not been the case in the Third World where there is already high urban unemployment. In Latin America during the decade 1950-'60 factory employment absorbed only about 9% of the growth in urban population.

Figure 18:5
GROWTH OF WORLD'S TEN LARGEST CITIES

City	1990 Population (millions)	Projected Population Year 2000 (millions)
Mexico City, Mexico	19.4	24.4
Sao Paulo, Brazil	18.4	23.6
Tokyo, Japan	20.5	21.3
New York City, USA	15.7	16.1
Calcutta, India	11.8	15.9
Bombay, India	11.1	15.4
Shanghai, China	12.6	14.7
Tehran, India	9.2	13.7
Jakarta, Indonesia	9.4	13.2
Buenos Aires, Argentina	11.6	13.1

Source: Todaro, Michael P. **Economic Development** (1994)

Today, urbanisation is recognised as bringing with it a number of problems. Not only will it often cause hardship and suffering to individuals, it will actually impede economic growth. As the economist Michael Todaro notes, *"migration in excess of job opportunities is both a symptom of and a contributor to Third World underdevelopment"*.

Among the problems of urbanisation are:

Employment and Unemployment Problems: Across the world, urban unemployment rates compare badly with rural unemployment rates.

Housing problems: Along with the spread of urbanisation has come the problem of slums.

- Today, slums represent one third of the urban population in the Third World. In Africa in the late 1980s, 92 out of every 100 new households established in urban areas were in shanty towns or slums.

- Many cities are unable to provide services for the numbers of people they now have living in them. Cairo caters for 9.1 million people, using a water and sanitation system built for 2 million.

Rural depopulation: Rural areas loose their most able, literate and innovative individuals to urban centres. Migrants to urban areas tend to be men and women aged between 15 and 24. It is generally the most educated that go. While in the past most migrants were the poorest of the rural poor, the growth of a modern industrial sector in most cities means that migrants come from all socio-economic strata.

This 'brain-drain' has a number of consequences:

- Agriculture gets left to the oldest and the weakest sections of the population. This can lead to conservatism in agricultural methods and an increase in subsistence farming.

- The loss of the younger (more fertile) population means a decline in birth rates and the preponderance of older people means an increase in the death rates, thereby increasing depopulation.

Dealing with the problems of urbanisation is not easy. Focusing on improving the conditions of squatters and people in slums can lead to real or perceived bias towards urban areas and can help cause internal migration. This in turn can have a detrimental effect on a country's chances of industrial development. Yet a rural bias may mean not dealing with huge urban poverty, slums and squatter camps. Simply trying to deal with migration as a problem of a country's economic policy ignores the dynamic aspects such as family links and perceived cultural superiority of cities.

Figure 18:6
SLUMS AND SQUATTER SETTLEMENTS AS A PERCENTAGE OF URBAN POPULATION, (1983)

City	Slums as % of City Population
Latin America	
Bogota, Columbia	60%
Mexico City, Mexico	46%
Caracas, Venezuela	42%
Middle East and Africa	
Addis Ababa, Ethiopia	79%
Casablanca, Morocco	70%
Kinshasa, Zaire	60%
Cairo, Egypt	60%
Ankara, Turkey	60%
Asia	
Calcutta, India	67%
Manila, Philippines	35%
Seoul, South Korea	29%
Jakarta, Indonesia	26%

Source: Michael Todaro, **Economic Development**, (1994)

Internal Migration in Ghana

In 1988 a study was published about the nature, causes and effects of internal migration in Ghana, by the geographers, Kasanga and Avis. They looked at migration from the Wa area of the Northern District of Ghana to two prosperous towns in the South: Techiman in the Brong Ahafo region; and Obuasi in the Ashanti region.

Most migrants first left their home area quite young. 97% of all the migrants they spoke to in Techiman, and 100% in Obuasi first left home between the age of 15 and 30.

When asked why they left home, most responded that they were searching for wealth. Almost all of the best off people were in the two towns. 60% of those questioned in the two towns had 4 or less dependants to feed. In the Wa area, 60% of those interviewed had 5 or more dependants, with almost 10% having 17 or more.

The second most important reason for moving was the presence of relatives. People were either travelling to join their husbands or immediate family, or were going to an area where there was some link, an area they had heard stories about, where there was someone to stay with and someone to help organise a job. Another major reason for migration was the search for independence and to see new places. Part of this was the prestige of living in an urban area.

It is clear from this that simple economic explanations involving 'push' and 'pull' factors cannot account for the links which enable migration and for cultural factors (such as the search for independence and the prestige of town life) which encourage it.

At least some of the factors involved in this system date to the colonial era. The prestige of the town is dated from this era, as is the bias towards developing the South of the country to the neglect of the North. The people of the Northern region were regarded by the colonial government as *"an amiable but backward people, useful as soldiers, policemen and labourers in the mines and cocoa farms; in short fit only to be heavers of wood and drawers of water for their brothers in the colony and Ashanti"*. The result of this was forced movement of people from the North to work in the South (setting up cultural links), a lack of any meaningful development of the north and a lack of investment in education in the North. Post-colonial development has been based on urban industrialisation, restricting wage earning capabilities to cities and urban areas.

Kasanga, R.K., & Avis M. R. ***Internal Migration and Urbanisation in Developing Countries***; Findings from a Study in Ghana (1988)

"Refugees are Inconvenient"

Refugees and internally displaced persons flee because they have no choice. In recent years, the numbers of refugees in the world has risen dramatically. It is hard to gauge the extent of the growth of the refugee crisis in the world. This is because some estimates are used by governments who wish to down play the problem, while others include all sorts of migrants under the heading of refugee. In 1951, when the UNHCR was founded, there were an estimated 1.5 million refugees in the world (the real figure was probably higher). By 1980 this figure had risen to 8.2 million. The current estimates range from 14.5 million to 22 million. To that we must add the figures for internally displaced people, estimated at about 26 million. This gives a total of something like 50 million people forced to flee their homes and their lives.

Table 18: 7

ESTIMATED NUMBER OF PERSONS OF CONCERN WHO FALL UNDER THE MANDATE OF UNHCR, 1994, BY REGION

Region	Total of Concern
Africa	11,816,000
Asia	7,921,500
Europe	6,520,100
Latin America	184,600
North America	925,500
Oceania	51,200
Total	27,418,900

Source: **UNHCR by Numbers,** UNHCR January 1995

Figure 18:8

ORIGIN OF MAJOR REFUGEE POPULATIONS AND PEOPLE IN REFUGEE LIKE SITUATIONS (TWENTY LARGEST GROUPS)[1]

Origin[2]	Main Countries of Asylum	Total
Afghanistan	Iran, Pakistan	2,745,200
Rwanda	Zaire, Tanzania, Burundi	2,257,000
Former Yugoslavia[3]	Croatia, Germany	843,900
Liberia	Cote d'Ivoire. Guinea	794,200
Iraq	Iran	702,100
Somalia	Ethiopia, Kenya	546,000
Eritrea	Sudan	422,400
Sudan	Uganda, Zaire	398,600
Burundi	Tanzania, Zaire	389,200
Viet Nam	China, Hong Kong	341,600
Azerbaijan	Armenia	299,000
Angola	Zaire, Zambia	283,900
Sierra Leone	Guinea, Liberia	275,100
Mozambique	South Africa	234,500
Chad	Sudan	211,900
Myanmar	Thailand, Bangladesh	203,900
Armenia	Azerbaijan	201,500
Ethiopia	Sudan	188,100
Mali	Mauritania, Algeria, Burkina Faso	72,700

Notes:

1. Does not include 2.9 million Palestinian refugees who are not under UNHCR mandate.
2. Many refugees are in countries which do not supply a breakdown by country of origin.
3. This figure does not represent all the refugees from former Yugoslavia, as many are in countries which do not provide data to the UNHCR and many more are Internally Displaced People.

Source: **UNHCR by Numbers,** UNHCR January 1995

While some refugees make it to countries where they can apply for asylum and may, in time, be allowed to live a normal life (albeit in an unfamiliar country, with an unfamiliar language and unfamiliar ways), many refugees end up living in camps. In the short term these camps may be set up in a matter of days (as happened in Goma during the Rwandan refugee crisis). Without proper facilities they may be breeding grounds for disease and despair. In the early days of the crisis in Goma, thousands of people were dying every day from Cholera and other diseases.

In the medium term refugee camps become settled. They become slum cities of dependent people. Rudimentary facilities are provided and people settle into a routine. Basic food and some other necessities are provided. What health services and education are provided are usually quite rudimentary and so the children grow up without the benefit of proper education and proper health care. Some camps are closed camps where people are not allowed to leave. These are basically prison camps.

Sometimes people are left outside their country of origin for long periods. Refugees from the Afghan war are still one of the largest groups of refugees in the world. About 5.6 million people fled Afghanistan after the Soviet Union invaded in 1979. In 1995, years after the Soviet Union ceases to exist, there are still 2.7 million Afghans in Iran and Pakistan. Some of the 5 million Palestinians without a country have been stateless for 40 years.

The Western world is fond of saying that the best solution for the refugee crisis is for refugees to be settled as near to their home as is possible. There are many reasons for believing that this is true. It is also possible that this belief is used by Western governments to ensure that they do not have to be affected by the refugee crisis. Hence Africa, which has 10% of the world's population, has 43% of those people the UNHCR is concerned with. The world's poorest countries, which are often unable to provide for their own populations, are required to provide what minimal support they can to foreign nationals while the Western world puts up barriers to make it more difficult for asylum seekers to reach their shores.

Some definitions . . .

▼▼ REFUGEE:

A Refugee is *"any person who, owing to a well founded fear of being persecuted for reasons of race, religion, nationality, membership of a particular social group or political opinion, is outside the country of his [or her] nationality and is unable or owing to such fear is unwilling to avail himself [or herself] of the protection of that country"*. This (rather narrow) definition is the one found in the **United Nations Convention Relating to the Status of Refugees,** 1951.

The word 'refugee' is normally used in a much wider sense to mean those who have had to flee their country of origin through fear. Other organisations have wider definitions than the UN one. The Organisation of African Unity includes people *"fleeing external aggression, internal civil strife, or events seriously disturbing to the public order"*. A definition used by Central American nations includes *"persons who have fled their country because their lives, safety or freedom have been threatened by generalised violence, foreign aggression, internal conflicts, massive violations of human rights or other circumstances which have seriously disturbed public order"*.

While Ireland has signed the UN convention, until recently she has had no Refugee legislation. A Bill introduced in 1995 gives a slightly broader definition of 'refugee' than the UN definition. The Bill also ensures that someone whose life may be in danger in a particular country (irrespective of their status as a refugee) will not be returned to that country. There is also a category of 'programme refugee'. These are people in refugee-like-situations who are invited to Ireland even if, individually, they would not fit into the UN definition. This is the category that the Bosnian community in Ireland fall into. The Irish Refugee Bill is regarded by many as being among the best in Europe.

In Britain the Asylum and Immigration (Appeals) Act 1993 is the law covering asylum applications. It relies on the UN Convention definition of a refugee, stating: *"no removal or application of the Immigration Rules may be contrary to the UK's obligations under the Convention"*.

▼▼ MANIFESTLY UNFOUNDED APPLICATIONS:

Some countries have experienced difficulties in processing the number of applications for asylum that they receive. This gave rise to demands for a category of applications called Manifestly Unfounded Applications. Originally this was defined by the UNHCR as applications which are *"clearly fraudulent or not related to the criteria for the granting of refugee status"*. The EU Council of Ministers re-defined this in 1992 to include, among other things, those who lie during their application. This provision does not reflect the realities of the decisions made by refugees who arrive in a country tired, terrified and desperate not to be returned home. Despite this, the European Union countries agreed in December 1992 to provide for Manifestly Unfounded Applications. This may result in people who have valid claims being returned to danger on a procedural technicality.

▼▼ INTERNALLY DISPLACED PERSONS (IDPs):

Some people are forced to flee their homes for the same reasons refugees flee but never cross the borders of their country. According to the UN definition these people are not officially refugees. Instead they are referred to as 'Internally Displaced Persons' (or IDPs for short). They are refugees in all but name.

▼▼ UNHCR:

In 1951 the United Nations set up a High Commissioner to deal with the refugee crisis in the world at that time. The post was a temporary one lasting for three years. Today the Office of the High Commissioner for Refugees (or UNHCR) still exists.

Europe and Refugees

As refugees are fleeing from persecution, it is vital that they be afforded an opportunity to apply for asylum in a safe country. In the last few years movement towards a European Political Union has focused attention on 'harmonising' asylum policies across Europe. Unfortunately, in the search for a common immigration and asylum policy, European governments have exhibited a tendency to move towards a 'lowest common denominator', i.e., they choose the worst policies, because they are the only ones everyone will agree on.

In 1985 the Schengen Agreement was drafted. This was an agreement on a common border policy for a number of European countries. In March 1995 the Agreement came into effect for France, Germany, Benelux, Portugal and Spain. Italy, Greece and Austria are hoping to adopt the agreement. This allows for increased policing of borders and for Carrier Sanctions. Some non-Schengen countries, including Britain, already have carrier sanctions (see above).

In 1990 the Dublin Convention produced a list of criteria by which member states would decide which country was responsible for processing an asylum application. This means that if someone comes to Ireland via England they will be returned to England to have their application assessed there. There is no basis in international refugee law for this provision. The UNHCR has emphasised *"none of [the internationally accepted principles relating to asylum] suggest - much less prescribe - that the right to seek asylum has to be exercised in a particular country, or that a person escaping persecution would forfeit his right to seek asylum if he does not exercise it in the first country whose territory he has entered"*. This practice may result in someone who would receive asylum in one country being sent to a 'safe third country' which does not recognise human rights abuses in their country of origin and subsequently returns them to danger.

A set of resolutions (usually called the London Resolutions) were adopted by the Council of Ministers in December 1992. Resolutions are not legally binding on EU countries, but countries do feel obliged to work in accordance with them. Among the London Resolutions was one on 'Manifestly Unfounded Applications' which re-defined this category (see definitions above). Although Ireland had no legal obligation to adopt this new definition, it was written into her Refugee Bill against the advice of agencies who work with refugees. This could lead to refugees being returned to danger without their case being properly investigated.

Individual countries have also taken steps on their own accord. The Irish government, upon discovering that a large number of Cubans were applying for asylum in Ireland, imposed a transit visa obligation on Cubans thereby preventing people getting to Ireland to apply for asylum. The number of Cuban asylum seekers fell from 240 for the year 1994 to 5 in the first six months of 1995.

Further movements towards 'harmonising' European asylum policies are expected in the near future. If the past efforts are anything to go by, each step towards harmony will be a further brick in the walls of 'Fortress Europe'.

What's it got to do with me?

It is common for people in the West to look at the refugee crises in the Third World and ask, "If these people want to kill each other, what's it got to do with me?". These feelings are re-enforced by the media who talk of 'ethnic conflicts' using 'traditional weapons'. This makes it appear that these conflicts are purely internal matters. Very often this is not the case.

The genocide in Rwanda left between half a million and one million people dead. In its aftermath millions of people fled into Zaire, Tanzania and Burundi fearing reprisals. In January 1995 there were still 2.3 million refugees from Rwanda, making it the third biggest refugee population in the world. This conflict was presented as a conflict between ethnic groups, the Hutus and the Tutsis. The genocide was perpetrated, we were told, using a traditional weapon: the machete. Most of this is far from the truth.

The genocide in Rwanda was not isolated from the rest of the world. The weapons in Rwanda came from the outside: from France; Belgium; China and others. The machetes, which the media portrayed as a traditional weapon, were bought from China specifically for the genocide. France continued to supply weapons to the Rwandan government while they were massacring people. For example, the massacres began on April 6th 1994. On 25th of May a shipment of arms, arranged by the French government, arrived in Goma (Zaire) en route to Rwanda. Dr. Jean Herve Bradol an aid worker from a French agency in Rwanda said, *"France's role in this country and France's responsibility are overwhelming. The people carrying out the massacres today, who are putting this planned, systematic policy of extermination into effect, are financed, trained and armed by France..."*

When France intervened to set up a safe area in South West Rwanda to protect the refugees they also protected those who were guilty of genocide. Amnesty International claim that many weapons were not confiscated, and that those taken were left unguarded so people could take them back easily. Those people who were imprisoned by the French were released from prison before the UN force came to take over.

Despite the reported effects of their intervention, the French government claimed it as a success. The vice-president of the Defence Committee in the French National Assembly said, *"from a strictly military viewpoint, Operation Turquoise is positive. Under the impetus of its government, France has shown that it has the means [to undertake] a rapid and effective intervention. Friendly countries on the black continent, and with who we have, sometimes signed treaties of military assistance can be reassured: we have just proved we are capable of acting in Africa. Fast and well."*. In other words, France was more interested in showing French-speaking African governments that it would support them than it was in human rights.

France is a member of the European Union, an ally of Ireland and of Britain. Failure to condemn makes other governments accomplices.

Five Testimonies

"If we speak out, they kill us. If we are suspected of speaking out, they disappear us. And if we keep our mouths shut, they think we're hiding something. So they kill us for that too."

MANILO ARGUETA. writer, El Salvador

"He was a student of economics at the university. He was going to work; he left the house at two o'clock in the afternoon, but then he was taken by a group of heavily armed men. We know this from a boy who works waxing cars at the university. He was there, and he told us. Since then we have denounced this to the police; we've looked for him in hospitals, in all the detention centres. We even went to the morgue to look for him. Yesterday it was eleven months since my son "disappeared"; we've tried every means to locate him. He was the sole support of our house; he left a little one of nine months old. It's not possible that they just "disappear" people like that. It's just as if the earth opened and swallowed them up."

Mother, Guatemala

"We were there in the house when we heard something like a bomb explosion. Then we saw a child who fell terribly wounded. She was just an infant, about a month old. We really got scared at that point; so we decided to leave, to run away. We set out by foot, and when it grew dark, we kept walking. Finally we got to a shelter where we stopped to rest. I don't recall the time when the soldiers fell on us. I stepped out of the shelter with my children when we heard the shooting. My children ran away from me, I guess because they were scared. I realised then that I had lost my children. This is one of my worries. I don't have my three children any more; and they are part of my body."

Mother, El Salvador

"We made lists. This was the manifest: name, sex, age. When the captain came for us, we went quickly to the bus, squeezed into the front with all our luggage on one seat as he told us to. A man asked who could speak English. It was dark. He told us to be silent or we would be shot. We held our breath. There wasn't a sound on that crowded bus.

As we approached the plane made a huge noise, like a C-130. It opened at the back, a mouth. We were thrown in like packets. The pilot ordered stop just as the last of our group was in. Hundreds of us sat on the floor, a huge string tied around us, our babies on our laps. Many were sick.

We arrived at Clark Field, Philippines, at 1.30 AM. Everyone was quiet. We were handed medicine, blankets, mattresses. People were everywhere. There was much red tape: name, sex, age"

TRAN THI NGA, bookkeeper, Viet Nam

"This is a detention camp and we are treated as prisoners. It seems that I just ran out of one prison to get to another. With 1,433 other refugees, I have been put in an ill-smelling windowless warehouse, used as a temporary detention ward. I need air more than anything else - air and space. I often cannot breathe. When suffocated by the sultry heat and lack of air, I usually wonder if I will get out of this camp alive. For a whole week, in spite of an awful backache, I had to sit day and night on the damp cemented floor, in the midst of heaps of luggage and people, before I could get a little space to lie down at night, with my knees under my chin."

Vietnamese Woman, closed camp, Hong Kong

▼ References

S.Castles and M.Millar (1993) **The Age of Migration,** Basingstoke, Macmillan.

W.Gould and A.Finlay (eds.1994) **Population Migration and the Changing World Order,** Chichester, J.Wiley.

P.Harrison (1993) **Inside the Third World,** London, Penguin.

J.Jackson (1986) **Migration,** Harlow, Longman.

M.Todaro (1994) **Economic Development,** London, Longman.

UNHCR (1993) **The State of the World's Refugees,** New York, Penguin.

P.Weyland (1993) **Inside the Third World Village,** London, Routledge.

PUTTING YOU IN THE PICTURE

Colm Regan and Roger Robinson

"It so happens that to every understanding, sooner or later an action corresponds. Once man perceives a challenge, understands it, and recognises the possibilities of response, he acts. The nature of action corresponds to the nature of his understanding. Critical understanding leads to critical action..."
Paulo Freire (1974) **Education for Critical Consciousness**, London, Sheen and Ward.

INTRODUCTION

In applying the work of Brazilian educator Paulo Freire to the situation of Western societies, Robin Richardson highlighted four key moments in the development of critical consciousness:

- *naming* - a description of what the problem is - of what it is that hurts
- *reflecting* - an account of the background and causes of the problem
- *acting* - a set of behaviours whose purpose is to remove, solve, manage or adapt to the problem
- *valuing* - a vision of the ideal situation which would exist in the absence of the problem, and in the light of which the problem was defined and described in the first place.

Development education seeks to create the circumstances in which such critical consciousness and the moments which underpin it can be realised. Development education seeks to create the situation where people do not simply respond naively or emotionally to a situation, it seeks to build an informed basis for effective and long-term responses to injustice and underdevelopment. Development education is about learning of environmental, economic, social, cultural and political issues within the world at both local and global levels. And it is also about discussing and debating the nature of that world and how it might be transformed into one which is more just.

In this chapter, we seek to introduce some of the groups/organisations which are active on these issues within Britain and Ireland. By definition it will be impossible for us to list or describe them all and the huge variety of actions and campaigns in which they are involved. Instead we have chosen to illustrate some which are reflective of the broad overall approach to both education and campaigning and which give a flavour of the methodologies which are used or advocated. A list of organisations from which additional information can be obtained is included at the end.

LEARNING ABOUT THE ISSUES

Throughout England, Scotland, Wales and Ireland, there are a huge variety of groups/organisations whose aim is to assist people in understanding and responding to issues of injustice, underdevelopment and inequality. Individually and collectively, they organise courses and workshops, publish newsletters and educational resources, lobby governments, companies and agencies, organise exhibitions, letter writing campaigns etc. Understanding the issues and the root problems and the complexities which lie behind them is vitally necessary as part of the process of taking effective action. Too often, the media and many agencies offer overly simplistic understandings and solutions, frequently reducing action to those of fund-raising, charity and welfare alone.

In England and Wales, a major source of information and action is the network of Development Education Centres and educational organisations which come together in the **Development Education Association** (DEA - see below). In Scotland, they come together in the **Scottish Forum for Development Education in Schools (SIFDES)** and in the **International Development Education Association of Scotland (IDEAS)**. In Ireland, **Dóchas** brings together the bulk of Irish development agencies while **NODE (Network Outreach in Development Education)** represents the regional One

World Centres and groups and **Development Education for Youth (DEFY)** those youth organisations active in development and justice issues. In Northern Ireland they come togheter in **The Northern Ireland Development Education Forum.** For all these groups education is a central and vital part of the struggle for world justice. Below we include some representative examples of the work of such groups and some of the approaches they adopt. It provides a flavour of the different styles of work in development education in these islands.

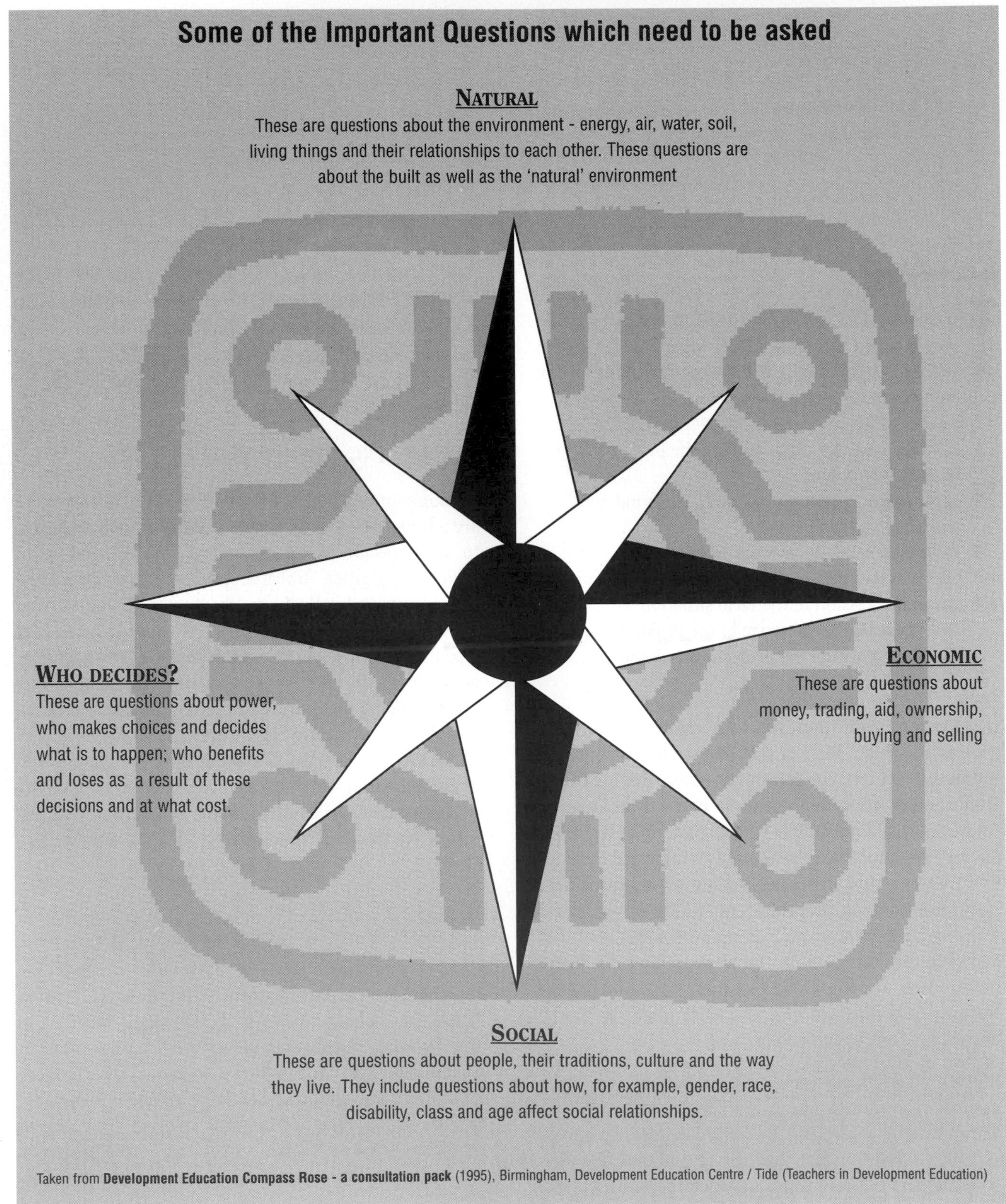

Some of the Important Questions which need to be asked
NATURAL
These are questions about the environment - energy, air, water, soil, living things and their relationships to each other. These questions are about the built as well as the 'natural' environment
WHO DECIDES?
These are questions about power, who makes choices and decides what is to happen; who benefits and loses as a result of these decisions and at what cost.
ECONOMIC
These are questions about money, trading, aid, ownership, buying and selling
SOCIAL
These are questions about people, their traditions, culture and the way they live. They include questions about how, for example, gender, race, disability, class and age affect social relationships.

Taken from **Development Education Compass Rose - a consultation pack** (1995), Birmingham, Development Education Centre / Tide (Teachers in Development Education)

Linking the Local and the Global

Section 3 - Activity Sheet

NEWSPAPER ARTICLE NO.1

TRAVELLERS TOLD TO BREAK LINKS WITH THE PAST

Some people living in West Belfast believe it is now time for Travellers to change their way of life. They were speaking almost three years after a community of Travellers moved on to public land in West Belfast.

A person who drives past this site on the Monagh Road everyday told me, "I have no pity for the Travellers because they always bring dirt and rubbish to their camps. This area was clean and tidy before they came here. Travellers always cause problems no matter where they live."

One of the Travellers living on the site said, "most people think that we want to pile up rubbish on our camp and make a mess. The fact is that our rubbish is not collected as it is from other people's homes. We would like to live in a place that is clean and safe."

The Travellers have an electricity supply for only a few hours a day on their site and no running water. Another problem is that they do not have a washing area which makes it difficult to get their children ready for school in the morning. A woman with four children who lives on this site said, "most people do not know how bad things really are for us here."

NEWSPAPER ARTICLE NO.4

TRAVELLERS IN KARNATAKA FORCED TO CHANGE THEIR WAY OF LIFE

A community of Travellers called the Budubudike from the state of Karnataka have had to give up their old way of life. For hundreds of years these Travellers moved around from village to village without ever settling in one place. As a member of this community said, "we used to tell people their fortunes, share stories and play instruments. In return we would be given food and shelter for the night."

All of this changed however when people began to see the Travellers as being lazy and living off charity. They were no longer given food or welcomed into people's homes. One of the older Travellers said, "we were not beggars living off other people. Everyone used to be glad to have us visit their village. When we told someone their fortune they would believe what we had to say. Now we can no longer travel from place to place as we used to do."

The Travellers have taken over public land 30 km from Bangalore, the capital city of Karnataka. Most members of their community have taken up farming as a way to make a living. Many of their new neighbours however are trying to drive them off this land. They do not want to share land with the Travellers because of the way they lived in the past. The Travellers believe that they do not have the same rights as everyone else even after they have been forced to change their way of life.

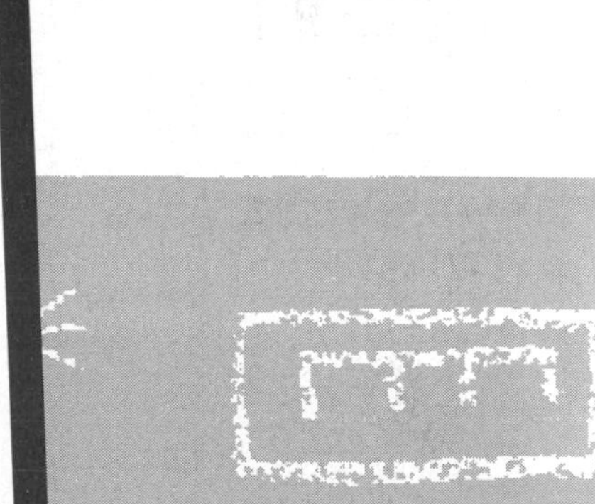

Primary Issues: **Northern Ireland and India: an active learning Resource for Key Stage 2** (1995), Belfast, One World Centre

Using the Pack TO THE FULL

further questions

CASE STUDIES

All three Units suggest ways of using case studies. Here are some more suggestions for discussion:

SCOTLAND

'A Wee Bit of Clout': Glasgow Unemployed Women's Forum

Do you think men and women experience unemployment differently?

Do you think the groups network together effectively?

What can your group learn from this case study?

'I Spy Strangers': Broom Women's Group goes to Westminster

Margaret says:'We can't get away (from these issues), because we're living them.' How far are ordinary people experts?

What did the women gain from going to Westminster?

What lessons do you think political parties should learn from the Broom women's experience?

What can your group learn from this case study?

A4 'Putting a Value on Us': Glenfield Housing Association

Has the group been effective?

Does it matter who owns your house? What benefits and / or disadvantages are there for tenants between housing association and council ownership?

Could the housing association have been set up without Scottish Homes support?

What can your group learn from this case study?

A5 Finding Local Solutions: Gairloch Childcare Group

Has the group been effective?

What has been helpful and unhelpful in the group's relationship with the council's development worker? What constraints have been on him?

Groups are said to network better in the Highlands than in Scottish cities. Why should this be?

What can your group learn from this case study?

SOUTH AFRICA

Reaching the Core:Community Participation in Townships

What is democracy? Which do you think is more democratic - South Africa or Scotland?

Do you think the first majority rule government will be able to maintain this level of local democracy?

Does your group exercise the influence of the street committees? Do you need to?

What can your group learn from this case study?

Maintaining the Momentum: Women's Representation and Majority Rule

What is the best way of translating women's issues into government?

Do you think UK political parties can learn anything from the ANC Women's League? If so, how can we go about persuading them?

No black person in South Africa has ever voted in government elections. What practical advice would you give them so that after majority rule they can avoid the kind of exclusion felt by the Broom women?

What can your group learn from this case study?

B4 Track Two

The information on this sheet does not ostensibly involve women. Why not?

What skills do you think are necessary for people representing the various communities involved in One City processes?

What can your group learn from this case study?

Photographs and Cartoons

Visual images are great 'levellers': everyone reacts to them, and everyone's reaction to them is equally valid. The photographs have been carefully chosen as discussion-starters, and Unit One suggests ways of using them. Try using the cartoons in the Units, too, as 'icebreakers' to introduce the 'heavier' topics. For example, use the cartoon 'I just want to tell you my house is damp' in Unit Three as a way of starting a discussion on 'blocks' to changing things: has anyone in the group had a similar experience?

Asking Questions

Taken from Scottish Education and Action for Development (nd) **Knowhow: a SEAD skills study pack,** Edinburgh.

page from Banulacht (1994) **Making Connections: Women Developing Links for Change,** Dublin.

A OVER-POPULATION
The main reason for underdevelopment is over-population. Throughout the Third World birth rates far exceed death rates, family sizes are big and better health-care programmes have reduced the mortality rate. Nothing can be done until the rate of population growth is drastically reduced.

B
...control most of world trade and investment and while the world remains like this, little change is possible.

C COLONIALISM
Colonialism is a major problem. Not only did it create economic, social and political problems but it also left a deeply ingrained psychological impact which most Third World countries find difficult to overcome.

D LACK OF CAPITAL
Lack of capital for investment, for financing development is the single biggest cause of underdevelopment. What they need is massive injections of capital, financial aid and loans to fund much-needed development.

E TECHNOLOGY
Third World countries just don't have the proper know-how or technology to develop themselves. They desperately need our help.

F IGNORANCE
Superstition, ignorance and the survival of old-fashioned attitudes impede development. Without proper education and positive attitudes, development will remain a dream.

G HEALTH
Poor health ensures that people will not have the physical ability or energy to undertake development. The eradication of health problems is a vital first step on the road to development.

H INJUSTICE
How can we have development when injustice remains dominant within poorer countries and between rich and poor countries?

I CORRUPTION
Corruption and incompetence remain central problems for most Third World countries. The governments of these countries just don't care about their people – just about lining their own pockets.

J ENVIRONMENT
The environment provides a major obstacle. Lack of rain, too much rain, high temperatures, typhoons, hurricanes etc all combine to produce an environment which will not support high levels of development.

The Development Education Association

The Development Education Association (DEA) is an umbrella body set up in 1993. It was formed in response to a need to support and promote the work of all those engaged in bringing about a better public understanding in the UK of global and development issues. The membership of the DEA includes the overseas development agencies, over 40 local development education centres (DECs), media organisations and broadcasters, local education authorities and teachers' centres, religious and youth organisations, peace, human rights and solidarity groups, overseas linking and exchange organisations, trade union and adult education organisations, environmental bodies, universities and colleges as well as community and youth groups.

The key aims of the DEA are:

- to provide an information and support base for members
- to facilitate networking and co-operation at local, national and international levels
- to act as a forum for the development of educational ideas and practice
- to lobby local and national government as well as educational and national curriculum bodies to recognise the importance of development education.

For further information on the DEA, write to Information Officer, Development Education Association, Third Floor, 29-31 Cowper Street, London EC2A 4AP.

What is NODE?

Node stands for Network Outreach in Development Education and is a network of groups and development education centres throughout Ireland. NODE has been established to increase the level of development education activity in Ireland. This it does in three ways:

NETWORKING - providing opportunities for groups to meet, share and learn from their experiences
TRAINING - offering training in areas identified by groups involved in the network
SUPPORT - offering support to newly established groups through both training and networking.

NODE can be contacted through Cómhlámh, 10 Upper Camden Street, Dublin 2.

National Committee for Development Education

The NCDE was set up by the Tanaiste and Minister for Foreign Affairs in 1994 as part of the Irish Government's official overseas development assistance programme. The Committee is made up of both elected and appointed individuals from those sectors with an interest and involvement in development education. In co-operation with other agencies and structures involved in development and education, NCDE seeks to promote awareness and understanding among Irish people on development issues, especially as they relate to developing countries.

NCDE provides a support service to those active in different sectors of development education work as well as undertaking pro-active projects in the formal and non-formal sectors. NCDE also provides a resources support service.

NCDE can be contacted at 16-20 Cumberland Street, Dublin 2 - tel 662 0866.

"The realities of racism and intolerance effect all our lives - diminishing our humanity, moulding our attitudes, endangering the prospects for peace on our island, our continent and our world. The portrayal of the majority of peoples of the world through stereotyped images; the portrayal of young people in our communities as vandals, victims or saints; these are part of one and the same problem - the problem of prejudice. The future of our world depends, at one level, on consciously changing the attitudes of people towards greater tolerance, respect for difference and belief in equality for all. Every basic national and global issue - from global hunger to Travellers' rights to youth unemployment - is fundamentally a question of changing attitudes."

Introduction to **Ireland - All Different All Equal: an anti-racism and equality education pack**

All Equal All Different - Challenging Racism, Xenophobia, Intolerance and Anti-Semitism.

The European youth campaign against racism and in favour of tolerance and respect for difference is part of the work of the Council of Europe. It is part of a broader plan to combat racism, xenophobia, anti-Semitism and intolerance - all of which have grown in Europe in recent decades. The Council of Europe is an inter-governmental organisation which brings together 36 countries from Western, Central and Eastern Europe. It was set up in 1949 to protect human rights and to promote democracy.

The ***All Different All Equal Campaign*** is a campaign of activities at local, regional, national and international level including music festivals and events, education and training seminars, media action, women's groups actions, materials production and dissemination and youth trains etc.
To illustrate some of the approaches of the campaign we have chosen two pages from the Irish education pack produced in association with the National Youth Council of Ireland.

For more information about the All Different, All Equal Campaign, contact

COMMISSION FOR RACIAL EQUALITY,
Elliot House
10/12 Allington Street,
London SW1E 5EH

NATIONAL YOUTH COUNCIL
OF IRELAND,
3 Montague Street,
Dublin 2.

Let's Discriminate Discretely

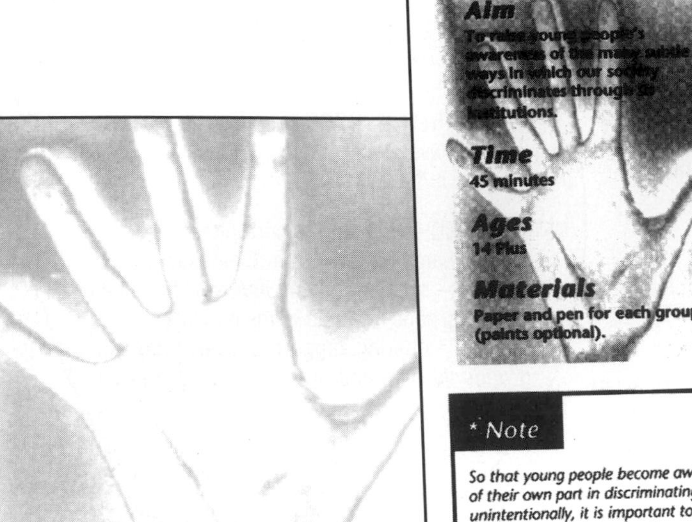

Aim
To raise young people's awareness of the many subtle ways in which our society discriminates through its institutions.

Time
45 minutes

Ages
14 Plus

Materials
Paper and pen for each group, (paints optional).

*** Note**

So that young people become aware of their own part in discriminating unintentionally, it is important to include the Family among the institutions treated.

What to do...

- Form groups of about 4-5 people. Each group is to represent a particular institution in Irish society: Family, Education, Media, Politicians, the Legal system, Church, Unions, Youth Clubs, Pubs and Discos, etc.

ROUND 1

- Call out one group who have been discriminated against in Irish society, eg, Travellers, Gays, Black People, Refugees, the Unemployed or a religious minority. The small groups have 5 minutes to think up devious ways that their institution could possibly discriminate against such people, ***without breaking the law***.
- After 5 minutes each of the institutions reports on what ways it thought up.
- Appoint a Scorekeeper and award points. The sub-groups take turns to report one item at a time. Award 2 points per item, 3 for extra subtlety; no points for something already said by another group. As a group reports each answer, one other group may 'rob' one of the points by quickly giving a way of countering that type of discrimination. Whichever group gains most points leads.

ROUND 2

- The members get up and move to the next institution. The leader calls another minority for the institutions to 'pick on' and to defend. Again report and give point. It is important that the young people also think of ways of countering the discriminations suggested.

ROUND 3

- Continue for a third and fourth round according to the time and energy of the group. Whichever group has gained most points wins.
- If time allows invite the young people to act out or paint situations of these forms of discrimination taking place, and of the counter measures.

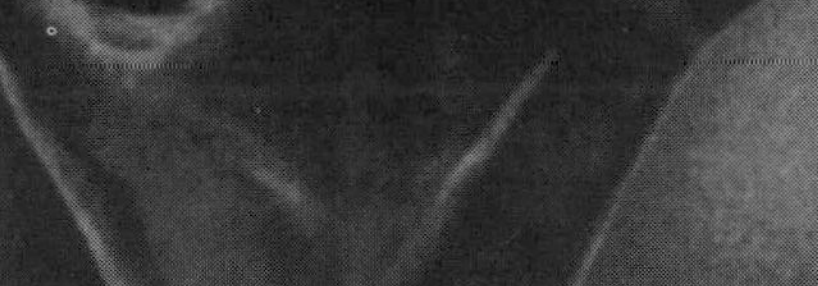

Discussion
* Suggestions

Do many of these ways of discrimination actually happen? Should they be allowed to continue? Is there anything we can do locally to change these? eg, have a positive Traveller poster on the wall, gather facts and get publicity for them...Brainstorm together.

ALTERNATIVELY

Call out examples of discrimination from the Examples for the Leader (on page 24) or others you are aware of, and award points for the group which proposes the best way of stopping that discrimination.

Taking it Further

Invite a member of a group which is discriminated against to speak to the club about their own experience, and how things could change.

Examples for the leader:

While the following do involve generalisations, they are a guide for you as to how discrimination could actually happen in Ireland. Their purpose here is to help the leader stimulate the imagination of participants to understand the subtlety of discrimination and the need for measures to counter discrimination.

Education:
We won't make our schools welcoming places for them to be in. We won't employ them. They won't be shown in the school books, nor will pupils be taught about their special identity. Everyone must be the same, act the same, dress the same, learn the same things. We will put them in separate schools, or separate classes, separate playgrounds. There will be nowhere else for them to go during religion class.

Banks and Insurance Companies.
We will delay their applications, charge extra premiums, not understand their accents, ask extra questions, require AIDS tests and that they sign a form declaring their sexual identity, require a fixed address. The door at the top of the wheelchair ramp will be locked to keep the heat in.

Family:
We will keep our children away from them. We will keep them away from our home. If our brother or sister dates with one, or plans to marry one, they won't have our support. We will call them crude names and tell jokes about them. We will blame them for trouble and crime in the area.

Churches.
We'll call for charity towards them, not justice. We'll make it hard for them to attend or teach in our schools. We won't train our ministers about their special needs. We won't let them use our premises for meetings. We won't include them in groups we praise. We'll cough or 'em' before referring to them. We will be quiet when they are attacked. We will not fit hearing-aid loop systems or have wheelchair ramps in our churches.

Politicians:
We will make it difficult for them to qualify for grants. We will raise other issues before theirs. We won't legislate to protect their rights. We will not intervene on their behalf or accept invitations to their meetings. If any of us is one of them they had better hide it.

Media:
We won't interview them or employ them or show photos of them doing good things. We'll spell their names incorrectly. We'll throw in the bin any press releases from their organisation. We'll show the charity of others towards them, but not their work for themselves. We won't publish articles standing up for them or broadcast programmes showing their uniqueness or their abilities and achievements. We won't let them make programmes.

The Police System:
We will respond quicker to calls from other groups. We will always wear our hat talking to them. We will stop them on the street and ask where they are going. We will be fussy when they fill in forms. We will check their cars over - lights and tyres, the works. They don't make very strong witnesses in court.

CAMPAIGNING ABOUT THE ISSUES

"The case for putting poor people first is not only the strong moral imperative to do so, powerful though this is. It is...also the way to achieve the objectives of protecting the environment and increasing production. Putting people first does not have to be a slogan divorced from the world of economic and environmental realities, but a way of re-entering it. The aim is to establish a virtuous circle of grassroots initiatives, instead of the vicious circle of poverty, inappropriate development and environmental destruction."

Ben Jackson (1990) ***Poverty and the Planet: A Question of Survival,*** London, Penguin.

In this section we profile some of the organisations and groups which have become active in campaigning for change and some of the methodologies they employ. The examples include *One World Week, The World Development Movement, The Campaign Against the Arms Trade, Pax Christi, Cómhlámh (The Irish Association of Returned Development Workers), Cafod, Trócaire, Greenpeace, Friends of the Earth, The Pesticides Action Network, Oxfam, and Amnesty International.*

"Asking Questions About Campaigning"

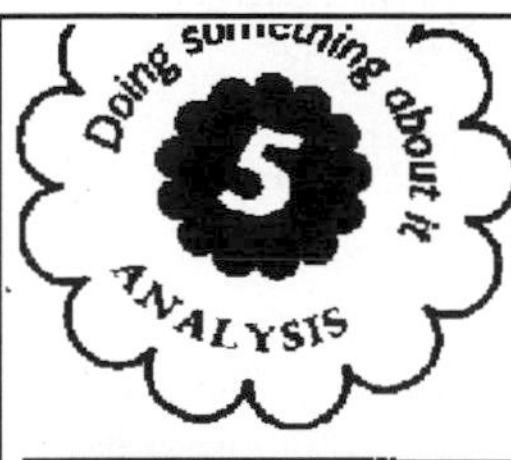

Non-Violent Action

AIM

That young people experience building peace as 'active' not 'passive'.

AGE

Over 16 years.

TIME

45 minutes.

MATERIALS

Paper, markers, poster-sheets, blue-tack.

WHAT YOU NEED TO DO

ICEBREAKER

■ Divide the group in two. One group sits on the floor, linking each others arms tightly, in peaceful protest.

■ The second group are police officers whose aim is to physically move those sitting-in. They may in no way hurt those sitting. They try lifting, gently dragging, etc. Remind them that TV cameras are watching.

■ The sitting group let their bodies be limp, except for their clasped arms. They do not argue.

Part One

■ In small groups the participants begin by brainstorming:

- *What kind of non-violent action young people take within their families when there is conflict...* sulk, stop talking, stop cleaning their bedroom, play the music loudly etc ?
- *What kind of non-violent action their parents take when there is conflict with children...* grounding, reducing pocket money etc ?
- *What types of 'non-violent action' exist in the wider society ?* (Prompt the group with current examples such as the Irish Press being occupied; the road being blocked at Moate, in objection to the allocation of a council house to a Traveller family; the Dunnes Store strike; the Shell boycott etc).

■ Each type of action is written on a separate card.

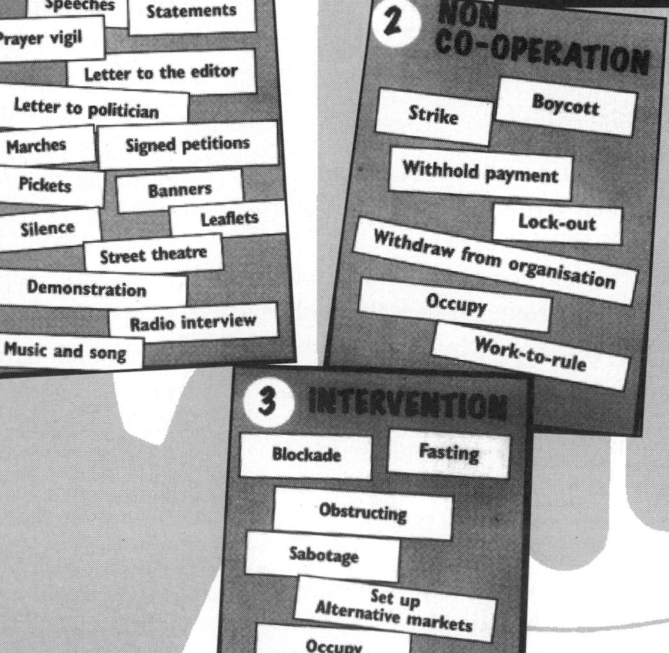

The Arms Trade - The Need for a European Code of Conduct

In January 1995, 3 non-government organisations - the *British American Security Information Council, Saferworld* and the *World Development Movement* in co-operation with Marc Weller of Cambridge University and Francoise Hampson of Essex University - developed a framework for a code of conduct for the European arms industry. It seeks to translate into practical measures the general code proposed by the European Council of Ministers in June 1991.

Briefly stated this code outlines eight criteria which should govern the export of arms from Europe taking into account the internal and regional situation of the purchasing country; the purchasing country's human rights record and attitude to terrorism and the effect the purchase of arms will have on the country's economy. The limitations of the Council of Ministers proposals are that they are not binding on governments and there is no agreement on how they should be interpreted. The latter point is crucial for it leads to considerable variation in the approaches of different EU states. The UK continues to export Hawk jet fighters to Indonesia whilst Italy and Portugal have self-imposed embargoes on the same country because of its poor human rights record.

The translation of the Code into a series of specific and enforceable practical proposals has been put forward by the three organisations listed above. A full copy of the proposed Code can be obtained, free of charge (SAE's please), from *Comhlámh,* 61 Lower Camden St., Dublin 2 or *World Development Movement,* 25 Beehive Place, London SW9 7QR.

These organisations encourage people to obtain a copy of the Code, read it and then write to TD's/MP's/MEP's requesting them that they aquaint themselves with the proposals and act upon them in the name of those who suffer at the hands of the arms trade today or those who may suffer in the future unless positive action is taken now.

It is important that urging the EU to act does not let national governments off the hook, so supporting national campaigns on specific issues is equally necessary.

Two organisations who have vigorously campaigned against the arms trade ate *The World Development Movement (WDM)* and the *Campaign Against the Arms Trade (CAAT).*

Laser Weapons

Weapons for the specific purpose of inflicting permanent blindness are expected to become operational within the next five years. Laser rifles are capable of inflicting permanent blindness at a range of up to one kilometre via a silent, invisible laser beam which burns the retina and causes haemorrhaging.

Blindness is a particularly severe form of a permanent injury. Their use would have widespread implications for civilians as well as military. Intentional blindness as a method of warfare causes long-term damage and suffering and should be abhorrent to all right thinking people.

For further information on these weapons and on what you can do about them, contact ***Pax Christi*** in either Dublin (52 Lower Rathmines Road, Dublin 6) or London (9 Henry Place, London N4 2LH).

"Up in arms with the PM"

WDM is currently urging the British Prime Minister to review Britain's arms export policy. The move follows John Major's belated ban on arms export to Nigeria (following the 1995 murder of Ogoni activist and leader Ken Saro-Wiwa and eight colleagues) and the government's continuing failure to consider a purchasing country's human rights record when exporting arms.

For example, WDM's is urging the Prime Minister to extend the ban to cover existing military equipment orders which have still to be delivered to Nigeria. WDM argues that if the ban is not extended, Nigeria's military ruler General Abacha could receive a hefty hamper filled with outstanding orders which could include the likes of Italian spotter planes, German trucks and up to 30 orders of 'non-lethal' military equipment from Britain.

For further information about *WDM* or to obtain a copy of *Gunrunners Gold:* **how the public's money finances arms sales,** write to 25 Beehive Place, London SW9 7QR.

The Campaign against arms trade (CAAT) has a long and often lonely history of work against the arms trade in Britain.

- CAAT is currently calling for the closure of the Defence Export Services Organisation which helps organise the sale of British weapons abroad and for an end to Government involvement in arms exhibitions.
- CAAT is calling for a register of all applications for UK arms export licences to be available for public inspection to enable comment and, if appropriate, parliamentary debate before a contract is signed. This would complement the UN register (see chapter 14).
- CAAT is calling for the effects of the arms trade on development to be taken into account when arms export applications are considered.
- CAAT is calling for an immediate ban on the supply of military, parliamentary and police equipment to governments with records of sustained human rights abuse. Training of military, security and police personnel from these countries should also be ended.
- CAAT believes no arms or other equipment should be supplied to the military, security or police forces of countries involved in armed conflict.
- CAAT argues that getting out of the arms export business could mean more not less jobs - but only if serious planning and investigation of the alternative starts now.

For more information about *CAAT,* write to them at 11 Goodwin Street, Finsbury Park, London N4 3HQ.
For information on the arms trade in Scotland, contact *Commonweal,* 41 George IV Bridge, Edinburgh EH1 1EL.

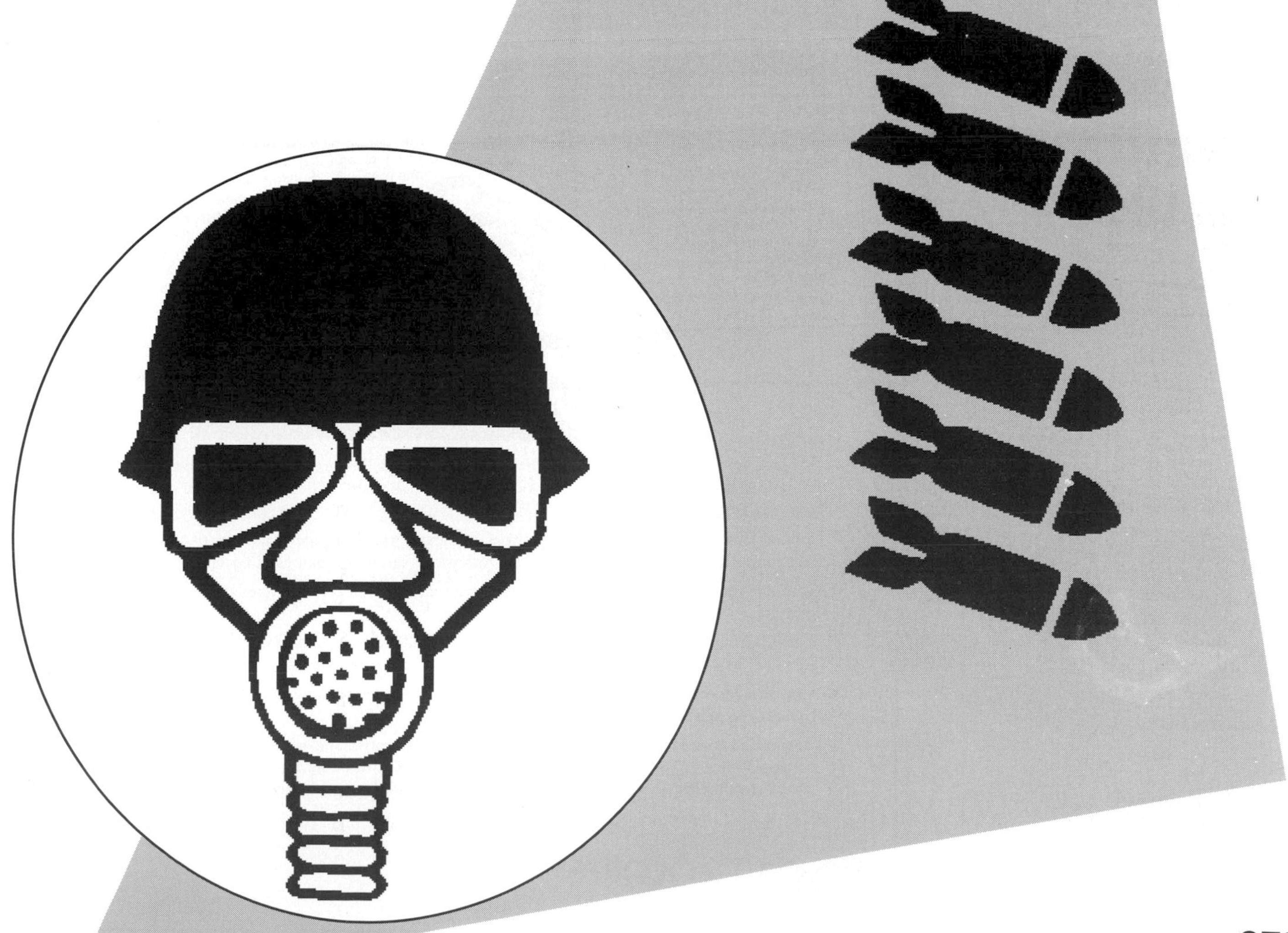

Campaigning on Landmines.

Over the past number of years, a large number of organisations have campaigned against the manufacture and export of landmines which have inflicted huge suffering and underdevelopment on millions of people. Groups such as *The Mines Advisory Group, Trócaire* and *CAFOD* have been active in this area.

For additional information, please contact the *Mines Advisory Group,* 54A Main Street, Cockermouth, CA13 9LU, United Kingdom; *Trócaire,* 169 Booterstown Avenue, Blackrock, Co.Dublin, Ireland or 50 King Street, Belfast BT1 6AD; *CAFOD,* Romero Close, Stockwell Road, London SW9 9TY, England.

UK switch to landmine ban likely

David Fairhall
Defence Correspondent

BRITAIN looks set to change its policy on the production and use of anti-personnel landmines in favour of a complete ban.

The unexpected U-turn comes as the United Nations launches a fresh effort to control a worldwide plague of 100 million landmines that are killing and maiming 2,000 people a month, mostly civilians. The British shift has been prompted in part by signs that the United States is preparing to renounce these weapons.

A spokesman at the Ministry of Defence said a Commons statement on the issue

14 US generals have declared a ban 'humane and militarily responsible'

clined to eliminate such weapons. Gulf war commander General Norman Schwarzkopf and the former Nato supreme commander, General John Galvin, are among 14 retired US generals who have signed an open letter to President Clinton declaring a total ban "not only humane but also militarily responsible".

British diplomats accepted that Britain's former stance opposing a ban had come under great pressure. But one source suggested that the prevailing view at the Geneva conference favoured a more pragmatic approach.

The aim of the meeting is to revise the 1980 inhumane weapons convention to tighten curbs on the design, sale and use of anti-personnel mines.

Given the objections raised by China, and to a lesser extent by India, Pakistan and Russia, Britain believes it better at the conference to concentrate on limited objectives that may attract univers support, such as prohibitin non-detectable min necessary modi stocks

Guardian Monday 22 / 4 / 1996

LANDMINES ACTION SHEET

There are more than 23 million refugees in the world today. Many have run from war, others from human rights abuse or other persecution. They are waiting across borders for news of peace. They want to go home.

But once there is peace or the chance of a safe return one deadly danger can stop refugees going home: anti-personnel mines (APMs).

There are over 100 million landmines strewn across the world today. In Cambodia one in every 236 people is an amputee, in the United States it is only one in every 22,000.

What is an anti-personnel mine?

There are four main types of APM:
1: blast
2: fragmentation
3: directional and
4: bounding.

Some types of mine, such as the Italian **"Valmara"** are both fragmentational and bounding.

Blast mines (like the **Soviet PMN**) are the most common. They are activated by pressure.

Fragmentation mines are either packed with fragments of metal (like ball-bearings) or have an outer case which breaks into fragments when they explode. One easily recognisable mine is the **"Valmara"**, which was made by the Italian company Valsella. It looks a bit like a very small Dalek. It is a bounding fragmentation mine which leaps 0.5m when activated. Anyone standing within 30 metres is killed, and it causes injuries to anyone within 100 metres.

△ Valmara

The most common directional mine is the American **"Claymore."** This is activated by tripwire and sprays 700 ballbearings at a height of two metres in an arc.

Anti-personnel mines can be buried slightly underground, placed on stakes or scattered above ground. Some are placed by hand, others are dropped by helicopter or light aircraft.

One of these scatterable mines is the **"butterfly,"** particularly common in Afghanistan. This has two wings and is the size of a hand. In one wing is liquid explosive which will blow up when the mine is picked up. The mine is very attractive to children who often think it looks like a toy. It is capable of blowing a child's arm off.

◁ Butterfly Soviet PFM-1

Who is most at risk from anti-personnel mines?

More civilians than soldiers are injured by anti-personnel mines.

Collecting firewood is a high-risk activity in a mined area - this is what many women in particular are doing when they are hit. Also in the top ten high-risk activities is simply playing.

Farming, walking along paths, grazing animals and visiting graveyards all become dangerous when the area is mined.

△ POMZ Stake mine

What happens if you are hit by an anti-personnel mine?

Some people are killed immediately by the force of the blast or loss of blood. But many suffer horrific injuries - if you tread on a mine the blast forces earth and pieces of your shoe up into your leg, causing traumatic wounds which very easily become infected. Amputation of one or more limbs is just about the only effective treatment.

Why don't people just avoid the areas where there are mines?

It is very difficult to know where mines are. They are buried, or they are designed to blend into the background. If you look at a field there is no way of telling whether it is mined or not.

One of the aims of planting mines is to deny access to land which is useful, so mines are often laid around wells, in good farming land, or around villages. If you are in a city where there is no food, do you stay there and starve or do you risk crossing a minefield to find food? People make these choices every day in mined areas.

Why is CAFOD concerned and what is CAFOD doing?

Anti-personnel mines make it difficult for refugees to go home, and they make long-term development and the post-war rebuilding of a country much more difficult. Their presence means that people are denied access to land, transport and water. Scarce health resources are diverted to care for victims of mines. CAFOD spends money on projects to clear mines and rehabilitate landmine victims when it could be spent on long-term development projects. We support, for example, the work of the Mines Advisory Group clearing mines in Angola.

What can I do?

- Sign and send the enclosed post card to the Government, calling for a total ban on the production and use of landmines worldwide. Give copies to your friends and ask them to do the same. More postcards are available from any Trócaire office.
- Support Trócaire's campaign to ban these inhumane terror weapons and to provide increased aid for demining. Ask to be put on our mailing list for updates on the landmines campaign.
- Contact your TD/MEP to press for resolute government action on landmines at the UN and among our EU partners.
- Watch out for TV programmes and press reports on landmines. A number of videos are available for hire from Trócaire. Contact the campaigns office.
- Run a landmines event in your area to publicise the effects of these weapons and raise public awareness. Trócaire can provide resource materials.
- Organise a petition in your school, college, workplace or parish and ask as many people as possible to sign it. A sample sheet is enclosed. Contact Trócaire if you need more forms, or photocopy this one. When it is complete send your petition to Trócaire and we will forward it to the Government.

TRÓCAIRE
169 Booterstown Avenue, Blackrock.

Campaigning on African Issues

A Scottish Charter for Africa - SCIAF

The people of Sub-Saharan Africa are 9% of the world's population but receive little more than 1% of its income. Rapid advances have been made in many countries in the past 40 years in terms of life expectancy, literacy, nutrition and health care. Yet these gains, achieved in large part through the struggles of African people themselves, are under threat.

Literacy rates in Sub-Saharan Africa still lag behind those of other developing countries.

40 million Africans are currently displaced from their hoomes by military conflict or environmental disaster.

Africa's debt burden has tripled since 1980 and debt repayments now outstrip total spending on health and education.

Efforts to increase exports by 25% have been rewarded by a 30% reduction in income due to falling international prices.

We live in an interdependent world where our lifestyle and actions have an effect far beyond our own borders. Our companies and financial institutions have links with many developing countries, including those in Africa.

Scots have a tradition of individual generosity towards the poor and disadvantaged. We believe that all Scots, irrespective of race, religion or political opinion, want to see their efforts achieve a world where the dignity of every human being is respected. As part of SCIAF's Solidarity with Africa Campaign, we are encouraging Scots to:

- Sign the Charter for Africa
- Commit themselves to action on behalf of Africa
- Change their lifestyles.

"As members of one extended family, we hear your concern that we in Europe are allowing Africa to slip to the margins of our political, social and economic agenda...we undertake to listen more closely to your voice...and to engage our governments and the European Community...to counter this marginalisation in Africa. We undertake to do this in obedience to God and out of love for you."

Council of Churches for Britain and Ireland.

Greenpeace - Making a World of Difference

'We can make a difference'. That's the thought that inspired a handful of North American activists when, in 1971, they sailed their small boat into a US atomic test zone off Amchitka, Alaska. They believed that you should stand up for what you believe in, however formidable the challenge and however small your voice. So Greenpeace was born.

The following successes, won over the last two decades give us all hope for the future. Without Greenpeace, how many of these battles would have been won? Through its campaigning, Greenpeace helped:

- Restore Antarctica to its status as the last wilderness continent after an eight year campaign which consumed half our funds.
- to establish a whale sanctuary in the Southern Ocean, protecting the great whales from commercial whaling all round Antarctica.
- Stop the French government testing nuclear weapons in the Pacific.
- End large scale driftnetting which once stripped our oceans bare.
- Stop the killing of baby seals for commercial gain.
- Alert governments to the alarming rise in children's asthma caused by car emissions.
- Persuade the European community to reduce pollution in the North Sea including a ban on the UK dumping of industrial waste.
- Campaign internationally for a ban on ozone destroying chemicals winning an agreement to phase out CFCs in Europe by 1995.

For more information on Greenpeace and its various campaigns, contact them at *Greenpeace Ireland,* 44 Upper Mount Street, Dublin 2; *Greenpeace UK,* Canonbury Villas, London N1 2PN.

Campaigning for Human Rights

Action for Justice

Oxfam has recently launched a campaign linking human rights and poverty right across the development spectrum. They invite people concerned about any or all of these issues to join in their campaign which highlights key dimensions of human rights issues.

JOIN THE OXFAM CAMPAIGN

EVERY PERSON HAS A BASIC RIGHT TO:

Enough to eat
Denied: 800 million people go hungry.

A livelihood
Denied: One in four of the world's people lives in abject poverty.

An education
Denied: 31% of people in the third world are illiterate.

Clean water
Denied: More than a billion people are at risk from dirty water. 25,000 die each day.

A home
Denied: Millions of children live on the streets of the world's cities.

Health care
Denied: 10% of children in the third world die before the age of five.

A safe environment
Denied: Pollution and environmental disaster threaten millions of the world's poorest people.

Equality of opportunity
Denied: For reasons of race, sex, religion or nationality, people are exploited or ignored.

Protection from violence
Denied: 90% of war casualties are civilians. 100 million landmines lie waiting.

A say in their future
Denied: Poor people are the last to be heard and the first to suffer.

KNOWLEDGE IS POWER

You could make yourself a more effective campaigner for rights by doing some more reading.

THEY HAVE RIGHTS

The world agrees. Rights are internationally recognised, and endorsed by almost every government there is.

But the world still hasn't done enough.

Yet we can. Together we can call to account those in power. We can campaign for the rights that millions are denied.

For additional information, contact **Oxfam**
in England at 274 Banbury Road, Oxford OX2 7DZ;
in Scotland at Floor 5, Fleming House, 134 Renfrew Street, Glasgow G3 6ST;
in Northern Ireland at 52-54 Dublin Road Belfast BT2 7HN
and in Ireland at 19 Clanwilliam Terrace, Dublin 2.

"The candle burns not for us, but for all those whom we failed to rescue from prison, who were shot on the way to prison, who were tortured, who were kidnapped, who "disappeared". That's what the candle is for..."

Peter Benenson, founder of Amnesty International

Amnesty International and Human Rights

> *"The efforts of Amnesty International and other human rights organisations had a direct, immediate and personal effect on the Turkish Government - and for those of us who were in prison, the interest shown in us brought warmth and hope."*

Iiker Demir, a 39 year old Turkish journalist who spent seven years in jail after the military coup of 1980.

Amnesty International is one of the world's best known and most successful human rights organisations. Most well known are Amnesty's letter writing campaigns for the release of prisoners of conscience detained throughout the world. But Amnesty International is also involved in a wide variety of other campaigns for the abolition of the death penalty, the legal recognition of Covenants to promote and protect particular human rights for example and it also publishes a yearly international human rights report which details the human rights situation in most countries.

Amnesty International members can also become active on human rights issues within their own countries. Over the years Amnesty International has identified a number of key areas where local members can make a positive contribution to the situation in their own country in ways that still preserve the fundamental principles of the movement.

For example:

- they mount national and local human rights education programme in schools, universities and the community at large;
- they campaign for the general abolition of the death penalty in their own country (normally the principle of international action on individual cases is respected);
- the sections, groups and members campaign to get their government to ratify international human rights treaties and bring domestic laws into line with international human rights standards (special international approval is needed for such initiatives);
- the sections and groups in the country translate, stock and distribute the international reports on every country in the world - including their own.

Through public work on behalf of victims in other countries, Amnesty International members show that human rights are universal and that ordinary people anywhere in the world can help to combat torture, executions and other abuses, wherever they occur.

With the aim of preventing their own country from contributing to human rights violations elsewhere local members:

- intercede to help prevent asylum-seekers being sent back to countries where they would risk becoming prisoners of conscience or being tortured or executed;
- take a stand against the transfer of military, police or security equipment and expertise to countries where they are used to detain prisoners of conscience or inflict torture or carry out executions.

You can contact Amnesty International in Ireland at 48 Fleet Street, Dublin 2 and in Britain at 99-119 Rosebery Avenue, London EC1R 4RE.

AN IRREVERENT GLOSSARY

written to challenge the notion that definitions are neutral and to encourage discussion

AID: Some see aid as a direct link between those in the West and our brothers and sisters in the Third World. Others see it as part of the process through which the rich world takes nine pounds from the poor world for every pound it gives and still manages to feel good about itself. It is classed as either *Official Development Aid* (ODA) donated by the government or voluntary aid donated by private donors. Official aid is either spent on projects in the Third World *(Bilateral Aid)* or given to multinational organisations such as **UNICEF** *(Multilateral Aid).*

BIO-DIVERSITY: Biological diversity. A large variety of species of life. Many plants and animals can provide resources (such as medicine) to humans. Many of those which could have done so have been wiped out due to the actions of humans in the last forty years. The decrease in bio-diversity is therefore an untold loss.

BRETTON WOODS: Home to an agreement which enslaved millions. Bretton Woods is a location in New Hampshire USA. At a conference in Bretton Woods in July 1944 the members of the ***United Nations*** set up the *International Monetary Fund* and the *International Bank for Reconstruction and Development (The World Bank).* The two institutions were originally set up to promote international trade and to aid development. Many see them as essential to ***development*** today and in the future, others argue they are little more than the leg-breakers of whole societies on behalf of international loan sharks.

CULTURE: To a sociologist culture is the values, norms and beliefs of a society. For others it is a more general notion of the music, art and literature of a country. Some feel that the culture (values and beliefs) of poorer countries helps to keep them poor as they do not have a Western entrepreneurial spirit. Others feel that this is a red herring. Some feel that Third World cultures are under attack from a barrage of Western ideas and fashions which are presented through a Western dominated media. This is called *cultural imperialism.* Others point to the increasing availability of Third World music and culture in the West as part of a growth in a global culture. Together with the increase in global political institutions and global economic activity this process is referred to as *Globalisation.*

DEVELOPMENT: Economist Richard Douthwaite suggests that development is a global process through which a few get rich, most become poor and the earth gets destroyed. This process is also known as *mal-development.* A small group of global optimists still believe that there is some possibility of increasing living standards and opportunities for all the people on the planet. They continue to refer to this as development. For yet others such as geographer Keith Buchanan, *development* has become one of the great dirty words of modern society.

DEVELOPMENT EDUCATION: focuses on issues of human and global development in an educational and participative way. It seeks to encourage people to ask questions about their everyday world and their links with the wider world. Not to be confused with fund-raising or public relations - telling 'them' what a good job we're doing and how much it costs.

ECOSYSTEM (ECOLOGICAL SYSTEM): A functioning community of living things and their environment. An ecosystem should be a well balanced system incorporating the recycling of waste elements and the conversion of energy into forms used by other members of the ecosystem (i.e. food). Together all ecosystems form the ecosphere of the planet.

FAMINE: Conventionally thought of as mass starvation due to lack of food in an area. First the economist Amayarta Sen pointed out that famines usually happen in places where there is food available. Then, when famine had been re-defined as mass starvation, social researcher Alex de Waal pointed out that many people do not die of starvation in a famine but of disease and that this can have more to do with a lack of clean water than a lack of food. The only thing that people seem able to agree on is that famine generally has little to do with drought or floods and a lot to do with whether people are allowed access the food available. It's worth remembering the saying of the Dinka people *'the Dinka don't starve, someone has to starve them."*

FAO: United Nations Food and Agriculture Organisation.

GATT (GENERAL AGREEMENT OF TRADE AND TARIFFS): The GATT was another ***Bretton Woods*** institution. Its role in regulating world trade was often felt to be detrimental to the Third World. It was replaced by the *WTO (World Trade Organisation)* in the early 1990s. This fulfils essentially the same role in much the same way. GATT/WHO approves of free trade but only on our terms and only when it doesn't threaten our interests.

GENDER BLINDNESS: A disease which affects not the eyes but the mind. Many feel that in looking at development certain measures tend to be blind to the different effects on the situations of men and women. For example, in looking at household ***poverty*** we do not see how resources are distributed within the family. Household poverty is, then, a gender blind measure. ***GNP*** per capita and ***history*** are often accused of being gender blind.

GLOBALISATION: For some the process of bringing the people of the world closer together in a common agenda, for others the process of dividing the world's people even more by imposing Western values, economics and institutions whilst telling those who lose out that they've never had it so good.

GDP (GROSS DOMESTIC PRODUCT): See ***GNP.***

GNP (GROSS NATIONAL PRODUCT): The sum of goods and services bought for private consumption, plus government spending, plus net exports (exports minus imports), plus business investment. *Gross Domestic Product* does not take exports and imports into account. *GNP per capita* measures the amount of GNP in a country divided by the number of people in that country. GNP has in the past been used as a measure of economic activity but is widely regarded as a poor measure of development. For this reason, many government agencies continue to use it as a development indicator. American Cartoonist Mike Peters makes distinction between the Gross National Product as defined above and the *Really Gross* National Product such as defence spending.

G - 7: The group of seven leading industrial countries - some of whom actually run the world, others of whom like to think they run the world and one or two of whom used to run the world.

HISTORY: One of the most contentious of all concepts, history is the story of the past as told by those who won. Generally defined as a written reconstruction of man's past, magazine writer John Leo suggests that the word denotes the past as written by men (His -story). He suggests using the phrase and concept *his 'n' herstory* as a substitute.

IMAGINATION: Sociologist C. Wright Mills suggests that a skill people need to develop is imagination. When looking into a cup of coffee try not to see brown liquid, instead see a web of unequal social relations. What is in the cup is not simply liquid, but part of the reason for poverty (unequal trade relations). See also ***Development and Development Education.***

IMF: See ***Bretton Woods.***

INDUSTRIALISATION: Industrialisation is the process through which there is a growth in the importance of the secondary or manufacturing sector. It is often presented as synonymous with ***Modernisation*** or ***Development.*** Western societies are often thought of as now being *post-industrial.* A post-industrial society is one in which knowledge in more important than property, and the service sector is more important than manufacturing. For people who argue this, industrialisation is sometimes seen as a step on the road to *post-industrial* (or the 'new' modern) society. See also ***Populism.***

INFANT MORTALITY RATES: The number of deaths in the first year of life per 1000 live births, usually calculated for a particular country in a particular year. This means a country with 50,000 children born alive in a given year, of which 500 die before their first birthday, will have an infant mortality rate of 10. For many one of the most important and most sensitive measures of *development.*

INTERNATIONAL BANK FOR RECONSTRUCTION AND DEVELOPMENT: See ***World Bank.***

LESS-DEVELOPED WORLD: a polite phrase used to describe those countries which are not yet 'fully developed' like us but who, if they adopt the right policies, might just become as developed as us. See ***Third World.***

LIFE EXPECTANCY: The average life span of people calculated on a country by country basis. Like all averages it is a crude measure which may not be a good snapshot of the situation. For example, if you include all infant mortality in your calculations then the average will be lower than if you exclude infant mortality. Life expectancy includes ***infant mortality*** and is more correctly known as known as *life expectancy at birth.* For those who make it past infancy, their life expectancy may increase, hence on average you may expect to live longer at five than you do at birth.

MALNUTRITION: Inadequate dietary intake of one or more necessary components of a healthy diet. Generally this takes the form of protein deficiency, but it can also take the form of vitamin or mineral deficiency. If the body does not get enough energy from carbohydrates and fats to carry out its activities it will turn protein into energy.

MULTI NATIONAL CORPORATIONS (MNCS): See ***Trans National Corporations.***

NGO (NON-GOVERNMENTAL ORGANISATION): More common term for charity or voluntary organisations. *NGDOs* (Non-Governmental Development Organisations) are NGOs who work specifically on development or Third World issues.

POPULISM: A focus on development as a process which must come from the people who are themselves developing. It is often seen as opposition to ***Industrialisation,*** as it does not see development as necessarily requiring a growth in large industry or a change to manufacturing. Not popular in many official circles.

POST-INDUSTRIALISATION: See ***Industrialisation.***

POVERTY: Another contested concept. First attempts to measure it were made by Seebohm Rowntree, also famous for his chocolate. Sociologist Peter Townsend claims that poverty has to be understood in relative terms, i.e. people must be thought of as being poor when compared to the norm for society. This is known as ***relative poverty.*** He measured poverty in terms of whether people could afford to engage in normal activities. The economist Amayarta Sen pointed out that a person starving to death in an area affected by ***famine*** could feel perhaps that they had quite a lot compared to the people around them. Did their relative affluence mean they were not in poverty? This is called ***absolute poverty.***

RIGHTS: The concept of rights which we hold in the West is generally seen as coming from Thomas Jefferson who wrote that all men are created equal and endowed by their creator with certain rights including the right to life, liberty and the pursuit of happiness. Jefferson himself kept slaves. In the modern world, human rights are listed in the ***UN*** Universal Declaration of Human Rights. The notion of rights is often criticised by those who feel that it is an attempt to impose Western values on the world. Others feel that there is not enough focus on the economic human rights mentioned in the Declaration, such as the right to a job. Others would like to see rights extended to include non-human animals.

SOUTH: The South can mean both a direction and the ***Third World.*** Some point out that the Third World is only South when you are in the North and that Australia is in the South. Others claim that this doesn't matter since the Far East is only in the East if you are in the West and how far away it is depends on whether you are in London or the Lebanon. Some refer to the 'social South' and the 'geographical South' while others use the phrase Majority World. Its all part of the highly political debate on how to refer to the poor and powerless of the world. See also ***Third World***

STRUCTURAL ADJUSTMENT: Cuts in government spending which the ***Bretton Woods*** Institutions require before giving Third World countries loans. Also known by some as *austerity packages.* They are seen either as a means of trying to make less developed countries more competitive in the global market and thereby richer, or as a means of ensuring that the rich get their money while the poor pay the price.

THIRD WORLD: Originally the non-aligned and former colonised nations during the cold war. For some the phrase is not sufficient as it implies a separation between the rich nations and the poor nations which belies the links through which poverty and wealth are created. Other phrases used include under-developed, less developed, and Southern. More recently the phrase *Majority World* has been suggested.

TRANS NATIONAL CORPORATIONS (TNCs): Companies that have branches in more than one country. MNC (Multi National Corporation) implies the company operates in many countries, where TNC implies the company has a base where its profits return to. Some argue that TNCs are essential to development as they invest in a country and bring modern ideas and technology. Others claim that they are part of the process through which wealth is extracted from the poorer countries.

UNDER DEVELOPED WORLD: See ***Third World.***

UNITED NATIONS: A world organisation set up to help the nations of the world to work for peace after the Second World War. The real power in the UN lies in the Security Council, which contains the victors of that war plus rotating other members. Currently there is some debate about how the UN should be reformed. Some argue that the balance of world power has shifted since the 1940s, and that the composition of the Security Council should change. This is usually the point of view of those who feel they would be on the new Security Council were there to be such a change.
For many the UN is an overblown bureaucracy which has failed miserably in recent years; others object to the fact that its voting is based on one country, one vote and that this is too much like democracy (especially when 'we' have to pay the bills!); for others the UN is an excellent institution which would function well if they let it.

UNCTAD: United Nations Conference of Trade and Development.

UNDP: United Nations Development Programme.

UNEP: United Nations Environmental Programme.

UNESOC: United Nations Educational, Scientific and Cultural Organisation.

UNFPA: United Nations Population Fund.

UNHCR: United

UNICEF: United Nations (International) Children's (Emergency) Fund.

UNIDO: United Nations Industrial Development Organisation.

UNWRA: United Nations Works and Relief Agency (for Palestinian refugees).

URBANISATION: The development of towns and cities.

U5MR (UNDER FIVE MORTALITY RATE): The number of children who die before the age of five for every 1,000 live births. So a country with 2,000 live births of which 140 die before the age of five, will have a U5MR of 70.

WHO: World Health Organisation

World Bank: See ***Bretton Woods.***

WTO (World Trade Organisation): See ***GATT.***

Women in Africa - active agents for change

SOME DEVELOPMENT EDUCATION RESOURCES

Compiled by Marie Cullen, Rachel Hayhow, Colm Regan and Roger Robinson

10 TITLES FOR STARTERS!

In this section we have chosen 10 titles which we feel will introduce many of the issues highlighted in 75:25. The books are of a general nature, are reasonably priced (for the most part!) and are readily available. The one title we would nominate for the general reader has to be Paul Harrison (1993ed.) **Inside the Third World,** London, Penguin, which comes highly recommended.

Susan George (1988) **A Fate Worse Than Debt,** London, Pelican.
Paul Harrison (1993) **Inside the Third World,** London, Penguin.
——————— (1992) **The Third Revolution: Population, Environment and a Sustainable World,** London, Penguin.
Kevin Watkins (1995) **The Oxfam Poverty Report,** Oxford, Oxfam.
Ben Jackson (1990) **Poverty and the Planet: A Question of Survival,** London, Penguin.
Paul Vallelly (1992) **Promised Lands: Stories of Power and Poverty in the Third World,** London, Fount/Christian Aid.
John Madeley, Dee Sullival and Jessica Woodroffe (1994) **Who Runs the World,** London, Christian Aid.
John Grindle (1992) **Bread and Freedom: Basic Human Needs and Human Rights,** Dublin, Gill and Macmillan/Trócaire.
Ronald J.Sider (1990) **Rich Christians in an Age of Hunger,** London, Hodder and Stoughton.

25 TITLES FOR AFTERS!

The titles in this section have been chosen because they provide more indepth and extended analysis of key global and justice issues. Many of them (but by no means all) are academic in nature and thus not for the fainthearted! However, many of them are ideal for additional reading and research especially for projects or articles and should be in the local library. If not, why not ask for them to be ordered?

Wolfgang Sachs (1992) **The Development Dictionary**, London, Zed Books.
Sean McDonagh (1994) **Passion for the Earth,** London, Chapman.
Donal Dorr (1992 revised ed.) **Option for the Poor,** Dublin, Gill and Macmillan.
Will Hutton (1996) **The State We're In,** London, Vintage.
John Darby (1995) **Northern Ireland: Managing Difference,** London, Minority Rights Group.
J. Cleves Mosse (1993) **Half the World, Half a Chance: An Introduction to Gender and Development,** Oxford, Oxfam.
Duncan Green (1991) **Faces of Latin America,** London, Latin American Bureau.
Tony Gibson (1991) **Taking the Neighbourhood Initiative,** London, Department of the Environment.
Alan Gilbert (1994) **The Latin American City,** London, Latin America Bureau.
Robert Chambers (1993) **Challenging the Professionals,** London, Intermediate Technology Publications.
Ian Smillie (1995) **The Alms Bazaar: Altruisn Under Fire Non-Profit Organisations and International Development,** London, Intermediate Technology Publications.
Sarah J. Tisch and Michael B. Wallace (1994) **Dilemmas of Development Assistance,** London, Westview Press.
Ramashray Roy and R.K.Srivastava (1986) **Dialogues on Development,** New Delhi, Sage.
UN/NGO Group on Women and Development (1991 to 1994) **Women and Development Series** (6 titles), London, Zed Press.
A.P.Thurwell (1995- 5th ed.) **Growth and Development,** Basingstoke, Macmillan.
John Toye (1993) **Dilemmas of Development,** Oxford, Blackwell.
A. Webster (1990) **Introduction to the Sociology of Development,** Basingstoke, Macmillan.
Bruce Rich (1994) **Mortgaging the Earth,** London, Earthscan.
Denis Goulet (1971) **The Cruel Choice,** New York, Atheneum Press.
D.C.Korten (1995) **When Corporations Rule the World,** London, Earthscan.
Herman E. Daly and John B.Cobb Jr. (1990) **For the Common Good: Redirecting the Economy towards Community, the Environment and a Sustainable Future,** London, Green Print.
David Hicks and Charles Townley (1982) **Teaching World Studies: an introduction to global perspectives in the curriculum,** London, Longman.
Jenny Pearce (1992) **Poverty and Power: Latin America after 500 Years,** London, Cafod.
T.Allen and A.Thomas (eds.) **Poverty and Development in the 1990s**, Oxford University Press
M. Todaro (1994) **Economic Development,** London, Longman.

GETTING THE 'FACTS'

One of the great mythologies about tackling world development and justice issues is that it is very difficult to get access to the "facts". Nothing could be further from the truth! Today's reality is that we are drowning in "facts" and it's very difficult to sort them all out and to choose between different, competing, and often contradictory, sets of facts. The titles listed below provide much of the "stuff" of development education and will provide all you might need by way of basic information. Some of them look formidable and incomprehensible but don't be put off - they are, in fact, easy enough to access. Most of them can be consulted at many of the Resource Centres listed on pages 293 - 294 and it is possible to photocopy relevant sections. Some organisation will even do it for you and forward the information (SAEs always help).

United Nations Development Programme (1994) ***Human Development Report,*** Oxford University Press.

Published annually by the United Nations Development Programme, it focuses on human development. Provides an alternative set of measures of human development to the economic; has been the subject of debate and controversy (this is discussed in various editions) and is a mine of really useful information. Annual editions take a particular theme eg. 1995 focused on women, 1994 on human security and peace. A must!

UNICEF (1994 and 1995) ***State of the World's Children Report,*** Oxford University Press.

Published annually, it is one of the most accessible and user friendly sources of information and focuses on issues as they affect children. Again, normally has an annual theme eg. 1996 highlighted children in war and 50 years of child focused work; 1995 on social development. Well worth the effort!

Instituto del Tercer Mundo (1993/94) ***Third World Guide,*** Montevideo, Uruguay.

And now for something completely different - the world as seen and described from the Third World. An expensive annual blockbuster packed with articles and statistics, usually from a 'radical' and often 'Third Worldist' perspective. Argumentative, political and engaged and, as a result, highly enjoyable. Covers most of the basic issues - not a gripping read but useful for dipping. Should be available for review in your local DEC or development agency.

World Bank (1995) ***World Development Report,*** Oxford University Press.

The 'old man' of them all - the world according to the World Bank. As you would expect, chock full of revealing and useful basic statistics - the first few tables are the ones most regularly cited. Again, has a regular annual theme eg. 1995 - Workers in an Integrating World; 1990 (one of the best to date!) focused on poverty. Regularly stuffy and hard to read, it is, nonetheless, a vital basic source.

Bread for the World Institute (1995) ***State of World Hunger,*** Silver Springs.

Published annually by the Bread for the World Institute in the United States, it is a must for those interested in this vital topic. Not only does it provide annual statistical updates, it also contains articles and reviews - usually from a 'committed' standpoint. Looks at hunger and poverty, organising against hunger, population etc. globally including in the US. Almost a gripping read!

Actionaid (1995) ***The Reality of Aid,*** Earthscan, London.

Subtitled 'an independent review of international aid', it reviews aid issues and trends, country by country and provides a general overview as well. Is part of the broader NGO debate on international aid. Very useful for summary facts and figures in a usable format. Regularly contains Third World comments and views.

Organisation for Economic Co-operation and Development (1994) ***Development Co-operation: Development Assistance Committee Report,*** Paris.

Facts on aid for the afficionados! The basic source of information on the aid world. Designed for insomniacs, it is, nonetheless, an important reference point. Can be approached with caution through your local NGO.

Ruth Sivard (1991-93) ***World Military and Social Expenditures,*** World Priorities, Washington.

The annual statistical and analytical report on one of the world's most useless and lunatic creations - the arms trade. Has the distinct advantage of comparing and contrasting military and social expenditure. Readable, well designed and easily used. A great resource for project work! High on our list!

United Nations (1995) ***The World's Women 1995: Trends and Statistics,*** New York.

First published in 1991, this is a basic reference source on women in development and is supported by seven UN organisations. Gathers statistics under different headings - population growth, health, work, education etc. - and contains useful and usable graphs and case studies (the 1995 edition has a brilliant case study of women in mathematics!). Heavy in presentation and tone. Still it's well worth some time and effort.

UNHCR (1996) ***The State of the World's Refugees,*** New York, Penguin/UNHCR. The basics on the situation of the world's refugees with detailed figures, overviews and analysis.

Development Education Resources - a taster!

All the pages in 75:25 would not be enough to list all of the resources now available in development education and allied areas. In this edition we have chosen to list and briefly describe some of them. We have chosen them on the basis that they exemplify broad approaches and themes and are indicative of the full range. There's no better way to see what suits your own needs (as distinct from those of the publishers!) than to nip down to your local Resource Centre and have a browse. We apologise if we have not included your favourite resource (or those of your favourite agency!) but space and cost inhibits us.

PRIMARY SCHOOL LEVEL

Pakistan: Change in the Swat Valley (1994), Action Aid, ages 7-14 - one of several such studies, this photopack looks at daily life in a remote family community, and how and why the area is changing.

Eritrea: Africa's Newest Country (1993), Oxfam, 5-11 - excellent pictures contrast two communities and their daily routines, encourages children to make connections betweeen this area and their own.

The Big City Pack (1994), Oxfam, 5-11 - photo material on four cities - Dakar, Phnom Penh, Santiago and Glasgow with activities for challenging stereotypes and making connections.

Mapping Our World (1993), Oxfam, 9-13 - this has a broader focus - it challenges assumptions about how the world looks by providing a variety of maps, and questionning who made them and for what purpose.

Go Bananas (1995), Oxfam, 6-13 - introduces the concept of world trade by following the production and distribution of one commodity.

The Whole World Cake (1994), 8-11 - imaginatively uses the list of ingredients to look at the lives of people in the South producing a range of foods for consumption in the North.

Clean Water: a right for all (1995) UNICEF, 5-11 - Looks at issues of water supply and quality in Britain and other parts of the world.

Doorways (1992), Save the Children, 9-13 - a good example of how photopacks can provide source material for a wide range of ages. The photos can introduce the wide variety of housing worldwide while the case studies bring out complex issues of injustice and inequality in housing.

In all of the above resources an active approach to learning leads on to suggestions onhow to act for change. Other resources which focus on preparing young people for active citizenship include:

Team Planet: An Action Pack on our World and Ourselves (1994), Mary Immaculate College/Trócaire and in Northern Ireland by Southeastern Education and Library Board/Trócaire - a carefully graded programme covering ages from 4 to 12 focused on environment and development issues. Key concepts tackled include nurturing (things I need, things which need me), dependence (habitats and food), interconnections (nature, the great recycler, wasting away) and sustainable development (trees, earthlinks). Contains teacher and student pages as well as 20 photographs.

Festa (1996), Trócaire, 4-12 - focuses on Brazil, it includes sections on land, poverty and wealth, indigenous peoples.

Our Changing World (1995), Save the Children, 4-7 - a poster pack which encourages young people to think about the past and their choices and hopes for the future. Contains examples of people acting to improve their own communities.

Educating for the Future (1994), World Wildlife Fund, 8-14 - a handbook for teachers wanting to make concerns for the future more explicit in the classroom. It provides both practical activities and theoretical support.

Viva! (1992), Cafod, 7-11 - resource focused on Latin America and built around three stories, those of Marcio in Brazil, Lucia in Peru and Miguel in Guatemala (with full colour posters for each). The final section looks at the idea of discovery, exploration, Christopher Columbus, conquest and slavery.

Making it Real: Introducing a global dimension in the early years (1995), DEC, Birmingham, 2-5 - simple practical ideas for bringing a global dimension to work with under fives. Full of easy-to-use imaginative activities for nurseries, playgroups, family centres etc.

Start with a Story: supporting young children's exploration of issues (1991), DEC, Birmingham, 4-7 - explores the use of stories as a way of encouraging young people to discuss complex or difficult issues. Issues covered include the environment (rainforests and endangered species) and buildings (do people everywhere have a right to a home?).

Around the Garden in 80 Ways (1994), DEC, Birmingham, 7-11 - uses plants and botanical gardens to raise development issues. Case studies focus on cotton and the wages of cotton pickers, jute in Bangladesh and musical instruments made from plant materials.

Try to See it My Way (1995), Sightsavers International/DEC, Birmingham, 7-11 - shows what visually impaired people can do and achieve. Highlights the common issues facing people living in our society and overseas. Includes a tape, containing interviews with visually impaired children and adults from Britain and Kenya.

Themework - a global perspective in the primary curriculum in the 90s (1991), DEC, Birmingham, 7-11 - the book explores four themes and how they can be approached across the curriculum - What is a Country?, Roots and Journeys, Images and Change.

Windows on the World (1992), Columban Fathers and Sisters, 4-12 - this series has four programmes focused on the following themes - Valuing Ourselves and Others; Naming Ourselves and Others, Heroes and Heroines; and Stories and Storytelling. Contains lesson plans, activities, poems, art and drama ideas and worksheets.

Primary Issues: Northern Ireland and India: an active learning resource for Key Stage 2 (1995), One World Centre Belfast, 7-11 - explores the links, parallels and differences between issues such as the Travellers in Northern Ireland and India.

Talking Drum (1996 SCIAF/Christian Aid, 4-9 - classroom ideas for teachers of 4-9 year olds based on stories from India, Nigeria, China and Peru.

POST-PRIMARY SCHOOLS

Handle with Care (1994), CAFOD, 11-16 - a teacher's resource book exploring a Christian response to development and the environment.

Refugees: we left because we had to (1995), British Refugee Council, 14-18 - focuses on refugees, who they are, why do they leave their homes, what has happened to them in the past and what may happen in the future? Background information, case studies and activities.

People on the Move (1996), Concern, 14-18 - this pack includes five units focused on the theme of migration. Contrasts betweeen the local and global experience of migration are explored through case studies from Ireland and overseas.

The Fair Trade Mini Company (1995), Irish Fair Trade Network, 14-16 - written for students who wish to run a fair trade mini-company. It contains information on fair trade and gives step by step guidelines on the running of a mini company using fair trade products.

Fair Shares: a discussion pack on poverty for post-primary schools and youth groups (1991), Combat Poverty Agency, Dublin, 14-18 - a pack containing a handbook with worksheets, 40 black and white photos plus photo activities and four colour posters.

Where we live: exploring local/global environment (1992), DEC, Birmingham, 11-16 - a text book for students on events in the world's environment; uses case studies and activities to make the links. Development issues and sustainable development are explored throughout.

Can You be Different? resources for understanding internationalisation and cultural change in communities (1994), DEC, Birmingham, 11-16 - Taiwan is used as a case study to examine the pressures on countries to 'Westernise'. It looks in detail at two communities and how they are affected by links with other nations and cultures. A teacher's handbook consisting mainly of pupil pages.

Peacemaker (Module One of the Sedekah Peace Programme) and **Power to Hurt** (Module Two) (1991 and 1993), Irish Commission for Justice and Peace and the Irish Council of Churches, 11-16 - two modules on the broad themes of peace and violence. Each contains lesson plans and worksheets.

Ayida: Change and Development in Nigeria (1995), Oxfam, 11-14 - explores what development means to young people living in a small Nigerian village.

Mangla: a study of change and development in Mirpur, 'Azad' Jammu Kashmir and Pakistan (1995), South Yorks DEC, 11-18 - takes the definition of development further and is quite challenging. It provides a wealth of material for examining aspects of change in the area of the Mangla Dam and linking them to experiences in Britain.

The Final Frontier?: land, environment and pastoralism in Kenya (1994), Leeds DEC, 11-16 - active learning materials offering stimulating ways of exploring issues of land use and economic difficulties for Masai pastoralists.

Colonialism, Slavery and the Industrial Revolution: a case study - the Empire in South Yorkshire 1700-1860 (1992), South Yorks DEC, 11-14 - This pack is rare in that it provides documents for learning about Britain's part in the historical basis of world inequality.

Focus for Change: class, gender and race inequality and the media in an international context (1992), Reading International Support Centre, 14 to adult - a wide selection of materials with challenging visual images and quotations on the role of the media in maintaining inequality. Has a broader appeal that just for classrooms and can be used with a variety of groups.

Famine: Remembering Our Past... Remembering Our Future? (1995), Ulster Folk and Transport Museum/National Famine Museum/Trócaire, 13/14 plus - This pack produced to mark the 150th anniversary of the Great Famine in Ireland provides the opportunity to explore similarities and differences between hunger and famine in the past and present. Contains posters, a famine timeline, boardgame, briefing papers and activity notes.

In Search of El Dorado (1996), Trócaire, 12-16 - a textbook designed for junior secondary geography focused on the history and geography of Brazil. Specific issues examined include land distribution, urbanisation, migration, environmental destruction and indigenous people.

Nuncamas - Never Again: teaching about human rights and responsibilities (1993), Amnesty International/Trócaire, 14 plus - an introductory resource highlighting the issues themselves plus case study material and ideas for taking action.

The Backbone of Development: resources and ideas for understanding the role of women in economic development (1994), DEC, Birmingham, 11-16 - What work do women do? What issues do they face in economic development? Who has the power and how will things change? These are the central questions asked in this photopack, which focuses on case studies from Nepal and Taiwan.

Fala Favela (1991), Movimento do Defesa do Favelados (Brazil) with SCIAF/CAFOD/ TRÓCAIRE etc., 11 plus - this photopack explores life in one favela or shanty town in Sao Paulo, Brazil. It highlights the struggle of the community there as well as the actions of the favelados to create change.

Food Matters (1992), DEC, Birmingham and Trócaire, 12-16 - this student's text raises many issues about hunger and poverty. It considers food as a basic need and a human right and examines the causes of famine in Ethiopia.

TEACHERS' HANDBOOKS

Simon Fisher and David Hicks (1985) **World Studies 8-13: A Teacher's Handbook,** Oliver and Boyd - basic activities for introducing and exploring global issues with over 80 practical suggestions.

Graham Pike and David Selby (1988) **Global Teacher Global Learner,** Hodder and Stoughton - Comprehensive introduction to the theory and practice of global education, contains a wide variety of practical classroom suggestions.

Susan Fountain (1995) **Education for Development: A Teacher's Resource for Global Learning,** Unicef/Hodder and Stoughton - examines six major themes at a variety of levels - Interdependence, Images and Perceptions, Social Justice, Conflict and Conflict Resolution, Change and the Future and Taking Action.

YOUTH AND ADULT RESOURCES

Development Education for Youth (DEFY) (1996) **Challenges for Change: Development Education in 'Disadvantaged' Youth Work,** Dublin - examines both theory and practice in pursuing development education amongst marginalised youth in Ireland. Practical youthwork activities included.

Irish Congress of Trade Unions/Trócaire (1993) **Forging Links:Trading Places: You and Your Union's Role in Global Solidarity,** Dublin - a practical handbook focused on the role of trade unionists in the development and justice fields, contains case studies of action, practical groupworking and organising skills as well as suggestions for using resource materials.

The Irish Jesuits, The National Conference of Priests of Ireland, The Catechetical Association of Ireland, Trócaire (1991) **In Words and Deeds - 100 Years of Catholic Social Teaching: A Poster Pack,** Dublin - an activity based pack focusing on a range of key themes such as Human Dignity and Equality, Solidarity, Peace, Structures of Sin etc.

Banúlacht (1994) **Making Connections: Women Developing Links for Change,** Dublin - a development education resource designed for use by educators and trainers in women's community and adult education groups; makes connections between local and global issues and covers topics such as development, oppression, debt etc. from a gender perspective.

Scottish Education and Action for Development **Using Knowhow: Learning from Case Studies of Community Empowerment in Scotland and South Africa,** Edinburgh - a "practical down-to-earth look at some development issues facing people in Scotland and the so-called "Thrd World"; contains three units, one for discussion, one for research and one for practical action.

One World Week (1995) **Young People Imagine,** Dublin and London - the practical guide to support One World Week in both Britain and Ireland (each place has a different theme and timing) - a set of activities focused on the theme of the Week - in 1995 it was Young people imagining the future in Ireland and in Britain.

National Youth Council of Ireland/Council of Europe (1995) **All Different All Equal: An Anti-Racism and Equality Education Pack,** Dublin - pack produced in support of the Europe wide All Different All Equal Campaign focused on such themes as Belonging and Difference, Understanding Racism, Justice Issues and Change - includes Irish Language activities.

Colm Regan, Scott Sinclair and Martyn Turner (1988) **Thin Black Lines** and (1994) **Thin Black Lines Rides Again,** Birmingham, DEC - two collections of cartoons on development issues plus a range of suggestions for using them in learning situations. Both editions contain over 100 cartoons from all over the world.

SCIAF (1995) **Prayers from around the World,** Glasgow - a collection of prayers for use in liturgies and reflection sessions on themes such as health, refugees, street children and poverty.

CAFOD (1992) **Viva!: a resource pack for youth groups,** London - produced as part of Cafod's Latin America Campaign, this resource is structured around a series of six workshops and a Fiesta - the workshops cover topics such as getting to know Latin America, culture, traditions and lifestyles, hopes and dreams, drugs, youth and homelessness etc.

CAFOD (1989) **Renewing the Earth: Study Guide for Groups,** London - structured around six meetings, this resource provides information, activities and reflections and prayers on themes such as people and environment, poverty and care for the earth, managing resources, working for renewal and our common future.

Anne Hope and Sally Timmel (1984) **Training for Transformation: A Handbook for Community Workers,** Zimbabwe, Mambo Press - this handbook is in three volumes and all the activities contained in it have developed as a result of work with groups in Africa. Part One focuses on the theory, a derivation from Paulo Freire; Part Two introduces skills necessary for participatory education and for breaking the 'culture of silence' while Part Three deals with social analysis and critical awareness.

It's Not Fair: a handbook on world development for youth groups (1993), Christian Aid/Trócaire, 14 plus - a collection of activities and simulation games exploring world development issues including trade, food, debt, conflict, refugees, human rights etc.

CAFOD (1993) **The Refugee Campaign - 1. Study Guide for Adult Groups, 2. Stay With Us: Worship Resources, 3. Road to Emmaus: A Pilgrimage,** London - three resources produced as part of a focus on the plight of refugees around such themes as Who is a Refugee?, Why are there Refugees?, The Search for Asylum plus Biblical Texts, Quotations, Poems/Drama and Prayers. Also contains detailed ideas and suggestions for organising your own pilgrimage.

SCIAF (1995) **The Horn: People, Poverty and Environment** - a CD-Rom packed with text, maps and photographs which covers eight distinct themes about life and development in the Horn of Africa. Contains general introductory materials as well as case study material for older groups.

There are, of course, a huge range of other resources including slide packs, videos, simulation games, cd-roms etc. - it would be impossible for us to list them all here. Detailed lists and updated references can be had from most of the organisations listed on pages 293 - 294.

Finally!

A useful resource which examines development education within the EU is NGDO - EU Liaison Committee (1994) **Education for Change: Grassroots Development Education in Europe,** Brussels (copies can be obtained from Dóchas).

SOME USEFUL ADDRESSES

In Ireland:

Dóchas
59 Deerpark Road, Mount Merrion, Co.Dublin - tel. 01 288 6141
(see also the full listing of Dóchas member agencies on page 296)

Network Outreach in Development Education (NODE)
c/o Cómhlámh, 10 Upper Camden Street, Dublin 2 - tel. 01 475 1998

National Committee for Development Education (Resource Centre)
16-20 Cumberland Street, Dublin 2 - tel. 01 662 0866

Development Education for Youth (DEFY!)
3 Montague Street, Dublin 2 - tel. 01 478 4122

Combat Poverty
8 Charlemont Street, Dublin 2 - tel. 01 478 3355

Focus Point (homelessness)
14a Eustace Street, Dublin 2 - tel. 01 671 2555

Pavee Point (Travellers' issues)
46 North Great Charles Street, Dublin 1 - tel. 01 878 0255

Tullamore Resource Centre
Bridge Street, Tullamore, Co.Offaly - tel. 0506 53303

Galway One World Centre
2 Church Yard, Galway - tel. 091 65589

Trócaire Resource Centres
12 Cathedral Street, Dublin 1 - tel 01 874 3875
9 Cook Street, Cork - tel. 021 275622
169 Booterstown Avenue, Blackrock, Co.Dublin - tel. 01 288 5385

Oxfam in Ireland
19 Clanwilliam Terrace, Dublin 2 - tel. 01 661 8544

Action Aid
Unity Buildings, 16 Lower O'Connell Street, Dublin 1 - tel. 01 878 7911

World Education Project
St. Angela's College, Lough Gill, Sligo - tel. 071 45485

World Development Centre
25 O'Connell Street, Waterford - tel. 051 73064

Midlands Development Education Project
The Old Library, Church Street, Portlaoise, Co.Offaly - tel. 0502 61185

Kerry Action for Development Education
Tralee Teachers' Centre, Collis-Sandes House, Oakpark, Tralee, Co.Kerry - tel. 066 28255

In Northern Ireland

One World Centre
4 Lower Crescent, Belfast BT7 1NR - tel. 0232 241 879

Derry Development Education Centre
13a Pump Street, Derry BT48 6JG - tel. 504 269 183

Trócaire Resource Centre
50 King Street, Belfast BT1 6AD - tel. 0232 238 586

Oxfam
52-54 Dublin Road, Belfast BT2 7HN - tel. 0232 230 220

In Scotland

Poverty Alliance
102 Buchanan Street, Glasgow G1 2LL - tel. 0141 353 0440

SEAD
23 Castle Street, Edinburgh - tel. 0131 225 6550

Justice and Peace Scotland
65 Bath Street, Glasgow - tel. 0141 333 0238

Commonweal
41 George IV Bridge, Edinburgh EH1 1EL - tel. 0131 225 1772

SCIAF
5 Oswald Street, Glasgow G1 4QR - tel. 0141 221 4447

In England

Development Education Centre (Birmingham)
Gillett Centre, 998 Bristol Road, Birmingham B29 6LE - tel. 0121 472 3255

CAFOD
2 Romero Close, Stockwell Road, London SW9 9TY - tel. 0171 733 7900

Oxfam (Education in England)
4 Bridge Place (4th floor), London SWV 1XY - tel. 0171 931 7660

Save the Children Fund
17 Grove Lane, Camberwell, London SE5 8RD - tel. 0171 703 5400

Action Aid
Hamlyn House, Macdonald Road, Archway, London NI9 5PG - tel. 0171 281 4101

UNICEF(UK)
55 Lincoln's Inn Fields, London WC2A 3NB - tel. 0171 405 5592

Catholic Institute for International Relations
Unit 3, Canonbury Yard, 190a New North Road, Islington, London N1 7BJ - tel. 0171 354 0883

Intermediate Technology Development Group
Myson House, Railway Terrace, Rugby CV21 3HT - tel. 01788 560 631

Latin American Bureau
1 Amwell Street, London EC1R 1Ul - tel. 0171 278 2829

Third World First
217 Cowley Road, Oxford OX4 1XG - tel. 01865 245 678

Development Education Dispatch Unit
151 Cardigan Road, Leeds LS6 1LJ - tel. 01132 784 030
(dispatches the development education materials of many development education centres).

Development Education Association
Third Floor, 29-31 Cowper Street, London EC2A 4AP - tel. 0171 490 8108
(The DEA can forward the addresses of many development education centres throughout Britain and also co-ordinates the work of other groups working in various sectors such as youth work.)

Africa Music has heavily influenced western music in the past three decades

Development Education Centre, Birmingham

- ▼ DEC is a small educational charity which focuses on awareness of development issues and the global dimensions of such issues in our own locality and in other parts of the world
- ▼ DEC is the focus for a network of creative educational activity related to development education
- ▼ DEC is a source of information, resources and ideas through its project work and through its Resource Centres

At the core of DEC's work is the idea of partnership focused upon development education. This has led to the creation of TIDE - Teachers in Development Education - a network of teachers involved in a variety of projects usually in partnership with other organisations. The majority of such partnerships have been local but some have involved links with others throughout Britain as well as Irelaand, Ghana, Spain and Japan. Most of DEC's work revolves around projects which strongly emphasise the involvement of teachers and, through them, students in both design and delivery. This has facilitated the emergence of a wide variety of work with the overall objective of making development education part of the mainstream educational agenda.

Some of the core ideas which underpin DEC's work include:

- development education is a response to major global issues such as those discussed in 75:25 but it is equally concerned with educational issues - for example, the building up of skills, the application of analysis and an awareness of the influence of attitudes and skills.
- the process of understanding the issues involves recognising and appreciating different views, an awareness of the dynamics of change as well as recognition of underlying similarities in economic, social, environmental and political issues internationally. This has implications for how we learn and teach about these issues.
- an appreciation of global issues is pivotal to our own political literacy and such literacy is central to citizenship in the context of modern society, the speed of change and the process of globalisation.
- in that sense, development education is a political response to the process of globalisation and to the need for individual and collective questionning of the nature of that process and its impact on people and the environment as well as the economy.

Given that much of DEC's work is with teachers and for teachers, priority is often given to the immediate needs of the curriculum and the interests of young people over that of our own understanding of the issues. The publication of 75:25 represents the starting point for a number of initiatives aimed at addressing the issue of understanding.

Some DEC projects

Around the Garden in 80 Ways - a project in partnership with the Botanical Gardens to make use of plants from different parts of the world.

Costa Rica Link - an experimental project making use of the Internet, linking a small group of schools with environment / development projects in Costa Rica.

Decisions on Development - a project designing decision making exercises around development case studies for 'A' level geography.

Developing Geography Ghana - a project which involved a group of teachers visiting Ghana and then developing materials for trialing. This project also involved a group of Ghanaian teachers.

Forward Thinking - a project to develop a document in partnership with the Local Authority highlighting children's entitlement to development education.

Handworth: Ten Years On - a project to explore issues relating to human rights and participation linked to events in the Handsworth area of Birmingham now and ten years ago.

Khulna - a project to create a video pack featuring long term community based health and development projects in Khulna, Bangladesh.

Look Out, There's a World About - a programme involving Birmingham's Environment Centres and Museum Service in offering development education activities for groups of children at their centres.

Try to See it My Way - a project exploring strategies for teaching about issues of sight and blindness, both in a global and local context.

DÓCHAS is the Irish Association of Non-Governmental Development Organisations and represents the bulk of non-governmental development organisations in Ireland. Dóchas aims to provide a forum for these organisations to meet together and to develop common understanding and action on important global justice and development issues. It regularly speaks on behalf of Irish NGOs on issues as diverse as Irish Government Policy, the European Union's relations with Third World countries, trade, human rights, humanitarian assistance etc. Dóchas meets regularly with Government Departments and organisations with a view to impressing on them its member agencies' experiences and perspectives on such issues.

Dóchas is administered by an Executive Committee and has three working groups - the Development Education Working Group, the Development Policy Working Group and the Development Aid Working Group. Each group has its own programme of research and action aimed at strengthening the vision and impact of the NGO movement in Ireland generally.

DÓCHAS MEMBER AGENCIES (Summer 1996)

Action from Ireland (AFrI)
2nd Floor, 16 Harcourt Road, Dublin 2 - tel. 478 5100

Christian Aid
Christ Church, Rathgar Road, Rathgar, Dublin 6 - tel. 496 6184

Church Missionary Society Ireland
Overseas House, 3 Belgrave Road, Rathmines, Dublin 6 - tel. 497 0931

Church of Ireland Bishops' Appeal (CIBA)
103 Anglesea Road, Ballsbridge, Dublin 4 - tel. 668 4029

Comhlamh
10 Camden Street, Dublin 2 - tel. 478 3490

Concern Worldwide
52-55 Camden Street, Dublin 2 - 475 4162

Development Education for Youth (DEFY!)
3 Montague Street, Dublin 2 - tel. 478 4122

Gorta
12 Herbert Street, Dublin 2 - tel. 661 5522

Irish League of Credit Unions International Development Foundation
Castleside Drive, Rathfarnham, Dublin 14 - tel. 490 8911

Interculture Ireland
10a Lower Camden Street, Dublin 2 - tel. 478 2046

Irish Commission for Justice and Peace (ICJP)
169 Booterstown Avenue, Blackrock, Co.Dublin - tel. 288 5021

Irish Council for Overseas Students (ICOS)
41 Morehampton Road, Dublin 4 - tel. 660 5233

Irish Foundation for Co-operative Development (IFCD)
84 Merrion Square, Dublin 2 - tel. 676 4783

Irish Missionary Union (IMU)
Orwell Park, Rathgar, Dublin 6 - tel. 497 1770

Methodist World Development and Relief Committee (MWDRC)
3 Fountain Ville Avenue, Belfast, BT9 6AN - tel. 0232 320 078

One World Centre for Northern Ireland
4 Lower Crescent, Belfast BT1 1NR - tel. 0232 241 879

Refugee Trust
4 Dublin Road, Stillorgan, Co. Dublin - tel. 283 4256

Self Help Development
Hacketstown, Co.Carlow, tel. 0508 71175

Support for Afghan Further Education (SAFE)
9 Sandycove Avenue West, Sandycove, Co.Dublin - tel. 280 4178

Trócaire
169 Booterstown Avenue, Blackrock, Co.Dublin - tel. 288 5385

Voluntary Service International (VSI)
30 Mountjoy Square, Dublin 1 - tel. 855 1011

War on Want
1 Rugby Avenue, Belfast BT7 1RD - tel. 0232 232 064